Valuation for Mergers, Buyouts, and Restructuring

Valuation for Mergers, Buyouts, and Restructuring

Enrique R. Arzac

Graduate School of Business
Columbia University

WILEY

John Wiley & Sons, Inc.

Acquisitions Editor   *Leslie Kraham*
Marketing Manager   *David Woodbury*
Senior Production Editor   *Norine M. Pigliucci*
Design Director   *Maddy Lesure*
Program Assistant   *Jessica Bartelt*
Production Management Services   *Pine Tree Composition*

This book was set in Times Roman by Pine Tree Composition and printed and bound by Hamilton Printing. The cover was printed by Phoenix Color.

This book is printed on acid free paper. ∞

Library of Congress Cataloging-in-Publication Data
Arzac, Enrique R.
  Valuation : mergers, buyouts and restructuring / Enrique R. Arzac.
    p. cm.
  Includes bibliographical references (p.) and index.
  ISBN 0-471-44944-X (cloth : alk. paper)
  1. Corporations—Valuation—Textbooks.   2. Consolidation and merger of corporations—Textbooks I. Title.

HG4028.V3A79 2005
658.1'62—dc22

Printed in the United States of America

10 9 8 7 6 5 4 3 2 1

To Alicia, Martin, my Mother and
in memory of my Father

Preface

This book presents a comprehensive approach to corporate valuation. It treats in detail the valuation of mergers, acquisitions, and leveraged buyouts, and the assessment of asset restructuring options and recapitalization plans. It contains valuation procedures and examples for the different types of transactions and contractual arrangements commonly encountered in practice. It also discusses the theoretical underpinnings and the research evidence that justifies the recommended procedures.

The book is intended as the core text for corporate valuation courses taught to finance majors in undergraduate and MBA programs.

The book assumes that readers are familiar with basic accounting and finance concepts. The mathematical requirement is limited to basic algebra with the exception of a few sections on option pricing applications that use calculus notation. Mathematical details have been relegated to notes at the end of the book.

VALUATION PROCEDURES

The reader will find assistance and procedures to undertake the following tasks:

- Valuation of stand-alone companies and business units from the points of view of the acquirer and the seller, with procedures for testing assumptions and results.

- Valuation of a merged firm involving the combination of two or more companies or business units, including expected share price impact, valuation of synergies, accretion-dilution analysis of earnings, and scenario analysis.

- Valuation of foreign firms in developed and emerging markets and how to treat foreign exchange translation, inflation, and country risk.

- Assessment of the value creation potential of business units and their restructuring options.

- Structuring and valuing leveraged buyouts and the recapitalization of troubled companies.

- Valuation of contingent clauses and agreements commonly included in the terms of a transaction.

- Valuation of real options in mergers and acquisitions involving postponement, entry, foothold, and exit options.

TOOLS

In addition to the description and examples of the procedure to follow in each task, the book provides a detailed treatment of the required tools of analysis:

- How to estimate the cost of capital for public and private companies from developed and emerging markets.

- How to perform discounted cash-flow valuation.

- How to estimate and apply valuation multiples.

- How to estimate the sustainable debt of a company and the debt capacity of a highly leveraged transaction.
- How to compute economic value added for companies and business units.
- How to value companies with changing capital structures.
- How to value financial and real options.

SOFTWARE

Most of the valuation analyses treated in this book can be performed using generally available spreadsheet software. Specialized computations can be carried out with the software contained in the Valuation Aids CD-ROM included with this book. In particular, Valuation Aids has programs for estimating the equity premium and valuing financial and real options.

In addition, DealModeler^{TM}, a comprehensive financial modeling Excel workbook, is available for purchase from the publisher. It generates accounting closing statements, stand-alone and consolidated pro-forma financial statements, and the valuation of mergers, acquisitions, and buyouts using discounted cash flow and accretion-dilution analysis. DealModeler^{TM} is not required to reproduce the spreadsheets presented in this book or to apply its procedures.

ACKNOWLEDGMENTS

A number of colleagues from the academic and professional communities have generously read parts of the manuscript and made helpful criticisms and suggestions. In particular, I would like to thank David Beim (Columbia University), William Comfort (Citigroup Venture Capital), John Donaldson (Columbia University), Frederic Escherich (former Managing Director at J.P. Morgan), Joseph Gallagher (Credit Suisse Asset Management), Kathleen McGahran (Columbia University and Pelham Associates), James McVeigh (Banc of America Securities), William Priest (Steinberg Priest Sloane Capital Management), and Joel Stern (Stern Stewart & Co.).

At John Wiley & Sons, I am grateful to Leslie Kraham, my editor, for her support and wise counsel, and to Jessica Bartelt, for her editorial guidance. I am also indebted to the following people for their insightful reviews of the manuscript: Chao Chen (California State University–Northridge), Robert B.H. Hauswald (University of Maryland), David Lins (University of Illinois at Urbana–Champaign), Lloyd Levitin (University of Southern California), Timothy A. Thompson (Northwestern University), and Pieter A. Vandenberg (San Diego State University).

Thanks go as well to my son, Martin Arzac (UBS Investment Bank), who reviewed the manuscript from the investment banker's perspective, and to my wife, Alicia, for her forbearance and unfailing support.

Enrique R. Arzac

Brief Contents

Part One   The Tools of Valuation

1. A User's Guide   3
2. Forecasting and Valuation of Free Cash Flows   9
3. The Equity Premium and the Cost of Capital   35
4. Metrics and Multiples   63
5. Economic Value Added   77
6. Valuation with Changing Capital Structure   89
7. Debt Capacity for Acquisition Financing   107
8. Valuing Entry and Exit Options   121

Part Two   Mergers, Acquisitions, and Buyouts

9. Mergers and Acquisitions   143
10. Deal Making with Differences of Opinion   179
11. Special Offer Structures: Price Guarantees and Collars   195
12. Acquisitions in Developed and Emerging Markets   205
13. Leveraged Buyouts   221

Part Three   Recapitalizations and Restructuring

14. Recapitalization of Troubled Companies   243
15. Asset Restructuring   265

Appendix A.   Financial Options   A–1
Appendix B.   Valuation Aids Software   A–7
Appendix C.   Answers to Selected End-of-Chapter Problems   A–9

Technical Notes   TN–1

References   R–1

Index   I–1

Contents

Part One   The Tools of Valuation

1.   A User's Guide   3

1.1   Valuation of Stand-alone Firms and Business Units   3
          1.1.1   Free Cash-flow Valuation   3
          1.1.2   Cost of Capital   3
          1.1.3   Valuation Multiples   4
1.2   Economic Value Added   4
1.3   Valuation with Changing Capital Structure   4
1.4   Valuation in Developed and Emerging Markets   4
1.5   Mergers and Acquisitions   5
1.6   Deal Design and Special Offer Structures   5
1.7   Leveraged Buyouts   5
1.8   Recapitalization of Troubled Companies   5
1.9   Asset Restructuring   6
1.10   Real Options: Valuing Entry and Exit Options   6
          1.10.1   Financial Options   6
1.11   Technical Notes and Problems   6
1.12   Valuation Aids   6

2.   Forecasting and Valuation of Free Cash Flows   9

2.1   Free Cash Flows   9
2.2   Building a Financial Model   9
2.3   Enterprise Valuation   14
2.4   Continuation Value   17
          2.4.1   Forecast Consistency   17
          2.4.2   Sensitivity to Parameter Estimates   19
          2.4.3   Competitive Advantage Period   20
          2.4.4   EBITDA Multiples   21
2.5   An Equivalent Approach: Valuing the Cash Flow to Equity   21
          2.5.1   Decomposition of Free Cash Flows: Cash Flows to Equity
                    and Debt   21
          2.5.2   Equity Valuation   22
          2.5.3   Debt Valuation   23
          2.5.4   Financial Policy and Dividends   23
2.6   Some Practical Aspects   24
          2.6.1   Choosing the Valuation Method   24
          2.6.2   Personal Taxes and Enterprise Value   25
          2.6.3   Enterprise Value in Tax Imputation Countries   27
          2.6.4   Balance Sheet Adjustments   27
          2.6.5   Cash and Marketable Securities   28

2.6.6   Mid-year Discounting   29
2.6.7   Dealing with Equity-linked and Other Securities
         in the Capital Structure   29
2.6.8   Restructuring Expenses   29

2.7   Analysis of Results: The Value of Franchise and Growth   30
2.8   Summary   32
      Problems   P–1

3.   The Equity Premium and the Cost of Capital   35

3.1   Estimating the Cost of Capital   35
3.2   The Cost of Equity   36
      3.2.1   The Capital Asset Pricing Model Approach   36
      3.2.2   Choosing the Riskless Rate   36
      3.2.3   Estimating the Equity Premium: Historical Analyses   38
      3.2.4   Time Varying Equity Premium   41
      3.2.5   Prospective Equity Premium   41
3.3   The Cost of Equity of Large Capitalization Companies   47
3.4   The Cost of Equity and Leverage   47
3.5   Beyond the Capital Asset Pricing Model   50
      3.5.1   The Original CAPM   50
      3.5.2   The Fama-French Three-factor Model   51
      3.5.3   Arbitrage Pricing Theory   53
      3.5.4   Liquidity and Expected Returns   54
3.6   The Cost of Equity of Small Capitalization Companies   55
3.7   Estimating the Cost of Equity: A Detailed Example   58
3.8   The Cost of Debt and Other Components
      of the Capital Structure   58
      3.8.1   Investment-grade Debt   58
      3.8.2   High-yield Debt and Preferred Stock   60
      3.8.3   Convertible Securities, Warrants, and Other Options   61
3.9   Estimation of the Cost of Capital in Practice   61
3.10 Summary   62
      Problems   P–1

4.   Metrics and Multiples   63

4.1   The Use of Multiples in Valuation   63
4.2   Using Comparables: An Example   65
4.3   Multiples and Continuation Value   65
4.4   Relationships Among Valuation Multiples   68
4.5   Adjusting Multiples for Leverage and Growth   70
4.6   The Franchise Factor in Valuation Multiples   73
4.7   Normalizing P/E Ratios by the Growth Rate   76
4.8   Summary   76
      Problems   P–1

5.   Economic Value Added   77

5.1   Measuring Value Creation   77
5.2   Relation to Free Cash-flow Valuation   78

5.3   A Detailed Example of EVA Valuation   80
5.4   The Sources of Value: Franchise and Growth   82
5.5   Economic Value-added and Market Value   84
5.6   Some Empirical Evidence   86
5.7   Summary   87
        Problems   P–1

6.   **Valuation with Changing Capital Structure   89**

6.1   Leverage Changes and Enterprise Value   89
6.2   Adjusted Present Value and the Value of the Tax Shield   90
6.3   A Detailed Example of APV Valuation   92
6.4   Valuing an Acquisition with Leverage Above Target   94
6.5   Recursive WACC Valuation   95
6.6   Compressed APV   97
6.7   Uncertain Leverage: A Recursive APV Model   99
6.8   Valuing Equity as an Option   102
6.9   Summary   105
        Problems   P–1

7.   **Debt Capacity for Acquisition Financing   107**

7.1   Financial Interdependencies   107
7.2   Financing Growth   108
7.3   Growth via Acquisitions   111
7.4   Sustainable Debt   111
7.5   The Target Debt Ratio Assumed in WACC Valuation, Debt Capacity,
        and Interest Coverage   113
7.6   Debt Capacity in Leveraged Buyouts and Recapitalizations   114
7.7   The Debt Capacity Multiple in Practice   119
7.8   Summary   119
        Problems   P–1

8.   **Valuing Entry and Exit Options   121**

8.1   Net Present Value and Options   121
        8.1.1   Accounting for Flexibility   121
        8.1.2   Option Pricing   123
8.2   A Continuous-time Model of Free Cash Flows   124
8.3   Valuation in Discrete and Continuous Times   128
8.4   Valuing a Going Concern in Continuous Time   129
8.5   Valuing the Entry Option   130
8.6   Entry and Exit Options   132
8.7   Valuing Foothold and Growth Options   133
        8.7.1   Foothold Investment with an Expansion Option   133
        8.7.2   Valuing Foothold and Expansion Options   135
8.8   Allowing for Uncertain Costs in Foothold Investments   137
8.9   Sensitivity of DCF Values in the Presence of Real Options   138
8.10   Summary   139
        Problems   P–1

Part Two   Mergers, Acquisitions, and Buyouts

9. Mergers and Acquisitions   143

9.1   Value Creation and Mergers   143
9.2   Legal Form of the Transaction and Tax Considerations   143
9.3   Examples of Tax Consequences   145
9.4   Tax-free Reorganizations   146
9.5   Merger Accounting   147
9.6   Premiums and the Iron Law of M&A   148
        9.6.1   All-cash Offer   152
        9.6.2   Share Exchange   152
        9.6.3   Cash and Share Offer   153
9.7   Break-even Synergies   153
9.8   Premiums and the Acquirer's Foothold   154
9.9   Accretion-dilution Analysis   155
9.10   Free Cash-flow Valuation: Total versus Incremental Free
        Cash Flows   156
9.11   Comprehensive Merger Example   157
        9.11.1   Terms of the Merger   160
        9.11.2   Building the Financial Model of the Merger   161
        9.11.3   Accretion-dilution Analysis   161
        9.11.4   Free Cash-flow Valuation   169
        9.11.5   Sensitivity and Scenario Analysis   171
9.12   Summary   176
        Problems   P–1

10. Deal Making with Differences of Opinion   179

10.1   Sources of Disagreement in Deal Making   179
10.2   Risk Shifting   181
10.3   Staged Financing   182
10.4   Earnout Agreements   184
10.5   Valuing Earnouts by Straight DCF   185
10.6   Earnouts as Options on Future Cash Flows   186
        10.6.1   Earnouts with Thresholds   186
        10.6.2   Earnouts with Thresholds and Caps   188
        10.6.3   Earnouts Based on Average Performance   188
        10.6.4   Valuing the Seller's Repurchase Option   189
        10.6.5   Valuing Multiyear Earnouts   189
10.7   Perpetual Earnouts and Class Shares with Threshold   190
10.8   Summary   193
        Problems   P–1

11. Special Offer Structures: Price Guarantees and Collars   195

11.1   Special Offer Structures   195
        11.1.1   Risk Arbitrage   195
        11.1.2   Guarantees   195
11.2   Valuing Price Guarantees   196
        11.2.1   Commodity Price Guarantees   199
11.3   Valuing Offers with Price Collars   200

11.4   Additional Features in Price Collars   202
    11.4.1   Walk-away Rights   202
    11.4.2   Top-up Rights   203
    11.4.3   Fixed Exchange Ratio with Collar   203
    11.4.4   Weighted Average   203
11.5   Summary   203
    Problems   P–1

12.   Acquisitions in Developed and Emerging Markets   205

12.1   The Global Capital Market   205
12.2   Translating Foreign Currency Cash Flows   205
12.3   The Cost of Capital in Developed Capital Markets   206
12.4   Valuing Emerging-market Companies   208
    12.4.1   Translating Free Cash Flows to the Acquirer's Currency   209
    12.4.2   Value to the Acquirer   212
    12.4.3   Nominal and Real Cash Flows and the Cost of Capital   214
    12.4.4   Value to the Seller   214
12.5   On the Nature of the Country Risk Premium   216
12.6   Post-emergence Systematic Risk   217
12.7   Summary   218
    Problems   P–1

13.   Leveraged Buyouts   221

13.1   The Rationale for LBOs   221
13.2   Financing LBOs   223
13.3   Robust Financial Structures   224
13.4   Computing the Returns to Investors   225
13.5   Option Pricing of Warrant Kickers   227
13.6   Debt Capacity and Affordable Price   227
13.7   Returns to Investors and the Private-equity Discount   229
13.8   A Detailed LBO Example   232
13.9   Mezzanine Financing   236
13.10   APV Valuation   239
13.11   Summary   240
    Problems   P–1

Part Three   Recapitalizations and Restructuring

14.   Recapitalization of Troubled Companies   243

14.1   Dealing with Financial Distress   243
14.2   Framework for Recapitalizations   243
14.3   Out-of-court Workouts and Bankruptcy   245
    14.3.1   Out-of-court Workouts   245
    14.3.2   In-court Reorganization   246
    14.3.3   Prepackaged Bankruptcy   246
    14.3.4   Liquidation   246

14.4   Accounting Treatment   247
    14.4.1 Troubled Debt Restructuring   247
    14.4.2 Asset Impairment   247
    14.4.3 Fresh-start Accounting   247
14.5   Tax Considerations   248
14.6   Valuing Recapitalization Securities   249
    14.6.1 The Southland LBO   249
    14.6.2 The Recapitalization Plans   250
    14.6.3 Valuing the New Debt Securities   251
    14.6.4 Valuing Equity   254
    14.6.5 Recovery   255
14.7   Valuing Recapitalization Rights and Options   257
14.8   Summary   263
    Problems   P–1

15. Asset Restructuring   265

15.1   Asset Restructuring and the Value Gap   265
15.2   Is There a Diversification Discount?   265
15.3   Share Repurchases   267
15.4   Asset Disposition   267
15.5   Tax and Accounting Treatment   269
    15.5.1 Private Sales, IPOs, and Carve-outs   269
    15.5.2 Spin-offs   270
    15.5.3 Tracking Stock   270
15.6   Sum-of-the-parts Valuation   271
15.7   Headquarter Costs and Benefits   279
15.8   Summary   280
    Problems   P–1

Appendix A. Financial Options   A–1

A.1   Financial Options in M&A Valuation   A–1
A.2   European Calls and Puts and American Calls   A–1
A.3   American Puts   A–2
A.4   Warrant Pricing Model   A–2
A.5   Asian Options   A–3
A.6   Knockout (Barrier) Options   A–4
A.7   The Put-call Parity   A–4
A.8   Stock Options Paying a Known Dividend Yield   A–5
A.9   Dilution Adjustment in Warrant Valuation   A–5
    Problems   P–1

Appendix B. Valuation Aids Software   A–7

Appendix C. Answers to Selected End-of-Chapter Problems   A–9

Technical Notes   TN–1

References   R–1

Index   I–1

Valuation for Mergers, Buyouts, and Restructuring

Part One

The Tools of Valuation

Chapter 1

A User's Guide

This book is organized in three parts. Part One contains the main methods used in valuation of companies and their business units; Part Two applies these methods to the valuation of mergers, acquisitions, and leveraged buyouts; and Part Three deals with recapitalization and restructuring analyses.

This chapter provides a guide to the use of the book. Readers interested in getting a detailed grounding on the different aspects of transaction valuation can follow the order of presentation of the book. Those using the book as a reference on valuation of particular transactions can read selected chapters as explained next.

1.1 VALUATION OF STAND-ALONE FIRMS AND BUSINESS UNITS

1.1.1 Free Cash-flow Valuation

The valuation of a stand-alone company or one of its business units is a common practical problem. Chapters 2 and 4 (Sections 4.1 to 4.3) provide the background necessary to perform this type of valuation. Chapter 2 introduces financial modeling and the valuation approach followed in the book, and it should be read first, even by those already familiar with the methods of free cash-flow valuation, since it provides the foundation upon which the rest of the book is based as well a common terminology.

Chapter 2 presents a self-contained description of valuation based upon discounting the free cash flows generated by the enterprise. It shows how to compute free cash flows and the weighted average cost of capital (WACC) in order to obtain the value of the enterprise, which is the value of the claims held by equity-holders as well as bond-holders. From the enterprise value one can calculate the value of equity by subtracting the value of the outstanding net debt. This chapter also shows how to value equity directly from the cash flows available to equity-holders and discusses under what conditions each approach is appropriate.

In addition to the mechanics of valuation, Chapter 2 includes sections on sensitivity analysis, the examination and testing of the determinants of value and how to incorporate the effect of personal taxes on valuation, as well as the balance sheets adjustments that need to be made to complete the valuation of a company or a business unit.

1.1.2 Cost of Capital

Chapter 3 provides a detailed discussion of the state-of-the-art approach to estimating the costs of equity and debt. In particular, the several approaches used in practice for estimating the equity premium and the cost of equity are surveyed and a procedure for estimating the prospective equity premium implicit in current stock prices is presented. In addition, this chapter deals with a number of technical aspects such as the proper way of adjusting the cost of equity for leverage and the additional premium required by investors from small capitalization companies. An spreadsheet containing an Equity Premium Calculator is included in the enclosed Valuation Aids CD-ROM. It permits calculating the prospective equity premium weekly with generally available capital market data.

1.1.3   Valuation Multiples

Chapter 4 discusses the use of multiples in valuation. In particular, the use of EBITDA (earnings before interest taxes depreciation and amortization) multiples to complement and test the results of discounted cash-flow valuation. The spreadsheet Equivalent Multiple Calculator included in the Valuation Aids CD-ROM permits computing one type of multiple from another for a given set of company characteristics and to decompose multiples into their franchise and growth factors.

1.2   ECONOMIC VALUE ADDED

A number of firms around the world have adopted the economic value added (EVA)[1] approach to incentive compensation. This has led many of those companies to integrate their valuation methods with EVA accounting in order to follow a unified approach to investment decisions and managerial incentive compensation. Chapter 5 shows how to value companies by discounting yearly EVA in a way consistent with free cash-flow valuation and how to use the EVA approach for examining and testing the sources of value. The EVA approach is applied in Chapter 15 to the valuation of restructuring decisions.

1.3   VALUATION WITH CHANGING CAPITAL STRUCTURE

The assumption of constant leverage ratio commonly made and adopted in Chapter 2 is often not met in practice. Chapter 6 examines the valuation of firms with changing capital structure. It shows that valuations made by discounting cash flows at WACC with constant weights are quite robust to large fluctuations in the debt ratio. In addition, for those situations in which leverage departures from their initial values are persistent, Chapter 6 introduces alternative valuation procedures and discusses when the use of each of them is appropriate. These procedures are: 1) Adjusted present value (APV), and two extensions of it: compressed APV and recursive APV, and 2) an option-pricing model for the valuation of equity with uncertain debt retirement. Recursive APV and option pricing of equity can be made with the provided spreadsheet model HLF Value Calculator.

1.4   VALUATION IN DEVELOPED AND EMERGING MARKETS

Chapter 2 deals with the valuation of a domestic company in a developed capital market. The expansion of the global economy has made common need the valuation of foreign acquisitions. This requires dealing with the translation of foreign currency cash flows and the estimation of the relevant cost of capital. In addition, issues of high inflation and potential devaluation need to be addressed and, if the company is located in an emerging market, an allowance for country risk needs to be made. These issues are dealt with in Chapter 12, which provides the appropriate extension of the valuation model introduced in Chapter 2.

---

[1]EVA® is a registered trademark of Stern Stewart & Co.

1.5   MERGERS AND ACQUISITIONS

Those readers particularly interested in the structure and valuation of a merger transaction can go directly to Chapter 9 after having read Chapter 2.

Chapter 9 examines the analysis and valuation of mergers and acquisitions, including the legal form of the transactions and its accounting and tax treatments. It shows how to apply valuation tools and concepts to (a) estimating how the terms of the merger affect the shareholders of the bidder and the target, (b) estimating the value of expected synergies, and (c) testing the robustness of the assumptions upon which the transactions are predicated.

1.6   DEAL DESIGN AND SPECIAL OFFER STRUCTURES

The parties to a transaction often disagree about the value of the asset in question. Chapter 10 discusses contractual arrangements that allow the parties to agree to disagree by establishing that the final price of the transaction be contingent on the realization of certain performance values, such as the attainment of a level of revenue or EBITDA. These contractual arrangements are generally called earnouts and are properly conceptualized and valued as options. This chapter discusses a number of arrangements made in negotiating stakes in new ventures, buyouts and acquisitions and shows how to value them using option pricing techniques.

Chapter 11 examines in detail merger structures with price guarantees and collars and shows how to value them with option pricing techniques. (The software for this purpose is included in the Valuation Aids CD-ROM.)

1.7   LEVERAGED BUYOUTS

Readers interested in the structure and valuation of leveraged buyouts should refer to Chapter 7; Chapter 9, Sections 9.2 to 9.4; and Chapter 13. Chapter 7 provides an introduction to the concept of debt capacity and the relationship between growth and financing sources, as well as a detailed discussion of the concept of sustainable debt and its determination. In particular, it presents a model for estimating the debt capacity of a leveraged buyout or a leveraged recapitalization. Computation of debt capacity can be made with the Debt Capacity Calculator included in the Valuation Aids CD-ROM.

Chapter 9 deals with the legal form of acquisitions and its tax treatments. Further discussion of the financial structure and valuation of LBOs is made in Chapter 13, which deals with the determination of the financial sponsor's affordable bid and the estimation of the expected returns to the sponsor, management, and other suppliers of capital.

1.8   RECAPITALIZATION OF TROUBLED COMPANIES

Chapter 14 is a continuation of Chapter 13. Recapitalizing a distressed company is similar to structuring an LBO in the sense that both use all the debt capacity they can realistically manage and that the cash flow available to subordinated holders is in the distant future. Chapter 14 presents the basic framework for recapitalizations, discusses the options available in and out of court and examines their tax consequences. It shows how to carry out realistic analyses of debt capacity and how to value the several instruments offered in exchange for the existing claims, both of which are essential elements of any recapitalization plan.

1.9 ASSET RESTRUCTURING

Chapter 15 deals with sum-of-the-parts valuation and restructuring actions for increasing shareholder value and closing the value gap, including asset sales, spinoffs and carve-outs and shows how to use EVA concepts and valuation to develop a restructuring plan. This chapter applies many of the concepts and analyses developed in Chapter 9 and should be read after having studied the latter. It complements Chapter 14 because recapitalizations under distress often require sale of assets and restructuring operations.

1.10 REAL OPTIONS: VALUING ENTRY AND EXIT OPTIONS

As usually applied, the discounted cash flow approach fails to properly value the option to exit the business under poor realizations of cash flows or the option to further invest in the business when future conditions warrant it. Chapter 8 deals with the valuation of entry and exit options, as well as valuation of the option to establish a foothold in a potential market before deciding whether or not to carry out a full-scale expansion. This is done by applying option pricing theory. Chapter 8 presents the option pricing models and illustrates their application. In addition, it shows how to examine the robustness of the discounted cash flow (DCF) valuation in the presence of real options. Computing the value of real options can be carried out using the provided spreadsheets Real Option Calculators I and II.

1.10.1 Financial Options

In addition to the specialized models computed with the real option software, a number of real options can be valued by the direct application of models developed for the valuation of financial options. Appendix A reviews the valuation of a number of common financial options (European, American, and Asian calls, puts, warrants, and knock-out options) and illustrates their application and computation with the Financial Options Calculator included in the Valuation Aids CD-ROM.

1.11 TECHNICAL NOTES AND PROBLEMS

Chapter notes are collected at the end of the book. They deal with technical aspects, extensions, and proofs of some assertions made in the main text. Their study is not required to understand the main text or to successfully apply its valuations procedures. Most notes use simple algebra, with the exception of the notes to Chapter 8 and Appendix A, which require familiarity with differential calculus.

Review problems are included at the end of each chapter. They are meant to reinforce and complement the concepts presented in the main text. Solutions to selected problems are provided at the end of the book.

1.12 VALUATION AIDS

The enclosed CD-ROM contains Excel spreadsheets useful in valuation practice. The following calculators are included: equity premium, equivalent multiples, debt capacity, highly levered firm valuation, financial options, and real options I and II. They can be used to reproduce many of the calculations made in the book and so solve end-of-chapter problems. These calculators are described in Appendix B.

In addition, DealModeler[TM], an integrated financial modelling Excel workbook for preparing pro-forma financial statements and performing valuation of mergers, acquisitions, and leveraged buyouts is available for purchase from the publisher (ISBN 0-471-66660-2). The software is similar to those used by investment bankers and appraisal professionals and it contains the main valuation procedures described in this book. DealModeler[TM] is not required to reproduce the spreadsheets presented in the book or to apply its procedures.

Chapter 2

Forecasting and Valuation of Free Cash Flows

2.1 FREE CASH FLOWS

In this chapter, we study how to determine the value of a company or a business unit. By value we mean the price investors would be willing to pay in a competitive capital market. Pricing an asset is done by comparing its free cash flows to those derived from other assets of similar risk available to investors.[1]

Why do we find it necessary to refer to a cash flow that is "free"? In practice, the term cash flow has many uses. For example, accountants define the cash flow of a company as the sum of net income plus depreciation and other non-cash items that are subtracted in computing net income. However, that cash flow is not available for distribution to investors when the firm plans to reinvest all or part of it to replace equipment and finance future growth. Free cash flow is the cash available for distribution to investors after all planned capital investments and taxes.

The free cash flows generated by an enterprise can be decomposed into two components: (a) The after-tax cash flows corresponding to equity-holders and (b) the after-tax cash flows available to pay bond-holders. However, the aggregate magnitude of free cash flows is independent of the debt-equity mix adopted by the firm; the latter determines only the allocation of free cash flows among classes of security holders. In the following sections, we study how to estimate aggregate free cash flows and how to value them and their components.

2.2 BUILDING A FINANCIAL MODEL

Direct estimation of free cash flows can be made by projecting their individual components (such as operating income, depreciation, and capital expenditures) from current accounting data. A preferred alternative is to develop a financial model of the company made up of a complete set of pro-forma (forecast) financial statements: income statements, balance sheets, and cash-flow statements. This assures that the assumptions about the individual line items of the forecast are consistent with each other and permits a variety of analyses in addition to the computation of free cash flows.

---

[1]The groundwork for the valuation methodology presented in this chapter was laid out in Miller and Modigliani (1961). Joel Stern (1974, 1975) developed the practical implementations of this method and introduced the term "free cash flow." For an empirical analysis of free cash-flow valuation as a predictor of market value see Kaplan and Ruback (1995).

We now show how to create a financial model and derive its free cash flows. For this, we use a case based upon data from the paper industry. In December of 2002, a diversified paper company undergoing restructuring was considering the sale of its specialized packaging unit that we shall call Paktech International (PI). PI designed and manufactured high-performance packaging products, filters, pressboard, and circuit boards. PI could be attractive to another specialized paper product company or could stand on its own as an independent company.

The first step in forecasting free cash flows is to translate the business plan of the company into a set of pro-forma financial statements. PI's forecasting assumptions for the next 5 years are provided in Exhibit 2.1. The growth of dollar sales was expected to decrease from 8.5% in 2003 to 6% in 2007 and thereafter (about 3.5% real growth).[2] Initial growth was based upon an anticipated mild economic recovery and the elimination of excess capacity caused by industry consolidation, which was expected to increase volume and firm up prices. The long-term growth forecast recognized that industry consolidation would produce stronger competitors and a more challenging long-term environment for PI products.

EBITDA (earnings before interest, taxes, depreciation, and amortization) was expected to be about 14% of sales during the forecast period and beyond as the planned increase in selling expenses was to be offset by a decrease in the cost of goods sold. Fixed assets were projected to decrease from 43.2% of sales to 41.1% to reflect equipment upgrade and planned operating efficiencies. Book and tax depreciation were estimated accounting for the accelerated depreciation permitted for tax purposes by the U.S. Tax Code. Working capital assumptions were maintained at their historical levels, which were consistent with industry practice and PI's inventory policy. PI's financial policy was defined in terms of a target net debt ratio of 35%, expressed as the ratio of net debt to the market value of net debt and equity. Total debt was projected at about 2 times next year's EBITDA. Net debt was defined as interest-bearing liabilities minus cash and marketable securities. In addition, dividend distributions of excess cash were projected.

Exhibits 2.2 to 2.4 present the pro-forma income statements, balance sheets, and cash-flow statements, which follow directly from the forecasting assumptions contained in Exhibit 2.1. The reader is referred to Note N2.1 for details about the calculation of each line item.

The pro-forma financial statements provide the elements needed to compute the free cash flows available to all security holders. This is done in Exhibit 2.5. First, net interest expense after tax is added to net income to obtain unlevered net income, which is so named because it is the net income that would result if the company carried no debt. For example, the unlevered net income forecast for 2003 is:

$$\text{Unlevered Net Income}_{2003} = \text{Net Income}_{2003}$$
$$+ (1 - \text{Tax Rate}_{2003})(\text{Interest Expense}_{2003} - \text{Interest Income}_{2003})$$
$$= 8,950 + (1 - 40\%)(4,518 - 46) = 8,950 + 2,683 = \$11,633 \text{ million.}$$

This calculation eliminates the deduction of interest expense and its tax shield because net interest is part of the free cash flow corresponding to all the security holders.

---

[2]Dollar sales growth is made up of volume growth and price increases, the latter being at least in part due to inflation. The resulting projection is usually referred to as a "nominal" projection because it has embedded an inflation assumption. A "real" projection is one that expresses all future figures in dollars of constant purchasing power. It is usually preferred to make the projections in nominal terms and account for inflation through the discount rate, although it is possible to express the projections in real terms. Chapter 12 discusses the valuation of companies in high-inflation economies.

EXHIBIT 2.1	*Packtech International. Historical Data and Forecasting Assumptions*					

($000)	Historical	Forecast for Fiscal Years Ending 12/31				
	2002	2003	2004	2005	2006	2007
Operations:						
Unit Sales Growth	5.4%	6.1%	6.1%	5.6%	4.6%	3.6%
Price Growth	2.0%	2.3%	2.3%	2.3%	2.3%	2.3%
Growth Rate of Sales	7.5%	8.5%	8.5%	8.0%	7.0%	6.0%
Cost of Sales (Excl. Dep. & Amort.) as % of Sales	78.0%	78.0%	77.5%	77.5%	77.5%	77.5%
Sales, General & Administrative Exp. as % of Sales	7.1%	7.0%	7.0%	7.5%	7.5%	7.5%
Research & Development as % of Sales	0.9%	1.0%	1.0%	1.0%	1.0%	1.0%
EBITDA as % of Sales	14.0%	14.0%	14.5%	14.0%	14.0%	14.0%
Growth Rate	8.5%	8.5%	12.4%	4.3%	7.0%	6.0%
Capital Expenditures and Depreciation:						
Capital Expenditures (Net of Disposals)	16,100	18,964	23,568	23,874	24,965	26,524
Net Property, Plant & Equipment (PP&E)	92,243	98,153	106,772	113,114	119,548	126,469
% of Sales	43.19%	42.36%	42.47%	41.66%	41.14%	41.06%
Book Depreciation	12,268	13,054	14,948	17,533	18,530	19,603
% of Net PP&E	13.3%	13.3%	14.0%	15.5%	15.5%	15.5%
Tax Depreciation	13,467	14,330	16,016	18,438	19,486	20,614
% of Net PP&E	14.6%	14.6%	15.0%	16.3%	16.3%	16.3%
Working Capital:						
Cash Balance as % of Sales	1.6%	1.6%	1.6%	1.6%	1.6%	1.6%
Accounts Receivable as % of Sales	8.9%	8.9%	8.9%	8.9%	8.9%	8.9%
Days Receivable	32	32	32	32	32	32
Inventories as % of Cost of Sales	15.1%	15.1%	15.0%	15.0%	15.0%	15.0%
Inventory Days on hand	55	55	55	55	55	55
Other Current Assets as % of Sales	0.35%	0.35%	0.35%	0.35%	0.35%	0.35%
Accounts Payable as % of Cost of Sales	10.6%	10.8%	10.8%	10.8%	10.8%	10.8%
Days Payable	39	39	39	39	39	39
Accrued Expenses as % of Sales	1.15%	1.15%	1.15%	1.15%	1.15%	1.15%
Tax Payable as % of Current Income Tax	0.37%	0.37%	0.37%	0.37%	0.37%	0.37%
Other Current Liabilities as % of Sales	0.41%	0.41%	0.41%	0.41%	0.41%	0.41%
Debt, Interest, Dividends and Taxes:						
Short-term Debt & Curr. Portion of LTD as % of Total Debt	16.67%	16.67%	16.67%	16.67%	16.67%	16.67%
Total Debt as a Multiple of Next Year EBITDA	2.04	1.92	1.97	1.96	1.97	1.97
Interest Rate on Debt		6.84%	6.84%	6.84%	6.84%	6.84%
Interest Rate on Cash and Marketable Securities		1.35%	1.35%	1.35%	1.35%	1.35%
Dividends Paid	100% of excess cash and marketable securities					
Tax Rate on Income	40%	40%	40%	40%	40%	40%

| EXHIBIT 2.2 | *Packtech International. Pro-Forma Income Statements* |

($000)	Historical	Forecast for Fiscal Years Ending 12/31				
	2002	2003	2004	2005	2006	2007
Sales	213,580	231,734	251,432	271,546	290,554	307,988
Cost of Sales	166,592	180,753	194,860	210,448	225,180	238,691
Gross Profit	46,988	50,982	56,572	61,098	65,375	69,297
Sales, General & Administrative Expenses	15,164	16,221	17,600	20,366	21,792	23,099
Research & Development	1,922	2,317	2,514	2,715	2,906	3,080
EBITDA	29,901	32,443	36,458	38,016	40,678	43,118
Depreciation	12,268	13,054	14,948	17,533	18,530	19,603
EBIT	17,633	19,388	21,509	20,484	22,148	23,516
Interest Expense		4,518	4,791	5,132	5,468	5,803
Interest Income		46	50	54	59	63
Pretax Income		14,916	16,769	15,406	16,739	17,775
Current Income Tax		5,456	6,280	5,801	6,313	6,705
Deferred Tax		510	427	362	383	405
Net Income		8,950	10,061	9,244	10,043	10,665

| EXHIBIT 2.3 | *Packtech International, Inc. Pro-Forma Balance Sheets* |

($000)	Historical	Forecast for Fiscal Years Ending 12/31				
	2002	2003	2004	2005	2006	2007
Assets						
Current:						
Cash and Marketable Securities	3,417	3,708	4,023	4,345	4,649	4,928
Accounts Receivable	19,009	20,624	22,377	24,168	25,859	27,411
Inventories	25,158	27,294	29,229	31,567	33,777	35,804
Other Current Assets	752	816	885	956	1,023	1,085
Total Current Assets	48,337	52,442	56,515	61,036	65,308	69,227
Property, Plant & Equipment	129,496	148,460	172,028	195,902	220,866	247,390
Less: Depreciation	37,253	50,307	65,255	82,788	101,318	120,921
Net Property, Plant & Equipment	92,243	98,153	106,772	113,114	119,548	126,469
Other Noncurrent Assets:	9,352	9,352	9,352	9,352	9,352	9,352
Total Assets	149,931	159,947	172,639	183,502	194,209	205,048
Liabilities						
Current:						
Short-term Debt & Current Portion of LTD	11,008	11,673	12,503	13,321	14,139	14,988
Accounts Payable	17,659	19,521	21,045	22,728	24,319	25,779
Accrued Expenses	2,452	2,661	2,887	3,118	3,336	3,536
Taxes Payable	20	20	23	21	23	25
Other Current Liabilities	869	943	1,023	1,105	1,182	1,253
Total Current Liabilities	32,008	34,817	37,481	40,293	42,999	45,580
Long-term Debt	55,041	58,365	62,517	66,607	70,694	74,939
Deferred Income Taxes	1,209	1,719	2,146	2,508	2,891	3,296
Total Liabilities	88,258	94,902	102,144	109,408	116,584	123,815
Common Stock and Retained Earnings	61,674	65,045	70,495	74,093	77,624	81,234
Total Liabilities and Net Worth	149,931	159,947	172,639	183,502	194,209	205,048

EXHIBIT 2.4   *Packtech International. Pro-Forma Cash Flow Statements*

($000)	Historical 2002	2003	2004	2005	2006	2007
		Forecast for Fiscal Years Ending 12/31				
Funds from Operating Activities						
Net Income		8,950	10,061	9,244	10,043	10,665
Depreciation		13,054	14,948	17,533	18,530	19,603
Deferred Tax		510	427	362	383	405
Decrease (Increase) in Current Assets		(3,815)	(3,758)	(4,199)	(3,968)	(3,640)
Increase (Decrease) in Current						
Liabilities except Debt		2,145	1,833	1,995	1,888	1,732
Decrease (Increase) in Net Working Capital		(1,670)	(1,925)	(2,205)	(2,080)	(1,908)
Funds From Operations		20,845	23,511	24,934	26,876	28,765
Funds for Investment						
Capital Expenditures		18,964	23,568	23,874	24,965	26,524
Funds to (from) Financing						
Decrease (Increase) in Debt		(3,989)	(4,982)	(4,908)	(4,905)	(5,094)
Dividends		5,579	4,611	5,646	6,512	7,056
Total Funds to (from) Financing		1,590	(371)	738	1,607	1,962
Increase (Decrease) in Cash		290	315	322	304	279
End-of-Year Cash & Marketable						
Securities	3,417	3,708	4,023	4,345	4,649	4,928

EXHIBIT 2.5   *Paktech International. Enterprise Valuation as of 12/31/2002*

($000) Year-end	2002	2003	2004	2005	2006	2007
Net Income		8,950	10,061	9,244	10,043	10,665
Net Interest after Tax		2,683	2,845	3,047	3,245	3,444
Unlevered Net Income		11,633	12,906	12,290	13,289	14,109
Change in Deferred Taxes		510	427	362	383	405
NOPAT		12,143	13,333	12,652	13,671	14,514
Depreciation		13,054	14,948	17,533	18,530	19,603
Change in Net Working Capital		(1,670)	(1,925)	(2,205)	(2,080)	(1,908)
Capital Expenditures		(18,964)	(23,568)	(23,874)	(24,965)	(26,524)
Free Cash Flow		4,564	2,788	4,106	5,156	5,685

Valuation

WACC	8.48%			
PV{FCF} @	WACC	17,300		
Continuation Growth Rate	6.0%			
Continuation Value				242,855
PV{Continuation Value} @	WACC	161,648		
Enterprise Value		178,948		

Not accounting for the tax benefit from debt at this stage does not mean it is ignored. The tax shield of debt is accounted for in the cost of capital used to value free cash flows.

The next step is to add back changes in deferred taxes and depreciation because both are non-cash items that were subtracted in the computation of net income.

Deferred taxes are generated when, as under U.S. GAAP (Generally Accepted Accounting Principles) accounting, firms are permitted to choose a depreciation method for reporting purposes that can be different from the one allowed by the tax code. The latter usually permits accelerated depreciation, which may be faster than the estimated loss in the value of the assets. Using a slower depreciation schedule for financial reporting results in a higher reported income tax liability. The difference between the higher tax computed for reporting purposes and the actual tax liability is then booked as a deferred tax liability, which is to be reduced in the future if and when book depreciation exceeds tax depreciation.[3] Depreciation is subtracted for the purpose of determining taxable income, but it does not constitute a cash outlay because the latter occurred at the time of the purchase of the assets being depreciated.

Unlevered net income plus changes in deferred taxes gives net operating income after taxes (NOPAT). Free cash flow is obtained adding depreciation to NOPAT and subtracting planned capital expenditures (capex) and increases in net working capital.[4] PI's free cash flows (FCFs) for the years 2003 to 2007 are shown in Exhibit 2.5.

We further note that, since Net Income = (1 − Tax Rate) (EBIT − Net Interest Expense),

$$\text{Net Income} + \text{Net Interest Expense after Tax} = (1 - \text{Tax Rate})\text{EBIT},$$

which means that one can estimate unlevered net income starting from net income as in Exhibit 2.5 or starting from EBIT (Earnings Before Interest and Taxes). The first approach is commonly followed in practice because projections of financial statements usually precede valuation. Deriving free cash flow from net income is also more accurate when taxes are not proportional to EBIT as it is often in practice. The unlevered net income of Paktech can be derived from EBIT as follows:

($000)	2003	2004	2005	2006	2007
EBIT	19,388	21,509	20,484	22,148	23,516
Tax on EBIT @ 40%	7,755	8,604	8,194	8,859	9,406
Unlevered Net Income	11,633	12,906	12,290	13,289	14,109

2.3 ENTERPRISE VALUATION

A going concern would normally operate for many years beyond the period for which it is possible to make an explicit cash flow forecast. That is why, in practice, the approach followed in forecasting free cash flows is to divide the forecast into: (1) an initial period over which an explicit forecast is made, and (2) the estimation of the value of the going con-

---

[3]At that time, the excess of actual over accounting taxes will be offset with debits against deferred taxes. For a growing firm with continuous addition to depreciable assets subject to accelerated depreciation, accounting taxes will keep on exceeding actual taxes and the deferred taxes account will increase over time.

[4]Changes in net working capital do not include changes in cash and marketable securities. They are treated separately. See below on the definition of net debt and Section 2.6.3.

cern at the end of that period. The latter is usually referred to as the horizon value, terminal value, or continuation value. We shall call it "continuation value," except when it is planned to sell the business at the end of the forecast period, in which case we shall call it "exit value." The length of the forecast period is chosen somewhat arbitrarily, usually between 5 and 10 years. The purpose it to incorporate all the changes in the cash flow that cannot be assumed to follow a smooth pattern, such as significant lumpy capital expenditures and asset disposals, reductions of operating expenses, turn-around consequences, and/or atypical growth, and the effect of the economic cycle.

Because of competition and imitation, most firms tend to regress to the industry norm. Managers quickly adopt successful innovations made by competitors, and competitive advantage tends to be short-lived. In addition, the ability to forecast the future is limited, and the forecast quickly converges to growth assumptions based upon industry growth and the maintenance of market share. These assumptions are then built into a capitalization multiple or formula that is used to estimate continuation value.[5] Therefore, the value of future free cash flows is computed as follows:

Value of expected future free cash flows	=	Present value of free cash flows during explicit forecast period	+	Present value of continuation value at the end of explicit forecast period

The value of the enterprise is the present value of the free cash flows available to all security holders computed at the weighted average cost of capital (WACC) of the firm.[6] We shall refer to this valuation approach as the "enterprise method." Exhibit 2.5 applies the enterprise method to the valuation of Paktech International.

WACC is computed weighting the cost of equity and the after-tax cost of debt by the target debt and equity ratios, which in this case are 35 and 65%, respectively:[7]

$$\text{WACC} = \frac{(1-t)rD + kS}{D + S} = (1 - 40\%)(7.15\%)(35\%) + (10.74\%)(65\%) = 8.48\% \quad (2.1)$$

where D and S stand for the values of net debt and equity, D/(D + S) is the target debt ratio, r is the cost of net debt, and k is the cost of equity. The cost of net debt is computed after tax in order to capture the tax shield resulting from the tax deductibility of interest expense, which is not accounted for in the free cash flows. The cost of net debt of Pakteck was 7.15% before taxes, and the tax rate was 40%.[8,9] Equation (2.1) is an approximation to the yearly cost of capital because initial and future debt ratios are likely to depart from the target. Fluctuations of the debt ratio about its target have a small effect on enterprise value because changes in the tax shield over time tend to offset each other. Significant, persistent departures from a target debt ratio can have a material effect on enterprise value and require special treatment. This is done in Chapter 6.

---

[5]Chapter 4 contains a detailed discussion of capitalization multiples and formulas.

[6]A formal justification if this statement is provided in Note N2.3.

[7]Numbers do not add up because of rounding.

[8]The cost of net debt is estimated as the average net interest expense during the forecast period ($5,088 million) divided by average net debt ($71,145 million).

[9]The marginal tax rate of a corporation can be substantially lower than the statutory rate. See Graham (1996), and Graham, Lemmon, and Schallheim (1998). DeAngelo and Masulis (1980) noted that the ability of the firm to shelter income by borrowing is reduced by the use of other tax shields such as accelerated depreciation. Also, some tax systems allow for partial deduction of interest on equity for tax purposes, see Section 2.6.2.

The several approaches available for estimating the cost of equity are discussed in detail in Chapter 3, including a justification of the procedure used in this book. A summary of the computation of Paktech's cost of equity follows. The cost of equity is computed using a two-factor model that allows for a premium for the nondiversifiable risk of the company and a premium for its small size, itself a proxy for reduced liquidity. That is,

$$k_{paktech} = \text{Return on a riskless asset} + \text{Market equity premium} \times \beta + \text{Size premium}$$

The yield of the 10-year Treasury note measures the return required by investors from a relatively safe asset, including a premium for expected inflation. As of 12/17/02, the yield on 10-year-Treasury note was 4.07%. The second term measures the premium required by investors from a large capitalization company. It is made up of the premium required from a well-diversified portfolio (the market equity premium) scaled by a coefficient β, which measures the contribution of the stock to the risk (variance) of such a diversified portfolio. The prospective market equity premium implied in the level of the Standard & Poor's 500 (S&P 500) index and consensus growth expectations as of 12/17/02 was about 5.08%. The β coefficient of Paktech is based upon comparable companies, that is, specialized paper product companies of similar size. This value, adjusted for the degree of leverage planned for Paktech, is $\beta = 0.706$. Finally, Paktech's small size makes it subject to an additional premium to account for its reduced liquidity.[10] Firms of Paktech's size have historically been subject to an additional premium of about 3.08%.

Putting these numbers together yields Paktech's cost of equity:

$$k_{Paktech} = 4.07\% + (5.08\%)(0.706) + 3.08\% = 10.74\%$$

The present adjustment for size assumes that the company is going to trade on its own via an IPO. A strategic buyer would impart it own liquidity to the cash flow of the acquisition and may not require a size premium. On the other hand, a private equity buyer would assume more illiquidity and demand a higher cost of equity.[11]

The expected free cash flows to all security holders for the years 2003 to 2007 are discounted back to the beginning of fiscal year 2003 at 8.48%. The reader should verify that the present value of the 2003 to 2007 free cash flows PV{FCF} equals $17,300 million. The next step is to value the going concern as of year-end 2007.

Here, we are going to assume that Paktech will continue to grow at an average (nominal) rate of 6% per year for the indefinite future, such that the continuation value (CV) of the enterprise at the end of year 2006 can be determined by a constant growth perpetuity (more on continuation value in the next section):

$$CV = \frac{FCF_{2007}(1 + g)}{WACC - g} = \frac{(5.685)(1.06)}{0.0848 - 0.06} = \$242.855 \text{ million} \qquad (2.2)$$

where $FCF_{2007} = \$5.685$ million is the free cash flow in year 2007, and $g = 6\%$ is the growth rate of the cash flows. Adding the present value of continuation value $(242.855)/(1.0848)^5 = \$161.648$ million to the present value of the 2003 to 2007 free cash flows yields $178.948 million as the value of the enterprise.

To obtain the value of equity one subtracts outstanding net debt from the enterprise value. Recall that net debt equals interest-bearing liabilities minus cash and marketable

---

[10]The size premium is a proxy for a number of factors in addition to reduced liquidity, including underestimation of the beta coefficient of small companies and the effect of the return on human capital. The nature and estimation of the size premium is discussed in Chapter 3, Sections 3.6 and 3.7.

[11]The cost of capital in private equity transactions is examined in Chapter 13, Section 9.6.

securities. Cash and marketable securities are not valued by discounting free cash flows because interest income is not part of EBITDA and FCF. Cash and marketable securities are most properly considered as an offset to outstanding debt.[12] PI's net debt at the beginning of 2003 was $62.632 million. Hence,

$$\text{Value of Equity} = \text{Enterprise Value} - \text{Value of Net Debt}$$
$$= \$178.948 - \$62.632 = \$116.316 \text{ million.}$$

*2.4 CONTINUATION VALUE[13]

2.4.1 Forecast Consistency

One important requirement in the estimation of continuation value is consistency between the forecast for $T + 1$, the first year after the explicit forecast period, and the assumed long-term growth rate. Hopefully, the end of the explicit forecast has converged toward the free cash flow that corresponds to the steady-state growth assumed in the computation of continuation value, but this may not be so if a significant decrease in the growth rate is assumed after the explicit forecast period. In particular, lower growth implies lower net investment and higher free cash flow. Whenever $FCF_T(1 + g)$ does not provides a good estimate of FCF_{T+1}, a normalized estimate is required to take into account the net investment (capital expenditures and increases in working capital in excess to depreciation) needed to support the assumed growth rate.

A simple way to control for consistency is based upon the return on capital (ROC) on new investment. While obtaining a precise estimate of the rate of return on new investment to take place several years ahead is difficult, an estimate of future ROC is required to arrive to the growth forecast because only investments expected to yield a positive spread of ROC over WACC should be planned for. In order to obtain the relation between FCF, growth, and ROC, let us express FCF in terms of its determinants: NOPAT, net investment, and growth as done in Miller and Modigliani's (1961) original contribution. Denote net investment by ΔC.

Furthermore, since it seems reasonable to assume that after the explicit forecast period the company will maintain approximately constant asset turnover ratio (asset/sales) and NOPAT margin (NOPAT/sales), ΔC becomes a constant fraction of NOPAT. Denote it $b = \Delta C/NOPAT$, usually referred to as the plowback ratio. Before proceeding we warn the reader that introducing ROC into the analysis can lead to error if the effect of inflation is not properly taken into account.

For example, it may appear natural to conclude that under the stated assumptions

$$FCF_t = NOPAT_t - \Delta C_t = (1 - b)NOPAT_t \tag{2.3}$$

and

$$NOPAT_t = NOPAT_{t-1} + (ROC)bNOPAT_{t-1} = (1 + bROC)NOPAT_{t-1} \tag{2.4}$$

which means that the growth rate of NOPAT and FCF is $g = bROC$. It would then follow that one can test the consistency of the FCF forecast with the assumed rate of growth by calculating the ROC implied by the continuation value given by Equation (2.2) and comparing it to the ROC expected from new investments. For example, substituting Paktech's forecast into the solution for ROC from Equations (2.3) and (2.4) yields:

---

[12]Balance sheet adjustments, including the adjustment for cash and marketable securities are discussed in Sections 2.6.2 and 2.6.3.

[13]Sections marked with an asterisk may be skipped on a first reading.

$$FCF_{2007} = 5.685 \text{ million}, \quad NOPAT_{2007} = 14.514 \text{ million}, \quad g = 6\%$$
$$ROC = g \div (1 - FCF_T/NOPAT_T) = 0.06 \div (1 - 5.685/14.514) = 9.86\%$$

In words, expecting that free cash flows grow at 6% after the explicit forecast period requires that future investment opportunities yield approximately 9.86%. However, this is not correct! In fact, the correct ROC on future investment is just 8.38%, a really big difference.

The problem with the plowback growth expression g = bROC is that is only correct when both g and ROC are expressed in real terms (that is, dollars of a given year that have constant purchasing power). The reason is that Equation (2.4) does not take into account that $NOPAT_{t-1}$ will grow at the rate of the inflation without further *net* investment. $NOPAT_t$ is made up of last year's earnings inflated by inflation plus the return on new net investment. That is, the proper expression of $NOPAT_t$ when the inflation rate i > 0 is

$$NOPAT_t = NOPAT_{t-1}(1 + i) + ROC^R bNOPAT_{t-1}(1 + i) \tag{2.5}$$

where ROC^R is the *real* return on capital. Note that $ROC = (1 + ROC^R)(1 + i) - 1$ or $ROC^R = (ROC - i)/(1 + i)$. Substituting this last expression into Equation (2.5) yields

$$NOPAT_t = NOPAT_{t-1}(1 + i) + (ROC - i)/(1 + i)bNOPAT_{t-1}(1 + i)$$
$$= (1 + bROC - bi + i)NOPAT_{t-1}$$

which means that the correct *nominal* rate of growth of NOPAT is g = bROC − bi + i, not bROC.[14] Hence, taking into account that inflation is projected at i = 2.3% in Exhibit 2.1, the correct nominal ROC implied by the valuation made in Equation (2.2) is

$$ROC = [g + i(1 - FCF_T/NOPAT_T) - i] \div (1 - FCF_T/NOPAT_T)$$
$$= [(0.06 + (0.023)(1 - 5.685/14.514) - 0.023] \div (1 - 5.685/14.514)$$
$$= 8.38\% \text{ not } 9.86\%$$

And the correct conclusion is that expecting that free cash flows grow at 6% after the explicit forecast period requires that future investment opportunities yield approximately 8.38% nominal or (8.38% − 2.3%)/1.023 = 5.94% real. If the expected ROC is lower than 8.38%, either planned investment needs to be higher than b = (g − i)/(ROC − i) = (6% − 2.3) ÷ (8.38% − 2.3%) = 61% of NOPAT or the growth rate needs to be lower than 6%.

A way to salvage the plowback formula is to recognize that it applies only when the analysis is carried out in real terms and write it as $g^R = bROC^R$. In particular, it applies in its simple form when inflation is zero for which nominal and real terms are the same. For example, let us use this expression to calculate the implied real return on capital in real terms:

$$ROC^R = g^R \div (1 - FCF_T/NOPAT_T) = [(g - i)/(1 + i)] \div (1 - FCF_T/NOPAT_T)$$
$$= (6\% - 2.3\%)/(1.023) \div (1 - 5.685/14.514) = 3.62\% \div 0.6083 = 5.95\%$$

such that ROC = (1.0595)(1.023) − 1 = 8.38% as calculated before.

Instead of testing the assumed growth rate via the implied return on capital, we can begin with a forecast of g^R and ROC^R, estimate $b = g^R/ROC^R$ and substitute b into Equation (2.3) to obtain[15]

$$FCF_T = (1 - g^R/ROC^R)NOPAT_T. \tag{2.6}$$

---

[14]See Bradley and Jarrell (2003) for a detailed derivation of the correct nominal rate of growth of NOPAT.

[15]This approach is recommended by Copeland, Koller, and Murrin (2000) although these authors use b = g/ROC with g and ROC expressed in nominal terms.

For example, for Paktech $FCF_{2007} = (1 - 3.62\%/5.95\%)(14.514) = \$5.684$ million. However, this would make the continuation value entirely dependent on the estimate of the future ROC^R. In practice, a combination of both approaches works best: Start with a careful projection of normalized income, accounting and tax depreciation, capital expenditures, and changes in working capital that correspond to the projected long-term growth rate, and compare the resulting FCF to that produced by Equation (2.6).

2.4.2   Sensitivity to Parameter Estimates

Misestimation of growth, profit margins or the cost of capital can have significant effects on the estimated value of the enterprise. Value is particularly sensitive to the growth rate assumed to hold after the explicit forecast period because continuation value commonly accounts for a large percentage of the enterprise value and more so when, as in the case of Paktech, the explicit forecast period is only 5 years long. This is so because the length of the latter determines how much future value is to be accounted by the continuation value. The sensitivity of Paktech's enterprise value to changes in WACC and the continuation growth rate is shown in Exhibit 2.6.[16]

These results can be verified by changing WACC and the growth rate in Exhibit 2.5. While the sensitivity of value to changes in WACC is significant, the most pronounced changes correspond to changes in the growth rate, which should be tested for consistency with the long-term growth rate of the industry and the attainable market share of the firm.

In practice, some companies control for excessive optimism in forecasting long-term growth by assuming no real growth after the explicit forecast period but making the latter long enough to capture the growth than can be reasonable expected. One food company uses a forecast period of 10 years in valuing potential acquisitions.

Afterwards, it assumes no further real growth (free cash flows grow at the rate of inflation). The rationale for choosing 10 years is that the first 5 years are likely to be years of investment to develop the acquisition and establish a market position and will not produce the long-term profitability that justifies the acquisition. The second half of the forecast period is the one in which the company should begin to reap the benefits from growth and an established market position. The target is not considered worthwhile if the growth attained over the 10 years is not sufficient to justify the cost of the acquisition.

Growth affects value when the firm is expected to maintain its ROC above WACC beyond the explicit forecast period, but it has no effect on value when future investment merely breaks even. This is taken into account in the following specifications of continuation value. Additional analysis of the effect of growth on enterprise value is made in Section 2.7.

EXHIBIT 2.6	*Paktech International Value Matrix ($000)*		
		Growth Rate	
	5.0%	6.0%	7.0%
8.00%	152,961	222,609	431,552
WACC 8.48%	131,430	178,948	290,614
9.00%	114,047	147,611	214,738

---

[16]The interpretation of sensitivity analyses is discussed in Chapter 9.

2.4.3 Competitive Advantage Period

In his pioneering work on free cash-flow valuation, Joel Stern (1974) proposed defining a time horizon, H, over which the market has confidence that ROC > WACC and after which ROC = w, such that further growth creates no value and is irrelevant. Stern's horizon H can be interpreted as the period of competitive advantage, over which the company may be expected to grow and generate returns in excess to its cost of capital.[17]

When the explicit forecast ends at T = H, continuation value is obtained substituting $ROC^R = WACC^R$ in Equation (2.6) and that expression into Equation (2.2). Taking into account that $WACC - g = (WACC^R - g^R)(1 + i)$, we can write Equation (2.2) for the break-even case as follows:

$$CV = \frac{(1 - g^R/WACC^R)NOPAT_{T+1}}{(WACC^R - g^R)(1 + i)} = \frac{NOPAT_{T+1}}{WACC^R(1 + i)} = \frac{NOPAT_{T+1}}{WACC - i} \quad (2.7)$$

which is independent of the rate of growth of NOPAT.

There is much confusion in the literature and valuation practice about how to value the enterprise in the break-even case. Note that if i = 0, continuation value equals $NOPAT_{T+1}/WACC$, but this formula is commonly recommended and applied when inflation is positive leading to a significant underestimation of value because it implies that real free cash flows decrease at the rate i, which often is not the intended forecast.[18]

An alternative to the assumption that the firm breaks even at the end of the explict forecast T is that positive spread continues for a number of years until H > T such that the firm earns $ROC^R > WACC^R$ and grows at g^R, then

$$CV = \sum_{t=1,H-T}\left[\frac{(1 - g^R/ROC^R)NOPAT_T(1 + g^R)^t}{(1 + WACC^R)^t}\right] + \frac{NOPAT_T(1 + g^R)^{H-T+1}}{(1 + WACC^R)^{H-T}WACC^R}$$

$$= (1 - g^R/ROC^R)NOPAT_T\frac{(1 + g^R)}{(WACC^R - g^R)}\left[1 - \frac{(1 + g^R)^{H-T}}{(1 + WACC^R)^{H-T}}\right] \quad (2.8)$$

$$+ \frac{NOPAT_T(1 + g^R)^{H-T+1}}{(1 + WACC)^{H-T}WACC^R}$$

The working of this expression cannot be illustrated with the case of Paktech because it is assumed to essentially break even immediately after T. Note that $ROC^R =$ 5.95% ≈ $WACC^R$ = (8.48% – 2.45%)/1.0245 = 5.89%.[19] Instead, assume that its WACC is only 7.65% or $WACC^R$ = 5.08% and that the company is expected to maintain ROC^R = 5.95% during 10 years after the explicit forecast period such that T = 2007 and H = 2017 and that $ROC^R = WACC^R$ = 5.08 afterwards. Furthermore, let NOPAT grow at g^R = 3.62% through 2018, then continuation value would equal

$$CV = (1 - 0.0362/0.0595)(14.514)\frac{(1.0362)}{(0.0508 - 0.0362)}\left[1 - \frac{(1.0362)^{10}}{(1.0508)^{10}}\right]$$

$$+ \frac{14.514(1.0362)^{11}}{(1.0508)^{10}(0.0508)} = \$309.7 \text{ million.}$$

---

[17]We examine competitive advantage and value creation in Chapter 5.

[18]See Bradley and Jarrell (2003) for more on this confusion and its implications.

[19]While NOPAT grows at the rate of Paktech's price growth, WACC is corrected at the inflation rate of the economy that is the compensation demanded by investors. The consensus long-term inflation forecast was 2.45% in December 2002.

EXHIBIT 2.7	*Paktech International Implied EBITDA Multiples from Continuation Value Estimates*		

		Growth Rate		
		5.0%	6.0%	7.0%
	8.00%	4.4	6.6	13.2
WACC	8.48%	3.8	5.3	8.9
	9.00%	3.3	4.4	6.6

This value is intermediate between $295.9 million, the continuation value when break-even is attained at the end of the explicit forecast period T, and $401.7 million, the value when the spread $ROC^R - WACC^R = 5.95\% - 5.08\% = 0.87\%$ persists forever.

2.4.4   EBITDA Multiples

A common approach used in practice to gauge continuation value is to combine DCF with valuation multiples. Exhibit 2.7 shows the EBITDA multiple implied by the continuation value resulting from combinations of WACC and the growth rate.

The EBITDA multiple is computed dividing continuation value by the EBITDA forecasted for year 2008 at the assumed growth rate.[20] The intersection of WACC = 8.48% and growth = 6% implies an EBITDA multiple equal to 5.3x. This value can be compared to the multiples implied by the market values of other "comparable" companies to determine the reasonability of the assumed valuation inputs. Future multiples will depend on the state of the economy and the industry at the time but a large discrepancy of the implied EBITDA multiple from the current industry average would require justifying and further proving the valuation assumptions in addition to verifying that the discrepancy is not just caused by different accounting practices.

2.5   AN EQUIVALENT APPROACH: VALUING THE CASH FLOW TO EQUITY

2.5.1   Decomposition of Free Cash Flows: Cash Flows to Equity and Debt

We now proceed to decompose the free cash flows into two components and to value each of them separately. In Exhibit 2.8, we derive the cash flows corresponding to equity-holders from the pro-forma income statements. They are obtained adding to net income non-cash items, subtracting capital expenditures and increases in net working capital, and adding the increase in debt, which it is a source of cash for equity-holders.

The net after-tax cash flow to bond-holders is computed next. For valuation purposes, it is simpler to compute all cash flows on an after-tax basis. Thus, the firm is seen as paying bond-holders after-tax interest minus the increase in debt (although bond-holders receive pre-tax interest). The sum of the equity and debt components of the free cash flows is shown on the last line of Exhibit 2.8. Note that it equals the free cash flows

---

[20]The multiples of Exhibit 2.7 are called *forward* multiples as opposed to *trailing* multiples. The latter are based upon last-year earnings. Valuation multiples and their application to the valuation of Paktech are discussed in Chapter 4.

| EXHIBIT 2.8 | *Paktech International. Free Cash Flow Decomposition* |

($000)

	2003	2004	2005	2006	2007
Net Income	8,950	10,061	9,244	10,043	10,665
Depreciation	13,054	14,948	17,533	18,530	19,603
Deferred Tax	510	427	362	383	405
Decrease in Net Working Capital	(1,670)	(1,925)	(2,205)	(2,080)	(1,908)
Capital Expenditures	(18,964)	(23,568)	(23,874)	(24,965)	(26,524)
Increase in Net Debt	3,699	4,667	4,586	4,601	4,815
Cash Flow to Equity-holders	5,579	4,611	5,646	6,512	7,056
Net Interest after Tax	2,683	2,845	3,047	3,245	3,444
Increase in Net Debt	(3,699)	(4,667)	(4,586)	(4,601)	(4,815)
Cash Flow Paid to Debt-holders, After Tax	(1,015)	(1,822)	(1,540)	(1,356)	(1,371)
Free Cash Flow to All Security-holders	4,564	2,788	4,106	5,156	5,685

computed in Exhibit 2.5. In fact, by construction, the sum of the cash flows corresponding to equity-holders and bond-holders always adds up to the free cash flow of the enterprise.

2.5.2 Equity Valuation

The valuation of the cash flows corresponding to equity-holders (to be referred to as the "equity method") is presented in Exhibit 2.9. First, the expected cash flows to equity holders for the years 2003 to 2007 that were computed in Exhibit 2.8 are discounted back to the present at the cost of equity to the firm, that is, at 10.74% (not at WACC!). The reader should verify that the present value of the 2002 to 2007 cash flows is $21.523 million. The next step is to value the going concern as of year-end 2007. Here, as in Section 2.2, it is assumed that Paktech will continue to grow at an average nominal rate of 6% per year for the indefinite future, such that its equity value can be estimated by the constant-growth perpetuity:

$$CV = \frac{CF_{2007}(1 + g)}{k - g} = \frac{(\$7.056)(1.06)}{0.1074 - 0.06} = \$157.856 \text{ million}$$

where CF_{2007} = $7.056 million is the cash flow to equity in year 2007, g = 6% is the growth rate of the cash flows, and k = 10.74% is the cost of equity. The value of equity is

| EXHIBIT 2.9 | *Paktech International. Equity Valuation as of 12/31/2002* |

($000)

	2002	2003	2004	2005	2006	2007
Free Cash Flow to Equity		5,579	4,611	5,646	6,512	7,056
Cost of Equity	10.74%					
Continuation Value Growth Rate	6.0%					
Continuation Value						157,856
PV of Equity Cash Flows	21,523					
PV of Continuation Value	94,793					
Equity Value	116,316					

attained by adding the present value of the continuation value $157.856/(1.1074)^5 =$ $94.793 million to the present value of the 2003 to 2007 cash flows. This gives $116.316 million.

2.5.3   Debt Valuation

The valuation of cash flow corresponding to debt-holders is presented in Exhibit 2.10. The cash flows are expressed in terms of the net after-tax cash payments made by the firm to debt-holders. The cash flows for the years 2003 to 2007 and the net debt balance in 2007 were computed in Exhibits 2.8 and 2.3, respectively.

Note that the value of net debt is the initial net debt in year 2003. This is because future debt changes have zero net present value.[21] Hence, the value of net debt is simply the initial net debt.[22] Adding the value of net debt to the value of equity gives the value of the enterprise:

$$\text{EV} = \text{Value of Equity} + \text{Value of Net Debt}$$
$$= 116.316 + 62.632 = \$178.948 \text{ million.}$$

This is the value obtained via the valuation of the aggregate free cash flows made in Exhibit 2.5. Hence, valuing the aggregate free cash flows at WACC and valuing their components at their respective discount rates are equivalent valuation procedures. This will always be so as long as the same financial policy (debt ratio) is assumed in both calculations.[23]

2.5.4   Financial Policy and Dividends

Cash flows are distributed to equity holders via dividends and share repurchases. Exhibit 2.4 shows that Paktech planned to distribute $5,579 million to equity holders in 2003 as dividends such that retained earnings would equal $8,950 − 5,579 = \$3,371$ million. In practice, companies follow rather stable dividend policies and do not adjust dividend payout to short-term variations of their cash flows. Changes in retained earnings and share repurchases make the difference. The valuation model implicitly assumes that if the firm

---

EXHIBIT 2.10   *Paktech International. Net Debt Valuation as of 12/31/2002*

($000)

	2002	2003	2004	2005	2006	2007
Free Cash Flow to Net Debt		(1,015)	(1,822)	(1,540)	(1,356)	(1,371)
Cost of Net Debt After Taxes	4.29%					
Net Debt Balance in 2007						84,999
PV of Net Debt Cash Flows	(6,263)					
PV of Net Debt Balance	68,895					
Net Debt Value	62,632					

---

[21]This is shown in Note N2.2. It is also shown there that the value of the cash flow received by debt-holders valued at the pre-tax rate interest rate is also equal to the value of the initial debt.

[22]Note, however, that when the coupon rate is below or above the cost of debt, the value of debt is below or above its face value and it needs to be marked to market.

[23]See Note N2.2 for a proof.

pays out less than its available cash flow, the funds retained are invested in nonspecified zero-net present value projects financed with the same debt ratio assumed in the valuation. If the firm expects to be able to reinvest free cash flows in additional positive net present value projects, the original valuation is incomplete should be revised. Alternatively, if the firm plans dividends in excess to the cash flows corresponding to equity, it would need to issue debt and/or equity. The latter actions have zero net present value and would not alter the valuation results if the firm stays within its target debt ratio. Additional borrowing without an increase in equity would move the firm away from its target debt ratio. As noted in Section 2.3, temporary departures will not materially affect the valuation results and are to be expected in practice. They produce small changes in the tax shield that tend to offset with each other as the debt ratio fluctuates around its target. On the other hand, permanent departures from the original target debt ratio imply a different financial policy and require a readjustment of the valuation model.

When valuing a business unit, the cash flow to equity generated by the unit is the *net* cash flow effectively transferred to headquarters. Actually, the unit normally transfers the cash flow before taxes to headquarters, and headquarters takes care of taxes and financial transactions such as borrowing and paying interest. Net, headquarters retains the cash flow accruing to equity, which can be thought of as an intercompany dividend.

2.6 SOME PRACTICAL ASPECTS

2.6.1 Choosing the Valuation Method

Although mathematically equivalent, the enterprise method offers a number of advantages over the equity method and, with some exceptions, is the preferred method in practice. Some of the advantages of the enterprise method are:

- It explicitly values the assets under management.
- It can be naturally applied to valuation of the firm as a whole and to its individual businesses.
- It is consistent with the capital budgeting procedures used by most corporations. In fact, the value of the enterprise can be thought of as the aggregate value of all its activities.
- It is simpler to implement, in particular with respect to the implication of the financial policy of the firm, which is subsumed in the WACC.
- It is consistent with economic value-added valuation and incentive compensation schemes. And, as such, it can be more easily linked to the drivers of value creation.[24]

Free cash flows can be discounted at the after-tax WACC or at the pre-tax WACC. The first approach is the one used in practice and developed in this chapter. Discounting at pre-tax WACC requires defining free cash flows as the cash flows *received* by security holders, which should include pre-tax interest payments. Note N2.3 shows that both methods give the same result.

The equity method is particularly useful in valuing financial institutions for which equity is a small fraction of the assets, and small errors in estimating the value of the latter would have a disproportionate impact on the value of equity.[25] The enterprise method

---

[24]The economic value added approach to valuation is discussed in Chapter 5.

[25]The valuation of banks and insurance companies is discussed in Copeland et al. (2000).

based on WACC can lead to erroneous valuations when the capital structure changes over time. For those cases an alternative method called "adjusted present value" is studied in Chapter 6.

The cost of capital should be applied to discounting *expected* free cash flows. The expectation should allow for the probability of downside realizations of cash flows, and these should not be taken into account in the cost of capital. Doing a casual "most likely" estimation of free cash flows and increasing the cost of capital to account for downside cash-flow risk is not recommended. In enterprise valuation, there is no substitute for a careful study of the possible scenarios faced by the company and their cash-flow consequences.

*2.6.2 Personal Taxes and Enterprise Value

So far we have ignored the effect of personal taxes on asset values. This is the correct approach when the tax rates on personal income from debt and equity are the same or income is effectively not taxed. The latter would happen if the price-setting investors, that is, the marginal investors, faced the same rates on income from stock and debt or are tax-exempt institutions or individuals who offset dividend income with interest expense or use one of the several tax-deferral vehicles allowed by the U.S. tax code to postpone tax on dividend and interest income.[26] However, the empirical evidence on the effect of personal taxes on asset values is ambiguous and does not allow ignoring personal taxes off-hand. We show in Note N2.5 that WACC discounting is still valid when personal taxes affect asset prices but that the cost of equity needs to recognize the effect of personal taxes on capital income as follows

$$k = \frac{(1 - t_B)}{(1 - t_S)}r_f + \beta[R_m - \frac{(1 - t_B)}{(1 - t_S)}r_f] \tag{2.9}$$

where t_B is the personal tax rate on interest income, t_S is the personal tax rate on stock income,[27] r_f is the riskless rate of interest, and R_m is the expected return on the market portfolio.[28] Equation (2.9) would result in a lower (greater) cost of equity than $r_f + \beta(R_m - r_f)$ depending on if β is lower (greater) than one. Note that this relation has to do with a measurement problem and not with the economics of a change in the tax law. A reduction of the tax on dividends will unequivocally decrease the cost of capital, but Equation (2.9) simply recognizes personal taxes under an existing tax regime that has already affected the return on the market portfolio.

The problem with estimating Equation (2.9) is that the values of t_B and t_S for the marginal investors are not known. Casual observation suggests that t_B is much lower than the statutory rate on income. For example, in January 2003, 10-year AAA-rated tax exempt municipal bonds traded at 3.76% while 10-year Treasury notes traded at 4.06%. This suggests that marginal investors were indifferent between $(1 - t_B)(4.06\%)$ and 3.76%, or that $t_B \approx 7.6\%$, but the higher yields of municipals may be caused, in part, by their lesser liquidity. The implied tax rate varies with maturities and over time. In fact, in January 2003, 2-year municipals traded at 1.54% versus 1.74% for 2-year Treasuries, which implied $t_B \approx 11.5\%$. Performing this last calculation over the last 2 years yields values between 10 and

---

[26]See Miller and Scholes (1978) and Hamada and Scholes (1985).

[27]As in Miller (1977), t_S is defined as the effective tax rate that would produce the same present value of tax payments as the actual taxes.

[28]Valuation under different tax regimes is treated in Sick (1990) and Taggart (1991).

20%. Let us assume $t_B \approx 20\%$. To estimate t_S, note that the payout ratio of the S&P 500 in January 2003 was 51%, close to its long-term average and that capital gains were taxed at 20% at that time. Since capital gains are taxed only when realized, a 10-year deferral would reduce their present value to about half. Therefore, t_S for the marginal investors would be about $(20\%)(0.51) + (10\%)(0.49) \approx 15.1\%$.[29]

Using the above estimates we obtain $(1 - t_B)/(1 - t_S) \approx (1 - 20\%)/(1 - 15.1\%) = 94\%$. Substituting this value into Equation (2.9) gives the following estimates of Paktech's after-personal-tax cost of equity and WACC:

$$k_{Paktech} = (0.94)(4.07\%) + [9.15\% - (0.94)(4.07\%)](0.706) + 3.08\% = 10.66\%$$
$$WACC_{Paktech} = (1 - 40\%)(7.15\%)(35\%) + (10.66)(65\%) = 8.43\%.$$

That is, allowing for personal taxes in the present case and under the 2002 U.S. tax law decreases the cost of equity from 10.74 to 10.66% and WACC from 8.48 to 8.43%. This adjustment has a small effect on the valuation results. Substituting 8.43% for WACC in Exhibit 2.5 yields an enterprise value equal to $182.8 million and an equity value equal to $182.8 − $62.6 = $120.2 million, which are 2.2% and 3.4% higher than the values calculated in Section 2.3. The reader may find these results counterintuitive. Personal taxes, being higher on income from bonds than on income from stock, make the tax shield of debt less attractive. Therefore, it would seem that since the tax shield is actually worth less the value of the firm should decrease.

However, even without the adjustment made in Equation (2.9), WACC recognizes that the tax shield is worth less because investors gross up the cost of debt to account for the higher taxes they pay on interest received. On the other hand, although investors take into account that the return on equity is taxed at a lower effective rate and value equity accordingly, the cost of equity and WACC calculated in Section 2.3 do not recognize the lower after-tax return on equity that investors demand from Paktech. This is done by Equation (2.9).

In May 2003, the U.S. Congress reduced the tax rates on both dividends and long-term capital gains to 15%.[30] That change should produce portfolio reallocations and adjustments on taxable and tax-exempt interest income, as well as changes in the identity of the marginal investors. Let us gauge the effect of the rates reduction on the cost of capital letting $r_B \approx 15\%$, the present value of the rate on capital gains to be about 7.5%, and $r_S \approx (15\%)(0.51) + (7.5\%)(0.49) = 11.33\%$. Hence, $(1 - t_B)/(1 - t_S) \approx (1 - 15\%)/(1 - 11.33\%) = 95.9\%$ in Equation (2.9). In addition, the before-personal taxes required return on the market and the size premium should decrease by about $100\% - (1 - 15.1\%)/(1 - 11.33\%) = 4.3\%$, recognizing that the effective tax on stock income would be reduced from about 15.1% to about 11.33%. Substituting in Equation (2.9) yields

$$k_{Paktech} = (0.959)(4.07\%) + [(0.957)(9.15\%) - (0.959)(4.07\%)](0.706)$$
$$+ (0.957)(3.08\%) = 10.28\%$$
$$WACC_{Paktech} = (1 - 40\%)(7.15\%)(35\%) + (10.28\%)(65\%) = 8.18\%$$

Let us now consider the error committed by ignoring personal taxes under the new tax regime. Suppose the required market return and the size premium become $(0.957)(9.15\%) = 8.76\%$ and $(0.957)(3.08\%) = 2.95\%$, respectively, and that $r_f = 4.07$. Then, ignoring the adjustment made in Equation (2.9) would yield

---

[29]A similar calculation is made by Brealy and Myers (2003); it ignores the possible effect of state taxes.

[30]This was done via the Jobs and Growth Tax Relief Reconciliation Act.

$$k_{Paktech} = 4.07\% + (8.76\% - 4.07\%)(0.706) + 2.95 = 10.33\%$$

$$WACC_{Paktech} = (1 - 40\%)(7.15\%)(35\%) + (10.33\%)(65\%) = 8.22\%$$

In conclusion, although the 2003 reduction of the tax rates on dividends and capital gains will have a material effect on the cost of capital of corporations ($8.43\% - 8.18\% = 25$ basis points in the case of Paktech), once the required return on the market portfolio and the small cap premiums adjust to account for the lower tax rates, ignoring the adjustment for personal taxes would result in a small error in the cost of capital (a 4 basis point overestimation in the case of Paktech).

*2.6.3   Enterprise Value in Tax Imputation Countries[31]

A number of countries[32] allow shareholders a deduction on their dividend tax based upon the income tax paid by the firm. That is, the corporate tax is imputed as paid on behalf of the shareholder. Denote the imputation tax rate by t_I, then a dividend Div is grossed up by the imputation rate to $Div/(1 - t_I)$ and the personal rate applying to dividends t_{Div} is reduced to $t_{Div} - t_I$. Hence, the after-tax dividend becomes

$$Div - Div\frac{(t_{Div} - t_I)}{(1 - t_I)} = \frac{Div(1 - t_{Div})}{(1 - t_I)}$$

Since $(t_{Div} - t_I)/(1 - t_I)$ is the effective tax rate on dividend income, the effective tax rate on stock income becomes

$$t_S = p\frac{(t_{Div} - t_I)}{(1 - t_I)} + (1 - p)t_{cg} \qquad (2.10)$$

where p is the payout ratio of the firm and t_{cg} is the effective tax on capital gains. t_I is usually the corporate tax rate.

Equation (2.10) provides the estimate of t_S needed in Equation (2.9) to calculate the cost of equity, which substituted into WACC permits enterprise valuation to proceed as in Section 2.3. Note that if $t_{Div} < t_I$ the shareholder would receive a rebate from the tax authority. However, most governments are not that generous and set the personal tax at $max(t_{Div} - t_I, 0)$.[33] Suppose the shareholder receives a dividend of €10, and the firm pays corporate tax at a 30% rate. Then, the shareholder is deemed to have received a gross dividend of €10 ÷ (1 – 30%) = €14.29 and pays taxes at the rate $max(t_{Div} - 30\%, 0)$. This means that many taxpayers, including tax-exempt investors, will pay no tax on net dividends (or, equivalently, pay 30% on gross dividends) and keep the €10 cash dividend. For these investors, the effective tax rate on stock income would be very low. For example, Equation (2.10) gives $t_S = 4\%$ for p = 40%, $t_{cg} = 10\%$ and $t_{Div} \approx t_I$.

2.6.4   Balance Sheet Adjustments

It is common for a company to have assets and liabilities that will escape discounted cash-flow valuation. In general, any asset and liability that has no cash-flow consequences

---

[31]This section follows Cooper and Nyborg (2000). For additional refinements, with specific application to Germany and Austria, see Husmann, Kruschwitz, and Löffler (2001) and Bogner, Frühwirth, and Shwaiger (2002), respectively.

[32]For example, Australia, Austria, Croatia, Denmark, Finland, Germany, Italy, Mexico, Norway, Spain, Venezuela, U.K., and New Zealand. On the other hand, Belgium, Denmark, Japan, Netherlands, Sweden, and Switzerland have tax regimes similar to the U.S. regime.

[33]For example, rebates are made in Australia but were eliminated in the U.K. in 1999.

registered in the projections will be missed by the discounted cash-flow method. The final result of a valuation study should include a careful analysis of the balance sheet, and additional due diligence directed to identifying and pricing omitted items is essential. On the assets side of the balance sheet, one should look for such items as unutilized land, equipment, inventories, patents, legal claims and other rights that do not produce cash flow in the projection. For example, suppose the company bought real estate some years ago for an expansion that did not take place but the property was kept and does not have an expected use in the future. The analyst should proceed to make sure that property taxes and any other incidental expenses associated with this property are excluded from the cash-flow projection and then establish its disposal value net of selling expenses and taxes. This value should be added to the enterprise value generated by discounting free cash flows.

Long-term investments should also receive special consideration. Investments with a recurring cash flow would normally be accounted for in the free cash flow of the enterprise and affect the growth forecast and the risk factored in the cost of capital. They require no adjustment. However, equity investments that do not pay dividends will escape free cash-flow valuation. Even when dividends are received, discounting them as part of the enterprise's total free cash flows is not advisable when their expected growth or systematic risk are too different from the core business. In such cases, it is better to exclude after-tax dividends from free cash flows and value the investments separately, for which market prices may be available. In doing so, the analyst should consider if the estimate of the company's systematic risk should be adjusted to reflect the exclusion of long-term investments.[34]

Similarly, a careful examination of the liability side of the balance sheet, and of off-balance sheet items that have not reached the level of probability required for accounting recognition will reveal the need for adjusting downward the enterprise value. Contingent liabilities depending on the outcome of litigation or potential liabilities such as those related to previous disposals of toxic waste should be taken into account even when their value would be no more than an educated guess. Other contingent liabilities include guarantees given to buyers of securitized assets such as receivables. Similarly, contracts depending on contingencies such as earnout agreements should be valued and accounted for.[35] Also, unrecorded underfunded pension liabilities should be added to the value of debt. The surplus in overfunded pensions should be added to the enterprise value net of the tax applicable to the recovery. Finally, the definition of debt includes both capitalized and, when material, non-capitalized (operating) leases, with lease payments excluded from EBITDA and the capitalized value of all the leases included as part of debt.

2.6.5 Cash and Marketable Securities

The amount of cash and marketable securities varies widely among firms and over time. Corporations keep cash balances for transactions and precautionary motives, including cash kept in connection with the maintenance of bank credit lines. But the ultimate goal is to invest available cash in liquid marketable securities.[36] The interest earned on cash and

---

[34]See Chapter 9, Section 9.11.4 on sum-of-the-parts valuation.

[35]The use and valuation of earnouts, holdbacks, and other contingent contracts are treated in Chapters 10 and 11. Earnouts, like minority interest, options, and warrants, are equity claims and should be subtracted from the value of equity in order to arrive at the value of common equity.

[36]When treating cash as a costly inventory, the optimal cash balance is the one that accounts for the trade off between the interest forgone and the cost associated with selling marketable securities to replenish the cash balance. In practice, transaction costs are relatively small and the policy of corporations is to invest in marketable securities as much of the available cash as possible.

marketable securities is not part of the free cash flow as defined in Section 2.1 and, therefore, it is not part of the enterprise value calculated in Section 2.2. This requires adding cash and marketable securities to the valuation of the enterprise as another balance sheet adjustment. However, in practice, cash is treated as a reduction of debt, and the enterprise value is defined as equal to the value of equity plus the value of net debt. This approach has the advantage of producing a value of free cash flows (the enterprise value) consistent with the value produced by valuation multiples such as EBITDA multiples.[37] Future changes in cash and marketable securities have zero net present value and so have no effect on enterprise value. However, if maintaining a significant float of *non-interest-earning* cash is required, it should be considered part of the working capital necessary to operate the business and only the amount of cash and marketable securities in excess to this float should be treated as an offset to debt.

2.6.6 Mid-year Discounting

The valuations made in the previous sections assumed that cash flows become available at the end of each year. In practice, cash flows develop over the year and may exhibit a seasonal pattern. When there is significant intra-year variation in the occurrence of cash flows it may be desirable to reduce the length of the forecast time-unit to a quarter or a month. Practitioners sometimes assume the cash flow takes place in the middle of the year as an approximation to the case in which the cash flow occurs continuously over time at a constant rate.[38] The adjustment for mid-year discounting involves replacing each present value factor $(1 + r)^{-t}$ by $(1 + r)^{-(t - \frac{1}{2})}$ or, equivalently, multiplying the valuation that assumes end-of-year cash flows by $(1 + r)^{\frac{1}{2}}$. For example, the enterprise value of Paktech adjusted for mid-year discounting is: $(\$178.948)(1.0848)^{\frac{1}{2}} = \$186.381$ million.

2.6.7 Dealing with Equity-linked and Other Securities in the Capital Structure

In addition to straight equity and debt, a number of other securities are often part of the capital structure of the company to be valued. These include convertible bonds and preferred stock, straight preferred stock, warrants, and other options such as executive stock options and stock appreciation rights, and minority interests. These securities will be discussed in more detail in Chapter 3 dealing with the estimation of the cost of capital. It will be seen there that all of them can be assigned, sometimes after an adequate decomposition, to either straight equity or to straight debt. The valuation of common equity requires valuing and subtracting from the enterprise value all the outstanding claims of the other security holders. Thus, in addition to debt claims, one needs to value the outstanding equity-linked securities, warrants and other options, and minority interests. For options lacking an observable market price, option-pricing techniques may be required. Section 14.7 of Chapter 14 shows how to value options claims on common equity.

2.6.8 Restructuring Expenses

It is often the case that an acquirer needs to incur additional expenses related to the transaction and to restructuring of operations. Change of control may trigger severance

---

[37]The use of multiples in valuation is studied in Chapter 4.

[38]If the cash flow arrives at the constant rate c, its present value calculated with continuous discounting at the rate $\ln(1 + r)$ can be shown to be approximately equal to $c(1 + r)^{-\frac{1}{2}}$.

payments to departing executives and changes in operations may require significant up-front expenses. The share of these expenses borne by the buyer should be taken into account in the valuation of the target. In addition, the cash-flow consequences of restructuring actions that impact operations should be incorporated into the projections. These details as well as the tax consequences of the form chosen for the transactions, whether a merger, an asset purchase, or a purchase of stock are treated in Chapter 9.

2.7 ANALYSIS OF RESULTS: THE VALUE OF FRANCHISE AND GROWTH[39]

Obtaining the DCF value of a company is just the beginning of the valuation exercise. The DCF value is usually generated after making a number of assumptions about revenue growth, operating margins, and the cost of capital. Some of these assumptions are relatively harmless and have a small effect on enterprise value. But dissipation of the competitive advantage implied in the assumed operating margins or the lack of realization of the growth rate upon which the projections are based can cut the DCF value by half.

Once the DCF value is attained, the analyst should carefully reexamine its components and assumptions. A useful approach is to decompose the DCF value into three parts: (1) reproduction value; (2) value of the present earning power of the enterprise; and (3) value of the expected growth opportunities.

(1) Reproduction value: The reproduction value of the firm's assets measures the cost of entry into the business by an acquirer and its potential competitors. It is an estimate of the cost of the "do-it-yourself" alternative that can be compared to the asking price for the target. It indicates not only what the acquirer can do on its own as an alternative to purchasing the target but also what potential entrants need to spend in order to enter the business. The assets to consider include hard assets, patents and other intangibles related to know-how, as well as the cost of recruiting and training management and the necessary labor force, and having the new company up-and-running in order to match the production and marketing capability of the target. How to estimate reproduction value? One approach is to start with the balance sheet of the target and estimate the cost of replacing the relevant items. This, plus an estimate of the cost of hiring and training management and labor and the set-up cost associated with bringing the operation up to speed would give a reasonable estimate of the cost of reproducing the target's assets. It should be noted that these estimates are simple guesses, even when estimating the replacement value of a tangible asset such as an aged-plant. The costs of reproducing a clientele or a brand are difficult to gauge and can be left out of the reproduction value estimate. They are not ignored but considered when evaluating the earning power of the target.

For the purpose of the following illustration let the reproduction value of Paktech be equal to capital invested less cash, assuming negligible non-capitalized set-up costs. From Exhibit 2.3 we estimate the reproduction value of Paktech at $128.9 million.[40]

---

[39]The original decomposition between earning power and the value of growth is due to Miller and Modigliani (1961). Bruce Greenwald formulated the decomposition outlined in this section. See Greenwald et al. (2001). The concept of earning power has a long tradition and it goes as far back as court opinions at the turn of the 19th century [Dewing (1953), pp. 287–288]. Graham and Dodd (1934) further developed and applied it. Lebowitz and Kogelman (1990) used the concept of franchise in their analysis of P/E multiples (see Chapter 4, Section 4.6 below). Brealey and Myers (2003) discuss the value of growth, which they call "present value of growth opportunities."

[40]Estimated as the sum of shareholders' equity plus net debt plus deferred taxes. The estimation of the capital invested in the firm is discussed in Chapter 5.

(2) Present earning power: The next component of value is the current level of free cash flow generated by the company in excess to its reproduction value. It is estimated assuming that the company will have no real growth in the future. Doing this requires adjusting the projections of capital investment, increases in net working capital and depreciation, because these three items would decrease if the firm does not experience volume growth. If profits margins are maintained, the revised forecast is obtained by simply reducing the growth rate of sales in Exhibit 2.1 to 2.3%, PI's rate of price inflation, and recalculating Exhibits 2.2 to 2.4.[41] It also requires adjusting earnings for any transitory components. In the words of Graham and Dodd (1934, p. 429), the objective is to base the estimation of earning power on "actual earnings, shown over a period of years, with a reasonable expectation that they will be approximated in the future, unless extraordinary conditions supervene."

Exhibit 2.11 calculates the enterprise value under no real growth following the method developed in Section 2.3. It shows that the value of Paktech with no volume growth would be $133.4 million. This calculation assumes that both prices and costs increase at the same rate. If that were not the case because competition or regulation would not permit passing all cost increases to prices, the rate of price growth would be lower than the rate of cost increases and result in a reduction of the EBITDA margin and free cash flows.

From the no-real-growth value, we subtract reproduction value to obtain the *current franchise value* of the company. This value is an estimate of what the company is worth

---

EXHIBIT 2.11   *Paktech International. Enterprise Valuation under No-Real Growth as of 12/31/2002*

($000) Year-end	2002	2003	2004	2005	2006	2007
Net Sales		218,492	223,518	228,659	233,918	239,298
EBITDA		30,589	32,410	32,012	32,748	33,502
Depreciation		12,308	13,289	14,764	14,918	15,231
EBIT		18,281	19,121	17,249	17,830	18,271
Taxes		7,312	7,649	6,899	7,132	7,308
Unlevered Net Income		10,968	11,473	10,349	10,698	10,963
Change in Deferred Taxes		481	380	305	308	314
NOPAT		11,450	11,853	10,654	11,006	11,277
Depreciation		12,308	13,289	14,764	14,918	15,231
Change in Net Working Capital		(462)	(332)	(566)	(575)	(589)
Capital Expenditures		(12,610)	(15,663)	(15,094)	(15,915)	(17,249)
Free Cash Flow		10,687	9,146	9,758	9,434	8,670

Valuation

WACC	8.48%						
PV{FCF} @	WACC	37,850					
Continuation Value Growth	2.3%						
Continuation Value							143,491
PV{Continuation Value} @	WACC	95,509					
Enterprise Value		133,359					

---

[41]Problem 2.2 at the end of this chapter asks the reader to do so.

over and above what it would cost to enter the business without an established clientele. It measures the value of the present competitive advantage of the company or, equivalently, the value of its clientele. Paktech's franchise value is 133.4 – 128.9 = $4.5 million.

A number of questions should be asked in connection with a material franchise value: Is the advantage sustainable? What are the barriers to entry that justify paying a price for the target in excess to the cost of entry? The assumptions underlying the cash-flow projections should be revised if these questions cannot be satisfactorily answered. In the case of Packtech, the justification of its enterprise value depends on its ability to real-ize the growth assumption.

(3) Growth opportunities: The difference between the DCF value of the enterprise and its no-growth value is the value of the assumed growth opportunities. Without doubt, this is the less reliable component of enterprise value, particularly because it depends on the ability of the firm to grow and produce returns in excess to its cost of capital. The growth assumption should be subject to careful scrutiny. Is the growth assumed to take place within the core competency of the firm by expansion of the total market for its prod-ucts, or does it depend mainly on an increase of the company's market share? How vul-nerable is the projected growth to competitors' actions, technological change, and changes in consumer tastes? Is the growth assumed to take place outside the present franchise, with the present business considered a platform for new products or for penetrating new markets? An acquirer should be cautious of paying for non-core growth. Growth assumed to take place outside the established competency of the target is likely to have zero or close to zero net present value. Paktech's value of growth opportunities is the difference between its DCF value and its no-real growth value: 178.9 – 133.4 = $45.5 million.

Summarizing, the DCF value of Paktech can be decomposed as follows:

Reproduction value	$128.9 million
Value of current franchise	4.5
Value of growth	45.5
Enterprise value	$178.9 million.

This analysis reveals that expected growth accounts for 25% of Paktech's valuation. Note that in this case, the value of growth takes place during the explicit forecast period because, as we saw in Section 2.4.1, Paktech essentially breaks even after 2007. In Chap-ter 4, this result will be compared to that produced by a complementary valuation ap-proach based on valuation multiples from comparable firms.

The present decomposition is different from the one discussed in Section 2.4.3. There, the value of the firm was divided over time, before and after return break-even, with the projection allowed to grow until the end of the explicit forecast period and as-sumed to attain break-even returns afterwards. Here, the partition is done in present value from the beginning of the forecast and the firm can have ROC ≠ WACC before and after the end of the explicit forecast.

2.8 SUMMARY

This chapter presented a synthesis of the basic valuation approach used in this book. Essentially, a firm or business unit is conceived as generating after-tax free cash flows for distribution to equity- and debt-holders. These cash flows are valued at the after-tax weighted average cost of equity and debt and the result is the value of the enterprise that comprises the value of equity and the value of net debt. The latter made up of all interest bearing liabilities minus cash and marketable securities. Spontaneous liabilities are not part of the value of the enterprise. They constitute an offset to the working capital carried by the firm to support its operations. Whatever cost these liabilities have is already built into the computation of operating income. The total value of the enterprise is obtained by adding balance sheet adjustments to the enterprise value resulting from free cash-flow discounting. These adjustments are made to account for items not affecting cash flows and therefore not reflected in the discounted value of free cash flows, such as idle assets and contingent liabilities.

The value of equity results from subtracting the value of net debt from the enterprise value. It was shown that, equivalently, equity can be valued discounting the cash flow to equity at the cost of equity but that, with the exception of financial institutions, the enterprise method should be preferred.

We examined the effect of personal taxes on valuation and showed that WACC discounting is still valid when personal taxes are taken into account but that the estimation of the cost of equity needs to be adjusted. However, the magnitude of the adjustment is not known as it depends on unavailable tax data from price-setting investors. We noted that under the U.S. tax law in force in early 2003 as well as the changes introduced in May 2003, the effect on valuation of allowing for personal taxes in the cost of capital would be relatively small.

A necessary complement of DCF valuation is its decomposition into the value of the business at the present level of free cash flows and the value of growth. Comparison of these values to the cost of entry into the business and the nature of the barriers to entry can help gauging the reliability of the valuation results.

In addition, the valuation output can be subject to sensitivity and scenario analyses by changing the underlying assumptions one at a time and in combination. The application and interpretation of these tests are made in Chapter 9, Section 9.11.5.

PROBLEMS

2.1 A firm sells a used piece of equipment for $150,000. The equipment was originally acquired for $500,000 and is 80% depreciated for tax purposes at the time of the sale. The firm's marginal tax rate is 30%. What is the after-tax cash flow produced by the sale?

2.2 Using the forecasting assumptions of Exhibit 2.1 and the line-item formulas detailed in Note N2.1, reproduce Exhibits 2.2 to 2.5 on a worksheet. (Note that slight differences may result because of rounding.)

2.3 Using the spreadsheet developed in Problem 2.2 change the growth of sales assumptions and reproduce Exhibit 2.11.

2.4 GCL Industries is an industrial conglomerate undergoing restructuring. As part of its restructuring program GCL is considering the sale of its low-growth Fleet Meat Packing unit. Fleet is in the high volume–low margin meatpacking business. Fleet's volume sales are not expected to increase in the future and the long-term growth of dollar sales is projected at 3% per year. Operating projections and other pertinent data are presented below. Estimate the price GCL may get for Fleet as of January 1, 2005.

Fleet Meat Packing Co., 2005–2009 Projection

	Actual	Forecast				
	2004	2005	2006	2007	2008	2009
		million $				
Sales	2,223.2	2,245.6	2,284.2	2,308.0	2,550.0	2,616.7
EBITDA margin	2.55%	2.57%	2.65%	2.71%	2.71%	2.71%
Depreciation	29.0	32.6	34.2	32.9	32.0	31.5
Increase in deferred taxes	0.5	1.6	2.2	2.9	2.5	2.5
CAPEX + Net WC increase	38.7	41.8	42.2	33.4	32.5	32.5

Miscellaneous data:

- Corporate tax rate: 40%.
- GCL estimates that the buyer can finance the acquisition with 50% debt that can be raised at 7%.
- The beta of companies in Fleet's industry with similar capital structures is 1.32. The yield on 10-year Treasury notes is 4.5%, the equity risk premium is about 5% and the micro-cap size premium is about 3.3%.
- Valuation multiple: An examination of comparable companies yielded an average EBITDA multiple equal to 5.6 times current (2004) EBITDA.

2.5 A prospective buyer of Fleet Meat Packing Co. would like to finance the acquisition entirely with equity capital and not use debt financing in the future. The buyer would like to determine the maximum price to pay for Fleet. The buyer has estimated that the beta coefficient in the absence of debt would be 0.66 and that the cost of equity should allow for a micro-cap size premium equal to 3.3%. Furthermore, the riskless rate is 4.5%, the equity premium is 5% and the corporate tax rate is 40%. Value Fleet under this financial structure. Is the result different from that obtained in Problem 2.4? Why?

2.6 The buyer of Problem 2.5 is also considering the possibility of financing the acquisition with an alternative structure designed to maintain the interest coverage ratio at 5.05 times. (Interest coverage is here defined as the ratio of EBITDA to interest expense.) The costs of debt and equity would be 7 and 14.4%, respectively, and the tax rate would be 40%. How much can the buyer afford to pay for Fleet Meat Packing Co. under this financing plan? Compare your result to those obtained for the previous two problems and explain the differences, if any.

2.7 TPI Inc., a manufacturer of computer storage devices, is planning to go public at the end of 2004. The purpose of the initial public offering is to retire debt and liquefy the position of some of its original investors. Future growth will be financed by TPI's internally generated cash flow and the additional borrowing made possible by the expected increase in the company debt capacity.

The company has put together the following projection:

($ millions)	2005	2006	2007	2008	2009
EBIT	24.8	28.0	32.0	34.0	37.0
Depreciation	5.8	7.6	9.2	10.2	11.0
Increase in deferred taxes	0.8	0.6	0.7	0.7	1.0
Capital expenditures	18.2	12.2	14.3	14.3	12.0
Net working capital change	(0.8)	(0.8)	1.0	1.8	0

After 2009, EBIT is expected to grow at 8% per year, capital expenditures will equal depreciation and working capital will be self-financed.

Currently, TPI has net debt of $112 million, but its CFO has already negotiated retiring $53 million with the proceeds of the equity issue and refinancing the rest at 8%. As a consequence, TPI is expected to begin 2005 with its net debt reduced to $59 million and its interest coverage ratio (here defined as EBIT-to-interest) increased to about 5.25. The CFO plans to maintain the coverage ratio at that level afterwards and expects to raise future debt at an interest rate of about 8%. As far as the debt-ratio is concerned, the goal is to keep it at about 26% of enterprise value. The CFO believes that debt ratio would be consistent with the target coverage ratio.

TPI's corporate tax rate is 40%. Its cost of equity is estimated accounting for risk and its relatively small size (its beta for the planned capital structure equals 2.0, the Treasury yield is 4.5%, the equity premium is 5%, and the micro-cap size premium is 3.3%). TPI's has issued 10 million shares to its present owners and plans to issue 5 million new shares in the IPO, bringing the total number of shares outstanding to 15 million.

On the basis of the share prices of recent IPOs and other companies in the industry and the growth prospects of TPI, the investment bankers have suggested a preliminary IPO price based upon a P/E multiple of 13 to 14 times TPI's 2004 earnings. Underwriter fees are expected to be 5% of gross proceeds and additional issue expenses to amount to $600,000.

Your task is to value TPI as of the beginning of year 2005.

a. Estimate the value of TPI's share of common equity.
b. Compute and interpret the prospective (i.e., with respect to next-year-earnings) price-earnings multiple implied by your valuation at the *beginning* of 2005 and compare it to the investment bankers' range.
c. Check if a debt ratio in the mid 20s is consistent with maintaining an EBIT interest coverage ratio of about 5 times.
d. Would the proceeds of the IPO be sufficient for retire $53 million of debt?

For simplicity, assume that all debt financing for each year is raised at the beginning of the year such that beginning-of-year debt and average debt are the same.

2.8 Consider the following four-year projections for Square Peg, Inc.:

($ millions)	2005	2006	2007	2008	
EBIT	100	120	150	190	rate=3%
Depreciation	30	40	50	55	
Increase in deferred taxes	2	3	4	4	rate = 3%
Capital expenditures	92	63	64	69	
Net working capital change	(5)	(5)	15	15	constant

After 2008, EBIT and deferred taxes are expected to grow at the inflation rate of 3%, capital expenditures will equal depreciation and net working capital will not change.

In addition, Square Peg's tax rate is 40%, its WACC is 11%, and its debt amounts to $650 million and is projected to grow to $820 million by the end of 2008. The interest rate on debt is 9.5%. This rate is expected to apply to future borrowing as well. Square Peg has 35 million common shares outstanding.

a. Estimate the free cash flows of Square Peg for the *five* years 2005 to 2009 and compute the enterprise value as of year-end 2004.
b. Estimate the value per share of Square Peg's equity.
c. Compute and interpret the prospective (i.e., with respect to next-year-earnings) price-earnings multiples implied by your valuation at year-end 2004 and year-end 2008. (Hint: Construct the pro-forma income statements for 2005 and 2009.)

For simplicity, assume that all debt financing for each year is raised at the beginning of the year such that beginning-of-year debt and average debt are the same.

2.9 3DS Industries is considering a 35% carve-out of its retail unit, the Storr Family Stores. Your task is to estimate the share price 3DS may be able to get for Storr as of January 1, 2005. You have available the following operating projections:

Storr Unit, 2005–2009 Projections (million $)

	2005	2006	2007	2008	2009
Sales	4,700.5				
Growth rate of sales	5.0%	5.0%	5.0%	5.0%	5.0%
Cost of sales	72.5%	72.5%	72.5%	72.5%	72.5%
Operating expenses	26.9%	26.8%	26.7%	26.6%	26.6%
EBIT	28.2				
Depreciation	30.6	36.2	40.9	42.1	37.0
Increase in deferred taxes	2.1	2.2	2.3	2.3	2.3
Capex + NWC increases	45.0	49.5	50.0	45.0	40.0

3DS intends to put net debt equivalent to 50% of Storr's enterprise value on the balance sheet. Debt will pay 7.9% interest. 3DS intends to capitalize the company with 10 million shares and issue 3.5 million to the public. In addition, on the basis of data for comparable companies, Storr's equity beta for that leverage is estimated to be about 1.2. The corporate tax rate is 40%. The riskless interest rate is 4.5%. The equity risk premium is 5%, and, because of its size, Storr would be subject to a micro-cap size premium of 3.3%. Finally, an examination of companies comparable to Storr yielded an average trailing EBITDA multiple equal to 5.5 times current EBITDA. This multiple can be used to estimate Storr's continuation value as of the end of 2009.

2.10 In the spring of 1999, the pricing of Internet companies was a matter of debate among finance practitioners and academics alike. Take the case of AOL, which on April 22, 1999 closed at 148$^{11}/_{16}$, consensus had a next-year earnings estimate of $0.53 per share and forward P/E = 281 as well as 49.5% annual nominal earnings growth for the next 5 years. Assume that AOL's annual growth decreases to 28% during the following 5 years and then settles down to the average long-term growth of 8%. AOL's 5-year growth consensus was about 2% higher than the long-term nominal growth of earnings forecasted at that time for the S&P 500 as a whole. In addition, assume that after 10 years AOL will start a 51% dividend payout (about the same as the long-term average of the S&P 500). Value AOL share by discounting future dividends. Assume a cost of equity of 10%. Interpret your results.

How many times AOL needs to growth its real earnings over ten years to justify your result? Assume 2.5% annual inflation.

2.11 On July 26 of 2002, AOL-Time Warner stock closed at $10.90, had a next-year consensus earnings estimate of $0.99 per share and forward P/E = 11, as well as 18.5% annual nominal earnings growth expected for the next 5 years. Assume that AOL-Time Warner's annual growth decreases to 10% during the following 5 years and then settles down to the average long-term growth of 4%. AOL-Time Warner's 5-year growth consensus was about 1.5% higher than the long-term nominal growth of earnings forecasted at that time for the S&P 500 as a whole. In addition, assume that after 10 years AOL-Time Warner will start a 51% dividend payout. Value AOL-Time Warner share by discounting future dividends. Assume a cost of equity of 12%. Interpret your results.

Cost of Capital.
CAPM Formula.

Est. Risk Premium

Chapter **3**

The Equity Premium and the Cost of Capital

3.1 ESTIMATING THE COST OF CAPITAL

In this chapter, we study how to estimate the components of the cost of capital: the cost of equity and the cost of debt. These are the opportunity costs of the providers of capital to the firm, measured by the return they can attain investing their funds in alternative assets of equivalent risk. The costs of equity, debt, and hybrid combinations of debt and equity are considered.

The cost of equity of a corporation is one of the fundamental concepts of corporate finance and an essential input to most practical valuation problems. In spite of considerable research, the cost of equity remains a most elusive quantity. In fact, several approaches have been proposed to estimate the cost of equity and the implementation of each of them varies widely in practice. In Section 3.2, we evaluate some of the proposed approaches and put forward guidelines for the estimation of the cost of equity. The main problem in estimating the cost of equity is agreeing on the proper risk premium, also called *equity premium* that investors demand for holding equity instead of government bonds. Since this is a controversial subject we discuss the several approaches to estimating the equity premium in some detail, perhaps more than the reader may want to consider at this point. We conclude that the cost of equity is not as high as simple analysis of the historical record would suggest. We show that both the historical record, financial theory, and prospective estimates based upon present stock prices and growth expectations, all indicate that the future equity premium in developed capital markets is likely to be between 3 and 5% but that it can vary significantly over time and, at times, be outside this range. In summary, we recommend using the prospective premium embedded in today's stock prices as a way of tracking the equity premium and show how to calculate it.

In other sections, we deal with the difference between the cost of equity of large capitalization and small capitalization companies, examine the role of liquidity in asset pricing, and provide the size premium to add to the cost of equity for small capitalization companies. In addition, we consider the technical issue of how to adjust the cost of equity for leverage. The chapter concludes with guidelines for estimating the cost of the other components of the capital structure such as straight debt, hybrid securities and warrants, and the computation of the weighted average cost of capital.

Estimating the cost of capital in the global capital market and in emerging markets in particular requires further extensions. These are made in Chapter 12. The cost of equity of private equity investments is treated in Chapter 13.

3.2 THE COST OF EQUITY

The discount rate on any given asset, that is, the rate that makes the present value of the *expected* cash flows equal to its price, is a quantity not directly observable. The estimation of the rate applicable to equity is further complicated by our limited ability to estimate expected future cash flows. Each of the approaches discussed in this section is essentially a way around this major difficulty. We first outline the basic approach to estimating the cost of equity, and then we examine alternative ways of estimating its components.

3.2.1 The Capital Asset Pricing Model Approach

The capital asset pricing model (CAPM) provides the framework for the most common method of estimating the cost of capital. In general, there is agreement among academics and practitioners that the required return on equity has to allow for the higher risk of holding stock as compared with the risk of holding high-grade corporate bonds or Treasury securities. Empirical evidence supports the proposition that investors are, on average, risk averse, and that equities are riskier than Treasury securities. One of the implications of the CAPM is that the required return on a stock is given by a riskless interest rate r_f, plus a risk premium that depends on the amount of nondiversifiable risk contributed by the stock to the *market portfolio* (the portfolio of all available assets). Specifically, the stock risk premium is equal to the market risk premium scaled by its β coefficient, which accounts for the nondiversifiable risk of the stock[1]:

$$k = r_f + \text{Market Risk Premium} \times \beta \qquad (3.1)$$

One should note that the choice of the appropriate proxy for the market portfolio is not obvious and that, in addition, the choice of the riskless rate and the proper estimation of the stock beta are not free from controversy. Furthermore, one can argue that there is no risk-free asset in practice. Even Treasury bills have risky real (inflation adjusted) returns. Fortunately, asset-pricing theory is sufficiently robust in this respect because it does not require the existence of a truly risk-free asset. In fact, Equation (3.1) holds with r_f replaced by r_z, the return on an asset uncorrelated with the market portfolio that is called a *zero-beta asset*.[2] The yield on a long-term Treasury security is a reasonable approximation to the return on that asset.

Furthermore, CAPM is essentially a single-period model that applies to the multiperiod valuation problem only under rather stringent assumptions. As such, it should be understood to provide a guideline for the estimation of the cost of equity rather than the definitive recipe.

3.2.2 Choosing the Riskless Rate

The CAPM approach to estimating the cost of equity requires a riskless (or zero-beta) rate as input. In valuing a company, a division of a company, or a long-term investment project, one has to discount free cash flows that extend over many periods into the future. If a short-term riskless rate is chosen, the equity premium consists of a *term premium* reflecting the longer maturity of equity cash flows and a pure *risk premium* reflecting their risky

---

[1] An introduction to CAPM is provided in most finance textbooks. A detailed discussion of the CAPM and its extensions is provided in Elton and Gruber (1991).

[2] See Black (1972).

nature. Alternatively, if a long-term riskless rate is chosen, the equity premium measures only the pure risk premium associated with equity.

Estimating the appropriate riskless rate is not a straightforward matter. In particular, an *ad-hoc* adjustment has to be made in order to estimate the short-term riskless rate by the 1-year Treasury bill rate if the cost of capital is to be based upon a short-term rate. Short-term rates are affected by monetary policy to a greater extent than long rates. For example, a tight monetary policy such as that followed in the early 1980s in the United States would result in high Treasury bill rates and produce an inverted yield curve. At that time, the long rate was lower than the short rate because the market expected inflation to subside and short-term interest rates to decrease in the future. Under such circumstances, basing the estimate of the cost of equity for long-term valuations on the yield on bills plus a historic risk premium over bills would lead to an overestimation of the cost of equity and an underestimation of present values. Similarly, during a recession, the short-term rate is likely to be below its expected long-term level if the monetary authority follows an easy-money policy, and using the short rate would lead to underestimation of the cost of equity. The bill rate provides useful information for estimating next-year cost of equity but not the long-run cost of equity. In theory, the cost of equity should be allowed to vary from year to year along the term structure of interest rates and the equity premium should be allowed to change each year as well, but using different rates to discount each year's cash flow is not practical given the present state of valuation practice.[3]

Two approaches have been suggested for estimating the riskless rate. The first involves subtracting an estimate of the average bond/bill return spread from the prevailing long-term government bond rate. For example, subtracting 1% from the yield of 10-year Treasury notes on April 23, 2003 yields 3.03% as the expected future yield on bills, well above the 1-year bill rate of 1.31% on that date. This approach requires adding the premium of the return of common stock over *bills* to the adjusted value of r_f in order to estimate the required return on the market portfolio. For example, for an equity premium of 6.4%,[4] the return required on the market portfolio would then be 3.03% + 6.40% = 9.43%.

The second approach consists of simply making r_f equal to the yield to maturity of an outstanding long-term Treasury security. The choice of the maturity of the bond depends on the length of the cash flows being discounted, and shorter maturities should be used for evaluating capital budgeting projects of shorter life, but a long-maturity bond is the reasonable choice for valuation of companies or business units and is the one most often made in practice. For example, on April 23, 2003, the 10-year Treasury note yielded 4.03%. Adding it to the equity premium over 10-year government notes (for the present example 6.4% − 1% = 5.4%) yields a required market return equal to 9.43%. This result is identical to that of the adjusted bill rate approach as both give the same result for $\beta = 1$. In symbols, the first approach estimates the cost of equity as follows:

NO.

$$k = [r_{LTerm} - (\hat{r}_{LTerm} - \hat{r}_{Bill})] + (R_m - \hat{r}_{Bills})\beta$$

$$= [r_{LTerm} + (R_m - \hat{r}_{LTerm})\beta] - (\hat{r}_{LTerm} - \hat{r}_{Bills})(1 - \beta),$$

where the term in brakets is the value of k under the second approach and the second term equals zero for $\beta = 1$. The hat "^" denotes a historical average and R_m denotes the return required on the market portfolio. The two approaches yield close results but for large values of β.

---

[3]Ang and Liu (2002) show how to discount free cash flows with time-varying discount rates.

[4]The equity premium is estimated in Section 3.2.5 below.

Returning now to the lack of existence of a truly riskless asset and the need to estimate the expected return on a zero-beta asset, it should be noted that empirical research have found that the Treasury bill rate is too low an estimate of the zero-beta return.[5] This suggests that the long-term rate may be a better approximation to the return on a zero-beta asset than the short-term rate estimated as outlined above.[6]

While the 30-year bond would seem the most appropriate benchmark for valuation of long-term cash flows, recent developments in the Treasury market suggest using the 10-year note as the benchmark. This is so because the Treasury's decision to retire the longest maturity bonds outstanding has reduced the liquidity of these bonds and made the 10-year note the preferred benchmark. Since the yield of 10-year notes is usually lower than the yield of 30-year bonds, it is combined with a higher equity premium when computing the cost of equity. Therefore, the use of a 10-year rate produces estimates of the cost of equity that are very close to those obtained on the basis of longer maturity bonds. The more liquid 10-year Treasury benchmark the one adopted in this book.

3.2.3   Estimating the Equity Premium: Historical Analyses

One way to estimate the equity premium is from historical data. The rationale for this approach is that if expectations are unbiased, the realization of returns should permit estimating the discount rate and risk premium investors applied to valuing equity. If one further assumes that the investors' required risk premium is stable over time, its historic average can be used to estimate the risk premium required for the future. Unfortunately, there seem to be no agreement on the best way to use historical data to estimate the risk premium. Let us examine some of the more controversial aspects.

The average of the yearly differences between realized returns on a market index such as the S&P 500 index and a government security (Treasury bill or long bond) is the established way to compute the historic premium. However, there is not agreement about the length of the period to use. Should one use the series from 1926 to the present or a subset of it?[7] Why starting in 1926 and not before? In fact, return series going as far back as 1802 are available.[8]

The argument for using post–World II data is that extraordinary events such as the Great Depression and World War II may have temporarily affected investors' attitudes toward risk and the holding of equity. In fact, empirical research has found significant long-term negative autocorrelation in stock returns.[9,10] Other arguments for using recent data

---

[5]For example, Black, Jensen, and Scholes (1972).

[6]Strictly, the long-term rate should be corrected for systematic risk because long-term bond returns have a small but positive beta coefficients (about 0.07). However, this correction is small and mostly offset by the corresponding increase in the equity premium, which must then be measured against the slightly lower zero beta return. Grinblatt and Titman (2002) suggest using LIBOR (London Inter Bank Offer Rate) as the risk-free rate. That would require computing the equity premium with respect to LIBOR.

[7]1926 was the starting date of the seminal compilations made by Fisher and Lorie (1964) and Ibbotson and Sinquefield (1976) as well as of the Ibbotson Associates annual updates. See Ibbotson Associates (2002).

[8]See Schwert (1990), Siegel (1992), and Wilson and Jones (2002). Dimson, Marsh and Staunton (2002) computed returns and premia over the period 1900 to 2000.

[9]See, for example, Porterba and Summers (1988) and Lo and MacKinlay (1988).

[10]The mean-reverting movements in the equity premium seem have taken place only in the 1926 to 1958 period and no autocorrelation or seasonal influences have been detected in the post-1959 period. Moreover, the forecast error in the post-1959 period is the lowest. See Chinebell, Kahl, and Stevens (1994).

EXHIBIT 3.1	*Historic Returns and Equity Premia in the United States, 1802–2002*

STOCKS

	Nominal Return		Real Return	
	Arithmetic Average	Geometric Average	Arithmetic Average	Geometric Average
1802-2002	9.5%	8.1%	8.2%	6.7%
1900-2002	11.4%	9.5%	8.2%	6.1%
1926-2002	11.8%	9.7%	8.5%	6.4%
1982-2002	13.2%	12.0%	9.8%	8.6%

BONDS

	Nominal Return		Real Return	
	Arithmetic Average	Geometric Average	Arithmetic Average	Geometric Average
1802-2002	5.2%	5.0%	4.0%	3.6%
1900-2002	5.2%	4.9%	2.2%	1.7%
1926-2002	5.9%	5.5%	2.9%	2.5%
1982-2002	13.0%	12.3%	9.6%	8.8%

EQUITY PREMIUM

	Nominal Return		Real Return	
	Arithmetic Average	Geometric Average	Arithmetic Average	Geometric Average
1802-2002	4.38%	3.01%	4.28%	3.06%
1900-2002	6.23%	4.37%	5.94%	4.33%
1926-2002	5.90%	4.03%	5.61%	3.88%
1982-2002	0.20%	–0.20%	0.24%	–0.23%

SOURCES: Updated from Siegel (2002) and Dimson et al. (2002).

for estimating the equity premium are not difficult to construct. For example, investors seem to have underestimated the effect of inflation on bond returns prior to 1980 and demanded low returns on bonds, which may have resulted in an exaggerated risk premium.[11]

Since there will always be some arbitrariness in the choice of a date of change in regime, one can argue that the best estimate of the equity premium is that based upon a period that includes stock market crashes, bubbles, depressions, world wars, stagflation, and other extraordinary phenomena. In this respect, choosing the longest period available would seem best. The arithmetic average risk premia in the United States over 1802 to 2002, 1926 to 2002, and two recent subperiods are presented in the Exhibit 3.1. For comparison, geometric averages are included.[12] The equity premium averaged 4.4% from 1802 to 2002. This value is 1.5 to 1.8% lower than the average premiums in the periods 1900 to 2002 and 1926 to 2002 but 4.2% above the premium observed in 1982 to 2002. Historical data is available for other countries as well. Dimson, March, and Staunton

---

[11]Siegel (1993) advanced this hypothesis. Blanchard (1993) made a somewhat similar interpretation of this phenomenon. He found a significant decrease in the equity premium after the seventies.

[12]Geometric averages are compound annual returns. For the difference between arithmetic and geometric mean equity premiums see Note N3.1.

(2002) compiled stock and bond returns for sixteen countries for the period 1900 to 2000 and found arithmetic and geometric mean equity premia across these countries to be 5.6 and 4.7%, respectively. If there is a conclusion to be drawn from this barrage of numbers is that the equity premium is not an immutable constant but a magnitude that changes over time depending on the volatility of stock returns and attitudes toward risk.

There is further difficulty with the use of historic risk premia. Their values may be biased upward because of what Brown, Goetzmann, and Ross (1995) have called the survivorship bias.[13] They note that the stock markets in Austria, Britain, France, Germany, Holland, and the United States were all in operation at the beginning of the 19th century but that only the British and American markets did not suffer major interruptions or disruptions and thus yielded continuous price data. They argue that conditional expected returns on a market that has survived overstates unconditional expected returns. Brown et al. derive the expected return on markets that exhibit price paths above a minimum level such that the market ceases to trade. They show that the expected return conditional on survival is $r_m^* = r_m(2 - \pi)\pi^{-1}$, where r_m is the unconditional expected return and π is the probability that the stock market will survive over a very long period of time. This result implies that the unconditional (unbiased) equity premium is equal to $r_m - r_f = r_m^*(2 - \pi)^{-1}\pi - r_f$. Substituting $r_m^* = 8.2\%$ and $r_f = 4.0\%$ from Exhibit 3.1 yields

Probability of survival	Unconditional equity premium
66%	0.04%
80%	1.47%
90%	2.71%
100%	4.20%

That is, if investors were predominantly risk averse, the probability of long-term survival of the U.S. stock market has to have been greater than 66% in order to generate a positive risk premium. Of course, for a probability of survival of 100% the mean risk premium (4.2%) would be an appropriate estimate of the unconditional risk premium. However, it is difficult to accept that the survival of any stock market was virtually certain during the last two centuries. A probability of long-term survival as high as 90% implies an equity premium of 2.7%. This suggests that estimates of the equity premium of the order of 3 to 4% are reasonable and to be expected.[14] Li and Xu (2002) have recently argued that the Brown et al. model exaggerates the magnitude of the bias because the probability of market failure becomes negligible as markets mature. Their model implies that the average annual survival bias over a century of about 1% or less. Even if the survival bias is, in fact, small, one can still conclude that the long-term historic unconditional equity premium in the United States was not much higher than 4%.

Finally, there are strong theoretical reasons to expect the equity premium to be smaller than the average premium observed over 1926 to 2001. Mehra and Prescott (1985) have argued that the high-equity premium observed over the period 1889 to 1978 cannot be reconciled with an asset pricing model in which economic agents exhibit positive rates of

---

[13]See also Jorion and Goetzmann (1999).

[14]Another important implication of Brown et al. survival model is that a return time series of surviving markets will exhibit long-term negative autocorrelation of the sort found in the studies cited in footnote 9 above, even if returns follow a random walk.

time preference. They concluded that the equity premium over the riskless rate cannot exceed 0.35% and the real riskless rate should be about 3% above the observed rates in the United States. Since these results are so inconsistent with observations, they called them "a puzzle." A number of modifications and extensions of the Prescott-Mehra analysis have been proposed in the literature in order to produce results more in line with observations.[15] Constantinides, Donaldson, and Mehra (1998) have proposed a persuasive generalization. They examine the risk premium and the riskless rate in a model in which a borrowing constraint prevents the young from investing in equities and show material increases in the equity premium and decreases in the real riskless rate for realistic parameters values. Still, their results suggest that an equity premium of less than 4% is consistent with theory.

3.2.4   Time Varying Equity Premium

The assumption that the risk premium follows a stationary random walk is one of convenience. Existing theory imposes no restriction on the behavior of the risk premium over time. In fact, it suggests that the risk premium is a function of such variables as the level of wealth, investor preferences, and market risk, all of which can and do change over time. However, models of the relation between expected return and market risk over time have not yielded stable results that can be used in valuation practice.[16] Another complication in the study of the time behavior of the risk premium is that it is affected not only by the evolution of expected stock returns but by changes in the riskless rate proxy as well. It has been pointed out that the equity premium puzzle discussed above actually is a real interest puzzle. This is because the relatively high historic equity premium is more a product of very low real return on government bonds during the 20th century than the result of unusually high real returns on equity.[17] Hence, in order to study variations of the equity premium over time, one needs a model of both the expected returns on equity and on fixed-income assets. This was done by Blanchard (1993).

Blanchard developed a dynamic model of the expectations of real returns on stocks and bonds. He found that the risk premium during the 1930s and 1940s was unusually high rising from 3 to 5% in the early 1930s to more than 10% in the 1940s. Afterwards, it started a gradual decline with some relatively minor fluctuations and reached between 2 and 3% by the early 1990s. His results are consistent with the survival-adjusted estimates of the long-term historical average premium calculated above. Furthermore, recent research provides evidence of a structural shift in the volatility process of stock returns that took place after 1940. It shows that, after accounting for such a shift, the equity premium over the yield on long-term Treasury bonds was about 4% for the period after 1940, and can be less than 3% in the future.[18]

3.2.5   Prospective Equity Premium

From the simple version of the dividend growth model [Williams (1938), Gordon (1962)], one can estimate the cost of equity for an individual firm by solving for the discount rate that makes the present value of future dividends equal to its price. That is,

---

[15]See Kocherlakota (1996) and Cochrane (1997).

[16]See, for example, Merton (1980) and Glosten, Jagannathan and Runkle (1993).

[17]See Siegel (1993).

[18]Mayfield (1999). Pástor and Stambaugh (2001) find evidence of a second shift after 1992, and suggest that the risk premium after 1992 could be as low as 2.4% over the yield on Treasury bills.

$$P_0 = \sum_{t=1,\infty} D_0 (1 + g_t)^t (1 + k)^{-t} \tag{3.2}$$

where P_0 is the present price of the stock, D_0 is the current dividend, g_t is the expected growth rate of dividends in year t, and k is the shareholder's required return or cost of equity capital to the corporation. For constant g_t, Equation (3.2) becomes

$$P_0 = \frac{D_1}{k - g} \tag{3.3}$$

where $D_1 = D_0 (1 + g)$. Solving Equation (3.3) for k yields

$$k = \frac{D_1}{P} + g, \tag{3.4}$$

which gives an estimate of the cost of equity equal to the dividend yield expected for next year plus the expected growth rate of dividends.

Applying Equation (3.4) to an individual company requires estimating its expected growth rate. This is, in most cases, a rather subjective exercise. For example, as of December 27, 2002, Exxon's dividend yield was 2.7%, and Zacks Investment Research's consensus 5-year EPS growth for Exxon was 8.1%. Assuming that Exxon's dividend payout remains constant over time and substituting into Equation (3.3) the dividend yield and the growth rate results in k = 2.7% + 8.1 = 10.8% as Exxon's cost of equity.[19] Note, however, that this estimate is based upon the extrapolation of the 5-year growth consensus into the indefinite future. A more reasonable assumption is that the long-run nominal growth rate of Exxon will approach that of the economy as a whole. Assume the latter to be 4.5% nominal[20] and that Exxon's growth rate approaches it linearly from year 6 to 10. Then, one can substitute the initial share price and dividends, and the assumed growth rate into Equation (3.2) and solve for k to obtain k = 7.6%. Thus, a change in the assumption concerning long-term growth resulted in a 3.2% reduction in the cost of equity. Similar calculations are performed for other oil companies in Exhibit 3.2. The problem with this approach is that the long-term dividend growth rate of an individual company cannot be estimated with any degree of precision. Hence, the dividend growth model is not likely to produce reliable estimates of the cost of equity of individual companies. Moreover, its application becomes even more difficult for non-dividend-paying stocks as it requires estimating their future dividend payout.

A more useful and common application of the DCF method is for estimating the required return on a diversified market portfolio such as that making up the S&P 500 index, which can then be used to calculate the market equity premium needed for applications of the CAPM model.[21] This is so because it is possible to make plausible assumptions about the long-term evolution of earnings and payouts for the economy as a whole. Dividing Equation (3.3) by the earning per share expected in the first year (EPS_1) from such a portfolio and solving for k results in the following alternative expression for Equation (3.4):

$$k = \frac{P_1}{PE_1} + g, \tag{3.5}$$

---

[19] Since dividends are paid quarterly, a more precise calculation requires solving for k such that $k = (D_1/P)[(1 + k)^{0.75} + (1 + k)^{0.5} + (1 + k)^{0.25} + 1]/4 + g$. The solution for Exxon's data gives k = 10.9%.

[20] For 2.0% real growth and 2.45% expected long-term inflation, the long-term nominal growth of the economy is $(1.02)(1.0245) - 1 = 4.5\%$. See discussion of Exhibit 3.3 below.

[21] A number of authors and investment banks have used variations of this approach. See, for example, Malkiel (1979).

EXHIBIT 3.2	*Cost of Equity of Individual Companies Using the Dividend Growth Model as of 12/27/2002*				
	Price 12/27/02	Dividend Yield	Growth Forecast*	Cost of Equity (1)	Cost of Equity (2)
Chevron-Texaco	$65.90	4.2%	6.9%	11.1%	9.1%
Exxon-Mobil	34.64	2.7%	8.1%	10.8%	7.6%
Royal Dutch	43.41	2.9%	8.5%	11.4%	7.9%
British Petroleum	39.70	3.6%	7.4%	11.0%	8.5%

*Five-year EPS consensus forecast compiled by Zacks Investment Research.

where $p_1 = D_1/EPS_1$ is the payout ratio expected during the first year and PE_1 is the prospective price-earnings multiple.

In practice, however, earnings and, to some extent, dividends may be expected to grow at different rates in the short run and the long run. For example, when the economy is in a recession, the earnings of firms in cyclical industries are depressed, and analysts tend to forecast significantly higher rates of earnings growth as the economy comes out of the recession and earnings recover toward their normal level. This has led practitioners to rely on Equation (3.2), the variable growth version of the DCF model, which for the present purposes can be written as follows:

$$P_0 = p_1 E_1 (1 + k)^{-1} + p_2 E_1 (1 + g_2)(1 + k)^{-2} \ldots \tag{3.6}$$

where $p_t = D_t/E_t$, E_t denotes earnings at time t such that $E_t = E_0(1 + g_1)\ldots(1 + g_t)$ for rates of growth of earnings g_t, $t = 1, \ldots$ Dividing through by E_1 yields the following expression for the 1-year forward price/earnings multiple of the market:

$$P_0/E_1 = p_1(1 + k)^{-1} + p_2(1 + g_2)(1 + k)^{-2} \ldots \tag{3.7}$$

The prospective equity premium is now defined as the difference between the rate of return required by investors on a market portfolio [k, the solution to Equation (3.7)], and the estimate of the risk-free rate. Hence, to estimate the prospective equity premium, one first needs to solve Equation (3.7) for k. The other components of Equation (3.7) are estimated as follows: (a) Earnings growth during the first five years is the analysts' consensus forecast;[22] (b) dividend payout adjusts linearly from its current value to its long-term average at the end of the first 5 years; (c) during the following 5 years, that is, from year 6 to 10, earnings growth converges linearly to its historical long-term average; (d) thereafter, payout and growth equal their long-term averages. The values beyond year 10 are summarized by the present value of the constant growth perpetuity that here equals $p_{10} \Pi_{t=1,11}(1 + g_t)^t/(k - g_{11})$. This procedure accounts for the slow adjustment of dividends, which imparts cyclical behavior to the payout ratio. High payouts are observed during recessions when earnings are depressed but dividends are not reduced proportionally.

---

[22]As compiled by Zacks Investment Research, Inc. and First Call Corporation. The latter is available, for instance, from http://finance.yahoo.com or from http://www.thomson.com/financial.

Afterwards, as earnings rebound, payout tends to decrease.[23,24] In addition, it recognizes that rational investors would not extrapolate into the indefinite future the growth rates expected to prevail during the first 5 years. Initial growth rates may be lower than expected for the long run when the economy is expected to go into a protracted recession, or higher than expected for the long run when the economy is expected to enter into an expansionary phase.[25]

The implementation of this model depends on a number of inputs that are subject to estimation error. For example, the 5-year consensus earnings growth depends on a sample of analysts' opinions. In addition, the expected long-term growth of earnings required by the model cannot be precisely estimated. The simple average of historical growth rates has high variance and its compounding would produce upward biased estimates of long-term dividends [Blume (1974)]. In addition, the observed growth rates are subject to the survivor upward bias discussed in Section 3.2.3. This means that Equation (3.7) can give only an indication of the likely magnitude of the equity premium and not a precise estimate. A number of empirical studies have documented optimistic bias in analysts' earning forecasts.[26] However, Equation (3.7) would yield unbiased estimates of the equity premium if investors price stocks in accordance with analysts' opinions. On the other hand, if analysts' growth expectations exceed the true (but unobserved) market expectations about future growth, Equation (3.7) would itself generate an upward biased estimate of the equity premium. Thus, it seems reasonable to conclude that Equation (3.7) yields an upper bound to the equity premium.

To illustrate the procedure, let us obtain the prospective equity premium estimate as of December 19, 2001. First, we need to solve for k in Equation (3.7). We use the following inputs: The forward P/E[27] of the S&P 500 index (21.8); its current dividend payout (63.24);[28] the analysts' consensus nominal growth of S&P 500 earnings for the next 5 years (12.75%); the long-term average payout ratio (51%); and an estimate of the expected real long-term growth of S&P 500 earnings. For this we use 2%, the average compound rate (geometric mean) for the period 1955–2000,[29] in order to account for (a) the upward bias produced by compounding the simple arithmetic average and (b) survivorship bias. Substituting these values into Equation (3.7) and solving for k yields a real required return on equity equal to 5.55% or, for a long-term inflation rate of 2.55%,[30]

---

[23]In applying a rather similar approach Cornell, Hirshleifer and James (1997) excluded non-dividend paying stocks from the S&P 500 portfolio. We did not do so because we use the analysts' consensus growth estimate of the aggregate earnings of the S&P 500 index, which already takes into account the higher rate of growth of non-dividend paying stocks, and the aggregate payout ratio is measured with respect to total earnings, including those of non-dividend paying stock.

[24]Note N3.2 argues that the computation of the required return on equity using this model is valid when share repurchases are expected and may change the long-term dividend payout ratio.

[25]Extrapolating the 5-year growth consensus indefinitely into the future would result in higher estimates of the risk premium. See Harris and Marston (1992, 1999) for a different approach to estimating the prospective equity premium.

[26]See, for example, Butler and Lang (1991).

[27]Computed with respect to next year consensus earnings.

[28]From *Business Week*, December 31, 2001. As of December 19, 2001, the trailing S&P 500 index was 46.5 and its dividend yield was 1.36%.

[29]The average payout ratio and growth rates are computed from data supplied in Council of Economic Advisers (2001) in http://w3.access.gpo.gov/eop/.

[30]The long-term inflation forecast is compiled quarterly by the Federal Reserve Bank of Philadelphia and is available from http://www.phil.frb.org/econ/spf/index.html.

$(1.0555)(1.0255) - 1 = 8.24\%$ nominal return. The prospective equity premium is computed subtracting from 8.24% the annually compound 10-year Treasury note yield: 8.24% − 5.16% = 3.08%.[31]

The estimate of the equity premium increases somewhat if one takes into account the systematic risk of long-term Treasuries. Since the beta of long-term Treasuries is about 0.07, the riskless rate can be estimated from the equation for the expected return on bonds:

$$5.16\% = r_f + (0.07)(8.24\% - r_f)$$

which yields $r_f \approx 4.92\%$. That is, the riskless rate is about 24 basis points lower that the long-term yield and the prospective equity premium is then about 3.32%. Thus, the adjustment for systematic risk of the Treasury rate is small and can be omitted without loss. In fact, reducing the riskless rate results in an increase in the equity premium with an immaterial overall effect on the cost of equity.

The spreadsheet Equity Premium Calculator solves Equation (3.7) and calculates the equity premium for a given set of inputs, which the reader can use to verify the calculations outlined above. The inputs necessary to estimate the equity premium are generally available. Figure 3.1 show the prospective equity premium computed weekly from March 2002 to August 2003 using data reported by *Business Week* and First Call. The weekly data are: dividend payout ratio, forward P/E multiple, consensus 5-year growth rate of earnings and 10-year Treasury yield. Expected inflation is obtained from the Federal Reserve Bank of Philadelphia.

The equity premium during this period went from 2.83% (March 2002) to 6.44% (March 2002) with a mean of 4.83%. It experienced a significant increase as stock prices followed a downward trend in spite of the expected increase in corporate earnings over the next 5 years. As of the end of December of 2002, the equity premium stood at 5.08%,

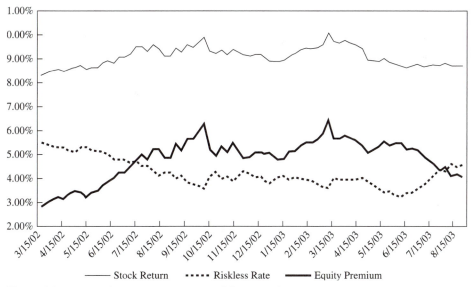

Figure 3.1 Required Stock Returns, Treasury Yields and Prospective Equity Premia. March 2002–August 2003

---

[31]Problem 3.5 at the end of this chapter guides the reader through the computations outlined in this section.

225 basis points above its level in late March of 2002 and further increased during the first quarter of 2003 apparently because of investors' apprehension about geopolitical uncertainty. At the end of August 2003, it had fallen from its previous peak to 4.10%, about the same as the long-term historical average shown in Exhibit 3.1.

Fama and French (2002) used Equation (3.5) and dividend data from 1872 to 2000 to calculate the equity premium with respect to the annually compound 6-month commercial paper rate. They calculated a premium of 3.54%. For the period 1950 to 2000, they obtained a premium equal to 2.55%. These numbers are of the same order of magnitude as those produced by our prospective estimates prior to the recent upsurge of the equity premium.[32]

The DCF methodology can be applied to the expectation data compiled for other countries. Claus and Thomas (2001) aggregated growth consensus data for individual companies in Canada, France, Germany, the United Kingdom, as well as the United States and, applying a version of the multiple-stage dividend growth model,[33] obtained average equity premiums with respect to the 10-year government note yields. Exhibit 3.3 summarizes their results for the 5-year period 1994 to 1998. It shows that the average equity premium for these countries was between 0.9 and 3.44%, with the highest value corresponding to the United States. Earlier computations carried out by the author [Arzac (1993)] that included Italy as well yielded similar results. Dimson et al. (2002) adjusted their 16-country risk premium estimate for unanticipated cash flows and changes in volatility and obtained a forward estimate of 4%.

Graham and Harvey (2001) provide an alternative estimation of the ex-ante equity premium from a quarterly survey of chief financial officers of U.S. corporations who were asked their expectation about the return on the S&P 500 for the next 10 years. Graham and Harvey found that the spread between the expected return and the 10-year Treasury note yield was between 3.6 and 4.7% from the second quarter of 2000 to the third quarter of 2001.

In conclusion, the long-term historical analysis of the equity premium, prospective estimates, and theoretical reasons lead us to conclude that the equity premium in the United States and other developed capital markets is between 3 and 5% and that, at times,

EXHIBIT 3.3	*Prospective Equity Premium in Developed Capital Markets Spread over 10-Year Government Bond Yield, 1994–1998*			
	Period	Average	Range	
Canada	1994 1998	2.40%	1.65%	2.71%
France	1994 1998	2.19%	1.70%	2.53%
Germany	1994 1997	1.99%	1.30%	2.28%
Japan	1994 1998	0.90%	−1.04%	1.99%
United Kingdom	1994 1998	2.77%	2.09%	3.34%
United States	1994 1998	3.44%	2.51%	4.06%

SOURCE: Claus and Thomas (2001)

---

[32]Another estimation of the equity premium based upon an extension of (3.15) made by Jagannathan, McGrattan, and Scherbina (2000) found an even more dramatic reduction of the equity premium since 1970.

[33]Claus and Thomas state the dividend growth valuation model in terms of accounting variables such as book value and earnings in excess to the cost of equity of the company. Chapter 5 discusses this valuation approach.

EXHIBIT 3.4	*Cost of Equity of Individual Companies Using the Capital Asset Princing Model (as of 12/17/2002)*		

10-year U.S. Treasury note yield			4.07%
Market risk premium			5.08%

	Beta Unadjusted	Beta Adjusted*	Cost of Equity
Chevron-Texaco	0.48	0.66	7.4%
Exxon-Mobil	0.43	0.62	7.2%
Royal Dutch	0.78	0.85	8.4%
British Petroleum	0.64	0.76	7.9%
Dell	1.78	1.51	11.8%
Gateway	2.26	1.83	13.4%
Hewlett-Packard	1.53	1.35	10.9%
IBM	1.45	1.30	10.7%

*Adjusted Beta = 0.34 + 0.66 Unadjusted Beta

---

it can be significantly lower or higher. The required return on equity varies over time depending on changes in interest rates, return volatility, and attitudes toward risk.

3.3 THE COST OF EQUITY OF LARGE CAPITALIZATION COMPANIES

Exhibit 3.4 contains examples of the estimation of the cost of equity for individual companies as of December 17, 2002. The cost of equity was computed substituting into the CAPM expression (3.1) the 10-year Treasury note yield, the equity risk premium, and the company's beta coefficient. For the equity premium, we used the prospective estimate as of that date, which was 5.08%.

The beta coefficients are from Standard & Poor's Compustat Services. They are based upon the last available 60 monthly returns. The *unadjusted* beta coefficient is the slope that results from regressing the stock rate of return on the S&P 500 rate of return. The slope is then adjusted for regression toward the mean in order to provide a better estimate of the future beta by using Blume's (1971) adjustment: Adjusted Beta = 0.34 + 0.66 Unadjusted Beta. These adjustment coefficients are commonly used in practice and are derived by regressing the estimated values of beta on the values estimated in the previous period.[34]

3.4 THE COST OF EQUITY AND LEVERAGE

A number of valuation problems require estimating the cost of capital of firms with no debt. Also, adjustments for differences in debt ratios are often required when using data from comparable companies. In this section we review how the beta coefficient changes

---

[34]See Merrill Lynch, Pierce, Fenner & Smith Inc. (1998). Beta coefficients are also provided by Bloomberg, Ibbotson Associates and others. These services adjust beta for regression toward the mean. All services but Bloomberg estimate betas with 60 monthly observations. Bloomberg uses 104 weekly observations. Estimates based upon monthly observations seem to provide slightly better statistical predictions when judged by R^2. See Bartholdy and Peare (2001).

Ignore
Formula

↓

(P.48-44)

with leverage and find out how to estimate the cost of equity from data of firms with similar operating asset riskiness but different debt ratios. We shall use the following well-known property of portfolio betas: The beta coefficient of a portfolio of n assets each with weights $w_1, \ldots w_n$, is the weighted average of the beta coefficients of the individual assets. That is, $\beta_P = w_1\beta_1 + \ldots + w_n\beta_n$.[35] Since the return on the enterprise assets is equal to the return on a portfolio of its net debt and equity claims, the beta coefficient of the firm's levered assets is

$$\beta_A = \frac{D}{D + E}\beta_D + \frac{E}{D + E}\beta_E \qquad (3.8)$$

where A, D, E denote levered assets, net debt and equity, respectively. Inverting this equation yields $\beta_E = (1 + D/E)\beta_A - (D/E)\beta_D$, which shows how the systematic risk of equity increases with leverage. For $\beta_D = 0$ (β_D is zero for risk-free debt and about 0.08 for high-grade debt), Equation (3.8) becomes

$$\beta_A = (1 + D/E)^{-1}\beta_E \qquad (3.9)$$

or

$$\beta_E = (1 + D/E)\beta_A. \qquad (3.10)$$

Since we have not explicitly accounted for corporate taxes, it would seem that Equation (3.8) yields the beta coefficient of the unlevered firm only in the absence of taxes, which is the case for which the value of the firm with or without debt is the same.[36] Let us analyze this matter in more detail. Under corporate taxation, the value the enterprise is made up of two components: the value of the unlevered assets and the value of the interest expense tax shield,[37] and β_A is a weighted average of their corresponding betas. That is, the value of the enterprise is

$$V_A = D + E = V_U + PV(TS) \qquad (3.11)$$

where V_U is the value of the assets of the unlevered firm, PV stands for present value, and TS for the tax shield, and

$$\beta_A = \frac{D + E - PV(TS)}{D + E}\beta_U + \frac{PV(TS)}{D + E}\beta_{TS} \qquad (3.12)$$

where $V_U = D + E - PV(TS)$ has been substituted in and the beta of tax shield β_{TS} equals β_D because the yearly tax shield is proportional to net debt. For the case considered by Hamada (1972) in which net debt is constant and risk-free, $PV(TS) = trD/r = tD$, $\beta_D = 0$ and Equation (3.12) collapses to

$$\beta_A = \frac{D + E - tD}{D + E}\beta_U \qquad (3.13)$$

Solving Equations (3.8) and (3.13) for β_E in terms of β_U yields

$$\beta_E = [1 + (1 - t)D/E]\beta_U. \qquad (3.14)$$

---

[35]This follows from the property of the covariance of a sum of random variables. See Elton and Gruber (1991), for example.

[36]This is Modigliani and Miller's (1958) Proposition I. See Ch. 6 below.

[37]This is shown in Chapter 6, Section 6.3.

However, Equation (3.14) is a special result that applies only when the level of net debt is constant and the tax shield is riskless. In fact, although Equation (3.14) is commonly used in practice in order to adjust for differences in leverage, it is not appropriate when net debt changes over time. In particular, it does not apply in the important case in which the firm maintains a constant net debt ratio and cash flows are discounted at WACC. For this case, Miles and Ezzell (1985) noted that, when the firm adjusts its net debt over time to a fixed proportion of its value, the *level* of net debt is perfectly correlated with the value of the firm. Thus, the tax shield has the same risk as the value of the firm and, therefore, the same beta. Substituting $\beta_{TS} = \beta_A$ in Equation (3.12) results in $\beta_A = \beta_U$. Hence, it follows from Equation (3.8) that the beta of equity is

$$\beta_E = (1 + D/E)\beta_U - (D/E)\beta_D, \tag{3.15}$$

and $\beta_U = (1 + D/E)^{-1}[\beta_E + (D/E)\beta_D]$ gives the unlevered or asset beta for given observed equity and debt betas. For riskless debt such that $\beta_D = 0$,[38]

$$\beta_E = (1 + D/E)\beta_U \tag{3.16}$$

which, in practice, is a suitable approximation to Equation (3.15) given the small beta of corporate bonds. Inverting Equation (3.16) yields

$$\beta_U = (1 + D/E)^{-1}\beta_E. \tag{3.17}$$

Equation (3.16) was derived without assuming a specific tax regime, which means that it is valid when the tax shield is not affected by personal taxes as well as when it is.

EXHIBIT 3.5   *Unlevered Cost of Capital as of 12/17/2002*

| 10-year U.S. Treasury note yield = | | | 4.07% | | |
| Market risk premium | | | 5.08% | | |

	Levered Beta	Net Debt[1]	Market Equity[2]	Unlevered Beta[3]	Cost of Capital
Chevron-Texaco	0.66	12.9	58.2	0.54	6.8%
Exxon-Mobil	0.62	4.0	173.4	0.61	7.2%
Royal Dutch	0.85	15.2	112.0	0.75	7.9%
British Petroleum	0.76	21.0	30.9	0.45	6.4%
Dell	1.51	(3.49)	72.1	1.59	12.2%
Gateway	1.83	(0.36)	0.96	2.92	18.9%
Hewlett-Packard	1.35	(3.40)	54.7	1.44	11.4%
IBM	1.30	20.5	130.7	1.12	9.8%

Notes:
[1]Book interest bearing debt minus cash in $ billion.
[2]Shares outstanding times share price in $ billion.
[3]Beta unlevered according to (3.17).

---

[38]Miles and Ezzell (1985) assumed riskless debt and allowed for the fact that, when leverage adjusts at the end of each period, the first period cash flow is riskless. In that case, β_A is the weighted average of β_U and the beta of the riskless first-period tax shield, which is zero. The weight of β_U is then V_A minus the value of the first-period riskless tax shield $trD/(1 + r)$ divided by V_A. Thus, $\beta_A = [1 - trd(D + E)^{-1}(1 + r)^{-1}]\beta_U$ and $\beta_E = [1 + (1 - tr(1 + r)^{-1})D/E]\beta_U \approx (1 + D/E)\beta_U$ for r small. Note that with continuous adjustment of the capital structure $r \to 0$ and Equation (3.16) results.

In conclusion, in the common case of firms following constant target net debt ratios such that discounting at WACC is warranted, the adjustment of comparable betas for differences in leverage has to be done using Equation (3.15) or (3.16) and not the commonly used Equation (3.14). The latter will overestimate the unlevered beta for any observed equity beta.

Exhibit 3.5 computes the unlevered cost of capital for the companies of Exhibit 3.4. Note that net debt is defined as all interest bearing debt minus cash and marketable securities. Hence, the resulting beta coefficients correspond to the unlevered assets of the firm excluding cash and marketable securities and Equation (3.17) still applies.[39]

*3.5   BEYOND THE CAPITAL ASSET PRICING MODEL[40]

3.5.1   The Original CAPM

So far, the estimation of the cost of equity has been based on the notion that investors demand compensation for bearing nondiversifiable risk and that such compensation can be measured by multiplying the market risk premium by a measure of the nondiversifiable risk of the stock. This intuitive notion received a theoretical foundation in the mid-1960s with the development of the capital asset pricing model (CAPM).[41] The basic model and a number of its extensions have been subject to empirical tests during the last four decades. In this section, we briefly survey the results from empirical research and its implications for valuation practice.

Testing the CAPM is inherently difficult because it involves the relationship between the expected return on a security and the expected return on a market portfolio and neither expectation is directly measurable.[42] Most tests of the theory proceed in two steps: First, the beta coefficients are estimated from a time series for each stock by running the regression

$$R_{jt} = \alpha_j + \beta_j R_{mt} + u_{jt}, \tag{3.18}$$

where R_{jt} is the return of stock j in month t, R_{mt} is the return on a value weighted portfolio such as the S&P 500 index or a more comprehensive index, α_j and β_j are the constant coefficients to be estimated, and u_{jt} is a random residual.[43]

The second step consists of estimating a cross-section regression (across the firms in the sample) of the following equation

---

[39]Consider the case when net debt equals –C, such that C is the net cash position of the company. Then a portfolio made up of equity minus net cash has value U = E – C and its beta equals $\beta_U = (E\beta_E - C\beta_C)/(E - C) = (1 - C/E)^{-1}\beta_E$ because $\beta_C = 0$. Note that when net debt equals zero in Equation (3.15), $\beta_E = \beta_U$.

[40]Sections marked with an asterisk may be skipped on a first reading.

[41]J. Treynor (1961), Sharpe (1964), Lintner (1965) and Mossin (1966). Since its creation, the single-period CAPM has been refined and extended in a number of directions. For example, Mayers (1972) allowed for non-marketable assets and Arzac and Bawa (1977) showed that the model holds in the presence of safety-first investors. Merton (1973) derived the continuous-time version of the CAPM.

[42]Roll (1977) has argued that the CAPM is untestable. His argument is based upon the mathematical fact that for any set of risky assets a mean-variance efficient portfolio exists such that the expected returns of all securities are linearly related to their betas calculated with respect to that portfolio. Then, if the market portfolio chosen for the empirical tests happens to be mean-variance efficient, the test will hold even if the theory is not valid. On the other hand, if the chosen market portfolio is not mean-variance efficient the test will reject CAPM even when it is true. Thus, the tests of CAPM are actually tests of the mean-variance efficiency of the market portfolio.

[43]The beta services referred in footnote 34 estimate beta coefficients by carrying out these regressions.

$$R_j = a_0 + a_1\hat{\beta}_j + a_2F_{1j} + a_3F_{2j} + \ldots + v_j, \tag{3.19}$$

where R_j is the average monthly return of stock j, $\hat{\beta}_j$ is the estimate of β_j from the regression of Equation (3.18), F_{ij} represents other characteristics of the stock such as stock variance, firm size, and book-to-market ratio, v_j is the regression residual, and a_0, a_1, a_2, ... are the constants to be estimated.[44]

The results from regression (3.19) permit testing the validity of the CAPM and Equation (3.1), which is the basis of the main procedure used in practice for estimating the cost of equity. If the CAPM holds, a_0 should equal the risk-free return, a_1 should equal the equity premium, and a_i for i > 1 should be zero because beta is the only determinant of the stock risk premium in the CAPM. The first tests of the CAPM found the predicted linear relationship between average stock returns and beta to hold but with an intercept that was higher than the short-term riskless rate. The regression line was flatter and showed a smaller beta effect than predicted by the original CAPM. However, these results are consistent with Black's (1972) generalization of CAPM that includes borrowing restrictions. The cost of equity estimation procedure developed in this chapter is consistent with this finding.

3.5.2   The Fama-French Three-factor Model

Recent research has found that other factors [the F_j's in Equation (3.17)] are significant determinants of average return and result in a much weaker relationship between average return and beta. In particular, Fama and French[45] found that two other factors account for most of the variance in average stock returns: (1) The size of the firm measured by market capitalization. Average returns are higher for small capitalization firms even after accounting for their higher betas.[46] Size can be interpreted as a proxy for liquidity. (2) Average returns are higher for stocks with higher book-to-market ratios.[47] Firms with poor prospects tend to have high book-to-market ratios and would face higher cost of capital (they would need to provide higher expected returns to investors). Thus, this ratio can be interpreted as a proxy for relative distress. These findings led Fama and French to propose estimating the cost of equity with the three-factor model: (1) the traditional CAPM factor (the return on a market portfolio minus the return on Treasury bills); (2) the return on a portfolio of small capitalization stocks minus the return on a portfolio of large capitalization stocks; and (3) the return on a portfolio of high book-to-market stocks minus the return on a portfolio of low book-to-market stocks. Fama and French show that these factors explain better the cross-section variation of stock returns than the simple CAPM. The improvement comes at a price because practitioners would need to estimate three types of beta coefficients for each stock and three different risk premia (the factors). This tasks has been simplified by availability of up-to-date series of factor returns maintained by Kenneth French and available at his website.[48]

---

[44]The design of these regressions is more complicated than this simple description. Researchers need to take into account a number of econometric complications that can bias the regressions results, including that $\hat{\beta}_j$ is an estimate and thus it is measured with error and that the regression residuals themselves may be correlated. See Fama and MacBeth (1973).

[45]Fama and French (1992), (1993) and (1996).

[46]That small capitalization stocks had higher rates of returns that can be explained by the CAPM was found by Banz (1981). The "small cap" effect has been found to hold in several others countries as well.

[47]See Statman (1980).

[48]http://mba.tuck.dartmouth.edu/pages/faculty/ken.french/data_library.html.

Let us illustrate the estimation of the cost of equity with the three-factor model. The model postulates that the risk premium over the risk-free rate demanded by investors from firm j is given by

$$R_j - r_f = \beta_j(R_m - r_f) + s_j \, SMB + h_j HML \qquad (3.20)$$

where R_j is expected return on the stock of firm j, R_m is the expected return on the market portfolio, r_f is the riskless interest rate, SMB (small minus big) is the difference between the returns on a portfolio of small stocks and a portfolio of big stocks, HML (high minus low) is the difference between the returns of a portfolio of high book-to-market stocks and a portfolio of low book-to-market stocks. β_j, s_j, and h_j are the factor sensitivities or loadings, of which β_j is the CAPM beta coefficient.

In order to estimate the risk premium applying to a particular stock, we need to use historical data on the returns on the stock, the riskless rate, and the three factor returns. Kenneth French's website provides all the needed data except for the company returns, which can be computed from stock and dividend data available from various sources.[49] For example, the linear regression of Dell's excess returns on the three factors, using the three-year monthly returns ending in December 2002, gives[50]

$$\beta_{Dell} = 1.476, \quad s_{Dell} = 0.0634 \quad \text{and} \quad h_{Dell} = -0.661$$

The averages of the annualized factors returns during 1926 to 2002, obtained from French's website, are Market Factor = 7.48%, Size Factor = 2.59% and Book-to-Market Factor = 6.13%. Hence, the estimate of Dell's risk premium is

$$\begin{aligned}
\text{Dell Risk Premium} &= 1.476 \times 7.48\% + 0.0634 \times 2.59\% - 0.661 \times 6.13\% \\
&= 11.04\% + 0.16\% - 4.05\% = 7.15\%.
\end{aligned}$$

That is, according to the three-factor model, Dell's stock is subject to a risk premium of 11% because of its correlation with the market return, it has no exposure to the size factor, and it gets a credit of 4% for its negative exposure to the book-to-market factor, which proxies the additional return required from distressed firms.

Since the risk-free interest rate used to compute the factors is the Treasury bill rate, one must add the risk premium to the bill rate to obtain the cost of equity of Dell. As discussed in Section 3.2.2, a rough estimate of the future average bill rate is obtained by subtracting 1% from 3.83%, the 10-year Treasury note rate on December 30, 2002, which gives 3.83% – 1% = 2.83%. Therefore, the three-factor model estimates the cost of equity of Dell at k = 2.83% + 7.15% = 9.98 which is 1.8% lower than the CAPM estimate obtained in Exhibit 3.5 with the prospective equity premium as of December 2002.

As with CAPM's estimates, the three-factor model estimates of the cost of equity are imprecise.[51] The values of the factor coefficients and the factor returns are very sensitive to the choice of the estimation period. For example, estimating Dell's coefficients using the last five years of monthly data gives $\beta_{Dell} = 1.207$, $s_{Dell} = -0.00198$ and $h_{Dell} = -0.844$, a risk premium of 3.85% and a cost of equity of only 6.68%.

There are a number of difficulties with the three-factor model as developed to date. Besides the high instability exhibited by its results, it is based on historical data, which

---

[49]In http://chart.yahoo.com/d for example.

[50]The coefficient estimates can be calculated with any of the available statistical packages or using MS Excel's array formula "Linest."

[51]Fama and French (1995) investigated the imprecision of cost of equity estimates and found that standard errors of 3% are typical of CAPM and the three-factor model.

does not necessarily reflect investors' expectations and forward attitude toward risk. In fact, its statistical relationship is based upon data from 1963, and there is no assurance that it will continue to hold in the future. In particular, because it is not based upon a model derived from economic or behavioral principles. In fact, the Fama and French results have not remained unchallenged in the literature. Daniel and Titman (1997) tested the validity of their factor model taking into account that if it is correct, returns should be explained by the sensitivities to size and book-to-market and not by the characteristics (factors) themselves. For example, one would expect that the returns of stocks with low market capitalization and higher sensitivities with respect to market capitalization should have higher returns than other low market capitalization stocks, however, they found that both of such returns were insensitive to their factor coefficients and tended to have returns similar to each other. They also found that the returns were insensitive with respect to the coefficients of the book-to-market variable. Moreover, Kothari, Shanken and Sloan (1995)[52] noted that the effect of the book-to-market variable is magnified because of selection bias in the data.[53] More importantly, they found no significant book-to-market effect when the ratio was obtained from an alternative data set of S&P 500 stocks. They also pointed out that the estimation of betas for the test should be based upon annual returns in order to reduce measurement errors that tend to understate the betas of small-cap stocks. In conclusion, Kothari et al. found a statistically significant relationship between average returns and beta but they also found a modest size effect. A reasonable conclusion is that, in spite of the differences between these studies, all show that beta is not the only factor determining the required return on equity at least for small-cap firms for which CAPM underestimates their risk.

Another possible explanation of the observed book-to-market effect is that investors incorrectly extrapolate past earnings growth. Lakonishok, Shleifer, and Vishny (1994) suggest that investors are overly optimistic about firms that have done well in the past (those with low book-to-market ratios) and are overly pessimistic about firms that have done poorly (those with high book-to-market ratios). This would result in low returns for low book-to-market stocks and high returns for high book-to-market stocks. If the book-to-market effect detected in the past was, in fact, driven by mispricing, one would expect it not to be observed in the future as investors can decrease their portfolio risk and increase their expected returns by choosing low-beta high book-to-market stocks thus forcing the effect to disappear.

3.5.3   Arbitrage Pricing Theory

The foundation of multi-factor return models is the *arbitrage pricing theory* formulated by Ross (1976). Chen, Roll, and Ross (1984) found that the following four factors explain expected returns: the level of industrial activity, the rate of inflation, the spread between short- and long-term interest rates, and the spread between the yields of low- and high-risk corporate bonds.[54] They also found that the market index did not add to the

---

[52]See also Kothari and Shanken (1998) and Loughran (1997).

[53]Fama and French's book-to-market variable was obtained from the Compustat database, which tends to exclude distressed firms that fail, while the surviving firms are likely to exhibit higher returns. However, Kim (1997) has shown that the survivor biases cannot account for much of the book-to-market effect found by Fama and French.

[54]An application of the APT factor model to the estimation of the cost of equity of public utilities is made in Elton, Gruber and Mei (1994).

explanatory power of the regression. Their finding is not surprising because macro-economic factors are fundamental explanations of expected return, including the return on the market portfolio. In fact, the market portfolio is proxy for the complex of factors that affect expected returns. However, the macroeconomic factors considered by Chen et al. do not seem to account for the size effect. Jagannathan and Wang (1996) found that the growth rate of aggregate per capita labor income is a significant factor in the explanation of expected returns in addition to those found by Chen et al. This factor accounts for the role of human capital, which is omitted from the common proxies of the market portfolio. Jagannathan and Wang found that the return on small-cap stocks are more sensitive to changes in per capita labor income than the return on large-cap stocks, which implies that the CAPM beta underestimate their systematic risk. This result provides further confirmation of the need of allowing for a small-cap premium in estimating the cost of equity of small-cap companies.

3.5.4 Liquidity and Expected Returns

Amihud and Mendelson (1986, 1988) found that less liquid stocks provide higher average returns than more liquid stocks. They measured liquidity by the bid-ask spread of the stocks and found that average returns increase with the bid-ask spread. They reasoned that investors price securities net of trading costs and thus require higher returns for holding less liquid stocks in order to get compensation for the higher costs of trading and found their hypothesis to be consistent with empirical data. They found that the bid-ask spread has a significant effect in a cross-section regression that included the beta coefficient. They also found high correlation between the bid-ask spread and size, and that the latter was insignificant in the presence of the bid-ask spread.[55] Amihud and Mendelson's findings suggest that the small-cap effect is at least in part a correction of expected returns for higher transaction costs, and should be taken into account in estimating the cost of equity of small capitalization companies. The findings of Daniel and Titman and Jagannathan and Wang are consistent with this view.

The role of liquidity as a factor in the pricing of assets is receiving increasing attention in academic research. Simon Hodrick and Moulton (2002) characterize liquidity in terms of three dimensions: time, price, and quantity. Thus, a perfect liquid asset is one that can be traded immediately without reducing its price at the desire quantity. Trading less liquid assets require sacrificing some of these three attributes and imposes a trade-off among them. While there is not general agreement about how to measure liquidity, it is usually characterized by a function of the bid-ask spread and trading volume. For example, Amihud (2002) proposed measuring liquidity by the ratio of the stock absolute daily return to its daily dollar volume as a measure of the price impact of the order flow.

Huberman and Halka (1999), Chordia, Roll, and Subrahmanyam (2000) and Jones (2002) found a systemic component of liquidity affecting the cross-section of stock returns. Pástor and Stambaugh (2001) found that the stocks with lower liquidity are more exposed to aggregate liquidity fluctuations and that stocks with small market capitalization are the most exposed to liquidity fluctuations. These stocks tend to have high liquidity betas, while the liquidity betas of large capitalization stocks are not significantly different from zero. Furthermore, they estimated the average liquidity premium for the lowest-size decile stocks to be 4.1%.

---

[55]See also Brennan, Chordia and Subrahmanyam (1996).

3.6   THE COST OF EQUITY OF SMALL CAPITALIZATION COMPANIES

We now show how to account for the effect of size on the cost of equity. Size is introduced as a proxy for omitted factors in the CAPM equation. It attempts to account for the fact that smaller firms tends to be less liquid, have higher default risk and their limited trading results in downward biased beta estimates.[56]

Exhibit 3.6 presents the small-cap premia estimated by Ibbotson Associates (2002) using the market capitalization decile portfolios developed by the Center for Research in Security Prices of the University of Chicago with the stocks listed on the NYSE, AMEX and NASDAQ. Figure 3.2 plots the size premia against the midpoint of the size ranges shown in Exhibit 3.6.

Consider, for example, the fourth decile. It contains 230 companies and accounts for about 3.45% of total market capitalization. Its average return during 1926 to 2001 was 14.44%, 1.79% in excess to the return on the S&P 500 index of 12.65%. However, part of its higher return was caused by its higher equity premium, which is estimated multiplying its beta coefficient minus one (the beta coefficient of the S&P 500 index) times 7.42%, the realized equity premium during the period, or 0.13 × 7.14% = 0.96%. Thus, the premium attributable to size is the difference 1.79% − 0.96% = 0.83%.[57]

For example, the size premium corresponding to Paktech International based upon its equity value calculated in Chapter 2 equal to $116.316 million can be obtained from Exhibit 3.6 by linear interpolation between midpoints as follows:

$$\text{Paktech Size Premium} = 3.46\% + (2.41\% - 3.46\%)/[^1\!/_2(100 + 270) \\ - {}^1\!/_2(55 + 100)] \times [116.316 - {}^1\!/_2(55 + 100)] = 3.08\%$$

Note that because the size premium is an input to the cost of equity, its value has to be approximated in order to calculate the value of equity or, more precisely, the size premium has to be solved simultaneously with the value of equity as done in the valuation of Paktech.

The size premiums shown in Exhibit 3.6 accounts for the size effect and also for the underestimation of the betas of small cap companies.[58] Beta coefficients are usually estimated using monthly return data, which for small-cap companies trading in thin markets does no reveal their full sensitivity to market movements. Researchers have attempted to correct for this bias in a number of ways. For example, Kothari, Shanken and Sloan (1995) estimated betas using annual returns reasoning that such returns should better reflect investors' valuations of small cap stocks. An alternative approach is to regress the following equation:

$$R_{jt} - r_{ft} = \alpha + \beta_t(R_{mt} - r_{ft}) + \beta_{t-1}(R_{mt-1} - r_{ft-1}) + u_t \qquad (3.21)$$

on monthly returns.[59] That is, the lagged excess market returns are added as a regressor in order to capture the delayed effect of market movements on the measured return of small-cap companies. Then the systematic risk of the stock is estimated by Sum $\beta = \beta_t + \beta_{t-1}$.

---

[56]More generally, Berk (1995) has pointed out that size is a proxy for omitted determinants of return as well as an offset for estimation error.

[57]Some numbers in Exhibit 3.6 do not add up because of rounding. Ibbotson Associates estimated the equity premium as the difference between the arithmetic return on the S&P 500 index and the return on 20-year government bonds.

[58]Size and estimated betas are highly correlated. This has led researchers to think that size might be a better proxy for the true beta than the estimate itself. See, for example, Chan and Chen (1988).

[59]This procedure was proposed by Dimson (1979) and is suggested by Ibbotson, Kaplan and Peterson (1997). See also Fama and French (1992).

EXHIBIT 3.6 *Average-Size Premia, 1926–2001*

Size	Number of Firms	Percentage of Capitalization	Capitalization Range as of 9/2001 million $ Greater than	Up to	Beta	Arithmetic Average Return	Return Difference	Equity Premium × Beta Diff.	Size Premium 1926–2001
Large-Cap	**391**	**81.63%**	**5,300**		**0.93**	**11.98%**	**-0.67%**	**-0.52%**	**-0.15%**
Decile 1	183	69.78%	12,400		0.91	11.69%	-0.96%	-0.68%	-0.28%
Decile 2	208	11.85%	5,300	12,400	1.04	13.27%	0.62%	0.29%	0.33%
Mid-Cap	**735**	**11.94%**	**1,200**	**5,300**	**1.12**	**14.25%**	**1.60%**	**0.88%**	**0.72%**
Decile 3	228	5.88%	2,600	5,300	1.09	13.94%	1.29%	0.70%	0.59%
Decile 4	230	3.45%	1,700	2,600	1.13	14.44%	1.79%	0.96%	0.83%
Decile 5	277	2.60%	1,100	1,700	1.16	14.92%	2.27%	1.22%	1.04%
Small-Cap	**1,265**	**4.84%**	**270**	**1,200**	**1.22**	**15.70%**	**3.05%**	**1.63%**	**1.42%**
Decile 6	341	2.08%	700	1,100	1.18	15.37%	2.72%	1.36%	1.36%
Decile 7	386	1.48%	460	700	1.24	15.66%	3.01%	1.75%	1.26%
Decile 8	538	1.28%	270	460	1.28	16.66%	4.01%	2.07%	1.94%
Micro-Cap	**2,822**	**1.58%**	**—**	**270**	**1.36**	**18.63%**	**5.98%**	**2.67%**	**3.30%**
Decile 9	766	0.94%	100	270	1.34	17.61%	4.96%	2.55%	2.41%
Decile 10	2,056	0.64%	—	100	1.42	21.11%	8.46%	3.13%	5.33%
10a	650		55	100	1.43	19.28%	6.63%	3.17%	3.46%
10b	1,330		—	55	1.41	24.82%	12.17%	3.02%	9.15%

SOURCE: Stock, Bonds, Bills and Inflation Valuation Edition © 2002 Yearbook. © 2002 Ibbotson Associates, Inc. All rights reserved. Used with permission.

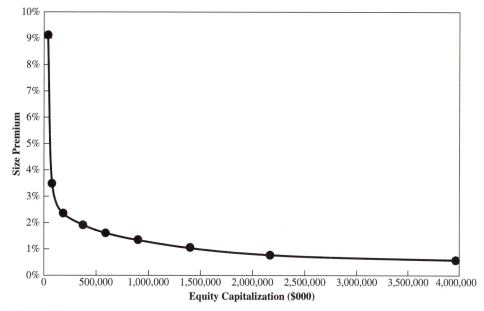

Figure 3.2 Average Size Premia 1926–2001

Unbiased estimates of small-cap betas would reduce the correction for size. However, all commercially available sources of beta provide betas based upon the simple regression of the stock excess return on the market excess return and use weekly or monthly data. This means that they are biased downward for other than large-cap stocks and that the larger correction for size given in Exhibit 3.6 should be used in order to correct for both size and beta estimation bias.

EXHIBIT 3.7	*Cost of Equity of Small Capitalization Companies (as of 5/2002)*

10-year U.S. Treasury note yield			5.32%			
Market risk premium			4.04%			
	Beta Unadjusted	Beta Adjusted*	CAPM Cost of Equity	Market Cap	Size Premium	Cost of Equity
First Data	1.04	1.03	9.47%	30,517	0.00%	9.47%
Concord EFS	1.48	1.32	10.64%	16,112	0.00%	10.64%
Paychex Inc.	0.72	0.82	8.61%	13,331	0.00%	8.61%
Equifax	0.52	0.68	8.08%	4,148	0.58%	8.66%
Iron Mountain	0.76	0.84	8.72%	2,738	0.75%	9.47%
Global Payments	1.13	1.09	9.71%	1,333	1.08%	10.79%
Nco Industries	1.38	1.25	10.37%	651	1.61%	11.99%
First Service	0.55	0.70	8.16%	333	2.02%	10.18%
Caminus	1.45	1.30	10.56%	196	2.38%	12.94%
Teamstaff	0.63	0.76	8.37%	99	3.25%	11.62%
Innotrac	1.08	1.05	9.57%	74	3.86%	13.43%
Outlook Group	0.38	0.59	7.71%	17	10.35%	18.05%

*Adjusted Beta = 0.34 + 0.66 Unadjusted Beta

Exhibit 3.7 shows the effect of the size premium on the cost of capital of companies of different size, where we have set to zero the size adjustment for large cap companies and use interpolation on Exhibit 3.6 to calculate the size premium for the smaller companies.

Exhibit 3.7 combines the prospective equity premium with the historical size premia. Ideally, one should use prospective estimates of size premia as well, but they are not available at the present time. Also, the adjustment for size is an imperfect proxy for the liquidity premium because it is unable to adjust for different degrees of liquidity of companies of the same size. In particular, not all firms with same market capitalizations have the same liquidity because the stationary blocks of shares held by insiders and other long-term investors vary across firms and can be particularly large in small companies. The availability of liquidity betas for individual stocks that can be used to adjust a market-wide liquidity premium has to wait for the development and estimation of a generally accepted model of asset pricing that incorporates systematic liquidity. In the meanwhile, making the size premium equal to zero for large-cap stocks and increasing it with size is a reasonable approach consistent with recent research, in particular with the results of Pástor and Stambaugh (2001).

3.7   ESTIMATING THE COST OF EQUITY: A DETAILED EXAMPLE

We now estimate the cost of equity of Paktech, the company valued in Chapter 2. Because Paktech has no stock pricing record upon which to base its cost of equity one needs to rely on a set of comparable companies. Appropriate comparable companies are those with similar products and size, because the beta coefficient depends on the industry and the size of the company. Paktech is a small cap company with capitalization in the middle of the lower tenth-size decile (see Exhibit 3.6). Exhibit 3.8 shows data for four small-cap companies. Their median unlevered beta coefficient is adjusted for Paktech's target leverage, and the size premium is that computed for Paktech in the previous section. For comparison, the size premia of comparable companies are also shown.

3.8   THE COST OF DEBT AND OTHER COMPONENTS OF THE CAPITAL STRUCTURE

The sources of financing of a company normally include a number of other securities in addition to common equity. Senior debt, leases, subordinated debt, convertible debt, preferred stock, convertible preferred stock, warrants, and other stock options can be part of the capital structure of the firm. Hence, a natural question is how the cost of these sources of financing can be factored into the cost of capital of the firm. Let us consider each of these instruments in turn.

3.8.1   Investment-grade Debt

The yield spread of noncallable investment-grade debt over government debt of the same *duration*[60] is made up of a systematic risk component plus a negligible default risk premium. Thus, the promised yield to maturity of corporate bonds provides a close estimate of the cost of debt. Note that, if the outstanding debt of the company is used to estimate the cost of debt, its coupon rate should be disregarded and its current market yield should be used instead. If, as is common, the debt of the company is not actively traded, the current

---

[60]*Duration* is the average number of years it takes to receive the asset's *discounted* cash flows. See Sundaresan (2001) for a detailed discussion of duration concepts and valuation of fixed income securities.

EXHIBIT 3.8 *Cost of Equity of Paktech International, Inc. (as of December 2002)*

10-year U.S. Treasury note yield = 4.07%
Market risk premium = 5.08%

	Market Equity[2]	Beta	Adjusted Beta	Net Debt[1]	Debt-to-Equity	Unlevered Beta[3]	CAPM Cost of Equity	Size Premium[4]	Cost of Equity
Caraustar Inc.	262.0	0.75	0.835	476.0	1.82	0.296	8.3%	2.21%	10.5%
Fibermark Inc.	49.0	0.15	0.439	302.0	6.16	0.061	6.3%	6.70%	13.0%
Glatfelter Co.	589.0	0.42	0.617	203.0	0.34	0.459	7.2%	1.67%	8.9%
Rock-Tenn Company	467.0	0.90	0.934	466.0	1.00	0.468	8.8%	1.82%	10.6%
Wausau-Mosinee Paper Co.	581.0	0.72	0.815	159.0	0.27	0.640	8.2%	1.68%	9.9%
Mean						0.406			
Median						0.459			
Paktech International, Inc.	116.3		0.706		0.54	0.459	7.66%	3.08%	10.7%

Paktech's cost of equity = riskless rate + market risk premium × beta + size premium
= 4.07% + 5.08% × 0.706 + 3.08% = 10.7%

Notes:
[1] Book interest bearing debt minus cash in $ million.
[2] Shares outstanding times share price in $ million.
[3] Beta unlevered according to Equation (3.17).
[4] Interpolation on Exhibit 3.6 premia.

yield on long-term debt of comparable rating or interest coverage should be used. In fact, it is always preferable to estimate the cost of debt from the yield on current new issues rather than from seasoned issues.[61] This same rate also measures the cost of debt over the long-term of short-term, revolving credit lines or floating-rate debt because it measures the expected cost of short-term debt rolled over time. This is so even if the debt in question is floating and has a cap and/or a floor, once the costs of the latter are factored in as they should be.[62] The cost of *leases* (capital or operating) is also measured by the cost of long-term debt because leases displace debt capacity.

3.8.2   High-yield Debt and Preferred Stock

The quoted yield to maturity of high-yield debt is the *promised* yield that results from assuming that all the promised coupon and principal payments will be made. Estimating the cost of high-yield debt on the basis of its promised yield to maturity overestimates the true cost of high-yield debt by the default risk premium.[63] The appropriate estimate is given by the computation of the *expected* yield to maturity based upon expected payments, which are lower than promised payments because of the lower cash flows to be received by bond-holders in the event of default. In practice, estimates of the probability of default and the recovery under default for specific issues are rough approximation at best.[64] Instead, Copeland et al. (2000) suggest approximating the expected yield of high-yield debt by the yield to maturity of BBB-rated debt, which contains a much smaller default risk than high-yield debt. This is a suitable approximation although is may underestimate the true cost of high-yield debt in the measure that the latter has higher systematic risk that BBB-rated debt.[65]

A note of caution is required. The use of the expected yield as the cost of high-yield debt in the computation of WACC assumes that the cash flows to be valued are true unconditional free cash flows, that is, based upon a projection that gives appropriate weight to downside realizations. Otherwise, the use of the expected yield would result in an overestimation of the enterprise value. Furthermore, using the expected yield in the computation of WACC assumes that the tax shield is reduced in the same proportion. However, the tax shield may be different when the probability of capturing the tax shield times the promised yield does not equal the tax shield of the expected yield.[66] These difficulties

---

[61]This in order to avoid the tax effect on discount or premium of seasoned bonds as noted by Modigliani and Shiller (1979).

[62]Arbitrage-free pricing requires that the cost of collared (cap plus floor) floating-rate debt rate plus the cost of the collar has to be equal to the cost of an unrestricted floating-rate debt. See, for example, Smith (1989). While minor departures may exist and can be exploited by traders and companies, they will not have a material effect on the estimation of the cost of capital for valuation purposes.

[63]Schaefer (1977) discusses the limitations of the promised yield to maturity.

[64]The historical default rates of high-yield debt are examined in Altman (1989) and Asquith, Mullins and Wolff (1989).

[65]Kaplan and Stein (1990) estimated the beta coefficient of high-yield debt in highly leveraged transactions to be between 0.54 and 0.89. However, as these authors pointed out, the debt in highly leveraged transactions may have different risk characteristics than other lower-grade debt. Previous work by Blume and Keim (1987) found no significant difference between the betas of high-grade and high-yield debt and Cornell and Green (1991) reported a beta coefficient of only 0.25 for low-grade debt.

[66]Let r_P and r_E be the promised and expected yield, respectively, p be the probability of tax shield utilization, and t be the corporate tax rate. Then, the expected after-tax cost of debt is $r_E - ptr_P$, which equals $(1 - t)r_E$ only if $pr_P = r_E$. For a further discussion of this issue, see Grinblatt and Titman, *op cit.*, pp. 478–479.

make the use of WACC for valuing free cash flow less desirable when the probability of default is significant. The adjusted present value method presented in Chapter 6 is more appropriate in that case.

The cost of perpetual straight (noncallable, nonconvertible) preferred stock can be estimated as the ratio of the promised dividend to the market price of the stock, compound to an annual rate when the dividend is paid quarterly. The cost of preferred stock would normally be higher than the cost of fixed-rate debt because of its subordination to the latter. In particular, in highly leveraged structures, the cost of preferred stock can contain a significant default premium and should be reduced to its *expected* cost as in the case of high-yield debt. The rate of BBB-rated debt provides a suitable approximation. Although the dividends of regular preferred stock are not tax-deductible, the dividends of trust-preferred issues are, which makes the consideration made above about the value of the tax shield under default apply to these issues as well.

3.8.3   Convertible Securities, Warrants, and Other Options

Convertible bonds and preferred stock pay lower interest or dividend because they contain warrants[67] on the company stock. A simple way to deal with the cost of these issues is to split them into two components: a straight bond or preferred stock and the warrant(s). The value of the straight component is the present value of the interest coupons or dividends and its maturity principal discounted at the rate for a corresponding straight security, which is also the cost of the straight component. The value of the warrant component is the difference between the proceeds or market value of the convertible issue and the value of the straight component. A reasonable approximation is to treat the value of the warrant as part of the equity and assign the cost of equity to it.[68]

Callable bonds and preferred stock have higher costs than their noncallable counterparts because of the interest put option they contain. Ignoring transaction costs, the purchase of the put by the company is a zero-net present value transaction such that the callable security plus the value of the put equals the value of a noncallable security. Thus, for the purpose of valuing the enterprise, one can use as cost the yield on a noncallable security. When available, the yield of a noncallable convertible bond can be used to price the equivalent callable convertible plus its put. Then, this latter price minus the value of its straight component gives the value of the embedded warrant.

3.9   ESTIMATION OF THE COST OF CAPITAL IN PRACTICE

A survey of methods of estimating the cost of capital in practice conducted by Bruner, Eades, Harris, and Higgins (1998) among 27 highly regarded corporations and 10 leading investment banks found that:

- Discounted cash flow with WACC discounting is the dominant valuation technique.

- WACC is based upon market- not book-value weights.

---

[67]A warrant is a call option upon exercise of which the company issues additional shares and is valued as a regular call option with an adjustment for dilution. See Appendix A.

[68]The systematic risk of the warrant can differ from that of the stock. Its beta can be estimated using the option version of the capital asset pricing model. See Copeland and Weston (1988). However, the difference will not be material but for the case in which warrants are a large portion of the capital structure.

- The after-tax cost of debt is predominantly based upon marginal pretax costs, and the marginal or statutory tax rates.
- The CAPM is the dominant model for estimating the cost of equity.
- A majority uses the long Treasury rate as the risk-free rate.
- 48% of the corporate respondents used an equity premium of 6% or lower, and 11% used a premium lower than 4.5%. 4% used the average of historical and prospective premia. 10% of the investment banks used 5%, 50% used 7.0 to 7.4%.

Another survey conducted by Escherich (1998a) of over 200 companies found that most firms rely on discounted cash flow analysis, estimate the cost of equity based upon the CAPM, and use an equity risk premium between 5 and 7%.

The large variance in the responses indicates that there is still significant disagreement on how to measure the equity premium. Furthermore, the surveys made no reference to adjustments for reduced liquidity. One would expect that, as the evidence summarized in this chapter becomes better known, the use of lower equity premia and adjustments for reduced liquidity would become the norm.

3.10   SUMMARY

Estimating WACC for a given target debt ratio requires estimates of the cost of equity and the cost of straight debt. Equity is defined as common equity and other equity-like securities such as warrants, warrants embedded in convertible securities, options, and minority interests. Debt includes straight debt of senior and subordinated nature, as well as the debt component of convertible debt, each with its own cost weighted by its value. Preferred stock of regular or trust-preferred type is treated as part of debt but weighted separately when its dividend is not tax-deductible.

This chapter has presented the main approaches used to estimate the cost of equity and discussed some of their shortcomings. It has taken issue with the indiscriminate use of a large-equity risk premium popularized by finance textbooks. Instead, an equity premium over the yield on long-term government bonds in the 3 to 5% range is recommended for large capitalization companies from developed capital markets. This is supported by prospective estimates of the equity premium derived from consensus expectations, by the longest historical record available, as well as by the theory of asset pricing. The equity premium can vary significantly over time, as it did during March 2002 to August 2003. The prospective approach suggested in this chapter is incorporated into the Equity Premium Calculator included in this book's Valuation Aids CD-ROM. It permits tracking down the value of the equity premium on a weekly basis.[69]

In addition, procedures for adjusting the cost of equity for leverage and liquidity were presented. The latter based upon the observed small-cap premia that range from 0.7% for mid-cap companies to about 9% for micro-cap companies.

---

[69]See Appendix B.

PROBLEMS

3.1 Explain the nature of the survivorship bias and why it results in higher observed equity premiums for those markets that survived over the long run such as the U.S. and U.K. stock markets.

3.2 Verify the calculation of Exxon's cost of equity as of December 27, 2002 made in Exhibit 3.2. Use the dividend growth model and the following data and assumptions: stock price = $34.64, dividend yield = 2.7%, next 5-year growth of EPS = 8.1%, earnings growth over years 6 to 10 decreases linearly to 4.5%, dividend payout remains constant. What are the limitations of this estimate?

3.3 Consider the following data on the S&P 500 index on October 14, 1987, just before the crash of 1987:

Index	305.2
P/E	21.2
Dividend yield	2.9%
Payout	61.4%
Beta	1.0
Equity premium over long Treasury rate	4.0%

In addition, the long-term Treasury bond rate was 9%, and the consensus forecast of long-term inflation was 4.5% per annum.

a. What is the expected real growth rate of earnings implied by the S&P 500 P/E ratio according to Equation (3.5) of the dividend growth model? Do you think the implied growth rate was sustainable in the long run?

b. Suppose that the consensus forecast of nominal earnings and dividend growth of the S&P 500 for the next 5 years was 16 or 11% in real terms. Furthermore, since the long-term real growth of earnings and dividends in the American economy had been about 2%, allow dividend growth to drop to 2% after the 5th year and stay at that level in the future. How can you use these and the above data to estimate the prospective risk premium of equity over long-term Treasury bonds using Equation (3.7)?

3.4 Recalculate the equity premium with the data of Problem 3.3 allowing for gradual convergence toward trend values of growth and payout as done in Section 3.2.5. (You can use the spreadsheet Equity Premium Calculator.) Interpret the difference of your result with respect to your answer to Problem 3.3.

3.5 Verify the value of the prospective equity premium as of December 19, 2001 as computed in Section 3.2.5 using the data there provided. First, verify that the values of undiscounted terms in Equation (3.7) are as shown in the fourth column of the following exhibit. Second, write the discounted expression in terms of $(1 + k)^t$ and equate it to the observed P/E multiple. Use the value of a constant-growth perpetuity for truncating Equation (3.7) at the end of year 10. Note that year-one growth is embedded in the forward multiple.

n	Real Growth	Compound Growth	Payout	Payout × (1 + Compound Growth)
1	0.00%	0.00%	60.79%	0.608
2	9.95%	9.95%	58.34%	0.641
3	9.95%	20.88%	55.90%	0.676
4	9.95%	32.91%	53.45%	0.710
5	9.95%	46.12%	51.00%	0.745
6	8.36%	58.34%	51.00%	0.808
7	6.77%	69.05%	51.00%	0.862
8	5.18%	77.81%	51.00%	0.907
9	3.59%	84.19%	51.00%	0.939
10	2.00%	87.87%	51.00%	0.958
11	2.00%	91.63%	51.00%	0.977

3.6 Use the Equity Premium Calculator to estimate the equity premium as of December 17, 2002 with the following data:

S&P 500 forward P/E (next 12 months) 16.4
Consensus 5-year earnings growth rate 12.23%
Consensus long-run expected inflation 2.45%
10-year Treasury note yield 4.07%
Expected long-term real growth rate of earnings 2.0%
Current payout rate 51.1%
Long-term dividend payout rate 51%
Sources: First Call, Federal Reserve Bank of Philadelphia, and *Wall Street Journal*.

3.7 The beta coefficient of the stock of a company is 1.32. Its average market value net debt ratio is 50%. What is its unlevered beta coefficient?

3.8 The following exhibit contains estimations of beta coefficients, market capitalization and net debt for a number of paper companies. Adjust their estimated betas for regression toward the mean (see Section 3.3) and estimate their average unlevered beta coefficient.

Paper Industry Capital Structure and Beta Coefficients
as of December 2002 (Million US$ except as noted)

	Levered Beta[1]	Market Equity[2]	Net Debt[3]
Abitibi-Consolidated[4]	1.14	4,374	5,770
Bowater Inc.	0.70	1,928	2,278
Domtar Inc.[4]	0.95	3,356	2,655
Georgia-Pacific Corp.	1.59	2,822	12,905
International Paper Co.	0.87	16,931	11,823
Meadwestvaco Corp.	0.99	4,186	4,809
Packaging Corp. of America	0.35	1,874	688
Pope & Talbot, Inc.	0.70	186	226
Temple-Island Inc.	0.93	2,149	1,772
Weyerhaeuser Co.	1.06	10,070	14,041

[1]Regression of company returns on S&P 500 returns, unadjusted.
[2]Shares outstanding times share price.
[3]Book interest bearing debt minus cash and marketable securities.
[4]Canadian dollars.
SOURCES: Companies's 10-Ks and 10-Qs and Deutche Bank Securities.

3.9 Verify the estimation of Paktech cost of equity made in Section 3.7. Do it step by step starting from the levered beta coefficients of the comparable companies.

Chapter 4

Metrics and Multiples

which relates to
- FV
- Equity Value.

4.1 THE USE OF MULTIPLES IN VALUATION

In Chapter 2, a company was valued in relation to the pricing of fixed-income securities and a market portfolio of equities by discounting free cash flows at WACC. A more direct approach often used in practice relies on valuation multiples such as price-to-earnings, price-to-book, enterprise value to EBITDA, and enterprise value to revenues. These multiples are calculated as the ratio of value to some normalizing metric such as net income, EBITDA or revenues. For example, the EBITDA multiple is obtained dividing the value of the enterprise by EBITDA and it expresses enterprise value-per-dollar of EBITDA.

Although valuation based upon multiples is only indicative and not a substitute for a careful projection and valuation of free cash flows, it has a role as a complement and check of DCF valuation. Empirical research on the forecasting performance of the DCF approach and valuation multiples derived from comparable companies suggests that each contains useful information and that relying on both approaches in combination is likely to produce more accurate estimates of value than each in isolation.[1]

Multiples are estimated from the prices of other companies with characteristics comparable to the company being valued. Usually, these *comparables* are companies in the same industry. Since the ultimate purpose of a valuation multiple is to provide the value of the expected cash flow of a company, a comparable must have similar expected growth and risk. Even scale is a factor in choosing comparables because size is a determinant of value.[2] True comparables are not always available. Firms in the same industry are the usual source of comparables but they may be in different growth cycles that the company being valued. Precedent transactions in the same industry, when available, are likely to be a better match if the targets had similar expected growth and margins.

Multiples can be applied to current or next-year estimates of earnings in order to obtain the present value of the enterprise or of its equity, or can be used to estimate continuation value in discounted cash flow valuation. In either case, they provide a useful complement to DCF and a check on the assumptions made in projecting cash flows. They also provide a quick estimate of value before proceeding to the more detailed discounted cash flow valuation.

The most commonly used multiple is the price-earnings (P/E) ratio obtained by dividing the share price of a comparable company by its earnings per share (EPS). When applied to the EPS of the company being valued it yields an estimate of its share price. For

---

[1]See Kaplan and Ruback (1995). Liu, Nissin, and Thomas (2002) examine the performance of multiples in relation to observed prices in ten countries.

[2]See Chapter 3, Section 3.6.

example, suppose that the average P/E multiple computed with respect to the last-twelve-month (LTM) EPS for a number of comparable companies is 20, and that the LTM EPS of the company being valued is $2.8. Then, the share price of the latter is estimated at 20 × $2.8 = $56. Multiples based upon LTM earnings are called *trailing* multiples. Alternatively, one can divide current prices by estimates of the EPS of comparable companies for the following 12 months in order to obtain *forward* or *prospective* multiples. A forward multiple is multiplied by an estimate of earnings for the following 12 months. A forward multiple can give a better estimate of value because it incorporates expectations about the future that may be better related to future cash flows than historical earnings or cash flows.

P/E multiples can differ from company to company because of differences in accounting practices in addition to differences in growth and risk. For example, depreciation and amortization charges depend on previous write-ups of assets and on if the firm used pooling or purchase accounting in their acquisitions.[3] Differences in the amount of net debt also lead to differences in interest expense and earnings. Correcting for these differences can be laborious and yield unreliable results. Particularly when applying multiples to foreign companies with different accounting standards than the comparable companies. In order to overcome some of these difficulties, practitioners rely on the more robust EBITDA metric.

EBITDA multiples, sometimes referred as "cash flow multiples,"[4] are obtained dividing the enterprise value (the value of equity and net debt) of comparable companies by their EBITDA. When applied to the target company's EBITDA, this multiple yields an estimate of its enterprise value. Whenever rental expense is a high component of costs, as in the case of a consumer retail business with leased stores, rental expense is added back to EBIT together with interest, depreciation, and amortization to produce EBITDAR (earnings before interest, taxes, depreciation, amortization, *and* rental expense) in order to get a metric that is not affected by the portion of the assets financed via operating leases. In addition, capitalized operating leases have to be added to net debt in order to compute the enterprise value of a comparable company, and the application of an EBITDAR multiple produces an enterprise value that includes the capitalized value of operating leases.[5]

Revenue multiples are calculated dividing enterprise value by revenues. They are used to value companies for which no earnings are expected in the near term, such as turn-around situations or fast-growing companies that sacrifice profits in the short term in order to capture market share. They can also be used to gauge the value of a company with no reliable cost information, particularly if the acquirer is confident of being able to impose its own cost structure. However, by moving up on the income statement from net income to EBITDA and then to revenue, one may ignore valuable information. Choosing the multiple to apply in a particular situation can be made only after a careful study of the company, its industry and the quality of the available information.

Another useful multiple is the price-to-book ratio (P/B). It can be used to gauge the value of companies for which book value provides a reasonable estimate of the replace-

---

[3]Pooling accounting has been discontinued in the United States as of July 2001. See Chapter 9.

[4]Strictly, EBITDA is only a measure of gross cash flow. Recall that "free" cash flow accounts for taxes, capitals expenditures and changes in net working capital.

[5]The rental expense is made up mostly of a depreciation charge and interest expense, which as such must be added back to EBIT to attain EBITDAR. See Chapter 9 for a detailed valuation of a consumer retail business, including the capitalization its operating leases. Note that leases that are capitalized according to GAAP (capital leases) are already part of net debt and most of their payments are included in the depreciation charge and interest expense, but for a small residual related to insurance and maintenance that is a proper charge to EBITDA.

ment value of the assets in place. Hence, a P/B of 2 times measures the value of the going concern as being twice the value of its book equity. Price-to-book ratios are useful for valuing financial institutions because they follow more comprehensive mark-to-market accounting practices than industrial companies. Price-to-book ratios can be computed by dividing the share price by book equity per share or, for enterprise value to book ratios, by dividing the enterprise value by the book value of equity and net debt.[6]

In the next section, we use multiples to value Paktech International, the company valued in Chapter 2 with the discounted cash-flow approach.

4.2   USING COMPARABLES: AN EXAMPLE

Exhibit 4.1 shows valuation multiples for companies comparable to Paktech International. They are all small-size (small-cap and micro-cap) companies in the packaging industry that are followed by security analysts and have forward earnings estimates. Trailing multiples are computed dividing current prices by actual earnings and revenues. Forward multiples are computed dividing current values by estimates of 2003 earnings and revenues. In addition, expected EBITDA growth rates and margins are provided. As it is usually the case, the number of comparable firms is small and choosing median rather than mean values for valuation is advisable in order to avoid the effect of extreme sample values. An examination of these companies reveals that each differs in one or more characteristics form Packtech.

For example, Rock Tenn has EBITDA growth and forward margin on sales equal to 10.9% and 11%, respectively, compared to Paktech's growth and margin of 6.0% to 8.5% and 14% to 14.5%. That is, Paktech is expected to grow less but maintain a higher margin. On the other hand, while the target debt ratio of Paktech is 35%, Rock Tenn debt ratio is 50%. Fibermark is the closest comparable to Paktech in terms of products and technology. It is expected grow at a faster rate than Paktech's as it recovers from its flat performance during 2002 but it has similar EBITDA margins. In addition, it has significantly more leverage than its peers. Its forward EBITDA multiple is 5.2x. These discrepancies are typical in comparable analysis as no company is the same and expected free cash flows tend to vary from company to company. That is why comparable analysis should be seen as only indicative and is not a substitute for careful forecasting and valuation of free cash flows.

Exhibit 4.2 shows the valuation of Paktech using multiples. The application of revenue and EBITDA trailing multiples provides an enterprise value range of $169 to $188 million. The forward multiples yield $178 million, which coincides the DCF enterprise value calculated in Chapter 2. On the other hand, the P/E forward multiple gives a value of equity of $105 million or 9.5% lower than that calculated in Chapter 2.

4.3   MULTIPLES AND CONTINUATION VALUE

Multiples can be used for gauging continuation value. Discounted cash flow is particularly useful in capturing expectations about future cash flows that depart from expectations about the firm's comparables. However, competition tends to compress margins and growth opportunities, and sub-par performance spurs corrective actions. This means that, with the passage of time, a firm's performance tends to converge to the industry norm, at

---

[6]Price-to-book multiples can be expressed in terms of the spread between return on capital and the cost of capital, the growth of capital, and the period during which the spread is expected to be maintained. See Chapter 5, Section 5.4.

EXHIBIT 4.1 Paktech International. Industry Comparable Companies as of 12/23/2002

($ million)

	Market Equity[1]	Net Debt[2]	Revenue 2002	Revenue 2003	EBITDA 2002	EBITDA 2003	Net Income 2002	Net Income 2003
Specialized paper products:								
Caraustar Inc.	262	476	932	960	88	113	(4)	14
Fibermark Inc.	49	302	394	410	57	67	4	10
Glatfelter Co.	589	203	544	622	125	142	44	55
Rock-Tenn Company	467	466	1,437	1,489	174	170	27	40
Wausau-Mosinee Paper Co.	581	159	954	1,028	108	149	23	49

Multiples

	Trailing Multiples			Forward Multiples			EBITDA Growth[3]	EBITDA Margin Trailing	EBITDA Margin Forward
	P/E	EBITDA	Revenue	P/E	EBITDA	Revenue			
Specialized paper products:									
Caraustar Inc.	NM	8.4	0.79	18.7	6.5	0.77	7.0%	9%	12%
Fibermark Inc.	12.3	6.2	0.89	4.9	5.2	0.86	15.0%	14%	16%
Glatfelter Co.	13.4	6.3	1.46	10.7	5.6	1.27	0.2%	23%	23%
Rock-Tenn Company	17.3	5.4	0.65	11.7	5.5	0.63	10.9%	12%	11%
Wausau-Mosinee Paper Co.	25.3	6.9	0.78	11.9	5.0	0.72	22.0%	11%	14%
Mean	17.0	6.6	0.91	11.6	5.6	0.85	11.0%	14%	15%
Median	15.3	6.3	0.79	11.7	5.5	0.77	10.9%	12%	14%

Notes:

[1] Shares outstanding times share price.

[2] Book interest bearing debt minus cash and marketable securities as of 9/30/2002.

[3] Next 5 year consensus growth estimate.

SOURCES: Companies's 10-Ks and 10-Qs, Deutche Bank Securities (2002), UBS Warburg (2002), and First Call's and Zack's consensus estimates.

EXHIBIT 4.2   *Valuation of Paktech International as of December 2002*[1]

($000)

	Revenue		Net Income[2]	EBITDA	
	2002	2003	2003	2002	2003
	213,580	231,734	8,950	29,901	32,443
Multiple	0.79	0.77	11.7	6.3	5.5
Enterprise value	168,728	178,435		188,376	178,437
Equity value			104,715		

[1]Data from Exhibits 2.1, 2.3, 2.5 and 4.1.
[2]Net income not available for 2002.

---

which time valuation according to comparable multiples is reasonable. Let us apply the forward EBITDA multiple to a projection of EBITDA for 2008: $EBITDA_{2007}$ (1 + growth rate) = ($43.118)(1.06) = $45.705 million. The continuation enterprise value is then 5.5 × $45.705 = $251.4 million.

Another way to use the observed valuation multiple (5.5x) is to compare it to the multiple implied by the DCF valuation. The EBITDA multiple implied by the DCF continuation value is equal to Continuation Value/$EBITDA_{2008}$ = $242.9/$45.705 = 5.3x.

Exhibit 4.3 combines the continuation value based upon the EBITDA multiple with the free cash flow projected in Exhibit 2.3. Their present value gives an enterprise value equal to $184.6 million. When using an EBITDA multiple to compute continuation value it is useful to estimate the growth rate implied by the valuation. This is done equating the DCF formula for continuation value to the value of the EBITDA multiple, and solving for the growth rate. That is,

$$CV = \frac{FCF_{2007}(1 + g)}{WACC - g} = EBITDA_{2007}(1 + g)M_{ebitda}$$

where M_{ebitda} denotes the forward EBITDA multiple. Hence,

$$g = WACC - FCF_{2007}/(EBITDA_{2007}M_{ebitda}) \qquad (4.1)$$

and the continuation value of Paktech implies a continuation growth rate equal to g = 8.48% − 5.685/[(43.118)(5.5)] = 6.1%, which is almost the same as the growth rate

---

EXHIBIT 4.3   *Valuation of Paktech International as of December 2002,*[1]
Combining Discounted Cash Flows and Valuation Multiple

($000)

		2002	2003	2004	2005	2006	2007	2008
Free cash flow			4,564	2,788	4,106	5,156	5,685	
EBITDA								45,705
EBITDA multiple								5.5
Continuation value							251,378	
PV{FCF} @ WACC =	8.48%	17,300						
PV{Continuation value}		167,320						
Enterprise value		184,620						

[1]Data from Exhibits 2.3 and 4.2.

assumed in computing the DCF continuation value. In practice, these two rates can differ substantially and that should lead the analyst to reexamine the assumptions about the determinants of the growth rate of the industry and the company being valued. A crucial consideration in using a comparable multiple to estimate continuation value is the evolution of the industry toward the end of the explicit forecast period. Consideration should be given to whether the industry is in a growth stage that will taper down with the passage of time or its growth is likely to persist into the future. Only in the second case, the current multiples can be extrapolated to estimate continuation value. A second consideration is if the company in question can be expected to have a different growth rate from the rest of the industry after the explicit forecast period.

In summary, applying EBITDA multiples to the valuation of Paktech yielded an enterprise value in the $178–$188 million range. The DCF calculated in Chapter 2 estimated enterprise value at $179 million. Applying the comparable revenue multiples yielded an enterprise value between $179 and $188 million. On the other hand, applying the comparable P/E ratio to pro-forma 2000 net income yielded a value of equity of $105 million that, when added to the initial net debt, gives an enterprise value equal to 105 + 62.6 = $168 million. These differences are common and ought to be expected in valuation practice. Lack of perfect comparability, differences in the accounting of earnings across companies and errors of estimation all contribute to produce a range of values rather than a point estimate.

As with DCF estimates, the enterprise values calculated in Exhibits 4.2 and 4.3 must be subject to the balance sheet adjustments described in Section 2.6.2.

4.4   RELATIONSHIPS AMONG VALUATION MULTIPLES

Valuation multiples based upon measures of gross cash flow or operating income such as EBITDA and EBIT are often preferred by practitioners to price-earnings multiples. This is particularly so when valuing divisions of companies, or businesses that have experienced recapitalizations or asset write-ups. The proliferation of multiples has led to some confusion about what is the appropriate standard against which to compare them. In particular, although multiples from comparable companies can be estimated from financial and market data, they are not directly applicable when the company valued has a different capital structure or growth prospect. In addition, it is often desirable to be able to compare a proposed cash flow multiple with readily available price-earnings multiples.

In this section, we derive the relationship among P/E, EBITDA, EBIT, and revenue multiples of a company in terms of the following parameters: tax rate, interest rate, debt ratio, depreciation rate, and EBITDA margin. For a given valuation multiple, these parameters summarily characterize the earnings and net income of the firm. They permit computing a pro-forma income statement of the firm and the relevant balance sheet items from which to compute the other equivalent valuation multiples.

Consider, for example, that the EBITDA multiple for a given firm has been estimated from a set of comparable companies as being equal to $M_{ebitda} = 5.17$. In addition, let the earnings of the firm be characterized by the following parameters:

$$\delta = \text{Depreciation/Sales} \qquad = 5\%$$
$$m = \text{EBITDA/Sales} \qquad = 14\%$$
$$d = \text{Net Debt/Enterprise Value} = 50\%$$
$$r = \text{cost of Net Debt} \qquad = 11\%$$
$$t = \text{corporate tax rate} \qquad = 40\%$$

Taking into account that M_{ebitda} = Enterprise Value/EBITDA and using the above data, we can build a common-size income statement normalized to have sales equal to $100:

Sales	$100.00
EBITDA	14.00
Depreciation	5.00
EBIT	9.00

In order to compute net income we need to determine interest expense. That is, $r \times$ Net Debt. We know that Net Debt = $d \times$ Enterprise Value, Enterprise Value = $M_{ebitda} \times$ EBITDA and EBITDA = $m \times$ Sales. Hence,

$$r \text{ Net Debt} = rd \, M_{ebitda} \text{EBITDA} = 0.11 \times 0.50 \times 5.17 \times 0.14 \times 100 = \$3.98.$$

Now we can complete the income statement:

EBIT	$9.00
Interest Expense	3.98
Income before taxes	5.02
Taxes	2.01
Net Income	3.01

All the numbers required to compute the multiples equivalent to M_{ebitda} = 5.17 are available. That is,

$$M_{P/E} = \frac{\text{Value of Equity}}{\text{Net Income}} = \frac{(1 - d) \text{ Enterprise Value}}{\text{Net Income}}$$
$$= \frac{(1 - 0.50)(5.17)(14)}{3.01} = 12.0.$$

Furthermore, from EBIT = $(1 - \delta/m)$EBITDA and EBITDA = mSales, one gets the equivalent EBIT multiple: $M_{ebit} = M_{ebitda}/(1 - \delta/m) = 5.17/(1 - 0.5/0.14) = 8.04$ and the equivalent revenue multiple: $M_{rev} = (0.14)(5.17) = 0.72$.

When the initially available multiple is an EBIT or a revenue multiple, one proceeds in the same way as with the EBITDA multiple, obtaining the enterprise value and the amount of net debt and interest expense, from which the income statements and the other multiples are computed. When, as it is common, the available multiple is a P/E multiple obtained from a set of comparables, the computation of the enterprise value and the income statement is slightly more complicated because it requires solving the following two equations for Net Income and Net Debt:

$$\text{Net Income} = (1 - t)(\text{EBIT} - r \text{ Net Debt})$$
$$\text{Net Debt} = d(M_{P/E} \times \text{Net Income})/(1 - d),$$

where $(M_{P/E} \times \text{Net Income})/(1 - d)$ = Enterprise Value. Substituting the previously computed value of EBIT and the company's parameters yields:

$$\text{Net Income} = (1 - 0.4)(9 - 0.11 \times \text{Net Debt})$$
$$\text{Net Debt} = 0.5(12 \times \text{Net Income})/(1 - 0.5).$$

Solving for Net Income and Net Debt gives Net Income = $3.01, Net Debt = $36.16 and Interest Expense = $0.11 \times 36.16 = \$3.98$. Now we can proceed as above to complete the income statement and compute the other multiples. Actually, once the enterprise value has been obtained one can directly compute the equivalent multiples.

In Note 4.1 we derive the relationship among the P/E, EBITDA, EBIT, and revenue multiples in terms of parameters listed above. The formulas permit obtaining any three multiples from the fourth for reasonable estimates of the parameter values. The formulas are a summary of the pro-forma income statement derived above. They are not substitutes for direct estimation of the multiples from the financial statements of comparable companies. But they permit a quick and ready computation that can be used to assess the reasonability of a proposed multiple. The EBITDA multiple (trailing or forward) as a function of the P/E multiple (trailing or forward, respectively) is given by the following expression:

$$M_{ebitda} = \frac{(1 - \delta/m)M_{pe}}{(1 - d)/(1 - t) + rd\,M_{pe}} \tag{4.2}$$

Solving (4.2) for M_{pe} in terms of M_{ebidta} yields

$$M_{pe} = \frac{(1 - d)M_{ebitda}}{(1 - t)(1 - \delta/m - rdM_{ebitda})} \tag{4.3}$$

Similarly, Equations (4.2) and (4.3) can be restated to give the EBIT multiple M_{ebit} and the revenue multiple M_{rev}. For example, from Equation (4.2) one gets $M_{ebit} = M_{ebitda}/(1 - \delta/m)$ and $M_{rev} = mM_{ebitda}$.

Example 1

For $M_{pe} = 12$, $t = 40\%$, $d = 50\%$, $\delta = 5\%$, $m = 14\%$ and $r = 11\%$, Equation (4.2) gives $M_{ebitda} = 5.17$, $M_{ebit} = 8.04$, and $M_{rev} = 0.72$. Alternatively, suppose that one is given $M_{ebitda} = 5.17$ and wants to check it against the P/E comparables. Then, for the parameter values of this example, Equation (4.3) gives $M_{pe} = 12$. These are the same results obtained above via the detailed computation of the income statement.

The spreadsheet Equivalent Multiple Calculator included in the Valuation Aids CD-ROM permits calculating the equivalent multiples for a given initial multiples and the values of the parameters δ, m, d, r and t. It does so by computing Equations (4.2) and (4.3) as well as the implied income statement.

*4.5   ADJUSTING MULTIPLES FOR LEVERAGE AND GROWTH[7]

Equations (4.2) to (4.3) hold only when both leverage and growth are kept constant in passing from one multiple to another. However, when comparing the same or different multiples across firms one must account for different levels of leverage and growth. Changes in debt change the tax shield of the company, and different rates of growth determine the level of free cash flows. Each, and particularly the second, can have a significant effect on valuation multiples.

The best way to identify the proper multiples is to choose comparable companies with similar: (a) rates of expected growth, which in practice limits the comparables to those followed by analysts; (b) leverage; and (c) size. Unfortunately, the number of comparable companies that satisfy these conditions can be very small in practice, particularly in the case of small-cap companies. An alternative is to use valuation theory to adjust the observed multiples of similar size companies for changes in leverage and growth.

---

[7]Sections marked with an asterisk may be skipped on a first reading.

In this and the next sections, we provide two models for adjusting multiples for changes in leverage and growth. Here, we begin with the effect of leverage. In order to account for differences in leverage, we need a theory of valuation that accounts for the effect of corporate taxes. Following Modigliani and Miller (1963), the value of the levered firm is

$$\text{Net Debt} + \text{Equity} = \text{Equity}_0 + t(\text{Net Debt}) \tag{4.4}$$

where

$$\text{Equity}_0 = \frac{(1 - t)\text{EBIT}}{\rho} = \frac{(1 - t)(1 - \delta/m)\text{EBITDA}}{\rho} \tag{4.5}$$

is the value of equity of a firm with no leverage, and ρ is its capitalization rate (cost of equity). These expressions are based upon the assumption that the firm produces a constant stream of earnings in perpetuity. Growth will be introduced later on in this section.[8]

Equations (4.4) and (4.5) can be substituted into the definitions of the EBITDA and P/E multiples to express these multiples as a function of the net debt multiple, M_d (debt to EBITDA):

$$M_{\text{ebitda}} = \frac{D + E}{\text{EBITDA}} = \frac{(1 - t)(1 - \delta/m)\text{EBITDA}/\rho + tD}{\text{EBITDA}} \tag{4.6}$$

$$= \frac{(1 - t)(1 - \delta/m)}{\rho} + tM_d$$

$$M_{\text{pe}} = \frac{\text{Equity}}{\text{Net Income}} = \frac{\text{Equity}_0 - (1 - t)D}{(1 - t)[(1 - \delta/m)\text{EBITDA} - rD]} \tag{4.7}$$

$$= \frac{\rho^{-1} - M_d(1 - \delta/m)^{-1}}{1 - rM_d(1 - \delta/m)^{-1}}$$

respectively. These expressions permit adjusting the multiple for a change in the debt multiple or, equivalently, a change in the net debt ratio. (Note that $M_d = d(\text{Enterprise Value})/\text{EBITDA} = dM_{\text{ebitda}}$.) They can also be used for passing from a P/E multiple of comparable firms to the EBITDA multiple of another firm with different leverage.

Suppose that the P/E multiple of firm A is available, that this firm has a net debt multiple M^A_d and that one wants to value firm B using an EBITDA multiple. B has a net debt multiple M^B_d but is otherwise comparable to A. First solve Equation (4.6) for ρ^{-1}:

$$\rho^{-1} = M^A_d(1 - \delta/m)^{-1} + [1 - r^A M^A_d(1 - \delta/m)^{-1}]M^A_{\text{pe}} \tag{4.8}$$

Since expression (4.4) gives $\rho^{-1} = E_0/[(1 - t)(1 - \delta)\text{EBITDA}]$, which is the P/E multiple of the unlevered firm in the absence of growth, one can interpret Equation (4.8) as the unlevering of the P/E multiple. Substituting Equation (4.8) into (4.6) yields the EBITDA multiple corresponding to B's leverage:

$$M^B_{\text{ebitda}} = M^A_d + (1 - t)(1 - \delta/m - r^A M^A_d)(M^A_{\text{pe}}) + t(M^B_d - M^A_d) \tag{4.9}$$

which for $M^A_d = M^B_d$ provides an alternative but equivalent expression to Equation (4.2). Equation (4.9) can be rewritten to yield the P/E multiple of company A that corresponds to the EBITDA multiple of company B:

---

[8]Multiples can be adjusted for size by incorporating the size premium to the estimate of ρ.

$$MA^{A}_{pe} = \frac{M^{B}_{ebitda} - M^{A}_{d} - t(M^{B}_{d} - M^{A}_{d})}{(1 - t)(1 - \delta)/m - r^{A}M^{A}_{d}} \qquad (4.10)$$

that reduces to Equation (4.4) for $M^{A}_{d} = M^{B}_{d}$, after taking into account that $M_{d} = d\, M_{ebitda}$.

Example 2

Let $M^{A}_{pe} = 14$, $M^{A}_{d} = 3$, $r^{A} = 10\%$, $t = 40\%$, $\delta/m = 5\%/15\% = 1/3$. Then, M^{B}_{ebitda} for $M^{B}_{d} = 5$ is $M^{B}_{ebitda} = 6.87$. Also, substituting these values into Equation (4.7) yields the new P/E multiple $M^{B}_{P/E} = 18.70$.

The Equivalent Multiple Calculator gives the changes in the valuation multiples that correspond to changes in the net debt multiple and generates the corresponding pro-forma income statement.

If the available multiple is M^{A}_{ebitda}, it can be unlevered to obtain $\rho^{-1} = M^{A}_{ebitda} - tM_{d}/[(1-t) \times (1 - \delta/m)]$. Furthermore, since ρ is the cost of capital of the unlevered firm and, as such, it can be derived from the capital asset pricing model (CAPM) following the well-known procedure for unlevering beta.[9] Thus, one can follow one of two alternative procedures in order to obtain the EBITDA and P/E multiples for a firm B consistent with the valuation of another firm A. One can start from either A's P/E multiple and unlever it or from A's CAPM cost of equity and unlever it. The resulting value of ρ is then substituted into Equation (4.6) and/or Equation (4.7) in order to account for B's leverage.

A common situation in valuation via multiples is that comparable companies have significantly different net debt ratios. In that situation, one can unlever the sample multiples using Equation (4.8), average them, and relever the comparable average to the leverage of the company being valued via Equations (4.6) and (4.7).

The correction for leverage just developed assumes no growth and that changes in the cost of debt resulting from changes in leverage are negligible. Let us now deal with the case of differing rates of growth and allow for changes in the cost of debt as a function of leverage. Let B be the company to be valued and A be a comparable company. Denote B's cost of capital and expected growth rate[10] w^{B} and g^{B}, respectively. Let A's EBITDA multiple, cost of capital, and growth rate be M^{A}_{ebitda}, w^{A}, and g^{A}, respectively. (The cost of capital of each firm w = WACC captures the effect of changes in leverage in the costs of net debt and equity.) The other characteristics such as depreciation and capital expenditures to sales are assumed to be equal in the two firms. It is shown in Note 4.2 that the multiple of B can be calculated as follows:

$$M^{B}_{ebitda} = \frac{M^{A}_{ebitda}(w^{A} - g^{A})/(1 + g^{A})}{(w^{B} - g^{B})/(1 + g^{B})} \qquad (4.11)$$

The forward multiple is attained by dividing Equation (4.11) by $(1 + g^{B})$. Alternatively, if one starts with an original forward estimate of M^{A}_{ebitda}, B's forward multiple adjusted for leverage and growth is $M^{B}_{ebitda} = M^{A}_{ebitda}(w^{A} - g^{A})/(w^{B} - g^{B})$.

For a sample of comparables, the numerator of (4.11) would be the average of the corresponding expressions for the comparable firms. Differences in leverage are captured in Equation (4.11) via the cost of capital calculated as in Chapter 3. Furthermore, from Equation (4.11), one can calculate EBIT, revenue, and P/E multiples using the expressions of Section 4.4 above. The following example shows that the effect of leverage and growth on the valuation multiple can be substantial.

---

[9]See Chapter 3, Section 3.4.

[10]In this model the rates of growth of sales, earnings and cash flow are the same.

Example 3

Let trailing $M^A_{ebitda} = 9$, $w^A = 9.88\%$, $g^A = 7\%$, and $w^B = 9.09\%$, $g^B = 6\%$, then trailing $M^B_{ebitda} =$ 8.31, and the corresponding forward multiple is 7.84. Furthermore, let $d^B = 30\%$, $r^B = 9.3\%$, $t = 40\%$, $\delta/m = 5\%/15\% = 1/3$. Then, Equation (4.3) yields B's trailing P/E multiple adjusted for leverage and growth equal to

$$M^B_{pe} = (1 - 0.3)(8.31/[(1 - 0.4)(1 - 1/3 - (0.093(0.3)(8.31))] = 22.29$$

and the corresponding forward multiple equal to 21.03.

The Equivalent Multiple Calculator gives the changes in the valuation multiples that correspond to changes in the net debt ratio and the growth rates and generates the corresponding pro-forma income statement.

A note of caution: The above adjustments were made under the assumption that both comparables and the firm being valued will maintain constant growth in perpetuity. As such, the results are highly sensitive to the growth assumptions.

Also, errors in estimating WACC will result in significant changes in the adjusted multiples. In fact, correcting the multiples for leverage and growth is essentially an exercise in DCF valuation that can be done better by following the method presented in Chapter 2. The attractiveness of multiples as a quick check on the reasonability of DCF valuation is somewhat lost once modeling assumptions are introduced. One should always keep in mind that a "comparable" multiple is highly sensitive to growth and leverage and, as such, is likely to provide poor valuation estimates when the company being valued has significantly different leverage and growth prospects.

*4.6   THE FRANCHISE FACTOR IN VALUATION MULTIPLES

In Chapter 2, we introduced the concept of franchise as a measure of the value created by a company in excess to the reproduction value of its assets. The same notion can be applied here in order to get a better understanding of the assumptions made when applying valuation multiples. The following expressions are based upon the plowback equation $g = bROC$, which as we saw in Section 2.4.1 is valid only when expressed in real (inflation adjusted) terms when inflation is non-zero. To simplify notation we do not explicitly designate the variables as being real but they should be understood to be so.

Let us begin with the forward EBIT multiple $M_{ebit} =$ Enterprise Value/$EBIT_1$ and restate the constant growth perpetuity to yield the following expression for M_{ebit}:[11]

$$M_{ebit} = (1 - t)[\frac{1}{w} + \frac{(ROC - w)}{w\,ROC} \times \frac{g}{(w - g)}] \tag{4.12}$$

or, alternatively, $M_{ebitda} = (1 - \delta/m)M_{ebit}$ for the EBITDA multiple.[12] Working from first principles as in footnote 11 or, simply assuming no debt in Equation (4.12) one can write a similar expression for the P/E multiple:

$$M_{pe} = [\frac{1}{k} + \frac{(ROE - k)}{k\,ROE} \times \frac{g}{(k - g)}] \tag{4.13}$$

---

[11]Note that Enterprise Value = $(1 - t)EBIT_1(1 - b)/(w - g)$, where $b = g/ROC$ is the retention ratio. Dividing through by $EBIT_1$ adding and subtracting 1/w yields the following expression for the forward EBIT multiple:
$M_{ebit} = (1 - t)\{1/w + (1 - g/ROC)/(w - g) - 1/w\} = (1 - t)\{1/w + [w(ROC - g) - ROC(w - g)]/[wROC(w - g)]\} = (1 - t)\{1/w + (ROC - w)g/[wROC(w - g)]\}$.

[12]A similar decomposition of P/B ratios is made in Chapter 5, Section 5.4.

where k is the cost of equity. The second term within brackets in Equations (4.12) and (4.13) is made up of two factors that can be interpreted as the *franchise* and *growth* factors, respectively. As pointed out by Leibowitz and Kogelman (1990),[13] the P/E multiple will equal 1/k in the absence of either a franchise factor (return spread) and or real growth. Similarly, $M_{ebit} = (1 - t)/w$ and $M_{ebitda} = (1 - \delta/m)(1 - t)/w$ correspond to zero spread and/or no real growth (that is, growth at the inflation rate). The interaction between franchise and growth is illustrated in Figure 4.1. It depicts the values of the P/E ratio for the case in which k = 12% and various combinations of ROE and growth. Note that for ROE = k, $M_{pe} = 1/k$. In Figure 4.1 $M_{pe} = 1/12\% = 8.33\%$.

The decomposition of a multiple into its components permits a critical analysis of the valuation assumptions implicit in comparables and in the pricing of a specific company. The same questions posed about DCF valuation in Chapter 2 are applicable here: Is the franchise sustainable in view of present and potential competition, likely changes in technology and the evolution of the economic cycle? Is the growth factor implicit in the multiple consistent with the growth of the economy and the industry, over the economic cycle, and in the long run?

Although the ROC and ROE included in Equations (4.12) and (4.13) may not be directly observable, they can be calculated from the observed EBIT, EBITDA and P/E multiples. From Equations (4.12) and (4.13), one can solve for the implied ROC and ROE, respectively, as follows:

$$ROC = [w^{-1} - (M_{ebit}(1 - t)^{-1} - w^{-1})(w - g)g^{-1}]^{-1} \qquad (4.14)$$

$$ROE = [k^{-1} - (M_{pe} - k^{-1})(k - g)g^{-1}]^{-1} \qquad (4.15)$$

If the enterprise value multiple is based upon EBITDA, substitute $M_{ebit} = (1 - \delta/m)^{-1} \times M_{ebitda}$ in Equation (4.14).

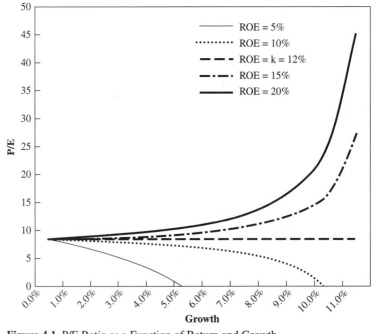

Figure 4.1 P/E Ratio as a Function of Return and Growth

---

[13]Leibowitz and Kogelman provided the interpretation of M_{pe} given in this section.

Example 4

Let k = 11%, WACC = 9%, ROE = 24%, ROC = 11.45%, g = 6%, and t = 40%. Then, from Equation (4.13):

$$M_{pe} = \frac{1}{0.11} + \frac{(0.24 - 0.11)}{(0.11)(0.24)} \times \frac{(0.06)}{(0.11 - 0.06)} = 0.09 + (4.92)(1.20) = 15.0,$$

Similarly, from Equation (4.12):

$$M_{ebit} = (1 - 0.4)[\frac{1}{0.09} + \frac{(0.1145 - 0.09)}{(0.09)(0.1145)} \times \frac{(0.06)}{(0.09 - 0.06)}]$$

$$= 6.67 + (0.6)(2.38)(1.2) = 9.53.$$

Furthermore, if depreciation and EBITDA to sales are $\delta = 5\%$ and m = 15%, respectively, $M_{ebitda} = (1 - 0.05/0.15)M_{ebit} = (2/3)(9.53) = 6.35$. Verify that under no real growth such that g = 0%, $M_{pe} = 9.09$, $M_{ebit} = 6.67$ and $M_{ebitda} = 4.44$.

Suppose that $M_{pe} = 15.0$ is observed but not ROE. One can solve for the implied ROE by computing Equation (4.15). That is, ROE = $[0.11^{-1} - (15 - 0.11^{-1})(0.11 - 0.06)0.06^{-1}]^{-1} = 24\%$. Then, one proceeds to decompose M_{pe} as in Equation (4.13) as follows

$$M_{pe} = 9.1 + (4.92)(1.2) = 9.1 + 5.9 = 15x.$$

That is, the multiple without franchise and growth would be 9.1x. The spread of ROE over the cost of equity adds 4.92, which is magnified by the growth factor to (4.92)(1.2) = 5.9.

The same calculation permits decomposing EBIT and EBITDA multiples. The Equivalent Multiple Calculator computes the implied return and the franchise and growth factors for P/E, EBIT and EBITDA multiples.

Example 5

Let us consider the assumptions underlying the application of a comparable multiple to Paktech. In order to do so, recall Paktech's comparable forward EBITDA multiple from Exhibit 4.1, and the projected long-term operating characteristics and WACC from Chapter 2: $M_{ebitda} = (5.5)(1.023) = 5.63x$ (to express the forward multiples in term of real EBITDA), real g = 3.62%, $\delta = 6.36$, m = 14% and real w = real WACC = 5.89%. Substituting these values into Equation (4.14) yields ROC = 5.94% or a spread ROC – w = 0.05%. Equation (4.12) yields the following decomposition:

Multiple without franchise and/or growth		5.56
Franchise factor	0.141	
Growth factor	× 1.572	
	0.222	
Scale factor [(1 – t)(1 – δ/m)]	× 0.327	0.07
EBITDA multiple		5.63

This means that when $M_{ebitda} = 5.63x$, growth does not contribute value beyond the explicit forecast period. Hence, the application of the comparable multiple to valuing Paktech's continuation value would be valid as long as the company is able to maintain break-even returns (ROC – WACC ≈ 0) in the future. The reader can verify the calculations made in the present example by entering the appropriate inputs into the franchise module of the Equivalent Multiple Calculator.

4.7 NORMALIZING P/E RATIOS BY THE GROWTH RATE

In practice, analysts compare the P/E ratio of a company to its expected growth rate. Often, P/Es are normalized dividing them by expected growth rates to produce PEG ratios. The purpose is to compare growth normalized P/E multiples in order to see if the high P/E multiple of a company can be justified by its growth rate. Presumably, the multiples of two companies can be compared once the effect of their respective expected growth has been removed. The company with the lowest growth adjusted multiple would be considered "cheap." This rough adjustment can be misleading. Consider the forward P/E of a constant growth firm: $P/E_1 = p/(k - g)$, where p is the dividend payout ratio, k is the cost of equity, and g is the growth rate. Then, two firms with the same payout and cost of capital should have the same growth adjusted P/E multiple but this is not so. $P/E_1/g = p/(k - g)/g$ will not be equal for firms with the same payout and cost of equity because $(k - g_1)/g_1 \neq (k - g_2)/g_2$ for $g_1 \neq g_2$ such that $k - g \neq g$. For example, let p = 50% and k = 10% for both companies, g_1 = 6% and g_2 = 8%. The P/E_1 = 0.5/(0.10 − 0.06) = 12.5, PEG_1 = 12.5/6 = 2.08, P/E_2 = 0.5/(0.10 − 0.08) = 25, PEG_2 = 25/8 = 3.13.

A true normalization can be made by noting that for g = 0, $(P/E_1)_{g=0}$ = p/k and p = $k(P/E_1)_{g=0}$. Hence, $P/E_1 = k(P/E_1)_{g=0}/(k - g)$ and $(P/E_1)_{g=0} = P/E_1(1 - g/k)$ yields the appropriate normalization. Consider two companies with the same payout and cost of equity but different P/E ratios and growth rates. Let $(P/E)_A$ = 30, g_A = 10% and $(P/E)_B$ = 20, g_B = 8%. k = 12% for each company. Then, $PEG_A = (P/E)_A/(100g_A)$ = 30/10 = 3 and $PEG_B = (P/E)_B/(100g_B)$ = 20/8 = 2.5. Thus, normalizing P/E ratios dividing by the growth rates shows that company A is priced at a higher normalized P/E ratio than company B. On the other hand, the true normalization gives $(P/E)_{g=0,A}$ = 30(1 − 10/12) = 5 and $(P/E)_{g=0,B}$ = 20(1 − 8/12) = 6.7, which shows that once growth is properly removed the P/E multiple of A is actually lower than the P/E multiple of B. In conclusion, normalizing by 1/g can be misleading and PEG ratios should be interpreted with care if used at all.

The reader would have recognized that normalizing by either (1 − g/k) or 1/g are not generally valid because they fail to account for varying rates of growth over time. Capturing this more realistic case would require doing a detailed discounted cash flow valuation.

4.8 SUMMARY

This chapter has examined the various multiples used in valuation practice and showed how they can be applied to complement DCF valuation. Multiples are derived from companies that are somehow comparable to the company or business unit being valued. Publicly traded companies and data from precedent acquisitions are the typical sources. Comparability is usually associated with the industry of the company being valued but the essential factors determining the value of a multiple are its franchise value or spread over the cost of capital and the expected growth of the cash flows.

In particular, we showed how to estimate comparable multiples and how to apply them to value a company, including their use in estimating continuation value in DCF valuation. In addition, we studied the relationship among the several multiples. We showed how a multiple can be estimated from the value of another multiple and how to adjust multiples for differences in debt ratios, cost of capital and growth.

Decomposing multiples into their franchise and growth factors is a useful way to understand the assumptions about future cash flows and competitiveness that are implicitly made when applying a given multiple. In practice, the P/E multiple is divided by growth in an attempt to make it comparable across companies but the meaning of PEG ratios is ambiguous and should be interpreted with care.

Comparable multiples for private equity valuation are discussed in Chapter 13.

PROBLEMS

4.1 Consider the following data:

End of Year	1	2	3	4	5
		(million $)			
Profit after taxes	5	6	8	10	11
Free cash flow	0	0	0	5	8
Continuation value of equity					120
Stockholders' required return on equity = 17%.					

    a. What is the value of equity as of the beginning of year 1? What is the P/E multiple with respect to year-1 earnings implied by your valuation? What is the P/E multiple with respect to year-5 earnings assumed in the estimation of continuation value? Explain the difference between the initial and the terminal multiples. Are they comparable?

    b. What is the growth rate of profit after taxes assumed for year 6 and beyond? State the assumptions needed in order to answer this question. Estimate the P/E multiple with respect to year-6 earnings.

4.2 Sometimes, it is claimed that stocks are fairly priced when earnings yields equal the yield on high-grade corporate bonds. The earnings yield is defined as per share profits divided by price. Compare this rule of thumb with the earnings yields implied by the dividend-growth model.

4.3 Consider a company with a forward P/E multiple equal to 18x, tax rate 40%, debt ratio 30%, cost of debt 9%, depreciation to sales 4%, and EBITDA to sales margin 10%. Answer the following questions using the formulas derived in this chapter or the Equivalent Multiple Calculator.

    a. What are the equivalent EBITDA and Revenue multiples?

    b. How would the three ratios change for a net debt ratio equal to 20%? For a net debt ratio equal to 40%? Assume that changes in the cost of debt are negligible.

    c. Assume the multiples computed for a net debt ratio of 30% correspond to a large-cap firm with a growth rate of 8% and a cost of equity computed from a riskless rate of 5.64%, an equity premium of 3.5%, and a beta coefficient equal to 1.4. Consider the application of the above multiples to pricing a mid-cap firm with the same beta, 7.8% growth rate, 35% net debt ratio, cost of debt of 9.1%, and a size premium of 0.7%.

    d. Interpret the results obtained in a through c.

4.4 The P/E multiple of Consumer World Inc. is 15x. In addition, its cost of equity = 12%, growth rate = 7%, and tax rate = 40%. Decompose the P/E multiple into a no-growth component and the franchise and growth factors.

4.5 Compute the equivalent EBITDA multiple for Consumer World Inc. as per the data of Problem 4.4. In addition, assume depreciation/sales = 4%, EBITDA/sales = 8% and WACC = 9%.

4.6 British Telecommunications (BT) went public in December 1984. American Depository Receipts (ADRs) consisting of 10 BT shares were sold to U.S. investors. BT's provided local, national and international telecommunications services in the UK, and was a supplier of telecommunication equipment and information services. BT was very much like the predivestiture ATT system with 50% of its revenues obtained from local communications (Bell unit's type) business. Consider the following data:

British Telecommunications Pro-Forma Income Statement 1985
(million £)

	UK GAAP	Change	US GAAP
Net Operating Income	1,875	–7	1,868
Interest expense	395		395
Income before taxes	1,480		1,473
Provision for taxes	53	192	727
Net income	95		746
Preferred dividend	41		41
Net income attributable to ordinary shareholders	904		705
Number of shares (million)	6,000		6,000
Earnings per share	15.1		11.8

Additional Data

1984 Bell units' avg. P/E	8.0
1984 ATT's P/E	13.7
Dollar/Sterling rate	$1.22

The main difference between EPS according to U.K. and U.S. GAAP derived from the calculation of deferred taxes. In the United Kingdom, provision was made for deferred taxes which were considered likely to become payable in the foreseeable future, whereas in the United States, provision for all deferred taxes is required. Other less important differences had to do with pension costs and the treatment of extraordinary items.

How would you price BT's ADRs on the basis of the data provided above?

4.7 Interpret the following price-earning and price-to-book ratios according to the discussion of the size premium made in Chapter 3, Section 3.7.

Price-Earning Multiples and Price-to-Book Ratios of Small Capitalization Companies

Market Cap Range ($ million)		Price-Earnings Multiple	Price-to-Book Ratio
996	2605	22.3	7.1
756	995	18.0	3.4
604	755	17.1	3.7
484	604	16.3	3.1
393	483	15.3	4.5
332	392	15.5	3.0
276	332	14.4	3.0
223	275	12.4	2.2
165	222	9.0	1.9
5	164	6.4	2.0

SOURCE: Heartland Advisors. Breakdown of Russell 2000 companies as of 12/15/1998.

⌐ **4.8** The following exhibit contains data for a number of paper companies as of December 2002. Use
√   them to estimate trailing and forward revenue, EBITDA and P/E multiples of each company. Compute means and medians.

Paper Industry Data as of December 2002 (Million US$ except as noted)

	Market Equity[1]	Net Debt[2]	Revenue		EBITDA		Net Income	
			2002	2003	2002	2003	2002	2003
Abitibi-Consolidated[3]	4,374	5,770	5,321	6,421	914	1,441	194	221
Bowater Inc.	1,928	2,278	2,581	3,255	277	390	(125)	(60)
Domtar Inc.[3]	3,356	2,655	5,559	6,031	831	1,026	146	320
Georgia-Pacific Corp.	2,822	12,905	24,259	25,565	2,325	2,735	284	467
International Paper Co.	16,931	11,823	24,980	26,584	3,307	3,975	548	914
Meadwestvaco Corp.	4,186	4,809	7,487	8,002	864	1,241	(70)	210
Packaging Corp. of America	1,874	688	1,761	1,903	304	381	52	108
Pope & Talbot, Inc.	186	226	540	589	26	52	(17)	0
Temple-Island Inc.	2,149	1,772	4,631	5,155	516	641	77	158
Weyerhaeuser Co.	10,070	14,041	18,551	19,018	2,265	2,560	173	487

[1]Shares outstanding times share price.
[2]Book interest bearing debt minus cash and marketable securities.
[3]Canadian dollars.
SOURCES: Companies's 10-Ks and 10-Qs and Deutche Bank Securities.

Chapter 5

Economic Value Added

5.1 MEASURING VALUE CREATION

This chapter examines the economic value added (EVA)[1] approach to valuation and discusses the similarities and differences between EVA and free cash flow. EVA is not just a restatement of DCF but an important complement that should have a place in every analyst's toolkit. While the applicability of the EVA concepts is wide-ranging and includes the design of managerial compensation systems, in this book we are interested in the use of EVA for estimating the sources of value creation and valuing strategic and restructuring decisions.[2]

Firms create value by investing in projects with returns in excess of their cost of capital. The value created by the firm is thus the difference between the present value of its future cash flows and the capital invested. In this context, the term "economic value-added" refers to a periodic measure of the value created by the firm. It is obtained by subtracting from operating income after taxes the cost of capital utilization. This measure has been found useful in evaluating the performance of companies and their business units and in developing incentive compensation schemes for aligning the interest of managers with those of the owners. It also provides a useful interpretation of free cash-flow valuation.

Economic value-added is referred to as "economic profit" in the economics literature, and some of the accounting and control literature has long recognized the cost of the total capital employed as a cost element [e.g., Schneider (1954)].

Solomon (1965) provided a detailed discussion of the measurement of divisional "residual income," which he defined as "the excess of earnings over the cost of capital." However, the modern literature on value creation stems from the seminal article of Miller and Modigliani (1961) on valuation of shares and its practical implementation by Stern (1974).[3] More specifically, the recent interest in economic value added is in a great measure the result of the work of Joel Stern and G. Bennett Stewart III [see Stewart (1991)] who developed a detailed practical approach to measuring and using economic value added for performance evaluation and incentive compensation. The EVA approach to valuation has also become part of the security analysts' tool kit.[4]

---

[1]EVA® is a registered trademark of Stern Stewart & Co.

[2]The role of EVA in managerial compensation and the effect of the latter on shareholder value creation are discussed in Stewart (1991).

[3]A number of authors have contributed to the refinement and applications of the value creation approach. They include Fruhan (1979), Alberts and McTaggart (1979), Rappaport (1981), Arzac (1986), and Copeland, Koller, and Murrin (2000). Ohlson (1995) reintroduced the "residual income" model in the accounting literature.

[4]See, for example, Jackson (1996) and Milunovich and Tsuei (1996).

According to the EVA approach a firm creates value for its shareholders *in a given period* if net operation profits after taxes (NOPAT) exceeds the after-tax cost of the invested capital (C):

$$\text{EVA} = \text{NOPAT} - w\text{C} > 0,$$

where EVA is the economic value added during the period and w is WACC. That is, as in previous chapters, $w = k(1 - d) + (1 - t)rd$, where k = cost of equity, r = cost of debt, t = corporate tax rate, and d is the target debt ratio defined as the value of interest-bearing net debt to the total market value of net debt and equity. Essentially, the EVA approach allocates to each period part of the total net present value of a project or a firm as measured by the present value of free cash flows. At any given time, equity-holders will experience additional value if there is an unanticipated increased in expected future EVAs. Such changes have present value equal to the increased in unanticipated future free cash flows. The mechanics of EVA and its relation to FCF are examined next.

5.2   RELATION TO FREE CASH-FLOW VALUATION

The following example illustrates the relationship between EVA and FCF valuation: Consider a business unit that has a 5-year life with no residual value and is expected to have the following operating profits:

	2004	2005	2006	2007	2008
EBITDA	$200	$325	$375	$210	$140
Depreciation	100	160	160	60	
NOP	100	165	215	150	140
Taxes (at 40%)	40	66	86	60	56
NOPAT	60	99	129	90	84

where NOP stands for Net Operating Profits before taxes. In addition, assume that at the end of 2003 the business unit starts with $300 of capital,[5] and capital expenditures of $180 will take place at the end of 2004. Both investments are depreciated over 3 years by straight-line depreciation such that the capital at the end of each year is projected as follows:

	2003	2004	2005	2006	2007	2008
Capital invested	$300	$180				
Depreciation		100	160	160	60	
Year-end capital	300	380	220	60	0	0

Let the cost of capital be 10% per year so that the capital charge in each year is 10% times the capital invested at the beginning of the year. Subtracting the capital charge from NOPAT yields the following economic value-added projection:

	2004	2005	2006	2007	2008
NOPAT	$60	$99	$129	$90	$84
Capital charge	30	38	22	6	0
EVA	30	61	107	84	84

---

[5]Cumulative goodwill amortization, if any, is added to invested capital. See Note N5.1 for corrections to accounting numbers.

The reader should verify that the present value of the yearly EVAs is $267.61. That is, the $300 invested in the business unit are worth to its owners $300 + $267.61 = $567.61.

This result is equivalent to that produced by FCF valuation.[6] In order to confirm it, let us first compute the free cash flows by adding depreciation and subtracting capital expenditures (Capex) from NOPAT:

	2004	2005	2006	2007	2008
NOPAT	$60	$99	$129	$90	$84
Depreciation	100	160	160	60	
Capex	(180)				
Free cash flow	(20)	259	289	150	84

The value of the business unit as of the beginning of 2004 is the present value of its future free cash flows discounted at WACC = 10% or $567.61. That is, shareholders investing $300 attain a net present value equal to $567.61 − $300 = $267.61, which is precisely the present value of the yearly EVAs previously computed.

The equivalence is preserved with the passage of time. Assume that 2004 has passed and that investors have contributed the negative free cash flow of 2004 such that capital invested at the end of 2004 equals $380. Then, the present value of the future economic value added is $264.37 and the value of the unit is $380 + $264.37 = $644.37. This same value is obtained discounting the free cash flows corresponding to 2005 to 2008. Moreover, the equivalence persists if the cash-flow forecast were to change as it can be verified by changing EBITDA in the above tables.

The equivalence is maintained even when depreciation for tax purposes is different from depreciation for reporting purposes. For example, let the investments made in the example above belong to a 3-year class for tax purposes and be depreciated by 33.33%, 44.45%, 14.81% and 7.41% over 4 years, respectively, as per the accelerated depreciation method permitted by the U.S. Tax Code. Then depreciation and taxes are:

	2003	2004	2005	2006	2007	2008
Capital invested	$300	$180				
Depreciation		100	193	124	49	14
Year-end capital	300	380	187	63	14	0
EBITDA		$200	$325	$375	$210	$140
Depreciation		100	193	124	49	13
NOP		100	132	251	161	127
Actual taxes (at 40%)		40	53	100	64	51
Book taxes		40	66	86	60	56
Deferred taxes		0	13	(14)	(4)	5

The difference between book and tax taxes is accounted for as deferred taxes. The yearly changes in deferred taxes are added to NOPAT and to FCF in order to offset the non-cash taxes produced by the accounting depreciation method used by the firm. For the present example, the adjustment for deferred taxes will add $0.61 to both valuations.

---

[6]A general proof of the equivalence between EVA and FCF valuation is contained in Note N5.2.

$0.61 is the present value of the additional tax shield provided by accelerated depreciation. In fact, the reader can verify that, after adding changes in deferred taxes to NOPAT, EVA and FCF become:

	2003	2004	2005	2006	2007	2008	NPV	Firm Value
EVA	(300)	30	74	93	80	89	268.22	568.22
FCF	(300)	(20)	272	275	146	89	268.22	568.22

This example illustrates both the similarity and difference between EVA and FCF. Both measure total value created, but, in addition, EVA allocates the value created to the year in which it takes place.

5.3   A DETAILED EXAMPLE OF EVA VALUATION

In this section, we provide a detailed illustration of valuation of a company with the economic value added approach. The company to be valued is Paktech International, which was already valued in Chapter 2 by free cash-flow discounting. The computations are shown in Exhibit 5.1. In order to value the enterprise, one begins calculating unlevered net income for the explicit forecast period. Then, adjustments are made for non-cash items such as deferred taxes to obtain NOPAT (see complete list of adjustments in Note N5.1). The capital charge is computed by applying the cost of capital (WACC) to the capital invested in the year. Paktech's capital invested at the beginning of the forecast period (2003) was $128.9 million (equal to total assets minus cash and spontaneous (non-interest bearing) liabilities plus deferred taxes at the end of 2002). The capital invested in each year is

---

EXHIBIT 5.1   *Paktech International. Economic Value Added Valuation as of 12/31/2002*

($000)

Year-end		2002	2003	2004	2005	2006	2007
EBITDA		29,901	32,443	36,458	38,016	40,678	43,118
Depreciation		12,268	13,054	14,948	17,533	18,530	19,603
EBIT		17,633	19,388	21,509	20,484	22,148	23,516
Taxes	40%	7,053	7,755	8,604	8,194	8,859	9,406
Unlevered net income		10,580	11,633	12,906	12,290	13,289	14,109
Deferred taxes			510	427	362	383	405
NOPAT			12,143	13,333	12,652	13,671	14,514
Capital charge @ WACC =	8.48%		10,935	11,578	12,473	13,197	13,920
Economic value added			1,208	1,755	180	474	594
PV{EVA} @	8.48%	3,483					
Continuation EVA value							69,909
PV{Continuation EVA value}		46,533					
Total PV of EVA		50,016					
Beginning capital		128,932					
Enterprise value		178,948					
Invested capital (year-end)		128,932	136,512	147,056	155,602	164,117	172,946
Depreciation			13,054	14,948	17,533	18,530	19,603
Change in defered taxes			510	427	362	383	405
CAPEX and incr. in net WC			20,634	25,492	26,079	27,045	28,431

computed in the usual way: initial capital plus capital expenditures and increases in net working capital minus depreciation.

The estimation of the initial capital is based upon adjusted accounting numbers and is at best an approximation but it has no effect on the value of the enterprise. This is so because a high level of initial capital implies lower yearly value-added and vice versa. This is not to say that the estimation of the initial capital is irrelevant. In fact, the meaning of the yearly value-added calculation depends on a reasonable estimation of the initial capital and its changes over time. However, the present value of the enterprise yielded by EVA valuation is always equal to the value of the enterprise calculated by discounted FCF no matter what initial value of capital is assumed. This is illustrated in Exhibit 5.2, which shows the present value of the yearly value added and the continuation value for several assumed values of initial capital. In all cases, the value of the enterprise is equal to $178.9 million, the value computed in Chapter 2.

The estimation of continuation economic value added is done calculating the present value of continuation NOPAT from the beginning of 2008 and subtracting from it the present value of the future capital charges. That is,

$$\text{Continuation EVA} = \text{NOPAT}_{2007}(1 + g)/(w - g) - \text{PV\{Capital Charge\}} \quad (5.1)$$

where, as before, g and w are the future growth rate and WACC, respectively. And

$$\begin{aligned}\text{PV\{Capital Charge\}} = &(\text{Capex} + \text{Increase in Net Working Capital} \\ &- \text{Depreciation})_{2007}(1 + g)/(w - g) \\ &+ \text{Invested Capital}_{2007}\end{aligned} \quad (5.2)$$

The nature of these formulas is straightforward: Equation (5.1) states that present value of future EVAs can be decomposed into the present value of future NOPATs and the present value of capital charges. But the latter is simply the present value of all the capital to be invested and this value is computed in Equation (5.2). Note that NOPAT and Capex + Increase in Net Working Capital – Depreciation are allowed to grow at the same rate as the projected growth of free cash flow. In the following section, we derive an equivalent formula [Equation (5.7) below] that gives continuation EVA in terms of ROC.

The estimation of the continuation value of EVAs done in Equations (5.1) and (5.2) [or, equivalently, in Equation (5.7) below] is the only computation consistent with the FCF model presented in Chapter 2. Furthermore, when the continuation value of the FCF model is based upon an EBITDA multiple, the growth rate in Equations (5.1) and (5.2) has to be the growth of FCF implied by the multiple, which is given by Equation (4.1).

EXHIBIT 5.2	*Paktech International.*
	Sensitivity of Value Split Between
	the Present Values of Yearly Value
	Added and Continuation Value

Initial Capital	PV{EVA}	PV{Cont. EVA Value}	Enterprise Value
128,932	3,483	46,533	178,948
40,000	33,221	105,727	178,948
60,000	26,533	92,415	178,948
80,000	19,845	79,102	178,948

Note that when no real growth is assumed after the explicit forecast period, g has to be fixed at the expected inflation rate implied in WACC. Setting g = 0 but letting WACC at its nominal value (inflation premium included) in Equations (5.1) and (5.2) implies that future real EVAs and FCFs will *decrease* at the rate of inflation. Security analysts sometimes make this assumption when computing continuation value of EVAs. Some authors, including Modigliani and Cohn (1979) and, more recently, Ritter and Warr (1998) have noted that such a treatment is a manifestation of money illusion because it ignores that earnings and cash flows grow at nominal rates that depend on the rate of inflation.

Incorrect specification of continuation value can lead to different values of the enterprise depending on if FCFs or EVAs are discounted.[7] From the analytic equivalence of these two models we know that consistent calculation of continuation value is always possible.

It should be noted that the balance sheet adjustments discussed in Sections 2.5.2 and 2.5.3 apply to EVA valuation as well. Finally, one may justifiably ask what is the use of EVA valuation if it gives the same final result as the more established FCF valuation. The answer is that, for a reasonable estimate of the initial capital, EVA valuation provides an estimation of the expected resolution of value creation during the explicit forecast period. This is particularly useful when evaluating strategies for asset restructuring as we do in Chapter 15.

5.4 THE SOURCES OF VALUE: FRANCHISE AND GROWTH

In Chapter 2, Section 2.7, the value of Paktech was decomposed into the value of its current franchise and the value of its growth opportunities. Here we examine the components of enterprise value in more detail. As in Sections 2.4.1 and 4.6, we rely on the spread between the return on capital and the cost of capital and use the plowback growth formula $g = bROC$, which in its simple form is only valid when expressed in real (constant dollar) terms or in the absence of inflation. For that reason, in this and the following sections all the rates, earnings and cash flows are expressed in real terms, that is, corrected for inflation.

As in Chapter 2 let us express the enterprise value in terms of free cash flows:

$$V = FCF_1(1 + w_1)^{-1} + FCF_2(1 + w_2)^{-2} + \ldots \qquad (5.3)$$

where $FCF_t = NOPAT_t - \Delta C_t$. $NOPAT_t$ is adjusted for deferred taxes and ΔC_t represents net investment (capital expenditures and increases in net working capital minus depreciation). Furthermore, let ROC_t be the return on capital invested such that $NOPAT_t = ROC_t \times C_{t-1}$. To keep notation simple, let $w_t = WACC_t$ be constant through time. Substituting these definitions in Equation (5.3) yields the following formula due to Miller and Modigliani (1961):

$$V = \frac{NOPAT_1}{w} + \sum_{t=1,\infty} \frac{(ROC_t - w)\Delta C_t}{w(1 + w)^t} \qquad (5.4)$$

This expression is the present value counterpart of the decomposition of valuation multiples done in Chapter 4, Section 4.6. The first term of Equation (5.4) is the value of the assets in place, which is the value of the firm when future investment just breaks even ($ROC_t = w$) or in the absence of real growth such that $\Delta C_t = 0$ for all t. In that case, only depreciation is reinvested and ROC_t is maintained. This means that (real) $NOPAT_t =$

---

[7]See, for example, Penman and Sougiannis (1998), Lundholm and O'Keefe (2001) and Penman (2001).

$NOPAT_1$ of all t. The second term represents the value created by net investment at a return in excess to what investors can obtain investing elsewhere. Investors demand at least $\Delta C_t w$. If the firm invests ΔC_t at a spread $ROC_t - w > 0$, then each year from the time of the addition of ΔC_t, the firm would generate EVA equal to $\Delta C_t \times (ROC_t - w)$. The value of this perpetuity at time t is $[\Delta C_t \times ROC_t - w)]/w$, which is brought to present value dividing it by $(1 + w)^t$. The sum of all the future additions to value constitutes the present value of the growth opportunities of the firm.

Equation (5.4) also includes the case of shrinking capital, that is, one for which $\Delta C_t < 0$. Negative net investment occurs for example when gross investment is less than depreciation. This is not necessarily non-optimal since the firm may face a shrinking market and positive net investment may be possible only at negative spread. [The product $\Delta C_t \times (ROC_t - w)$ will be positive if $\Delta C_t < 0$ and $ROC_t - w < 0$.] This is the harvesting situation.

Example 1

(a) Consider a firm with $NOPAT_1 = \$140$, $\Delta C_t = 0$, and cost of capital equal to 7%. Then its enterprise value is equal to $\$140/0.07 = \$2,000$.

(b) Assume ΔC_t is expected to be positive in future years but to yield just the cost of capital. Then V is still \$2,000 because growth opportunities just break even and have zero NPV.

(c) Consider instead the case in which the firm expects to make only one additional expansion equal to $\Delta C_4 = \$500$. The expansion would take place at the end of year 4 and yield ROC = 9% for the indefinite future with a cost of capital of 7%. The present value of this growth opportunity is $(ROC_4 - w)\Delta C_4/[w(1 + w)^4] = (9\% - 7\%)(500)/[0.07(1.07)^4] = \$109$. The enterprise value in this case is the sum of the value produced by the assets in place plus the value of the growth opportunities. That is, \$2,109.

(d) If the ROC in the expansion described in (c) is expected to be only 5%, the growth opportunity is worth –\$109 and would bring down the enterprise value from \$2,000 to \$2,000 – \$109 = \$1,891.

Suppose that the firm does not reinvest depreciation (Dep_t) and that the latter adequately measures the shrinking of productive capacity, then Equation (5.4) becomes

$$V = \frac{NOPAT_1}{w} - \sum_{t=1,\infty} \frac{Dep_t(ROC - w)}{w(1 + w)^t} \tag{5.5}$$

which, taking into account that now $NOPAT_t = NOPAT_1 - \sum_{j=1,t} Dep_j ROC_j$, it yields

$$V = \sum_{t=1,\infty} \frac{NOPAT_t + Dep_t}{(1 + w)^t} \tag{5.6}$$

because it corresponds to a harvesting situation in which all the operating cash flow is free for distribution.

Example 2

Let $NOPAT_1 = \$100$, $Dep_t = 0.1 \times NOPAT_t$, assets and $NOPAT_t$ shrink at 5% per year and w = 10%. Then, the enterprise value is given by a perpetuity growing at the negative rate of 5% and it equals $\$110/(10\% + 5\%) = \$733$.

An additional interpretation of Equation (5.4) can be made for the case in which NOPAT and C grow at a rate g. In that case Equation (5.4) can be written as follows:

$$V = NOPAT_1[\frac{1}{w} + \frac{(ROC - w)}{wROC} \times \frac{g}{W - g}] \tag{5.7}$$

where (ROC – w)/(wROC) and g/(w – g) can be called the *franchise factor* and the *growth factor*, respectively.[8] Equation (5.7) shows that value creation via growth requires maintenance of a positive return spread. No growth or growth at zero spread simply results in $V = \text{NOPAT}_1/w$.

If the firm invests at a negative spread, i.e., if $\text{ROC}_t – w < 0$, it destroys shareholder value and the present value of growth opportunities is negative. This case can be called "perverse growth" because the firm can increase its value by merely bringing net investment to zero.

Example 3

Let $\text{NOPAT}_1 = \$100$, g = 3%, ROC = 10% and w = 7%. Then the value of the assets in place is $100/0.07 = $1,428.6, the franchise and growth factors equal (10% – 7%)/[(7%)(10%)] = 4.2857 and 3%/(7% – 3%) = 0.75, respectively, and the value of growth opportunities is $100 \times 4.2857 \times 0.75 = $321.4. The enterprise value is $1,428.6 + $321.4 = $1,750. You can check this result using the formula for the value of a growing perpetuity. Since the firm is growing at only 3%, it can fund its expansion via retained earnings, which would limit NOPAT payout to 1 – g/ROC = 1 – 3%/10% = 70% or $0.7 \times \text{NOPAT}(1 + g)^{t-1}$. Hence, the value of the enterprise is (0.7)(100)/(7% – 3%) = $1,750. That is, Equation (5.7) partitions the value of a growing firm into the value produced by the asset in place and the value of its growth opportunities. In addition, it shows what contribution to the latter is made by the franchise factor or return spread and what contribution is made by future growth.

5.5   ECONOMIC VALUE-ADDED AND MARKET VALUE

For the simple valuations models outlined in the previous section it is possible to specify a linear relationship between market value and yearly measures of value creation. One such a model results from assuming that both FCF and capital grow at a constant rate. Then, substituting $\text{NOPAT}_1 = \text{ROC} \times C_0$ into Equation (5.7) yields the following ratio of enterprise value to capital invested:

$$\frac{V}{C} = 1 + \frac{\text{ROC} - w}{w - g} \tag{5.8}$$

V/C is the ratio of enterprise value to the book value of the assets.[9] V is the enterprise value, that is, the market value of net debt (D) and equity (E), ROC = NOPAT/C is the return on invested capital, and g is the grow rate such that g < w. As in the previous section, Equation (5.8) summarizes the basic meaning of value creation analysis: V/C is greater, equal, or less than unity as ROC is greater, equal, or less than w, and represents the cases in which the firm creates value, just breaks even or destroys value. Note that Equation (5.8) can be written as V/C = (ROC – g)/(w – g). Hence, for small g, V/C ≈ ROC/w.

Example 4

Let ROC be 19%, g = 9%, w = 13%. Substituting these values into Equation (5.8) yields

$$\frac{V}{C} = 1 + \frac{19\% - 13\%}{13\% - 9\%} = 2.5.$$

---

[8]See Chapter 4, Section 4.6 and compare Equation (5.7) to expression (4.11) for the EBIT multiple.

[9]When C is measured by the replacement value of the assets, this ratio is referred as Tobin's q after Tobin (1969).

While apparently different, Equation (5.8) is nothing else than a restatement of the familiar perpetual growth valuation formula. In fact, substituting the definitions of V, w and ROC into Equation (5.8) permits rewriting it as follows:

$$E = \frac{NOPAT_1(1 - t)rD_0 - g(C_0 - D_0)}{k - g} \tag{5.9}$$

Note that the first two terms equal net profits after taxes and $g(C_0 - D_0)$ is the growth of capital to be financed by equity. Thus, the denominator equals dividends when the growth of equity is financed via retained earnings and Equation (5.9) is an alternative expression of the dividend growth model.

Most firms are not expected to be able maintain a positive return spread indefinitely. Competition in the marketplace exerts downward pressure on product prices and product innovations and changes in tastes tend to erode competitive advantage. Barring a continuous stream of successful new products, the typical firm will not be able to maintain its competitive advantage in the marketplace forever and will see its return spread shrink over time. One simple way of capturing this phenomenon is by truncating the duration of the positive spread period at some finite time horizon T [as in Stern's (1974) model]. After that point, the firm is assumed to break even. A break-even firm is one that just manages to pay the cost of all the factors of production, including capital. This situation is similar to that of a firm in long-run competitive equilibrium in which excess profits have been removed by competition. Note that the market value and the invested capital of that firm will be the same when the return spread is zero. In fact, referring to Equation (5.8) we note that V/C = 1 if ROC = w for all t. Now, let us assume that the firm maintains ROC > w for t < T and that ROC = w thereafter. Then, one can show that Equation (5.8) becomes[10]

$$\frac{V}{C} = 1 + \frac{ROC - w}{w - g}[1 - \frac{(1 + g)^T}{(1 + w)^T}] \quad \text{if } g \neq w \tag{5.10}$$

and

$$\frac{V}{C} = 1 + \frac{T(ROC - w)}{1 + w} \quad \text{if } g = w \tag{5.11}$$

Note that Equation (5.10) allows for the case in which g > w because growth after T does not contribute to value when ROC = w. Equation (5.10) also applies to a firm that begins with a negative spread, i.e., ROC < w, and manages to break even after time T. In that case V/C < 1.

The models examined in Section 5.4 and the present one specialize to the valuation of equity and can be written in terms of share price P, book equity per share B, return on equity ROE, and cost of equity k. For example, Equation (5.10) can be restated to give the following expression for the price-to-book ratio:

$$\frac{P}{B} = 1 + \frac{ROE - k}{k - g}[1 - \frac{(1 + g)^T}{(1 + k)^T}] \quad \text{if } g \neq k \tag{5.12}$$

Example 5

Let ROE = 15%, g = 8%, k = 10% and the duration of the ROE – k spread T = 12 years. Substituting these values into Equation (5.12) gives:

---

[10]As with so many aspects of valuation theory, this formula was already mentioned by Miller and Modigliani (1961). See their footnote 15.

$$\frac{P}{B} = 1 + \frac{15 - 10}{10 - 8}[1 - (1.08/1.10)^{12}] = 3.29$$

That is, the equity of the company has a value equal to 3.29 times its book equity.

Example 6

Equation (5.12) can be used to get an estimate of the period during which a company is expected to maintain its competitive advantage or positive return spread. Consider IBM in February of 2002. Its P/B was 8.5, the 5-year consensus real growth of earnings was 9.27%, and its historic 5-year average real return on equity was 25.27%. In addition, its beta coefficient was 1.15, and the real 10-year Treasury note rate was 2.49%. Hence, for an equity premium of 3.5%, IBM's real cost of equity was k = 2.49% + (3.5)(1.15) = 6.52%. With these data we can ask for how long investors assumed that IBM could maintain a return spread equal to its historic average, that is, equal to ROE − k = 25.27% − 6.52% = 18.75%. Substituting these numbers into Equation (5.12) results in the following expression in terms of the period of competitive advantage T:

$$8.5 = 1 + 18.75\%/(-2.75\%)[1 - (1.0927/1.0652)^T], \quad \text{or} \quad T = 29 \text{ years}$$

5.6 SOME EMPIRICAL EVIDENCE

One interesting property of this admittedly simple model is its linearity in the return spread. That is, for g and T constant (or T sufficiently large), Equation (5.10) can be written as

$$V/C = a + b\,ROC = a + b\,NOPAT/C$$

or

$$V/C = a' + b'\,EVA/(wC)$$

where a′ = a + bw and b′ = bw. O'Byrne (1996) estimated both linear models with 7,546 observations from the Stern-Stewart Performance 1000 database for 1983 to 1993 and obtained the following results:

$$V/C = 0.81 + 9.88\,NOPAT/C, \quad R^2 = 0.33$$
$$V/C = 1.88 + 1.12\,EVA/(wC), \quad R^2 = 0.31$$

where the values of the correlation coefficient (R^2) mean that the regressions explain 33% and 31% of the variance of V/C, respectively. The unexplained variance is caused by other factors affecting value and not captured by this simple model, including variations across firms in the expected duration of their competitive advantage, the expected growth rate and the cost of capital (although the EVA/(wC) term captures some of the effect of variations in w). These two specifications are basically indistinguishable. Their coefficients are highly significant,[11] and both are consistent with the EVA version of FCF valuation in the sense that, to some extent, the market extrapolates futures cash flows based upon ROC or EVA/C. However, these results do not go beyond the traditional accounting model in which value is explained by earnings or the accounting return on investment.[12]

O'Byrne also estimated a more refined specification of the valuation model. He perceptibly noted that investors are likely to weigh more the effect on value of positive EVA

---

[11]The t-statistics are t(a) = 41, t(b) = 61, t(a′) = 174, t(b′) = 58. O'Byrne did not reported t values. They were calculated from other statistics reported in his article.

[12]See Eaton, Harris and Ohlson (1992).

than that of negative EVA because they would expect that a negative EVA situation would eventually be turned around. Thus, O'Byrne split the EVA/(wC) regressor into two variables. One variable containing the positive values or zero otherwise. The other containing the negative values or zero otherwise. In terms of Equation (5.10), O'Byrne's specification assumes that investors expect the period of competitive advantage (positive spread) to be longer that the period of competitive disadvantage (negative spread). In addition, O'Byrne added to the regression model the term ln(C) in order to account the effect of size and included industry dummies. He found that the modified EVA model accounts for 56% of the variance in V/C. Another study by Biddle et al. (1997) found that once the same adjustments are made to the NOPAT equation, it explains 49% of the variance. However, as pointed out by O'Byrne (1999), adding capital as a regressor to the NOPAT equation essentially converts it into an EVA model.

5.7   SUMMARY

This chapter has shown that EVA valuation is a restatement of free cash-flow valuation that provides an estimate of the expected realization of value during the explicit forecast period. Although estimating yearly EVAs is not needed for the strict purpose of valuing a firm or business unit, it permits linking valuation to strategic decision making in a natural way by showing when value is created or destroyed by the present business strategy and how changes to the latter may affect the value of the enterprise. In Chapter 15, we use the EVA framework to value asset-restructuring decisions.

EVA can play an important role in management compensation and act as a powerful incentive to capital efficiency and value creation.[13] Firms adopting EVA as a compensation metric will find it useful to adopt the EVA approach for valuing acquisitions and capital budgets.

---

[13]See Stewart, *op cit.*

PROBLEMS

5.1 Value TPI Inc. using the EVA approach with the data of Problem 2.7 and compare your result to the answer to Problem 2.7. Assume that initial capital is $70 million.

5.2 Recalculate the value of TPI Inc. using the EVA approach for an initial capital of $90 million, compare it to your result in 5.1.

5.3 Invested capital is $100 million. ROC is expected to be 20% for the next 10 years and drop to 10% afterwards. The cost of capital is 10%. The firm is expected to grow at 5% per year. What is the enterprise value? The firm has received a $100 million acquisition offer for its equity plus the assumption of its outstanding net debt that equals $40 million. What do you recommend to its stockholders?[14]

5.4 Consider the case in which initial equity capital is $100 million, ROE = 25%, the cost of equity is 15%, the duration of the positive spread is 10 years, and expected growth during this period is 30%. Note that required additional equity is 120% of net income (why?). Assume the target's net debt and dividend payout ratios are both 50%. This means that the firm will need to issue additional stock if it wants to maintain its current debt-to-equity ratio and undertake all its value creating investment opportunities because retained earnings will not be sufficient to finance its equity requirements. Equation (5.12) still applies to the present case (why?). Use it to estimate the value created by the firm.

5.5 Compute the enterprise value and the required capital investment as a fraction of NOPAT for ROC = 25% for 10 years and ROC = 10% thereafter, WACC = 10%, g = 15%, and initial invested capital equal to $100 million.

5.6 Capital invested amounts to $100, ROC = 10%, and WACC = 15%. ROC will remain at 10% during the next 5 years; afterwards it will increase to 15%, and it will stay at that level. The firm is expected to grow at 5% per year throughout. The firm has received an acquisition offer of $50 million for the enterprise free of debt. What would you recommend to its stockholders?

5.7 Mr. N. N. Miller, an important stockholder of SCN has asked you, a member of the investment banking firm of Bauer & Smith, to determine if his conjecture has any merit. Miller claims that SCN is underpriced because of its poor management and lack of clarity. He says that stockholders would gain if the company were split into two separate companies, one for each of its two business units: Paper Clips and Breakfast Tea. In his opinion, these two units would trade at a higher value after a spin-off or could be sold separately at good prices to potential acquirers and the proceeds distributed to the stockholders of SCN. He is thinking about attempting a takeover bid for SCN.

The current price of SCN stock is $36.7 per share. There are 200 million shares outstanding. Your own research on the matter has produced the following information:

Expected Performance After Split

	Paper Clips	Breakfast Tea
Return on equity first ten years	10%	30%
Return on equity thereafter	10%	cost of equity
Earnings at the end of first year (millions)	$320	$270
Earning retention rate	40%	80%
Current net debt (millions)	$2,290	$1,227
Beta of equity (levered)	0.7	1.1
Equity premium over riskless rate	4.0%	4.0%
10-year Treasury note yield	4.8%	4.8%

[14]In this and the following problems, all the rates are expressed in real terms.

Is Mr. Miller correct? Why? How much should potential acquirers be willing to pay for each of the two business units if sold separately?

5.8 North American Labels, Inc. is made up of two business units: Pinkerton and Pipedream. Great Dane Capital (GDC) has identified North American as a possible takeover target. Estimates of the expected performance of each unit after acquisition, break-up, and resale are as follows:

	Pinkerton	Pipedream
Invested capital (millions)	$2,000	$1,000
Growth rate	5%	10%
ROC (= NOPAT/Invested capital)		
First ten years	10%	20%
Thereafter	10%	12.8%
Net debt ratio	35%	30%
Beta (levered)	1.0	1.2
Cost of debt	7.0%	7.0%
Tax rate	40%	40%
10-year Treasury note yield	4.3%	4.3%
Equity premium over riskless rate	3.5%	3.5%

North American stock is trading at $35 per share and there are 100 million shares outstanding. What is the maximum share price GDC can afford to pay for North American if it estimates that it needs 6 months to carry the transaction through break up and resale of the units and it needs to make a 20% return over that period (that is, a 44% annualized return) on the capital invested to justify acquiring the equity of North American. Assume that the cash generated during the 6 months GDC would hold the assets goes to pay the deal expenses.

Chapter 6

Valuation with Changing Capital Structure

6.1 LEVERAGE CHANGES AND ENTERPRISE VALUE

This chapter examines the valuation of firms with changing capital structure. Temporary departures from a target debt ratio take place in the normal course of business because of internal changes or the lumpiness of external financing. Some departures are large and take time to correct. In principle, a firm may stick to its target debt ratio by continuously issuing or retiring equity and/or debt. However, a number of factors lead to departures from the company's desired target. They include economies of scale in financing that result in a relatively large issue of a particular instrument, acquisitions financed entirely with debt or equity, and increased indebtedness because of gradual deterioration of the business and its cash flow. Leveraged buyouts (LBOs) and some recapitalizations result in temporary high levels of debt. Some firms incur in high levels of debt in order to repurchase their own shares and fend-off unwanted takeovers; other recapitalizations are made to salvage a business in trouble. Another case of high level of debt to be reduced over time is project financing. Firms that in the past have embarked in significant debt reductions include Du-Pont, Eastman Kodak, Owens Corning, Southland, ATT, and most LBOs. The valuation method presented in this chapter also applies to firms that plan to increase their debt ratio over time in order to maintain or increase their dividend payout or repurchase their own shares.

An increase in the debt ratio affects the value of the firm in two ways: (1) value increases by the additional value of the interest tax shield, and (2) the tax-shield gain is partially offset by the increase in the cost of equity because leverage magnifies systematic risk. Thus, small fluctuations in leverage do not have a significant impact on the value of the firm and free cash flows can be discounted at a WACC based upon the target debt ratio of the firm. We show in Note N6.1 that fluctuations in the debt ratio around its target have less than a 1% effect on enterprise value. More specifically, for a firm with a target debt ratio of 40% that pays 12% interest on its debt and 40% corporate income taxes, yearly fluctuations of ±50% it its debt level would change its enterprise value by less than 0.5%, and a ±10% yearly fluctuation would result in a change smaller than 0.1%. However, for large persistent deviations from the target debt ratio, the tax-shield change may dominate the increase in the cost of capital and have a significant effect on the value of the firm. On the other hand, high leverage may increase the cost of potential financial distress or reduce the competitive flexibility of the firm and offset the tax-shield gain.

In order to value a firm that plans a large increase in leverage, proceed in two steps: First, perform a formal valuation as described below ignoring the possible cost of reduced financial flexibility or potential financial distress. Afterwards, compare the gain of additional leverage with the potential cost of reduced financial flexibility or potential financial distress. This last analysis is, of necessity, mostly qualitative and must include strategic considerations such as competition and the mobility of the firm assets.

In this chapter we show how to value a firm under three alternative debt policies that do not maintain a constant debt ratio. (1) The first case is one in which the *level of debt* is expected to follow a predetermined trajectory independent of the value of the firm. This case requires using a variation of the DCF valuation procedure called *adjusted present value* (APV). (2) In the second case, the *debt ratio* is expected to follow a predetermined set of values, but the *level* of debt in each year adjusts with the value of the enterprise to maintain the planned debt ratio during that year. This case can be valued discounting each year cash flow at the WACC applicable to that particular year. Discounting is somewhat more complicated than when the debt ratio is constant over time and WACC is constant. It requires starting from the continuation value at the end of the explicit forecast period and iterating backward to compute the value of the enterprise in each year. We call this method *recursive WACC*. Fortunately, discounting in this case can be reduced to discounting each year's sum of FCF and tax shield at the cost of capital of the unlevered firm. This alternative procedure is called *compressed adjusted present value*. (3) Furthermore, in high-leverage situations such as LBOs, debt reduction is a function of uncertain cash-flow realizations and results in a debt ratio that is itself uncertain, further complicating the valuation problem.[1] Handling this case requires a variation of APV called *recursive adjusted present value*. These variations may seem unnecessarily confusing at this point, and the reader may hesitate before undertaking the rather tedious task of going through the mechanics of each. However, such an undertaking would provide the tools for dealing with the most common departures from standard WACC valuation.

6.2   ADJUSTED PRESENT VALUE AND THE VALUE OF THE TAX SHIELD

Myers's APV rule[2] provides a straightforward procedure for valuing a firm with predetermined changes in the level of debt. It does so by partitioning cash flows into more easily valued components such that the value of the leveraged firm is made up of the value of the firm without debt plus the value of its tax shield. This result is quite general. We shall show it allowing for personal taxes. At the cost of burdening the argument with additional notation we provide an explicit examination of the role of personal taxes in APV valuation. Consider the after–personal taxes free cash flow (FCF) *received* by investors in a given period:[3]

$$[\text{Cash flow to Equity}] + [\text{Cash flow to Debt}] = [(1 - t_S)((1 - t)(\text{EBIT} - r\text{Debt})$$

$$+ \Delta\text{Deferred Taxes} + \text{Depreciation} - \text{Capex}$$

$$- \Delta\text{Net Working Capital}) + \Delta\text{Debt}] + [(1 - t_B)r\text{Debt} - \Delta\text{Debt}]$$

$$= (1 - t_S)[(1 - t)\,\text{EBIT} + \Delta\text{Deferred Taxes} + \text{Depreciation} - \text{Capex}$$

$$- \Delta\text{Net Working Capital}] + [(1 - t_B) - (1 - t_S)(1 - t)]\,r\text{Debt}$$

$$= (1 - t_S)\,(\text{Unlevered FCF}) + \text{Tax Shield after Personal Taxes}$$

---

[1]The debt covenants of leveraged buyouts or firms recapitalized under distress commonly forbid distributing excess cash to shareholders or reinvesting it in non-liquid assets. Excess cash can either be invested in marketable securities (at a rate well below the cost of the firm's debt) or, sometimes obligatorily, used to retire debt. In cases in which the cash flow is below the minimum amortization requirements, the firm may be able to use revolving credit facilities, issue new debt, or renegotiate the terms of existing debt.

[2]See Myers (1974). This is the original statement of the adjusted present value approach, itself based upon the work of Modigliani and Miller (1958).

[3]Note that the cash flow *received* by debt holders is before subtracting the tax shield of interest expense. In Chapter 2, Section 2.5.1, FCF was defined as the cash flow *paid* by the firm taking into account the tax it saved on its interest expense. See also Note N2.3.

where Unlevered FCF is before–personal taxes as defined in Chapter 2, and Δ denotes an increase during the period. t_S and t_B are the tax rates on personal income from stock and bonds, respectively, and t is the corporate tax rate.[4]

Thus, to value the FCFs of the firm one can simply value the Unlevered FCFs discounted at $(1 - t_S)\rho$, the after–personal tax cost of capital of the unlevered firm, and adds to it the value of the tax shield discounted at $(1 - t_B)r$, the after–personal tax cost of debt (because the occurrence of the tax shield has essentially the same risk as debt when debt levels are predetermined). Hence, the enterprise value at $t - 1$ is the sum of[5]

$$V^U_{t-1} = \frac{\text{Unlevered FCF}_t + V^U_t}{(1 + \rho)}$$

and

$$\text{Tax Shield}_{t-1} = \frac{[(1 - t_B) - (1 - t_S)(1 - t)]\, rD_{t-1} + \text{Tax Shield}_t}{1 + (1 - t_B)r}$$

where V^U_t is the value of a firm with no debt and D_{t-1} denotes debt. These expressions also apply in tax imputation countries with t_S given by Equation (2.4) of Chapter 2. The second expression adjusts the present value of the unlevered free cash flow by the present value of the debt tax shield. We shall refer to this valuation method as *original* APV in order to distinguish it from its recent variations.

When FCF_t and D_t are constant perpetuities the enterprise value becomes

$$\frac{\text{Unlevered FCF}}{\rho} + t_e D,$$

where $t_e = 1 - (1 - t_S)(1 - t)/(1 - t_B)$ is the effective tax advantage on corporate debt defined by Miller (1977).

When incomes from stock and bonds are taxed at the same rate or not taxed at all, $t_S = t_B$, and value of the tax shield at time $t - 1$ is simply tD_t. As discussed in Section 2.6.2, the effective personal tax rates for the marginal investor are lower than the statutory rates and $t_S < t_B$. Therefore, $t_e < t$ and the value of the tax shield is lower than tD_t. For example, for the rough estimates calculated in Section 2.6.2, $t_e = 1 - (1 - 0.15)(1 - 0.40)/(1 - 0.20)$ = 36.25%, which suggests that allowing for personal taxes decreases the value of the tax shield by about 9.4%. Were dividend taxes to be eliminated completely and t_B to stay at about 20%, then $t_e = 25\%$ and the value of the tax shield would be reduced by about one-third from current levels. On the other hand, ρ would also decrease not needing to make up for the tax on stock income.

Note that in APV valuation, debt can vary arbitrarily as no assumption about leverage is made to arrive to the partition of the free cash flows. However, while one may be able to estimate the level of debt for the next few years at a fair degree of approximation, a reasonable assumption about its long-run level is needed. This is done letting debt settle down to a constant target leverage ratio after a transition period. One can then estimate continuation value by discounting the continuation cash flow at the WACC that corresponds to the planned target debt ratio (or, alternatively, by using a valuation multiple from companies in the industry that approximately follow the planned debt ratio).

---

[4]As in Chapter 2, Section 2.6.2, and Miller (1977), t_S is defined as the effective tax rate that would produce the same present value of tax payments as the actual taxes. ΔDebt is not taxed at t_S because it provides an offsetting tax shield on the capital gains produced by new investment.

[5]For the unlevered free cash flow write $V^U_{t-1} = [(1 - t_S)FCF_t + V^U_t - t_S(V^U_t - V^U_{t-1})]/[(1 + (1 - t_S)\rho]$ and solve for V^U_{t-1}.

6.3   A DETAILED EXAMPLE OF APV VALUATION

In Chapter 2, Paktech International was valued using two alternative methods: (1) the value of the enterprise was attained discounting the free cash flows available to all security holders at WACC, and (2) equity was valued discounting the cash flows corresponding to equity-holders at the cost of equity. In both cases, it was assumed that the firm maintained the same financial policy represented by a target debt ratio of 35%. An acquirer following such a financial policy could pay up to $179 million for the enterprise, of which $63 million would be debt.

Consider now the case in which the owner of Paktech plans to spin it off to its shareholders[6] with only $20 million of debt, which the new entity would increase gradually to achieve a target debt ratio of 35%. The reason for such a more conservative policy could be limited access to the debt market at that time and legal limitations on the transfer of parent debt to the spin-off.

The APV approach is now applied to the valuation of Paktech. We initially ignore the effect of personal taxes. Let us assume that Paktech starts with $20 million of net debt at 7.15% interest, maintains the same level through year-end 2005, increases debt to $30 million at year-end 2005, $40 million at year-end 2006, and finally attains a 35% debt ratio at year-end 2007 ($85 million). The cost of capital of the unlevered firm is computed from the data on Exhibit 3.9:

$$K^U_{Packtech} = \text{riskless rate} + \text{market risk premium} \times \text{unlevered beta} + \text{size premium}$$
$$= 4.07\% + 5.08\% \times 0.459 + 3.08\% = 9.48\%.$$

Exhibit 6.1 shows the APV valuation. The unlevered free cash flow is the same as that computed in the WACC valuation of Chapter 2. The valuation proceeds as follows: The cash flows during the first five years are partitioned between the unlevered free cash flow discounted at the unlevered cost of equity, and the tax shield discounted at the cost of debt. The results are $16.8 million and $3.0 million, respectively. The continuation value at the end of 2007 is as calculated in the WACC valuation of Paktech. That is, once the firm attains its target debt ratio, the enterprise value is attained discounting free cash flows at WACC. This value is brought to present value at the beginning of 2003 by discounting it at the *unlevered* cost of capital for 2003 to 2007.[7] This yields $154.4 million at the beginning of 2003. Adding the three components of value gives a value of the enterprise equal to $174.2 million or $4.7 million lower than that resulting from assuming a constant debt ratio throughout. The difference is due to the lower tax shield attained under the present financial policy.

Suppose that instead of a spin-off, the company could be sold in an auction and consider a potential acquirer planning the same financial policy shown in Exhibit 6.1. Would such an acquirer be able to buy Paktech without the additional tax shield of higher debt? It would not if other potential buyers that can attain the same operating cash flow and finance the acquisition with more debt. On the other hand, imperfections in the market for corporate control and superior ability to extract free cash flow from the target may permit the acquirer to offer more than other potential buyers even without the benefit of higher leverage.

---

[6]That is, via a share distribution to stockholders. Spin-offs are discussed in Chapter 15.

[7]The reader may wonder why we are not discounting the continuation value back to the present at WACC. The reason is that using WACC would allow for an additional tax shield during 2003 to 2007 leading to double counting. Note that the tax shield during that period is calculated and valued separately.

EXHIBIT 6.1	*Paktech International. Adjusted Present Value Valuation as of 12/31/2002*

($000)

Year-end		2002	2003	2004	2005	2006	2007
Net Sales		213,580	231,734	251,432	271,546	290,554	307,988
EBITDA		29,901	32,443	36,458	38,016	40,678	43,118
Depreciation		12,268	13,054	14,948	17,533	18,530	19,603
EBIT		17,633	19,388	21,509	20,484	22,148	23,516
Taxes	40%	7,053	7,755	8,604	8,194	8,859	9,406
Unlevered net income		10,580	11,633	12,906	12,290	13,289	14,109
Deferred taxes			510	427	362	383	405
NOPAT			12,143	13,333	12,652	13,671	14,514
Depreciation			13,054	14,948	17,533	18,530	19,603
CAPEX & NWC incr.			20,634	25,492	26,079	27,045	28,431
Unlevered free cash flow			4,564	2,788	4,106	5,156	5,685
Net debt at year-end		20,000	20,000	20,000	30,000	40,000	84,999
Interest @	7.15%		1,430	1,430	1,430	2,145	2,860
Tax shield			572	572	572	858	1,144
Unlevered cost of equity	9.48%						
PV FCF 2003–2007 @	9.48%	16,827					
Continuation value @ WACC	8.48%						242,855
PV '07 Cont. value @	9.48%	154,391					
PV Tax shield @	7.15%	2,958					
Enterprise value		174,176					

We now recompute the APV value of the enterprise allowing for the effect of personal taxes. Once again, we use the rough estimates calculated in Section 2.6.2: $t_B = 20\%$, $t_S = 15\%$ and compute the *unlevered* the cost of equity with Equation (2.9):

$$k^U_{Paktech} = (0.94)(4.07\%) + [9.15\% - (0.94)(4.07\%)](0.459) + 3.08\% = 9.35\%.$$

Substituting this value, the effective tax rate $t_e = 36.25\%$ (calculated in Section 6.2), the after–personal tax cost of debt $(1 - t_B)r = (1 - 20\%)(7.15\%) = 5.72\%$, and WACC = 8.42% (calculated Section 2.6.2) into Exhibit 6.1 and recomputing the value of the enterprise results in

PV of FCFs	$ 16.888 million
Continuation Value	155.329
PV of Tax Shield	2.472
Enterprise Value	$174.690

which is 0.3% above the estimate attained in Exhibit 6.1. This is so because the decrease in the value of the tax shield is more than offset by the recognition that the cost of equity, that is, the opportunity cost to the equity investor, is in this case lower because of personal taxes. You will recall that we obtained a similar result in Section 2.6.2 when we allowed for personal taxes for valuing Paktech using a constant WACC. As noted there, personal taxes can be ignored in enterprise valuation under the tax regime in force in the United States in mid-2003. This conclusion applies to APV valuation as well. However, the elimination of dividend taxes would magnify the effect of personal taxes on interest income and require explicit incorporation of personal taxes in APV valuation. Presently, the valuation procedure developed in this section applies in countries with tax imputation systems that shelter most of the dividend income (tax imputation is treated in Section 2.6.3).

6.4   VALUING AN ACQUISITION WITH LEVERAGE ABOVE TARGET

Consider now financing for the acquisition of Paktech with leverage above its long-term target. An acquirer finances the acquisition with a loan of $88.4 million at 7.15% (implying a 49% debt ratio), and uses the company's cash flow to retire debt and bring the debt ratio to 35% in 5 years. Exhibit 6.2 shows the APV valuation under this financial policy. Proceeding as in the previous section, one obtains $181.5 million for the enterprise value

---

EXHIBIT 6.2 *Paktech International, APV Valuation of Acquisition Financed with Leverage above Target as of 12/31/2003*

($000)

Year-end		2002	2003	2004	2005	2006	2007
Net Sales		213,580	231,734	251,432	271,546	290,554	307,988
EBITDA		29,901	32,443	36,458	38,016	40,678	43,118
Depreciation		12,268	13,054	14,948	17,533	18,530	19,603
EBIT		17,633	19,388	21,509	20,484	22,148	23,516
Net interest expense			6,323	6,268	6,337	6,316	6,218
Income before taxes			13,066	15,242	14,146	15,832	17,298
Taxes	40%		5,226	6,097	5,659	6,333	6,919
Net income			7,839	9,145	8,488	9,499	10,379
Depreciation			13,054	14,948	17,533	18,530	19,603
Deferred taxes			510	427	362	383	405
Capex and NWC incr.			20,634	25,492	26,079	27,045	28,431
Available for debt retirement			770	(972)	304	1,367	1,955
Net debt		88,422	87,652	88,624	88,321	86,954	84,999
Interest @	7.15%		6,323	6,268	6,337	6,316	6,218
Tax shield			2,529	2,507	2,535	2,526	2,487
Net income			7,839	9,145	8,488	9,499	10,379
Interest after taxes			3,794	3,761	3,802	3,789	3,731
Unlevered net income			11,633	12,906	12,290	13,289	14,109
Deferred taxes			510	427	362	383	405
NOPAT			12,143	13,333	12,652	13,671	14,514
Depreciation			13,054	14,948	17,533	18,530	19,603
Capex and incr. in net working cap.			20,634	25,492	26,079	27,045	28,431
Unlevered free cash flow			4,564	2,788	4,106	5,156	5,685
Unlevered cost of equity	9.48%						
PV FCF 2003–2007 @	9.48%	16,827					
Continuation value @ WACC	8.48%						242,855
PV '07 Cont. value @	9.48%	154,391					
PV Tax shield @	7.15%	10,282					
Enterprise value		181,500					

or about $2.6 million above the value the firm would have under a constant debt ratio of 35%. The difference is caused by the additional interest tax shield produced by higher debt.[8]

This valuation is subject to two qualifications: First, it does not take into account the possible cost of reduced financial flexibility that may affect the competitive ability of the firm and eventually result in loss of revenues. Second, it assumes that the firm is a public company and therefore enjoys the cost of equity of publicly traded equity. Were the firm to be taken private, its cost of capital would increase by an additional premium for lack of marketability. The pricing of private companies is treated in Chapter 13.

It should also be noted that the borrowing capacity of Paktech is limited by its inability to generate much cash for debt retirement. In fact, Paktech is not a good candidate for a highly leveraged acquisition using limited equity. The determination of debt capacity for leveraged buyouts is discussed in Chapter 7.

6.5   RECURSIVE WACC VALUATION

In applying APV, it is common to discount the tax shield at the cost of debt. This is the approach followed in Sections 6.3 and 6.4. It is based upon the assumption that the debt level is certain. Certain debt implies that the tax shield is proportional to interest expense and has the same risk. However, future debt levels are rarely known in advance. For example, when the firm adheres to a constant debt ratio, debt financing is proportional to the value of the firm and its level is uncertain. In that case, the tax shield has the same risk as the unlevered cash flow of the firm. Miles and Ezzell (1980) have shown that allowing for this additional risk in the APV model is equivalent to discounting unlevered free-cash flows at WACC. That is, when the firm maintains a constant debt ratio, APV and WACC valuation are one and the same.

Recursive WACC valuation permits valuing firms that expect to follow known but variable debt ratios, such that the level of debt depends on the value of the firm within each year. The debt ratio itself can change over time but predictably so, and it is assumed to stay constant within each year. The level of debt changes during the year as free cash flow evolves to next-year value, and debt is reset next year to satisfy the new debt ratio. Assuming the debt ratio takes known values simplifies the valuation of firms with changing leverage and provides an alternative to valuation according to APV with known debt.

Once one assumes that within each year the debt ratio stays constant and the amount of debt varies with the value of the firm, it follows that the tax shield has the same risk as the value of the firm and that one can discount the free cash flow of each year at WACC.[9] However, WACC has to be allowed to change according to changes in the debt ratio and the cost of equity. Exhibit 6.3 illustrates this approach by valuing Packtech for the financial policy assumed in Section 6.4. When the debt ratio is the magnitude projected, one simply computes the beta of equity, the cost of equity, and the WACC corresponding to each year, and obtains the value of the enterprise recursively. The starting point is the continuation value at the end of 2007, which is equal to $242.855 million and is calculated as before, assuming that the firm has attained its target debt ratio. Then, one computes the value of the enterprise as of the beginning of year 2007, which is (242.855 +

---

[8]Discounting the tax shield at the cost of debt rather than at WACC results in a additional small increase in present value.

[9]This is formally shown in Note N6.2.

EXHIBIT 6.3 *Paktech International, Inc., Recursive WACC Valuation of Acquisition Financed with Leverage above Target as of 12/31/2003*

($000)

Year-end		2002	2003	2004	2005	2006	2007
Net Sales		213,580	231,734	251,432	271,546	290,554	307,988
EBITDA		29,901	32,443	36,458	38,016	40,678	43,118
Depreciation		12,268	13,054	14,948	17,533	18,530	19,603
EBIT		17,633	19,388	21,509	20,484	22,148	23,516
Net interest expense			6,323	6,268	6,337	6,316	6,218
Income before taxes			13,066	15,242	14,146	15,832	17,298
Taxes	40%		5,226	6,097	5,659	6,333	6,919
Net income			7,839	9,145	8,488	9,499	10,379
Depreciation			13,054	14,948	17,533	18,530	19,603
Deferred taxes			510	427	362	383	405
Capex and incr. in net working cap.			20,634	25,492	26,079	27,045	28,431
Available for debt retirement			770	(972)	304	1,367	1,955
Net debt		88,422	87,652	88,624	88,321	86,954	84,999
Interest @	7.15%		6,323	6,268	6,337	6,316	6,218
Tax shield			2,529	2,507	2,535	2,526	2,487
Net income			7,839	9,145	8,488	9,499	10,379
Interest after taxes			3,794	3,761	3,802	3,789	3,731
Unlevered net income			11,633	12,906	12,290	13,289	14,109
Deferred taxes			510	427	362	383	405
NOPAT			12,143	13,333	12,652	13,671	14,514
Depreciation			13,054	14,948	17,533	18,530	19,603
Capex and incr. in net working cap.			20,634	25,492	26,079	27,045	28,431
Unlevered free cash flow			4,564	2,788	4,106	5,156	5,685
Riskless rate	4.07%						
Equity premium	5.08%						
Size premium	3.08%						
Unlevered equity beta	0.459						
Debt ratio			49%	46%	43%	41%	38%
Relevered equity beta			0.90	0.85	0.81	0.78	0.74
Relevered cost of equity			11.71%	11.46%	11.28%	11.09%	10.91%
WACC			8.08%	8.17%	8.24%	8.32%	8.40%
Continuation value @ WACC	8.48%						242,855
Enterprise value		180,891	190,951	203,763	216,444	229,285	242,855

5.685)/(1.0840) = $229.285 million. The enterprise value as of the beginning of 2006 is (229.285 + 5.156)/(1.0832) = $216.444 million. Proceeding backward in time toward the beginning of year 2003, one gets $180.891 million for the present value of the enterprise and $180.891 − $88.422 = $92.469 million as the value of equity. The reader can verify that the same result is attained by recursively discounting the cash flow to equity at the time-varying cost of equity and adding initial net debt.

In practice, financial projections do not contain the planned debt ratios, which are the values needed to compute WACC. Instead debt is expressed in dollar amounts as a function of expected cash-flow generation. This complicates the calculation of the enterprise value in each year because the debt ratio implied by the amount of debt and the cost of capital have to be solved for each year simultaneously with the value of the enterprise. As before, let us start from the continuation value at the end of 2007. The next step is to calculate the value of the firm at the end of 2006 to be attained by discounting at WACC the free cash flow generated during 2007 plus the continuation value. However, WACC itself depends on the value of the firm to be calculated because the latter combined with the debt amount planned for the beginning of 2007 determines the debt ratio to use in the estimation of WACC. This means that the value of the firm and WACC have to be solved for simultaneously. This is done solving the following four equations:

$$EV_{2006} = (5.685 + 242.855)/(1 + WACC_{2007})$$
$$\beta_{2007} = [1 + 86.954/(EV - 86.954)](0.459)$$
$$k_{2007} = 4.07\% + \beta_{2007}(5.08\%) + 3.08\%$$
$$WACC_{2007} = (86.954/EV)(1 - 40\%)(7.15\%) + (1 - 86.954/EV)\,k_{2007}$$

in order to calculate the value of the enterprise, the beta coefficient of equity, the cost of equity and WACC. The first equation gives the present value of the enterprise at the end of 2006. The second equation relevers the beta coefficient of equity as per the formula derived in Section 3.4 of Chapter 3. The third and fourth equations compute the cost of equity and WACC for 2007 in the usual way. These equations can be solved by entering into a spreadsheet the data of Exhibit 6.3 and allowing for circular calculation in Excel. Exhibit 6.3 shows that the solution is EV_{2006} = \$229.285 million, β_{2007} = 0.78, k_{2007} = 11.09% and $WACC_{2007}$ = 8.40%, and that the debt ratio during 2007 equals 38%.

The next step is to calculate the value of the firm at the end of 2005, which is given by $(5.156 + 229.285)/(1 + WACC_{2006})$. Once again, we need to solve the system of equations shown above, now for an initial debt of \$88.321 million. The final result is EV_{2005} = \$216.444 million. Iterating backward in this way yields the present enterprise value EV_{2002} = \$180.891 million.

Admittedly, valuation with time-varying cost of capital is not simple. This is why it is often incorrectly done in practice, and we felt that a detailed outline of the proper procedure was required. However, the reader would be glad to know that the same result can be attained by a straightforward approach that discounts cash flows at a constant rate. This is done next.

6.6   COMPRESSED APV

Note N6.2 shows that the enterprise value can be computed either by discounting the free cash flow at a time varying WACC or by discounting the free cash flow plus the tax shield at the pre-tax WACC. It also shows that pre-tax WACC is constant over time and equal to the unlevered cost capital of the firm. This equivalence of the two valuation approaches was already mentioned in Note N2.3 for the case of constant leverage. Note N6.2 shows that it holds for time-varying leverage.

The resulting method is called *compressed APV* because, instead of discounting the unlevered FCF at the unlevered cost of capital and the tax shield at the cost of debt as commonly done in APV, it discounts both cash flows at the unlevered cost of capital. The equivalence between discounting FCF at WACC and FCF + Tax Shield at pre-tax WACC has long being known (see Note N2.3). That the pre-tax WACC is equal to the unlevered cost of capital and the simplification it affords for the case of time-varying debt ratio are results due to Ruback (2002).[10]

Calculating compressed APV requires computing the unlevered free cash flow and the tax shield for each year and discounting both at the unlevered cost of capital. For continuation value one assumes as before that the debt ratio attains its target value at the end of the explicit forecast period. The valuation is performed on Exhibit 6.4, which yields an

---

EXHIBIT 6.4   *Paktech International, Inc., Compressed APV Valuation of Acquisition Financed with Leverage above Target as of 12/31/2002*

($000)

Year-end		2002	2003	2004	2005	2006	2007
Net Sales		213,580	231,734	251,432	271,546	290,554	307,988
EBITDA		29,901	32,443	36,458	38,016	40,678	43,118
Depreciation		12,268	13,054	14,948	17,533	18,530	19,603
EBIT		17,633	19,388	21,509	20,484	22,148	23,516
Net interest expense			6,323	6,268	6,337	6,316	6,218
Income before taxes			13,066	15,242	14,146	15,832	17,298
Taxes	40%		5,226	6,097	5,659	6,333	6,919
Net income			7,839	9,145	8,488	9,499	10,379
Depreciation			13,054	14,948	17,533	18,530	19,603
Deferred taxes			510	427	362	383	405
Capex and incr. in net working cap.			20,634	25,492	26,079	27,045	28,431
Available for debt retirement			770	(972)	304	1,367	1,955
Net debt		88,422	87,652	88,624	88,321	86,954	84,999
Interest @	7.15%		6,323	6,268	6,337	6,316	6,218
Tax shield			2,529	2,507	2,535	2,526	2,487
Net income			7,839	9,145	8,488	9,499	10,379
Interest after taxes			3,794	3,761	3,802	3,789	3,731
Unlevered net income			11,633	12,906	12,290	13,289	14,109
Deferred taxes			510	427	362	383	405
NOPAT			12,143	13,333	12,652	13,671	14,514
Depreciation			13,054	14,948	17,533	18,530	19,603
Capex and incr. in net working cap.			20,634	25,492	26,079	27,045	28,431
Unlevered free cash flow			4,564	2,788	4,106	5,156	5,685
Unlevered cost of equity	9.48%						
PV FCF 2003–2007 @	9.48%	16,827					
Continuation value @ WACC	8.48%						242,855
PV '07 Cont. value @	9.48%	154,391					
PV Tax shield @	9.48%	9,673					
Enterprise value		180,891					

---

[10]Ruback calls the approach "the capital cash flow method" because the cash flow being discounted is the cash flow *received* by the suppliers of capital. Stewart Myers suggested the name "compressed APV." Discounting the tax shield at the unlevered cost of capital has been proposed by Kaplan and Ruback (1995) and Inselbag and Kaufold (1989).

enterprise value equal to \$180.891, the same as that attained in Exhibit 6.3 allowing WACC to change over time. This illustrates the important simplifying property of compressed APV.

In the present case, the value attained by allowing WACC to change or, equivalently, by using compressed APV is lower than the value obtained with original APV in which the debt tax shield was discounted at the cost of debt. This is so because compressed APV assigns a lower value to the debt tax shield. The difference increases with the spread of the unlevered cost of capital over the cost of debt.

*6.7   UNCERTAIN LEVERAGE: A RECURSIVE APV MODEL[11]

The APV models used in the previous sections assume that either the level of debt or the leverage ratio is known with certainly. This is a reasonable assumption as long as uncertain departures from the assumed levels are not large. In fact, as pointed out in Section 6.1, even large fluctuations *around* a target debt ratio have small effects on present value. When debt changes are a function of uncertain cash flows as is common in the case of high leverage, the tax shield becomes uncertain and its precise valuation is more complex. WACC valuation takes care of the case in which the change in debt approximates a constant debt ratio. APV applied to predetermined debt levels provides a good approximation in most other cases as long as cash flow uncertainty is not too high. Compressed APV deals with the case in which the debt ratio changes in a predicted way. None of these approaches deal with the case in which debt reduction depends on uncertain cash flows and results in an uncertain debt ratio. In fact, Myers's original APV rule does not strictly apply when debt reduction is uncertain. Specifically, the correct APV rule for highly leveraged firms (HLFs) needs to allow for uncertain leverage in valuing the tax shield.[12]

We now examine two approaches to the valuation of HLFs that explicitly account for uncertain leverage: First, we develop a recursive APV valuation formula for the value of the firm and compare it to alternative valuation methods. In particular, we examine the robustness of the original APV rule, which assumes predetermined debt levels. We show under what conditions original APV performs almost as well as recursive APV. Another approach to HLF valuation is to treat equity as a call option on the value of the firm. We develop an option-pricing model and illustrate its use. The option-pricing approach is conceptually more appealing than APV because it avoids explicit valuation of the tax shield. In practice, however, using both APV and option pricing is likely to result in better valuations of HLFs than relying on a single approach.

The financial policy modeled in this section is that of a firm planning to reduce its leverage over a number of periods by applying its free cash flow to paying interest and debt reduction. This is done in practice by retiring debt or reducing the refinancing of maturing debt. A gradual process of debt reduction, rather than a single-step recapitalization, is consistent with Myers's (1984) pecking order theory[13] and with the cash flow signalling hypothesis of leveraged buyouts in which firms revert to more conventional financial

---

[11]Sections marked with an asterisk may be skipped on a first reading. This section is based upon Arzac (1996).

[12]That the cost of debt is not appropriate for discounting the tax shield when debt is contingent on the realization of the firm's cash flows was recognized by Myers (1974) for the case in which the firm maintains a constant debt ratio. Miles and Ezzell (1980) solved the valuation problem under a constant debt ratio.

[13]Managers are reluctant to issue equity and prefer to rely on internally generated funds first and choose debt over equity when external financing is needed.

policies in the years following the buyout, after having used debt to pre-commit cash flows and achieve a higher valuation.[14]

We now obtain the expression for the value of the enterprise when the debt ratio is uncertain and debt reduction in any given period is a function of the random cash flow realization during that period. Denote by $P_{0,T}$ the value of the first T unlevered free cash flows plus the tax shields and by $P_0[V_T]$ the present value of the time-T continuation value V_T. Enterprise value can then be written as

$$V_0 = P_{0,T} + P_0[V_T]. \tag{6.1}$$

We show in Note N6.3 that when the debt ratio is uncertain $P_{0,T}$ can be computed forward in time with the following recursion

$$P_{0,t} = P_{0,t-1} + \frac{E[Y_t]}{(1 + \rho)^t} + \frac{\tau r}{(1 + r)}(D_0 - (1 - \phi)P_{0,t-1}), t = 2, \ldots, T, \tag{6.2}$$

where $P_{0,1} = E[Y_1](1 + \rho)^{-1} + \tau r D_0(1 + r)^{-1}$, Y_t denotes the uncertain unlevered free cash flow, $E[Y_t]$ is the expectation of Y_t, ρ is the unlevered cost of capital, r is the interest rate on debt, τ is the corporate tax rate, D_0 is the initial level of net debt, and ϕ is the dividend yield expressed as a fraction of the levered cash flow.[15]

The continuation value V_T is computed assuming that the firm is expected to maintain a constant leverage ratio from time T onwards, once debt has been reduced. V_T is obtained by discounting the post-time-T cash flows at the corresponding WACC denoted by w or by applying an EBITDA multiple to projected EBITDA.

Equations (6.1) and (6.2) provide a way to compute the value of a HLF. First, Equation (6.2) is solved recursively forward in time from t = 1 to T in order to obtain the value of first T cash flows $P_{0,T}$. The present value of the continuation value at time T is then added to $P_{0,T}$. Furthermore, when the post-time-T cash flows can be assumed to grow at a constant rate g, Equation (6.1) becomes:

$$V_0 = P_{0,T} + \frac{E[Y_{T+1}]}{(1 + \rho)^T(w - g)} \tag{6.3}$$

A closed-form solution to difference Equation (6.2) can be obtained for special cases such as when $E[Y_t]$ grows at a constant rate g. Then, $E[Y_t] = E[Y_1](1 + g)^{t-1}$ and Equation (6.3) becomes

$$V_0 = [\frac{p^T - a^T}{(1 + \rho)(p - a)} + \frac{p^T}{(w - g)}] E[Y_1] + \frac{(1 - a^T)D_0}{(1 - \phi)} \tag{6.4}$$

where $p = (1 + g)/(1 + \rho)$ and $a = 1 - (1 - \phi)\tau r/(1 + r)$.

Equations (6.1) and (6.2) and formula (6.4) can be computed using the spreadsheet HLF Value Calculator included in the Valuation Aids CD-ROM.

Example 1

Consider the valuation of a HLF that starts with an initial debt ratio of 72%, pays no dividend and plans to reduce its debt ratio to 35% via a recapitalization at the end of the 5th year. Until then, all

---

[14]See Arzac (1992) and Chapter 13.

[15]In practice, $\phi = 0$ because debt covenants in highly leveraged transactions preclude dividend payments.

EXHIBIT 6.5   *Data for Recursive APV Valuation*

$$E[Y_1] \quad \ldots \ldots \ldots \ldots \$ \quad 150 \text{ million}$$
$$g \quad \ldots \ldots \ldots \ldots \quad 4.0\%$$
$$D_0 \quad \ldots \ldots \ldots \ldots \$1,500 \text{ million}$$
$$\tau \quad \ldots \ldots \ldots \ldots \quad 40.0\%$$
$$r \quad \ldots \ldots \ldots \ldots \quad 11.0\%$$
$$\rho \quad \ldots \ldots \ldots \ldots \quad 13.90\%$$
$$w \quad \ldots \ldots \ldots \ldots \quad 12.47\%$$

---

the cash flow will go to debt reduction. Exhibit 6.5 contains the data assumed for this example. Substituting the parameter values into Equation (6.4) yields $V_0 = \$1,906$ million. Use the HLF Value Calculator to confirm this result.

Example 2: Valuation of Paktech with temporary high leverage.

Exhibit 6.6 contains the relevant data from Exhibit 6.2. Exhibit 6.7 presents the computation of Equations (6.2) and (6.3). The closed-form formula cannot be used in Paktech's case because cash flows do not grow at a constant rate.

Recursive APV gives an enterprise value equal to $181.6 million and an equity value equal to $93.2 million. These values are almost identical to those produced by original APV. In fact, original APV would give a close approximation to recursive APV in most practical situations. On the other hand, compressed APV tends to underestimate the value of the tax shield when leverage is uncertain. In the case of Paktech, the underestimation is only 0.75% of the value of equity. But the error increases with the spread between the unlevered cost of capital and the cost of debt, and the time it

---

EXHIBIT 6.6   *Paktech International Data for Recursive APV Valuation of Paktech*

$$E[Y_1] \text{ to } E[Y_5] \quad \ldots \ldots \ldots \text{ see Ex. 6.2}$$
$$\text{Continuation value } g \quad \ldots \ldots \ldots 6.0\%$$
$$D_0 \quad \ldots \ldots \ldots \$88,422$$
$$\tau \quad \ldots \ldots \ldots 40.0\%$$
$$r \quad \ldots \ldots \ldots 7.15\%$$
$$\rho \quad \ldots \ldots \ldots 9.487\%$$
$$w \quad \ldots \ldots \ldots 8.48\%$$

EXHIBIT 6.7   *Paktech International. Recursive APV Computation*

t	0	1	2	3	4	5
$E[Y_t]$		4,564	2,788	4,106	5,156	5,685
$P_{0,t}$	0	6,529	11,041	16,235	21,751	27,145
V_T with assumed growth	6.0%	—	—	—	—	242,988
$P_{0,T}$	27,145.2					
$P_0(V_T)$	154,494					
$V_0 = V_{0,t} + P_0(V_T)$	**181,638.9**					
$S_0 = EV - D_0$	**93,216.9**					

takes for leverage to settle down to a long-term target. This is so because compressed APV ignores that, under uncertain debt reduction, the tax shield is negatively correlated with the unlevered free cash flows and should therefore be discounted at a rate lower than ρ.[16] The following example shows that the differences in value can be significant.

Example 3

Let us compute the enterprise value and the value of equity according to the following inputs and a 10-year leverage adjustment period:

$E[Y_1]$ . . . . $60 million

G 6.50%

D_0 . . . . $1,000 million

τ 40.0%

r 8.0%

ρ 20.0%

w 9.0%

The reader can verify that the following results attain:

	Enterprise Value	Value of Equity
Recursive APV	$1,251	$251
Original APV	1,231	231
Compressed APV	1,162	162

That is, while the underestimation produced by original APV with respect to recursive APV is $20 million or 8% of the value of equity, compressed APV underestimates the enterprise value by $89 million or 35% of the value of equity.

---

*6.8   VALUING EQUITY AS AN OPTION[17]

This section examines an alternative partition of the cash flow that does not require explicit valuation of the tax shield. This is accomplished by valuing equity as an option.[18] Under the financial policy stated above, for the case in which a fraction ϕ of the cash flow Y_t is paid as dividend and the rest goes to bondholders, the cash flows of the firm can be partitioned into the cash flows received by bondholders:

$$\{(1 - \phi)Z_1, (1 - \phi)Z_2, \ldots, (1 - \phi)Z_{T-1}, (1 - \phi)Z_T + \min[D_T, V_T]\} \quad (6.5)$$

and the cash flows received by shareholders:

$$\{\phi Z_1, \phi Z_2, \ldots, \phi Z_{T-1}, \phi Z_T + \max[V_T - D_T, 0]\} \quad (6.6)$$

---

[16]When all free cash flow goes to debt amortization, the debt level and the debt ratio depend on the uncertain cash flow and shortfalls increase debt and the tax shield. This means that the tax shield is negatively correlated with FCFs and that ρ is not the correct rate to use. It can be shown that $\mathrm{cov}[\tau r D_t, Y_t] = -\tau r \, \mathrm{var}[Y_t]$. This means that the tax shield has to be discounted a rate lower than ρ.

[17]This model is a revision of a similar option-pricing model proposed in Arzac (1996).

[18]For an introduction to option pricing see Chapter 8. For a detailed treatment see Hull (2002).

where $Z_t = Y_t + \tau r D_{t-1}$ is the cash flow of the levered firm at time t, $D_T = D_0 - \Sigma_{t=1,T}((1 - \phi)Z_t - rD_{t-1})$ is the debt outstanding at time T, and V_T is the continuation value of the firm at time T. Equation (6.5) says that bondholders receive all the cash flow available for distribution after dividend payments[19] and receive either the due balance D_T or the value of the enterprise if $D_T < V_T$. Equation (6.6) says that shareholders get the dividends payments if any and keep the equity left after payment of the debt balance. That is, shareholders have the option to default if $V_T - D_T < 0$. They have a call on the enterprise with strike price equal to D_T.

Initial debt equals the value of Equation (6.5). With the notation introduced in Section 6.7, we can write the value of the cash flows received by bond-holders as $(1 - \phi)P_{0,T}$ and, since the value of $\min[D_T, V_T]$ is the present value of continuation value minus the shareholders' call on the enterprise, the value of initial debt is

$$D_0 = (1 - \phi)P_{0,T} + P_0(V_T) - c(V_T, D_T, T) \qquad (6.7)$$

where $P_{0,T}$ is the value of the first T cash flows of the levered firm, and c is a call option on the enterprise value V_T with strike price D_T and expiration date T.

Since shareholders receive the cash flows that do not go to bond-holders, the initial value of equity is equal to the dividends received plus the call on the enterprise:

$$S_0 = \phi P_{0,T} + c(V_T, D_T, T) \qquad (6.8)$$

Taking into account that D_0 is known, one can substitute Equation (6.7) into Equation (6.8) to eliminate $P_{0,T}$ and obtain:

$$S_0 = (1 - \phi)^{-1}[\phi(D_0 - P_0(V_T)) + c(V_T, D_T, T)] \qquad (6.9)$$

The enterprise value can then be computed from:

$$V_0 = D_0 + S_0 = (1 - \phi)^{-1}[D_0 - \phi P_0(V_T) + c(V_T, D_T, T)] \qquad (6.10)$$

If, as it is common in HLFs, $\phi = 0$, Equations (6.9) and (6.10) collapse to

$$S_0 = c(V_T, D_T, T) \qquad (6.11)$$

$$D_0 = V_T - c(V_T, D_T, T) \qquad (6.12)$$

Equation (6.12) is the well-known expression for the value of risky debt noted by Black and Scholes (1973) and further developed by Merton (1977), which is particularly appropriate for HLFs in which bond-holders receive all the available free cash flows until a recapitalization takes place. For the typical HLF, a significant portion of the outstanding debt becomes due at some time T, which is the natural time for the equity-holders' call option to expire. The tax shield is valued in Equation (6.9) through its contribution to reducing the exercise price D_T.

The model makes the simplifying assumption that equity-holders cannot default on their debt prior to T and, therefore, it assumes that the firm can refinance interim cash shortfalls [in particular, unpaid interests are added to the outstanding debt when $(1 - \phi)Z_t < rD_{t-1}$]. This is not unrealistic because, in practice, HLFs can tap credit lines or additional subordinated financing in order to cover temporary cash shortfalls.[20] In addition, the model assumes that the tax shield is lost upon default, as one would expect in most cases.

---

[19]Normally, dividend payout would not be allowed by the debt covenants and $\phi = 0$.

[20]Allowing for the possibility of premature expiration of the equity-holders' call would require valuing equity as a compound option in which minimum amortization and interest payments have to be made at each period in order to keep the next period option alive.

Equation (6.9) contains a call with uncertain exercise price because D_T depends on the previous realizations of the cash flow. This call can also be interpreted as an option to exchange an uncertain asset (D_T) for another (V_T). Margrabe (1978) and Fisher (1978) have shown that the Black and Scholes formula permits valuing this type of call when applied to a suitable transformation of the variables. Their result applies to the present case under the standard assumptions leading to the Black and Scholes formula as set out in Merton (1973b). When applied to the call in Equation (6.9), the Fisher-Margrabe formula becomes:

$$c(V_T, D_T, T) = P_0[V_T]N(d_1) - P_0[D_T]N(d_2) \qquad (6.13)$$

where $N(.)$ is the standard cumulative normal distribution function,

$$d_1 = \frac{\ln(P_0[V_T]/P_0[D_T]) + \tfrac{1}{2}\,v^2 T}{v\sqrt{T}}, \quad d_2 = d_1 - v\sqrt{T} \qquad (6.14)$$

and $v^2 = v_1^2 - 2v_{12} + v_2^2$,[21] where v_1 is the volatility of $P_0[D_T]$, v_2 is the volatility of $P_0[V_T]$ and v_{12} is the covariance between $P_0[D_T]$ and $P_0[V_T]$.

In order to compute Equation (6.13), we need to specify the stochastic processes driving V_T and D_T. This is done making free cash-flow uncertainty a function of revenue uncertainty such that the volatility of revenue imparts volatility and covariance to V_T and D_T. The estimation of v and computation of Equation (6.14) are made with an algorithm included in the spreadsheet HLF Value Calculator. The required inputs are those needed for the computation of recursive APV plus the volatility of revenue.[22] An estimate of the volatility of revenue can be attained by taking one-sixth the difference between the maximum and minimum values that the growth rate of revenues can assume in any given year.[23] This is consistent with the assumption that the growth rate of revenue is normally distributed.

Example 4

Let us apply the option-pricing model to valuing Paktech International. The inputs to enter to the HLF Value Calculator are those of Exhibit 6.6. Free cash flow after 2007 is assumed to maintain the margin on revenue (2.38%) projected for that year, and the volatility of revenue is allowed to vary from 10 to 30%. Exhibit 6.8 shows the enterprise and equity values of Paktech as well as the implied volatility of the equity option.

These values are only slightly above the original APV value computed in Exhibit 6.2 at low levels of volatility. However, as one would expect from the option nature of equity, the option value increases at higher values of volatility. For example, when revenue volatility is 30%, the volatility of the option is 37% and the option pricing model yields enterprise and equity values that are 3.0 and 6.5% higher than the APV values. This is why it is advisable to use option pricing to value highly leveraged firms when volatility is high. Option volatility is higher when the volatility of revenue and the cash flow margin on revenue are both high.

---

[21]The Fisher-Margrabe formula holds when constant volatility is replaced by the average volatility over the remaining life of the option.

[22]The technical details of the volatility model are contained in Note N8.8.

[23]This implies that the growth rate interval has 99% confidence. One would take one-forth of the maximum–minimum growth rate difference, if the interval had 95% confidence. See Chapter 8, Section 8.2, for details.

EXHIBIT 6.8	*Option Valuation of Paktech International*
	Sensitivity of Option Value to Volatility Estimate

Revenue	Volatility Option	V_0	S_0
10%	13%	$181,643	$93,221
15%	19%	181,814	93,392
20%	25%	182,630	94,208
25%	31%	184,333	95,911
30%	37%	186,833	94,461

6.9   SUMMARY

This chapter examined the valuation of firms with changing capital structure. Four models were presented and illustrated: (i) The original APV model for valuation of firms with predetermined debt levels; (ii) the compressed APV model for valuation of firms with predetermined debt ratios; (iii) a recursive APV model for valuation when the debt ratio itself is uncertain; and (iv) an option pricing model.

The models developed in this chapter apply to the valuation of firms undergoing financial restructuring, as well as to leveraged buyouts and project financing. In these situations, firms deploy all or a significant portion of their cash flow to debt reduction and their leverage ratio is uncertain. Explicit allowance for this characteristic led to a recursive formula for the value of HLF that results from applying the adjusted present value approach to uncertain tax shields. This formula was used to evaluate the robustness of the original APV rule and of compressed APV. The HLF equity was also modeled as a call option with uncertain exercise price, which provides a natural way of dealing with uncertain leverage by capturing the value of the default option possessed by equityholders.

Although recursive APV provides a useful benchmark against which to evaluate the various discounted cash flow approaches when leverage is uncertain, in most cases it does not result in a significantly improvement over original APV. Original APV also gives results that are very closed to those produced by option pricing at low levels of volatility. Option pricing is most appropriate when the volatility of revenue and the cash-flow margin on revenue are high. In conclusion, either recursive or original APV applied in conjunction with option pricing offer the best approach to the valuation of highly leveraged firms, with compressed APV used in those cases in which leverage follows a variable but predictable target.

PROBLEMS

6.1 Discuss the reason for switching to standard WACC valuation to compute the continuation value in APV discounting.

6.2 Obtain the original APV of TPI Inc. using the data of Problem 2.7, and compare your result to that obtained using WACC in the solution to Problem 2.7. Project interest expenses on the basis of the EBIT coverage ratio. For continuation value, use the enterprise value calculated with WACC for a 26% debt ratio. Unlever beta using Equation (3.17).

6.3 Assume TPI plans to reduce net debt to $100 million, pay 8% interest, keep debt at that level through 2009 and then switch to a 26% debt ratio via another equity issue. Use original APV to estimate the enterprise value and the share price it can attain on the initial IPO. How many shares would TPI need to issue to bring the present debt of $112 million down to $100? Interpret the implied P/E ratio. Compare your results to the answer to Problem 2.7.

6.4 Use compressed APV to recompute the enterprise value of TPI under the financial policy of Problem 6.3. When would compressed APV be the correct valuation approach?

6.5 Use HLF Value Calculator to compute Equations (6.2) and (6.3), and Equation (6.4) with the data of Exhibit 6.5.

6.6 Use HLF Value Calculator to value the HLF of Exhibit 6.5 using the option pricing model in Equation (6.14) for a volatility of revenue equal to 10%, 15%, 20%, 25%, and 30%. Assume first-year revenue equals $850 and free cash flow equals $-20 + 0.2$ Revenue.

6.7 Verify the values attained in Example 3 of Section 6.7 for recursive, original, and compressed APV.

Chapter 7

Debt Capacity for Acquisition Financing

7.1 FINANCIAL INTERDEPENDENCIES

The ability to finance a cash acquisition usually depends on the debt capacity of the merged company or, in the case of a leveraged buyout, of the target itself. This chapter presents a review and some extensions of financial concepts and techniques that are used in practice to assess the debt capacity of a company. We begin by examining financial requirements in relation to growth with the purpose of understanding the way the financial system of a company works. After that, we deal with the determination of sustainable debt and its expression in terms of target interest coverage ratios and debt ratios. The chapter concludes with an examination of the debt capacity of leveraged buyouts and recapitalizations.

Basically, a firm's cash flow determines its internal capacity to finance growth. In addition, the firm can take advantage of the debt capacity created by the expansion of its assets. Under normal circumstances, the firm is able to increase its debt maintaining a target interest coverage ratio (EBITDA to interest expense) without shifting to a higher risk class. The debt policy of the firm, represented here by its target coverage ratio (or, equivalently, by its target debt ratio), determines equity requirements for a given growth rate. How the firm finances its equity requirements, how much via retained earnings and how much via new equity issues, depends on its dividend policy.

The process of determining the proper mix of debt, equity, new equity issues, and dividend payout is iterative. In order to obtain the financial mix necessary to finance a given investment plan (asset growth), one can begin with the desired interest coverage and dividend payout ratios and then estimate external equity requirements. Alternatively, one can begin with the planned coverage ratio and stock issues and find out the affordable dividend payout. Finally, one can let the coverage ratio adjust to planned dividend payout and stock issues. The three variables cannot be fixed simultaneously if a given rate of asset growth is to be attained. Otherwise, financial policy will determine the rate of asset growth independently of value creation considerations.[1] In summary, in the four-variable system: asset growth, interest coverage, stock issues, and dividend payout, management has three degrees of freedom, the fourth variable being determined by the choice of the other three. If the growth rate is given, management is left with the choice of two out of the three financial variables. If the financial policy is predetermined (e.g., stock issues are ruled out, and the dividend payout and interest coverage ratios are given), the sustainable rate of asset growth is also determined. Exhibit 7.1 summarizes the financial interdependencies described above.

---

[1]See Higgins (1977, 1981) for an examination of the sustainable growth rate implied by a given financial policy.

EXHIBIT 7.1 *Financial Interdependencies*

Know Linkage not actual graph.

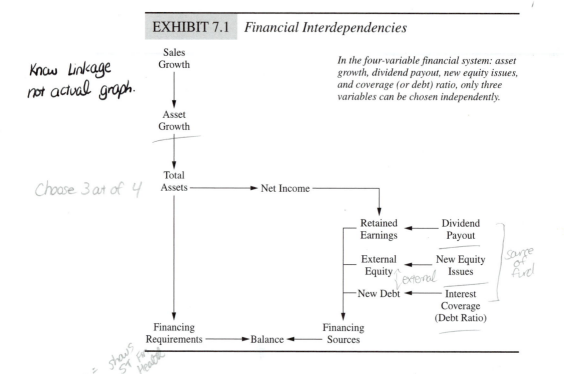

In the four-variable financial system: asset growth, dividend payout, new equity issues, and coverage (or debt) ratio, only three variables can be chosen independently.

Choose 3 at of 4

7.2 FINANCING GROWTH

Int. coverage rating = shows ST fin Health

 # times a company Can make interest payments before EBITDA →1.5

How interest coverage ratio = Debt promo

Significance ?

How from EBITDA to Debt.

The estimation of financial requirements for a planned growth rate is illustrated in Exhibits 7.2 and 7.3.[2] Exhibit 7.2 presents financial data of the IMT Corporation, including the characterization of its financial policy via its target dividend payout and interest coverage ratios. The implications of the planned growth rate are summarized in Exhibit 7.3. Let us begin by estimating the additional assets required. Since sales are expected to increase by $1,102.5 \times 10\% = \$110.25$ and the asset turnover ratio of the company is 0.84, the additional assets required to support additional sales are $\$110.25/0.84 = \$131.25$, of which $26.25 would come from spontaneous liabilities such as supplier credit (20% of assets), and the rest ($105) has to come from an increase in capital. On the other hand, EBITDA would increase by $14.57\% \times \$110.25 = \$16.06$, which, for an interest coverage ratio of 4.5 and an interest rate of 8.5%, would permit increasing debt by $\$16.06/(4.5 \times 8.5\%) = \$42$. To calculate the increase in retained earnings, we start with EBITDA = $14.57\% \times (\$1,102.5 + \$110.25) = \$176.7$, subtract depreciation = $3\% \times (\$1,102.5 + \$110.25) = \$36.38$ and interest expense = $\$176.7/4.5 = \$39.27$ and obtain income before taxes equal to $101.05. Thus, net income equals $(1 - 40\%) \times \$101.05 = \$60.63$ and retained earnings equal $(1 - 25\%) \times \$60.63 = \$45.5$. Therefore, a growth of 10% requires $105 of additional funds to finance asset expansion but, at that level of sales, the firm would generate only $42 + \$45.5 = \$87.5$ from additional debt and retained earnings if its target payout and coverage ratios are to be maintained. The firm can pursue one of several alternatives to close the financing gap. It can reduce its growth to a level compatible with its capacity to finance it under its current dividend and financing policies or it can alter the latter. For

---

[2]The estimation procedure followed in this section is strictly correct if all the variables are expressed in real terms, that is, adjusted for inflation. It provides a good approximation when done in nominal terms as long as the inflation rate is low.

EXHIBIT 7.2   *IMT Corporation. Financial and Operating Characteristics*

Gren

Balance Sheet
(Year-end 2002 in million $)

RE = 44.2

	Assets		Liabilities	
Current	$ 205.0	Other	$262.5	
		Debt	420.0	
			682.5	
Fixed	1,107.5	Equity	630.0	
	1,312.5		1,312.5	

Operating Data

Sales

Current	$1,102.5	
Planned growth	10.00% 7.02%	
EBITDA margin on sales	14.57%	17%
Depreciation/Sales	3.0%	
Spontaneous liabilities/Assets	20.0%	
Tax rate	40.0%	
Sales/Assets (asset turnover)	0.84	

14.57% × $110.25 = 16.06   *∆Sales*

Financial Policy   *Simplify Int Cov.*

Dividend payout ratio	25.0%	
EBITDA/Interest expense	4.5	
Interest rate on debt	8.5%	

(Interest Coverage Ratio)
= EBIT / interest expense

(1 - 25%)   25% (RE or SE)

Handwritten margin notes:
(As sales ↑ Assets ↑ How find Asset.
obligation? that arise automatically in operation when buy/sell goods on credit.
- Distinguish WIC assets & other Assets
- Reduce overall financing. Why? Earn ??   min REC / Inventory   Max Liability   firm happy B/c can hold $ longer   Instead pay in 90 days Now 60 days

example, reducing planned growth to 7.02% or $77.4 of sales would require $77.4/0.84 = $92.14 additional assets, of which $92.14 × 20% = $18.43 would be financed by spontaneous liabilities and the rest ($73.7) would need to be financed with debt and equity. Since EBITDA would increase by $74.40 × 14.57% = $11.28, the additional interest expense for a coverage ratio of 4.5x would be $11.28/4.5 = $2.51, and debt could be increased by $2.51/8.5% = $29.5. Proceeding in the same way as above, the reader can determine that net income would be $59.0 and retained earnings $44.2 such that the sum

EXHIBIT 7.3   *IMT Corp. Financing Planned Growth*

Balance Sheet Changes Resulting from Planned Growth
(Year-end 2003 in million $)

Additional assets needed to support			Retained earnings	$45.50
10% growth	*∆ Assets*	131.25	Debt increase	42.00
Minus spontaneous liabilities		26.25		87.50
Financing need		$105.00 *WRONG*	Deficit	17.50

Alternatives to support 10% growth		**Interest Coverage Ratio**
New equity issue	$17.50	4.5
Additional debt	$17.50	4.34
Sustainable growth‡	7.02%	4.5

‡Assuming no additional equity issues and maintenance of the target coverage ratio.

of the increase in debt plus retained earnings would add up to $73.7, the amount to be financed. That is why 7.02% is called the sustainable growth rate.

② Instead, the firm can allow its interest coverage ratio to decrease. For example, the firm can finance its planned 10% growth by borrowing the difference between its investment requirements and retained earnings, that is, $105 – $45.5 = $59.5. Then, debt would increase to $420 + $59.5 = $479.5, and the interest coverage ratio would become $176.7/(8.5% × $479.5) = 4.34, down from its 4.5 target. This could likely be done without materially increasing the cost of debt.[3] On the other hand, the coverage ratio would gradually decrease if the firm planned to grow at 10% beyond 2003, were to maintain its current dividend payout, and to finance the additional fund requirements with debt.

③ Alternatively, the firm can raise new equity by the amount $105 – $87.5 = $17.5 and preserve its target coverage ratio. In practice, however, management is reluctant to issue new equity because of the volatility of stock prices, the high cost of floating a new issue (issue costs plus possible underpricing) and, perhaps more importantly, dilution of control. (Stock prices tend to fall on announcement of equity issues because investors seem to interpret them as a negative signal about the firm's future.[4]) If stock issues are ruled out, the company is left with a three-variable system with only two degrees of freedom: Only two of the variables—growth, payout, and debt ratio—can be chosen, the other is determined by that choice.

The debt policy of the firm was defined in terms of the EBITDA interest coverage. One may as well have carried out the computations using the more common EBIT interest coverage ratio with the same results. In fact, note that

$$\text{EBIT} = \text{EBITDA} - \text{Depreciation} = (1 - 3\%/14.57\%)\,\text{EBITDA} = 0.7941\,\text{EBITDA}$$

Since, in the present case, depreciation equals 3% of sales and EBITDA equals 14.57% of sales. The corresponding EBIT coverage ratio is $0.7941 \times 4.5 = 3.57$. The calculation of new debt in terms of EBIT coverage follows similar steps to those undertaken above, first computing EBIT and then obtaining the additional debt. Although in this section it is a matter of indifference what multiple to use, normalizing debt capacity calculations in terms of EBITDA permits carrying out a unified analysis of valuation and financing in terms of EBITDA, which is the preferred valuation metric in practice. This is particularly so for the analysis of leveraged buyouts.[5]

A similar consideration applies to our choice of interest coverage over the debt ratio to carry out debt capacity calculations. The calculations could have been carried out in terms of the debt ratio with similar conclusions. In fact, the target debt ratio that corresponds to the target coverage ratio of 4.5 can be computed as follows:

$$\text{Target debt ratio} = \frac{\text{Debt}}{\text{Debt} + \text{Equity}} = \frac{\text{EBITDA}/(\text{Coverage ratio} \times \text{Interest Rate})}{\text{Sales/Asset Turnover} - \text{Spontaneous Liabilities}}$$

that, for the parameters of Exhibit 7.2, it equals

$$\text{Target debt ratio} = \frac{0.1457/(4.5 \times 0.085)}{(1 - 0.2)/0.84} = 40\%.$$

---

[3]Note, however, that the affordable dividend payout will decrease slightly because of the interest paid on the additional debt.

[4]See Asquith and Mullins (1983).

[5]Valuation multiples and leveraged buyouts are treated in Chapters 4 and 13, respectively.

Also, note that the profit margin on sales is

$$\frac{\text{Net Income}}{\text{Sales}} = \frac{(1 - \text{Tax rate})(\text{EBITDA} - \text{Depreciation} - \text{Interest Expense})}{\text{Sales}}$$

$$= \frac{(1 - 40\%)(14.6\% \times \text{Sales} - 3\% \times \text{Sales} - 14.6\% \text{ Sales}/4.5)}{\text{Sales}} = 5.0\%.$$

In order to use the target debt ratio rather than the target interest coverage ratio, we proceed as follows: Since the target debt ratio is 40% and the required capital is $105, debt can increase by $42 and the additional equity needs to be $105 – $42 = $63. However, net income would be 5% of $1,102.5 + $110.25 or $60.6 and maintaining a 25% dividend payout would leave only $45.5 of retained earnings, necessitating an equity issue for $17.5. Similarly, assume growth is only 7.02%, then the required additional capital is only $73.7 and can be financed with $29.5 of debt and $44.2 million of retained earnings.[6] It should be noted that we have made no reference to if the debt ratio is measured in accounting or market value terms. This is because at the margin, that is, in dealing with additional capital, the changes in book and market values coincide. If the long-term growth of the firm is already impounded into its stock price, enterprise value will increase by just the additional debt and equity amounts, and their ratio will correspond to the target debt-to-equity ratio. Actually, the analysis of capital requirements can be make by stating the debt ratio in accounting or market value terms with the same results as long as the other parameters are defined in a consistent manner. The fact that, in practice, definitions of the debt ratio vary widely makes it preferable to define debt capacity in terms of interest coverage ratios.

7.3   GROWTH VIA ACQUISITIONS

Financing of acquisitions is similar to financing internal growth. The acquisition brings additional assets with their own EBITDA and growth opportunities that increase the debt capacity of the acquirer. In addition, if the acquisition of the target's equity is made via a share exchange, the acquirer can more easily maintain its target coverage and debt ratios. There are cases in which the acquisition may bring additional cash flows rather than additional growth. In those cases, the acquisition may contribute to financing other emerging activities while maintaining financial balance. Other acquisitions, particularly hostile acquisitions, are usually made for cash. Whenever a significant cash component is involved, the acquirer has to decrease its interest coverage below its previous target. If the new level is sustainable, the acquirer may decide to maintain it in the future. More frequently, the goal is to return to the pre-acquisition interest coverage target. This has to be done via a combination of equity issues, reduced dividend payout, and divestments. The way this is done and how long it takes can have an impact on the ability of the company to finance future growth and face competition.

7.4   SUSTAINABLE DEBT

In previous sections, we examined financial policy in relation to growth and how financial policy needs to be changed in order to support a planned rate of growth. Now we consider how much debt can the firm undertake. We recognize that in practice, it is difficult if not impossible to determine what an optimal capital structure is. Instead, we provide guidelines for gauging debt capacity.

---

[6]See Problem 7.1.

Debt
1) sustainable

2) max.
- Distress
- Leverage
Buyout

In discussing debt capacity, it is useful to distinguish between two types of companies: (1) companies that have the freedom to choose a capital structure that is sustainable over time, and (2) companies that have to use debt capacity at its maximum during a transition period. The latter include leveraged buyouts and recapitalizations under distress and will be discussed in the following section. Here we examine the choice of sustainable capital structure by those companies that can do so.

The deductibility of interest expenses makes debt a desirable source of finance. The well-established way of gauging optimal capital structure begins with the tax advantage of debt and takes into account the costs of high leverage. These include loss of strategic flexibility, competitor predation,[7] and, at high levels of indebtedness, the possibility of financial distress and bankruptcy. The latter is usually gauged by considering adversity scenarios that may be faced by the company because of the economic cycle, competition, increases in input costs, or technological change. Where the optimum lies is not determined by a formula as it is difficult, if not impossible, to measure the magnitude of the different costs. In principle, companies with well-established market positions and strong cash flows are less likely to be subject to financial distress and can therefore borrow more than fast-growth firms or firms with a high proportion of intangible assets. This is so because the values of future growth and of intangible assets are more easily dissipated under financial distress.[8] In fact, food and chemical companies borrow more than software and pharmaceutical companies. However, in practice, companies do not seem to actively manage their capital structures and instead subordinate it to their investment and dividend policy and use debt as an offset to fluctuations of internally generated cash flows.[9] Actual leverage policy seems to obey the pecking order theory of capital structure[10] that recognizes that firms prefer to change dividends only gradually and seek external financing to fund positive NPV-investments only when internally generated funds are insufficient and, in that case, they issue debt before equity financing. Myers and Majluf (1984) have argued that pecking-order behavior is a consequence of asymmetric information, that is, of managers knowing more about their firms than outside investors who interpret equity issues as being made when managers think shares are overpriced.

In conclusion, firms with ample internally generated funds have considerable flexibility in choosing their capital structure and opt to carry low levels of debt. Thus, companies tend to end up with low debt ratios, high interest coverage, and their debt issues, if any, tend to be rated high-grade. On the other hand, companies with growth opportunities that cannot be fully financed by internally generated funds tend to issue more debt. It is for these firms that the analysis of the sustainable use of their debt capacity becomes particularly relevant.

A firm with a sustainable capital structure is a firm that can expect to refinance its debt with a reasonable degree of certainty and has to be concerned only with having sufficient funds to pay interest. The usual way of thinking about debt capacity is in terms of the coverage ratio (EBIT-to-interest) under conditions of adversity. For example, if the company wants to cover interest expense with 99.9% probability, it will admit a probability of shortfall of 0.1% in *a given year*.[11] That is,

---

[7]Competitor predation is examined in Bolton and Scharfstein (1990).

[8]Titman and Wessels (1988) found that debt ratios are negatively related to marketing, selling and R&D expenses.

[9]See, for example, Pnegar and Wilbricht (1989) and Baskin (1989).

[10]See Donaldson (1961) and Myers (1998).

[11]The probability of shortfall over a number of years is higher. For example, assuming independence of the growth rate of EBIT over time, the probability of default over ten years corresponding to a yearly shortfall probability of 0.1% is $1 - 0.999^{10} = 1\%$.

EXHIBIT 7.4	*Forward EBIT Interest Coverage Ratios for a Shortfall Probability of 0.1%*		
	Standard Deviation of EBIT Growth		
	10.0%	20.0%	30.0%
5%	1.42	2.43	8.54
EBIT 10%	1.39	2.28	6.36
Growth 15%	1.37	2.16	5.16
20%	1.35	2.06	4.40

$$\Pr\{EBIT \leq rD\} = 0.001. \tag{7.1}$$

Assuming the growth rate of EBIT is approximately normally distributed[12] and denoting its mean and standard deviation by g and σ, respectively, one can solve Equation (7.1) for the interest coverage ratio for the year and obtain[13]

$$\frac{EBIT_0(1 + g)}{rD} = [1 - 3.09\sigma/(1 + g)]^{-1} \tag{7.2}$$

Exhibit 7.4 gives the coverage multiple for various combinations of expected EBIT growth and standard deviation of growth.

For example, First Call consensus growth of New England Business Service, Inc. (NEB) for 1999 was 6.7% and the standard deviation of its growth rate during 1989 to 1998 was 23.4%. Substituting these values into Equation (7.2) yields a forward (1999) EBIT interest coverage multiple equal to 3.1. Since NEB's depreciation was 20% of EBITDA, the corresponding EBITDA interest coverage multiple was 3.1/0.80 = 3.9. This means that maintaining the EBITDA interest coverage at 3.9 times permitted NEB to redeploy depreciation toward asset replacement and pay interest with 99.9% probability. However, NEB had a forward coverage of 18.5 times EBITDA, which implies a shortfall probability of only 0.00001. This high-interest coverage is in accordance with the pecking order theory of capital structure. It means that NEB had unutilized debt capacity equivalent to 13.6 times EBITDA if it were willing to accept a probability of shortfall of 0.1% in any given year.[14]

Another related way for gauging the necessary coverage is to calculate the cash flows available for debt service under adversity scenarios that include a recession, competitors' unfavorable actions such as price wars, strikes, significant input cost increases, and delays in the introduction of key new products.[15]

7.5 THE TARGET DEBT RATIO ASSUMED IN WACC VALUATION, DEBT CAPACITY, AND INTEREST COVERAGE

In the enterprise valuation model, WACC is based upon a target debt ratio. Debt and interest expense are assumed to evolve through time in fixed proportion to the value of the firm. In practice, valuation is based upon projected financial statements that already

---

[12]See Chapter 10, Section 10.6.1 for a more general model.

[13]That is $\Pr\{EBIT \leq rD\} = F_N[(rD - EBIT_0(1 + g))/\sigma_{EBIT}]$, where $\sigma_{EBIT} = EBIT_0\sigma$. Hence, $rD/EBIT_0 - 1 = F_N^{-1}(0.001)\sigma/(1 + g)$ or $rD/EBIT_0 = 1 - 3.09\sigma/(1 + g)$ since $F_N^{-1}(0.001) = -3.09$.

[14]For an alternative shortfall approach to the analysis of debt capacity based upon rates of return see Leibowitz, Kogelman, and Lindenberg (1990).

[15]See Donaldson, *op ct.*

contain forecasts of debt levels and interest expense made before the value of the firm has been determined. Thus, valuation follows rather than initiates the construction of financial statements. Fortunately, the procedure followed in projecting the financial statements adheres quite closely to the assumptions of the valuation procedure. This is because financial officers, bankers, and rating agencies characterize financial policy in terms of debt capacity measured by interest coverage or, equivalently, the ratio of debt to EBITDA.

EBITDA interest coverage is directly related to enterprise value and to a value-based debt ratio. In fact, when all the components of the free cash flow are proportional to sales, FCF is proportional to EBITDA. Hence, when sales grow at the rate g, enterprise value equals $\mu EBITDA_1/(WACC - g)$, where $\mu = FCF_1/EBITDA_1$ and the EBITDA coverage ratio equals

$$c = \frac{EBITDA}{rD} = \frac{WACC - g}{\mu rd} \tag{7.3}$$

where g is the growth rate, D is net debt and d is the net debt ratio.

Equation (7.3) can be restated to yield two other common measures of debt capacity. Denote the ratios of depreciation to sales by δ and EBITDA to sales by m, then depreciation to EBITDA is δ/m and EBIT = $(1 - \delta/m)$EBITDA. Thus, the EBIT interest coverage multiple is $(1 - \delta/m)c$. Another measure of debt capacity is the debt capacity multiple defined as the ratio of net debt to EBITDA, that is, $1/(cr)$. This ratio is discussed in the following section and is used in Chapter 13 in conjunction with EBITDA valuation multiples.

For example, the forecast of Paktech International shown in Exhibit 2.1 assumes that FCF will be 13.2% of EBITDA from 2007 onwards (see Exhibits 2.2 and 2.5). Furthermore, WACC = 8.48%, d = 35%, and r = 7.15%. Equation (7.3) gives the implied coverage ratio for d = 35% as c = (8.48% − 6%)/(13.2% × 7.15% × 35%) = 7.5x and the debt capacity multiple as 1/(7.51 × 7.15%) = 1.86x. In fact, debt was projected in Exhibit 2.3 on the basis of an average debt to EBITDA multiple of 1.97x, which taking into account cash and marketable securities implies an average net debt to EBITDA multiple equal to 1.85x, as it can verified from Exhibits 2.2 and 2.3. From these exhibits one can also compute the average EBITDA to net interest coverage ratio and obtain 7.5x.

In conclusion, a financial projection based upon a target coverage ratio implies that the firm maintains an approximately constant debt ratio as it is assumed when discounting free cash flows a constant WACC.

7.6   DEBT CAPACITY IN LEVERAGED BUYOUTS AND RECAPITALIZATIONS

There are situations in which firms find it desirable to adopt high leverage during a transition period. These situations include *leveraged buyouts* (LBOs) financed mainly by borrowing against the acquisition's future cash flows; *leveraged recapitalizations,* in which companies borrow in order to retire most of their equity; and *workouts* of companies with excessive debt that have to be recapitalized with claims reduced to a level commensurate to their debt capacity.

The rationale for LBOs is provided by Jensen's (1986) free cash-flow hypothesis. It says that when managers can spend cash flow at their discretion rather than in the interest of the owners of the firm, investors are likely to value equity at less than its attainable value and an opportunity to reduce the valuation gap via restructuring exists. The use of debt reduces agency costs and restores the valuation of the enterprise by precommitting the distribution of future cash flows. Other situations leading to the use of high levels of debt are those in which management expects free cash flows to increase above the level expected by the market, even though cash flows were not misallocated in the past. A recapitalization with a share repurchase can then lead to a revaluation of the company. There are also cases in which managers buy business units in order to develop their full potential free from the constraints imposed by headquarters. The managers' main contribution is knowledge of the business and ability (human capital). Financing is usually provided by a sponsor who maximizes the use of leverage. In LBOs, the precommitment of cash flows to debt repayment signals to lenders and other investors the confidence that management and the sponsor have about the success of the enterprise. The sponsor's equity investment of 25% or more is a strong signal to lenders that the sponsor is confident about the future cash flows of the company, and thus debt investors require such a commitment from equity investors. Precommitment, together with the loss suffered by the sponsor in the event of default, produces the desired unambiguous signal that communicates the cash flows attainable by the buyout and results in the necessary valuation to make possible financing the acquisition.[16] However, once proper valuation for financing has taken place, management and the sponsor have no incentive to maintain high leverage and will strive to reduce the debt burden to a level sustainable in the long term.

A key difference between companies maintaining sustainable capital structures that do not fully exhaust their debt capacity and highly leveraged firms is that, while the first effectively choose how much debt they carry on their balance sheet, the second attempt to obtain as much financing as possible. For the latter, it is the lenders' criterion that determines debt capacity. Lenders determine debt capacity at the level that permits full debt service without refinancing during the period of senior debt amortization. That is, the cash flow of the company has to be sufficient to pay all cash interest and repay the principal to senior lenders. Refinancing normally takes place only after the senior debt has been retired and the company attains a level of leverage that is sustainable in the long run.

The capital structure of a highly leveraged firm is likely to have two or more layers of debt, each with decreasing order of priority: The most senior layer is the secured debt normally provided by a bank, although securities mimicking some of the characteristics of bank debt are sometimes issued to the public. The next layer is the subordinated debt, which can be subdivided into two or more tranches of different seniority such as senior subordinated and junior subordinated debt. Finally, below them there can be a layer of preferred stock, actually a form of debt but in its traditional form paying a dividend that may not be deductible for tax purposes.[17] Given the highly leveraged nature of this financial structure, banks require not only that interest be paid but often that principal be amortized over a number of years, from 3 to 7 years depending on market conditions and available liquidity. During this period, the borrower is not likely to be able to refinance the debt principal as it comes due, at least not at the secured level, although different independent tranches of secured debt with independent collateral can be structured in large transactions to permit partial refinancing. This is in contrast with financing of a well-established firm where the banks and other senior lenders generally stand ready to refinance the principal as a matter of course.

Requiring debt amortization as well as interest payment puts a higher hurdle on the borrower who is supposed to know more about its ability to service debt than the lenders. Since violations of the amortization schedule would trigger default, which can be very

---

[16]This argument is further developed in Arzac (1992). See also Chapter 13.

[17]In recent years, a form of preferred stock called "trust preferred" issued via a trust conduit effectively permits the tax deductibility of dividends.

costly to management and the equity sponsor, the high amortization requirements act as a screen and insure some degree of self-restraint on the part of the borrower. In addition, since significant amortization of debt would take place in a relatively short period of time, both borrowers and lenders need to have confidence on the realization of cash flows in the near term and determine borrowing capacity accordingly. During periods of high liquidity in the high-yield debt market, as that experienced in 1997, investment banks are able to issue securities to the public with the senior characteristics of bank loans, which are not necessarily amortizable for borrowers with high reputation and strong cash flows.

We shall now present a simple model that summarizes the lender's view of the debt capacity of a highly leveraged firm. In practice, debt capacity in these cases is measured as a multiple of EBITDA, which has the advantage of relating feasible debt financing to the appraisal of an acquisition. For example, if the debt capacity of a buyout target is determined to be 7 times EBITDA, and the purchase price is 10 times EBITDA, then equity has to be 3 times, from which one can quickly estimate the possible return to the equity investor as a function of time to exit and the estimated EBITDA exit multiple.[18]

The determination of debt capacity is a function of the rate of growth of revenues and of the sources and uses of cash that are also expressed as fractions of revenues. On the basis of such inputs, it is straightforward to express cash flows and debt amortization as a function of initial EBITDA and expected growth, and to determine how long it will take to amortize senior bank debt. If it takes longer than lenders require, it means that the debt capacity of the firm is lower than initially assumed. Estimating debt capacity is essentially an exercise in pro-forma forecasting. A typical set of parameters used in practice to estimate debt capacity in highly leveraged transactions is a follows:

Growth of sales	g	=	5.0%
EBITDA margin on sales	m	=	10.0%
Depreciation/sales	δ	=	1.5%
Other non-cash items/sales	η	=	0.2%
(Capital expenditures + increase in net working capital)/sales*	κ	=	2.0%
Cash balance/sales	h	=	0.2%
Interest on cash balances	r_h	=	4.5%
Tax rate	t	=	40.0%
Debt financing:			
$f = 35\%$ senior debt at	r_R	=	8.5%
$(1 - f) = 65\%$ subordinated debt at	r_B	=	10.0%
Amortization of senior by year	n	=	5
Net cash to senior amortization	a	=	100%

*Except cash balance.

Sales growth is an estimate of the average growth over the years of senior debt amortization, 5 years in this case. The growth rate depends on a projection of volume and prices as per a conservative analysis of the borrower's business plan. EBITDA margin is an estimate of the average margin over the period of senior debt amortization and depends on a projection of operating costs. Depreciation, other non-cash items such as deferred taxes, capital expenditures, increase in net working capital, and the cash balance are expressed as the average percentage of sales over the senior debt amortization period. The debt-financing parameters are the ones prevailing in the debt market. The numbers above

---

[18]This calculation is discussed in detail in Chapter 13.

illustrate a case in which senior lenders are willing to supply no more than 35% of the total debt financing and demand 8.5% cash interest with amortization over 5 years. Subordinated lenders would supply the remaining 65% of the debt as a high-yield tranche at 10% cash interest and will not receive principal repayment until after bank debt is retired. For this calculation, it is assumed that all available cash flow goes to senior debt amortization (a 100% *cash sweep*). The terms of the senior loan may allow for discretionary amortization over the amortization period or may prescribe the amounts to retire, based upon the expected cash flow for each year. The planned cash balance would, in practice, be kept at a minimum while satisfying the terms of the bank credit line, and will have a negligible impact on the debt capacity estimate. Since here the cash balance is assumed to growth with sales, its initial value is made equal to $h \times$ first-year sales/$(1 + g) = \$1.9$ million.

The cash flow and market parameters just presented imply a debt capacity for 4.4 times pro-forma EBITDA. For example, if first-year sales and EBITDA is expected to be $1,000 and $100 million, respectively, the company can borrow up to $440 million made up of a secured bank loan for $154 million at 8.5% and a high-yield loan for $286 million at 10%. This can be verified from the cash-flow computation presented in Exhibit 7.5. The top panel of Exhibit 7.5 presents the pro-forma income statements for 5 years and the cash flows available for senior debt retirement. The calculation is made starting with a total borrowing of $439 million distributed 35% senior and 65% subordinated debt. The second panel traces the balance of each tranche of debt. Senior debt decreases each year by the cash available for amortization and subordinated debt stays the same. It shows that the bank debt balance goes to zero in year 5 as required. This calculation started by assuming the solution to the debt capacity problem and verified that $439 million was the correct

---

EXHIBIT 7.5   *Cash Flow, Debt Amortization, and Debt Capacity*

	0	1	2	3	4	5
			Year			
Sales		1,000.0	1,050.0	1,102.5	1,157.6	1,215.5
EBITDA		100.0	105.0	110.3	115.8	121.6
Depreciation		15.0	15.8	16.5	17.4	18.2
Interest income		0.1	0.1	0.1	0.1	0.1
Senior interest expense		13.1	11.1	8.9	6.3	3.3
Subordinated interest expense		28.6	28.6	28.6	28.6	28.6
Income before tax		43.5	49.7	56.4	63.7	71.5
Provision for tax		17.4	19.9	22.6	25.5	28.6
Net income after tax		26.1	29.8	33.8	38.2	42.9
Depreciation and oth. non-cash		17.0	17.9	18.7	19.7	20.7
Capex+ Increase in Net WC&Cash		20.1	21.1	22.2	23.3	24.4
Available for debt retirement		23.0	26.6	30.4	34.6	39.2
Debt amortization:						
Senior		23.0	26.6	30.4	34.6	39.2
Subordinated		—	—	—	—	—
Cash balance:	1.9	2.0	2.1	2.2	2.3	2.4
Senior debt	153.7	130.8	104.2	73.8	39.2	—
Subordinated debt	285.5	285.5	285.5	285.5	285.5	285.5
Total debt	439.3	416.3	389.7	359.3	324.7	285.5
Interest coverage*		2.41	2.65	2.95	3.33	3.83

*EBITDA/Net Interest Expense

answer. The same spreadsheet model can be used to find the solution. One way to attain the solution is simple trial and error on the spreadsheet. For example, you should verify that starting with $300 million of debt, made up of $105 million of secured debt and $195 million of subordinated debt, permits retiring all the secured debt by the end of year 4 and results in an accumulation of cash of $94 million by the end of year 5. Therefore, the company can borrow more than $300 million. Alternatively, assume the company borrows $500 million, made up of $175 million of secured debt and $325 million of subordinated debt. In that case, the firm ends up with an outstanding secured debt balance of $40 million by the end of year 5, which it cannot retire until the following year. Trial and error should persuade you that only $439 million of debt permits retiring all the secured debt by the 5th year given the specified debt market requirements.

As you may have already concluded, there is no need to undertake time-consuming trial and error in order to estimate the debt capacity of a company. For example, available spreadsheet programs such as Excel permit solving for the amount of debt that would result in zero senior debt balance in any given year. The spreadsheet model Debt Capacity Calculator included in the Valuation Aids CD-ROM provides such a solution. An even simpler but less transparent way of computing the debt capacity of a highly leveraged firm is by use of the following formula:

Not on Exam

$$q = \frac{\gamma m^{-1}[\tau^n - (1 + g)^n]/(\tau - 1 - g)}{\tau^n f + (1 - t)r_B(1 - f)(1 - \tau^n)/(1 - \tau)} \tag{7.4}$$

where

$$\tau = 1 + (1 - t)r_R$$
$$\gamma = (1 - t)m + t\delta + \eta - \kappa + (1 - t)r_c h/(1 + g) - hg/(1 + g)$$

You should verify that for the parameter values used in the calculation of debt capacity on Exhibit 7.5, Equation (7.4) gives an EBITDA debt capacity multiple $q = 4.39$ or a total initial debt equal to $q \times EBTIDA_1 = \$439$, exactly the same value obtained on the spreadsheet. The derivation of Equation (7.4) is shown in Note N7.1. A hand-calculator program for this formula is provided in Note N7.2.

Exhibit 7.6 shows the debt capacity multiple for the same inputs used in Exhibit 7.5 and changes in the growth rate and debt amortization period. The debt capacity computed above is shown at the intersection of 5% growth and a 5-year amortization period. Increasing the amortization period to 7 years results in a debt capacity multiple equal to 5.54, while a growth rate of 7.5% with 7-year amortization results in a debt capacity of 5.95 EBITDA.

EXHIBIT 7.6	*Debt Capacity as a Function of Growth and Amortization Period*			
		Growth Rate		
		2.5%	5.0%	7.5%	10.0%
	3	2.93	3.00	3.07	3.14
	4	3.61	3.73	3.87	4.00
Senior	5	4.19	4.39	4.60	4.82
Amortization	6	4.71	4.99	5.29	5.61
Period	7	5.17	5.54	5.95	6.38
	8	5.58	6.05	6.58	7.15
	9	5.95	6.54	7.19	7.91

7.7   THE DEBT CAPACITY MULTIPLE IN PRACTICE

In a typical LBO, capital expenditures do not exceed by much depreciation and changes in deferred taxes. In fact, LBO candidates tend be those with limited investment requirements during the initial years because most of the cash flow needs to go to debt amortization. In addition, an aggressive management of inventories, receivables, and payables can permit self-financing of working capital needs. Finally, cash balances are kept to a minimum. When these conditions are expected, all net income after tax in Exhibit 7.5 becomes available for debt amortization, $\delta + \eta = \kappa$ and $h = 0$ such that γ in Equation (7.5) simplifies to $\gamma = (1 - t)(m - \delta)$. Even when these conditions are approximately met, the simplifying assumptions provide a first approximation to the debt capacity of the buyout based upon less information than required for the model of Section 7.6. Consider the previous example and assume that $\kappa = \delta + \eta = 1.7\%$ and $h = 0$. Then, $\gamma = 3.4\%$ and $q = 4.67$. Note that this value is somewhat higher than the estimate obtained in Section 7.7 because it assumes smaller capital expenditures.

A note of caution. Calculating debt capacity cannot be reduced to a simple mechanical exercise. The procedure outlined above provides a basis for understanding the principles of debt capacity determination and for carrying out a careful analysis of the robustness of the financial structure to adverse changes in the economic environment and internal execution. The projection of cash flows and feasible debt service has to be recalculated under scenarios of reasonable adversity. These stress tests should include price and volume pressure resulting from unfavorable competitive or macroeconomic developments, cost spikes in the case of crucial component parts or raw materials, and the effect of construction delays and process failures. Not all of these unfavorable factors would apply in each case, but the analyst should identify those that can result in material changes in cash flows and debt service. Realization will most likely differ from the projections, but every effort should be made to maintain financial flexibility and predictability during the initial years. Refinancing would be very costly if at all feasible if the LBO runs into financial difficulties during the 1st or 2nd year.[19]

7.8   SUMMARY

In this chapter, we examined the financing of a company as a system comprised of four variables: growth of assets, dividend payout, equity issues, and debt policy. The latter is represented by its interest coverage ratio or its debt ratio. Of these, one of the variables is determined by the choice of the other three. For example, if the firm is going to fund all of its positive net present value opportunities and has a predetermined dividend policy, the financing decision is reduced to the choice of debt and equity. If external equity financing is ruled out, the amount of debt is given. On the other hand, if the firm wants to maintain given coverage ratio and dividend payout and rules out external equity, growth is constrained to whatever rate is sustainable by the choice of these three variables, and asset growth may be constrained even if no dividends are paid. Changes in operating performance such as improvement in asset turnover and increases in the profit margins can decrease capital requirements and increase the internal generation of funds but those changes are limited by technology, managerial ability and competition.

The financial policy of a company can be assessed by the probability of cash shortfall. As a first approximation, this can be done estimating the probability that EBIT may be below interest expense in any given year, for which a simple formula was developed based upon the standard deviation of the yearly change in EBIT.

---

[19]For a discussion of contingency planning for meeting unexpected needs for funds see Donaldson (1969).

The criterion followed by lenders in determining the leverage of a highly leveraged transaction (HLT) was discussed and summarized into a spreadsheet model. Senior lenders usually demand that their loan be amortized within a specified number of years. Hence, the debt capacity of a HLT results from estimating how much debt can be serviced during that period such that all cash flows go to pay the interest and principal of the senior debt and the interest but not the principal of subordinated debt. The model summarizes the debt capacity of a highly leveraged firm as a multiple of EBITDA. This permits matching financing to the cost of an acquisition when the latter is expressed in terms of an EBITDA multiple as well.

The conceptual framework presented in this chapter permits a first approximation to the funding of company growth and the estimation of debt capacity. It should be followed by the construction, analysis, and testing of a detailed financial model what includes income statements, balance sheets, and cash-flow statements.

PROBLEMS

7.1 Refer to the data in Exhibit 7.2. Assume IMT's target debt ratio is 40% as calculated in Section 7.2 and verify that retained earnings for a growth rate of sales of 7.02% are $44.2.

7.2 Reproduce the top panel of Exhibit 7.3 (balance sheet changes) and verify that an EBITDA margin of 17% would permit financing growth at 10% under the financial policy summarized in Exhibit 7.2.

7.3 Jeffrey Wotsaf, the CFO of the Rapture Corporation, wants to estimate the EBIT interest coverage ratio that would keep the probability of EBIT falling short of interest expense at 0.1% (99.9% probability of interest coverage). He estimates that EBIT will grow at about 30% per year with a minimum growth of –5% and a maximum growth of 65%. However, Sharon Wirts, the treasurer, believes that EBIT will grow at about 5% with a minimum growth of –55% and a maximum growth of 65%, and would like to keep the probability of EBIT shortfall at 0.01% (99.99% probability of interest coverage). Estimate the target EBIT coverage ratio under each set of assumptions.

7.4 Use the spreadsheet model Debt Capacity Calculator to reproduce Exhibit 7.5.

7.5 Nigel Watt is considering the acquisition of the Oak Leather Company. Preliminary analysis of the company has produced the following data:

Growth of sales	5.0%
EBITDA margin	17.5%
Depreciation/sales	2.5%
Other non-cash/sales	0.2%
(Capex + Incr. in NWC)/sales*	3.0%
Cash balance/sales	0.1%
Interest on cash balance	4.5%
Tax rate	39.0%
Debt financing:	
40% Senior @	8.7%
60% Subordinated @	9.3%
Amortization of senior by year	5
Net cash to senior amortization	100%
First year sales	$17.630 million
First year EBITDA	$ 3.078 million
Initial cash balance	$ 0.230 million

*Excluding cash balance

The asking price for the company free of debt is $16 million. How much equity would Watt need to raise to meet the asking price?

7.6 Ruppert Kasten, a senior loan officer at First Delta Bank, is considering whether his bank should participate in the senior tranche for financing the acquisition of HLT Corp. At this point, he has summarized the projection made by the management of HLT who is part of the acquisition group. His intention is to determine (a) the debt capacity of HLT based upon management's projection and (b) how much debt can HLT carry if its growth were to be just half of that projection.

(Between 30 – 26)

Sub 9

Total Debt Cap = 32

Total Debt / EBITDA = 3.6

Why Small? Amortize most debt

my debt structure 100%

rely on Bank, thus no

borrow from High Yld mkt.

	2007
Growth of EBITDA	12.0%
Depreciation/EBITDA	41.0%
Other non-cash/EBITDA	1.0%
(Capex + Incr. in NWC)/EBITDA*	31.0%
Cash balance/EBITDA	0.02%
Interest on cash balance	5.0%
Tax rate	40.0%
Debt financing:	
75% Senior @	11.0%
25% Subordinated @	13.5%
Amortization of senior by year	7
Net cash to senior amortization	100%
First year EBITDA	$9.700 million
Initial cash balance	$0.015 million

*Excluding cash balance

Assumption

Out of Break: (250 mil of High Yld)

Easy to Project EBITDA

very small transaction, harder to finance. Why?

- B/c small company can't borrow from Public mkt.

- no liquidity in it

↳ No access to high yield mkt.

- Need to borrow from Bank

Chapter **8**

Valuing Entry and Exit Options

8.1 NET PRESENT VALUE AND OPTIONS

8.1.1 Accounting for Flexibility

The timing of an acquisition or the starting of a new venture is not often predetermined. In many cases, the investor has the choice between deciding right away whether to invest, not to invest, or postpone the decision until more information is obtained and more favorable conditions are attained. Similarly, once the investment has been made, it is usually possible to exit it when conditions become sufficiently unfavorable. There are cases in which a firm may enter a new product market or region by making a relatively small investment in order to establish a foothold and acquire the option to expand in the future if and when appropriate conditions are attained. While these cases can be and are usually valued using the discounted cash flow method presented in previous chapters, such valuations commonly ignore the value of the options involved. As usually applied, DCF valuation discounts *expected* free cash flows at a risk adjusted cost of capital and is therefore unable to capture the effect of altering the cash flows contingent on the occurrence of future events. In this chapter, we present a valuation approach, based upon option pricing techniques, that allows for the explicit valuation of waiting for entry, acquiring growth options, and exiting a business under unfavorable conditions.

Let us begin with a simple illustration of the approach and its difference from traditional DCF valuation. Consider whether or not to start a new venture with an investment cost of $4,000. The venture would generate a yearly real free cash flow of either $300 with probability p = 0.5 or $30 with probability 1 − p = 0.5 in the first year. The cash flows from that year on in perpetuity would remain at the level attained the first year. Furthermore, let us assume that cash flows are uncorrelated with the market (have β = 0) and, therefore, should be discounted at the real riskless rate, which is taken to be 3%. Since the expected yearly cash flow is $165, the value of the venture if investment takes place at time zero is $165/0.03 = $5,500 and its NPV = $5,500 − $4,000 = $1,500.

Consider now the possibility of waiting 1 year for the uncertainty concerning free cash flows to be resolved and then deciding whether or not to start the venture. Let the initial cost be the same as before. At this point, we assume that information about the economy and the market for the product would be sufficient to ascertain the future cash flows of the venture without the need of actually investing in it. Later on, we shall consider the case in which actual investment is required to learn about potential cash flows.

Obviously, if the expected free cash flows happen to be just $30 per year, the value of the venture would be just $1,000 and investment would not pay. However, if the expected free cash flows becomes $300 per year, the venture would be valued $10,000 and the NPV of the investment would be $6,000 1 year from today, with a value of $6,000/1.03 = $5,825 today. That would happen with probability 0.5 so, from the perspective of time zero, the NPV of the venture with the option to wait is 0.5 × $5,825 =

$2,912.5. That is, waiting 1 year increases the value of the option to invest in the new venture. This calculation assumes that the option to wait is available. Were the investment option to expire if the investment is not made at time zero, NPV would be $1,500, and the option to wait would have no value. In such a case, the standard NPV rule would apply and it would pay to start the venture right away. Such a situation would arise, for example, when time to market is crucial because the investment opportunity would be lost to a competitor if not undertaken right away.

A more realistic case is one in which learning about expected future cash flows requires actual investment in the venture but investment can be staged. Assume, for example, that instead of investing $4,000 right away, a pilot project can be started at the cost of $500 and that an additional $3,500 would be required in a year in order to generate free cash flows starting from the second year onward. The expansion would be undertaken only if the present value of future cash flows exceeds $3,500, that is, if the expected yearly free cash flow were $300, otherwise the venture would be scrapped. Let abandonment costs be $100. Then, the value of the foothold investment with option to expand is:

$$NPV = (0.5)(-500 - 100/1.03) + (0.5)[-500 + (300/0.03 - 3,500)/1.03] = \$2,607$$

Note that DCF proceeds by discounting backward along a decision tree. The tree structure of the last example and its valuation are shown in Figure 8.1. It shows that the optimal investment policy requires abandoning the venture at time one when expected future free cash flow is $30. The value of free cash flows in each branch is then weighted by its respective probability and discounted back to time zero, where the NPV of the foothold investment option is computed and the decision to proceed with the foothold is taken if NPV is positive.

In principle, it is possible to extend the DCF plus decision tree analysis to many periods and decisions and incorporate systematic risk by discounting each individual cash flow at the appropriate cost of capital. However, the information needed in terms of probabilities, expected cash flows, and the appropriate discount rates at the different branches of the tree would exceed the information that the analyst would have available in practice. For this reason, in this chapter we follow an alternative approach based upon option pricing theory. In doing so, we shall introduce a continuous-time model of free cash flows and apply principles of arbitrage pricing to the valuation of firms with entry, growth, and exit options. The continuous-time formulation is appealing because it allows capturing and applying in a clear and precise way the information about the probabilistic nature of the cash-flow process likely to be available in practice. We shall rely on simple cash-flow forecasting techniques and information about companies with comparable risk character-

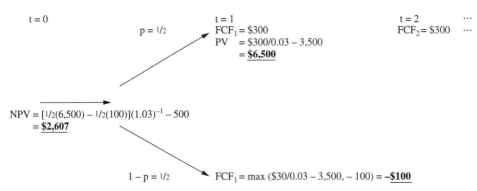

Figure 8.1 Valuation of Foothold Investment with a Growth Option

istics to define the cash flow process and its cost of capital. In addition, the continuous-time formulation leads to decision trigger points defined by state variables such as revenue or cash-flow levels rather than arbitrary points in time.

This chapter is organized as follows: First we provide the discrete-time option-pricing analog to the DCF valuation presented in this introduction. The purpose is to familiarize the reader with the principles of arbitrage pricing and show the equivalence between the DCF plus decision-tree approach and option pricing. In Sections 8.2 to 8.9, we develop a tractable free cash-flow model in continuous time characterized by the evolution of revenues and proceed to develop in successive stages valuation models incorporating entry, exit, and growth options. Throughout the chapter, we compare the option-pricing results with those attained using simple DCF based upon expected values and risk-adjusted discounting. In addition, we provide spreadsheet algorithms for option valuation of enterprise and equity values. The main text explains the nature of the models and illustrates their applications, with mathematical details confined to the chapter notes.

The approach followed in this chapter is an outgrowth and application of the valuation models used to value financial options, themselves extensions of the Black-Scholes formula for valuation of calls and puts on common stock. In Chapter 6, we used a modification of the Black-Scholes formula to value the equity of a highly leveraged firm with changing leverage. In this chapter, we deal with the effect of entry, exit, and growth options on the value of the firm.

Options on assets other than financial instruments are usually called *real options*. The literature on real options deals with the application of option pricing mainly to the valuation of capital budgeting decisions, which makes its results directly applicable to enterprise valuation. In recent years, the real options approach has made significant progress with applications to a wide number of specific capital budgeting decisions.[1] In addition, a theory of investment of the firm based upon option pricing that allows for entry, exit and growth options has been developed by Dixit (1989), Pindyck (1993), and others and synthesized in the work of Dixit and Pindyck (1994). Their contributions constitute the basis of the valuations models presented in this chapter.

8.1.2 Option Pricing

Using the terminology of option pricing, the first example of the previous section in which the decision to invest could be postponed is a *call option* with *strike price* equal to $4,000, and the question to consider is whether to exercise the option to invest at time zero or to wait a year and then decide. In year 1, the asset would be worth $300/0.03 − $4,000 = $6,000 if expected free cash flows are $300 per year and zero if they are $30 per year. Let us use the option-pricing approach to value the option today. For that, we need a spot market for the venture's cash flow. More specifically, we need a traded asset that is perfectly correlated with the cash flow of the venture such that it has the same risk characteristics. Such an asset would be available in a stock market characterized by the CAPM for example and, in the present case, it would have $\beta = 0$. Let this asset assume the value of either $10 or $100 in one year, each with probability 0.5 such that it would be priced at $55/1.03 = $53.40 at time zero.[2]

---

[1]Collections of such applications are included in Trigeorgis (1995) and Brennan and Trigeorgis (2000).

[2]The investment opportunity itself can be used as the perfectly correlated asset. Problem 8.4 asks the reader to value the same option using the cash flows the investment opportunity would generate if it were undertaken at time zero.

Now, consider a portfolio made up of an option to invest in the new venture and a short position of n units of the traded asset. Denote the time-zero value of the option to invest by c. Then, we can write the value of the portfolio at time zero as c − n($53.4) and its value 1 year hence as either $6,000 − $100n or −$10n. Note that the portfolio can be made riskless by choosing n such that 6,000 − 100n = −10n, that is, by shorting n = 66.67 units of the traded asset. In that case, the value of the portfolio at time 1 will be −$666.7, no matter what happens to the cash flows from the venture. Hence, the cash return of this portfolio is −$666.7 minus the initial investment. Since this portfolio requires an investment of c − 66.67($53.4) = c − $3,559.9, its cash return is −$666.7 − (c − $3,559.9) = $2,893.2 − c. Because the portfolio is riskless, its initial investment must yield the riskless rate. Hence we have the following equality:

$$2,893.2 - c = 0.03(c - 3,559.9),$$

or c = 3,000/1.03 = $2,912.6. Note that this portfolio is equivalent to borrowing −(2,912.6 − 3,559.9) = $647.3 at time zero (negative investment) and paying back $666.7, which includes $19.4 interest at a 3% rate.

The value of the investment option is the same as that attained by DCF under the assumption that a 1-year wait takes place before making the investment decision. Note that the valuation procedure consists in constructing a hedged portfolio that is riskless. It can be shown that any other value of the option would allow for riskless arbitrage profits. This is why this valuation procedure is often called *arbitrage pricing*.[3]

A similar calculation can be made to value the foothold option. Consider a portfolio made of the option to expand the venture at a strike price of $3,500 and a short position of n units of the traded asset. The value of such a portfolio in one year would be

$$(300/0.03 - 3,500) - 100n = 6,500 - 100n$$

if the cash flow from the venture turns out to be $300, and −(100 + 10n) if the cash flow is $30. To make it riskless, let n = 6,600/90 = 73.33. Since this portfolio requires an investment of c + $500 − ($55/1.03)(73.33) = c − $3,415.68, the value of the option must satisfy

$$-833.3 - (c - 3,415.68) = 0.03(c - 3,415.68)$$

or c = 2,685/1.03 = $2,607. This is the same value as the NPV calculated in Figure 8.1. Note that the investment cost takes into account that the buyer of the option must pay the foothold cost of $500 in addition to the value of the option. In addition, the buyer must commit to paying a cancellation fee of $100, which is accounted for in the value of the cash flow for the low return realization.

The above examples have shown that the introduction of options increases the value of the firm. This is generally so, with standard DCF giving the correct value only when flexibility is nonexistent or has negligible value.

8.2   A CONTINUOUS-TIME MODEL OF FREE CASH FLOWS[4]

In the rest of this chapter, we study entry and exit options in continuous time. With the exception of Section 6.8, in which we introduced an extension of the Black-Scholes, we have, so far, limited valuation analysis to discrete time. Discounting discrete-time free

---

[3]Problems 8.7 and 8.8 require showing the existence of riskless arbitrage profits for values of this option that depart from the option-pricing solution.

[4]The rest of this chapter requires familiarity with differential calculus notation.

cash flows extracted from pro-forma financial statements is sufficient for most valuation tasks. An exception is real-option analysis. Although some real options can be valued in discrete time on binomial trees (essentially a generalization of the valuation approach outlined in Section 8.1.2 above) or via simulation,[5] the continuous-time formulation offers a number of advantages for valuing entry and exit options: (1) It permits compact yet transparent modeling of the arbitrage pricing equation associated with options to enter or exit a business. (2) It is usually sufficient to capture the complexity of these decisions and to incorporate the relevant information: cost of total or foothold entry at different points in time, time evolution of free cash flows as a function of revenues and their volatility, and exit cost or proceeds. (3) A number of entry and exit options of going concerns have undefined expiration and do not lend themselves to a decision-tree representation but can be modeled in continuous time. (4) The general solution to the pricing equations is provided either in closed form or via numerical calculation. Both have been coded into easy-to-use spreadsheets (see Appendix B) to permit the analyst to concentrate on the nature of the economic problem rather than on formulating and solving its discrete-time representation if that is at all possible. The rest of this chapter presents the economic rationale for the pricing equations corresponding to the most common entry and exit options available to the firm, provides the solutions to the equations, and illustrates their practical use with examples. After studying this chapter, the reader will attain the necessary level of comfort and assurance to be able to routinely formulate entry and exit business options, select the appropriate inputs, and use the provided software. Mathematical details have been relegated to technical notes at the end of the book.

In the rest of this section, we model free cash flows as a function of revenues. We use the following notation:

Y	free cash flow of the enterprise
R	revenue
$c_0 + c_1 R$	operating costs, where c_0 and c_1 are constants
Capex	capital expenditures
ΔNWC	increase in net working capital
Dep	depreciation
ΔDefTax	increase in deferred taxes
τ	corporate tax rate
r_f	riskless rate
r_d	corporate borrowing rate
k	cost of equity of the firm such that $k = r_f + \pi\beta$, where π is the market equity premium, and β is the beta coefficient of the equity of the company or of comparable companies
w	weighted average cost of capital (WACC)

With this notation we can express the free cash flow as

$$Y = (1 - \tau)(R - c_0 - c_1 R) + \Delta\text{DefTax} + \text{Dep} - \text{Capex} - \Delta\text{NWC}$$

$$= (1 - \tau)(1 - c_1)R - (1 - \tau)c_0 + \Delta\text{DefTax} + \text{Dep} - \text{Capex} - \Delta\text{NWC}$$

For tractability we approximate ΔDefTax + Dep – Capex – ΔNWC by a constant. This permits writing Y as a linear function of revenue. That is,

$$Y = a + bR$$

---

[5]See Cox and Rubinstein (1985) and Hull (2002) for details on these approaches and Trigeorgis (1995) for applications.

where $a = - (1 - \tau)c_0 + \Delta DefTax + Dep - Capex - \Delta NWC$ and $b = (1 - \tau)(1 - c_1)$. The following analysis still applies if some of the constant cash-flow elements are made linear functions of revenue. For example, Capex can be allowed to be proportional to sales. Note that this specification permits free cash flows to be negative.

The uncertainty about R is represented by a random variable with a lognormal distribution. That is, we assume that the natural log of R (lnR) is normally distributed. A variable that has a lognormal distribution can take any value between zero and infinity and is fully characterized by the mean and standard deviation of lnR. The standard deviation of lnR is the *volatility* of R denoted by σ. σ is estimated from historical data about R, when available, and/or the analyst's forecast of the future variation of R. For example, σ can be approximated from the difference between an *optimistic estimate* R^+ of R, and a *pessimistic estimate* R^- of R such $Pr\{R^- < R < R^+\} = 1 - \theta$, where $1 - \theta$ is the level of confidence of the interval (R^-, R^+). For example, if the analyst considers that R^- and R^+ are essentially the lower and upper bounds of the revenue distribution, then $1 - \theta \approx 0$ and, since for the normal distribution most of the probability mass (99.9%) lies within 3.1 standard deviations around the mean, $\sigma \approx \ln(R^+/R^-)/6.2$. To illustrate, assume the likely range of R_t is (10, 100). Then, the volatility of R_t is approximately equal to $\ln(100/10)/6.2 = 37.1\%$. On the other hand, if the level of confidence of this interval is only 95%, that is, if it is considered that there is a 5% probability of larger deviations, $\sigma \approx \ln(100/10)/4 = 57.6\%$ because 95% of the probability of revenue lies within two standard deviations around its mean. There are cases in which historical data and/or consensus estimates of revenue growth for comparable firms or for the company itself permit estimation of the expected growth rate and its range (g^-, g^+). In that case, the volatility of revenue is estimated from $(g^+ - g^-)/(2s)$, where $s = 2.0, 2.6$, or 3.1 depending on if the level of confidence for the range of the growth rates is 95%, 99%, or 99.9%. For example, if revenue is expected to grow at a (continuous compounding) rate between -20% and 35% with 99% probability, its volatility is $(35\% + 20\%)/5.2 = 10.6\%$.

This characterization of R permits a tractable representation of the stochastic process followed by revenues and free cash flows. We shall assume that percentage changes in R, $d(lnR) = dR/R$ over a small time interval dt are given by

$$dR/R = \alpha dt + \sigma dz \qquad (8.1)$$

where α is the growth rate or *drift* of expected revenue. That is, $E(R_t) = R_0 e^{\alpha t}$, where E is the expectation operator. σ is the standard deviation of dR/R or volatility of R. dz is the change in z(t), which is given by $dz = \varepsilon(dt)^{1/2}$, where ε has zero mean and unit standard deviation. This implies that $E(dz)^2 = dt$. z(t) is called a *Wiener process* or *Brownian motion*. Equation (8.1) is a generalization known as an *Ito process* or a *geometric Brownian motion*. Since free cash flows are a function of revenues, changes in Y can be expressed by the differential

$$dY = bdR = b\alpha Rdt + b\sigma Rdz \qquad (8.2)$$

Geometric Brownian motion has been shown to provide a reasonable representation of the behavior of stock prices. It is frequently used to model the behavior of economic variables that assume non-negative values and grow over time but are subject to uncorrelated random changes about their expected growth rates.

Revenues and cash flows are expressed in real terms and, consequently, their rate of growth is real rather than nominal.[6] This implies that the nominal constant component of

---

[6]See Chapter 12 on real and nominal cash flows.

the cash flow increases with inflation over time. In addition, real cash flows have to be discounted at a real rate, namely at a cost of capital adjusted for inflation.[7]

Example 1

Consider a firm planning to enter the fluid handling business. Preliminary estimates result in the following processes for revenue and free cash flows: Initial revenue would be $R_0 = \$100$ million with an expected real discrete-time grow rate of the 5% per year. That is, $R_t/R_{t-1} - 1 = 5\%$ and the corresponding continuous-time growth rate is α such that $e^\alpha = 1.05$ or $\alpha = \ln(1.05) = 4.879\%$. Let the volatility of revenue be 15% and free cash flow be $Y = 0.3R - 20.0$ million.

Hence, we can write the motion of revenue as

$$dR = 0.04879Rdt + 0.15Rdz \tag{8.3}$$

Consider the change over a time interval Δt of a month such that $(\Delta t)^{1/2} = 12^{-1/2}$. Then, the monthly change in R_t obeys

$$\Delta R_t = 0.0041\,R_{t-1} + 0.0433\,R_{t-1}\varepsilon_t$$

such that $R_t = 1.0041\,R_{t-1} + 0.0433\,R_{t-1}\,\varepsilon_t$ and

$$Y_t = 0.3012\,R_{t-1} + 0.0130\,R_{t-1}\,\varepsilon_t - 20.0 \tag{8.4}$$

Figure 8.2 shows the sample paths of revenues and free cash flows and the expected revenue forecast produced by the above equations over 120 months, where ε_t are normal deviates with zero mean and unit variance.[8]

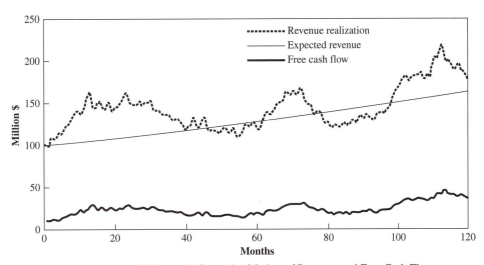

Figure 8.2 Sample Paths of Geometric Brownian Motion of Revenue and Free Cash Flow of Fluid Handling Business

[7]This assumes that the tax code allows for full indexing of inflation, which is not true in the case of the United States and most other countries' tax regimes. In particular, it ignores that depreciation may not preserve its real value and that nominal interest expense may be deductible. These two biases tend to offset each other.

[8]The computation was made on a spreadsheet using Excel's random number generator.

8.3   VALUATION IN DISCRETE AND CONTINUOUS TIMES

In order to value continuous-time cash flows we need to apply continuous-time discounting. In this section, we illustrate the latter and relate it to the discrete-time model of Chapter 2.

Example 2

Let us value the fluid handling business described by the cash flow process (8.4). Let the real cost of debt $r_d = 5.5\%$, the corporate tax rate $\tau = 40\%$, and w, the real WACC corresponding to the cash flows proportional to revenue, be equal to 7.46%.

First, we value the enterprise using the discrete time valuation model of Chapter 2. Real revenue grows at 5% per year from a starting level of $R_0 = \$100$ million. The cash flow margin is 30%, and there is an annual fixed cash-flow component of –$20 million. Exhibit 8.1 computes the enterprise value at $674.4. Note that the free cash flow has been separated into two parts: (1) The cash flow proportional to revenue, which has systematic risk and is discounted at 7.46%; and (2) the fixed cost component (–$20 million), which has negligible or no systematic risk and is discounted at the after-tax cost of borrowing, that is, at 3.30%.[9] The same discounting rate would apply to this component if it were random with fixed expectation as long as its changes were uncorrelated with the market.

EXHIBIT 8.1	*Discounted Cash Flow Valuation of Fluid Handling Business Enterprise Value as of 12/31/2003*

($million)

Free cash flow

Year-end	2003	2004	2005	2006	2007	2008
Revenues	100.0	105.0	110.3	115.8	121.6	127.6
Free cash flow	10.0	11.5	13.1	14.7	16.5	18.3
Fixed component	(20.0)	(20.0)	(20.0)	(20.0)	(20.0)	(20.0)
Proportional to revenue component	30.0	31.5	33.1	34.7	36.5	38.3

Valuation	Rate	PV				
PV{Fixed FCF} @ (1-t)rd	3.30%	(90.8)				
PV{Proportional FCF} @ WACC	7.46%	140.01				
Continuation value:						
Fixed FCF						(606.1)
Proportional FCF @ growth	5.00%					1,634.3
PV{Continuation value}:						
Fixed FCF	3.30%	(515.2)				
Proportional FCF @ growth	7.46%	1,140.5				
Enterprise value		$ 674.4				

---

[9]The value of the fixed-component of free cash flows is that of the loan the company could obtain with such cash flows at its borrowing rate r_d, while benefiting from the deductibility of interest expense. See Ruback (1986).

Similarly, using the continuous-time formulation of Y, we can compute the present value of free cash flows V(R) by integration as follows

$$V(R) = a\int_{0,\infty} \exp(-(1 - \tau)r_d t)dt + b\int_{0,\infty} E(R)\exp(-wt)dt$$

$$= a[-(1 - \tau)^{-1}r_d^{-1}\exp(-(1 - \tau)r_d t)]_{0,\infty} + bR_0\int_{0,\infty} \exp(-(w - \alpha)t)dt \qquad (8.5)$$

$$= \frac{a}{(1 - \tau)r_d} + \frac{bR_0}{w - \alpha}$$

where $(1 - \tau)r_d$ and w now denote the continuous-time equivalent rates. That is, $(1 - \tau)r_d = \ln(1.033)$ = 3.247%, and w = ln(1.0746) = 7.195%. Substituting these values and a = –20, b = 0.3, and α = 4.879% into Equation (8.5) yields an enterprise value of $679.4. This value is slightly higher than that computed in Exhibit 8.1 because the continuous-time formulation allows for the arrival of cash flows continuously through time rather than at the end of the discounting period.[10] A more general framework for continuous-time valuation is presented in the following section.

8.4   VALUING A GOING CONCERN IN CONTINUOUS TIME[11]

In order to value entry and exit options, we need to solve simultaneously for the value of the enterprise and the optimal entry and exit policy. This is so because the value of the enterprise is a function of that policy, which, in turn, is chosen to maximize the value of the enterprise. The option-pricing approach provides the appropriate framework for solving these simultaneous problems. This approach was introduced in Section 8.2 using simple discrete-time examples. Here we present the continuous-time model for valuing the going concern without entry and exit options. In the following sections, the model is generalized to account for the value of those options.

Consider the value of the firm V(R) as a function of revenue. As in Section 8.2, here revenue represents the basic underlying asset, and the value of the firm is treated as a derivative asset. In order to obtain V(R) we construct a portfolio made up of ownership of the going concern and a short position in n units of R, with n chosen so as to make the portfolio riskless. This assumes that the firm's cash flow is priced by the market, in other words, that it is possible to reproduce the cash flow via a portfolio of traded securities. Since the cash flow is linear in revenue, revenue itself is "spanned" by the market and a short position behaving as R can be constructed. In particular, the spanning property holds under the assumptions of the CAPM.

A hedged portfolio is made up of a long and a short position. The long position yields Ydt over a small time-interval dt, but the short position must pay the counterparty a "dividend" to make up the difference between the required return w and the rate of expected appreciation of the cash flow R, which is α.[12] That is, the portfolio must pay to the counterparty $(w - \alpha)Rdt$ per unit short. Hence, the portfolio yields $(Y - n(w - \alpha)R)dt$ plus the net capital gain dV – ndR. The total return on the portfolio is $[Y - n(w - \alpha)R]dt + dV$ – ndR = $[bR + a - n(w - \alpha)R]dt + dV$ – ndR. The latter is equal to the difference between the change in the value of the asset and the increase in the value of the short position. To remove the systematic risk associated with R, the short position n has be chosen so as to

---

[10]See Chapter 2 for the mid-year discounting adjustment sometimes made in discrete-time valuation to allow for the earlier arrival of cash flows.

[11]The following sections are based upon Dixit and Pindyck (1994). Earlier formulations along the same lines appeared in Marcus and Modest (1984) and McDonald and Siegel (1986).

[12]The reason why the counterparty would demand w and not k is that it can lever its investment at the same debt ratio as the firm.

hedge the stochastic component z(t). Denote this short position by $n = n^*$. Note that the hedged portfolio is not absolutely riskless because it still has the risk associated with the fixed component. This risk is not systematic, but it is a default risk similar to the risk of corporate debt cash flows, which have lower expectation than its promised values. Note that the value of a debt perpetuity of \$a per year is $a/[(1 - \tau)r_d]$. This cash flow has a certainty equivalent cash flow $a_{ce} = ar_f/[(1 - \tau)r_d]$. This is so because a_{ce} is the expected cash flow free of default risk that has the same value as a. Therefore, the total return of the portfolio has a certainty equivalent riskless return equal to $[bR + a_{ce} - n^*(w - \alpha)R]dt + dV - n^*dR$. This return should then equal the riskless return $r_f dt$ on its initial cost $(V - n^*R)$ and the following equality must hold

$$[bR + a_{ce} - n^*(w - \alpha)R]dt + dV - n^*dR = r_f(V - n^*R)dt \qquad (8.6)$$

It is shown in Note N8.2 that the solution to this equation has the following form:

$$V(R) = bR/(w - \alpha) + a/[(1 - \tau)r_d] \qquad (8.7)$$

This result was obtained by direct integration in Equation (8.5). While apparently redundant, this section has served to introduce the valuation approach that one must follow to value the entry option. This is done next.

8.5   VALUING THE ENTRY OPTION

When there is no option to defer entry, the entry (acquisition or start-up) decision is to do so if V(R) exceeds the cost of the acquisition. This is not necessarily the case when it is possible to wait in order to decide whether or not to enter the business.

Consider a target with value computed as in Section 8.3 conditional on revenue R. Let the entry cost (acquisition price) be \$I. Waiting for resolution of revenue and cash flow uncertainty has value to the acquirer because for a sufficient low value of R no acquisition would take place. On the other hand, at high values of R, the value of cash flow that would be forgone by delaying the acquisition would exceed the value of waiting. The same argument applies to the decision to start up a venture that would generate the cash flow Y(R). Hence the question to consider is what value of revenue is high enough to trigger entry.

As in Section 8.4, we need to construct a riskless portfolio that yields the riskless rate of interest. The portfolio is long one option to invest (acquire the firm) F(R) and short n units of R. The details are shown in Note N8.3. The solution to the resulting equation is the value of the deferral option:

$$F(R) = A_1 R^{\lambda_1} \qquad (8.8)$$

where λ_1 is the positive root of the quadratic equation

$$\tfrac{1}{2}\sigma^2 \lambda(\lambda - 1)dt + (r_f - w + \alpha)\lambda - r_f = 0 \qquad (8.9)$$

and

$$A_1 = (\lambda_1 - 1)^{\lambda_1 - 1}(I - a/[(1 - \tau)r_d])^{-(\lambda_1 - 1)}b^{\lambda_1}[\lambda_1(w - \alpha)]^{-\lambda_1} \qquad (8.10)$$

The optimal policy is to acquire the firm if and when $R \geq R_H$, where

$$R_H = \lambda_1(\lambda_1 - 1)^{-1}(I - a/[(1 - \tau)r_d])(w - \alpha)/b \qquad (8.11)$$

Furthermore, substituting the expression for R_H into Equation (8.7) gives the threshold in terms of the value of the firm

$$V(R_H) = \lambda_1(\lambda_1 - 1)^{-1}(I - a/[(1 - \tau)r_d]) + a/[(1 - \tau)r_d] \qquad (8.12)$$

That is, acquisition would pay if $V(R) \geq V(R_H)$. This expression shows the departure from the NPV rule when there is a deferral option. NPV prescribes to acquire (or start up) the firm as long as $V(R) \geq I$. Here, $\lambda_1 > 1$ (see Note N.8.2) and, thus, $\lambda_1/(\lambda_1 - 1) > 1$. Moreover, the constant a represents the fixed negative component of the free cash flow (see Section 8.2). Hence, it follows from Equation (8.12) that investing will take place only when $V(R) \geq V(R_H) > I$. Because of the option value of waiting, the value of the acquisition or start-up has to be higher than the entry cost in order to induce investment. This property may justify the practice of setting hurdle rates above the cost of capital.[13] The decision rule assumes that the cost of the investment does not change with R. Early exercise of the entry option may pay when the cost of entry increases over time because of bidding by competitors or other reasons.

Example 3

Refer to Example 2. Let I = $500 million be the cost of entry via the acquisition of an existing going concern or by building a manufacturing facility. In addition, let 3% be the continuous-time riskless rate. Example 2 showed that the business would be worth V(R) = $679 million if entry would take place immediately, giving a NPV = $679 – $500 = $179 million. Assume that the buyer can wait for more information about revenues and cash flows. Computation of Equations (8.8) to (8.12) gives[14]

$$\lambda_1 = 1.8406, \quad A_1 = 0.086, \quad R_H = \$189 \text{ million}$$

$$V(R_H) = \$1{,}828 \text{ million} \quad \text{and} \quad F(R_0) = A_1 R_0^{\lambda_1} = \$413 \text{ million}$$

That is, if the cost of entry stays at I = $500 million and there is an option to wait for more information, it pays to wait until potential revenues reach $189 million or, equivalently, until the value of the business reaches $1,828. The value of entry option at time zero is $413 million, which compares favorably with the NPV of $179 that would be attained by exercising the option immediately. The difference is the price that can be paid to have such an option versus immediate entry.

Example 4

Consider now a more realistic possibility. From Example 2 we know that immediately acquiring an existing going-concern for $500 million has a NPV = $179. Assume that if the acquirer were to forgo immediate entry, it would need to build its own facility at the cost of $750 million. In such a case, it would be able to do it at a time of its choice and only if the market develops favorably. Hence, the question to consider is what is the value of the option to wait, taking into account the higher cost of entry. Solving Equations (8.8) to (8.12) with the new data yields:

$$R_H = \$231 \text{ million} \quad \text{and} \quad F(R_0) = \$348 \text{ million}$$

That is, the firm should wait until potential revenues reach $231 million, and the value of the entry option under this policy is $348 million. This means that it would pay to wait for further resolution of revenue uncertainty in spite of the higher cost of entry. Note, however, that this calculation assumes that delaying entry would not diminish the entrant attainable revenue and growth. That may not be the case in a competitive industry. Starting revenues and the growth rate can be adjusted downward in calculating the value of the deferral option in order to reflect the effect of waiting on future revenues.

---

[13]See Summers (1987), who found that the average hurdle rate in a sample of companies was 17%, which exceeded by 13% the riskless rate, well in excess to the value of a reasonable equity premium. The use of hurdle rates to account for option value in capital investments is examined in McDonald (2000).

[14]The spreadsheet Real Options Calculator I provided these results. See Appendix B for details.

8.6   ENTRY AND EXIT OPTIONS

We now consider the value of a firm that has the option to delay entry and to exit the business after entry. Let us first consider the value of a going-concern with an exit option. From Section 8.4 we know that the value of the firm without option to exit is given by Equation (8.7). Note N8.4 shows that an additional term $B_2R^{\lambda_2}$ accounts for the value of the exit option. That is,

$$V(R) = B_2R^{\lambda_2} + bR/(w - \alpha) + a/[(1 - \tau)r_d]$$

Let R_L be the exit threshold such that the firm stops operations when R falls below R_L. In addition, let us introduce a lump-sum cost of exit equal to $\hat{E}$, which accounts for severance payments, contract cancellations and other closing costs. $\hat{E}$ would be negative when there is net recovery at exit. [$-\hat{E}$ must be less than V(R) and less than the cost of subsequent entry for otherwise infinite profits would be possible.]

Consider now the value of the deferral option with acquisition price $I. From Equation (8.8) the value of the deferral option is

$$F(R) = A_1R^{\lambda_1}$$

The valuation problem of the firm with both deferral and exit options is simplified by assuming that the abandoned firm can be restarted or reacquired for $I. This may not be the case in practice, but both the probability of reentry and the value of the reentry option would be very low at the exit threshold R_L, and no material bias is introduced by this approach when reentry is not possible. This assumption leads to a simple way of simultaneously computing the entry and exit thresholds and the value of the enterprise before acquisition. It is shown in Note N8.4 that the solution R_L, R_H, A_1, and B_2 satisfy the following equations.

$$A_1R_L{}^{\lambda_1} - B_2R_L{}^{\lambda_2} - bR_L/(w - \alpha) - a/[(1 - \tau)r_d] = \hat{E} \qquad (8.13)$$

$$\lambda_1A_1R_L{}^{\lambda_1-1} - \lambda_2B_2R_L{}^{\lambda_2-1} - b/(w - \alpha) = 0 \qquad (8.14)$$

$$A_1R_H{}^{\lambda_1} - B_2R_H{}^{\lambda_2} - bR_H/(w - \alpha) - a/[(1 - \tau)r_d] = -I \qquad (8.15)$$

$$\lambda_1A_1R_H{}^{\lambda_1-1} - \lambda_2B_2R_H{}^{\lambda_2-1} - b/(w - \alpha) = 0 \qquad (8.16)$$

This system of nonlinear equations can be solved on an Excel spreadsheet by a combination of (1) an enumeration search to identify a suitable initial solution, and (2) a local search using Excel's solver tool. Although not computationally efficient, this approach provides the solution using a software already available to most readers. The solution algorithm is included in the Real Options Calculator I.

Key assumptions of this model are that the cost of entry does not increase over time or as a function of revenues and that the cash flow process will not change if entry is delayed. This is not the case in many business situations. Delaying an investment can permit competitors to enter the market and attain first-mover advantages. If that were the case, the model can still be used to establish the value of an immediate entry while allowing for the benefit of exit if cash flows turn out to be disappointing. We illustrate this point with the following example.

Example 5

Let us add an exit option to Example 3 with exit costs equal to $\hat{E}$ = $50 million. To solve Equations (8.13) to (8.16) we input the data into the Real Options Calculator I and obtain:

$$\lambda_1 = 1.8406, \quad \lambda_2 = -1.4488, \quad A_1 = 0.0871, \quad B_2 = 30{,}810,$$

$$R_H = \$184 \text{ million} \quad \text{and} \quad R_L = \$31 \text{ million}$$

| EXHIBIT 8.2 | *Value of Entry, Deferral, and Exit Options of Fluid Handling Business* |

($million)

	Cost of Entry	Cost of Exit	Enterprise Value	Deferral Value	Exit Value	Entry Option	Revenue at Entry	Revenue at Exit
No deferral option	500	—	679	—	—	179	100	—
Exit option	500	50	718	—	39	218	100	31
Exit option	500	(200)	785	—	106	285	100	49
Deferral option	500	—	—	234	—	413	189	—
Deferral option	750	—	—	169	—	348	231	—
Deferral and exit options	500	50	—	200	39	418	184	31
Deferral and exit options	500	(200)	—	143	106	428	174	49

Substituting these values into the formulas for the value of the entry option and the value of the going concern yields

$$F(R_0) = A_1 R^{\lambda_1} = \$418 \text{ million}$$

$$V(R_0) = B_2 R_0^{\lambda_2} + bR_0/(w - \alpha) + a/[(1 - \tau)r_d] = \$718 \text{ million}$$

respectively. That is, the deferral option increases in value to $418 million (from $413 million in Example 3) when account is taken of the option to exit the business at low levels of revenue. Entry would take place when revenues increase to $184 million. As expected, the exit option allows entry at a lower level of revenues. Exit from the business would take place if revenue falls below $31 million. $V(R_0) = \$718$ million is the value the firm would have if entry is immediate, but there is an option to exit at the cost of $50 million. Note that this value exceeds by $39 million the value of the firm without exit and entry options. Although immediate entry is not optimal in the present case, it permits calculating the value added by exiting whenever $R < R_L$. Problem 8.9 asks the reader to recalculate the value of the deferral option with exit option when the entry cost is $750 million as in Example 4.

Suppose instead that exit results in a recovery (negative exit cost) equal to $\hat{E} = -\$200$ million. Then, Real Options Calculator I yields

$$\lambda_1 = 1.8406, \quad \lambda_2 = -1.4488, \quad A_1 = 0.0891, \quad B_2 = 82{,}264,$$

$$R_H = \$174 \text{ million} \quad \text{and} \quad R_L = \$49 \text{ million}$$

That is, the entry revenue threshold decreases and the exit threshold decreases. The value of the deferral option increases to $F(R_0) = \$428$ million, and the value of firm under immediate entry also increases to $V(R_0) = \$785$ million.

The values of the options considered in Sections 8.5 and 8.6 are summarized in Exhibit 8.2.

8.7 VALUING FOOTHOLD AND GROWTH OPTIONS

8.7.1 Foothold Investment with an Expansion Option

What is the value of a firm that has negative cash flows and no revenue but offers the uncertain possibility of capturing market share into a potentially growing and profitable market sometimes in the future? Technology and bio-technology start-ups fall into this category, as well as a variety of platform investments undertaken by venture capitalists and corporations alike. These firms or projects usually involve an initial phase of investment over a period of time followed by a decision to abandon the project or expand it via additional investments in order to attain scale and profits. Abandonment is an option available at any time during the initial phase or after the expansion decision. Whether to make the initial investment is also subject to decision and would be done only if the future prospects of the venture are attractive enough. In this section we present a valuation model for this type of firms and investments.

Entering a business or expanding into another region or country usually requires starting at a modest scale in order to learn the possibilities of the new market or to develop the necessary technology and products. Likewise, an extended period of research and development costs is common to many start-up ventures. During this initial period, the firm learns about the nature of the business and whether it is worthwhile to proceed to the next stage of full-scale production and marketing, which usually requires significant additional investments. Specific examples are: (1) Entry into a new market, region, or country via the acquisition of an established firm to have the option to expand in the future; (2) initial exploratory investment into a new business to have the option of undertaking full-scale penetration via additional investments or another acquisition (roll-up strategy); (3) acquisition of a technology company with no revenue or starting-up a new venture.

A simple way of valuing a foothold investment is to add to the cost incurred in the first stage the value of the option to growth at a future decision time T. The value of the foothold investment is then

$$-\sum\nolimits_{t=1,T} I_t e^{-w(t-1)} \int_{0,1} e^{-wx} dx + F_T e^{-wT} =$$

$$-\sum\nolimits_{t=1,T} I_t e^{-w(t-1)} w^{-1}(1 - e^{-w}) + F_T e^{-wT}$$

where I_t is the annual investment rate during the first stage (the foothold cost) that takes place from $t = 1$ to T, and F_T is the value of the growth option at T given by the solution to the entry/exit model of Section 8.6.

Example 6

Let $I_t = \$40$ million per year until year $T = 3$ and the rest of the data be as in the previous examples: The revenue expected at time T is $R_T = \$100 e^{(0.04879)(3)} = \$115.8$ million with real continuous-growth rate 4.879% and volatility 15% but entry can be postponed beyond T. The revenue of the business would generate an expected free cash flow equal to $0.3R - 20.0$ million. In addition, the continuous-time real riskless rate is 3%, the after-tax cost of debt is 3.247%, and WACC = 7.195%. Furthermore, assume that the cost of the expansion at time T is estimated at $500 million and that the cost of exit if revenues turn out to be disappointing would be $50 million. The Real Options Calculator I gives the value of the expansion option $F_T(R_T) = \$547.1$ million. Hence, the NPV value of the foothold investment is

$$-\sum\nolimits_{t=1,T} 40\, e^{-0.007195(t-1)} 0.07195^{-1}(1 - e^{-0.07195}) + 547.1 e^{-(0.07195)(3)} = \$340 \text{ million}$$

On the other hand, if the expansion has to take place at time T with no deferral option but with option to exit, the NPV of the foothold investment has to be computed taking into account the value of the firm at time T with exit option minus the entry cost. From the Real Options Calculator I we get $V(R_T) - 500 = 915.2 - 500 = \$415.2$ million. That is, the NPV of the foothold investment becomes

$$-\sum\nolimits_{t=1,T} 40\, e^{-0.007195(t-1)} 0.07195^{-1}(1 - e^{-0.07195}) + 415.2 e^{-(0.07195)(3)} = \$234 \text{ million}$$

Using the result from Example 2 the reader can verify that if the investment has to take place at time T with no postponement or exit options, the value of the foothold investment is only $-112 + (679 - 500)/(1.07195)^{-3} = \$33$ million. Furthermore, suppose that an additional initial investment $I_0 = \$60$ is required in order to start the foothold. Ignoring the expansion plus exit options, the NPV would be $-\$27$ million, while accounting for the second-stage options yields a value in the range $\$174 - \$280$ million depending on if the expansion has to be made exactly at time T or if it is possible to wait for additional information.

8.7.2 Valuing Foothold and Expansion Options

So far we have assumed that the foothold investment has to be initiated at time zero. Often this is not the case and the time of the foothold entry can be postponed until more information about future revenues is attained. Even during the foothold investment stage, expenditures can be stopped at low levels of expected revenues. The value of the foothold plus growth options requires valuing two compound options. The first-stage option is whether to make the foothold investment or to wait for additional information. The second-stage option involves the expansion decision once the first stage has shown satisfactory results. Throughout both stages there are available exit options when expectations about the future do no justify further investment. We call the first-stage option a *foothold option* and the second-stage option a *growth* or *expansion option.*

Let us denote potential revenue in the first and second stages by R_1 and R_2, respectively. The question to consider is what potential R_1 is high enough for a first-stage entry and what potential R_2 is high enough for a second-stage investment. Potential revenue is estimated via geometric Brownian motion as in previous sections. The motion is characterized by: (1) the attainable revenue at a given point in time, (2) its growth rate and (3) its volatility.

In order to solve the problem, one proceeds backwards starting from the solution to the second stage decision problem: Once the first stage is completed, the decision on whether or not to invest $\$I_2$ to expand and operate the business has to be made. This is the growth option. For the option to growth we shall use the solution to the entry and exit model of Section 8.6 with solution $F_2(R_2)$ given by Equations (8.13) to (8.16). Note that the value of the growth option $F_2(R_2)$ includes the option to exit the business at sufficiently low levels of revenues.

Since the solution to the second stage option is already available, it rests to solve for the value of the foothold option. This is the option to enter the market and invest over time $\$K$ (cumulative negative cash flow). At the completion of the first stage, the firm has the option to invest $\$I_2$ in order to establish and operate the full-scale going concern. During the first stage the firm receives no net positive cash flow. Although it is possible to interrupt expenditures and restart them at a later stage, the first stage requires a cost to completion equal to $K(t)$.

Following Majd and Pindyck (1987) model of "time to build,"[15] let the dynamics of $K(t)$ be given by

$$dK = -I_1 dt \tag{8.17}$$

such that I_1 is the rate of investment that can assume values in the interval $[0, I_{max}]$. This specification is designed to allow for learning with the remaining cost of the first stage declining with investment. As in previous sections, the motion of revenue is

$$dR = \alpha R dt + \sigma R dz, \tag{8.18}$$

with associated free cash flow $Y = bR + a$.

---

[15]See also Dixit and Pindyck (1994), pp. 328–332.

Let the value of the foothold option be $F_1(R_1, K)$. Its value depends on the firm following an optimal investment policy during the first stage. Denote the optimal policy by $I_1^*(R_1,K)$. It is shown in Note N8.5 that I_1^* provides a *bang-bang* solution with I_1 equal to either 0 or I_{max}, depending on if $R_1 < R_1^*$ or $R_1 \geq R_1^*$.

In order to value the foothold option, we proceed by considering the following portfolio: long the option to invest in the foothold and short n units of R_1. The value of this portfolio is $F_1(R_1, K) - nR_1$, which over the small interval dt has a change $dF_1(R_1, K) - ndR_1$. n is set equal to a value n^* that renders the portfolio riskless. Its return is made up of its change in value during dt minus the compensation required by the buyer of the short position, which is equal to $(w - \alpha)n^*Rdt$, and minus the outflow I_1dt that occurs while investment takes place. Equating the total return on the portfolio to the riskless return yields

$$dF_1 - n^*dR_1 - (w - \alpha)n^*R_1dt - I_1dt = r_f(F_1 - n^*R_1)dt. \qquad (8.19)$$

The solution to this equation needs to satisfy a number of conditions: (a) At completion, i.e., when $K = 0$, the firm gets the option to invest I_2 and operate the firm in the second stage, and (b) the value of the foothold option is negligible when $R_1 = 0$. In addition, Equation (8.19) must satisfy other technical conditions detailed in Note N8.5.

It is shown in Note N8.5 that the solution of Equation (8.19) when $R < R^*$ and $I = 0$ has the same form as Equation (8.8), that is $F_1(R, K) = A(K)R_1^{\nu_1}$. However, when $R_1 > R_1^*$ and $I_1 > 0$, Equation (8.19) is a second-order partial differential equation that lacks a closed-form solution and, therefore, it needs to be solved via numerical methods. The algorithm is detailed in Note N8.7 and can be computed using the Excel spreadsheet Real Options Calculator II.

Example 7

Let us reconsider Example 6 and allow for the option to postpone, stop, and reactive the foothold investment at the rate of $40 million per year. To do so we take into account that, from Example 5, the value of the expansion option is given by $F_2 = A_1R^{\lambda_1}$ and input the data in Exhibit 8.3 into the *Real Options Calculator II*.

The value of the option is $392 million.[16] That is, the option to manage the foothold investment by postponing, stopping and reactivating the foothold as conditions change increases the NPV of the foothold by $52 million over the value of the foothold when total immediate commitment to the first stage investment is required.

EXHIBIT 8.3   *Data for Valuation of Foothold and Expansion Options*

R	$ 100.000	Potential expected revenue at time zero
α	4.879%	Continuous-time growth rate of expected revenue
σ	15.00%	Volatility of revenue
K	$ 120.000	Foothold investment required
I_{max}	$ 40.000	Maximum annual rate of foothold investment
r_f	3.000%	Riskless rate of interest
wacc	7.195%	Weighted average cost of capital
A_1	0.0871	Constant of solution to expansion option $F_2 = A_1R^{\lambda_1}$
λ_1	1.8406	Power of solution to expansion option $F_2 = A_1R^{\lambda_1}$

---

[16]This value results from interpolating within the values generated by the Real Options Calculator II.

EXHIBIT 8.4	*Foothold Option: Optimal Investment Policy*		
Remaining Investment K	Critical Value R*	Remaining Investment K	Critical Level R*
	Million $		
120	221	22	90
110	211	20	86
101	200	18	81
91	191	17	77
83	181	14	74
76	172	13	70
68	164	12	67
62	156	11	63
56	148	10	57
52	141	8	55
47	134	7	49
42	128	6	45
38	122	5	40
35	116	4	35
32	110	2	27
29	104	1	19
26	99	0	0
24	94		

The Real Options Calculator II also gives the optimal investment policy: The foothold investment at a rate of $40 million per year when the remaining investment cost is $120 million should be started when the level of potential revenues exceeds $221 million but should be interrupted below that level of revenues. The optimal policy is contained in Exhibit 8.4. It gives for any remaining foothold investment K the critical value R^* such that additional investment takes place if and only if $R \geq R^*$. Note that the critical value R^* decreases as the remaining investment K becomes smaller, that is, as the expected time to exercise the expansion option gets closer.

*8.8 ALLOWING FOR UNCERTAIN COSTS IN FOOTHOLD INVESTMENTS[17]

A natural generalization of the first-stage model is to allow for the foothold cost to be a random variable $K̃ with expectation $K = E(K̃)$. This can be done with Pindyck's (1993) model of investment of uncertain cost. Let the dynamics of K(t) be given by

$$dK = -I_1 dt + \nu(I_1 K)^{1/2} d\zeta, \tag{8.20}$$

such that I(t) is the rate of investment that can assume values in the interval $[0, I_{max}]$, and $\nu(I_1 K)^{1/2} d\zeta$ represents technical cost uncertainty. $d\zeta$ is a Wiener process such that $d\zeta = \varepsilon(dt)^{1/2}$, where ε has zero mean and unit standard deviation. The parameter ν can be estimated from the variance of the cost to completion.[18]

---

[17]Sections marked with an asterisk may be skipped on a first reading.

[18]The proof is provided in Pindyck (1993) and Dixit and Pindyck (1994).

$$\text{var}(K^{\sim}) = (\frac{v^2}{2 - v^2})K^2 \tag{8.21}$$

As in the time to build model of the previous section, the first term of Equation (8.20) shows that the expected cost declines with investment. The additional term introduces uncertainty as a function of the level of investment and the expected cost to completion. Thus, uncertainty decreases as the expected cost to completion diminishes, and learning occurs when there is investment $(I_1 > 0)$. It its reasonable to assume that cost uncertainly is idiosyncratic to the firm and uncorrelated with the market, which means that $d\zeta$ can be diversified away.

As in previous sections, the motion of revenue is

$$dR = \alpha Rdt + \sigma Rdz \tag{8.22}$$

with associated free cash flow $Y = bR + a$.

As in Section 8.6.2, let the value of the foothold option be $F_1(R_1, K)$ and denote the optimal policy by $I_1^*(R_1, K)$. It is shown in Note N8.6 that I_1^* provides a bang-bang solution with I_1 equal to either 0 or I_{max} depending on if $R_1 < R_1^*$ or $R_1 \geq R_1^*$.

The foothold option is valued by constructing a portfolio with a long position in the option to invest in the foothold and short position of n units of R_1. The value of this portfolio is $F_1(R_1, K) - nR_1$ with change $dF_1(R_1, K) - ndR_1$ over the small interval of time dt. n is set equal to a value n^* that renders this portfolio riskless. Its return is made up of its change in value during dt minus the compensation required by the buyer of the short position, which is equal to $(w - \alpha)n^*Rdt$, and minus the outflow I_1dt that occurs while investment takes place. Equating the total return on the portfolio to the riskless return yields

$$dF_1 - n^*dR_1 - (w - \alpha)n^*R_1dt - I_1dt = r_f(F_1 - F_{1R}R_1)dt \tag{8.23}$$

The solution to this equation needs to satisfy a number of conditions: (a) At completion, i.e., when $K = 0$, the firm gets the option to invest I_2 and operate the firm in the second stage; (b) the value of the foothold option is negligible when $R_1 = 0$; and (c) when K is very large the value of the foothold option is also negligible. In addition, Equation (8.20) must satisfy other technical conditions described in Note N8.6.

Equation (8.23) is a second-order partial differential equation that lacks a closed-form solution and needs to be solved via numerical methods. Implementing the latter can be made with an algorithm based upon the implicit difference method, which does not lend itself to computation using Excel spreadsheets.[19] Schwartz and Moon (2000) used a similar model to value research and development investments.

8.9   SENSITIVITY OF DCF VALUES IN THE PRESENCE OF REAL OPTIONS

Let us reconsider the valuation of Paktech International made in Chapter 2. From Exhibit 2.4 we have that its DCF enterprise value is $178.95 million. A potential buyer would not consider paying more that this amount at least it expects to attain additional cost reductions or growth. The valuation was based upon a forecast of expected cash flows, themselves derived from a forecast of expected sales. Suppose the potential acquirer agrees with the calculation of Exhibit 2.4 but would like to consider exiting the business if and when there is a large revenue shortfall that puts in doubt the ability of Paktech to generate

---

[19]A FORTRAN program is provided in Press et al. (1992), pp. 854–860.

adequate free cash flows in the future. Would this consideration alter the value of Paktech to a prospective acquirer or is the standard DCF valuation of Exhibit 2.4 sufficient?

Essentially, the question posed can only be answered after allowing for the value of the exit option. In order to provide an estimate of the value of this option we first approximate the revenues and free cash flows of Paktech with the continuous-time model introduced in the present chapter. Let FCF be proportional to revenues. Then, a cash flow process $Y = bR$ with the same value as Paktech is given by the solution to $bR_0/(w - \alpha) = \$178.95$ million, where $R_0 = \$213.58$ million, real $w = \ln(1.0848/1.0245) = 5.7191\%$ and real $\alpha = \ln(1.06/1.0245) = 3.4064\%$ (for expected inflation equal to 2.45%). That is, the free cash-flow margin is $b = 0.019377$.

In order to value the exit option we need an estimate of volatility. Assume the optimistic and pessimistic estimates of revenue for 2004 are $300,000 and $130,000, respectively, with 95% confidence. Then, $\sigma = \frac{1}{4} \ln(300/140) = 19.05\%$. We also need the riskless rate $r_f = \ln(1.0407/1.0245) = 1.5689\%$.

Consider now the case in which the acquirer expects to be able to acquire Paktech for a net price of $162 million or 0.7x forward revenues, which is below its estimated value of $178.95 million. This would be so if the cash flows projected in Exhibit 2.4 are attainable by the buyer but not by the seller or other potential acquirers. Also, assume the acquirer estimates that exiting the acquisition in the future if the projections are not realized can be done with a net recovery of $60 million. The Real Options Calculator I gives the following solution:

Entry threshold = $R_H = \$379$ million

Exit threshold = $R_L = \$25$ million

Value of deferral option = $F(R_0) = \$57.1$ million

Value of immediate entry with exit option = $V(R_0) = \$193.8$ million.

The result says that, ideally, it would pay to wait before acquiring Paktech until its revenues reach $379 million. The value of such an option would be worth $57 million. However, this assumes that its acquisition price would stay at $162 million, which is highly unlikely because the DCF value of the company would increase as revenues increase. On the other hand, and more realistically, if no deferral option is available, immediate entry yields an enterprise value of $193.8 million with exit for $60 million if revenues fall below $25 million. That is, exit would take place at a revenue multiple of 2.40 times. Allowing for the exit option increases the value of Paktech to the acquirer by about $15 million.

The reader should verify that the value of the acquisition increases to $202 million if exit is expected to take place at an $80 million net price. In that case exit would take place below $34 million revenues or at a revenue multiple equal to 2.35x. In addition, the exit option becomes more valuable when volatility is higher. Assume again that exit can take place at $80 million but revenue volatility is 25%. Then, the value of the acquisition increases to $210 million, and exit would take place below $29 million revenues at a revenue multiple of 2.76 times.

8.10   SUMMARY

In this chapter, we introduced the principles of arbitrage pricing and showed how they can be used to value firms with real options. We developed a tractable free cash-flow model in continuous time that is characterized by the evolution of revenues, and proceeded to develop in successive stages models of valuation that incorporate entry, exit, and growth options. In addition, we provided spreadsheet algorithms for enterprise valuation when entry, exit and growth options are available.

The tractability of the cash-flow model resulted in simple, readily computable valuation models. On the other hand, its very simplicity may not permit dealing with additional complications one may want to consider. Still, the models of this chapter can play an important role in valuing firms with entry and exit options. In addition, these models can be used to gauge the robustness of standard DCF valuation to such options. Section 8.9 illustrated this type of application by considering how the value of Paktech, the company valued in Chapter 2, would vary when the option to exit after the acquisition is taken into account.

PROBLEMS

8.1 A new venture can be started at an investment cost of $1,200. The venture would generate a yearly expected real free cash flow of either $200 with probability $p = 0.5$ or $100, with probability $1 - p = 0.5$ in the first year. The cash flows from that year on would remain at the level attained in the first year in perpetuity. Furthermore, assume that cash flows are uncorrelated with the market (they have $\beta = 0$). The real riskless rate is 10%. What is the NPV of this venture if it is started right away?

8.2 Consider the possibility of waiting 1 year before deciding whether or not to launch the venture described in Problem 8.1 at the same initial cost of $1,200. Information about the economy and the market for the product would be sufficient to ascertain the future expected cash flows of the venture. What is the NPV of the venture?

8.3 Consider the case in which learning about expected future cash flows requires an actual investment in the venture but that the investment can be staged. Assume that in the venture described in Problem 8.1, instead of investing $1,200 right away, a pilot project can be started at the cost of $50, and that an additional $1,150 would be required in a year in order to generate free cash flows starting from the second year onward. The cost of abandoning the venture in year 1 would be $10. What is the NPV of the venture?

8.4 Review Section 8.1.2 and value the deferral option of the first example of Section 8.1.1 using the cash flows the investment opportunity would generate if it were undertaken at time zero. Note that the value of such an asset would be $5,500. Assume you short it and compute your liability in year 1 at the time of the occurrence of the first cash flow under each possible realization.

8.5 Let there be a traded asset with the same risk characteristics as the venture of Problem 8.2. Depending on if the venture expected free cash flow is $100 or $200, the traded asset would assume the value of either $1 or $2 in one year, each with probability 0.5. Value the option to invest in the new venture using the option pricing approach.

8.6 Value the foothold option of Problem 8.3 using the option pricing approach. Use the same traded asset as in Problem 8.5.

8.7 Refer to the call option of Problem 8.5 and assume you can sell it for $400. Show that you can realize a pure arbitrage profit and interpret your result.

8.8 Assume you can buy the option of Problem 8.5 for $320. Show how to realize a pure arbitrage profit and interpret your result.

8.9 Recalculate the value of the entry option in Example 4 of Section 8.5 for an entry cost of $750 million and compare it to the result of Example 4.

8.10 Consider entry into a business that, if made at the present point in time, would have a first-year revenue of $5 million. Revenue is expected to grow at a continuous-time real rate of 7% per year but growth can vary from −26% to 40% with 95% confidence. The volatility of revenue, that is, the standard deviation of the growth rate of revenue is expected to remain fairly constant over time. In addition, free cash flow as a function of revenue is estimated as having a fixed component of −$2 million plus 25% of revenue, both in real dollars. The continuous-time real risk free rate, after-tax cost of debt and applicable WACC are 3%, 5%, and 9%, respectively.

    a. What are the expected free cash flows in years 1 through 5?
    b. What is the value of the enterprise assuming that it has to be launched right away?
    c. What is the value created by the investment (NPV) if the initial entry cost is $30 million and no delay or exit options are available?

8.11 Refer to Problem 8.10. Assume that entry can be postponed but that the initial cost would then be $40 million in real dollars, with the rest of the data as before. What is the NPV of the investment, that is, the value of the entry option?

8.12 Assume that in Problem 8.11 it is possible to exit the business for a net recovery of $20 million if conditions turn out to be worse than expected. Value the entry option and compare it to the value obtained in Problem 8.11.

8.13 Consider an alternative to Problem 8.12 that consists of establishing a foothold in the market for a total cost of $18 million, at the maximum rate of $7.5 million per year. It would be possible to delay and interrupt the investment but the expansion into a full-scale operation cannot take place before the foothold investment is completed. The expansion would require an additional investment of $22 million and recovery in case of posterior exit would amount to $20 million. What is the value of the foothold option? Compare your result to that of Problem 8.12.

8.14 Consider the acquisition of Paktech International examined in Section 8.7. Let revenue volatility be 20% and assume that you are willing to bid $175 million for the enterprise but that you expect to be able to sell it for $100 million if revenue turns out to be disappointing. What is the value of Paktech now, and what is the exit revenue threshold?

Part Two

Mergers, Acquisitions, and Buyouts

Chapter 9

Mergers and Acquisitions

9.1 VALUE CREATION AND MERGERS

A merger should be attractive to the shareholders of the companies involved if it increases the value of their shares. Value creation may result from a number of factors such as economies of scale in production, distribution and management, a technology that can be best deployed by the surviving company, the acquisition of new channels of distribution, and cross-selling of each other's products. However, experience shows that merger synergies are difficult to attain and their size can be disappointing.[1] Acquisitions are sometimes made to redeploy excess corporate cash and avoid double taxation of dividends to shareholders, but the tax argument may lead the acquirer to overreach into areas beyond its competency.[2] Changes in technology and the globalization of markets have led to many recent mergers. These factors have created opportunities and, in many cases, the need to consolidate, and pushed the volume of transactions to $3.6 trillion in the year 2000. In the less favorable stock market and economic environment of 2002, the global volume of transactions fell to $1.4 trillion but deal activity started to pick up by mid-2003.

The chapter begins with an introduction to the legal, tax, and accounting aspects of mergers and acquisitions with emphasis in the choices available for structuring a transaction and their implications. The rest of the chapter shows how to apply the valuation tools studied in previous chapters to valuing expected synergies and testing the robustness of the assumptions upon which a transaction is predicated.

9.2 LEGAL FORM OF THE TRANSACTION AND TAX CONSIDERATIONS[3]

In a *merger,* the surviving company assumes all the assets and liabilities of the merged company, which ceases to exist as a separate entity. A merger requires approval of usually 50% of the shareholders of each firm. In an *acquisition,* the buyer purchases some or all the *assets* or the *stock* of the selling firm. Tax considerations, legal requirements, and the ability to attain shareholder approval determine the type of transaction chosen.

---

[1]See, for example, Jensen and Ruback (1983) and Sirower (1997). Morck, Schleifer and Vishny (1990) found that the stock market reacts negatively to diversifying acquisitions or when the bidder prior performance was poor. For the motives and merits of mergers in a historical context, see Wasserstein (1998), Chapters 6 and 7.

[2]In May 2003 the U.S. Congress reduced the tax rates on both dividends and long-term capital gains to 15%.

[3]The following three sections provide basic background on transactions structures and their taxation according to the U.S. Code. Wasserstein (1998, Chapters 16 and 17) discusses deal structure and negotiation. The tax treatment depends on the applicable tax law, which varies among countries. Useful references on the legal and tax aspects of merger and acquisition transactions, from the U.S. point of view but containing considerations applicable to other jurisdictions, are Gilson (1986), Herzel and Shepro (1990), Ginsburg and Levin (2002), Litwin (1995), and Scholes et al. (2001).

In a *stock purchase,* the acquirer becomes the main or sole shareholder of the target and the corporate entity of the latter is not affected, unless the target is subsequently merged into the acquirer. A stock purchase avoids tax at the corporate level, and the acquirer can use the net operating losses (NOLs) of the target, but the shareholders of the target are taxed on their capital gains.[4] On the other hand, the acquirer is not able to "step-up" (write-up) the basis of the target's assets for tax purposes. One advantage of a stock acquisition is that no assignment of existing contracts is required. A drawback is that the buyer needs to protect itself from the assumption of unexpected undisclosed liabilities. This is usually accomplished by holdbacks of the purchase price. However, contingent payments complicate the nature of the offer and are more common in acquisition from a corporate seller or from private companies.

An *asset purchase* avoids some of the difficulties associated with a stock purchase. In particular, it may avoid the assumption of potential liabilities. However, the purchase of the assets of an entire business may carry with it potential liabilities incurred by the target before the sale. On the other hand, an asset purchase may require obtaining consent to the reassignment of contracts from the customers and suppliers of the target. In an asset sale, the selling corporation is subject to corporate taxes, and the buyer can step up the basis of the acquired assets and amortize goodwill over 15 years for tax purposes,[5] but it is not allowed to use the NOLs of the target. While the sale of assets such as a division of a company does not require shareholder approval, the sale of substantially all of the assets of the target (typically 50% or more) usually requires shareholder approval.

The U.S. Tax Code allows the parties to elect treating a stock transaction as an asset purchase for tax purposes (Code Section 338 election). This results in the seller paying the corporate tax and the buyer being able to step up the basis of the acquired assets. This election may be attractive when the seller has accumulated operating losses or the target is a subsidiary of the seller.

A *merger* has legal consequences similar to an acquisition of stock. It generally avoids the reassignment of contracts and results in the assumption of the liabilities of the target. In addition, no minority shareholders remain because those target shareholders who voted against the merger must accept the approved consideration.[6] The most common form of merger is the *forward* merger, in which the target ceases to exist and is merged into the acquirer or a subsidiary of the acquirer (in which case it is called a triangular merger because it involves three entities). An alternative arrangement is to merge a subsidiary of the acquirer into the target such that the latter is the surviving entity. This is called a *reverse* subsidiary merger. The latter would usually avoid the transfer of contracts and licenses held by the target. Triangular mergers are commonly used for tax-free transactions. They maintain the assets of the target separated from those of the acquirer, and they usually do not require the approval of the acquirer's shareholders.

The tax consequences of the merger depend on if the consideration is in cash or stock or a combination of both. In a cash transaction, a forward merger is generally treated as a purchase of assets, but a reverse merger is generally treated as an acquisition of stock in order to avoid the reassignment of contracts. Asset purchases subject the seller

---

[4]However, part of the shareholders' gain would be classified as current income when depreciation and inventory valuation recapture taxes apply, and the U.S. Tax Code subjects the use of the target's NOLs by the acquirer to a number of limitations including the "continuity of business enterprise" test. See Ginsburg and Levin (2002).

[5]The value of the tax shield to the buyer would be greater if assets such as inventory or short-lived assets can be stepped up.

[6]Shareholders may be able to exercise appraisal rights. The Delaware Court does not give appraisal rights to the shareholders of a public company when the consideration is stock in another public company.

shareholders to taxation at the corporate and personal level. The double tax is reduced when the target has substantial NOLs and is not a problem when the target is not subject to tax at the corporate level as in the case of an S corporation.[7] In addition, if the target is an 80% or greater subsidiary, the proceeds can be distributed to the parent free of tax.

9.3   EXAMPLES OF TAX CONSEQUENCES

The following examples illustrate how the form of a taxable transaction may affect the net proceeds to the seller and the tax treatment of the buyer.

Example 1

Assume the buyer acquires a debt-free target for $100 cash, the target's tax basis in the assets is $40, the target shareholders' basis in the stock is $15, and the fair market value of the stock was $70 prior to the acquisition. Let the corporate tax rate be 40%, the personal tax rate on capital gains be 20%, and assume that all the gain to the seller is classified as capital gain and the buyer's price in excess to the target's basis is allocated to goodwill.

In a stock purchase, the seller pays no corporate tax, but its shareholders incur a taxable gain of $85, pay a tax of $17, and get net proceeds of $83. On the other hand, the buyer cannot step up the tax basis of the assets.

In an asset purchase, the target has a taxable gain at the corporate level of $60 and pays $24 tax. This leaves $76 for distribution to the target shareholders, who incur a taxable capital gain of $61, pay $12.2 tax, and get net proceeds of $63.8, or $19.2 less than under a stock purchase. The buyer benefits from the tax basis step-up of $60. Assume all of which is goodwill amortizable at $4 per year over 15 years, which results in $1.6 tax saving per year or a present value at 8% of $13.7, where 8% is the borrowing rate of the acquirer. Summarizing:

Stock Purchase	
Target Shareholders' net proceeds	$83.0
Asset Purchase	
Target Shareholders' net proceeds	$63.8
Value to the acquirer of basis step-up	13.7
Sum	77.5

That is, in the present case the seller will not agree to an asset purchase or a 338 election because the buyer cannot compensate it for the additional tax its shareholders will incur.

Example 2

Refer to Example 1 and assume the target has $58 of accumulated NOLs that would expire in 4 years. In a stock purchase, the acquirer can use the unexpired NOLs against future taxable income subject to an annual limitation and their expiration. Let the latter be $1.75 per year,[8] which discounted at 8% over 4 years gives a present value of $5.8. In an asset purchase, the target would have a gain of $100 − $40 − $58 = $2, pay corporate tax for $0.8, and distribute $99.2 to shareholders

---

[7]An S corporation is a limited liability corporation not subject to corporate income tax. It passes through its profits for the purpose of taxation to its shareholders, who pay personal income taxes on all the corporation income, independently of the amount distributed.

[8]U.S. Tax Code Section 382 limits the use of acquired NOLs to an amount given by the fair market value of the target's equity prior to the acquisition times the long-term tax-exempt interest rate. Assume the latter is 3%, then in the present case the limitation is $70 × 2.5% = $1.75 per year.

who would pay $19.84 of taxes and receive net proceeds of $79.96, $3.04 less than under a stock purchase. In summary,

Stock Purchase	
Target Shareholders' net proceeds	$83.0
Value to the acquirer of NOLs	5.8
Sum	88.8
Asset Purchase	
Target Shareholders' net proceeds	$79.96
Value to the acquirer of basis step-up	13.70
	93.66

Therefore, in the present case, the buyer can compensate the seller for the additional tax incurred by switching to an asset purchase. The seller would demand an increase in the consideration of $7.58, such that corporate tax would be $3.83, personal tax would be $20.75, and net proceeds would be $83. The buyer would be able to increase the tax basis by $7.58 and get an additional tax shield of $0.2021, which would add $1.73 to the value of the basis step-up. This means that the buyer's net cost of offsetting the seller's tax increase is $5.85 for a net gain of $13.70 − $5.80 − $5.85 = $2.05.

Example 3

Assume the target is a subsidiary of a corporate seller such that the target is able to distribute proceeds tax-free to the parent. As in Example 1, assume the tax basis in the stock is $15, the tax basis in the assets is $40, the target has no NOLs and the consideration is $100. Consider the case in which the transaction is a stock purchase but it is possible to treat it as an asset purchase for the purpose of taxation.[9] The reader can verify that the proceeds to the seller change as follows:

Stock Purchase	
Corporate seller's net proceeds	$66.0
Asset Purchase	
Corporate seller's net proceeds	$76.0
Value to the acquirer of basis step-up	13.7
Sum	89.7

In this case, the asset purchase election clearly dominates. This is so because the ("outside") tax basis in the stock is less than the ("inside") tax basis in the assets. Note that if, for example, the seller demanded $80 net proceeds, the consideration would need to be $100 + $4/(1 − 40%) = $106.67 pre-tax, but the buyer would be able to step up the asset basis by an additional $6.67 and increase its tax shield by $0.1779 per year for a present value of $1.52. Thus, the net cost to the buyer would be $5.15 and its net gain from the 338 election would be $8.55.

9.4   TAX-FREE REORGANIZATIONS

A stock merger is considered a tax-free reorganization (actually, the tax is deferred because the selling shareholders postpone the capital gain tax until the sale of the stock received in the transaction). The buyer cannot write up the target's assets or deduct goodwill for tax purposes but, subject to numerous limitations, may be able to use the target's NOLs. The tax-free nature of the stock transaction also applies to the sale of a subsidiary

---

[9]Under Code Section 338(h)(10).

for stock when the received stock is passed on to the sellers' shareholders.[10] Tax-free reorganizations must satisfy the continuity of interest requirement, which stipulates that a substantial part of the owners' interest in the target must be preserved in the transaction. This is accomplished by issuing common or preferred, voting or nonvoting stock for at least 50% of the target stock. In addition, the acquirer must continue the target's business or use a significant portion of the target's assets in a business.

Section 368 of the Tax Code lists three forms of tax-free reorganizations. Type A includes mergers and consolidations. In the first the acquirer absorbs the seller and in the second both firms are subsumed into a new entity. Type A requires that at least 50% of the consideration be paid in stock in order to satisfy the continuity of interest requirement with the exception of a reverse subsidiary merger that requires 80% percent to be paid in stock. Target shareholders get taxed on the gains resulting from the "boot" received (cash and other considerations not qualifying as stock).

The approval vote of the acquirer shareholders is required in mergers and consolidations but is not required in forward or reverse subsidiary mergers or in Type B or C reorganizations. In a Type B reorganization, the acquirer exchanges its own voting stock for *stock* of the target possessing at least 80% voting power and at least 80% of each class of nonvoting stock. In a Type C reorganization, the acquirer purchases at least 80% of the fair market value of the target's *net assets* using its own voting stock. However, when nonstock consideration is used, assumed liabilities are added to the market value used to determine the percentage of voting stock, which means than in practice the consideration in a Type C reorganization is 100% stock.

9.5   MERGER ACCOUNTING

There are three basic methods of accounting for mergers and acquisitions: purchase, pooling, and recapitalization accounting. In the United States, the Financial Accounting Standard Board has decided that all business combinations completed after June 30, 2001 use purchase accounting and that goodwill should not be amortized but should instead be tested for impairment. This change puts U.S. practice in harmony with international accounting standards, which generally prohibit the use of pooling accounting.

The pooling method was mainly used in the United States and was allowed only for mergers in which the consideration was in stock for more than 90% of the target voting stock. Under pooling, the target assets are accounted at their original book value and there is no recognition and amortization of goodwill. It should be noted that besides changing reporting practice, the choice of the accounting method has usually no effect on free cash flows and therefore no effect on the value of the enterprise. On this, the empirical evidence is rather conclusive.[11] Currently, standard accounting procedures in the United States, as well as abroad, require the recognition of goodwill. Goodwill is calculated as the difference between the value of the consideration paid for the target's equity and the fair market value of its net assets (assets minus liabilities).

An alternative to purchase accounting that avoids the recognition of goodwill is recapitalization accounting. This method is mainly relevant for acquirers that do not publish consolidated financial statements (such as LBO funds) and it is discussed in Note N13.2.

---

[10]This is accomplished via a "Morris Trust" structure that consists in spinning-off the subsidiary and subsequently merging it with the acquirer via a stock exchange. The use of this structure has to satisfy a number of restrictive tests. See Chapter 15, Section 15.5, on requirements for a tax-free spin-off.

[11]See the original work of Hong, Mandelker and Kaplan (1978) and the more recent update by Megginson (1996).

When the acquired entity is merged into or consolidated with the acquirer, the assets and liabilities of the acquiree are recorded into the books of the surviving entity. However, when the acquiree is maintained as a separate entity, as in the case of a stock acquisition not followed by a merger, the acquiree maintains its original set of books but consolidated financial statements must be prepared and goodwill, if any, must be recognized. In both cases, consolidated financial statements require establishing the accounting basis of the assets, accounting for goodwill, if any, and eliminating intercompany transactions. The following example illustrates the accounting treatment of a merger in purchase accounting.[12] Consider the case in which ABC Corp. acquires all the outstaying common stock of XYZ Inc. (50 million shares) at $30 a share. To simplify, assume that the book and tax bases of the assets are the same.

The first step is to establish the fair market value of XYZ assets. This is done in Exhibit 9.1.

The next step is the determination of goodwill (in thousands):

Purchase price	$1,500,000
Fair net asset value	1,253,472
Goodwill	$ 246,528

Consolidation is shown in Exhibit 9.2, which accounts for the fair value of the target assets, goodwill, and intercompany transactions. ABC investment in XYZ consisting of the acquisition of its stock is eliminated, and the goodwill calculated above is added to the consolidated balance sheet.

In a bargain purchase, the fair value of the net assets of the target exceeds the purchase price. This deficiency, called "negative goodwill," is allocated to reduce pro-rata the values assigned to the purchased assets, excluding cash, financial instruments required to be carried at fair value, receivables, inventories, other current assets, assets held for sale, and deferred tax assets such as NOLs. Any excess is reported as an extraordinary gain. For example, assume the purchase of XYZ was done at $22 a share for a total consideration of $1,100 million. The negative goodwill of $1,253.472 – $1,100 = $153.472 million results, which in the present case has to be allocated pro-rata to NPP&E, Intangible Assets, and Investments. These items add up to $1,652.797 million so that the subtraction is 153.472/$1,652.797 = $0.09286 per dollar or $3.587 million from Investments, $136.534 million from NPP&E, and $13.351 million from Intangible Assets. Since negative goodwill is fully absorbed, there is no residual to recognize as extraordinary gain.

9.6 PREMIUMS AND THE IRON LAW OF M&A

It is common for the acquirer to pay a premium over the share price of a publicly traded firm to induce the target shareholders to tender their shares. A premium is a payment in excess to the value improvements that the market has already impounded into the target pre-acquisition price. The size of the premium is ascertainable in the acquisition of publicly traded companies that have a quoted market value. The average acquisition premium paid for public companies during 1996 to 2002 was 31% in the United States and 34% in

---

[12]For a detailed discussion of current GAAP accounting for business combinations see Delaney, Epstein, Nach, and Weiss Budak (2001).

EXHIBIT 9.1 *XYZ, Inc. Balance Sheet as of December 31, 2004*

($000)

	Cost	Fair Value	Basis of Valuation
Current Assets			
Cash and marketable securities	14,000	14,000	Market value
Accounts Receivable	86,702	81,523	Present value, less allowance for uncollectible accounts.
Inventories			
Raw Materials	34,671	45,123	Replacement cost
Work in Process	18,790	19,342	Selling price, minus additional costs and normal profit
Finished Goods	70,415	85,457	Selling price, minus additional costs and normal profit
	123,876	149,922	
Other Current Assets	11,500	11,500	Appraisal value
Total Current Assets	236,078	256,945	
Investments	25,460	38,634	Market or appraisal value
Net Property, Plant and Equipment	987,234	1,470,381	Replacement cost. Appraisal value for land.
Intangible Assets	265,211	143,782	Appraisal value.
Total Assets	1,513,983	1,909,742	
Current Liabilities			
Short-Term Debt and Current Portion of LTD	43,784	42,512	Present value
Accounts Payable	56,234	54,318	Present value
Accrued Expenses	2,840	2,840	Present value
Taxes Payable	8,128	8,128	Present value
Long-term Debt	335,578	310,456	Present value
Deferred Income Taxes	8,561	8,561	
Total Liabilities	455,125	426,815	
Preferred Stock	249,870	229,455	Present value
Common Stock and Retained Earnings	808,988	1,253,472	Residual value
Total Net Worth	1,058,858	1,482,927	
Total Liabilities and Equity	1,513,983	1,909,742	

EXHIBIT 9.2 *ABC Corp. and XYZ, Inc. Consolidated Balance Sheet as of December 31, 2004*

($000)

	ABC	XYZ	Eliminations and Adjustments		Consolidated
			Debt	Credit	
Current Assets					
Cash and marketable securities	34,021	14,000			48,021
Accounts Receivable	196,032	81,523			277,555
Inventories	298,723	149,922			448,645
Other Current Assets	30,044	11,500			41,544
Total Current Assets	558,820	256,945			815,765
Investments	1,554,230	38,634		1,500,000	92,864
Net Property, Plant and Equipment	3,568,229	1,470,381			5,038,610
Intangible Assets					
Goodwill			246,528		246,528
Other	789,541	143,782			933,323
Total Assets	6,470,820	1,909,742			7,127,090
Current Liabilities					
Short-Term Debt and Current Portion of LTD	67,834	42,512			110,346
Accounts Payable	108,340	54,318			162,658
Accrued Expenses	4,567	2,840			7,407
Taxes Payable	12,690	8,128			20,818
Long-term Debt	1,890,450	310,456			2,200,906
Deferred Income Taxes	32,189	8,561			40,750
Total Liabilities	2,116,070	426,815			2,542,885
Preferred Stock	—	229,455			229,455
Common Stock and Retained Earnings	4,354,750	1,253,472	1,500,000	246,528	4,354,750
Total Net Worth	4,354,750	1,482,927			4,584,205
Total Liabilities and Equity	6,470,820	1,909,742	1,746,528	1,746,528	7,127,090

Europe.[13] Whether the premium is justified from the point of view of the shareholders of the acquirer depends on the value created by the merger. Hence, a crucial consideration in a merger is how the premium paid to the target shareholders will be recovered and, hopefully, exceeded by the additional value created by the merger. A sensible way to proceed in planning an acquisition bid is to first determine the value of the consolidated operation in order to arrive to the reservation price, that is, to the maximum price the bidder can pay before it dilutes the value of its own shareholders. However, in many cases the bidding process takes a dynamic of its own in which the desire to win takes precedence over consideration of shareholder value. It is suggestive that the control premium is much higher in hostile and competitive auctions than in friendly transactions. Winning an auction by paying an excessive premium generally results in lower share prices for the acquirer and becomes a "winner's curse."

Consider B's acquisition of T-Corporation. The share price and net income of each company prior to the announcement are as follows:

	B	T
Pre-announcement stock price	$30	$22
Net income (million)	$80	$37.5
Shares outstanding (million)	40	15
EPS	$2.00	$2.50
P/E	15	8.8
Market value (million)	$1,200	$330

How do the terms of this merger affect the shareholders of the acquirer and the target?[14] In order to answer this question, let C denote the merged firm and V_B, V_T, and V_C denote the value of the respective equities, such that the value of equity of the merged firm is

$$V_C = V_B + V_T + \text{Synergies} - \text{Cash},$$

where "Synergies" is the increase in the value of equity expected to result from the merger (from additional sales, economies of scale, or cost savings less merger expenses) and "Cash" is the cash and other non-equity component of the price paid for the target. V_B and V_T are the market values of the equities of the two firms prior to the merger announcement. In addition, let P_T denote the price paid for the target. The difference between this price and the value of the target is the premium, that is,

$$\text{Premium} = P_T - V_T.$$

The premium is the seller shareholders' gain. On the other hand, the acquirer shareholders' gain (loss) is:

$$\text{Acquirer's Gain} = \text{Synergies} - \text{Premium}.$$

That is, in a merger transaction the following "iron law" holds:

$$\text{Acquirer's Gain} + \text{Seller's Gain} = \text{Synergies}$$

---

[13]The passage of the Williams Act in 1969 is generally attributed with the increase in the premiums paid in the U.S. during the last three decades. The act requires the bidder to wait four weeks after the offer in order to buy shares of the target. This allows the management of the target to seek other bids or legal impediments to the takeover.

[14]The following framework was developed by Myers (1976). Gibbs (2001b) recommends a similar approach.

that simply says that the acquirer cannot give up more value to the seller than the acquisition will create without harming its own shareholders.

In order to compute the premium and the acquirer's gain, the price paid for the target needs to be determined. The calculation of P_T depends on whether the payment is in cash, stock, or a combination of both.

9.6.1 All-cash Offer

An all-cash acquisition is the simplest to evaluate. For example, assume the price paid by B for T is $30.8 a share (a 40% premium) and that the present value of synergies is estimated at $100 million. Then,

P_T = 15 million shares $\times$ $30.8 = $462 million.

Premium = $P_T - V_T$ = 462 – 330 = $132 million

Acquirer's Gain (Loss) = $100 – $132 = ($32) million

On a per-share basis, T shareholders gain $132 million/15 million shares = $8.8/share, and B's shareholders lose $32 million/40 million = $0.80/share.

9.6.2 Share Exchange

Consider a pure share exchange such that T shareholders receive 1.02667 shares of B for each share they own. Note that the exchange ratio times the pre-announcement value of B is 1.02667 $\times$ $30 = $30.8. Thus, it would appear that the stock swap has the same value as a $30.8 cash offer. However, this is not so because the price paid for the acquisition equals the exchange ratio times the share value of the *merged* firm. Obtaining the latter requires accounting for the dilution suffered by both sets of shareholders. Let n be the number of old shares of the acquirer and m the number of shares issued to the target shareholders, then a share of the merged firm is valued as follows:

$$p_c = \frac{V_C}{n + m} = \frac{V_B + V_T + Synergies - Cash}{n + m}$$

In the present case n = 40 million, m = 1.02667 $\times$ 15 million = 15.4 million, and Cash = 0. Assume as before that Synergies = $100 million. Then,

V_C = 1,200 + 330 + 100 = $1,630 million

n + m = 40 + 15.4 = 55.4 million

p_C = 1,630/55.4 = $29.42/share

$P_T = P_C \times m$ = $29.42 $\times$ 15.4 = $453.1 million

Premium = $P_T - V_T$ = 453.1 – 330 = $123.1 million.

That is, the exchange is valued at $453.1/15 = $30.21 per T's share (a 37.3% premium) and the gains to each set of shareholders are:

Seller's Gain = Premium = $123.1 million

Acquirer's Gain (Loss) = Synergies - Premium = 100 - 123.1 = ($23.1) million.

On a per-share basis, T's shareholders gain $123.1/15 = $8.21/share and B's shareholders lose $23.1/40 = $0.58/share.

This method permits the parties to estimate the costs and gains resulting from alternative merger terms prior to the merger announcement and its evaluation by investors. It is also useful even after the announcement of the merger agreement because it permits estimating the value of the offer if the merger takes place. The value of a share exchange is commonly computed after the announcement that a final agreement between the two firms has been reached. This is done multiplying the post-announcement share price of the acquirer times the number of shares given in exchange. However, this calculation does not yield the cost of the acquisition when there is uncertainty about the consummation of the merger because of regulatory review or other causes. In fact, there is always some probability that the merger may not take place and therefore the price of the acquirer may not fully reflect the value of the acquisition.

9.6.3 Cash and Share Offer

Assume B's offer is made up of $15 cash plus 0.541 shares of B per share of T. Also, maintain the assumption that synergies are worth $100 million. Then, the total cash payment is 15×15 million shares = $225 million and

$$V_C = 1,200 + 330 + 100 - 225 = \$1,405 \text{ million}$$
$$n + m = 40 + 15 \times 0.541 = 48.115 \text{ million}$$
$$p_C = 1,405/48.115 = \$29.201/\text{share}.$$

Therefore, the price paid for T is $P_T = p_C \times m + \text{Cash} = \$29.201 \times 8.115 + \$225 = \$462$ million or $462/15 = \$30.80$ per share. And the gains to the parties are:

$$\text{T's Gain} = \text{Premium} = 462 - 330 = \$132 \text{ million}$$
$$\text{B's Gain (Loss)} = 100 - 132 = (\$32) \text{ million}.$$

That is, a $15 cash plus 0.541 share exchange is equivalent to the $30.8 all-cash offer considered above, but the seller may find this offer more attractive if it permits deferring the capital gain taxes on the share component of the consideration.

9.7 BREAK-EVEN SYNERGIES

The analysis of the merger terms depends crucially on the value of the synergies that the merged firm is expected to attain. Estimating this value is difficult and always subject to uncertainty. That is why, as an intermediate step in the analysis, it is useful to estimate for what value of synergies the shareholders of the acquirer would break-even. Break-even attains when the value of the expected synergies equals the premium paid for the target. When this occurs, the post-announcement stock price of the merged firm, p_C, equals the pre-announcement stock price of the acquirer, p_B, and the price paid for the target is $P_T = mp_B + \text{Cash}$. Hence,

$$\text{Break-Even Synergies} = \text{Premium} = mp_B + \text{Cash} - V_T.$$

That is, the value of break-even synergies is simply attained by valuing the stock component of the consideration at the pre-announcement share price of the acquirer. For example, the synergy required for B's shareholders to break-even in the above cash and stock offer is

$$\text{Break-Even Synergies for B} = 8.115 \times \$30 + \$225 - \$330 = \$138.45 \text{ million}.$$

The value of break-even synergies is the hurdle the acquirer must overcome in order to justify the acquisition. Its meaning can be made more operational by expressing it in terms of the required increase in annual free cash flow or operating income. For example, for a corporate tax rate of 40%, real cost of capital of the target of 11% and merger expenses of $12 million, the justification of B's offer requires that real free cash flow increase by at least 11% of ($138.45 + $12) = $16.55 million in perpetuity. Assuming that the marginal increases in capital expenditures and net working capital are self-financed by the increases in depreciation and other non-cash items, the corresponding break-even increase in operating income is $16.55/(1 − 0.40) = $27.6 million. An alternative way of expressing break-even synergies is in terms of the required increase in net income. For example, since the pre-announcement P/E multiple of T equals 8.8x, the net income of the acquisition needs to increase by about ($138.45 + $12)/8.8 = $17.10 million or $17.10/(1 − 0.40) = $28.5 pre-tax for B to break-even.

9.8   PREMIUMS AND THE ACQUIRER'S FOOTHOLD

A potential acquirer planning to make a tender offer for the shares of the target can initially accumulate a *foothold* in the target by buying shares in the open market. By acquiring shares before the market becomes aware of the possibility of a bid, the bidder reduces the premium paid for the target and makes a profit in case of losing to a higher bidder. The size of the foothold is presently limited in the U.S. SEC rules require filing Schedule 13D-1 10 days after having acquired a 5% stake in the target.[15] The 10-day window gives the bidder the possibility of accumulating a foothold in excess to 5%. However, since the passage of the Hart-Scott-Rodino (HSR) Antitrust Improvement Act of 1976, the accumulation of meaningful footholds in large acquisitions has been severely restricted. As of February 2001, this law requires an additional filing with the Federal Trade Commission (FTC) and the Department of Justice, which must be made by the acquirer upon accumulating $50 million of the target's stock.[16] Moreover, the bidder is forbidden from acquiring any additional shares until after the FTC has reviewed the filing. In addition, the target receives a copy of this filing, and, since it is material information, it must announce its existence to the public. Therefore, for targets whose market value is over one billion, HSR filing limits the foothold below 5%.[17] It should be noted, however, that an LBO partnership or a 50%–50% joint venture between a partnership and a corporation are not subject to HSR filing.[18]

Returning to the example of the previous sections, consider the case in which B has acquired 0.72 million shares prior to its bid. This means that the cash and shares offer is for the 15 − 0.72 = 14.28 million shares held by the other shareholders or for 95.2% of the outstanding shares. In addition, only 0.952 × 8.115 = 7.725 million shares would be issued and the merged firm would end up with 40 + 7.725 = 47.725 million shares. Hence, break-even synergies require that:

---

[15]This is so by virtue of the 1968 Williams Act Amendments to the Security and Exchange Act of 1934. Jarrell and Bradley (1981) found that the average cash tender offer premium rose to 53% from 32% after the enactment of the Williams Act.

[16]Beginning in 2005, the reporting threshold will be adjusted each year to reflect changes in the gross national product during the previous year.

[17]If the acquisition is made for investment and not as a foothold in an acquisition, the HSR filing needs not to be made until it reaches a 10% stake and there is no dollar limit. If the investment turns out to be a foothold toward an acquisition, it can be considered a violation of antitrust and security laws.

[18]For example, in 1985 Carl Icahn announced in his Schedule 13D-1 that he had acquired a 20.5% stake in TWA. See Herzel and Shepro (1990) for additional details on this point.

$$V_B = V_C - (7.725/47.725)V_C \quad \text{or} \quad V_C = 1{,}200 \div (1 - 0.1619) = \$1{,}431.81.$$

The required value of the merged company has to be compared to the consolidated pre-merger value of the B and T minus the cash outlay, which is

$$1{,}200 - (0.72)(22) + 330 - (0.952)(225) = \$1{,}300.96.$$

Note that the value of the foothold has been subtracted from the per-merger value of the companies to avoid double counting. Break-even synergies are equal to $1,431.30 – 1,300.96 = $130.34 million. That is, break-even synergies decrease by 6% because the accumulation of a 4.8% initial foothold.

An ingenious way to go around the accumulation restriction is examined by Martin Arzac (1996). It was employed in the United Kingdom by Trafalgar House PLC in its 1994 attempt to take over Northern Electric PLC. Prior to the announcement of its takeover bid, Trafalgar purchased from its investment bank so called "contracts for differences" on shares of Northern Electric, as well as on some other utility firms, anticipating that upon announcement of its tender offer all utility shares would raise. The contracts stipulated that Trafalgar would receive the difference between the stock price and a specified strike price at maturity. Because they were cash contract without the right to purchase voting power they were not subject to the disclosure rules that in the United Kingdom apply to the purchase of target securities. The permissibility of using contracts for differences by bidders under U.S. law seems ambiguous and remains untested.[19]

9.9   ACCRETION-DILUTION ANALYSIS

Another way to size up the effect of the merger on the acquirer's shareholders is to compute the pro-forma earnings-per-share for the merged firm for the previous year and a number of years into the future. For example, the historical pro-forma EPS in the pure share exchange of the previous example is:

	B	T	C
Net Income (millions)	$80	$37.5	$117.5
Shares (millions)	40	15	55.4
EPS	$2.00	$2.50	$2.12
Accretion (Dilution)			$0.12
Accretion (Dilution) %			6%

On the face of it, this would appear to be an attractive merger for B's shareholders in contradiction to the calculation above that showed a loss of $23 million. Moreover, we have not taken into account the EPS impact of the expected synergies (assumed above to be valued at $100 million)! What is going on here? The answer is that this is just another case of a high P/E company acquiring a low P/E target.

When the P/E paid for the target is less than the P/E of the acquirer, EPS increase no matter what the economics of the merger is. When a company buys a low P/E company, it increases its earnings proportionally more than the increase in the number of shares, even when it pays a sizable premium over the pre-announcement stock price as in the present example. But it gets what it pays for. As we have seen in Chapter 4, low

---

[19]Martin Arzac (1996) examined the role of equity derivatives in an equilibrium model of takeovers and concluded that allowing the bidder to purchase equity derivatives on the target prior to the announcement of the bid would unequivocally increase the bid's probability of success.

multiples correspond to low earnings growth. The acquirer ends up with higher earnings in the short run but lower future growth. Of course, there is nothing wrong with higher EPS. Higher EPS attained without sacrificing their quality (that is, their expected growth) are likely to result in higher stock prices.

The moral of this example is that the simple accretion/dilution analysis can be misleading and should not be the only consideration in evaluating the terms of a merger. Investors would take into account that the earnings of the merged firm are a mixture of high and low growth earnings and, therefore, they would capitalize the new blended earnings at a weighted average of the P/E multiples of the original companies with their earnings as weights. For the present case, the applicable multiple would be $[(15)(80) + (8.8)(37.5)]/(80 + 35.5) = 13.02$, and the stock price of the merged company would then be $2.12 $\times$ 13.02 = $27.60, which is below $30, the pre-announcement price of the acquirer. The reader would note that we ignored the assumed value for the synergies which amounts to $100/55.4 = $1.81/share. Adding it to $27.60 results in a share price of $29.41 or a loss of 59 cents per share to B shareholders, comparable to the 58 cents loss estimated in Section 9.6.

A similar reservation applies to the calculation of break-even synergies based upon accretion/dilution analysis. Assume that the exchange ratio is 1.5 shares of B for each one of the 15 million shares of T such that 22.5 million shares are issued and the merged company ends up with a total of 62.5 million shares. Then, the pro-forma EPS become $117.5/62.5 = $1.88, and their dilution is $0.12 or 6%. This means that, in order to attain zero dilution, operating income has to increase by $0.12 $\times$ 62.5/(1 – 40%) = $12.5 million. However, an increase in the target's income that happens without a corresponding increase in its future growth would be capitalized at a lower P/E multiple than the multiple applicable to the acquirer. That would not bring the price of the merged company up to the pre-announcement level of the acquirer. This is why in the previous section we used the P/E of the target in calculating the required increase in pre-tax income. Only if future growth were expected to change as a consequence of the merger would it make sense to calculate break-even synergies on the basis of accretion-dilution analysis.

9.10 FREE CASH-FLOW VALUATION: TOTAL VERSUS INCREMENTAL FREE CASH FLOWS

Free cash-flow valuation as developed in this book is the fundamental method for valuing mergers and acquisitions. In combination with valuation multiples from comparable companies and precedent transactions, it provides a way of measuring the value creation of the transaction and establishing the reservation prices for the buyer and the seller. The value of the enterprise depends on the expectation of each party about future cash flows and, as such, the values assigned by the buyer, seller and competing buyers are likely to differ from each other. The discounted cash-flow method permits each party to estimate the value of the enterprise given its own assumptions about the operating policy planned for the enterprise. The buyer would take into account the potential synergies of operating the two businesses in combination, including cost savings and additional growth. The seller, on the other hand, would consider the value of the stand-alone operation and the value of the company in combination with possible merger partners. In the case of a privately-held seller, or a publicly-held company disposing of a business unit, the value of the going-public option can give a floor to the asking price, if such an option is available. A transaction would take place only if the acquirer can offer a price above the reservation price of the seller, which includes the price that competing buyers may be able to offer.[20] This is why, in estimating the size of its bid, the acquirer needs to value the company from the point of view of the seller and other potential buyers as well. Likewise, an informed seller should consider the value of its company to possible acquirers.

The value created by a merger results from additional efficiencies and growth of the target and synergies related to savings and cross-selling made possible by the integration of the operations of the merged firms. If these additional sources of free cash flow can be clearly identified and the per-merger price of the target does not already reflect these sources of value, one can proceed to value the resulting incremental free cash flow without the need to value the whole operation. This is so because the market has already priced the two firms pre-merger. Whenever possible, this is an attractive approach because it avoids the need of valuing the whole target or the merged firm itself, which can be a rather forbidding undertaking.

Unfortunately, in many situations it is not possible to limit the analysis to valuation of marginal cash flows. The case of a private company is an obvious one, but even when the target is public, the analyst is faced with the difficulty of identifying the truly marginal cash flows. These are the additional free cash flows to be produced in the future that are not impounded in the pre-merger price of the target or the acquirer. For example, assume that the acquirer expects to recover a significant fraction of the premium via cost savings but that investors already expect some of those saving to be attained by the stand-alone target and have impounded their value on the target's stock price. In that case, valuing such savings and adding them to the pre-merger value of the target to attain its post-merger value would yield an exaggerated value. Then, assuming that all the value of such savings is premium recovery would be wrong. Similarly, if the acquirer is already valued by the market taking into account its ability to reduce the costs of potential targets, valuing the incremental savings and adding them to the pre-merger values of the target and the acquirer would overestimate the value of the merged firm.

The same reasoning applies to the value of future growth opportunities than may be already impounded on the pre-merger prices. That is why, in many practical cases, one needs to value the whole target with the planned improvements and the whole merged firm as well. The flip side of this alternative is that in valuing the whole company one is ignoring that the market has already valued a great part of it. Estimation errors may lead the buyer to believe that the target is a bargain. This needs to be always kept in mind when interpreting valuation output.

The following example illustrates the valuation of the total cash flows of the target and the merged firm. Problem 9.6 presents a case that can be valued via the incremental cash-flow approach.

9.11   COMPREHENSIVE MERGER EXAMPLE

In this section, we examine a merger of two specialty retailers. The specialty retail industry has undergone significant consolidation in recent years and has a wealth of data and transactions upon which this example is based. In addition, valuation of retail companies requires careful treatment of operating leases, an important aspect often ignored in practice. We shall call the acquirer and the target CDH Group and Capitol Designs, Inc.,

---

[20]In Chapter 10 we discuss contractual arrangements that can produce agreement between the parties when there is a difference of opinion such that the offer price is below the reservation price of the seller.

| EXHIBIT 9.3 | *Comparable Specialty Retailers* |

	Revenue 2001	Revenue Growth 2001/02	Profit Margin 2001	EBITDA Margin 2001	EBITDAR[1] 2001	Enterprise Value[2] 2001
Large cap (> $4 bn):						
The Gap	$13,674	16.8%	6.4%	14.9%	$2,885	$35,390
Intimate Brands, Inc.	5,117	10.5%	8.5%	17.0%	1,135	9,591
Limited Inc.	10,105	4%	4.2%	10.8%	1,799	12,676
Abercrombie & Fitch	1,238	22%	12.8%	23.6%	368	4,771
Medium cap (> $1.2 bn):						
American Eagle Outfitter	1,094	9%	8.6%	15.5%	273	3,337
Talbots Inc	1,595	21%	7.2%	14.9%	316	3,336
Nordstrom	5,529	7%	1.8%	7.6%	469	4,166
Ross Stores	2,709	8%	5.6%	11.0%	427	3,232
Men's Wearhouse	1,334	11%	6.4%	13.3%	249	1,813
Ann Taylor Stores	1,233	14%	4.3%	11.7%	239	2,305
Small cap (> $0.27 bn):						
Chico's Fas Inc	259	77%	10.9%	20.1%	73	943
Claires Stores	1,060	17.1%	6.1%	14.6%	313	2,210
Bebe Stores	242	13.8%	12.2%	21.0%	77	864
Pacific Sunwear of Cal.	589	31.4%	6.8%	14.2%	155	1,234
Christopher & Banks	209	45.9%	12.2%	22.0%	65	676
Charlotte Russe	245	64.6%	7.8%	16.3%	72	847
Charming Shoppes	1,617	23.8%	3.2%	6.1%	235	1,693
The Wet Seal Inc.	580	10.4%	3.4%	8.5%	148	952
Cato Corp.	649	13.2%	6.0%	10.7%	104	669
Micro cap (< $0.27 bn):						
Goody's Family Clothing	1,251	3.0%	1.0%	3.3%	113	700
United Retail	420	11.3%	1.0%	3.5%	55	483
Mean	2,417	20.7%	6.5%	13.4%	456	4,376
Median	1,233	13.6%	6.4%	14.2%	239	1,813
Medians by capitalization						
Large cap	7,611	13.7%	7.4%	16.0%	1,467	11,134
Medium cap	1,464	10.0%	6.0%	12.5%	295	3,284
Small cap	580	23.8%	6.8%	14.6%	104	943
Micro cap	835	7.2%	1.0%	3.4%	84	591
CDH Group	1,126	3.1%	6.6%	12.4%	189	1,362
Capitol Designs	221	7.8%	5.9%	12.3%	37	396

Notes:

[1]EBITDAR = Earnings before Interest, Depreciation, Amortization and Rental Expense.

[2]Enterprise Value = Equity Capitalization + Adjusted Net Debt.

[3](Debt − Cash and Marketable Securities)/(Equity Capitalization + Net Debt).

[4](Debt + Capitalized Operating Leases − Cash and Marketable Securities)/(Equity Capitalization + Capitalized Operating Leases + Net Debt).

SOURCES: Companies' annual reports and 10Ks, Quicken.com, Zacks, First Call and Standard & Poors.

P/E Multiple		EBITDAR Multiple		Revenue Multiple		Consensus	Net Debt to	Adj. Net Debt	Beta
Trailing 2001	Forward 2002E	Trailing 2001	Forward 2002E	Trailing 2001	Forward 2002E	5-year growth	Enterprise Value[3]	to Enterprise Value[4]	Unlevered 6/2001
36.1x	32x	12.3x	12.5x	2.6x	2.6x	18.0%	5.0%	25.1%	0.81
18.4x	18x	8.4x	9.0x	1.9x	2.0x	15.6%	1.2%	23.9%	0.92
18.0x	18x	7.0x	7.7x	1.3x	1.4x	14.3%	−2.5%	47.0%	0.58
26.4x	23x	13.0x	10.8x	3.9x	3.2x	21.1%	−3.5%	14.5%	0.88
28.2x	28x	12.2x	11.5x	3.1x	2.9x	22.9%	−5.3%	20.8%	1.35
21.4x	19x	10.6x	9.0x	2.1x	1.8x	16.6%	1.2%	24.5%	0.62
26.2x	25x	8.9x	9.5x	0.8x	0.8x	12.2%	32.2%	40.7%	0.67
13.8x	13x	7.6x	7.6x	1.2x	1.2x	14.1%	1.4%	40.2%	0.68
14.5x	14x	7.3x	7.1x	1.4x	1.3x	20.4%	−3.5%	35.2%	0.97
20.9x	20x	9.6x	9.1x	1.9x	1.8x	19.3%	7.6%	54.9%	0.51
25.9x	22x	12.9x	9.2x	3.6x	2.6x	30.4%	−1.3%	10.2%	1.18
13.1x	14x	7.1x	7.3x	2.1x	2.2x	7.0%	7.8%	62.0%	0.44
29.9x	28x	11.3x	12.0x	3.6x	3.8x	19.1%	−10.1%	8.5%	1.75
19.7x	21x	8.0x	7.7x	2.1x	2.0x	22.2%	−4.3%	44.1%	0.67
25.3x	21x	10.3x	8.4x	3.2x	2.6x	26.0%	−5.2%	12.0%	1.72
28.1x	26x	11.7x	9.3x	3.5x	2.7x	26.4%	0.1%	31.4%	1.09
11.5x	11x	7.2x	7.2x	1.0x	1.0x	17.5%	10.2%	67.7%	0.18
19.9x	17x	6.5x	4.9x	1.6x	1.2x	21.5%	−15.5%	46.7%	0.56
12.6x	12x	6.4x	5.9x	1.0x	1.0x	NA	−20.3%	26.4%	0.48
17.9x	51.3x	6.2x	31.6x	0.6x	2.9x	15.0%	−92.9%	81.4%	0.14
27.0x	14.7x	8.8x	4.3x	1.1x	0.6x	NA	−48.0%	76.2%	0.11
21.7x	21.4x	9.2x	9.6x	2.07x	1.98x	18.9%	−6.9%	37.8%	0.78
20.9x	19.6x	8.8x	9.0x	1.87x	2.00x	19.1%	−2.5%	35.2%	0.67
22.4x	20.5x	10.4x	9.9x	2.23x	2.32x	16.8%	−0.6%	24.5%	0.85
21.2x	19.4x	9.3x	9.1x	1.61x	1.54x	18.0%	1.3%	37.7%	0.67
19.9x	20.7x	8.0x	7.7x	2.09x	2.15x	21.9%	−4.3%	31.4%	0.67
22.5x	33.0x	7.5x	18.0x	0.85x	1.72x	15.0%	−70.4%	78.8%	0.12
17.2x	22.3x	9.7x	7.5x	1.21x	1.26x	15.0%	2.1%	34.0%	0.69
24.0x	28.5x	14.6x	12.7x	1.79x	2.13x	NA	21.0%	38.7%	0.89

respectively, and consider CDH's proposal to acquire Capitol Design via a share exchange. CDH was a rapidly growing midsize regional mall-based retailer with $1.4 billion of revenues and $899 million market capitalization. It specialized in popular-priced fashion accessories and apparel for pre-teens and teenagers. Its target, Capitol Designs, sold private-label apparel, underwear, and sleepwear, swimwear, lifestyle, and personal-care products for fashion-aware, trend-setting young girls.

9.11.1 Terms of the Merger

At the time of CDH's offer, Capitol Design had revenues of $238 million and a market capitalization of $243 million. CDH planned to use Capitol Design's northwest coverage to enter the private-label segment and accelerate its national coverage. At the end of June 2001, the pre-merger announcement values of the companies were as follows:

	CDH	Capitol
Pre-announcement stock price	$32.75	$15.30
Pro-forma net income (million)*	$52.2	$10.1
Shares outstanding (million)	27.439	15.867
EPS	$1.90	$0.64
P/E (trailing)	17.2	24.0
EBITDAR multiple (trailing)	9.7	14.6
Market value of equity (million)	$899	$243

*For fiscal year ended 1/2002

Exhibit 9.3 shows the valuation of specialty retailers in June 2001. Both CDH and Capitol fell into the small-cap group ($0.27 billion to $1.2 billion capitalization). CDH traded somewhat below the median multiples of this group, but Capitol traded at the top of this group. In fact, the valuation of Capitol was already one of the highest in the entire industry, right there with such large-cap leaders as Abercrombie & Fitch. Such a rich valuation did not discourage CDH management from going after Capitol because it believed that, under its management, the concept and labels of Capitol Design would result in growth and profitability much beyond that already anticipated by the market. CDH believed that the revenue growth of Capitol would more than double during the next five years.

After preliminary discussions with Capitol management, CDH concluded that a stock offer valued at $20 per Capitol share, or an exchange ratio of 0.610687 shares of CDH per Capitol share would be appealing to Capitol's management and its board of directors. This signified a 30.7% premium over Capitol's stock price and a $74.6 million premium. In terms of 2001 valuation multiples, CDH offered 31x income, 15.0x EBITDAR, and 1.7x revenues, all at the upper end of the comparable multiples shown in Exhibit 9.1. The transaction is summarized in the statement of sources and uses of funds shown in Exhibit 9.4.

While Capitol had appealing products and high-growth potential, it required significant up-front expenditures in order to increase geographic coverage and attain market share. Financing of that magnitude was not available to Capitol in mid-2001. On the other hand, CDH had financial resources and ample growth-management experience.

Note that the calculation of the premium assumes that the price of CDH would not change. That is, that the $74.6 million premium plus transactions expenses estimated at $12.5 million would be recovered via synergies. The question then is if this premium can

EXHIBIT 9.4	*Capitol Designs. Sources and Uses of Funds at Closing*

($000 except share price)

Uses:		Sources:	
Offer Price per Share	$20	Cash in the Company	$1,875
Shares Outstanding	15,867	Cash from the Acquirer	10,585
Equity Purchase Price	$317,340	Short-Term Debt	12,993
Transaction Expenses	12,460	Long-Term Debt	53,432
Assumed Short-Term Debt	12,993	Stock-for-Stock	317,340
Assumed Long-Term Debt	53,432		
Total Uses	$396,225	Total Sources	$396,225

be recovered and how. This depends on the value of the synergies to be produced by the merger.

9.11.2   Building the Financial Model of the Merger

In order to evaluate the consequences of the merger, it is best to build a financial model of the merged firm starting from its balance sheet at the planned closing date. The process starts with the study of the historical operating characteristics of the acquirer and the target and their forecast. The operating characteristics include revenue growth, operating margins, depreciation, net working capital requirements and capital expenditures. Exhibit 9.5 summarizes the forecasting assumptions for the period 2003 to 2012 made by CDH's management for CDH and Capitol Designs. The most noticeable difference between these forecasts is the much higher volume growth projected for Capitol Design, as well as its higher operating margins from 2004 onward. These were expected to result from the intrinsic appeal of Capitol's private labels in combination with CDH's expansion plan.

In addition to operating characteristics, the planned financial policy of the merged company needs to be specified. In the present case, the acquisition was to be financed via a tax-free stock exchange so that no debt financing would be involved in the acquisition (but no amortization of goodwill for tax purposes would be allowed). Future borrowing was projected to keep the EBITDAR coverage of interest and operating lease payments at about 5x during the projection period. The corresponding net debt ratios were about 32% and 45% in market and book value terms, respectively.[21] The financial projections are summarized in Exhibit 9.6. They include capitalized operating leases that were the main source of financing for the planned store growth of Capitol Designs (see Note N9.1). The other debt items were planned to remain approximately constant over the forecast period. As in Chapter 2, combining the operating and financial projections yields the income, balance sheet and cash flow statements for the merged company shown in Exhibits 9.7 to 9.9. In addition, stand-alone financial statements for CDH and Capitol should be prepared. The latter taking into account the operating policy to be followed by the acquirer, transactions expenses and restructuring costs.

9.11.3   Accretion-dilution Analysis

The next step is to perform the accretion-dilution analysis of the EPS of the acquirer with and without the acquisition. The EPS of the merged company are calculated in Exhibit 9.7. From the forecasting assumptions for CDH, one can compute CDH's stand-alone

---

[21]Debt capacity and the relationship between coverage ratios and debt ratios are discussed in Chapter 7.

EXHIBIT 9.5 *CDH Group and Capitol Designs. Baseline Operating Assumptions*

	2003	2004	2005	2006	2007	2008	2009	2010	2011	2012
CDH Group										
Same store unit sales growth	3.0%	3.0%	3.0%	3.0%	3.0%	2.5%	2.0%	2.0%	2.0%	2.0%
New store unit sales growth	0.0%	1.0%	1.0%	1.0%	0.5%	0.5%	1.0%	1.0%	1.0%	1.0%
Unit Sales Growth	3.0%	4.0%	4.0%	4.0%	3.5%	3.0%	3.0%	3.0%	3.0%	3.0%
Price Growth	2.5%	2.5%	2.5%	2.5%	2.5%	2.5%	2.5%	2.5%	2.5%	2.5%
Nominal Sales Growth	5.6%	6.6%	6.6%	6.6%	6.1%	5.6%	5.6%	5.6%	5.6%	5.6%
Cost of Sales (% of Sales)	53.0%	53.0%	53.0%	53.0%	53.0%	53.0%	53.0%	53.0%	53.0%	53.0%
SG&A expenses (% of Sales)	36.0%	35.5%	35.5%	35.0%	35.0%	35.0%	35.0%	35.0%	35.0%	35.0%
Capex (net of Disposals) ($000)	63,176	75,000	84,783	88,004	95,774	90,059	97,644	95,748	101,854	108,215
Book depreciation ($000)	43,973	51,000	59,199	60,730	68,959	64,006	70,138	66,709	71,196	75,848
Tax depreciation ($000)	48,851	60,720	70,647	72,084	79,395	71,405	75,858	71,186	74,438	78,334
Accounts Receivable (% of Sales)	8.6%	8.6%	8.6%	8.6%	8.6%	8.6%	8.6%	8.6%	8.6%	8.6%
Inventories (% of COGS)	46.2%	46.2%	46.2%	46.2%	46.2%	46.2%	46.2%	46.2%	46.2%	46.2%
Accounts Payable (% of COGS)	22.6%	22.6%	22.6%	22.6%	22.6%	22.6%	22.6%	22.6%	22.6%	22.6%
Capitol Designs										
Same store unit sales growth	5.0%	10.0%	10.0%	10.0%	5.0%	3.0%	2.0%	2.0%	2.0%	2.0%
New store unit sales growth	13.0%	15.0%	15.0%	10.0%	10.0%	1.5%	1.0%	1.0%	1.0%	1.0%
Unit Sales Growth	18.0%	25.0%	25.0%	20.0%	15.0%	4.5%	3.0%	3.0%	3.0%	3.0%
Price Growth	2.5%	2.5%	2.5%	2.5%	2.5%	2.5%	2.5%	2.5%	2.5%	2.5%
Nominal Sales Growth	21.0%	28.1%	28.1%	23.0%	17.9%	7.1%	5.6%	5.6%	5.6%	5.6%
Cost of Sales (% of Sales)	51.0%	50.0%	48.0%	48.0%	48.0%	48.0%	48.0%	48.0%	48.0%	48.0%
SG&A expenses (% of Sales)	40.0%	40.0%	35.0%	35.0%	35.0%	35.0%	35.0%	35.0%	35.0%	35.0%
R&D (% of Sales)	3.0%	3.0%	3.0%	3.0%	3.0%	3.0%	3.0%	3.0%	3.0%	3.0%
CAPEX (net of Disposals) ($000)	35,500	44,500	43,000	43,000	43,000	35,000	35,000	35,000	35000	35,000
Book depreciation ($000)	8,392	12,460	16,910	19,908	23,615	24,377	26,020	25,782	26,545	27,294
Tax depreciation ($000)	10,658	17,725	23,116	25,655	28,587	27,884	28,324	27,421	27,782	28,184
Accounts Receivable (% of Sales)	4.5%	4.5%	4.5%	4.5%	4.5%	4.5%	4.5%	4.5%	4.5%	4.5%
Inventories (% of COGS)	31.4%	31.4%	31.4%	31.4%	31.4%	31.4%	31.4%	31.4%	31.4%	31.4%
Accounts Payable (% of COGS)	18.8%	18.8%	18.8%	18.8%	18.8%	18.8%	18.8%	18.8%	18.8%	18.8%

EXHIBIT 9.6 CDH Group-Capitol Designs Merger: Financial Projections

($000)

	2003	2004	2005	2006	2007	2008	2009	2010	2011	2012
Financing Assumptions										
Short-term Debt	$17,493	$17,493	$17,493	$17,493	$17,493	$17,493	$17,493	$17,493	17493	$17,493
Senior Debt	96,377	96,377	96,377	96,377	96,377	96,377	96,377	96,377	96377	96,377
Other Long-term Debt	100,000	100,000	100,000	100,000	100,000	100,000	100,000	100,000	100000	100,000
Subordinated Debt	7,700	7,700	7,700	7,700	7,700	7,700	7,700	7,700	07700	7,700
Preferred Stock	7,823	7,823	7,823	7,823	7,823	7,823	7,823	7,823	07823	7,823
Interest and Dividends										
Interest expense	$10,482	$20,382	$20,382	$20,382	$20,382	$20,382	$20,382	$20,382	$20,382	$20,382
Interest income	1,321	4,452	3,196	2,851	2,952	3,334	5,030	6,652	8,722	10,802
Preferred dividend	861	861	861	861	861	861	861	861	861	861
Common equity dividend	24,876	24,876	32,077	39,077	42,427	47,844	50,506	56,647	60,501	64,579
Operating Leases										
Operating Lease Payments	$58,644	$64,419	$70,735	$77,942	$84,931	$90,011	$95,030	$100,328	$105,921	$111,826
Capitalized Operating Leases	585,631	643,046	708,567	772,104	818,286	863,906	912,068	962,916	1016599	1,073,274

EXHIBIT 9.7 *Consolidated Income Statements: CDH Group—Capitol Designs*

($000)

	Historical	Fiscal Years Ending 1/31									
	2002	2003	2004	2005	2006	2007	2008	2009	2010	2011	2012
Total Sales	$1,398,930	$1,513,523	$1,675,395	$1,865,383	$2,066,018	$2,360,320	$2,396,870	$2,530,495	$2,671,571	$2,820,511	$2,977,754
Cost of Sales	742,795	796,408	876,892	965,018	1,065,920	1,163,703	1,233,637	1,302,413	1,375,022	1,451,680	1,532,611
Gross Profit	656,135	717,115	798,504	900,364	1,000,099	1,096,617	1,163,233	1,228,083	1,296,548	1,368,831	1,445,143
Sales, General & Admin. Expenses	496,727	556,386	611,367	659,847	723,106	791,112	838,904	885,673	935,050	987,179	1,042,214
Research & Development	2,268	8,638	11,068	14,181	17,442	20,560	22,022	23,250	24,546	25,915	27,359
EBITDA bef. Restructuring Exp.	157,140	152,090	176,069	226,336	259,550	284,945	302,306	319,159	336,953	355,738	375,570
Restructuring Expenses	0	45,500	0	0	0	0	0	0	0	0	0
EBITDA	$157,140	$106,590	$176,069	$226,336	$259,550	$284,945	$302,306	$319,159	$336,953	$355,738	$375,570
Depreciation	54,462	52,365	63,460	76,108	80,638	92,573	88,382	96,158	92,491	97,741	103,142
Financing Cost Amortization	0	1,780	1,780	1,780	1,780	1,780	1,780	1,780	0	0	0
EBIT	$102,678	$52,446	$110,829	$148,448	$177,132	$190,592	$212,144	$221,222	$244,462	$257,996	$272,428
Interest Expense		10,482	20,382	20,382	20,382	20,382	20,382	20,382	20,382	20,382	20,382
Interest Income		1,321	4,452	3,196	2,851	2,952	3,334	5,030	6,652	8,722	10,802
Pretax Income		43,285	94,899	131,261	159,601	173,162	195,096	205,870	230,732	246,336	262,849
Current Income Tax		13,824	30,567	43,455	54,506	60,340	70,452	75,676	85,916	92,511	99,248
Deferred Tax		2,732	5,731	6,753	6,541	5,894	4,172	3,069	2,339	1,713	1,292
Net Income		$26,728	$58,600	$81,054	$98,553	$106,927	$120,472	$127,125	$142,477	$152,113	$162,309
Dividends other than common:											
Preferred stock		861	861	861	861	861	861	861	861	861	861
Net Inc. Available to Common		25,868	57,739	80,193	97,693	106,067	119,611	126,264	141,617	151,252	161,449
Number of Shares (000)		37,129	37,129	37,129	37,129	37,129	37,129	37,129	37,129	37,129	37,129
EPS		$0.70	$1.56	$2.16	$2.63	$2.86	$3.22	$3.40	$3.81	$4.07	$4.35

EXHIBIT 9.8 Consolidated Balance Sheets: CDH Group—Capitol Designs

($000)

ASSETS	Historical 1/31/2002	Fiscal Years Ending 1/31 2003	2004	2005	2006	2007	2008	2009	2010	2011	2012
Current:											
Cash and Marketable Sec.	$23,175	$78,098	$56,062	$50,010	$51,788	$58,489	$88,253	$116,706	$153,009	$189,516	$229,639
Accounts Receivable	110,452	118,248	128,826	140,882	153,650	166,070	175,800	185,601	195,948	206,872	218,405
Inventories	324,410	345,969	377,576	412,002	450,886	488,670	517,503	546,354	576,813	608,970	642,920
Other Current Assets	31,570	33,520	36,053	38,844	41,810	44,710	47,258	49,892	52,674	55,610	58,711
Total Current Assets	489,607	575,834	598,517	641,738	698,133	757,940	828,814	898,553	978,444	1,060,969	1,149,675
PP&E and Capitalized Leases ...	465,526	564,202	683,702	811,486	942,489	1,081,264	1,206,322	1,338,966	1,469,714	1,606,568	1,749,783
Less: Depreciation	63,649	116,014	179,474	255,582	336,220	428,794	517,176	613,334	705,825	803,566	906,708
Net PP&E and Cap. Leases ...	401,877	448,188	504,228	555,903	606,269	652,470	689,146	725,632	763,889	803,002	843,075
Other Noncurrent Assets:	39,381	39,381	39,381	39,381	39,381	39,381	39,381	39,381	39,381	39,381	39,381
Goodwill	354,223	354,223	354,223	354,223	354,223	354,223	354,223	354,223	354,223	354,223	354,223
Capitalized Transaction Exp.	12,460	10,680	8,900	7,120	5,340	3,560	1,780	0	0	0	0
Total Assets	1,297,548	1,428,306	1,505,250	1,598,365	1,703,346	1,807,573	1,913,344	2,017,789	2,135,937	2,257,575	2,386,355

(continued)

EXHIBIT 9.8 *Consolidated Balance Sheets: CDH Group—Capitol Designs (continued)*

($000)

LIABILITIES	Historical 1/31/2002	Fiscal Years Ending 1/31									
		2003	2004	2005	2006	2007	2008	2009	2010	2011	2012
Current:											
Short-term Debt & Curr. LTD	17,493	17,493	17,493	17,493	17,493	17,493	17,493	17,493	17,493	17,493	17,493
Accounts Payable	163,211	174,511	191,277	209,589	230,418	250,629	265,553	280,357	295,987	312,489	329,910
Accrued Expenses	57,372	62,483	69,844	78,603	87,840	96,768	102,713	108,439	114,485	120,867	127,606
Accrued Liabilities	9,123	9,632	10,267	10,945	11,667	12,378	13,068	13,796	14,565	15,377	16,235
Taxes Payable	11,098	11,098	24,540	34,886	43,758	48,442	56,560	60,754	68,974	74,269	79,677
Other Current Liabilities	2,058	2,173	2,316	2,469	2,632	2,792	2,948	3,112	3,286	3,469	3,662
Total Current Liabilities	260,355	277,389	315,738	353,985	393,809	428,502	458,334	483,952	514,790	543,964	574,583
Long-term Debt:											
Senior Debt	86,377	96,377	96,377	96,377	96,377	96,377	96,377	96,377	96,377	96,377	96,377
Other Long-Term Debt	0	100,000	100,000	100,000	100,000	100,000	100,000	100,000	100,000	100,000	100,000
Subordinated Debt	7,700	7,700	7,700	7,700	7,700	7,700	7,700	7,700	7,700	7,700	7,700
Total Long-term Debt	94,077	204,077	204,077	204,077	204,077	204,077	204,077	204,077	204,077	204,077	204,077
Other Noncurrent Liabilities	3,214	3,214	3,214	3,214	3,214	3,214	3,214	3,214	3,214	3,214	3,214
Deferred Income Taxes	16,235	19,047	25,013	32,154	39,132	45,432	50,074	53,496	55,941	57,668	58,939
Total Liabilities	373,881	503,647	547,728	592,728	639,093	679,680	713,684	742,371	775,548	806,435	838,345
Preferred Stock	7,823	7,823	7,823	7,823	7,823	7,823	7,823	7,823	7,823	7,823	7,823
Common Stock and Ret. Earnings	915,844	916,835	949,699	997,815	1,056,430	1,120,071	1,191,837	1,352,566	1,352,566	1,443,317	1,540,186
Total Net Worth	923,667	924,658	957,522	1,005,638	1,064,253	1,127,894	1,199,660	1,275,419	1,360,389	1,451,140	1,548,009
Total Liabilities and Equity	1,297,548	1,428,306	1,505,250	1,598,365	1,703,346	1,807,573	1,913,344	2,017,789	2,135,937	2,257,575	2,386,355

EXHIBIT 9.9 *Consolidated Cash Flow Statements: CDH Group—Capitol Designs*

($000)

	Fiscal Years Ending 1/31									
	2003	2004	2005	2006	2007	2008	2009	2010	2011	2012
Funds from Operating Activities										
Net Income Available to Common	$25,868	$57,739	$80,193	$97,693	$106,067	$119,611	$126,264	$141,617	$151,252	$161,449
Depreciation	52,365	63,460	76,108	80,638	92,573	88,382	96,158	92,491	97,741	103,142
Financing Cost Amortization	1,780	1,780	1,780	1,780	1,780	1,780	1,780	0	0	0
Deferred Taxes	2,732	5,731	6,753	6,541	5,894	4,172	3,069	2,339	1,713	1,292
Change in current assets except cash	(31,304)	(44,719)	(49,273)	(54,617)	(53,105)	(41,110)	(41,286)	(43,588)	(46,018)	(48,583)
Chg. in current liabilities except debt	17,034	38,350	38,247	39,824	34,693	29,832	25,617	30,838	29,174	30,619
Change in Net Working Capital	(14,270)	(6,369)	(11,026)	(14,794)	(18,412)	(11,277)	(15,669)	(12,750)	(16,844)	(17,964)
Funds From Operations	68,475	122,341	153,808	171,859	187,902	202,668	211,603	223,697	233,862	247,918
Funds for Investment										
Capital Expenditures	(98,676)	(119,500)	(127,783)	(131,004)	(138,774)	(125,059)	(132,644)	(130,748)	(136,854)	(143,215)
Funds from (to) Financing										
Debt, Preferred & Minority Int.	110,000	0	0	0	0	0	0	0	0	0
Common Dividend Paid	(24,876)	(24,876)	(32,077)	(39,077)	(42,427)	(47,844)	(50,506)	(56,647)	(60,501)	(64,579)
	85,124	(24,876)	(32,077)	(39,077)	(42,427)	(47,844)	(50,506)	(56,647)	(60,501)	(64,579)
Increase in Cash	54,923	(22,035)	(6,053)	1,778	6,701	29,764	28,453	36,303	36,507	40,123
End-of-Year Cash & Marketable Sec.	$78,098	$56,062	$50,010	$51,788	$58,489	$88,253	$116,706	$153,009	$189,516	$229,639

| EXHIBIT 9.10 | *Accretion/Dilution Analyisis—Acquisition of Capitol Designs* |

Fiscal Years Ending 1/31

	2002	2003	2004	2005	2006	2007
Acquirer Stand Alone EPS	$1.90	$1.96	$2.15	$2.19	$2.56	$2.62
Consolidated EPS	$1.68	$0.70	$1.56	$2.16	$2.63	$2.86
Accretion (Dilution)		($1.26)	($0.59)	($0.03)	$0.07	$0.23
Accretion (Dilution) %		(64.4%)	(27.5%)	(1.5%)	2.7%	8.8%
Zero-dilution operating synergies ($000)		$75,755	$35,552	$1,934	NM	NM

income statement and its projected EPS.[22] The comparison of CDH's EPS without and with the acquisition of Capitol Designs is summarized in Exhibit 9.10. It shows that EPS were expected to fall by 64 and 28% during the first 2 years, respectively. This is because of three factors: the dilution resulting from the premium paid for Capitol, the initial restructuring expenses, and the additional expenses associated with CDH's planned expansion of Capitol. Eliminating dilution would require increasing operating income by $75.8 million in 2003 and $35.6 million in 2004. However, EPS were expected to be accretive after 2005 and increase by 23¢ or 8.8% by 2007. Note that in the present case, Capitol Designs was expected to grow faster than CDH's stand-alone business and at the same rate in the long run (see Exhibit 9.5), which means that the expected increase in EPS would be well received by investors. Note that here CDH would be buying a higher growth–higher P/E company, just the opposite of the case discussed in Section 9.9.

One can conclude that, given CDH's expectations, the merger should be beneficial to its shareholders. But how beneficial? A simple approach to this question is to capitalize future income or EBITDAR at an appropriate multiple. However, the choice of the earnings to capitalize is not obvious in the present case. Excluding restructuring expenses ($45.5 million in 2002) would not suffice because the planned growth of Capitol sales would demand stepping up expenses during the first two years. In addition, capital expenditures were expected to increase significantly during the initial years (see Exhibit 9.5) and that is not well captured by a multiple applied to a single-year earnings.

Exhibit 9.10 shows that EPS were expected to reach $2.86 in 2007, a point at which the initial expenditures would be digested and the fruit of the growth of Capitol would be attained. The choice of the multiple to capitalize these earnings is a matter of judgment. Since, after the period of rapid growth, Capitol's revenues were expected to approach those of CDH's retail business, it seems more reasonable to capitalize 2007 earnings at the multiple presently applied to the latter's earnings (17.2x) rather than to use the higher multiple at which Capitol was priced (24x). Hence, one would expect that the price of the merged company would reach 17.2 × $2.86 = $49 in 5 years from its pre-merger level of $32.75. Using security analysis terminology one can say that the long-term price target of the merger is about $49.

Pricing the stock at the time of the merger requires taking dividends into account (67¢ a share in 2003, which CDH expects to grow to $1.14 by 2007). However, a more effective way to value the company is via the free cash flow method introduced in Chap-

---

[22]See Problem 9.14 at the end for this chapter.

ter 2. In fact, the financial projections provide all the information needed to compute the expected free cash flows of the acquirer, the target and the merged company.

9.11.4   Free Cash-flow Valuation

In this section, the free cash flows of both CDH and Capitol Designs are valued following the procedure introduced in Chapter 2. The cost of capital of each is computed in Exhibit 9.11 following Chapter 3. Note that the cost of capital of Capitol was higher than that of CDH on two accounts: Capitol had higher systematic risk (beta), and its financing was projected using a lower debt ratio taking into account that its revenue growth mostly depended on new store openings and thus was riskier than the more established revenues of CDH. The size premium is calculated as in Chapter 3, Section 3.6, on the basis of the pre-merger market capitalization of the merged company.

Capitalized operating leases were taken into account in estimating the cost of capital and in calculating free cash flows and EBITDAR multiples. Operating leases are an off-balance sheet form of borrowing. Since they are a relatively small component of financing in most industries, the common practice of allowing their effect on valuation through operating expenses is acceptable. This is not the case of the specialty retail business where operating leases of stores constitute the bulk of financing. In fact, Exhibit 9.3 shows that the median net debt ratio of the 21 comparable retailers increases from –2.5 to 35.2% once operating leases are taken into account. Similarly, the net debt ratio of CDH increases from 2.5 to 34%. Note N9.1 shows the capitalization of the current and projected operating leases of CDH and Capitol Designs through 2007.

The valuation of Capitol Designs and CDH are presented in Exhibits 9.12 and 9.13. The valuation of the consolidated firms is done in Exhibit 9.14 using the sum-of-the-parts approach. That is, adding the value of the individual companies. This is the preferred approach in the present case because Capitol Designs is riskier and thus has a higher cost of capital. Since the cash flow generated by Capitol Designs is expected to grow faster than the cash flow contributed by CDH, the consolidated cost of capital increases over time. The alternative approach often followed in valuation practice would be to directly discount the consolidated cash flow of the merged company. The resulting valuation would be correct only if the betas and the debt ratios of the units were the same or if the units maintained their shares of value over time. Otherwise, valuation of the consolidated cash flow requires recomputing the cost of capital for each year because it would vary over time as the relative size of each unit changes. The sum-of-the-parts approach allows for

EXHIBIT 9.11 *Cost of Capital*		
	CDH Group	Capitol Designs
Long-Term Treasury yield	5.16%	5.16%
Equity premium	3.08%	3.08%
Size premium	1.21%	1.21%
Target debt ratio	35.0%	30.0%
Equity beta for target debt ratio	1.06	1.26
Cost of equity	9.62%	10.26%
Cost of debt	9.00%	9.00%
Tax rate	38.25%	38.25%
WACC	**8.20%**	**8.85%**

EXHIBIT 9.12 *CDH Group Discounted Cash Flow Valuation*

($000)   Fiscal Year Ending 1/31

			2003	2004
Net Income			$54,548	$59,755
Net Int.Exp.& Oper.Leases after taxes			26,113	27,716
Unlevered Net Income			80,661	87,471
Plus Deferred Taxes			1,866	3,718
NOPAT			82,526	91,189
Plus Depreciation and Amortization			43,973	51,000
Less Change in Net Working Capital			(11,910)	(14,897)
Less Capital Expenditures less Retirements			(92,351)	(106,101)
Free Cash Flow			**$22,238**	**$21,191**
EBITDAR			**$183,439**	**$202,078**
Continuation Value Growth Rate	5.50%			
Continuation EBITDAR Multiple	6.21 x			
Continuation Enterprise Value				
Cost of Capital	8.20%			
Present Value of Free Cash Flow through	2012	$234,423		
Present Value of Continuation Value		982,288		
Enterprise Value		1,216,710		
Plus Cash		33,760		
Enterprise Value plus Cash		1,250,470		
Minus Debt	487,187			
Minus Preferred Stock	7,823	(495,010)		
Equity Value		755,460		
Shares Outstanding (000)		27,439		
Equity Value per Share		$27.53		

the changes in the relative shares of the parts in the aggregate cash flow and provides the contribution of each part to the value of the merged firm.

In summary, the DCF valuation yields a value of $27.53 a share for CDH, $33.69 a share for Capitol Designs, and $34.75 a share for the merged company. These numbers suggest that acquiring Capitol Designs for $20 a share would be highly beneficial to CDH's shareholders and confirm the interpretation of the accretion-dilution analysis.

Note that pre-merger share price of CDH and Capitol Designs were $32.75 and $15.30. Why the differences? One possible interpretation is that the market had already impounded additional growth on the stock price of CDH, while the stand-alone valuation made in Exhibit 9.11 assumes modest volume growth. The difference between the share price of Capitol Designs and its DCF value is the result of the material increase that CDH plans to impart to its growth.

A final comment: The DCF valuation implies that the merged company would have an equity capitalization of about $1.3 billion. This would tend to increase the liquidity of its stock, reduce its cost of equity and potentially increase the value of the merged company's share. However, that would happen only if and when investors recognize that the merger makes sense and creates value beyond financial synergies. In fact, liquidity could

2005	2006	2007	2008	2009	2010	2011	2012
$61,008	$71,126	$72,886	$82,586	$86,082	$95,780	$101,138	$106,791
29,252	31,142	32,809	34,434	35,878	37,512	39,111	40,854
90,260	102,268	105,695	117,020	121,961	133,292	140,248	147,646
4,379	4,343	3,992	2,830	2,188	1,713	1,240	951
94,639	106,611	109,687	119,850	124,148	135,005	141,488	148,597
59,199	60,730	68,959	64,006	70,138	66,709	71,196	75,848
(16,258)	(15,128)	(16,569)	(14,091)	(16,590)	(16,269)	(18,264)	(19,344)
(117,936)	(120,600)	(127,444)	(123,494)	(132,943)	(133,015)	(141,199)	(149,754)
$19,643	**$31,612**	**$34,632**	**$46,271**	**$44,753**	**$52,429**	**$53,221**	**$55,347**
$215,415	**$237,055**	**$251,486**	**$265,507**	**$280,309**	**$295,936**	**$312,434**	**$329,852**
							2,160,755

shrink if the acquisition is a failure and the merged company actually decreases in value. A merger should not be predicated exclusively or mainly on potential financial synergies.

9.11.5   Sensitivity and Scenario Analysis

So far we have considered the effect of the merger under the baseline projections. These are subjective expectations of quantities that are probabilistic in nature. This is why in practice one considers the sensitivity of the valuation results to changes in the operating assumptions. A simple way to proceed is to change one variable at a time. Exhibit 9.15 shows the changes in the share value of Capitol Designs when each relevant operating assumption is changed by ±10%.

As expected, volume growth has a material effect on Capitol's value, so do cost of sales and SG&A (sales, general and administrative) expenses. Sensitivity analysis is useful for understanding the workings of the valuation model and allowing the analyst to refine the forecasting assumptions. However, it has well-understood limitations. A simple 10% change does not have the same meaning for all the variables. More importantly, many variables are interrelated. For example, lower capital expenditures are likely to

---

| EXHIBIT 9.13 | *Capitol Designs Discounted Cash Flow Valuation* |

($000)			Fiscal Year Ending 1/31	
			2003	2004
Net Income			($44,449)	($2,501)
Net Int.Exp.& Oper.Leases after taxes			8,800	15,056
Unlevered Net Income			(35,649)	12,555
Plus Deferred Taxes			0	0
NOPAT			(35,649)	12,555
Plus Depreciation and Amortization			10,172	14,240
Less Change in Net Working Capital			(2,616)	(4,561)
Less Capital Expenditures less Retirements			(58,829)	(70,815)
Free Cash Flow			**($86,922)**	**($48,580)**
EBITDAR			**$27,296**	**$38,410**
Continuation Value Growth Rate	5.50%			
Continuation EBITDAR Multiple	9.82 x			
Continuation Enterprise Value				
Cost of Capital	8.85%			
Present Value of Free Cash Flow through	2012	($6,743)		
Present Value of Continuation Value		698,843		
Enterprise Value		692,100		
Plus Cash		—		
Enterprise Value plus Cash		692,100		
Minus Debt	157,509			
Minus Preferred Stock	0	157,509		
Equity Value		534,590		
Shares Outstanding (000)		15,867		
Equity Value per Share		$33.69		

result in lower volume growth. Price changes are likely to affect volume growth. When price changes reflect expected changes in inflation, they should be accompanied by changes in the nominal cost of capital. Similarly, changes in R&D (research and development) expenditures and inventory policy may affect sales, and delays in account payable may result in an increase in the cost of sales.

Finally, there is no clear interpretation of the present value computation in sensitivity analysis because, according to financial theory, the enterprise value is determined by discounting *expected free cash flows* at a *risk adjusted* cost of capital. Systematic risk is accounted for in the cost of capital and the present value calculation has no clear meaning when the cost of capital is used to discount departures from expected cash flows. Each resulting present value is meaningful if one assumes that the changed assumptions yield expected free cash flows but one is left with the problem of selecting the "true" expected value out of all the variations considered in the analysis. Moreover, that is not what one normally has in mind when performing sensitivity analysis.

At this point, it is useful to refer to the possibility of using risk analysis in valuation. It was introduced years ago for the analysis of capital budgeting decisions.[23] It proceeds by assigning subjective probability distributions to the individual projections and deriving

---

[23]Hertz (1964) and Hillier (1963).

2005	2006	2007	2008	2009	2010	2011	2012
$30,667	$32,324	$32,733	$36,402	$39,330	$44,835	$48,864	$53,222
18,207	20,394	22,172	23,053	23,325	23,516	23,715	23,854
48,874	52,718	54,905	59,455	62,655	68,351	72,578	77,076
0	6,586	1,902	1,342	881	627	473	341
48,874	59,304	56,807	60,796	63,537	68,978	73,051	77,417
18,690	21,688	25,395	26,157	27,800	25,782	26,545	27,294
(5,116)	(6,336)	(6,057)	(2,841)	(2,385)	(2,518)	(2,658)	(2,807)
(75,368)	(73,941)	(57,512)	(47,184)	(47,863)	(48,581)	(49,338)	(50,137)
($12,919)	$715	$18,633	$36,928	$41,088	$43,662	$47,600	$51,767
$81,656	$100,437	$118,390	$126,811	$133,880	$141,344	$149,224	$157,544

1,631,431

the probability distribution of net present value via Monte Carlo simulation. That is done by drawing from the assumed distributions many cash-flow realizations and discounting them at the risk-free rate. This rate is used in order to avoid double counting for risk. (Remember that the risk-adjusted cost of capital applies only to *expected* free cash flows.) The final result is a distribution of present values. Unfortunately, this is as far as one can go with risk analysis because it is not possible to derive the relevant price from the distribution of present values. The distribution itself contains mainly diversifiable risk that is not priced in financial markets. In summary, risk analysis can be helpful in estimating

EXHIBIT 9.14 *DCF Valuation Summary*

	CDH Group	Capitol Designs	CDH Group and Capitol Designs
Enterprise Value	$1,216,710	$692,100	$908,810
Cash	33,760	0	33,760
Enterprise Value plus Cash	1,250,470	692,100	1,942,570
Minus Debt	495,010	157,509	652,520
Equity Value	755,459.97	534,590	1,290,050
Shares Outstanding	27,439	15,867	37,129
Equity Value per Share	**$27.53**	**$33.69**	**$34.75**

EXHIBIT 9.15	*Sensitivity of Capitol Designs Value*	
($/share)		
Change	**−10%**	**+10%**
Unit Sales Growth	−$6.03	$6.48
Price Growth	−0.91	0.91
Cost of Sales	30.26	−31.81
SG&A expenses	22.28	−22.45
R&D	1.90	−1.90
Capex	3.44	−3.44
Accounts Receivable	0.70	−0.78
Inventories	2.38	−2.63
Accounts Payable	−1.42	1.57
Restructuring expenses	0.19	−0.19

expected free cash flows but it does not provide a solution to the valuation problem. The latter requires discounting expected free cash flows at the cost of capital of the enterprise.

A common way to test the validity of a merger analysis is to consider a number of forecast scenarios. These alternative scenarios are usually formulated to bracket the baseline projection with pessimistic and optimistic projections. A scenario is a set of interrelated forecasting assumptions. The variables in each scenario are set to be internally consistent, such that faster growth recognizes the need for additional capital expenditures or that a reduction in price may lead to growth of sales. The scenario must also be externally consistent. The state of the overall economy and its evolution (expansion or recession, price level and interest rate changes, and the state of consumer sentiment), as well as technological change affecting the industry are basic underlying assumptions supporting each particular scenario. If revenue growth exceeds industry growth, the reaction of competitors to the increase in market share has to be taken into account. In addition, the financial implications of each scenario should be incorporated into the financial model. For

EXHIBIT 9.16   *Forecasting Scenarios for Capitol Designs Valuation*

	2003	2004	2005	2006	2007
Pessimistic					
Unit Sales Growth	3.0%	5.0%	15.0%	15.0%	10.0%
Price Growth	0.0%	0.0%	0.0%	0.0%	0.0%
Nominal Sales Growth	0.0%	0.0%	20.0%	35.0%	20.0%
Cost of Sales (% of Sales)	51.0%	50.0%	48.0%	48.0%	48.0%
SG&A expenses (% of Sales)	40.0%	40.0%	35.0%	35.0%	35.0%
R&D (% of Sales)	3.0%	3.0%	3.0%	3.0%	3.0%
Capex (net of Disposals) ($000)	20,000	30,000	35,000	35,000	35,000
Optimistic					
Unit Sales Growth	20.0%	30.0%	30.0%	30.0%	25.0%
Price Growth	2.5%	2.5%	2.5%	2.5%	2.5%
Nominal Sales Growth	25.1%	39.4%	38.9%	38.9%	38.9%
Cost of Sales (% of Sales)	51.0%	50.0%	48.0%	48.0%	48.0%
SG&A expenses (% of Sales)	40.0%	40.0%	35.0%	35.0%	35.0%
R&D (% of Sales)	3.0%	3.0%	3.0%	3.0%	3.0%
Capex (net of Disposals) ($000)	35,500	44,500	43,000	43,000	43,000

EXHIBIT 9.17	*Capitol Designs—Valuation of Scenarios*			
Scenario	Probability	Enterprise Value	Equity Value	Share Value
Pessimistic	21%	$209,196	$65,205	$4.11
Most Likely	54%	692,100	534,590	33.69
Optimistic	25%	1,091,732	932,679	58.78
Unconditional Value	100%	$690,598	$535,541	$33.75

example, the operating leases associated with opening new stores in the case of Capitol Designs should be accounted for and capital expenditures should be financed in a way consistent with the planned financial policy.

Consider the following scenarios for Capitol Designs: (1) A pessimistic scenario that assumes the state of the U.S. economy and consumer spending will further deteriorate during 2003 and will only begin to recover during the first half of 2004. (2) A most likely scenario corresponding to the baseline projection summarized in Exhibit 9.4 that assumes moderate resumption of economic growth in the first half of 2003. And (3) an optimistic scenario that assumes that consumer spending returns to pre-2001 growth early in 2003 and is followed by brisk economic expansion. Furthermore, let the odds of each scenario be 21%, 54% and 25%, respectively, and use the baseline forecast of Exhibit 9.4 as the most likely scenario. The assumptions corresponding to the pessimistic and optimistic scenarios change the first 5-year projections of Exhibit 9.5 as shown in Exhibit 9.16.

The free cash flows corresponding to each scenario can be weighted by the scenario probability in order to obtain the expected free cash flows of the enterprise. These cash flows can then be discounted at the cost of capital to obtain the value of the enterprise. Alternatively, one can compute the value of the enterprise and its equity by discounting each scenario's cash flows at the cost of capital. This is done in Exhibit 9.17. However, the interpretation of such values is subject to the same qualifications as the results from sensitivity analysis. In order to make sense of single-scenario cash flows discounted at the risk adjusted cost of capital one has to think of them as being expected values of free cash flows. Furthermore, they need to have the same systematic risk as that accounted for in the cost of capital. Then one can weigh each scenario's valuation by its own probability to attain the unconditional expected value of the company. The final result is the same as that produced by computing the unconditional free cash flows and discounting them at the cost of capital.

Exhibit 9.17 shows that the value of Capitol designs is very sensitive to the state of the economy. By being willing to pay $20 a share, CDH would be betting on the recovery of the U.S. economy in addition to its own ability to ignite growth on Capitol's business. The EPS computed in Exhibit 9.18 show that under the pessimistic scenario EPS would not catch up with its stand-alone level until after 2007.

EXHIBIT 9.18	*Accretion-Dilution Analysis: Scenario Analysis of Acquisition of Capitol Designs*					
	2002	2003	2004	2005	2006	2007
Acquirer Stand-Alone EPS	$1.90	$1.96	$2.15	$2.19	$2.56	$2.62
Consolidated EPS Pessimistic	1.68	0.67	1.49	1.87	2.21	2.28
Consolidated EPS Most Likely	1.68	0.70	1.56	2.25	2.91	3.10
Consolidated EPS Optimistic	1.68	0.70	1.58	2.27	2.89	3.33

EXHIBIT 9.19 *Capitol Designs Value Matrix*

		Cost of Capital				
		6.85%	7.85%	8.85%	9.85%	10.85%
	6.8 x	26.2	22.9	19.8	17.0	14.5
Continuation	7.8 x	31.7	27.9	24.4	21.3	18.4
Value EBITDAR	8.8 x	37.2	32.9	29.1	25.5	22.3
Multiple	9.8 x	42.6	38.0	33.7	29.8	26.3
	10.8 x	48.1	43.0	38.3	34.1	30.2
	11.8 x	53.6	48.0	43.0	38.3	34.1
	12.8 x	59.0	53.0	47.6	42.6	38.0

In addition, the baseline case can be valued for a number of alternative valuation parameters recognizing the approximated nature of the estimates of the cost of capital and valuation multiples. For example, Exhibit 9.19 shows that given the baseline scenario, the merger is value creating even under pessimistic valuation parameters. For the value of Capitol's common share to be below $20, the cost of capital would have to exceed 10%, and the continuation value would need to command an EBITDAR multiple lower than 8x. This is usually the case in valuation. DCF is less sensitive to the valuation parameters than to the determinants of free cash flows.

9.12 SUMMARY

In order to determine the value creation potential of a merger, one needs to perform a number of analyses:

(1) **The terms of the merger:** These include the form of payment whether in cash, stock, or a combination of both. The type of transaction adopted for tax purposes (whether a merger, a purchase of assets, or a purchase of stock), the tax consequences of the transaction for buyer and seller, and whether there are transferable net operating losses. The fees and expenses to be paid by the parties.

(2) **Financing the merger:** How the cash component of the price and the transaction expenses will be financed, whether from available cash in the target and/or the acquirer or with additional borrowing. What pre-merger debt and other claims such as preferred stock and warrants are assumed or exchanged and what claims are to be retired, at what cost and how will retirements be financed. This is summarized in a statement of sources and uses of funds.

(3) **Break-even synergies:** A first calculation of the value of the synergies net of transactions expenses necessary to maintain the share price of the acquirer at its pre-merger level. This is the value of the premium paid to the target shareholders.

(4) **Financial model of the merger:** A detailed analysis of the effect of the merger on shareholder value requires building financial models of the acquirer, the target, and the merged firm. The financial models should produce income statements, balance sheets, and cash flow statements for the forecast period for a given set of operating and financing assumptions. The financial models permits performing the following analyses.

(5) **Accretion-dilution analysis:** Calculation of EPS for the acquirer with and without the acquisition, including an estimate of the synergies required to break-even in those years in which the merger is dilutive.

(6) **Free cash-flow valuation:** Valuation of the stand-alone acquirer, the target and the merged firm. The target is valued under the operating assumptions assumed by the acquirer.

(7) Stress-testing and scenario analysis: Accretion-dilution and valuation computations should be tested for robustness, via sensitivity and scenario analysis.

The financial analysis of the merger is an iterative process that assists the buyer in carrying out due diligence, testing the consistency of the merger assumptions, formulating the terms of the offer, and reaching a decision. Negotiating an acquisition is a process of give and take as the parties get comfortable with each other and learn about their intentions. A flexible financial model will assist the acquirer during the negotiation process by showing the financial and value implications of alternative deal terms.

Reaching a final agreement may require the addition of earnouts, collars, escrows, and other contingencies to the terms of the merger in order to close the valuation gap separating buyer and seller. The formulation and valuation of such contingencies are studied in Chapters 10 and 11.

PROBLEMS

9.1 Assume the buyer acquires a debt-free target for $70 cash, the target's tax basis in the assets is $20, the target shareholders' basis in the stock is $35 and the fair market value of the stock was $55 prior to the acquisition. Let the corporate tax rate be 40%, the personal tax rate on capital gains be 20% and assume that all the gain to the seller is classified as capital gain and the buyer's price in excess to the target's basis is allocated to goodwill. The cost of debt to the buyer is 9%.

Calculate the net proceeds to the seller shareholders and the tax consequences to the buyer in a stock purchase and an asset purchase.

9.2 Refer to Problem 9.1. Assume the target has $80 of accumulated NOLs that would expire in seven years and the tax-exempt interest rate is 3%. Calculate the net proceeds to the seller shareholders and the tax consequences to the buyer in a stock purchase and an asset purchase.

9.3 Refer to Problem 9.1. Assume the target is a subsidiary of a corporate seller such that the target is able to distribute proceeds tax-free to the parent. Consider the case in which the transaction is a stock purchase, but it is possible to treat it as an asset purchase for the purpose of taxation. Calculate the net proceeds to the seller shareholders and the tax consequences to the buyer in a stock purchase and an asset purchase.

9.4 Refer to Section 9.5 and prepare the consolidated balance sheet for the case of negative goodwill. That is, assume the purchase of XYZ was done at $22 a share for a total consideration of $1,100 million and the fair value of XYZ's net assets is as shown in Exhibit 9.1.

9.5 GLD Corp. is investigating the possible acquisition of Stopper Systems Inc. The following data are available:

	GLD	Stopper Systems
EPS	$4.00	$2.20
Dividend per share	$1.20	$0.60
Number of shares	6,000,000	2,000,000
Stock price	$10.00	$5.00

The cost of equity of both GLD and Stopper Systems is 15%. The merged firm is expected to grow at 5% per year and to increase its dividend at 5% per year from the current aggregate dividend of the two companies. GLD plans to offer 0.6 shares of its own stock for every share of Stopper Systems.

a. What is the value of equity of the merged company?
b. What are the gains (losses) to each group of shareholders?

9.6 In the fall of 1987 the Bank of New York (BONY) offered to exchange 1.575 shares of BONY common stock, plus $15 in cash per common share of Irving Bank Corporation. 1987 data for each company were as follows:

	Irving	BONY
Pro-forma net income available to common*	$118 m	$153.5 m
Common shares (fully diluted)	18.391m	33.092m
Pre-announcement stock price	39.337	31.526

*After eliminating the effect of certain extraordinary items.

Calculate the following:

a. The 1987 pro-forma EPS of the combined entity assuming that the proposed exchange takes place.

b. The gains (losses) to each group of shareholders under the assumption that the combined entity is worth $300 million more than its original parts.

c. The increase in the value of the combined entity that has to take place in order to justify the acquisition from the point of view of BONY shareholders.

d. Assume BONY had accumulated a foothold of 2.8% at an average price of $29 a share prior to its bid and revise your estimate of (c).

9.7 Consider the acquisition by Gould Inc. of American Microsystems Inc. in a stock swap valued at about $200 million. American Microsystems, with sales of $129.4 million, was the largest commercial maker of custom semiconductors at the time.

Gould said it would issue 1.78 shares of its own common stock for each of American Microsystems 4,165,000 common and 150,000 preferred shares. Upon the announcement, Gould common closed at $24.125 a share, down 87½ cents a share and American Microsystems common was quoted at a bid price of $37.75 a share, up $11.125.

For the third quarter, Gould's profit rose 56% to $22.3 million, or 63 cents a share, from $14.3 million, or 41 cents a share, a year earlier. Sales increased 18% to $479.1 million from $405.1 million. For the third quarter, American Microsystems earnings doubled to $2.8 million from $1.4 million a year earlier. Revenue rose to $37.5 million from $35.8 million.

a. Estimate the gain and/or loss to Gould and American Micro's stockholders under the assumption that the acquisition does not create value. Treat American Micro's preferred as equivalent to common stock.

b. What value should the acquisition create in order to justify the transaction from the point of view of Gould's stockholders?

9.8 E-III Corp. is investigating the possible acquisition of Reluctant Inc. The following data are available:

	E-III	Reluctant
EPS	$2.00	$3.20
Dividend per share	0	$1.60
Number of shares	8,000,000	3,000,000
Stock price	$4.00	$8.00

The costs of equity are 17% for E-III and 15% for Reluctant. E-III plans to offer $5.00 cash and 1.5 shares of its own stock for each share of Reluctant.

a. Assume no synergy. What are the gains (losses) to each group of shareholders?

b. What synergy should the merged firm produce for the shareholders of E-III to break even?

9.9 In May of 1990 Lotus Development Corporation proposed a merger with Novell Inc. via a share exchange in which Lotus would exchange 1.19131 of its shares for every Novel share. Under the announced terms, Mr. Raymond Noorda, Novell's chairman, would become vice chairman of the merged company, while Lotus's Jim Manzi would remain as chairman, chief executive and president. The combination was hailed as redrawing the competitive balance in the personal computed software business by providing a challenge to the growing power of Microsoft. Fiscal year 1989 data for each company were as follows:

	Lotus	Novell
Net income available to common	$ 68.0 m	$ 48.5 m
Common shares	42.3 m	33.4 m
Stock price (pre-announcement)	$ 36.25	$ 42.875

a. Calculate the 1989 pro-forma EPS of the merged company assuming the proposed exchange took place.

b. What increase in the value of the merged company would have justified the transaction from the point of view of Lotus shareholders? Assume that the fees and expenses associated with the merger would have amounted to $40 million.

c. Evaluate the transaction from the point of view of Novell's shareholders.

9.10 On January 25, 1992, AB Volvo and Procordia AB surprised the business world by announcing that their boards had agreed to a merger. The merger was proposed by Mr. Pehr Gyllenhammer, the chairman of both Volvo and Procordia, and had been approved at meetings of the board of directors of each of the two companies. The merger was to be effected through a public offer by Procordia to Volvo's shareholders to tender their Volvo shares and convertible debentures in exchange for Procordia shares and convertible debentures. The new company would be called Volvo, have 105,000 employees and about Kr (Kronor) 115 billion ($20 billion) of revenues ranging from aerospace to foods and pharmaceuticals.

The agreement called for holders of each four Volvo Series A and Series B shares to receive nine Procordia shares of a corresponding class. Holders of each convertible debenture certificate in nominal amount Kr 385 pertaining to Volvo's 1987/95 loan, convertible to one Series B share at Kr 385, 2.4 million debentures outstanding, were offered one convertible debenture certificate in a nominal amount of Kr 385 issued by Procordia, plus Kr 43 in cash. Interest accrued to the date of payment would also be paid. Each debenture certificate could be exchanged for 2.25 Procordia Series B shares at a conversion price of Kr 190 per share. In other respects, the terms of the new Procordia's convertible debentures were the same as those applying to Volvo's debentures.

Holders of each convertible debenture certificate in nominal amount Kr 450 pertaining to Volvo's 1990/95 loan, convertible to one Series B share at Kr 450, 1.68 million debentures outstanding, were offered one convertible debenture certificate in a nominal amount of Kr 450 issued by Procordia, plus Kr 45 in cash. Interest accrued to the date of payment would also be paid. Each debenture certificate could be exchanged for 2.25 Procordia Series B shares at a conversion price of Kr 220 per share. In other respects, the terms of the new Procordia's convertible debentures were the same as those applying to Volvo's debentures. Additional details pertaining to the convertible debentures are provided below.

The offering was also subject to the required approval of a general meeting of Procordia's shareholders, and to the receipt of necessary permits from the authorities. It was planned to undertake negotiations with the government with respect to conversion of its holding of Series A shares in Procordia to Series B shares, with a view to reducing the percentage of the government's voting rights.

After full conversion, the offering would comprise 183.7 million Procordia shares. It was planned to eliminate Volvo's holding in Procordia by reducing the share capital. The number of shares in the new company would thereby become 338.7 million. If the offer were accepted, the Swedish government's holding of Procordia shares would be reduced from 34.2 percent to 25.6 percent.

The government's decision concerning the merger was expected to be influenced by the recommendation of the commission set up to advise Mr. Per Westerberg, the Minister of Industry and Commerce. The nine-member body, made up of financiers and industrialists, was to consider the industrial logic of the deal, as well as the advantages and disadvantages to Procordia's shareholders. By virtue of a 2-year old agreement between Volvo and Procordia, any increase in Procordia's share capital was subject to the approval of both Volvo and the government. Such a provision gave the government a *de facto* veto over the merger plan.

The capital stock of Volvo was made up of 77.6 million class A and B shares, of which 32.7 percent were A shares and 67.3 percent were B shares. The fully diluted number of shares was 81.7 million. A and B shares were equivalent in every respect except voting rights. Each A share was entitled to one vote and each B share was entitled to one-tenth of a vote. Volvo B shares were listed on stock exchanges around the world. In addition, they traded in the New York Stock Exchange in the form of ADRs. The price of Volvo's B shares increased by about 25% during the first 3 weeks of January on the strength of its restructuring and streamlining program. However, Volvo had losses in 1990 and 1991 and it was not expected to return to profitability until 1995 at the earliest, and it was experiencing cash flow problems. The dividend for 1992 was expected to be Kr 7.75 per share. B shares closed on January 24, 1991, just prior to the announcement at Kr 393 ($67.76 at a Kr 5.8 per dollar exchange rate). The volume of trading in Class A shares was very small. The prices of Class A and Class B shares were very close to each other. This was consistent with empirical studies showing that the value of voting power is only significant when the likelihood of a takeover battle is high.[24]

The capital stock of Procordia was made up of A and B class shares. Each A share carried one vote and each B share carried one-tenth of a vote. There were 253.562 million shares outstanding, of which 64.96 percent were A shares and 35.04 percent were B shares. The fully diluted number of shares was 255 million. Procordia shares were listed in the Stockholm and London stock exchanges. Procordia's annual dividend was Kr 2.85 per share. They closed on January 24, 1991, at Kr 212 ($36.55) up 8% during January. Trading volume in Class A shares was light. The prices of A and B type shares had historically traded at the same price or very close to each other.

Volvo held 100.096 million shares, or 39.5%, which gave it 42.7% of the voting rights. The Swedish Government (through Forvaltningsaktie-bolaget Fortia) owned 86.670 million shares, or 34.2% with 42.7% of the voting rights. But the new government headed by Prime Minister Carl Bildt had announced that it intended to sell its stake in Procordia as part of its privatization program.

Volvo Convertible Series

Series	87/95	90/95
Nominal amount (Kr)	924.0 m	754.6 m
Maturity	3/95	3/95
Interest rate (annual)	10.0%	12.5%
Conversion price (Kr)	385	450
Conversion number of shares	2.40 m	1.68 m
Price on 12/31/91	108%	110%
Swedish government note rate, year-end 1991	13%	
Corporate bond rate, year-end 1991	15%	
Volatilities based upon 1991 prices:		
Volvo B stock volatility	28.2%	
Procordia B stock volatility	21.7%	
Correlation between Volvo and Procordia returns	85.0	

a. It seems reasonable to assume that the merger of an auto and aerospace manufacturer with a food and pharmaceutical company would generate no material operating synergies. Given this assumption, evaluate the proposed merger from the point of view of both Volvo and Procordia shareholders.

b. How would voting power be distributed among the government, Volvo's shareholders, and others after the merger, with and without changing the government's A class Procordia shares into B class?

c. Discuss the exchange terms offered to the holders of Volvo convertibles and the value of the warrants embedded in the new convertibles.

d. How do you expect the prices of Volvo and Procordia to respond to the merger announcement?

e. Assume you are a member of the advisory commission to the Minister of Industry. Would you recommend the approval of the proposed merger?

---

[24]The average difference in price between Class A and Class B shares for a sample of Swedish firms was between 1.4 and 6.1 percent during 1975–1985. See Rydqvist (1987).

f. Assume the government informs Volvo that it is going to vote its shares against the proposed merger at the Procordia shareholders meeting. Design a revised proposal that, in your opinion, can be acceptable to both Volvo and Procordia shareholders.

9.11 On August 11, 1983, T. Boone Pickens and a consortium of investors began purchasing shares of Gulf Oil for $39. On February 22, 1984, Pickens announced a partial tender offer at $65 per share. ("A rich oilman conducting piracy on the high seas will hurt all of us," lamented the chairman of another oil company.) Gulf turned to "white knight" Chevron for help. Your task is to figure out how much Chevron could afford to pay for Gulf. So far, you know that the pre-takeover bid price was $39. That price was based upon the assumption that real oil prices would not change very much in future years and the investment and operating policies of Gulf would stay the same. A take-over premium would make sense to Chevron only if it could implement cash flow-increasing changes in Gulf's policies. Two such actions were available to Chevron: (a) Reducing Gulf's ambitious exploration program (actually rationalizing the exploration program of the merged company) and (b) rationalizing administrative and distribution operations to generate additional cost savings. Preliminary calculations indicated that the merged company could expect to realize about $2 billion of additional after-tax free cash flow per year during the first 8 years by a combination of (a) and (b) above. However, reduction of the exploration program would result in a decrease in after-tax free cash flow of about $350 million per year after the 8th year. This reduction could be assumed to continue long enough to be treated as a perpetuity. In addition, a one-year implementation delay was expected and restructuring cost would amount to $1 billion. All the above estimates are expressed in dollars of 1984. In the spring of 1984, the long-term government bond rate was 12%, the AA corporate yield was 13.5% (both Gulf's and Chevron's bonds were rated AA), the corporate tax rate was 50%, Chevron's target debt ratio was 26%, and expected long-term inflation was estimated at 6%. Gulf's and Chevron's stock betas were both equal to 1.15. The prospective market equity risk premium over the long-term Treasuries was estimated at 4%. There were 165.3 million Gulf shares outstanding.

9.12 Your firm, First Energy Advisors, has been retained to review the valuation of the Gulf Oil Corporation made using the information provided in Problem 9.11. You are in charge of this assignment. You have been asked to pay particular attention to the long-term trends of the energy market. In the process of reaching your conclusion on the value of Gulf Oil you have access to the following information:

a. The original valuation implied that Chevron could bid up to $85 per share of Gulf.
b. The original valuation assumed that Gulf's $39 per share price reflected the market's assumption that it would maintain its current policy and that no significant changes would take place in the energy market in the future.
c. On the other hand, based upon your own research you have concluded that although the real price of oil would stay fairly constant through 1991, oil prices would increase faster than general inflation after 1991. You estimate that Gulf's stand-alone real cash flows from oil and gas production would increase at 4% per year after 1991 and will continue growing at that rate well into the 21st century because of the projected upward trend in oil demand and prices. Furthermore, you believe that the $39 per share price of Gulf already discounts the upward trend in oil prices projected for the 1990s and beyond.

Modify the valuation of Gulf to take into account your projection of the post-1991 growth of real free-cash flows from oil and gas exploration. What is the maximum price per share that Chevron should be willing to pay for Gulf Oil as per your new valuation?

9.13 The DCF valuation of Heavy Industries Inc.'s business plan results in an enterprise value of $100 million. The capital expenditure budget yields negative cash flows during the next three years and a net funding requirement of $35 million. Although the company has no net debt and could fund its capital needs by borrowing, it is considering placing a 50% stake with an industrial partner in order to get the non-financial benefits of the partnership. Discuss whether the company should place outstanding equity, new equity, debt, or a mixture of each, and the impact of each alternative on pricing and proceeds.

9.14 Refer to Sections 9.11.2 and 9.11.3 and prepare the stand-alone income statements for CDH Group for the years 2003 to 2007 and compute its EPS. The operating forecasting assumptions for CDH are provided on the first panel of Exhibit 9.5; its income statement for 2002 and the projected interest expense and income are as follows:

CDH Group Income Statements 2002 ($000, except EPS)

Total Sales	$1,160,863
Cost of Sales	617,582
Gross Profit	543,281
Sales, General & Administrative Expenses	409,035
EBITDA	134,246
Depreciation	46,321
EBIT	87,925
Interest Expense	3,967
Interest Income	1,864
Pretax Income	85,822
Income Tax @ 38.25%	32,827
Net Income	52,995
Dividends to other than common:	
Preferred stock	861
Net Income Available to Common	52,134
Number of Shares (000)	27,439
EPS	$1.90

CDH Group Interest Expense and Income 2003–2007 ($000)

	02003	2004	2005	2006	2007
Interest Expense	$4,429	$5,329	$5,329	$5,329	$5,329
Interest Income	1,924	2,854	3,165	3,089	3,322

Chapter 10

Deal Making with Differences of Opinion

10.1 SOURCES OF DISAGREEMENT IN DEAL MAKING

In an acquisition, the parties exchange cash flows. In a cash-purchase, the acquirer exchanges a certain, measurable amount of value for expected future cash flows. In a merger effected through an exchange of shares, the seller receives claims to the joint cash flows of the merged company and surrenders claims to the target's cash flows. Finance practitioners refer to these exchanges as *deals*. In fact, one can define a deal as an agreement among parties for the exchange of cash flows.

A deal distributes cash flows among the parties participating in the transaction by amount, time, and risk. A deal depends on the parties' appraisal of the values being exchanged.

In general, a deal can take place only if there is a difference of opinion among the parties about the value being exchanged, because both have to believe that the transaction makes them better off. The difference of opinion about value arises from different appreciation about its determinants. As Sahlman (1988) noted: (1) Because cash flows are uncertain and difficult to estimate and the discount rates to apply for valuing them are not precisely known, the parties may disagree about expected cash flows, their risks, and the appropriate discount rates to use. (2) The parties to a deal may be affected differently by the transaction because of wealth, portfolio composition, or tax exposure. (3) The parties would normally have different information about the determinants of future cash flows, as it is the case between entrepreneur and venture capitalist and between the buyer and the seller of a going concern. (4) There is a natural conflict of interest among the parties to a transaction in the sense that the terms of a deal and the information provided or withheld can direct cash flow away from one party to the other. (5) The terms of the deal can create incentives and disincentives that can affect the nature of the cash flows being exchanged.

A difference of opinion about value can make a deal possible. For example, if the seller's discount rate is 20% and the buyer's is 12%, there are potentially many prices to transact the cash flows. On the other hand, a difference of opinion may make the deal difficult if not impossible to realize. For example, if there is an agreement about expected cash flows but not their risk, the seller's discount rate can be 12% and the buyer's discount rate can be 20%, such that there is no single price that would satisfy both parties. However, transactions take place in practice even in the presence of strong differences of opinion about value. This is accomplished by structuring the terms of the deal in such a way that both parties find the terms consistent with their prior beliefs. Contingencies are added to the terms of the transaction in order to condition the distribution of cash flows on the realization of measurable future outcomes. Differences of opinion about value create both difficulties for the consummation of a deal as well as opportunities. The role of the deal-maker is to create a deal structure satisfactory to both parties. In this chapter, we consider the form and valuation of such contingent deal structures.

Example 1

The following example illustrates the role of a contingent assignment of cash flows in resolving differences of opinion about value.

On August 12, 1996, Delmarva Power of Delaware and Atlantic Energy of New Jersey announced their agreement to merge into a new holding company to be named Delmarva Power. The terms of the merger were as follows: (1) Delmarva shareholders would receive one share of common stock in the new holding company for each Delmarva share they owned. (2) Atlantic Energy shareholders would receive 0.75 shares in the new holding company for each share they held plus (3) 0.125 shares in class A stock for each share they held. Class A shares, commonly called tracking stock, represented 30% interest in the earnings of Atlantic Electric above $40 million a year. Atlantic Electric was the regulated subsidiary of Atlantic Energy that supplied electric service to consumers.

These terms did not provide for the usual proportional distribution of cash flows that results from an exchange of common equity. All common shareholders were to benefit from the earnings of the original Delmarva Power business, the earnings of the unregulated business of Atlantic Energy, the first $40 million of Atlantic Electric, and the remaining 70% above $40 million of the earnings of Atlantic Electric. However, the original Atlantic Energy shareholders were also to get 30% of the earnings of Atlantic Electric in excess to $40 million.

The purpose of such a merger structure was to resolve a difference of opinion about the value of the regulated business of Atlantic Energy.[1] Delmarva did not value Atlantic Electric so highly as the management of Atlantic Energy did because it doubted Atlantic Electric's ability to maintain profits as New Jersey proceeded to deregulate retail power supply. In fact, a simple swap of common shares would have required Delmarva to offer more than 0.75 shares of the merged company per share of Atlantic Energy in order to satisfy the seller, which Delmarva would have found unacceptable. That is, under a simple share exchange, the terms of the merger would have been unacceptable to one or the other party and no merger would have taken place. The final terms of the deal solved the valuation problem. According to them, Delmarva gave up 30% of Atlantic Electric's upside, but, in return, it issued fewer shares of the holding company to Atlantic Energy shareholders. These shareholders received a price that was in part contingent on the future performance of the regulated business. They received more of the upside of Atlantic Electric but bore proportionally more of the risk of its underperformance.

The solution of the valuation problem involved accommodating the term of the merger to the different valuations made by the parties. The magnitude and probability of the upside of Atlantic Electric seemed less to Delmarva than to Atlantic Energy. As a consequence, Delmarva's valuation of the terms of the merger was lower than the valuation of the same terms made by Atlantic Energy. The contingent value of the deal is different for each party. In this sense, the resolution of the valuation difference consists in agreeing to disagree and establishing a price that is contingent on the realization of a measurable outcome.

The terms of the Delmarva-Atlantic Energy merger illustrate the fundamental difference between a simple share exchange that proportionally distributes expected cash flow and risk and a nonproportional sharing arrangement. The latter allocates higher downside risk to the seller in exchange for higher upside return. As such, nonproportional sharing of cash flows has two desirable properties for the buyer. It *screens* out sellers that do not believe their own representations about future cash flows because it makes them bear the risk of future underperformance, and it provides a strong *incentive* for the seller to reach for the upside when the seller remains involved in the management of the target.

The class-A shares received by Atlantic Energy shareholders can be interpreted as a series of calls on the distribution of profits of Atlantic Electric, each with a $40 million exercise price. Section 10.7 below shows how to value class shares using option-pricing techniques.

---

[1] As many other utilities around the country, Atlantic Electric was saddled with "stranded costs"—an estimated $1.2 billion of above-market power purchase contracts it has entered into before deregulation.

Example 2

In general, risk gravitates towards the party expected to be able to control it or to know most about its true nature. In the previous example, the risk was transferred from the buyer to the seller. In other situations, the seller absorbs the risk of underperformance. For example, in acquisitions effected via a merger, with the selling shareholders receiving shares of the acquirer, the sellers are usually concerned about the risks outside their control, such as a significant fall in the share price of the acquirer. This can be particularly important when the volatility of the latter is high or there is a long lead-time between the shareholder approval of the merger and its consummation because of lengthy regulatory review. This type of risk can be addressed by making the share exchange ratio variable such that the value of offer is kept constant as the price of the acquirer shares varies. Normally, the ratio is allowed to float inside a collar around the share price of the acquirer, and to assume fixed values at each end of the collar.

In other circumstances, the concern is about the risk of price deterioration after closing because of the acquirer's inability to make the merger work. In order to allay this concern, the acquirer can provide contingent value rights (CVRs) to the selling shareholders effective for a period of time after consummation of the deal. CVRs guarantee the level of the acquirer share price against a limited shortfall. In a sense, these guarantees reassure the seller by making the share offer more like a cash offer. The reader has undoubtedly noticed that these guarantees involve options and should try to conceptualize their corresponding payoffs in terms of puts and calls. A detailed analysis and valuation of actual collars and CVRs using option-pricing techniques is made in Chapter 11.

10.2   RISK SHIFTING[2]

The above examples illustrated the use of risk shifting to solve the valuation problem. In the first example, rather than offering a proportional share of the merged cash flow below the acceptable limit to the seller, the acquirer shifted part of the risk of the target's underperformance to the seller. In the second example, by taking more of the risk perceived by the seller, the buyer was able to make a lower offer and still satisfy the seller. Risk shifting is a common feature of financial contracts. For example, a venture capitalist (VC) buying a stake in a start-up may demand convertible preferred stock or a bond plus warrants. The purpose of such an arrangement would be to allocate all or most of the available cash flows to the VC in downside realizations and limit the entrepreneur's participation to upside realizations.

Consider a start-up requiring $1,000 initial funding. Furthermore, assume that the VC estimates the venture would yield low cash flows with probability $p = 0.75$ and high cash flows with probability $1 - p = 0.25$:

Year	0	1	2	3
Cash flow	(1,000)			
$p = 0.75$		0	0	900
$1 - p = 0.25$		0	0	10,000
Expected cash flow	(1,000)	0	0	3,175

If the VC is going to finance the required $1,000 and expect a 40% IRR, the VC would demand $1,000/[3,175(1.4)^{-3}] = 86.4\%$ of the common equity. This arrangement imposes proportional sharing of the cash flows between the VC and the entrepreneur. Consider now an alternative financing arrangement that results in nonproportional sharing of

---

[2]This and the following section draw on Sahlman's (1988) work on the role of financial contracting in venture capital.

cash flows. Let the VC receive preferred stock with no dividend rights but with a liquidation preference of $1,000 and convertible at any time into common shares at a one-to-one ratio. That is, the VC receives a fixed claim on the cash flow of $1,000 plus a warrant (a call option) on the common equity with a $1,000 exercise price. The first question to consider is what fraction of the common equity would the VC receive upon conversion of the preferred stock in order to expect a 40% IRR from the venture.

The VC's required equity stake results from taking into account that the VC will convert his or her preferred stock into common stock if and when the high cash flows are realized. Hence, the VC needs to be able to convert the preferred stock into a fraction α of common stock such that

$$1,000 = [(900)(0.75) + \alpha(10,000)(0.25)](1.4)^{-3}$$

or $\alpha = 82.8\%$, versus the 86.4% share of the equity required under a simple common stock arrangement.

Note that the expected cash flow of the VC is $2,745 or $2,745/$3,175 = 86.4%, which is the same share yielded by the common stock arrangement. However, using convertible preferred stock differs from the latter in that it reduces the risk of underperformance borne by the VC, helps to screen out entrepreneurs with unrealistic projections, and motivates the entrepreneur who accepts the deal. In fact, the VC may be satisfied with a lower IRR and a smaller than 82.8% share of the expected cash flow under convertible preferred stock financing. In addition, the entrepreneur may hold a more optimistic view of the probability of low and high cash-flow realizations, for example, at $p = 0.25$ and $1 - p = 0.75$, respectively. The entrepreneur would therefore prefer the convertible preferred alternative. In fact, the entrepreneur's expected cash flow under pure common stock financing would be 13.6% of $[(0.25)(900) + (0.75)(10,000)] = $7,725 or $1,051. But under the preferred stock alternative his or her expected cash flow would be 17.2% of $7,500, or $1,290, which is substantially more.

10.3   STAGED FINANCING

We now discuss a rationale for staged financing in deals. In a venture capital transaction, the VC acquires a stake in a start-up in exchange for financing. Normally, financing is made in stages that provide the VC with successive stakes in the company. The key to understanding the VC's reason for staging financing is the concept of *resolution of uncertainty*. More information becomes available with the passage of time and gives the VC the *option to abandon* the project if the new information is not promising.[3] This option is valuable, and we know from option pricing theory that options are more valuable the greater the uncertainty. In fact, the abandonment option increases the net present value of the project. Hence, there is more value to distribute, and the venture capitalist can be satisfied with a smaller share of the equity when he or she has an abandonment option. This means that staged financing is also beneficial to the confident entrepreneur. By raising less financing in the initial stages when the project is less credible, the confident entrepreneur can keep a larger share of the company in later financing rounds when additional information about the value of the project becomes available. Also, having to demonstrate that the project merits additional financing is a powerful motivator for performance.

---

[3]The valuation of exit options was treated in Chapter 8.

EXHIBIT 10.1   *Hotmail Capitalization—Round I, January 1996*

Financing from:	$ Invested	Post-money Valuation	Pre-money Valuation	Acquired Ownership	Pre-Financing Shares Outstanding	New Preferred Shares	Total Outstanding Shares	Price Per Share
VC and other	$315,000	$2,000,000	$1,685,000	15.75%	10,490,272	1,961,089	12,451,361	$0.160625

Example 3

The initial stages in the financing of Hotmail,[4] the pioneer internet email service, illustrate the role of staged financing in resolving the valuation problem. The VC firm Draper Fisher Jurvetson (DFJ) provided 95% of the first-stage financing of Hotmail according to the capitalization table shown in Exhibit 10.1.

That is, the VC acquired 15% of Hotmail for $300,000, which implied a post-money valuation of $300,000/0.15 = $2 million, a share price of 16.0625¢, and a value of the entrepreneurs' stake equal to 10,490,272 shares $\times$ 16.0625¢ = $1.685 million.

DFJ received convertible preferred stock with liquidation preference and the right to convert at any time into common at a one-to-one rate. In addition, the VC obtained the right to purchase all or any of future equity offers on the same terms offered to others, thus receiving the option to make additional investments in the future. Problem 10.5 asks the reader to relate the first-stage valuation to the revenues and number of subscribers required at IPO time to provide the VC's required return.

According to Saber Bathia,[5] Hotmail co-founder, DFJ was willing to provide $1.5 million of second-stage financing at an enterprise valuation of $4.5 million, but he instead took only $750,000 at a $7.1 million valuation. Details are provided in Exhibit 10.2.

Comparing Exhibits 10.1 and 10.2 we see that stage financing increased the valuation of Hotmail from 16¢ to 51¢ a share. Moreover, by agreeing to take half of the funding during the second round, and take the risk of lower valuation in the third round, Bathia doubled the second-stage valuation from 24¢ to 51¢.

At this point, the reader has undoubtedly recognized the similarity between the value of staged financing and the value of real options discussed in Chapter 8. In fact, the example summarized on Figure 8.1 can be used to illustrate how the abandonment option increases the value of a start-up, and the real option valuation models detailed in Chapter 8 are directly applicable to staged-financing valuation.

EXHIBIT 10.2   *Hotmail Capitalization—Round II, August 1999*

	$ Invested	Post-money Valuation	Pre-money Valuation	Acquired Ownership	Pre-Financing Shares Outstanding	New Preferred Shares	Total Outstanding Shares	Price Per Share
Proposed:								
DFJ	$1,500,000	$4,500,000	$3,000,000	33.33%	12,451,361	6,225,681	18,677,042	$0.2409
Final terms:								
DFJ	$750,000	$7,122,168	$6,372,168	10.53%	12,451,361	1,465,517	13,916,878	$0.5118

---

[4]As described in Bronson (1999), Chapter 3, and Mahesh (1999).

[5]Quoted in Mahesh (1999).

10.4   EARNOUT AGREEMENTS

An *earnout agreement* is a financial contract whereby a portion of the purchase price of a company is to be paid in the future contingent on the realization of the target's future earnings. Its purpose is to solve the valuation problem and motivate performance. This type of contract shifts some of the risk of underperformance to the seller and has similar incentive properties to those of venture capital contracts.

Some of the advantages of earnout agreements are that they:

- Close the gap between bid and ask prices.
- Protect the buyer from surprises.
- Screen out sellers who misrepresent the earnings potential of their business.
- Provide incentives to the seller who stays as manager of the business.
- Diminish the buyers' up-front financial commitment.

Designing an earnout agreement to achieve the objectives of both parties is not easy. The following guiding principles should be observed:

- The payment should be a function of easily observable accounting numbers that are not subject to manipulation by either party.
- The agreement should avoid disincentives to long-term value maximization.

For example, the earnout contract may provide that, at the end of the 3rd year, the seller will be paid four times the 3rd-year EBITDA of the acquisition minus $10 million minus receivables older than 1 year if the amount is positive and zero otherwise. Basing the earnout payment on EBITDA assures the manager would attempt to increase revenues with high EBITDA margin and would not delay capital expenditures designed to increase profits beyond the earnout period in order to avoid depreciation charges. Excluding stale receivables discourages the seller from inflating receivables with credit to doubtful accounts. In addition, a holdback from the earnout payment may be retained and paid in 6 months after deducting uncollected credits. Limiting the earnout to a multiple of the excess of EBITDA over a threshold motivates the effort of the manager.

Difficulties in the implementation of earnouts usually arise from: (1) Vague definition of what constitutes earnings and, in particular, what costs should be charged against the earnout earnings. (2) Loose specification or misunderstanding about the accounting system to apply. (3) Problems in integrating the two businesses particularly when the seller's success depends on certain services being performed by the acquirer. (4) Lack of adaptation of the former independent CEO to a relation of dependency. In addition, the seller faces the risk of the buyer being unable to pay the earnout because of financial difficulties in the rest of the company. That is why some deals are structured to give the seller the right to regain control of the business if the acquirer is unable to fulfill its obligations. Given these possible complications, some attorneys advise their clients to avoid earnouts if possible.[6] However, the alternative to including an earnout in the terms of the deal may be no deal at all.

Earnout agreements are particularly useful in acquiring private firms difficult to value, but contingent payments arrangements have also been used in the acquisition of large public firms as well. For example, when GM acquired EDS and Hughes Electronics, it paid the acquisitions with tracking stock, the dividends of which were contingent on the profits of the acquisitions. The class-A shares given by Delmarva to Atlantic Energy

---

[6]See Litwin (1995).

shareholders are an earnout. Bruner (2001b) notes that the fraction of publicly traded deals containing earnouts has increased from 1.3% in 1985 to 3.4% in 1999, and that earnouts accounted from 15% to 88% of the consideration in those deals. Furthermore, Kohers and Ang (2000) found that the bidder's stock price reacted positively to the announcement of merger terms containing earnouts, and that a high percentage of managers stayed in the merged firm beyond the earnout period.

10.5   VALUING EARNOUTS BY STRAIGHT DCF

In valuing an earnout, one should take into account that it is essentially a participation in the cash flows of the company and that, as such, it shares their risk characteristics. In most cases, the purchase price is not wholly accounted by the earnout. The offer may also contain cash and notes. Valuing the purchase offer in such a situation requires accounting for the different risk of its several components. The following example illustrates the valuation procedure.

Example 4

Consider the acquisition of Power Track, a privately owned manufacturer of aerobic and body building machines. At closing on December 31st of 2003, Conrad Owens, its owner, would receive the following consideration from R-II Inc.: (a) A cash payment of $3 million due at closing. (b) An 8% annual coupon 4-year subordinated note issued by R-II, for $5 million with principal payable in four equal annual installments. (c) A contingent payment to take effect at the end of the 4th year equal to one times EBITDA. R-II would assume Power Track's net debt of $6.2 million. Under the terms proposed by R-II, Power Track would become a wholly owned subsidiary of R-II, and Mr. Owens would stay as its manager with a 4-year contract and competitive compensation. At the end of the 4th year, Owens would receive the contingent payment and retire. In addition, the following information is available:

- R-II's outstanding subordinated notes are priced to yield 9%.

- R-II's corporate tax rate is 40%.

- Mr. Owens is confident that under his management and with the support of R-II, Power Track's EBITDA would grow at 20% per year during the following 4 years from its current level of $4 million.

- R-II has determined that Power Track free cash flow should be discounted at a WACC equal to 12% in order to account for its systematic risk and debt capacity.

To estimate the cost of the offer to R-II Inc., we value separately each of its three components: (1) The cash payment, (2) the fixed-income cash flows, and (3) the earnout. Cash, of course, is simply counted. The note should be marked to market by discounting it at 9%, R-II's cost of debt, assuming that it qualifies for original issue discount (OID) amortization for tax purposes.[7] [Otherwise, the *after-tax* cash flows of the note should be discounted at R-II's *after-tax* subordinated borrowing rate, which is equal to $(1 - 40\%)(9\%) = 5.4\%$.] The earnout bears the cash-flow risk of the aerobic equipment business and should be discounted at the appropriate WACC because R-II would

---

[7]OID is the difference between the redemption price and the issue value of the security. Subject to a number of tests, the U.S. Tax Code allows the amortization of OID on a yield to maturity basis to be deducted from taxable income. OID is treated as interest income taxable to the holder of the note. The mechanics is illustrated in Note N10.1 and in Chapter 13, Section 13.9. A buyer with substantial NOLs may not be interested in OID imputation and may structure the transaction to make use of one of the exemptions provided in the tax code. See Ginsburg and Levin (2002).

EXHIBIT 10.3   *Power Track Inc. Valuation of Purchase Offer with Earnout*

($000)

(i) Cash payment   3,000

(ii) Subordinated note

Year		2003	2004	2005	2006	2007	
Balance		5,000	3,750	2,500	1,250	—	
Amortization			1,250	1,250	1,250	1,250	
Interest @	8%		400	300	200	100	
Cash flow			1,650	1,550	1,450	1,350	
Present value @	9%	4,894					4,894

(iii) Earnout

EBITDA (t = 0)			4,000	
EBITDA (t = 4) @	20%		8,294	
Earnout multiple			1x	
Earnout payment			8,294	
Present value @	12%			5,271
Value of R-II's offer for Power Track equity				13,166
Assumed net debt				6,200
Value of R-II's for the enterprise				19,366
EBITDA (t = 0)				4,000
Trailing EBITDA multiple at sale time				4.8x

---

be giving up an amount of cash proportional to EBITDA and the outlay would reduce its debt capacity.[8,9] Thus, each component has to be valued separately as shown in Exhibit 10.3.[10]

That is, R-II is offering $19.4 million for the enterprise or 4.8x trailing EBITDA, of which $13.2 million is the offer for the seller's equity in Power Track. Three observations are in order: The seller's after-tax cash flow can be different from R-II's. He may not be as well diversified as the public shareholders of R-II. In addition, his earnout lacks marketability. On the other hand, the seller may be more optimistic than R-II with respect to the growth potential of Power Track and may value the earnout on the basis of higher projected EBITDA. The relative strength of these factors would determine if the seller's valuation of the offer is lower or higher than the buyer's. Owens's decision to sell would depend on if his own valuation of the deal is higher than the value he can get on his own or by selling to a third party.

10.6   EARNOUTS AS OPTIONS ON FUTURE CASH FLOWS

10.6.1   Earnouts with Thresholds

Some earnouts are payable only above a certain performance threshold. For example, the earnout for Power Track could have provided for a payment of 5.34 times the excess of EBITDA over a $4 million threshold. The proper valuation of such an earnout needs to recognize that its contingent payoff is equal to zero if year-4 EBITDA is below $4 million and equal to 5.34 times ($EBITDA_{t=4}$ – $4 million) if this difference is positive. This is the typical payoff of a European call with payoff payable at expiration. In general, earnouts

---

[8]As seen in Chapter 7, lower EBITDA reduces debt capacity and the tax shield.

[9]Earnout payments are not tax-deductible but capitalized into the tax basis of the acquisition.

[10]Numbers do not add up because of rounding.

are options and should be valued as such. Earnouts with no threshold as the one in the previous example can be interpreted as calls with zero exercise price.

In order to value an earnout based upon EBITDA with threshold we need to model the process generating EBITDA. We do so by allowing for the possibility that EBITDA become negative. As in the cash-flow model introduced in Chapter 8, Section 8.2, let us approximate EBITDA by the following linear function of revenue R:

$$EBITDA = bR + a \qquad (10.1)$$

where b is the EBITDA margin and the constant a can be made negative to represent fixed costs and both can be allowed to change over time. For a simple earnout settled on the basis of EBITDA in the final year of the contract, all that is needed are the values of b and a on that particular year. Note that when a < 0, EBITDA assumes negative values at low level of revenues.

Equation (10.1) implies that the payoff of an earnout with multiple of EBITDA M and threshold H is

$$M \max[bR + a - H, 0] = Mb \max[R - (H - a)/b, 0] \qquad (10.2)$$

Hence, the value of the earnout is equal to Mb calls on revenue with exercise price $X = (H - a)/b$. Note that the exercise price is the revenue level that corresponds to the EBITDA threshold. For example, if the threshold is set at $EBITDA_{t=0}$, then $(H - a)/b = R_{t=0}$ and the value of the earnout settled at time T can be written as

$$Mb \max[R_T - R_0, 0] \qquad (10.3)$$

To calculate the value of the call, project $R_T = R_0(1 + g)^T$ at the growth rate g, present value R_T at w = WACC, estimate the volatility of R_T from the range of its growth rate, and compute the value of the call with the Black-Scholes formula.[11]

Let us illustrate the procedure by valuing the Power Track earnout with a $4 million threshold. Assume that the riskless annual interest rate is $r_f = 5\%$. Let present revenue be $98.68 million, EBITDA margin be 14%, and fixed costs be $9.815 million. Furthermore, let revenue grow at the expected rate of 7.0% per year and the growth rate have a range (−13%, 27%) with 95% confidence so that its volatility can be estimated at one-fourth of this range, or $\sigma = 10\%$.[12]

Exhibit 10.4 shows revenues and EBITDA over the 4 years of the earnout. Note that EBITDA at time 0 and at the end of year 4 are the same as in Exhibit 10.3. In addition, the value of the expected year-4 revenue at the 12% cost of capital of the target is

---

EXHIBIT 10.4   *Power Track Inc. Revenue and EBITDA Projections*

($000)

Year	2003	2004	2005	2006	2007
Revenue	$98,680	$105,588	$112,979	$120,887	$129,349
Revenue growth		7.00%	7.00%	7.00%	7.00%
EBITDA margin	14%	14%	14%	14%	14%
Fixed costs	$9,815	$9,815	$9,815	$9,815	$9,815
EBITDA	$4,000	$4,967	$6,002	$7,109	$8,294

---

[11]See Appendix A on financial options.

[12]See Chapter 8, Section 8.2 on the estimation of volatility.

$129.349/1.12^4 = \$82.204$ million. We now calculate the value of the call on revenue. The needed inputs are:

$$PV(R_4) = \$82.204, \quad X = \$98.68, \quad r_f = 5\%, \quad \sigma = 10\%, \quad t = 4 \text{ years}$$

Substituting these inputs into the call option spreadsheet of the Financial Options Calculator yields Call Value = $7.051 million. Thus, Equation (10.3) gives as the earnout value $(5.34)(0.14)(7.051) = \$5.27$ million. Note that simple DCF valuation yields a value of the earnout equal to $5.34 \times [(0.14)(129.349)/1.12^4 - (9.815 + 4)/1.05^4] = \$0.76$ million. DCF ignores the option value of the earnout, which protects the holder from low EBITDA realizations. Moreover, the earnout is more valuable the higher its volatility.

10.6.2   Earnouts with Thresholds and Caps

It is common for the buyer to cap the value of earnouts. For example, suppose the earnout valued in Section 10.6.1 is capped at $20 million. This makes it equal to a call spread made of the difference between the following two calls: The seller is long a call on EBITDA with $4 million exercise price and short a call on EBITDA with exercise price at $4 + \$20/5.34 = \$7.745$ million.[13] In terms of Equation (10.3), the seller is long $Mb = 5.34 \times 0.14 = 0.748$ calls on revenue with exercise price $X_1 = (4,000 + 9,815)/0.14 = R_0 = \$98.680$ and short 0.748 calls on revenue with exercise price $X_2 = (7.745 + 9.815)/0.14 = \$125.429$ million. Hence, the earnout is valued as follows:

$$\begin{aligned} \text{Earnout Value} = {} & 0.748 \, [\text{call}(PV(\text{Revenue}_4) = \$82.204, X_1 = 98.68, r_f = 5\%, \\ & \sigma = 10\%, t = 4) - \text{call}(PV(\text{Revenue}_4) = \$82.204, X_2 = \$125.429, \\ & r_f = 5\%, \sigma = 10\%, t = 4)]. \end{aligned}$$

The Financial Options Calculator gives $1.182 million as the value of the cap. Thus, the earnout is worth $0.748 \times (7.051 - 1.182) = \$4.39$ million. As with other options, the value of the cap would be higher the higher the volatility. Suppose the purpose is to have the value of the capped earnout equal to $5.27 million as before. Then the earnout multiple has to be increased and the exercise price of the cap recalculated. Setting the earnout multiple at 7.66 times yields an exercise price equal to $(4 + 20/7.66 + 9.815)/0.14 = \$117.328$ million, and a value for the call equal to $2.139 million. Thus, the earnout would be worth $(7.66)(0.14)(7.051 - 2.139) = \$5.27$ million.

*10.6.3   Earnouts Based on Average Performance[14]

Some earnouts depend on the average value of the performance measure over a number of periods. For example, let the earnout of Power Track be based upon 5.34 times the excess of the average EBITDA during 4 years over $4 million and the cap be fixed at $20 million. Averaging diminishes volatility and, therefore, the value of the earnout. Average options are called *Asian Options,* recognizing its initial use to hedge foreign exchange for Asian exporters. The Asian Option module of the Financial Options Calculator yields $2.444 million and $0.076 million, respectively, as the values of the long and short options on revenue. The value of the earnout is then $(5.34)(0.14)(2.444 - 0.076) = \$1.77$ million or $2.62 million less than the capped European-option earnout valued in the previous

---

[13]That is, the cap restricts the earnout payout to $5.34(\text{EBITDA} - 4) \leq 20$ million. This means that the cap on EBITDA is $4 + 20/5.34$.

[14]Sections marked with an asterisk may be skipped on a first reading.

section. Unaware buyers and sellers may believe that averaging increases the value of the earnout by making it "safer." But that intuition is incorrect because it ignores that the option nature of the earnout payoff makes it more valuable the higher its volatility.

10.6.4   Valuing the Seller's Repurchase Option

Suppose that the seller of Power Track can repurchase his company in case the buyer is unable to pay the earnout at maturity, and that the repurchase price is 75% of the total consideration already received from the buyer. In this case, the exercise price would be 75% of the cash received at closing and the undiscounted note service received in years 1 to 3, that is, $0.75 \times (3 + 4.65) = 5.7375$ million.[15] The value of the seller's equity was calculated in Section 10.6.1 as $13.166 million. The volatility of Power Track's equity can be estimated from comparables. Alternatively, one can estimate the volatility of equity from the volatility of EBITDA taking into account the effect of leverage. This procedure yields a volatility of equity equal to 73.5%.[16] With these data we can return to the call module of the Financial Options Calculator and obtain a value of the call equal to $9.88 million. Of course, the repurchase option would be exercisable only in the event of the buyer's default. Suppose the probability of the buyer default is estimated at 5%,[17] then the value of the repurchase option is $(0.05)($9.88) = 0.494 million. In summary, the value of the buyer's offer is the expected value that takes into account its default probability and the seller's repurchase option, or $(0.95)($13.2) + (0.05)($9.88 + $6.94) = 13.4 million, where $6.94 million is the present value of the cash payments to be made by the buyer prior to its default.[18]

10.6.5   Valuing Multiyear Earnouts

Sometimes earnouts are payable every year based upon performance matched against yearly targets. Suppose the earnout of Power Track is based upon the excess of EBITDA over yearly thresholds for the next four years. Exhibit 10.5 shows the thresholds, earnout multiples and call values.

   This earnout is the sum of four calls, each with its own exercise price and present value of revenues. For example, the 1st-year earnout is equal to $2.333 \times 0.14 = 0.327$ times the following European call:

$$\text{call}(PV(\text{Revenue}_{t=1} = \$94.275, X = \$98.679, r_f = 5\%, \sigma = 10\%, t = 1 \text{ year}).$$

---

[15]In practice, the repurchase price may be adjusted by the capital invested in the business by the buyer and other items.

[16]The volatility of EBITDA can be estimated by simulation: drawing normal deviates from the distribution of revenue, computing EBITDA from Equation (10.1) and computing the standard deviation of its growth rate. The simulation estimate of the volatility of Power Track's EBITDA is 50%. [For simulation procedures see Hull (2002), for example.] The volatility of the enterprise value (EV) can be approximated by the volatility of EBITDA. Furthermore, the volatility of EV is equal to $[d^2 \text{var(debt return)} + (1 - d)^2 \text{var(equity return)}]^{1/2}$, where d is the debt ratio and var(.) denotes variance. Since the volatility of debt is usually much smaller than the volatility of equity, we let it equal zero. (This assumption would tend to bias the volatility of equity upwards.) The debt ratio of Power Track was $6.2/(6.2 + 13.2) = 32\%$. Hence, vol (equity) = vol (EV)/(1 – d) = 50%/0.68 = 73.5%.

[17]The probability of default can be gauged from the spread of the company's debt over Treasuries. See Note N10.2.

[18]Cash + PV(Note Payments) = $3 + $3.94 = $6.94 million. Strictly, it would be more appropriate to use the final value of the buyer's offer in valuing the seller's call. This would require iterating the valuation until the input to the option and the final value of the offer coincide but the improvement would be immaterial.

EXHIBIT 10.5   *Power Track Inc. Valuation of Multiyear Earnout*

($000)

Year		2004	2005	2006	2007	2008
Revenue		$98,680	$105,588	$112,979	$120,887	$129,349
Revenue growth			7.00%	7.00%	7.00%	7.00%
EBITDA margin		14%	14%	14%	14%	14%
Fixed costs		$ 9,815	$9,815	$9,815	$9,815	$9,815
EBITDA		$ 4,000	$4,967	$6,002	$7,109	$8,294
Earnout threshold			4,000	5,000	6,000	7,000
Revenue PV @	12%		94,275	90,066	86,045	82,204
Revenue strike price			98,679	105,821	112,964	120,107
Revenue volatility	10%					
Riskless rate	5%					
Call value			3,939	2,834	2,231	1,753
EBITDA earnout multiple			2.333	3.333	4.333	5.333
Mutiple x Margin			0.327	0.467	0.607	0.747
Value of yearly earnout			1,287	1,322	1,353	1,309
Total earnout value		$ 5,271				

The Financial Options Calculator values this call at $3.939 million so that the value of the 1st year earnout is $0.327 \times 3.939 = \$1.283$ million.

*10.7   PERPETUAL EARNOUTS AND CLASS SHARES WITH THRESHOLD

Some earnouts, such as the class A shares received by Atlantic Energy shareholders that were discussed in Section 10.1 and other tracking stocks with threshold, provide yearly payouts for an undefined number of years and require the valuation of an infinite number of calls. Consider, for example, an earnout that pays 55.83% of the excess of Power Track's EBITDA over $9 million for the indefinite future. Furthermore, let us simplify the problem by assuming a constant long-term rate of revenue growth equal to 6%. One approach to valuing this earnout is to treat it as the sum of a large number of European options, each valued as in Exhibit 10.5. Since the value of a European option decreases when the present value of future revenue becomes small, the sum converges to the value of the perpetual earnout.[19] From Equation (10.3), we have that the payoff of the perpetual earnout is

$$\text{Mb} \sum_{t=1,\infty} \max[R_t - (H - a)/b, 0] \tag{10.4}$$

and the inputs for valuing the option on revenue for year t are:

$$PV(R_t) = R_0(1 + g)^t/(1 + w)^t = \$98.68(1.06)^t/(1.12)^t$$

$$X = (H - a)/b = (9.0 + 9.815)/0.14 = \$134.393$$

$$r_f = 5\%, \quad \sigma = 10\%, \quad \text{expiration date} = t$$

---

[19]The value of the yearly earnout tends to zero together with the present value of future revenue. For example, $PV(\text{Revenue}_{t=100}) = \$0.0545$ million, and the value of this earnout is only $4,265.

The value of this option is multiplied by Mb = (0.559)(0.14) to obtain the value of the earnout for year t. The sum of the calls on revenue converges to $67.42 million after t = 100,[20] and the value of the earnout equals (0.5583)(0.14)(67.42) = $5.27 million. Figure 10.1 shows the earnout value as a function of its duration. Another way to value a perpetual earnout is with the entry–exit model of Chapter 8, defining free cash flow as Y_t = $EBITDA_t$ − 9 = 0.14 × $Revenue_t$ − 18.815 and setting both the costs of entry and exit at zero. In terms of this model, the activity is entered whenever Y_t is positive and exited whenever Y_t negative. This accounts for the holder of the earnout capturing Y_t whenever it is positive.

To value the perpetual earnout using the exit–entry model, we enter the following inputs into the Real Options Calculator I:[21] zero entry and exit costs, riskless rate equal to 5% used for discounting the fixed component of the earnout ($18.815 million) that here is the exercise price of the option,[22] long-term rate of revenue growth equal to 6%, and WACC equal to 12%. The Calculator yields a value of $9.352 million or 55.83% × $9.352 = $5.23 million for the perpetual earnout.[23]

It makes sense to index the threshold of a perpetual earnout to inflation in order to keep it in proportion to nominal EBITDA. Otherwise the threshold would become insignificant with the passage of time. Let us reconsider the perpetual earnout of Power Track with threshold indexed to inflation and let expected inflation be 3%. Similarly, let us realistically assume that the fixed cost component in the EBITDA model of Equation (10.1) increases with inflation. Then the exercise price corresponding to year t become

$$X_t = (H_t - a_t)/b = (9.0 + 9.815)(1.03)^t/0.14$$

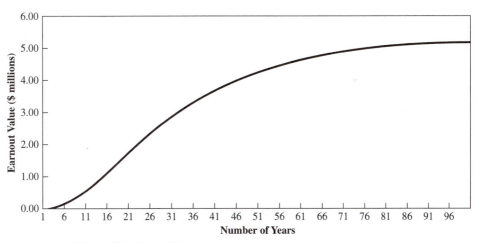

Figure 10.1 Value of Multiyear Earnout

---

[20]The computation can be performed attaching a data table to the call module of the Financial Options Calculator. Problem 11.17 asks the reader to perform this computation.

[21]The Real Options Calculator I transforms annual growth and interest rates into the continuous-time rates required by the model. It yields a slightly lower option value because of a different treatment of volatility. See Appendix A, Section A.2 on volatility assumptions.

[22]This is accomplished by setting $r_d = r_f$ and $\tau = 0$ in the Real Options Calculator I.

[23]See comment at the end of Note N8.7 on the stability of the solution given by the Real Options Calculator I when the entry and exit costs are set to zero.

Substituting this expression in the call option module of the Financial Options Calculator and recomputing the value of the perpetual earnout yields a value of the perpetual calls on revenue of \$2.5115 million and an earnout value of only $Mb(3.204) = (0.5583)$ $(0.14)(3.204) = \$0.250$ million. This is so because an increasing nominal threshold decreases the value of the calls. If the goal is to provide a value of \$5.27 million via the earnout, its multiple should be increased to $M = 5.27/[(0.14)(3.204)] = 11.75$.

Class shares sometimes include a threshold on net income. A typical formulation would establish that these shares pay dividend based upon the performance of a subsidiary to be operated as a semi-independent unit with its own GAAP accounting and independent auditors. The shares are accrued a certain percentage of the excess of the unit net income over a threshold, and the unit is expected to regularly pay a fraction of the excess to the class shareholders.

The valuation of these shares can be made with the following adaptation of the perpetual earnout model. Let depreciation and amortization be projected as a fraction δ of EBITDA, debt be projected as q times EBITDA, and τ denote the corporate tax rate. Using Equation (10.1), we can write net income as function of revenue

$$\text{Net Income} = (1 - \tau)(1 - \delta - r_d\, q)\, \text{EBITDA} \qquad (10.5)$$
$$= (1 - \tau)(1 - \delta - r_d\, q)(b\text{Revenue} + a)$$

Denote the shares' yearly accrual and payout θ and p, respectively, so that class shareholders would receive each year

$$p\theta \max(\text{Net Income} - H, 0)$$

or, substituting Equation (10.5) into this expression

$$p\theta(1 - \tau)(1 - \delta - r_d\, q)b \max[\text{Revenue} + ab^{-1} - H((1 - \tau)(1 - \delta - r_d\, q)b)^{-1}, 0].$$

This rather intimidating expression simply means that the value of each year dividend is equal to

$$p\theta(1 - \tau)(1 - \delta - r_d\, q)b \qquad (10.6)$$

European calls on revenue, each with strike price $X = -ab^{-1} + H((1 - \tau) \times (1 - \delta - r_d q)b)^{-1}$.

Example 5

Let us return to the sale of Power Track and assume that the seller receives Class A shares that give right to 35% of the excess of Power Track net income over \$2.246 million and that the yearly dividend payout is expected to be 75% of that excess. Furthermore, assume that depreciation is 8% of EBITDA and that the debt of Power Track is targeted at 1.55 times EBITDA. The rest of the data are as in Section 10.6. Hence,

$$(1 - \tau)(1 - \delta - r_d\, q) = (1 - 0.40)(1 - 0.08 - (0.09)(1.55)) = 0.468$$

$$p\theta(1 - \tau)(1 - \delta - r_d\, q)b = (0.75)(0.35)(0.468)(0.14) = 0.0172$$

$$X = -ab^{-1} + H((1 - \tau)(1 - \delta - r_d\, q)b)^{-1} = 9.815/0.14 + 2.246/[(0.468)(0.14)]$$
$$= \$104.387 \text{ million}$$

Recall that $R_0 = \$98.68$ million and $\text{EBITDA}_0 = \$4$ million. This means that Net $\text{Income}_0 = (0.468)(4) = \$1.872$ million so that the threshold is set at 20% above current income ($H = 1.872 \times 1.2 = \$2.246$ million). The inputs for the call module of the Financial Options Calculator for each year t are:

$$PV(R_t) = R_0(1 + g)^t/(1 + w)^t = \$98.68(1.06)^t/(1.12)^t$$

$$X = \$104.387, \quad r_f = 5\%, \quad \sigma = 10\%, \quad \text{expiration date} = t$$

Summing the calls with a data table over 150 years yields $160.253 million as the value of the calls on revenue, with 88% of the value attained during the first 50 years. Thus, the value of the class shares is $(0.0172)(160.253) = \$2.756$ million. Alternatively, the valuation can be performed using the Real Options Calculator I with zero costs of entry and exit. The inputs for the latter are:

$$R_0 = \$98.68, \quad b = 0.14, \quad a = (-\$104.387)(0.14), \quad \alpha = 6\%$$
$$r_d = r_f = 5\%, \quad \tau = 0, \quad w = 12\%, \quad \sigma = 10\%$$

Its output is $22.16 million, which multiplied by $(0.35)(0.75)(0.468) = 0.123$ yields $2.726 million as the value of the shares.

When the size of the transaction is large enough, as in the case of the Class A shares issued by Delmarva Power (see Section 10.1), the shares may be listed on an exchange and distributed to the shareholders of the seller. Alternatively, part of the shares may be sold to public shareholders with the proceeds used to pay cash to the shareholders of the seller. The above valuation provides an estimate of the IPO price of these shares.

10.8   SUMMARY

This chapter has examined ways of resolving value disagreement among the parties to a deal. We have seen how contingent contracts permit effecting a transaction in spite of a difference of opinion. Contingent contracts determine the allocation of future cash flows among the parties depending on the realization of mutually agreed and observable performance metrics. We examined the shifting of the risk of underperformance from the buyer to the seller via such instruments as convertible preferred stocks and bonds plus warrants and discussed the use of staged financing in venture capital financing. In both cases, we saw that contingencies provide options to the buyer (the venture capitalist "buys" a fraction of the enterprise) to increase his or her investment or abandon the venture. The abandonment option increases the value of the enterprise and the expected compensation of the seller. These options also accommodate the seller's more optimistic expectation that results in the seller's valuation of the enterprise being higher than that of the buyer. Since an optimistic seller would assign less value to the options given to the buyer, the seller would be more willing to do a deal that provides him or her with a higher equity participation.

We studied in detail the valuation of earnout agreements, which are financial contracts whereby a portion of the purchase price of a company is to be paid in the future contingent on the target's future earnings. In addition to the simple case in which the earnout is proportional to cash flow and can be valued with straight DCF, we valued a number of common earnouts using option pricing. In particular, we valued as call options earnouts that pay only when EBITDA exceeds a given threshold. We also showed how to value earnouts with caps and earnouts based upon average performance. It is common for the seller to keep a repurchase option in case the buyer defaults the earnout payment. This option is a call that can be exercised at the time when the earnout payment is due and depends on the value of the recaptured firm and the exercise price provided in the earnout contract. Since the exercise of this option depends on the buyer defaulting, the call value has to be weighted by the probability of default, which can be gauged from the yield spread of the company's debt over Treasuries.

We studied how to value multiyear earnouts of finite and infinite duration. Perpetual earnouts were valued in two alternative ways: as a convergent sum of a large number of calls and using the valuation model with entry and exit options presented in Chapter 8, which specialized in the case of earnouts to a model without entry and exit costs. Finally, the perpetual earnout model was applied to valuing class shares with a net income threshold.

PROBLEMS

10.1 Consider a start-up requiring $1,000 initial funding. Furthermore, let us assume that the venture capitalist estimates the venture would yield the following cash flows with probability p = 0.5 and 1 – p = 0.5, respectively.

Year	0	1	2	3
Cash flow	(1,000)			
p = 0.5		150	150	1,000
1 – p = 0.5		150	150	5,000
Expected cash flow	(1,000)	150	150	3,000

a. What proportion of the equity would the VC demand in a simple common stock capitalization in order to attain an expected IRR = 40%?

b. Consider now a financing arrangement that results in nonproportional sharing of cash flows. Let the VC receive a convertible preferred stock that pays a 15% dividend, has a $1,000 liquidation preference and is convertible at any time into common stock. What share of the common equity should the preferred stock convert into for the VC to attain a 40% IRR?

c. Assume the terms of the deal as calculated in a or b above but that the entrepreneur assigns probabilities p = 0.25 and 1 – p = 0.75 to the low and high realizations of cash flows, respectively. What are the entrepreneur's expected cash flows for the 3rd year under a common share arrangement and under a preferred stock arrangement?

10.2 (a) Consider a two-year venture requiring $2 million initial investment yielding $5 million (expressed in time-zero present value) with 50% probability or zero with 50% probability. What is its expected net present value of the venture and how much equity would the VC demand? (b) Assume that the initial investment can be reduced to $1 million and that it is possible to wait one year before deciding to invest the remainder ($1 million present value) or abandon the venture, depending on the information available at that time. At the end of the 1st year it will be known if the 2nd-year proceeds are going to have a time-zero present value of either $5 million or zero, each with 50% probability. What is the net present value of the venture under alternative (b). How much equity would the VC demand under each alternative?

10.3 Refer to Section 10.3 and calculate the equity stakes of the entrepreneurs and other employees after the first and the second rounds of financing of Hotmail.

10.4 Assume you are Hotmail's VC pondering whether to invest $300,000 in the first-stage of the venture. At this point in the negotiation, Mr. Bathia is offering 15% of the equity that, after successive rounds of financing, would be diluted to about one-third or 5% by the time the IPO becomes a possibility in 5 years. Furthermore, assume that for this type of transaction, taking into account the risk, lack of marketability of your stake, and the high value that you expect to add to the start-up, you require a 50% IRR on your investment. You estimate the IPO valuation would be made at five times revenue at least, with no debt outstanding. What is the value of the pre-money IPO required to provide your required return? The pre-money IPO is the value of the equity of the company before the IPO proceeds.

10.5 Refer to Problem 10.4 and your answer. In order to check the viability of your investment you want to estimate the number of subscribers required for supporting your valuation. Assume Hotmail will have no debt and will be valued at a revenue multiple equal to 5x. Start with internet advertising prices at $5 per CPM (cost per thousand impressions). You estimate that the average subscriber would check e-mail 200 days a year and would be subject to five ad impressions per visit. How many subscribers are required to support your minimum revenue target?

10.6 You are a venture capitalist considering a $2 million investment in Floating Line Electronics Apparatus, Inc. (FLEA) that is expected to require no additional capital through year 4. FLEA is expected to earn $1.5 million after taxes in year 4. You expect to get your initial investment plus your return at that time by selling your stock. In your opinion, FLEA should at that time be comparable to companies with equity priced at a 13 price-earnings multiple. FLEA has $1 million debt outstanding and plans to pay no dividends in year 1 through 4. There are already 500,000 shares outstanding that are owned by the entrepreneur and other investors. You require a 40% rate of return from this type of investment.

a. What equity participation (percent ownership) would you demand?
b. How many new shares need to be issued?
c. What price would you pay for each share now?
d. What is the implicit post-money valuation of the equity?

10.7 You have invested $1 million for a 25% equity stake in a new venture. Current sales are $8.1 million and EBITDA is 10% of sales. You expect to recover your investment plus return in 4 years via the sale of the company at an expected exit EBITDA multiple of 8x. No further equity issues are contemplated but the company will have $6 million of net debt at exit time. Fees and expenses will amount to 4% of the sale price of the enterprise (net debt plus equity). What growth rate of sales is needed in order to provide you with a 40% return? What return will you attain if sales grow at half the required rate and the exit EBITDA multiple is only 6x?

10.8 As the investment banker of TUV-TUV Systems, you are working on TUV-TUV's purchase of Balkan Audio from the sole owner Mr. Yenidge Sobranie. After several meetings with Mr. Sobranie, you have put together the following preliminary purchase terms: Mr. Sobranie would receive from TUV-TUV

1. A cash payment of $8 million at closing.
2. A 10-year $400,000 annuity.
3. A lump-sum payment at the end of the 3rd year equal to a multiple of third year EBITDA. This multiple is still subject to negotiation.
4. Balkan Audio would become a subsidiary of TUV-TUV with Mr. Sobranie staying as its president with a competitive salary for 3 years, at the end of which he would retire.

In addition, you have the following information:

a. TUV-TUV would assume Balkan's net debt of $15 million.
b. TUV-TUV has expressed willingness to pay for Balkan's equity (items 1 to 3 of the purchase terms) nine times current EBITDA of $4 million minus assumed net debt.
c. TUV-TUV's outstanding debt is priced to yield 9% and its tax rate is 40%.
d. The WACC of companies similar to Balkan is about 13%.
e. Balkan's EBITDA is expected to increase at 20% per year during the following 3 years.

At this point, you are giving the final touches to the earnout agreement (item 3 of the purchase terms). How high a multiple of 3rd-year EBITDA would be acceptable to TUV-TUV?

10.9 VASM is a privately owned manufacturer of light trailers that are sold to rental companies and individuals. Its sole owner, Mr. Benjamin Webster is presently considering a purchase offer from Prentice Works. The offer for the equity of VASM is as follows:

1. A cash payment for $5 million due at closing on March 31st, 2005.
2. A 7.5% annual coupon five-year subordinated note issued by Prentice Works for $7 million with principal payable at maturity. In addition, it was decided to elect not to amortize OID (original issue discount) for tax purposes, as it was permitted in the present case.[24]
3. An earnout agreement stipulating a payment to take effect at the end of the 3rd year equal to one-half times 3rd-year EBITDA.

Prentice Works will assume VASM's present net debt of $14.8 million. Furthermore, VASM would become a wholly owned subsidiary of Prentice, and Mr. Webster would stay as its president with a 3-year contract and competitive compensation, at the end of which he would retire.

---

[24]The U.S. Tax Code permits such an election when the coupon rate exceeds the yield of comparable U.S. Treasury obligations outstanding at the time of the transaction.

The following additional information is available:

Prentice Works' outstanding subordinated notes are priced to yield 9%.

Mr. Webster believed that he could make VASM's revenue grow at 10% per year during the fol lowing 3 years. Current revenue is $50 million. EBITDA = 0.15Revenue – 1.5 million such that current EBITDA is 6 million.

Companies with characteristics similar to VASM have a WACC of about 14%.

Prentice Works' corporate tax rate is 40%.

a. What is the value of the 7.5% $7 million note offered by Prentice Works?
b. What is the value of the earnout agreement?
c. How much is Prentice Works offering for the enterprise (net debt plus equity) of VASM?
d. What is the initial enterprise value EBITDA multiple offered by Prentice?

While Mr. Webster would take into account his salary as president of the subsidiary, as well as the tax consequences of the transaction, you should ignore these matters in answering the above questions.

10.10 Consider the following alternative earnout for VASM's Mr. Webster. The other components of the consideration stay the same. The earnout would pay 3.484 times the excess of 3rd-year EBITDA over $6 million. The riskless 3-year annually compound interest rate is r = 5%. The 95% confidence range of VASM's revenue growth is [–20%, 40%]. (Hint: estimate volatility as one-fourth of this range). What is the value of the earnout?

10.11 (a) What would the value of the earnout of Problem 10.10 be if it were capped at $10 million? (b) Redesign the earnout such that even with the cap it has the same value as in Problem 10.9.

10.12 Let the earnout of VASM be payable at the end of the 3rd year based upon the excess of the average EBITDA during the previous 3 years over $6 million and be capped at $10 million. Value the earnout for an earnout multiple equal to 3.484 and compare your result to that obtained in Problem 10.11. How can you keep the value of the earnout equal to the value calculated in Problem 10.9?

10.13 Assume the terms of the earnout are as specified in Problem 10.9. Suppose that the seller of VASM can repurchase his company in case the buyer is unable to pay the earnout at maturity, and that the repurchase price is 90% of the total cash consideration already received from the buyer. In this case, the exercise price would be 90% of the cash received at closing and the value of the note service received in years 1 to 2, assuming default occurs before the 3rd-year debt service. Also, as the value of the seller's equity, take the sum of the cash component, the present value of the subordinated note, and the value of the earnout calculated in Problem 10.9. Assume the volatility of VASM's equity is 30% and that the probability that the buyer will default is 5%. What is the value of Prentice Works' offer for the equity of VASM?

10.14 Suppose the earnout of VASM is based upon the 2.5 times the excess of EBITDA over a $6 million yearly threshold for the next 3 years payable at the end of every year. In addition, each yearly payment is capped at $2 million. What is the value of the earnout?

10.15 Suppose that Mr. Webster would instead receive a perpetual earnout in the form of Class A shares that would pay dividend based upon the performance of VASM, which would be operated as a semi-independent unit with its own GAAP accounting and independent auditors. Class A shares would receive 30% of the excess of VASM's net income over $3.5 million and are expected to have 75% yearly dividend payout. Last year net income was $2 million. EBITDA is projected to be a function of revenue as per Problem 10.9 with revenue growing at 10% per year and volatility of 15%. Furthermore, depreciation and amortization are projected at 10% of EBITDA and net debt at 3x EBITDA. The cost of debt is 9%, WACC is 14%, the riskless rate is 5% and the corporate tax rate is 40%. One million Class A shares would be issued, 50% of which would be sold to the public immediately with the proceeds after fees and expenses of 6% paid to Mr. Webster. The latter would keep 50% of the shares for 3 years after which he would be able to sell them in the open market. Estimate the IPO price of Class A shares and the value of Mr. Webster earnout. Hint: Use the Real Options Calculator I.

10.16 (a) Open the Financial Options Calculator. Save the copy to use under another name such as "Perpetual." Add a data table to the call option module of this copy and compute the value of the perpetual options of Section 10.6.5 over 150 years. Verify that your result agrees with that given in Section 10.6.5. (b) Use the same call program with the data table you have just computed to value the perpetual earnout of Problem 10.15. Compare it to the result you obtained using the Real Options Calculator I. Hint: Follow Excel's instructions to construct a data table.

10.17 Valuation of holdbacks: Consider now the case where part of the purchase price is held back by the buyer to be paid if and only if certain conditions are met. For example, refer to Problem 10.9 and suppose that instead including $5 million cash in its offer for VASM, Prentice Works offers $3 million cash at closing and puts $2 million in escrow for 1 year (yielding the Treasury Bill rate). This second amount would be paid to the seller in 1 year if and only if the first year EBITDA is equal to or greater than $6.66 million. Otherwise, the seller would forfeit any right to such a payment. Value the holdback in Prentice's offer.

10.18 It took Mike Strong, the new CEO of Colossus, 5 minutes into Martin Gustav's presentation to turn to Bob Marüs, the Vice President of Corporate Development, and say: "We are not a music store. Get rid of it...Nothing personal Martin." Martin Gustav had been working for the good part of the last 2 years in the development of a new internet-cum-video music delivery technology. Now $25 million later, the technology was ready for commercial launch.

Mike Strong had been recruited by Colossus' Board of Directors to restructure the 32-division conglomerate with businesses from fiber optics and industrial turbines to newspapers. Strong's mandate was to look for core competencies and return cash to shareholders in order to avoid a possible takeover. Thus, 1 week after assuming his post, he had axed the NetTune project among others.

This decision did not come as a surprise to Martin Gustav, who had already been planning to acquire the unit for himself and his associates because of what he perceived was a lack of understanding on the part of top management about NetTune. He figured that the VP of Corporate Development, with much bigger units to unload, would jump at a preemptive offer of about $15 million, and expected the transaction to be consummated by December 31st, 2003.

The problem was financing the buyout. Gustav realized that the leveraged financing applicable to traditional rust-belt companies did not apply to NetTune. He knew he could not count on bank debt and that his deal was too small for any kind of high-yield issue, particularly in a weak high-yield market. Also, discussion with All-Mighty Insurance was leading nowhere.

Between him, his NetTune associates, friends, and relatives he hoped to get $2 million cash. This, plus the stock appreciation rights he had in Colossus, plus the severance payments he planned to negotiate for his team, would bring the management's contribution to the acquisition price to only $3 million, of which he would contribute $1.5 million for half the management's stake. Moreover, the $12 million shortfall was just one of Martin's problems. He needed an additional $42 million to develop and operate the e-commerce site through December 31st, 2004 (order handling, billing and tracking, payroll, legal fees, lease charges, capital investments, working capital, advertising, and R&D). He estimated that with $3 million he would have the site operational by March 2004 and funded through June 2004. The final upgrade of the system, additional equipment, and a full-blown advertising campaign would come during the second half of the year and would require $42 – $3 = $39 million.

Rather than an alternative standard to MP3, the technology was completely flexible and could be set to allow a variety of standards, including MP3 and the standard recommended by the industry's Secure Music Initiative. In addition, delivery was compatible with a variety of playback devices available in the marketplace. Gustav expected to capture just a tiny fraction of the $12 billion U.S. music market during 2004 and hoped to position NetTune to benefit from the fast growth of the digital music market that was projected to exceed $1 billion by 2005. Gustav was already holding advanced discussions with three major music companies, as well as with a number of independent producers for distributing pirate-proof versions of their labels.

The court's affirmation of copyrights and injunction of Napster's CD swaps was a timely development for NetTune. Gustav projected that NetTune.com would hit $32.5 million of revenue by Christmas of year 2004 and at least $40 million for the full year April 2003 to March 2004. Allen Venture Partners (AV Partners) had expressed interest in supplying $8 million in total: $5 million for the acquisition and $3 million to launch the e-commerce site. Allen's funding would be structured as a subordinated note for $8 million paying 12% annual interest[25] plus 51% of the equity. The note and interest would be due on June 30, 2004. They further proposed to take the company public at the end of June 2004, assuming initial sales in the second quarter of 2004 (April–June) reached $7 million as projected, which would make credible the sales projection of $40 million for the year. The plan was to raise $80 million in a primary offering of common shares, which, after fees and expenses of 6%, would leave $75.2 million net proceeds. The proceeds would go to retire the outstanding debt, finance the expansion, and fund operating deficits until NetTune became cash positive by the third quarter of 2004. Both AV Partners and an investment banker brought in to discuss the IPO estimated that going public in June could be made at an enterprise value of four times full-year (April '04 to March '05) pro-forma revenues. This valuation was for the enterprise value post-IPO. It already included the net proceeds from the IPO, all of which were to be spent paying back the debt plus interest and making the operation viable. NetTune would be taxed at a 40% corporate profit rate but NOLs were expected to last until 2006.

All the above looked very appealing to the NetTune crowd. But Gustav still needed $15 – $3 – $5 = $7 million. Marüs (Colossus' VP) had indicated Colossus might be willing to provide bridge financing for the $7 million, assuming Allen Venture Partners put up $8 million. The note would be senior, secured by the assets (mainly pending patents) of NetTune, pay 10% annual cash interest,[26] and would come due on June 30, 2004. In addition, Colossus required 10% of the equity. The terms were onerous, but there was not much that Martin Gustav could do if he was going to have a shot at realizing his goal of attaining serious wealth while still young.

a. What percentage of the equity needs to be sold in the IPO?
b. How much can Martin Gustav expect to be worth at the IPO time?
c. What is the expected value of Allen Venture Partners' stake on June 30th, 2004 based upon the expected IPO value of NetTune? What is their expected return multiple (that is, how many times their investment multiplies) from January 1st, 2003 to June 30th, 2004.
d. How much can Gustav expect to pay Colossus in total for NetTune?
e. What is the allocation of the expected IPO proceeds? Allow 6% for fees and expenses.
f. Add the balance of the proceeds from the IPO minus the retirement of the outstanding debt to the cash balance of NetTune as of 6/30/2004 and project the cash balances through 12/31/2005. Assume 1¼% quarterly interest on cash balances.
g. Compute the EBITDA multiple implied by the IPO valuation with respect to 7/1/05 to 6/30/06 pro-forma numbers. Is the P/E multiple with respect to net income during the same period meaningful?

---

[25]The loan contract would specify that interest for a fraction of a year would be based upon compound interest. That is, the interest rate for a fraction f of a year would be computed according to the formula $(1 + \text{annual interest rate})^f - 1$.

[26]See previous footnote.

NetTune.com—Income and cash flow projection, 2004–2006 (millions)

	12/31/03	3/31/04	6/30/04	9/30/04	12/31/04	3/31/05	6/30/05	9/30/05	12/31/05	3/31/06	6/30/06
Revenues		$ 2.50	$ 7.00	$ 14.50	$ 8.50	$ 10.00	$ 18.30	$ 25.60	$ 34.40	$ 18.20	$ 26.20
Expenses		3.20	4.80	18.80	24.00	19.80	20.50	22.00	24.00	21.10	23.10
Operating income		(0.70)	2.20	(4.30)	(15.50)	(9.80)	(2.20)	3.60	10.40	(2.90)	3.10
Interest expense		to be determined									
Interest earned @	1.25%	0.04	0.02								
Net income before taxes		(0.66)	2.22	(4.30)	(15.50)	(9.80)	(2.20)	3.60	10.40	(2.90)	3.10
Non-cash interest		to be determined									
Depreciation			0.10	0.25	0.85	1.25	1.40	1.90	2.10	2.30	2.40
Other noncash				0.04	0.05	0.05	0.10	0.20	0.20	0.20	0.20
Capex and NWC incr.		(1.10)	(3.50)	(9.30)	(11.30)	(6.60)	(5.10)	(3.50)	(2.40)	(4.70)	(6.00)
Net IPO proceeds			to be determined								
Financial transactions			to be determined								
Cash surplus (deficit)	3.0	(1.8)	(1.2)	(13.3)	(25.9)	(15.1)	(5.8)	2.2	10.3	(5.1)	(0.3)
Cash balance	3.0	1.2	0.1	(13.3)	(39.2)	(54.3)	(60.1)	(57.9)	(47.6)	(52.7)	(53.0)

10.19 The core business of TVL Corporation is undergoing a difficult period. TVL bonds have been downgraded to BB rating in order to reflect the higher probability of default the company now faces. TVL is considering a very promising (high NPV, low risk) capital investment project that, if successful, would get it out of its current predicament. Financing the project would require issuing more high-yield debt at a substantial cost. TVL plans to attach a call provision to its bonds.

a. What is the role of the call provision in the specific case of TVL?

b. What determines the value of a call provision? How will the call provision affect the pricing of the issue?

c. Do you expect the call provision to be costly to TVL? Explain.

10.20 Georgetown Group was the 82.76% owner of DesignPlus.com, an internet site-design firm. Management owned 17.24% of the company. DesignPlus was capitalized with 12 million Series A shares, owned by Georgetown, and 2.5 million Series B shares owned by management. Series A shares had voting rights. Series B shares differed from Series A only in that they had no voting rights. DesignPlus had no debt and carried a negligible cash balance. In August 2000, Georgetown received an offer for DesignPlus from Morningside Partners at three times 2000 pro-forma revenues.

DesignPlus' revenues during the last 12 months ending July 31st were $9.5 million, of which $6.8 million were billed in the first 7 months of year 2000. DesignPlus management forecasted revenues for the whole calendar year 2000 at $12 million, of which 75% were already committed in signed contracts. Its clients included three Fortune-500 firms and a number of smaller companies, including two dot.coms with second-stage financing in place, which so far had paid invoices with acceptable delays. Georgetown started to finance the company in 1997 and had so far invested $15 million. The investments took place as follows: $3 million on July 30, 1997, $4 million on February 15, 1998, $4 million on November 20, 1998, and $4 million on October 27, 1999. The company was close to becoming cash-positive and Georgetown did not anticipate putting more money until the closing of the sale, expected to take place on October 15, 2000.

Morningside was building NetServices Inc., an internet service company to be made up of three acquisitions: a systems integration company, an advertising agency, and a front-end internet site-design firm. NetServices had just acquired two business partnerships: STL Consulting and Letts. STL was a system-integration firm with annual billing through July 31st of $20 million. In addition, Morningside had invested $75 million cash in NetServices for about 45% of the equity in common shares. The partners of STL received common shares in NetServices and were to run the company. In addition, NetServices had acquired Letts, an advertising agency, with $15 million of annual billing through July 31st. NetServices paid $15 million cash plus common shares for Letts. The value of the shares given to the partners of STL and Letts was determined on the basis of enterprise valuations at revenues multiples of 3.5x for STL and 2.5x for Letts applied to the last-12-month revenues ended July 31st, 2000. The shares were priced at the same price paid by Morningside for its own stake. A total of 25 million shares of NetServices were issued to Morningside and to the owners of STL and Letts. No debt was assumed by NetServices in these acquisitions.

NetServices proposed to acquire DesignPlus at 3x 2000 pro-forma revenue, and pay $19 million cash plus an equity stake in NetServices for Series A shares. Management would get common shares in NetServices. The new shares to both Georgetown and DesignPlus' management would be priced at the same "ground floor" price paid by Morningside for its NetServices shares.

NetServices' business plan for the joint operation of STL, Letts, and DesignPlus forecasted revenues of $180 million by the end of 2002, at which time an IPO would be feasible. The IPO proceeds would be used to finance international expansion via acquisitions. The IPO would take place at a pre-IPO equity value equal to 4.5 times revenues minus debt. (Pre-IPO equity is the value of the equity priced at the IPO price before adding the IPO proceeds.) End-of-2002 net debt was forecasted at $25 million. The pre-IPO fully diluted number of shares was estimated to be 30 million in order to account for additional stock to be given to employees as per the stock incentive plan of NetServices.

a. Build a capitalization table showing the distribution of the 25 million shares of NetServices among Morningside, STL, and Letts.

b. Build another capitalization table showing the shares issued to Georgetown and DesignPlus management, as well as the percent ownership of all the parties after the acquisition of Design-Plus.

c. What would the IRR of Georgetown's investment in DesignPlus be, assuming the IPO of Net-Services takes place as planned? Georgetown expected to exit 6 months after the IPO. Assume that no appreciation of the shares takes place between the IPO and the exit.

10.21 Refer to the previous question and consider the following alternative capitalization for DesignPlus: DesignPlus was capitalized with 12 million Series A shares, owned by Georgetown, and 2.5 million stock options issued to management giving the right to acquire 2.5 million of Series B shares at a strike price of $1.5 per share. Series A shares had voting rights. Series B shares differed from Series A only in that they had no voting rights. The options vested in 3 years but were fully exercisable in case of sale or change of control of the company. DesignPlus had no debt and carried a negligible cash balance.

In addition, the terms of the NetServices offer are changed as follows: NetServices proposed to acquire DesignPlus at 3x 2000 pro-forma revenue, and pay $19 million cash plus an equity stake in NetServices for Series A shares. Management would get 2.5 million options in NetServices with of the same intrinsic value as their stake in DesignPlus. The new options would vest in 3 years. The new shares and options would be priced at the same price paid by Morningside for its NetServices shares. Intrinsic value was defined as the difference between the share value of NetServices and the strike price of the options.

Recompute the return to the Georgetown Group.

Chapter 11

Special Offer Structures: Price Guarantees and Collars

11.1 SPECIAL OFFER STRUCTURES

The value of the consideration in a share-exchange offer depends on the market perception about the stock price of the acquirer and on the probability attached to the consummation of the merger. Shareholders can diversify away the specific risk of the buyer's stock, but value depends on the expected gains from the merger, which investors estimate on the basis of management declarations, their track record and credibility, and general economic and competitor analyses. In addition, investors have to estimate the probability of the merger going through and the effect on the possible synergies of delays because of regulatory review.

11.1.1 Risk Arbitrage

The uncertainty about the value of the offer attracts the activity of arbitrageurs. These are specialist in gathering and analyzing the information pertaining to the deal and estimating the probability of its consummation. Their goal is to profit from the spread between the offer "see-through" price and the market price of the target. In doing so, they provide liquidity to the market by standing ready to buy the stock of the target from investors unwilling to bear the risk that the merger may not take effect. A typical arbitrage consists in buying the target and shorting the acquirer in proportion to the exchange ratio of the offer. In this way, the arbitrageur hedges the risk of market fluctuations and guarantees the spread under any market condition as long as the deal goes through. In fact, the arbitrageur specializes in estimating the odds that the merger will take effect and is willing to bear that risk and be compensated for it. Arbitrage activity increases the price of the target and brings it closer to its see-through price. As the offer premium is impounded into the price of the target, shareholders become more willing to vote in favor of the merger or to sell the stock to the arbitrageurs, who have an economic interest in seen the merger through.[1] On the other hand, shorting of the acquirer stock by arbitrageurs can depress its price during the tender period and make the exchange offer less attractive.

11.1.2 Guarantees

Price guarantees and collars attached to an exchange offer can counteract the reduction of the see-through price produced by shorting activity. More generally, contingencies are added to the terms of a merger in order to induce agreement between buyer and seller. In

---

[1]See Note N11.1 for a description of merger arbitrage.

Chapter 10, we examined the use of earnouts for resolving disagreement about value between buyer and seller. Here we examine the role of price guarantees and price collars. These are similar to earnouts in that their value depends on the performance of an appropriate metric, which in the present case is commonly chosen to be the stock price. Sometimes the contingencies are added as protection to the buyer rather than to the seller and take the form of escrows and walk-away rights. These are discussed in Section 11.13 below.

A price guarantee provides a minimum price to the seller if the average price of the stock offered in exchange trades below the guarantee during some period following the consummation of the merger. A typical price collar varies the exchange ratio over a certain range of the stock price of the acquirer to provide a variable number of shares with a fixed value. In addition, merger terms may include walkway rights that give the seller (buyer) the option to terminate the merger agreement if the average price of the buyer (target) falls below a certain level.

Since contingent prices complicate the terms of the offer, they are used only in special circumstances such that their absence would most likely preclude the merger or require a too onerous fixed-exchange-ratio offer from the bidder. Fuller (2003) identified 354 (7%) offers with some form of price collar out of a sample of 4,916 mergers that took place between 1992 and 1997.

Both price guarantees and collars are offered by the buyer to the seller in order to insure the value of a stock consideration. Otherwise the resulting uncertainty may keep the price of the target materially below the value of the offer and be insufficient to generate the approval of the merger by the target shareholders. In particular, contingent terms are offered when the expected volatility of the stock consideration is high either because of its own nature or because of external factors that would delay completion of the merger. Also, there are cases in which the seller that is paid with stock is skeptical about the value of the upside that may result under the buyer's management. In deciding whether or not to add a guarantee to the offer, the buyer should compare the cost of the guarantee to the alternative increase in the cash component of the offer or in the premium that may be required by the seller.

Closing the perception gap about the future level of the merged firm's stock price seems to have been the reason for the price guarantee attached by Dow Chemical to the issuance of stock in Marion-Merrell-Dow (MMD) to the public shareholders of Marion Laboratories. The terms of this offer are examined in the following section. Another example is the price collar included in the ADR[2] offer made by Terra Networks for the stock of Lycos in 2000. Long regulatory review imparts volatility to the stock consideration over the time it takes to complete the merger. This is the case of bank mergers. Houston and Ryngaert (1997) report that 86 (41%) merger agreements contained price collars in a sample of 209 bank mergers that took place between 1985 and 1992. Furthermore, since a collar reduces the uncertainty of the value of the offer, it makes it more like a cash offer but preserves capital gain deferral for the seller and, under certain circumstances,[3] may allow the buyer to capture the net operating losses of the target.

11.2   VALUING PRICE GUARANTEES

Let us begin with the case of price guarantees, also called *contingent value rights* (CVRs). CVRs can have a material effect on the total value of the offer. A stock offer with a price guarantee is worth the value of the stock consideration plus a put with strike price at the price

---

[2]ADR are American Depository Receipts that represent shares of foreign companies and trade in U.S. stock exchanges.
[3]See Ginsburg and Levin (2002).

floor. Normally, the guarantee is limited to a certain reduction of the stock price, say to the first 10% fall from a floor. In that case, the value of the offer is equal to the value of the stock plus a put with strike at the floor minus another put with strike at the limit of the protection.

Example 1

Consider Dow Chemical's guarantee to Marion shareholders, which took the form of 92 million CVRs that stipulated that if the average price of MMD during the 90-day period prior to the maturity of the rights on September 18, 1991 was below $45.77 a share, Dow would buy the rights for cash by paying the difference between $45.77 and the average price of MMD's stock up to a maximum of $15.77 per right. Dow's CVR was a put spread. That is, Marion shareholders received at the time of the merger one share of MMD for each Marion share they held plus a put with a $47.77 strike price minus a put with a $30 (= $45.77 – $15.77) strike price. The second put recognizes that the guarantee was limited to a $15.77 price shortfall. In valuing these puts, one has to take into account that they are *Asian* options. These are options with payoff that is a function of the average price of the stock prior to expiration. Ignoring averaging and applying the simple Black-Scholes formula overestimates the volatility and the value of these options.[4]

Figure 11.1 plots the value of each put at expiration of the CVR and the average price of the stock at expiration represented by the 45° line. The investor is long the $45.77 put that is worth max $(45.77 - P_{avg}, 0)$, where P_{avg} is the average price at expiration. In addition, the investor is short a put worth max $(30 - P_{avg}, 0)$. The payoff of CRV at expiration is the difference between the payoffs of these two puts, represented by the grey area.

Let us value Dow's CVRs as of November 14, 1989, just prior to the consummation of the merger and their distribution to shareholders. The following inputs are required for the valuation of the Asian puts: MMD shares traded on a when-issue-basis at $25.175 on November 14; the annual yield of a Treasury note maturing September 1991 was 7.83%; volatility was 27.97%;[5] Marion's

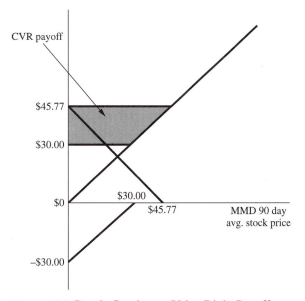

Figure 11.1 Dow's Contingent Value Right Payoff

---

[4]Asian options are discussed in Appendix A and can be valued with the Asian module of the Financial Options Calculator.

[5]Problem 11.1 of Appendix A provides the price data prior to the announcement of the merger for computing the historical volatility of Marion's stock price.

quarterly dividend was $0.09 and was expected stay at that level in the future; and the 90 calendar days prior to September 18 contained 63 trading days over which the average was to be determined in order to establish the value of the guarantee. In addition, one put had exercise price equal to $45.77 and the other put had exercise price equal to $30.

The Asian options module in the Financial Options Calculator yields put values of $15.91 when the exercise price is $45.77 and $4.60 when the exercise price is $30. Thus, the value of the guarantee was $15.91 − $4.60 = $11.31.

Historical volatility may underestimate the price uncertainty that would result during the months that follow the merger. However, because the value of CVR is given by the difference of two options, the error committed in estimating volatility is limited. For example, the reader can verify that increasing volatility to 35% decreases the value of the CVR by only 34¢.[6]

Dow's CVRs had an additional feature. At expiration of the guarantee, that is on September 18, 1991, Dow had the option of extending the guarantee for another year by increasing the floor to $50.23 and limiting the payment to $20.23. It would appear that, as of November 14, 1989, the longer price guarantee would be more valuable to investors. However, that would be so only if the CVR could not expire worthless on 9/18/91. More precisely, at that time Dow would extend the guarantee only if its value was less than the cost of canceling it. In other words, Dow has the option of exchanging an asset (a new CVR) for another (the settlement cost of the first CVR at its expiration). Valuing Dow's exchange option can be done via simulation. The steps are as follows: (1) Simulate the path of the stock price from 11/14/89 to 9/18/91, (2) compute $\min[\max(45.77 - P_{avg}, 0), 15.77]$ as the value of the first option at expiration, where P_{avg} is the simulated average price corresponding to the 63 trading days ending on 9/18/91, and (3) value the second CVR as Put(50.23) − Put(30) at the simulated price on 9/18/91 with expiration on 9/18/92 using the Asian option formula included in the Financial Options Calculator.[7] The value of the exchange option on 9/18/91 is the difference between (2) and (3) or zero, whichever is higher. Repeating these steps for 10,000 simulation trials, averaging the results and discounting the average to 11/14/89 gives only 17¢ as the value of the exchange option. Note N11.2 discuss the technical details of the simulation procedure.

In summary, as of November 14, 1989, the Dow's CVRs were worth about $11.31 − $0.17 = $11.14 per unit and their total value was $11.14 × 92 million = $1,024.9 million.[8] The decision whether or not to extend the guarantee was taken on 11/18/91 based upon the actual price average of the stock prior at that date and the value of the CVR if extended for an additional year. The average stock price during the 90 days prior to September 18, 1991 was $34.583 such that the value of each CRV was $45.77 − $34.583 = $11.187. On September 18, the stock price had fallen to $29.50. For this price, the Asian option formula gives $15.26 as the value of the extended CVR so that it did not pay to extend the guarantee and Dow decided instead to pay $11.187 for each right.

Example 2

A similar price guarantee was included in the terms of General Mills's acquisition of Pillsbury from Diageo plc, approved by the board of directors of both companies on July 16, 2000. The terms of the merger specified that General Mills would issue 141 million shares to Diageo and assume debt for $5.142 billion. In addition, an escrow fund was established by Diageo for $642 million plus interest. The escrow funded a contingent payment from Diageo to General Mills that

---

[6]The CVR decreases with volatility because the sensitivity of an option value to changes in volatility is higher the lower the exercise price and the value of the CVR is the difference between a put with high exercise price and a put with low exercise price.

[7]The put spread was calculated using the same volatility as above and a 7.95% interest rate, which was the forward rate implied by the yields of Treasury notes maturing in mid-September of 1991 and 1992.

[8]At that time, the CVR traded on the American Stock Exchange on a when-issue basis at $8.875. On several occasions Wall Street analysts recommended their purchase based upon the apparent underpricing of these rights.

would depend on the average stock price of General Mills during the 20 trading days preceding the first anniversary of the closing date. Diageo would pay General Mills the difference between the average stock price and $38 per share owned up to a maximum of $4.55 a share for a total of $4.55 × 141 millions shares = $642 million. In all circumstances, General Mills would receive the interest earned on the escrow fund.[9] The contingent payment permitted the parties to resolve the difference of opinion about the value of General Mills' shares.[10] Sometimes referred as a *clawback,* this contingency is equivalent to the CVR issued by Dow Chemical. In fact, the terms of this contingent payment can be restated as follows: Pillsbury received $642 present value (recall that it received the interest earned on the escrow fund), and would pay Diageo the shortfall of its 20-day average price from $42.55 up to a maximum of $4.55 a share. That is, Diageo was long a 1-year Asian put with a $42.55 exercise price and short another 1-year Asian put with a $42.55 − $4.55 = $38 exercise price. In summary, the contingent payment in this transaction was similar to the CVR issued by Dow Chemical and had to be valued in the same way.

The inputs required to value the first put are:

General Mills' stock price on 14/7/2000	$36.3125
Exercise price	$42.55
Time to expiration	1 year
Averaging period	20 days
One-year Treasury bill yield on 14/7/2000	5.78%
Annual dividend	$1.12
Volatility	24.63%

The Financial Options Calculator yields $6.68 as the value of this Asian put. The value of the second put is obtained by changing the exercise price to $38. It yields $3.80. That is, the value of the contingent payment is $6.68 − $3.80 = $2.88 per share or $2.88 × 141 million shares = $406 million in total as the value of price guarantee to Diageo.[11] In payment for the acquisition, General Mills was to issue 141 million common shares to Diageo, assume $5.142 million of debt and receive the escrow proceeds minus the settlement of the price guarantee in one year. In summary, the value of General Mills' offer for Pillsbury as of 14/7/2000 was:

Common stock = $36.3125 × 141 million shares	$ 5.120 billion
Plus: Assumed debt	5.142
Minus: Escrow account	(0.642)
Plus: Contingent value rights	0.406
Value of the offer	$10.026 billion

11.2.1   Commodity Price Guarantees

Sometimes the disagreement about value is based upon a different forecast about an external factor such as commodity prices. For example, in 1991 Apache made an offer for the

---

[9]General Mills, Proxy Statement Pursuant to Section 14 (a) of the Securities Exchange Act of 1934, August 22, 2000.

[10]See Bruner (2001a) for a discussion of this transaction.

[11]General Mills's Proxy Statement included a fairness opinion by Evercore Partners, which valued the guarantee at $396 millions or $2.81 per share as of July 14, 2000.

MW Petroleum subsidiary of Amoco that was below the price demanded by the latter.[12] The difference in valuation of MW Petroleum was caused by a more pessimistic view of the future of oil prices held by Apache. The price gap was closed via a price-support contract that required Amoco to compensate Apache for the shortfall in the average oil price from a specified level for each of the next 2 years following the transaction date. The total compensation was to be based upon preset levels of production and subject to a maximum price shortfall in each year. As with CVRs, these guarantees are Asian put spreads on the price of a barrel of oil. For each year, Apache was long puts with exercise price at the support level and short puts with exercise price at the support level minus the maximum shortfall allowed by the contract. The value of each year's price support scheme to Apache was equal to the preset production level times the put spread for that year.[13]

11.3   VALUING OFFERS WITH PRICE COLLARS

Offers structures with price collars have become common in recent years. Let us examine one in detail.

Example 3

On July 9, 1991, Borland International Inc. announced the acquisition of the Ashton-Tate Corporation in a stock swap. Ashton-Tate shareholders were to receive a fractional share of Borland stock with a market value $17.50 for each of their Ashton-Tate shares, subject to a collar of 0.346 shares and 0.398 shares. This was a 7% collar around Borland's average stock price over the 20 trading days ending on July 2, which was $47.275.[14] That is, Ashton-Tate shareholders would receive $17.50 in stock as long as Borland shares traded between an average of $50.58 and $43.97 during the 20 trading days preceding the consummation of the deal. If the average were higher (lower) than $50.58 ($43.97), Ashton-Tate shareholders would receive 0.346 (0.398) shares of Borland for each of their shares.

In order to interpret the nature of this offer, suppose the switch to a fixed exchange ratio would take place if the price at expiration (not its average) is higher that $50.58 or lower than $43.97. Then the value of this offer would be made up of the present value of $17.50 plus one call giving Ashton-Tate shareholders the right to buy 0.346 Borland shares at $50.58 minus a put giving Borland the right to sell to Ashton-Tate shareholders 0.398 Borland shares at $43.97. The respective payoffs of these options are max $(P_T - 50.58, 0)$ and max $(43.97 - P_T, 0)$, where P_T is the price of Borland at expiration. Figure 11.2 shows the payoff of this simplified collar.

However, the fixed exchange ratios become effective when the average price of Borland's stock during the 20-day averaging period is higher (lower) than $50.58 ($43.97). Moreover, a fixed exchange ratio becomes effective if one of the average period conditions is satisfied no matter what value P_T assumes and so the end-point adjustment to the fixed price is not an option in a strict sense. This means, for example, that if the average price is higher than $50.58 the payoff of the offer is $17.50 + 0.346 (P_T - \$50.58) = 0.346P_T$ even if $P_T < \$50.58$. Still, because of their close relations to actual options we shall refer to the end-point adjustments to the fixed price as a "call" and a "put."

No closed-form solution is available for valuing this type of collar but valuation by simulation on a spreadsheet is straightforward. The procedure is described in Note N11.3. It is based upon the price of Borland's stock ($47.375),[15] the exercise prices stated above, the expected time to

---

[12]This transaction is described in Luerhman (1995).

[13]Problem 11.3 requires the valuation of a commodity price guarantee.

[14]Borland's board approved the offer on July 3. Ashton-Tate's board approved the offer on July 8.

[15]The offer was valued *after* the announcement. Valuing the offer *before* a merger announcement would require estimating the post-announcement price of the acquirer taking into account the premium offered and the value of the synergies.

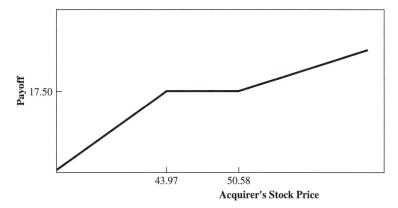

Figure 11.2 Payoff of an Offer with a Simplified Collar

expiration (estimated to be three months),[16] the Treasury bill interest rate (5.78%) and the volatility. The historical volatilities of Borland and Ashton-Tate prices were quite similar: 62% and 59% per year, respectively. We used 60.5%. Simulation yielded the following adjustments to the fixed price: call($50.58) = $4.50 and put($43.97) = $3.48.

In order to compute the value of the offer, one needs to take dilution into account:[17]

	Pre-merger	Post-merger	
		at exchange ratio	
		0.398	0.346
Ashton-Tate shares	24,792	9,867	8,578
Borland shares	16,223	16,223	16,223
Ratio of new to old shares		0.608	0.529

Therefore, the value of the exchange offer was:

$$17.50/1.0578^{92/365} + 0.346 \times 4.50/1.529 - 0.398 \times 3.48/1.608$$
$$= 17.25 + 1.02 - 0.86 = \$17.41,$$

where the long "call" value is multiplied by 16,223/(8,578 + 16,223) = 1/1.529, and so on in order to account for dilution. Note that the collar was worth only about 1.02¢ − 86¢ = 16¢ to Ashton-Tate shareholders.

Ideally, one wants to keep the terms of the offer relatively simple, and that is why it is best to design the collar such that the values of the put and the call offset each other and keep the value of the offer close to the price guaranteed inside the collar.[18] This is in contrast with CVRs that are designed with the explicit purpose of increasing the value of the offer.

---

[16]The settlement of the offer price takes place when the merger is consummated and that depends on satisfying conditions agreed by the parties and receiving appropriate regulatory approval. That is why the options attached to the collar are valued on the basis of the expected time to consummation. Instead, the options can be valued for a number of possible times to consummation, each with their own probability, and the option values so attained weighted by their respective probabilities.

[17]The reason for the dilution adjustment is that Ashton-Tate shareholders shared the cost of their upside (call) and the benefits of their downside (put) as shareholders of the merged firm. For example, if the stock price were greater than $50.58, Ashton-Tate shareholders would own 0.53/1.53 = 35% of the merged firm and "pay" 35% of the cost of the call. For more on dilution adjustments see the discussion of warrant valuation in Appendix A.

[18]While this is usually the case in practice, there are exceptions. Fuller (2003) reports instances in which the value of the options materially changed the price guaranteed within the collar.

Instead of simulation, the following more expedient analytic approximation can be used to value the collar: First, note that European options based upon the price at expiration are worth more than options with exercise based upon a price average because averaging reduces volatility. Second, traditional Asian options with payoff equal to max $(P_{avg} - 50.58)$ and max $(43.97 - P_{avg})$, where P_{avg} is the average price prior to the expiration, are worth less than options with exercise triggered by P_{avg} but with payoff that is a function of P_T. This suggests estimating the value of the end-point adjustments by taking the average of the values of the corresponding European and Asian options. In fact, this approximation gives values that are quite close to the simulation benchmark. For the present collar, the European and Asian options modules of the Financial Options Calculator yield the following values:

	European	Asian	Average
Call ($50.58)	$4.71	$4.26	$4.49
Put ($43.97)	$3.69	$3.34	$3.52

11.4 ADDITIONAL FEATURES IN PRICE COLLARS

11.4.1 Walk-away Rights

These rights give the seller the option to terminate the merger agreement if the average price of the acquirer falls below a specified value. Sometimes, the buyer gets the option to walk away from the merger if the average price of the target falls below a specified value. Walk-away options are sometimes included in offers with a fixed-exchange ratio. They are also attached to price collars with the walk-away prices being the end points of the collar. The seller may exercise the walk-away option if its own stock price is greater than the value of the offer, that is, higher than the applicable exchange ratio times the price of the acquirer's stock. The walk-away option can be interpreted as a seller's option to exchange (to return) the stock of the acquirer for its own stock. However, the averaging feature complicates the valuation of this option because there is no closed-form approximation available, and it requires the use of Monte Carlo simulation.[19] In practice, the specification of the decision rule to exchange one share for another is not precise because it depends on the price of the target as a stand-alone entity at the time of consummation of the merger. The stand-alone price is not observable because investors cannot assume that the walk-away option will be exercised with certainty and it has to be assumed. In fact, in practice most walk-aways are allowed to expire unexercised. It should be noted that walk-aways have a very small value relative to the total value of the offer because of their out-of-the-money nature and their dependence on the average price of the acquirer's stock prior to consummation of the merger.

In some cases, the walk-away is not triggered by the mere decrease in the price of the acquirer. It is also required that the price fall must exceed by some percentage the fall in the price of a specified group of comparable companies. This excludes price drops caused by market or industry factors and limits the walk-away option to changes specific to the acquirer.

What is the rationale for including walk-aways in the terms of a merger? One possible interpretation is that they complement material adverse change (MAC) clauses. For example, an adverse change in either the acquirer or the target may result in a large fall in the price of the acquirer or the target and permit the target or the acquirer to walk away from the merger.

---

[19]A modification of the simulation procedure outlined in Note N11.3 can be used to value this feature.

11.4.2   Top-up Rights

These rights give the buyer the option to avoid the target's walk-away by topping the offer with additional cash or stock consideration up to a specified level. The target may retain the right to walk away if the acquirer price falls below an even lower trigger point.

11.4.3   Fixed Exchange Ratio with Collar

In this offer structure, the exchange ratio is fixed over a range of the acquirer stock price, but the exchange ratio decreases to maintain a fixed value of the consideration if the average price prior to consummation of the merger exceeds the upper end of the range, and the exchange ratio is increased to maintain the value of the offer if the average price falls below the lower end of the range. Essentially, the issuer is short a put and long a call. These collars can be valued via simulation or using the analytic approximation presented in the previous section.

11.4.4   Weighted Average

In some cases, the price average of the collar is computed from a randomly selected lot from a number of consecutive trading days ending before the closing of the merger. In addition, the average is weighted by the daily volume of trading during those says. The purpose of these precautions is to protect the parties from extraneous temporary influences on the price of the acquirer. For valuation purposes, the averaging period is taken to have the length of the random sample.

11.5   SUMMARY

Price guarantees and collars are added to the terms of a merger in order to induce agreement between buyer and seller. A price guarantee (CVR) provides a minimum price to the seller if the average price of the stock offered in exchange trades below the guarantee during some period following the consummation of the merger. A typical price collar varies the exchange ratio over a range of the stock price of the acquirer to provide a variable number of shares with a fixed value. In addition, merger terms may include walkway rights that give the seller (buyer) the option to terminate the merger agreement if the average price of the acquirer (target) falls below a certain level.

CVR and price collars can have a material effect on the value of the offer and are valued using option pricing techniques. The valuation of CVR can be made with available Asian option formulas like the one included in the Financial Options Calculator. In other cases, simulation is required. This chapter has shown when and how to use the appropriate valuation technique.

PROBLEMS

11.1 Compute the volatility of Marion Laboratories' stock as of July 14, 1989, based upon the previous 52-week closing prices and dividend payments given in the following table. This estimate is used in Section 11.2.

Weekly Closing Prices of Marion Laboratories, July 15, 1988 to July 14, 1989

Week	Closing Price	Week	Closing Price	Week	Closing Price	Week	Closing Price
0	19.625	14	18.750	28	23.625	42	25.375
1	18.500	15	20.375	29	24.750	43	26.500
2	19.375	16	20.500	30	22.750	44	27.500
3	20.000	17	19.750	**31	23.500	45	27.375
4	19.000	18	19.375	32	22.750	46	27.250
5	18.750	19	19.500	33	23.375	47	26.500
6	18.750	20	19.625	34	23.375	**48	25.000
7	18.750	21	20.250	35	24.125	49	25.750
8	18.875	**22	19.750	36	24.375	50	23.500
*9	17.750	23	20.125	37	25.125	51	23.875
10	17.000	24	20.125	38	25.875	52	25.250
11	17.000	25	21.500	39	25.875		
12	17.375	26	22.125	40	26.625		
13	17.250	27	22.750	41	25.375		

*Quarterly dividend of $0.07 paid during this week.
**Quarterly dividend of $0.09 paid during this week.

11.2 Compute the volatility General Mill's stock as of July 16, 2000, using the data shown in the following table. This estimate is used in Section 11.3.

Weekly Closing Prices of General Mills, July 12, 1999 to July 10, 2000

Week	Closing Price	Week	Closing Price	Week	Closing Price	Week	Closing Price
0	42.0625	14	42.3750	28	30.2500	42	38.0625
1	42.1250	15	43.5938	29	30.3750	43	38.4375
2	41.4063	16	41.3438	30	30.4375	44	39.8125
3	41.0000	17	40.8750	31	32.0625	45	41.0000
4	41.6563	18	39.1875	32	33.0000	46	39.5625
5	41.5938	19	37.8750	33	32.3750	47	38.9375
6	42.9375	20	37.9375	34	31.3750	48	38.6875
7	42.5625	21	34.8125	35	34.5000	49	37.8750
8	41.6563	22	33.6875	36	34.2500	50	38.2500
9	41.5000	23	33.8750	37	36.1875	**51	38.2175
10	41.0938	24	35.7500	**38	35.6550	52	36.3125
11	40.3750	**25	33.9050	39	36.1875		
*12	42.1188	26	32.6875	40	36.1875		
13	40.1563	27	31.5000	41	36.3750		

*Quarterly dividend of $0.275 paid during this week.
**Quarterly dividend of $0.28 paid during this week.

11.3 Value the following gold price guarantee provided by the seller to the buyer of a gold mine as of August 17, 2001: The contract would pay 5 million times the difference between $265/ounce and the average price of gold over the trading days of the year ending August 16, 2002 if the average is less than $265, and up to a maximum of $75 million. In addition, the buyer would pay the seller 2.5 million times the excess of the average price over $300. Gold closed at $277.45 on August 17, 2001. Its 1-year historical volatility was 10.45%. The 1-year Treasury rate was 3.38% (annually compound) and the present value of the yearly cost of storage was estimated at $2 per ounce. Note that gold is essentially an investment asset with ample inventories and negligible chance of shortages and has no convenience yield (that is, the ownership of the physical commodity provides no benefit). Hint: In order to value the Asian options, treat storage cost as a negative dividend.

11.4 Refer to Section 11.3 and provide two alternative interpretations to the simplified version of Borland's collar offer in terms of European options. Use the put-call parity (see Appendix A) or a graph to show the equivalence of your representation to the one made in Section 11.3.

11.5 Consider the following terms contained in the merger agreement between Qwest Com and US West executed on July 18, 1999: US West shareholders were to receive common stock having a value of $69 so long as Qwest average stock price was between $28.26 and $39.90. Qwest average price was to be computed as the volume weighted average of the trading prices of common stock for the 15 consecutive trading dates randomly selected from the 30 consecutive trading days ending on the third trading day immediately before the date on which the conditions to the closing of the merger were satisfied, which was expected to happen by July 30, 2000. If the average price of Qwest were above $39.90, US West shareholders would receive, for each share of common stock they own, 1.72932 shares of Qwest common stock. If the average price of Qwest were below $28.26, US West shareholders would receive, for each share of common stock they own, 2.44161 shares of Qwest common stock.

Data as of July 16, 1999:

One-year Treasury bill rate = 4.71%
Qwest paid no dividend

	Stock Price	Number of Shares (millions)	Market Cap millions	Market Cap %	Volatility
Qwest	$35.00	747	$26,245	46.16%	60.2%
US West	60.25	508	30,607	53.84	32.5
			56,852	100.00%	

The historical returns of Qwest and US West were not correlated.

Value the collar offer using the Financial Options Calculator.

11.6 Some years ago, the Norton Simon company was created from the merger of Canada Dry, McCall's, and Hunt Foods. Later on, Norton Simon was acquired by Esmark, which in turn was acquired by Beatrice. The latter was eventually acquired by an LBO and broken up. Let us return to Norton Simon and consider the transaction leading to its creation as summarized by Wyser-Pratte (1982) and figure out the arbitrage opportunity. The terms of the three-way merger were as follows: Each shareholder of Canada Dry was to receive 0.6875 common shares of the new Norton Simon company plus 0.3125 shares of a new $1.60 preferred stock, which was immediately convertible into 0.875 of the new common. Canada Dry stock traded at $36. A share of McCall's, which traded at $37, was exchangeable for 0.6875 shares of Norton Simon common plus 0.3125 of the new $1.60 convertible preferred. Finally, each share of Hunt Foods, traded at $58, was exchangeable for 1.25 shares of Norton Simon plus 0.3125 of the $1.60 convertible preferred. Based upon the pricing of other convertible preferred outstanding, the Norton Simon convertible preferred were expected to trade at $40 a share. Note that Norton Simon common and preferred stocks were not trading at the time of the arbitrage decision. Your task is to find a safe way to make money out of this transaction. Specifically, look for a hedged way of acquiring the convertible preferred at a cheap price. How can you do it, and how much money can you make?

Chapter 12

Acquisitions in Developed and Emerging Markets

12.1 THE GLOBAL CAPITAL MARKET

A number of developments in international trade and finance have contributed to the integration of capital markets: Trade barriers have been lowered, capital controls have been removed in developed countries and many developing countries and tax harmonization and treaties have reduced the impact of different tax rates on trade and investment. In addition, floating exchange rates and free convertibility have facilitated the international flow of capital, and transactions costs associated with foreign portfolio investment have fallen as a consequence of advances in information technology and competition. These developments have facilitated global diversification and contributed to a reduction of the cost of capital of corporations. This is so because wider diversification reduces the standard deviation of portfolio returns beyond the level attained in a local market and reduces the risk premium required by investors. On the other hand, globalization makes stock markets around the globe move together and that offsets in part the gains from diversification.

In this chapter, we examine procedures for valuing acquisitions in developed and emerging capital markets.

12.2 TRANSLATING FOREIGN CURRENCY CASH FLOWS

Consider a U.S. company planning an acquisition in Germany. The usual valuation procedure would produce a forecast of the expected free cash flows of the target in euros, as shown in Exhibit 12.1, and translate them into dollars using a forecast of the future euro/dollar spot rates. This can be done by appealing to *interest-rate parity* theory. Interest-rate parity is the relation between forward rates and interest rate differentials between two currencies. For example, investors are able to invest €1 at the rate $r_{€1}$, in order to get $1 + r_{€1}$ in 1 year. Alternatively, they can buy dollars at the spot rate $S_o = \$/€$ and invest S_o dollars at $r_{\$1}$, in order to get $S_o(1 + r_{\$1})$ and, at the same time, buy euros forward at the 1-year forward $\$/€$ rate F_1, to realize $S_o(1 + r_{\$1})/F_1$ euros in 1 year. Hence, ignoring transactions costs, absence of arbitrage profits requires that $1 + r_{€1} = S_o(1 + r_{\$1})/F_1$. Since forward rates are predictors of future spot rates under floating rate regimes,[1] the future spot rate for year t, S_t, can be estimated from F_t. That is, by the expression

$$S_t = S_o(1 + r_{\$t})^t/(1 + r_{€t})^t.$$

---

[1]See, for example, Cornell (1977). The forecasting ability of forward rates has been called into question by the work of Fama (1984), among others. The evidence suggests that forward rates are not consistently unbiased predictors of future spot rate but are subject to small and erratic biases. See also Roll and Yan (2000). These authors argue that forward exchange rates are unbiased although noisy predictors of subsequent spot rates.

EXHIBIT 12.1	*Translating Euro Cash Flows into U.S. Dollars*					
		2004	2005	2006	2007	2008
Euro cash flows (millions)		€ 89.01	€ 93.12	€ 106.34	€ 123.17	€ 180.90
German interest rate		2.21%	2.61%	2.95%	3.30%	3.55%
U.S. interest rate		1.19%	1.72%	2.18%	2.75%	3.40%
Dollar/euro spot rate	1.1780					
Future spot dollar/euro rate		1.1662	1.1577	1.1518	1.1531	1.1695
Dollar cash flows (millions)		$103.81	$107.80	$122.48	$142.03	$211.56

Exhibit 12.1 shows the data and calculations required to translate the euro cash flows into dollars. For example, the forecast of the 2004 \$/€ spot rate S_{2004} = (1.178)(1.0119)/(1.0221) = 1.1662 \$/€.

12.3   THE COST OF CAPITAL IN DEVELOPED CAPITAL MARKETS

Once the cash flows have been expressed in the home currency of the acquirer, the cost of capital for discounting them is required. As in Chapter 3, according to asset pricing theory, the cost of equity of a large capitalization company is made up of the riskless rate plus a risk premium that is a function of the contribution of the asset to the risk of a well-diversified portfolio. In the global capital market, that portfolio is a global portfolio diversified over the investment opportunities available in the international capital market. The Morgan Stanley Capital International (MSCI) World Index is the proxy of the global portfolio adopted by practitioners and researchers.

In a world where investors can diversify globally but are restricted to consume domestically, the CAPM pricing equation applies to the global market when *purchasing power parity* (PPP) holds.[2] PPP states that if international arbitrage is possible, any given currency must have the same purchasing power in every country. These assumptions are obviously extreme and justified only by the need for tractability.[3] Investors' portfolio home bias limits global diversification.[4] On the other hand, restrictions to domestic consumption are only partial because high-net-worth individuals are able to consume a basket of home and foreign goods, including purchases abroad. With these qualifications in mind, let us see how far we can go implementing the global capital asset pricing model (GCAPM). As in Chapter 2, the required return on equity is given by

$$k = r_f + \text{Market Risk Premium} \times \beta \qquad (12.1)$$

where r_f is the local country riskless rate but the market risk premium is the difference between the required return on the global market portfolio and r_f, and β is the beta of the company with respect to the global market portfolio.

Let us examine the risk premium component of Equation (12.1). One expects the global equity premium to be smaller than the domestic equity premium simply because of

---

[2]Stulz (1981) showed that a sufficient condition for the CAPM to hold in an international context is that the world market portfolio and world consumption be perfectly correlated.

[3]Research by Roll (1979), Rogalski and Vinso (1977), and others found no evidence of persistent deviations from PPP. See, however, Engels and Hamilton (1990) and Logue (1995).

[4]See Cooper and Kaplanis (1994, 1995) and Karolyi and Stulz (2001).

the lower standard deviation of the global portfolio.[5] In order to obtain an estimation of the global equity premium, we first note that the beta of the U.S. market with the world market portfolio is close to unity, as one would expect because of the size of the U.S. stock market.[6] Therefore, the price of the U.S. portfolio in the global market has to be subject to the same equity premium as the global market portfolio. However, were one to use a historical premium based upon a long series dominated by pre-globalization returns, one would need to reduce it by at least 20%.[7] For example, Exhibit 3.1 of Chapter 3 shows that the U.S. long-term average equity premium since 1802 through 2002 was 4.4%, or 3.5% after a 20% reduction for the effect of globalization.[8] Instead, in Chapter 3 we recommended the use of prospective equity premium in order to track its temporal evolution. As of the end of August 2003, the prospective premium stood at 4.10%.

Let us now consider the estimation of the global company beta ($\beta_{Company/Global}$). The most reliable way to do so is to regress the company returns, or its comparable company returns when the first are not available, on the MSCI index returns. An alternative estimation can be obtained from the country stock market beta[9] with respect to the MSCI index ($\beta_{Country/Global}$) and the local company beta ($\beta_{Company/Country}$) from the equation

$$\beta_{Company/Global} = \beta_{Company/Country} \times \beta_{Country/Global} \qquad (12.2)$$

This estimation, although convenient when the components are already available, is less desirable than the direct estimation of the global company beta. Equation (12.2) assumes that there are no material covariance (off-diagonal) relationships between the company and the components of the global portfolio, which is not likely to be so for multinational firms residing in small countries because their returns may be more correlated with the global portfolio than with their domestic portfolio.[10] Equation (12.2) is more appropriate for a company operating mostly in its home market. Also, with a few exceptions, Equation (12.2) seems appropriate for U.S. companies.

Equation (12.1) applies to large capitalization companies. The size factor is also present in non-U.S. markets.[11] Thus a small-cap premium has to be added to Equation (12.1) when appropriate. See Chapter 3, Exhibit 3.7 for estimates of size premia using U.S. data.

---

[5]The standard deviation of annual returns was 11% lower for the MSCI index than for the U.S. stock market component of the index during 1970 to 1989. See C. Harvey (1991).

[6]The weight of the U.S. market in the MSCI index is about 30%. Harvey (1991) found that the beta of the New York stock market with the MSCI index was 0.97.

[7]This follows from the equality between the ratio of the U.S. equity premium to the variance of U.S. returns and the ratio of the global equity premium to the variance of the global portfolio returns. For the justification of this relationship see Stulz (1995).

[8]Using a model of time-varying ex-ante risk premium with data from the U.S., U.K., German, French, and Japanese markets, Bansal and Lunblad (2002) find that the global equity premium with respect to the one-month Eurodollar rate was about 2.5% during 1990 to 1998. The authors attribute the decline of the equity premium to the fall of the volatility of the world output growth in recent years.

[9]Country betas are computed in Harvey (1991), Table VI, for developed capital markets, and Lessard (1996), Table 2, for emerging markets but they are likely to increase over time as markets become more integrated.

[10]As in the case of Nestlé. See the estimation of its cost of equity in Stulz (1995).

[11]See, for example, Korajczyk and Viallet (1989) and G. Hawawini and D. Keim (1993, 2000). Dimson et al. (2002) note that the size premium reversed into a discount during the 1990s, but by 2001 the size premium had reestablished itself in the United States and the United Kingdom. Loderer and Roth (2001) estimated the discount for lack of marketability on P/E multiples in the Swiss market to be as high as 40% for small-cap companies. Chen and Xiong (2001) examine the discount of restricted shares in China and find that their price discount can be as high as 85%.

As in Chapter 3, the present method for estimating the cost of equity should be considered only an approximation motivated more by practical need than theoretical rigor. Purchasing power parity does not hold everywhere and, particularly, in the short run. PPP violations may lead investors in different countries to value more those assets that protect their real purchasing power, and thus attach premiums or discounts to the required return on particular assets. Those premiums or discounts have been shown to be a function of the covariances of the rates of return on the assets with exchange rates.[12] In fact, recent research suggests that currency risk is a factor priced by the market.[13] However, the currency risk premium seems to be a small fraction of the total premium, with most of the latter accounted by the equity premium and, as one would expect, the U.S. risk premium is almost totally made up by the equity premium.[14] For other countries, the currency risk premium seems to vary in magnitude and sign.

A final observation: Expressing the cost of equity in a currency other than dollars such as euros, may require more than simply changing the riskless rate to the euro benchmark when the company returns are correlated with the exchange rate.[15] However, the no-arbitrage pricing condition tells us that instead of discounting the euro cash flows at a euro rate, one can simply do the valuation in dollars and convert it at the euro/dollar spot rate. Although the choice of the reference currency for GCAPM pricing is somewhat arbitrary, expressing Equation (12.1) in dollars terms seems justified by the central role played by the U.S. capital market.

Example 1

Refer to Exhibit 12.1 and let the cost of capital to the U.S. acquirer be 9%. Then the value of the target's free cash flows is obtained discounting the cash flows translated into dollars at 9%. This yields $518.7 million. Note that this value does not depend on the home country of the acquirer. In fact, a German acquirer capable of realizing the same expected euro cash flows would also value them at $518.7 million or at $518.7 \div 1.178$ \$/€ = €440.3 million.

12.4   VALUING EMERGING-MARKET COMPANIES

In valuing an emerging-market company, the analyst usually faces additional uncertainty of a political and/or economic nature. In particular, inflation may be high and volatile, large devaluation of the currency can affect earnings and cash flows, and sovereign debt default may impede capital flows, repatriation of profits and access to foreign capital markets. In addition, industry and company data is scarce and less reliable.[16] All these factors would seem to impede credible valuations. However, it is shown in this chapter that valuation of emerging market companies differs only in degree from that of companies in developed capital markets. We present a straightforward extension of the valuation approach introduced in Chapter 2 and show how to apply it to value emerging-market companies. Let us consider the following example.

---

[12]See Solnik (1974) and Adler and Dumas (1983).

[13]Dumas and Solnik (1995) and De Santis and Gérard (1998). See also Schramm and Wang (1999) for an attempt to estimate the effect of currency risk on the cost of capital of specific companies.

[14]Similar results are reported by Koedijk, Cool, Schotman, and Van Dij (2001) using a sample of returns from several countries.

[15]This was pointed out by Ross and Walsh (1983) and further elaborated by O'Brien (1999).

[16]Pereiro (2002) surveys sources of valuation data for emerging markets and Latin America in particular.

Example 2

At the end of 1996, a manufacturer of automotive parts for original equipment manufacturers (to be called here AixCorp) was considering the acquisition of APSSA Ltd, a South African company in the same line of business. The product line of APSSA included seat fabrics, floor carpets, mats and other accessories. Preliminary estimates of the operating results of APSSA expressed in current rands were as detailed in Exhibit 12.2. Although the valuation of previous acquisitions in the United States and the Europe had not presented difficulties to AixCorp, the circumstances of the South African economy required special consideration. In particular, South Africa's persistent inflation was at about 8% per year, the rand was expected to continue to lose value with respect to the dollar, and there was uncertainty related to the future performance of the economy.

In order to determine the price to offer for APSSA, the acquirer was interested in estimating two values: (1) The value of the target to its own shareholders, and (2) the value of the target to the seller's shareholders. The offer price should dominate (2) but should not exceed and hopefully be significantly below (1). In the following sections, we establish these values and explain why they are likely to differ from each other.

12.4.1 Translating Free Cash Flows to the Acquirer's Currency

As in Chapter 2, we proceed by computing the unlevered free cash flows during the explicit forecast period. Here, the original cash flows are expressed in rands and have to be translated to U.S. dollars, the home currency of AixCorp. This is done in Exhibit 12.3. In order to translate the rand free cash flows into U.S. dollars, it is necessary to forecast the rand/$ spot exchange rates that are expected to prevail in future years. In Section 12.2, we showed how this could be done using interest rate parity. Here we shall follow an alternative approach based upon purchasing power parity that can be used when there is not enough information about interest rates for all the cash flow dates. The computation in Exhibit 12.3 assumes that the rand will devaluate with respect to the U.S. dollar according to purchasing power parity (PPP). That is, at the rate (1 + expected rand inflation)/(1 + expected dollar inflation) − 1. Although this relationship does not hold exactly, it

---

EXHIBIT 12.2 *APSSA Limited Income and Cash Flow Projections 1997–2001*

(Rand thousands)

		1997	1998	1999	2000	2001
Revenues		128,800	161,014	195,372	225,936	275,725
Cost of goods sold less depreciation		57,960	71,651	85,963	98,282	118,562
Sales, general and administrative expenses		17,388	22,558	28,654	34,972	44,622
EBITDA		53,452	66,805	80,754	92,682	112,541
Depreciation		6,440	6,820	7,915	8,222	8,450
Operating income		47,012	59,985	72,839	84,460	104,091
Net interest expense		2,673	3,340	4,038	4,634	5,627
Income before taxes		44,339	56,645	68,801	79,826	98,464
Provision for taxes @	40.0%	17,736	22,658	27,520	31,930	39,386
Net Income		26,604	33,987	41,281	47,895	59,079
Plus depreciation		6,440	6,820	7,915	8,222	8,450
Cash flow from operations		33,044	40,807	49,196	56,117	67,529
Net working capital increases		8,711	7,534	6,998	6,950	7,154
Capital expenditures		9,890	10,346	9,457	10,588	10,950
Net cash flow		14,443	22,927	32,741	38,579	49,425

EXHIBIT 12.3   *APSSA Limited Free Cash Flow and Exchange Rate Projection 1997–2001*

(Thousands)

		1997	1998	1999	2000	2001
Net income in rands		26,604	33,987	41,281	47,895	59,079
Net interest expense after taxes		1,604	2,004	2,423	2,780	3,376
NOPAT		28,207	35,991	43,703	50,676	62,455
Plus depreciation		6,440	6,820	7,915	8,222	8,450
Minus net working capital increases		8,711	7,534	6,998	6,950	7,154
Minus capital expenditures		9,890	10,346	9,457	10,588	10,950
Free cash flow in rands		16,046	24,931	35,163	41,360	52,801
Rand expected inflation rate	8.0%					
U.S. expected inflation rate	3.0%					
Rand/$ exchange rate		4.77	5.00	5.25	5.50	5.77
Free cash flow in U.S. dollars		3,363	4,984	6,704	7,520	9,156

describes a general tendency of exchange rates, and deviations from it by weaker currencies are less likely to be persistent than deviations among strong currencies. In fact, the rand/dollar exchange rate has moved along a trend related to the differential in rand/dollar inflation ratios. This is shown in Figure 12.1, which compares the rand exchange rate to the relative rand/dollar producer prices.

A natural question to consider at this point is how temporary departures from PPP in the rand affect present values in dollars. The following example shows such departures have a minor impact on present values.

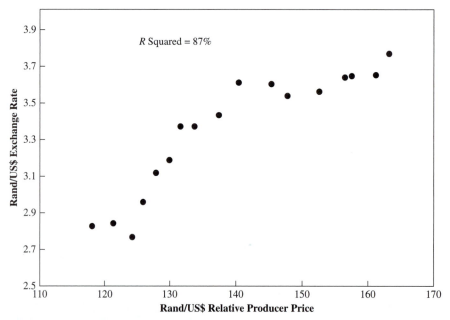

Figure 12.1 Rand Exchange Rate vs. Producer Prices, 1992 I–1996 I

Exhibit 3

Exhibit 12.4 presents two alternative scenarios. In Scenario 1, the rand devaluates by the relative differential in inflation rates. It approximates a floating rate regime fulfilling PPP. In Scenario 2, the rand rate is kept fixed for 2 years followed by an overshooting devaluation, with average over/undervaluation averaging zero over 5 years.

The present value of free cash flows is higher in Scenario 2 because the fixed exchange rate makes the initial dollar cash flows higher, but only by 0.5%. This example illustrates the typical effect of devaluation. It is usually triggered by an exchange rate that is out of phase with domestic prices. Domestic prices escalate while the exchange rate is kept fixed and results in higher dollar cash flows. This eventually leads to a forced devaluation that usually overshoots—sometimes by design as policy makers anticipate further price increases following the devaluation and attempt to gain a temporary competitive advantage in exports.

Analysts should not fall into the trap of extrapolating profits and cash flows from a period of overvaluation of the domestic currency because its exchange rate would not be sustainable. Some practitioners attach a "devaluation risk" premium to the cost of capital or reduce valuation multiples. However, there is no substitute for understanding the macroeconomic process driving free dollar cash flows over the exchange rate cycle. For that reason, a simple yet sensible approximation is to translate free cash flows into dollars by assuming the exchange rate adjusts to inflation according to PPP, as the process eventually returns to the rate that prevails in such a regime. That is not to say that opportunistic timing of temporary over or undervaluation of the exchange rates cannot be highly profitable in the short run. Experienced local and global companies have refined the art of timing remittances and of domestic vs. hard currency borrowing in order to minimize the effect of, or to profit from exchange rate fluctuations in weak currency countries.

EXHIBIT 12.4   *Exchange Rate Fluctuations and Present Values*

Scenario 1: Rand rate devaluates by the relative differential in inflation rates

		1997	1998	1999	2000	2001
FCF in 1997 rand (real) @ growth	5%	100.0	105.0	110.3	115.8	121.6
Rand inflation		8%	8%	8%	8%	8%
FCF in current rand (nominal)		108.0	122.5	138.9	157.5	178.6
Exchange rate rand/US$	4.5	4.7	4.9	5.2	5.4	5.7
US$ inflation	3%					
FCF in nominal US$		22.9	24.8	26.8	29.0	31.3
PV{US$ FCF} @ 16%	$86					

Scenario 2: Rand rate is kept fixed for two years and then devaluation overshoots

		1997	1998	1999	2000	2001
FCF in 1997 rand (real) @ growth	5%	100.0	105.0	110.3	115.8	121.6
Rand inflation		8%	15%	30%	18%	8%
FCF in current rand (nominal)		108.0	130.4	178.0	220.6	250.1
Exchange rate rand/US$	4.5	4.5	4.5	8.0	8.0	8.0
PPP exchange rate		4.7	5.3	6.6	7.6	8.0
Rand over (under) valuation	Avg = 0%	5%	17%	–17%	–5%	0%
FCF in nominal US$		24.0	29.0	22.3	27.6	31.3
PV{US$ FCF} @ 16%	$87					

In the example of Exhibit 12.4, it was assumed that the inflation effect is uniform over all the line items making up the cash flow. In practice, not all items adjust *pari passu* with inflation (the depreciation tax shield being one such an example). Also, the impact of the economic cycle was ignored. In practice, monetary instability is associated with fluctuations in real GDP and business profits and that should be taken into account when projecting expected cash flows.

From the above discussion one should not conclude that exchange rate fluctuations should be disregarded. There are cases in which such fluctuations can have an effect on value if the volatility they induce on cash flows can result in reduced financial flexibility or financial distress leading to loss of business and competitive advantage. In such cases, the firm should implement a hedging program and incorporate its cost to the cash flow projection.[17]

12.4.2   Value to the Acquirer

AixCorp's WACC was 9.6% and was trading at nine times forward EBITDA.[18] Furthermore, Aix's planned to finance its acquisition in the U.S. capital market, limiting more expensive borrowing in South Africa to financing temporary cash needs while maintaining cash balances at a minimum. As the reader must have already concluded, Aix's WACC and EBITDA multiple cannot be used to value APSSA. One needs to account for the global systematic risk of the target, the *country risk premium* demanded by investors for investing in South Africa and the target debt capacity. Aix felt that the APSSA could be financed with 40% debt, which would maintain its aggregate target debt ratio at that level. The beta of the South African stock market with respect to MSCI index was estimated in 0.74 at the time of the valuation. Although betas of local comparables were not available for APSSA, the seller, who also had a market debt ratio of about 40%, traded on the Johannesburg stock exchange and had a local beta equal to 1.55. This value was not entirely satisfactory because the seller was not a pure-play auto-parts supplier. An alternative was to use Aix's beta, which was a pure-play auto-parts supplier. That would be appropriate if the returns of auto-parts manufacturing had the same correlation with the local market index in South Africa and the United States. Substituting these estimates into Equation (12.2) one obtains a global beta for APPSA in the range $0.74 \times 1.55 = 1.147$ to $0.74 \times 1.19 = 0.881$. The midpoint is 1.014, which is lower than Aix's own beta and accounts for the diversification gain from foreign investment. Hence, the WACC for valuing APSSA, before allowing for the country risk premium, was

$$(0.60)(5.79\% + 3.2\% \times 1.014 + 2.7\%) + (0.40)(1 - 40\%)(9.2\%) = 9.25\%,$$

where 5.59% was the U.S. Treasury rate, 3.2% the prospective equity premium, 2.7% an estimate of the small-cap size premium at that time and 9.2% the cost of debt.

Next, we need to estimate the country risk premium. This premium can be gauged from the yield spread of the South African sovereign bonds over the same duration U.S. Treasury bonds. The longest maturity South African sovereign bond outstanding at the

---

[17]It has been pointed out that, in practice, the success of hedging programs in reducing cash-flow volatility has been mixed at best because of the large number of factors that affect it in addition to the exchange rate. See Copeland and Joshi (1996).

[18]Verify AixCorp's WACC using the following data: equity premium = 3.2%, beta coefficient = 1.19, long-term Treasury yield = 5.79%, small-cap size premium = 2.7%, cost of debt = 9.2%, tax rate = 40% and debt ratio = 40%.

end of 1996 was the $300 million, $8^3/_8$% 10-year non-callable bond maturing on 10/17/06, rated Baa2/BB+, which traded on 11/29/96 at 212 basis points spread over U.S. Treasuries. 2.12% is an estimate of the country risk premium, which is the additional return that investors demand for holding South African sovereign debt rather than U.S. Treasury bonds. Hence, adding the country risk premium to the previous estimate yields 9.25% + 2.12% = 11.37%.[19] This is Aix shareholders' required return on investment in South Africa. It accounts for: (1) the non-diversifiable business risk of the auto-parts business; (2) the benefits of debt financing and the offsetting effect of debt via magnification of business risk; (3) the small-cap nature of Aix, which requires it to offer an additional return to investors because of its reduced liquidity; and (4) the additional risk of investing in South Africa.

Exhibit 12.5 discounts the dollar cash flow obtained in Exhibit 12.4 at the cost of capital of 11.37%. Continuation value is computed assuming a real growth rate of 2% based upon estimates of the growth of the auto-parts business in South Africa, or $(1.02)(1.03) - 1 = 5.06$% dollar growth after allowing for dollar inflation. Thus, continuation value is estimated at $(9.156)(1.0506)/(11.37\% - 5.06\%) = \$152.478$ million.[20] Finally, Exhibit 12.5 calculates the forward EBITDA multiples dividing enterprise value at the end of 1996 and 2001 by EBITDA in 1997 and 2002 projected to growth at 5%, respectively. EBITDA numbers are from Exhibit 12.2. Since APSSA did not have local comparables, one can compare the implied multiples to Aix's own multiple of 9x. The higher initial multiple of APSSA seems justified by the significant growth expected during the forecast period. However, since most U.S. auto-parts manufacturers had single-digit EBITDA multiples at that time, one may ask if APSSA's multiple should not be lower in order to account for country risk. We should note, however, that the implied multiples already account for country risk. As discussed in Chapter 4, valuation multiples are both a function of the cost of capital with its allowance for risk and of growth. A multiple reduction for country risk may be more than offset by the higher growth opportunity offered by the emerging market.

EXHIBIT 12.5 *Enterprise Value of APSSA Limited*

($ 000)

		1997	1998	1999	2000	2001
Free cash flow		3,363	4,984	6,704	7,520	9,156
Continuation value with growth @	5.06%					152,478
Present value of free cash flows @	11.37%	22,124				
PV of continuation value @	11.37%	89,001				
Enterprise value		111,126				
EBITDA		11,204				19,515
Implied forward EBITDA multiple		9.9				7.4

---

[19]Note that the country risk premium was added to WACC in the present case. This is so because both equity and debt rates corresponded to the U.S. capital market. If the debt rate were the cost of borrowing in South Africa, it would have already included the country risk premium and the adjustment for country risk would apply only to the U.S.-based cost of equity component of WACC.

[20]Numbers do not add up because of rounding.

12.4.3   Nominal and Real Cash Flows and the Cost of Capital

In the previous section, APSSA Ltd. was valued translating its free cash flows into dollars and discounting them at the applicable cost of capital expressed in dollars. Alternatively, the original free cash flows in rands calculated in Exhibit 12.3 can be valued at the cost of capital expressed in rands. In order to attain the cost of capital applicable to rand cash flows, one needs to allow for the difference in expected inflation rates in the rand and the dollar. This is done according to the formula[21]:

$$\text{Rand WACC} = (1 + \text{Dollar WACC})(1 + \text{Rand Inflation})/(1 + \text{Dollar Inflation}) - 1$$
$$= (1.1137)(1.08)/(1.03) - 1 = 16.77\%$$

Continuation value is also computed allowing for the expected growth of future cash flows in rands, that is, at a rate equal to $(1 + \text{real growth})(1 + \text{rand inflation}) - 1$, which in the present case equals 10.16%. Exhibit 12.6 summarizes the cost of capital and rate of growth in nominal rands, nominal dollars and real terms. *Nominal* rates include inflation while *real* rates do not.

The first panel of Exhibit 12.7 shows the valuation of nominal rand cash flows. The second panel shows the valuation of real rand cash flows. The nominal cash flow in year t is corrected for inflation by dividing it by $(1.08)^t$, and is brought to present value at the real cost of capital, which is equal to 8.12%. Both procedures yield an enterprise value of 506 million rands, which converted to U.S. dollars at the spot exchange rate of 4.55 rand per dollar yields $111 million as in Exhibit 12.5.

12.4.4   Value to the Seller

The value of the target can be higher to the buyer than to the seller if the buyer has superior technology or distribution channels that allow it to attain higher growth and/or lower costs and so attain higher free cash flows. This can happen even within a developed capital market. In addition, a multinational firm may be able to minimize corporate taxes by the use of transfer prices and cost allocations as allowed in the different tax jurisdictions.

Barring product market imperfections, the value of an emerging market target in a perfect, fully integrated global capital market should be the same for the buyer and the seller. However, market imperfections may result in different valuations with the differ-

---

EXHIBIT 12.6	*APSSA Ltd. Nominal and Real Cost of Capital and Growth Rates*
Expected dollar inflation	3.0%
Expected rand inflation	8.0%
Cost of capital in U.S. dollars	11.37%
Cost of capital in nominal rands	16.77%
Real cost of capital	8.12%
Continuation value growth in dollars	5.06%
Continuation value growth in rands	10.16%
Real continuation value growth	2.0%

---

[21]This relation is a consequence of the Fisher (1930) effect that says that anticipated inflation is built into the required nominal rate by the relation $(1 + \text{real rate})(1 + \text{inflation rate}) = 1 + \text{nominal rate}$.

EXHIBIT 12.7	*Discounting Nominal and Real Rand Cash Flows*

(Thousands)

		1997	1998	1999	2000	2001
Discounting nominal rand cash flows						
Rand unlevered nominal free cash flows		16,046	24,931	35,163	41,360	52,801
Continuation value with growth @	10.16%					879,331
PV of free cash flows @	16.77%	100,665				
PV of continuation value @	16.77%	404,956				
Enterprise value in rands		505,621				

		1997	1998	1999	2000	2001
Discounting real rand cash flows						
Expected rand inflation rate	8.0%					
Rand unlevered real free cash flows		14,858	21,374	27,914	30,401	35,935
Continuation value with growth @	2.0%					598,458
PV of free cash flows @	8.12%	100,665				
PV of continuation value @	8.12%	404,956				
Enterprise value in rands		505,612				
Rand/dollar exchange rate	4.55					
Enterprise value in U.S. dollars		111,126				

ence depending on the opportunities available to investors and companies in the seller and buyer capital markets. Even if the seller trades in the local equity market, its cost of capital can be higher if it cannot access the global market either because of a self-imposed limitation or because of lack of reputation among foreign investors. Being restricted to the local market should not be a serious problem if local investors are globally diversified. However, if they are unwilling or unable to diversify internationally, they have to bear more risk and require additional compensation for it, such that the seller ends up with a higher cost of capital than a buyer from a developed capital market. In a completely segmented market, the cost of capital applicable to dollar cash flows should have a premium based upon the local equity premium times the local beta coefficient. However, it is difficult to gauge the prospective domestic equity premium from historical emerging market data,[22] and the method for estimating the prospective equity premium presented in Chapter 3 requires reliable consensus forecasts of earnings growth, which are not generally available for emerging markets.

Looking at the transaction from the point of view of the seller, the buyers' reservation price represents the price goal to be attained. For that, the seller should attempt to conduct an auction among several buyers each able to realize synergies and finance in the global market. Short of selling the company, the seller should carefully consider what it takes to tap the global capital market and reduce its own cost of capital.

Another case in which the value to the seller may be lower than to the buyer is when the seller is a privately held company not able to access the public market because of size or lack of reputation. Private equity values are normally subject to a further discount for lack of marketability.[23] On the other hand, a publicly traded acquirer can impart instant

---

[22]Dimson et al. (2002) estimate the historical equity premium of the South African market at about 6%.

[23]Private equity discounts are discussed in Chapter 13.

liquidity to an acquisition because its shareholders are able to trade in the public market the additional expected free cash flows from the purchase.

12.5 ON THE NATURE OF THE COUNTRY RISK PREMIUM

The sovereign bond spread accounts for the lower *expected* cash flows associated with the *promised* cash flows of a bond subject to default. That is, in the absence of default, bond-holders would receive the promised coupons and principal, but in the event of default they are likely to receive less. Thus, the expected cash flows of bonds subject to default are less than their promised cash flows. The yield to maturity based on of their promised cash flows is therefore higher than the yield corresponding to U.S. Treasury bonds in which expected cash flows equal promised cash flows. In this sense, the sovereign spread is a cash-flow correction, a correction made to the promised cash flows via the discount rate. Hence, when we increase the cost of capital by the sovereign bond spread, we are actually making a correction to the free cash flows to obtain a better estimate of expected cash flows. This seems reasonable because the forecast of cash flows of an emerging-market company is made conditional on the assumption that sovereign default does not occur.

It is uncommon for analysts to forecast cash flows for scenarios of no default and default and to weigh them by their respective probabilities, mainly because it is difficult if not impossible to estimate the latter.[24] The yield spread, on the other hand, is the capital market synthesis of both the probability that the country defaults or runs into financial distress such that the cash flow from the bond is reduced, and of the magnitude of such a reduction. Since it measures the return investors require in order to bear the probability and consequences of financial distress, it is a good proxy for the country risk premium that applies to emerging market companies. This assumes that firms are affected by sovereign financial distress. That is, that when the capital market is closed to the sovereign it is also closed to private companies. When companies are unable to refinance hard-currency borrowings they may default and end up producing reduced future cash flows.[25] Moreover, when a country runs into financial difficulties, it may take actions such as tax increases that reduce corporate profits. In addition, macroeconomic and political conditions may change dramatically following sovereign default and result in reduced free cash flows not properly accounted in the analyst's projections.

In conclusion, the purpose of adding the sovereign risk spread to the cost of capital is to correct for the upward bias in the free cash flow projection that ignores the consequences of default. In principle, no correction for "country risk" would be needed if the analyst were able to make unbiased estimations of expected cash flows that already take into account the probability of default.

In practice, the sovereign bond spread is computed from a bond with the same duration as the U.S. benchmark used to compute the cost of equity, which presently is the 10-year Treasury note. However, not all countries have long-term bonds outstanding, and that leads to the question of how appropriate it is to use the spread of a shorter duration. Contrary to what one would expect, empirical evidence from the U.S. high-yield market does not suggest that yield spreads increase with duration. On the contrary, the evidence

---

[24]As Lessard (1979) pointed out, a common approach in forecasting cash flows is to project the most likely (mode) rather than expected cash flows. For projects with significant downside because of economic uncertainty or expropriation risk the means will be lower than the modes of the cash flows.

[25]Empirical research by Bansal and Dahlquist (2001) suggests that two-thirds of the equity premium for emerging markets can be attributed to other factors than systematic risks, such as lack of credible commitment to keep the capital market open.

suggests high-yield spreads decrease with duration. This was noted by Johnson (1967) and confirmed in more recent research by Sarig and Warga (1989). Johnson called this phenomenon "crisis at maturity" and interpreted it to mean than the probability of default of a risky borrower and the default premium increase as the time to repay the principal gets near.

We should note, however, that first, the use of the sovereign risk spread to account for the downside of the cash flows ignores that the impact of sovereign default is not uniform across firms.[26] Second, there is some tentative empirical evidence that suggests that country risk is a factor determining security returns.[27] This would imply that a country risk premium would apply even to unbiased cash flow forecasts. Third, as it is well known, adjusting the cost of capital to correct cash flows penalizes future cash flows because of compounding. Finally, credit spreads are not available for every country or the outstanding issues are relatively illiquid and may contain an additional premium for reduced marketability.[28]

12.6   POST-EMERGENCE SYSTEMATIC RISK

In using Equation (12.2) to estimate the beta coefficient of an emerging market company, one must take into account that the betas of emerging market returns on the MSCI index vary over time. They were low during the decade 1986 to 1995, averaging 0.34. In addi-

EXHIBIT 12.8	*Post-emergence Systematic Risk*	
Country	Long-term estimates (ending 12/1995)	50-week estimates (ending 12/1995)
Argentina	−0.07	1.96
Brasil	0.35	2.42
Chile	0.12	0.65
China	−0.04	1.08
India	−0.03	0.08
Indonesia	0.19	0.79
Korea	0.52	−0.08
Malaysia	0.73	0.56
Mexico	0.70	0.83
Philippines	0.71	0.75
Taiwan	0.73	0.35
Thailand	0.34	0.72
Venezuela	0.18	−0.18
Average	0.34	0.76

SOURCES: Long-term estimate from Goetzmann and Jorion (1999).
50-week estimates from Lessard (1996).

---

[26]In fact, empirical evidence shows that there is not a one-for-one response of corporate spreads to changes in the sovereign spread. See Durbin and Ng (1999).

[27]See Bailey and Chung (1995). These authors found that credit spread on Mexican sovereign bonds is a factor determining the expected returns on the local stock market.

[28]A number of countries have gone through debt rescheduling and issued Brady bonds with principal collateralized with U.S. Treasury securities. Removing the Treasuries' cash flows from the promised cash flow of such bonds permits computing the *stripped* yield from which the country credit spread can be estimated.

tion, the high average return of 24.8% attained during that period is unlikely to persist in the future. Goetzmann and Jorion (1999) attribute the observed high returns and low systematic risk to the structural change associated with the reemergence of these markets and give persuasive arguments as to why the return relationship of emerging markets is likely to align itself with developed markets and result in a substantial increase in correlation. In fact, Exhibit 12.8 shows that the average beta estimated with the last fifty months ending December 1995 had already more than doubled. As globalization of the capital market continues, one would expect increased correlation among markets, increased country betas and increased global betas of individual companies.[29] Still, the net result of globalization should be a net decrease in the cost of capital of emerging market companies.[30]

12.7 SUMMARY

In this chapter we examined the valuation of companies in the global capital market. The main conclusions are as follows:

1. The cash flow of the company can be expressed in its own currency including expected inflation (nominal terms), its own currency without inflation (real, constant purchasing power terms), or the currency of the acquirer. Cash flow projections are better stated in the currency of the target in order to capture expected price level changes that can affect differently the several components of the cash flow. Translation to a foreign currency can be done with future spot exchange rates estimated either from the interest rates in each country (interest rate parity) or assuming devaluation according to the relative expected inflation rates in each country (purchasing power parity).

2. The cost of capital for discounting free cash flows depends on if the company is situated in a developed or an emerging market. The equity component of the cost of capital in developed capital markets is based upon a global equity premium, a global beta coefficient and a size premium. Given the magnitude and influence of the U.S. capital market in the global market, its prospective equity premium provides an estimate of the global premium. The prospective premium is based upon expectations about the future, which are incorporated into the price of U.S. equity and, as such, already summarize the expectations of global investors. On the other hand, the contribution to a global portfolio of a particular stock depends on the correlation of its home market with the global portfolio. For the U.S. market that correlation is close to unity and so is its beta coefficient. Hence, the equity premium of a particular U.S. stock can be estimated by multiplying the prospective market premium times the U.S. local beta. For other markets, one needs to account for the additional diversification effect from their reduced correlation with the world market portfolio. This can be done by direct estimation of the beta coefficient from the regression of the company's return on the return of the global portfolio (as represented, for example, by the MSCI index). Alternatively, the local beta can be multiplied by the beta of the local market with the global portfolio. This last approximation may not work well for highly diversified multinational companies, particularly when their local market is a small fraction of the global capital market.

3. The cost of capital of emerging market companies can be estimated in the same manner as in the case of developed market companies as far as the estimations of the equity and size premium are concerned, but such a cost should be subject to a further adjustment for country risk. The country risk premium is estimated from the spread of sovereign bonds over the international benchmark (U.S. treasuries for dollar issues, German government bonds for euro issues, Japanese government bonds for yen issues). This adjustment ap-

---

[29]This is confirmed by the research Bekaert and Harvey (2000).
[30]Stulz (1999).

plies to both the cost of debt and the cost of equity. It is essentially a cash flow adjustment made in order to correct free cash flows projections for the downside probability of financial distress in the emerging market. This is required whenever the cash flow projection is conditional on the no occurrence of default and is therefore upward biased. If the cost of debt already reflects country risk, then the country risk premium should be added only to the cost of equity component. In addition, the cost of capital should be adjusted for the difference in the inflation rates when passing from valuation in one currency to another.

PROBLEMS

12.1 Verify the calculation of future dollar/euro spot rates and the dollar cash flows made in Exhibit 12.1.

12.2 Verify the computation of the cost of capital for AixCorp's valuation of APSSA.

12.3 In the Fall of 1993, Leucaida, the owner of Bolivian Power Co. was planning a secondary offering of shares in the U.S. market.[31] Bolivian Power was in the business of generation, transmission, distribution, and sale of electricity in Bolivia. The Company had operated since 1925, and its shares were listed on NASDAQ until 1993 when it moved to the NYSE. The Company's first parent was Canadian International Power, which was acquired by the conglomerate Baldwin-United Corporation. In 1983, Baldwin-United declared bankruptcy, and Bolivian Power switched owners again when it was taken over by the U.S. insurance company, Leucadia National, as part of the deal in which Baldwin-United was bought by Leucadia. Until 1993, the insurance company owned 49.8% of Bolivian Power's stock.

Two companies dominated Bolivia's electric power industry: Bolivian Power and ENDE (Empresa Nacional de Electricidad). ENDE was the state-owned power entity that operated mainly thermal power stations and two hydroelectric power stations. Together, these two companies owned and operated 96% of the generating capacity in the country. In terms of distribution, Bolivian Power was the largest distributor of electricity in the country with a 42% market share.

Demand for electricity had been growing at about 5 to 6% per annum for Bolivia as a whole, at 3.5% for ENDE and 8.3% for Bolivian Power. Electricity demand was expected to grow at least at 7% per annum through the year 2000 and beyond of which Bolivian Power was expected to take the larger share. In addition, as a low-cost producer, Bolivian Power would benefit from the power needs of neighboring countries. Domestic demand and export growth would permit Bolivian Power to increase output at a rate above 8% for years to come. In fact, the terms of the 1990 concession required that the company increased its energy supply output by at least 6% per annum over the 40 years of the concession. Since the expected long-term inflation rate of the U.S. dollar at that time was 3%, the nominal growth of revenues and cash flows was about $(1.08)(1.03) - 1 = 11.24\%$.

In order to cope with the increase in demand, Bolivian Power's management was planning a number of expansion projects. The most important one was the Zongo Valley Project, a project that would cost $120 million over a 4-year period. The Zongo Project would add generating capacity, transmission capacity, and substations and distribution lines in La Paz. The financing of these expansions was to be partially funded by a $50 million loan guaranteed by the Overseas Private Investment Corporation (OPIC), an agency of the United States Government. Bolivian Power had no debt at the time and $16 million in cash and short-term investments.

At the end of September 1993, Bolivian Power share price was $24¼. On November 4, 1993, Bolivian Power Company registered its shares in preparation for the public offering of 1,250,000 primary shares and 750,000 secondary shares of common stock, with an over-allotment option of 15% of the offering.[32] 4,200,000 shares were expected to be outstanding after the planned offering of 1,250,000 shares. Fees and expenses were estimated as 5⅜% of gross proceeds. Leucadia's ownership of Bolivian Power's outstanding common stock would change from 49.8% to 17.1%. The primary offering would permit Bolivian Power to increase generating capacity to meet rising domestic and export demand. Exhibit A presents the income and cash flow projections.

The company's rates are indexed to the U.S. dollar and are automatically adjusted on a monthly basis to reflect changes in the exchange rate. Bolivian Power was subject to a 13% tax rate on profits. As of January 1, 1995, the rate would increase to 25%. However, the company recovered

---

[31]This problem is based upon the case *Bolivian Power Company Ltd.,* Columbia Business School, 1997, prepared by Martin E. Diaz, Columbia MBA 1995, and on Bolivian Power Company Limited, *Prospectus,* November 22, 1993.

[32]An over-allotment option gives the underwriter the option to acquire more shares of the offering if needed. This is sometimes referred to as the "green shoe option" because it was first used in an offering of the Green Shoe Co.

EXHIBIT A	*Bolivian Power Company Ltd. Consolidated Income Statement and Cash Flow Data*

In thousands of U.S. dollars, except for per share data
December 31st fiscal years

	1992 Actual	1993 Estimated	1994	1995	1996	1997	1998
			<-----------------Projected----------------->				
Income statement:							
Revenue	39,201	41,840	46,494	53,749	57,943	65,825	71,273
Operations	(28,874)	(29,930)	(35,988)	(39,352)	(35,255)	(35,133)	(39,951)
Depreciation	(3,268)	(3,400)	(3,324)	(3,579)	(5,402)	(8,444)	(8,782)
Other taxes	(1,231)	(1,240)	(1,114)	(1,263)	(1,362)	(1,547)	(1,675)
Operating income	5,828	7,270	6,068	9,555	15,924	20,701	20,865
Capitalized interest*	117	329	1,977	5,522	5,032	0	0
Interest income	1,016	1,240	1,570	1,385	1,200	1,140	1,520
Interest charges**	0	0	(1,215)	(3,936)	(5,847)	(6,094)	(6,094)
Pretax income	6,961	8,839	8,400	12,526	16,309	15,747	16,291
Income tax	(1,001)	(1,280)	(1,260)	(2,870)	(3,420)	(3,420)	(3,560)
Net income for common	5,960	7,559	7,140	9,656	12,889	12,327	12,731
Average shares	2,949	3,300	4,200	4,200	4,200	4,200	4,200
Earnings per share	2.02	2.29	1.70	2.30	3.07	2.94	3.03
Tax rate	14.4%	14.5%	15.0%	22.9%	21.0%	21.7%	21.9%
Cash flow data:							
Dividends	1,887	2,244	3,023	3,191	3,359	3,527	4,457
Dividends per share	0.64	0.68	0.72	0.76	0.80	0.84	1.06
Capital expenditures	6,891	7,000	40,726	47,722	22,943	8,448	9,024
Working cap. increases	(466)	0	244	2,380	4,669	1,715	516
Increase in debt	0	0	4,825	42,825	13,992	(7,081)	(674)

*Acrued interest on capital invested during construction added to the rate base.
**1994 includes financing expenses.

this tax through the rates it charged to consumers. In addition, it was entitled to include in its rates an amount equal to the excess of the rate of interest paid over 6% on debt financing. Hence, the effective cost of debt for Bolivian Power was only 6% but it did not enjoyed a tax shield because no effective tax savings resulted from interest payments given that corporate taxes were passed on to consumers.

The country risk premium was estimated at about 5%, on the basis of the spread between the yield of sovereign bonds of other South American countries and U.S. Treasury bonds. In addition, Bolivian Power (unlevered) beta was 0.45, the prospective equity premium was 3.5%, and the micro-cap premium was about 4.5%. In addition, multiples from Chilean companies and a number of similar US utilities were available. Exhibit B contains data on comparables. The U.S. Treasury yield was 6.8%.

Value the shares of Bolivian Power as of January 1st, 1994, taking into account the proposed equity issue and project financing. Compute the continuation value as of 1998, assuming perpetual growth and relate your results to the comparable EBITDA multiples of Exhibit B. Prepare cash-flow statements through 1998.

Hints:

1. Examination of the cumulated planned debt shows that it jumps from zero to $48 million by 1995, increases to $62 million, and falls to $54 million by 1998. Hence, discounting unlevered

EXHIBIT B	*Comparison of Selected Publicly Held Electric Utilities*		
	Bolivian Power Co.	Enersis S.A. (Chile)[1]	Endesa (Chile)[1]
Fiscal Year End	12/92	12/92	12/92
Last Financial Statement	9/93	6/93	6/93
BUSINESS DESCRIPTION	Electric generation and distribution utility in Bolivia. (100% Hydro)	Electric generation and distribution utility in Chile and Argentina	Electric generation utility in Chile and Argentina
CURRENT MARKET DATA			
Current Stock Price	$24.250	$19.75[3]	$0.41[3]
Shares Outstanding	2.900	125.2	8,002.0
Market Value	$70.325	$2,471.874	$3,280.820
Enterprise Value[2]	$54.118	$2,643.031	$4,147.220
LTM Price Range	$10.25–$26.75	$20.13–$22.00	$0.30–$0.42
Dividend Yield	2.8%	3.3%	6.6%
MARKET MULTIPLES			
Price / LTM EPS	9.5 x	22.8 x	18.5 x
Price / Book	91%	474%	160%
Enterprise Value / LTM Revenues	1.3 x	5.8 x	9.0 x
Enterprise Value / LTM EBITDA	5.8 x	24.6 x	11.7 x
LTM OPERATING DATA			
Revenues	$42.902	$459.124	$460.941
EBITDA	$9.337	$107.314	$353.674
Net Income	$7.514	$101.063	$177.488
EPS	$2.54	$0.02	$0.02
3-YEAR AVERAGE MARGINS			
Gross Margin	14.7%	22.7%	43.7%
EBITDA	24.0%	22.9%	63.6%
Net Margin	15.7%	32.3%	41.5%
3-YEAR GROWTH RATES			
Revenues	21.6%	0.1%	–7.2%
EBITDA	13.0%	9.0%	25.0%
EPS	11.9%	24.3%	45.2%
CAPITALIZATION AS OF	9/93	6/93	6/93
Cash	$16.207	$7.241	$147.500
Short Term Debt	$0.000	$104.201	$141.900
Long Term Debt	$0.000	$178.398	$1,013.900
Preferred Stock	$0.000	$0.000	$0.000
Common Equity (Book)	$76.977	$521.613	$2,044.300
Total Capitalization	$76.977	$700.011	$3,058.200

[1]All financials based on Chilean GAAP and converted into US dollars using June 30, 1993 exchange rate of Ch$404.65 for US$1.
[2]Defined as Market Capitalization plus Debt less Cash.
[3]Stock price as of 11/3/93 using current exchange rate of Ch$399.5 for US$1.

Chilgener (Chile)[1]	Central Vermont (US)	Idaho Power (US)	Green Mountain (US)
12/92	12/92	12/92	12/92
6/93	6/93	6/93	6/93
Electric generation utility in Chile and Argentina	Electric generation and distribution utility in Vermont (30% Hydro)	Electric generation and distribution utility in Idaho (35% Hydro)	Electric generation and distribution utility in Vermont (41% Hydro)
$3.63[3]	$21.50	$30.38	$33.50
193.0	11.4	36.7	4.5
$700.590	$245.165	$1,113.365	$149.142
$884.690	$377.991	$1,907.772	$226.279
$2.48–$3.43	$21.33–$25.63	$25.50–$33.00	$30.13–$36.63
3.7%	6.6%	6.1%	6.3%
14.0 x	13.5 x	16.0 x	13.8 x
120%	142%	173%	157%
5.0 x	1.4 x	3.6 x	1.5 x
11.6 x	6.8 x	9.3 x	7.3 x
$177.065	$278.058	$529.263	$146.653
$76.262	$55.505	$205.013	$31.112
$48.907	$18.072	$68.735	$10.654
$0.26	$1.60	$1.90	$2.43
26.4%	14.8%	26.7%	14.3%
37.2%	19.9%	38.6%	19.4%
20.4%	7.2%	12.0%	6.7%
−13.2%	9.1%	3.5%	−0.8%
7.1%	9.1%	−1.0%	11.1%
−7.5%	2.6%	−9.9%	5.3%
6/93	6/93	6/93	6/93
$9.400	$0.955	$7.586	$0.082
$21.700	$7.050	$0.465	$10.242
$193.500	$98.727	$694.206	$67.644
$0.000	$35.054	$107.787	$9.575
$583.700	$172.060	$642.049	$94.710
$777.200	$358.997	$1,877.844	$194.269

free cash flows at constant WACC is no correct. You may be tempted to discount the cash flows to equity at the cost of equity, but note that you cannot maintain the cost of equity constant when leverage changes. Rather than troubling yourself in trying to compute a changing WACC or a changing cost of equity you can value Bolivian Power using the APV method introduced in Chapter 6. In doing so, you should note that Bolivian Power does not benefit from a tax shield. (If you still insist in discounting FCF at a changing cost of capital that allows for changes in the capital structure you should review Sections 6.5 and 6.6 of Chapter 6, but you will get the same result as that attained using the original APV method. This is an unavoidable consequence of the fact that in the present case there is no tax shield to value.)

The trick here is to compute the correct unlevered free cash flow. For example, the unlevered FCF for the year 1994 is computed as follows:

Net income for common	7,140	From the income statement.
Capitalized interest	(1,977)	During construction the company is credited interest on investment, which is added to the rate base. That interest becomes part of net income but it is a non-cash item and should be excluded for cash flow computation.
Interest income	(1,570)	Interest income is subtracted because it is not part of the unlevered free cash flow. However, note that here it is taken out before taxes because the company effectively pays no taxes.
Plus 6% interest on debt	290	This is 6% $\times$ cumulated debt, before taxes. Recall that the company pays the first 6% only.
NOPAT	3,883	
Depreciation	3,324	From the income statement.
Capex	(40,726)	From Exhibit A.
Net working capital increases	(244)	Same
Unlevered free cash flow	(33,763)	

2. To compute EBITDA add depreciation to NOPAT. For example, EBITDA for 1994 is computed as follows: $3,883 + 3,324 = 7,207$.

3. From the enterprise value, you have to subtract net debt to obtain the value of equity. However, the company had no debt at the beginning of 1994 and had cash and marketable securities for $16 million.

4. Now you have to divide the value of equity by the number of shares. How many shares to use? Hope this problem offers no difficulty because from now on you are on your own!

12.4 In 1991 Petöfi Printing Company was the leading packaging company in Hungary.[33] Since its privatization by the Hungarian State Property Agency in 1990, capital expenditures had been adequately funded by its internally generated cash flow. However, by the end of 1991, management had identified substantial opportunities in the introduction of new packaging products, including flip-top box packaging. In order to fund the introduction of these products, the existing shareholders determined to make a private placement of common shares. The company's investment bank had obtained an

---

[33]The data for this problem is based upon materials prepared by Ralph White, Columbia MBA '93, and Petöfi's 1992 offering memorandum.

expression of interest from two institutional investors, and some existing shareholders were expected to contribute additional equity on the same basis. Petöfi's pro-forma financial statements are summarized in Exhibits A and B (see pp. P–7 and P–8). Since packaging was deemed a strategic sector under The Foreign Investment Act, Petöfi enjoyed a 100% tax holiday that expired in September 1995. Thereafter, Petöfi's would pay a rate that was 40% of the standard rate (40%) until September 2000.

Compute Petöfi's free cash flows in current Hungarian forints (HUF) and take inflation into account to express them in HUF of the end of 1991, that is, in HUF of constant purchasing power. Examine the resulting cash flows and decide how to value them, if at WACC or APV discounting. What is the value of the tax shield for APV valuation?

12.5   Valuing the private placement of Petöfi's common shares mentioned in Problem 12.4 was complicated by the fact that Petöfi's shares did not trade in the Budapest Stock Exchange, nor they had a local comparable among the 22 equities traded on the exchange. This means that any estimation of Petöfi's cost of capital had to rely on international valuation parameters plus an adjustment for country risk. Relevant capital market data at the time were as follows:

30-year U.S. Treasury bond yield	7.55%
3-year U.S. Treasury note yield	5.90%
3-year U.S.$ Hungarian gov. bond yield	9.50%
U.S. expected inflation rate	3.30%
HUF/$ exchange rate	78.3
U.S. equity premium	3.2%

The following data about comparable companies were available.

a. Beta coefficients and debt-to-equity ratios of the following packaging companies:

Company	Beta	Debt/Equity
Engraph	0.99	0.29
Sonoco	1.07	0.14
David Smith	0.99	0.06
Low & Bonar	1.03	0.13

b. Their corporate tax rate was about 40%.
c. The median EBITDA trailing multiple at the end of 1991 from six North American and UK publicly traded packaging companies was 7.9x, and the median EBITDA multiple from six international acquisitions of packaging companies during 1990–1991 was 7.3x.

In addition, Petöfi's cost of capital needs to account for its micro-cap nature and include a premium for lack of marketability. For such a small company, this premium is hard to gauge. At that time micro-cap U.S. firms had premia of about 4.5%. Finally, even after allowing for its micro-cap nature, one needs to allow for the fact that Petöfi was still private and further reduce its value below that of a publicly traded micro-cap stock. Empirical evidence compiled in the United States over a number of years suggests a private equity discount on enterprise value of about 20%, and recent research on other developed and emerging markets indicates the existence of significant discounts for lack of marketability.[34]

---

[34]See footnote 11 above, Chapter 13, Section 13.8, and the references therein.

EXHIBIT A *Petőfi Printing Company Ltd. Projected Income and Cash-flow Statements*

HUF (Hungarian Forint) millions
Fiscal year ending December 31

	1991	1992	1993	1994	1995	1996	1997	1998	1999	2000
Sales	2,667	3,398	6,255	8,332	9,770	10,837	10,625	10,422	10,724	11,399
EBITDA	354	475	949	1,308	1,553	1,744	1,714	1,697	1,759	1,865
Depreciation and amortization	(68)	(118)	(234)	(244)	(262)	(286)	(313)	(341)	(367)	(394)
EBIT	286	357	715	1,064	1,291	1,458	1,401	1,356	1,391	1,471
Investment income	17	21	24	27	29	31	33	35	37	39
Interest income	85	27	37	82	134	206	297	376	467	583
Interest expense	(109)	(79)	(94)	(80)	(56)					
Pre-tax profit	279	326	682	1,092	1,398	1,695	1,731	1,767	1,895	2,092
Extraordinary items		(39)								
Tax rate	0.0%	0.0%	0.0%	0.0%	4.0%	16.0%	16.0%	16.0%	16.0%	22.0%
Profit tax	0	0	0	0	(56)	(271)	(277)	(283)	(303)	(460)
Net income	279	287	682	1,092	1,342	1,424	1,454	1,485	1,592	1,632
Dep & Amort	68	118	234	244	262	286	313	341	367	394
Exchange gain	6									
Cash from operations	353	404	916	1,336	1,604	1,710	1,767	1,825	1,959	2,026
Sale of assets			52							
Capex & Net WC increase	(475)	(1,516)	(509)	(450)	(548)	(516)	(479)	(463)	(468)	(504)
Cash flow bef. fin. transactions	(122)	(1,112)	459	886	1,056	1,194	1,288	1,362	1,491	1,522
Financial transactions:										
ERBD debt drawdown		499								
Debt repayments	(160)	(60)	(174)	(255)	(299)					
Share capital increase	174	674								
Dividends paid	(108)		(68)	(219)	(268)	(285)	(291)	(297)	(318)	(326)
Net cash flow		1	217	413	489	909	997	1,065	1,173	1,196
Starting cash balance	190									
Ending cash balance	82	83	300	713	1,202	2,111	3,108	4,173	5,346	6,542
HUF inflation rate	37.5%	24.0%	14.0%	11.0%	9.0%	7.5%	6.5%	5.5%	5.0%	5.0%

EXHIBIT B *Petőfi Printing Company Ltd. Projected Summary Balance Sheets*

HUF (Hungarian Forint) millions
Fiscal year ending December 31

	1991	1992	1993	1994	1995	1996	1997	1998	1999	2000
Current assets	789	908	1,790	2,829	3,872	5,159	6,271	7,446	8,825	10,336
Fixed assets	1,423	2,766	2,813	2,729	2,674	2,661	2,623	2,552	2,451	2,332
Total assets	2,212	3,674	4,603	5,558	6,546	7,819	8,894	9,998	11,276	12,668
Current liabilities	463	525	1,016	1,351	1,565	1,699	1,611	1,527	1,531	1,618
Long-term debt	157	668	534	299	0	0	0	0	0	0
Shareholder equity	1,592	2,480	3,053	3,908	4,982	6,121	7,284	8,471	9,745	11,050
Total liabil. and equity	2,212	3,674	4,604	5,558	6,546	7,819	8,894	9,998	11,276	12,668
HUF inflation rate	37.5%	24.0%	14.0%	11.0%	9.0%	7.5%	6.5%	5.5%	5.0%	5.0%

    a. Estimate Petöfi's unlevered cost of capital as of December 1991.

    b. Estimate Petöfi's enterprise and equity values.

    c. Petöfi has 23.194 million shares outstanding and planned to issue 6.604 million shares in the private placement. Issue fees and expenses were expected to be 5.88% of gross proceeds. Estimate Petöfi's share price and net proceeds.

12.6   Value Petöfi by discounting U.S. dollar cash flows.

12.7   Value Petöfi by discounting nominal HUF cash flows.

Chapter 13

Leveraged Buyouts

Why LBO?
ROE
Debt Capacity of LBO

13.1 THE RATIONALE FOR LBOs

This chapter deals with the financial structure and valuation of leveraged buyouts (LBOs) and other leveraged recapitalizations. In an LBO transaction, a group of investors finance the acquisition of a corporation or division mainly by borrowing against the target's future cash flows. The buyout is organized and effected by the *promoters*, which include a *sponsor* and, often, existing management as well. When the latter is an important part of the promotion group, the LBO is called a management buyout (MBO). The sponsor is usually an LBO equity fund or the merchant-banking arm of a financial institution. It provides the core equity and effectively controls the acquisition.

LBOs contribute to the better allocation of resources in the economy by improving the performance of the acquired firms.[1] The expected gains lead promoters to pay a premium over the public value of the target, to the public shareholders benefit. Empirical research shows stock prices tend to go up at the time of buyout announcements. One study found that prices went up by about 30% from 40 days prior to the day of the buyout proposal, after adjustment for general market movements, and by 22% in the 2 days surrounding the announcement of the initial proposal.[2]

LBOs are financed mainly with secured bank debt and unsecured subordinated debt. LBOs worth more than about $400 million may be able to raise subordinated debt in the public high yield market. Small transactions rely on secured bank debt and the private placement of subordinated debt that is likely to include an equity participation or "kicker." In between these polar cases lie many combinations of secured and subordinated debt structures. By changing the relative participation of debt and equity in the capital structure, an LBO redistributes returns and risks among the providers of capital. In addition, the total expected return can be greater than that of the original company because of larger tax shields and the realization of additional operating gains.

Why do LBOs take place? Most advantages attainable by an LBO are available to a public corporation. However, it is the ability to act quickly in appraising and structuring a transaction that gives buyout specialists a competitive advantage over other buyers, including large corporations with several levels of decision making. Corporations welcome LBO promoters' interest when they are in the midst of restructuring via asset disposition. In the case of private firms, the sellers' ability to extract a higher price can be limited by information barriers. On the other hand, an informed LBO acquirer may be willing to buy the private firm as a platform over which to execute add-on acquisitions and participate in the consolidation of an industry. Or it may buy the firm as an add-on acquisition if it already has a platform in place. The ultimate goal is an IPO or a sale to a strategic buyer once the consolidated company has realized sufficient economies of scale.

---

[1] See Lichtenberg and Siegel (1990).
[2] DeAngelo and DeAngelo (1987).

For a buyout to take place, its promoters must believe that they can increase free cash flows above the level expected by the seller. Promoters would want to organize an LBO only if they expect to reap a significant gain from the transaction. Such a gain would result from a disposition of free cash flow that produces value in excess of the buyout price. The promoters get the net present value of the transaction via their equity participation. The value they retain is an increasing function of the value placed on future cash flows by other investors. Hence the importance of a credible signal that unambiguously conveys the promoters' commitment to generate and distribute free cash flow to investors. In this respect, high leverage performs an important role in addition to financing the acquisition. Interest payments, together with a loss suffered by the promoters in the event of default, produce the desired unambiguous signal that communicates the cash flows attainable by the buyout and induces a valuation consistent with the promoters' financing need.[3]

The cash flow signaling hypothesis is consistent with the observed trend toward reduction of indebtedness after the buyout.[4] Once the signal has been made and the proper valuation for financing the transaction has taken place, the promoters have no incentive to maintain high leverage, particularly if the there are states of nature in which the firm may default.

Signaling free cash flow with debt can be made without taking the company private through a leveraged recapitalization. Management can use leverage to signal its commitment to distribute free cash flow to investors and improve the valuation of the company (sometimes, in order to avoid a hostile takeover). As in an LBO, committing cash flow to debt service is a credible signal because management exposes itself to job termination and loss of capital in the event of default.

Why is the use of debt to signal higher free cash flows adopted by some firms and not by others? The answer lies in the nature of the LBO transaction, which involves firms the promoter considers to be operating below their potential. On the other hand, companies that do not expect a significant increase in free cash flow would know they could not possibly profit from reallocating cash flow to debt service. The recapitalization of these companies would simply change the labeling of their payout from dividends to interest, and may require forgoing positive net-present-value projects in order to generate cash for debt service.

Debt-induced tax savings can provide another incentive for promoters to choose debt financing. However, questions have been raised concerning the significance of corporate taxes as a determinant of capital structure in general and LBO financing in particular.[5] If the main motivation for the change in capital structure is capturing additional tax savings, one has to explain why the capital structure change was not made before undertaking the LBO,[6] and why high leverage is not more pervasive. Moreover, the tax-saving hypothesis is inconsistent with firms reducing their indebtedness following a leveraged buyout or recapitalization.

Empirical research by Kaplan (1989b) shows that the market-adjusted premium paid to pre-buyout shareholders is significantly related to the buyout tax savings. Kaplan points out that, although tax savings may be a proxy for other buyout gains, the finding is

---

[3]See Arzac (1992) for an elaboration of this argument.

[4]Kaplan (1993) found that LBO companies decrease debt levels and increase coverage ratios after their initial financing but their debt remains at a higher level than both their pre-buyout level and the median public-company level.

[5]Jensen and Meckling (1976) and Auerbach (1989).

[6]Amihud (1989). Gilson, Scholes and Wolfson (1988).

consistent with investors anticipating the tax savings and forcing the promoters to pay for them in the purchase price. This result does not imply that taxes are the driving force of LBOs, because if expected tax savings are captured by pre-buyout shareholders, the promoters would lack an incentive to undertake the buyout in the absence of other expected gains. Tax savings can be a significant factor in explaining the purchase premium but only as a by-product of an LBO transaction driven by other forces. On the other hand, assuming the promoters' expectations about future cash flows are predominantly correct, one can compare pre- and post-buyout performance in order to test if expected value creation is the driving force of LBOs. The empirical evidence is consistent with the hypothesis that promoters' expectations about future cash flow are an important determinant of LBOs.[7]

What is an ideal LBO candidate? Desirable characteristics are: (a) A firm with predictable revenues and cash-generating capacity. (b) Competent management that understands the demands imposed by the financial structure of the LBO as the focus shifts to cash generation and debt retirement. (c) The nature of the company's assets is also important, particularly the possibility of reducing working capital and the resale market for the company as a whole or for some of its assets, which can provide future financing and an exit to the promoters' investment.

Where do the candidates come from? (1) A large firm that wants to sell a unit for lack of fit but cannot find a corporate buyer. At that point, the management team may come up with a buyout offer or the corporation itself may suggest it to the managers. Often, the seller hires an investment banker to run an auction and private equity acquirers may be invited to participate. (2) The management of the LBO candidate approaches an LBO fund or bank, or the latter approaches management with the idea of organizing an LBO for the firm because either party believes the company would become more valuable under the LBO organization.

LBOs are transitory forms of ownership. During the buyout period, management attempts to improve operations, and the sponsor looks for a transfer of ownership to a more permanent owner. Exit can be made via (a) an IPO to recapitalize the firm once debt has been reduced to a manageable level; (b) sale to strategic buyers of all or part of the original company; or (c) another LBO to provide some liquidity to the sponsor and higher ownership to management.

13.2 FINANCING LBOs

LBO financing is provided by (a) secured debt financing from banks, insurance companies, and other institutional investors; (b) the high-yield public market, made up of mutual funds, insurance companies, pension funds, and endowments funds; and (c) sellers willing to accept debt for part of the price.

LBO financing is expressed in terms of debt to EBITDA. The feasible financing mixture changes over time depending on market liquidity. Before the development of the high-yield market, the typical financial structure contained about 5 times EBITDA of debt and about 1.5 times EBITDA of equity for a purchase price of 6.5 times EBITDA. This structure is still common in small transactions that do not justify access to the public high-yield market. With secured debt supplied by banks, and subordinated debt supplied by insurance companies. In these structures, subordinated lenders would normally get equity participation to supplement below-market coupon interest.

---

[7]See Bull (1989), Kaplan (1989a) and Lichtenberg and Siegel (1990).

The typical financial structure changed in the 1980s with the development of the high-yield market. Secured financing accounted for about 3 times EBITDA, high-yield financing accounted for between 2.5 and 3 times EBITDA, and equity for about 1.5 EBITDA, for a purchase price between 7 and 8 times EBITDA. More recently, secured "bank loans" were securitized and placed with a variety of institutional investors.

The financing mode changes when the liquidity of the high-yield market becomes scarce as during 1998 to 2003. When high-yield financing is not available, the gap is partly filled by so-called *mezzanine financing* provided by insurance companies and mezzanine funds. These investors demand a higher compensation for their role in enabling the transaction, which usually involves warrants or other forms of equity in addition to interest on subordinated notes. Sponsors are then required to put more equity and accept lower returns. As a consequence, bid prices and the number of LBO transactions fall. For example, if secured-bank financing supplies 3 times EBITDA, mezzanine investors supply 1 time, and equity sponsors supply 2 times, the affordable purchase price is only 6 times EBITDA.

Subordinated lenders with up to 40% of the capital of the LBO are very much like equity holders and, as such, demand returns commensurate to their equity risk. They also demand compensation for the reduced liquidity of their investment. Given that subordinated financing has the risk and compensation of equity, one must consider why it is denominated debt and not equity. Some of the reasons are: (a) Debt increases the tax shield provided by interest payments. (b) Debt commitments force management to assume a credible risk on its own. A manager who is not able to service debt may lose his or her job and reputation. Since management's participation and appraisal of the prospect of the business is usually crucial to the planning and management of the LBO, it is essential for subordinate lenders to be able to discriminate between pretenders and competent, well-informed managers. And (c), not all the cash paid to lenders over time is in the form of interest. Repayment of principal is important because it permits lenders to recoup their investment tax-free. However, there are limits to how much debt can be carried by an LBO because management needs some degree of flexibility to operate the business, and the process of renegotiating debt terms can be very costly when many lenders are involved. The determination of debt capacity in highly leveraged transactions was discussed in detail in Chapter 7, and it is illustrated in Sections 13.6 and 13.9 below.

13.3 ROBUST FINANCIAL STRUCTURES

Strip financing was common prior to the development of the high-yield public market. Under a strip financing arrangement, each investor receives a percent participation in both the debt and the equity of the LBO. Strip financing makes the LBO less vulnerable to disagreement between different security holders in case the business does not turn out as expected. A lender who tries to enforce a covenant may bring the company to bankruptcy and dilute his or her equity stake. Even if the company is forced to appeal to the protection of Chapter 11, strip-holders are likely to be more amenable to debt restructuring because they would be less likely to suffer from the transfer of claims among security-holders. The strip arrangement is also consistent with the need to provide an equity kicker to the lender in order to supplement the low coupon interest affordable by the LBO.

The development of the high-yield market has diminished the attractiveness of strict strip structures. Marketing strips for billion-dollar deals may not be possible, given the need to attract many investors with varying interests and portfolio needs. In addition, coordination in the event of default would be too costly if there are many strip-holders. A standardized bond with, perhaps, an attached warrant is a simpler product to market. A bond-plus-warrant structure can approximate the incentive properties of a strip structure and can be in the interest of both the promoters and the other investors to issue. Lenders accepting a below-market interest rate on their loans in exchange for equity kickers will find their interest aligned with the promoters' if the kickers are sufficiently large. So will senior lenders whose claims are exposed to the threat of bankruptcy proceedings of unforeseen duration and consequences. These investors will prefer that all other investors have an incentive to avoid premature liquidation or protracted bankruptcy proceedings. Thus, by inducing interest alignment that minimizes conflict under default, promoters can reduce the cost of financing.[8]

It should be noted that in a number of actual transactions, mezzanine financing is provided by the same institutions participating in the private-equity fund that promotes the transaction. In addition, a number of LBO firms in the United States and in Europe manage both equity and mezzanine financing partnerships, with the latter supplying subordinated debt to their buyouts. In transactions financed by an equity fund and a mezzanine fund with common investors, the capital structure resembles a strip arrangement.

13.4   COMPUTING THE RETURNS TO INVESTORS

During the initial years of a buyout, free cash flows go to pay interest and amortize secured debt. No cash is available for distribution to equityholders. Subordinated lenders usually receive cash interest and, when the latter is below market, their original investment is bought at a discount to its principal value or they receive part of the equity. From their point of view, the relevant cash flow is the *total* cash flow they expect to receive, that is, that obtained from coupon payments, principal repayment, and equity participation at exit time, if any. The computation of the total return is illustrated in the following example.

Example 1

Let the LBO purchase price be $210 million, of which $60 million is secured debt, $100 million is subordinated debt with a below-market coupon interest of 6% plus 27% of the equity, and $50 million is invested by the sponsor for 73% of the equity. Assume the free cash flows generated during the first 5 years go to pay interest and amortize the secured debt in its entirety and that cash balances are negligible. Furthermore, let expected year-5 EBITDA equal $49.5 million and assume that the company is expected to be sold for 8 times EBITDA or $396 million net of fees and expenses. Then, the cash flows and the return to subordinated holders are as follows:

Year	0	1	2	3	4	5
			($ millions)			
Bond price	−100					
Coupon		6	6	6	6	6
Principal						100
Equity kicker						80
Total cash flow	−100	6	6	6	6	186
Blended IRR	17.3%					

[8] See Arzac (1992).

Thus, the sponsor receives no cash flow until exit time and its return is computed as follows:

Year	0	1	2	3	4	5
			($ millions)			
Initial investment	−50					
Exit proceeds						216
Return multiple (216/50)	4.3x					
IRR	34.0%					

The equity kicker brings the return to a level acceptable to the mezzanine investor. In general, the kicker compensates for the inferior coupon interest of a bond (which is not bought at its fully discounted value). Kickers are common in other situations besides LBOs. For example, a convertible bond has low coupon interest because of its conversion feature, which is a warrant on the firm's equity. Similarly, the warrants are the kicker in a unit of straight bonds plus warrants.[9]

Warrants are also used to increase the return to some of the equity investors on upside realizations of cash flows. For example, the equity can be shared 80%/20% between the sponsor and management, but management may get warrants with a sufficiently high but attainable exercise price as an additional incentive.[10]

In LBOs, the kicker can be common equity or a mixture of stock and warrants or warrants alone. Common equity would normally have voting rights. Although voting rights and board seats can be given to warrant-holders or bond-holders, the rights of shareholders to guide the management of the firm are more clearly recognized in the law. On the other hand, the possibility that the debt claims of a common shareholder be treated as equity in bankruptcy (equitable subordination), can make non-voting shares or warrants a preferred alternative for the lender.

When the warrants have a negligible exercise price, they are worth as much as common stock. However, due accounting has to be made for dilution in order to provide the lenders with their required equity participation. For example, if the participation has to be 20% of the exit value of equity, and this participation is to be provided via warrants of negligible exercise price giving right to one share per warrant and there are n = 20 million shares outstanding, then m warrants are required as follows:

$$\frac{m}{n + m} = 20\%, \quad \text{or} \quad m = \frac{0.2}{0.8}n = 5 \text{ million.}$$

This calculation can be easily generalized to the case of positive exercise price and more than one share per warrant. For example, if each warrant gives the right to purchase two shares for $0.75 each, the expected net value of the kicker at exit time has to be $7 million, and the expected IPO value before the exercise money from the warrants is $200 million, the number of warrants to be issued is given by the solution to the equation:

$$\frac{2m}{n + 2m}(200{,}000{,}000 + 1.50m) - 1.50m = \$7{,}000{,}000,$$

that is, for n = 20 million, m = 393,258.

---

[9]A warrant is a call option upon the exercise of which the firm issues new shares to the warrant holder. See Appendix A.

[10]See Section 13.5 below. The valuation of contingent incentive contracts is treated in Chapter 10.

*13.5   OPTION PRICING OF WARRANT KICKERS[11]

When the exercise price of the warrants is material, their required number has to be calculated using option pricing. To illustrate, consider the following example.

Example 2

On February 25, 2003, the HLT Corp. wanted to issue $100 million of 7-year debt at par with 8% annual coupon interest (100,000 bonds of $1,000 par value each, with principal to be repaid in 2010). The lenders demanded that HLT attach 7-year warrants to the bonds to raise the effective yield to 13%, the yield required by the market on this type of issue, such that each warrant entitled the holder to buy one share of HLT for $15. In order to price the warrants and estimate their required number the following inputs are needed:

- The yield on a 7-year government note, which was 4% (annually compound rate).
- The share value of HLT Corp., estimated at $10 a share.
- The volatility of the rate of return of HLT, estimated at 60% per annum.[12]
- The common shares outstanding, which were 20 million.

First, we need to find the required kicker. To do so we discount the bond cash flows at 13%:

Year	1	2	3	4	5	6	7
Bond cash flow ($million)	8	8	8	8	8	8	108

which gives $77.89 million. Hence, the present value of the warrants has to be $100 - 77.89 = 22.11 million and the number of warrants to issue is m = $22.11 million ÷ warr, where warr is the value of each warrant. m and warr have to be solved for simultaneously. This is achieved substituting 22.11/warr for m in the warrant pricing formula.[13] For example, 22.11/warr can be entered in the warrant module of Financial Options Calculator. The other inputs are: stock value = $10, exercise price = $15, time to expiration = 7 years, volatility = 60%, interest rate = 4%, and shares outstanding = 20 million. The solution is warr = $5.201 and m = 4.2508 million. That is, the value of the kicker is m × warr = 4.2508 × 5.201 = $22.11 million as required, and 42.508 warrants need to be attached to each bond.

13.6   DEBT CAPACITY AND AFFORDABLE PRICE

The price to bid for an LBO depends on the debt capacity of the company and the return required by the sponsor. We saw in Chapter 7 that debt capacity is a function of the business model of the LBO and its financial expression in terms of revenue, costs and capital investment projections. Debt capacity is an estimate of how much the company can borrow against its expected cash flow and still be able to amortize senior debt and pay interest to both senior and subordinated debt. The use of debt capacity determines how much is left to equityholders at exit time. The present value of exit equity plus debt capacity is the *affordable price* for the buyout. The valuation process is summarized in Exhibit 13.1.

---

[11]Sections marked with an asterisk may be skipped on a first reading.

[12]Not being publicly traded, HTL Corp. does not have a price history from which to estimate its volatility. An estimate of it can be obtained from comparable companies or, directly, from subjective estimates as discussed in Chapter 8, Section 8.2 and footnote 17 of Chapter 10.

[13]See Appendix A, Section A.7.

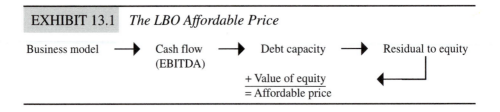

EXHIBIT 13.1 *The LBO Affordable Price*

The above process should be iterated under a variety of scenarios, including adversity in demand and costs triggered by economic conditions and competition, in order to establish the robustness of the structure. The affordable price for a robust financial structure is then compared to the price demanded by the seller or an estimate of the price other bidders might be able to offer. If the affordable price is below the required bid, the buyer can consider changes that would increase debt capacity and decrease equity requirements. Other bidders may be able to offer a higher price because they are in a better position to create value from the acquisition. On the other hand, that possibility may lead the sponsor to consider changes in its business plan that may increase cash flow and debt capacity. Such changes may involve, for example, the sale of less productive assets to those better fitted to manage them or a strategic partnership to attain synergies. Even when the affordable price seems sufficient to get the target, further iterations on the nature of the operations and assets retained may result in higher expected returns. Of course, the concept of affordable price is only a guideline, and the buyer would not bid more than necessary to satisfy the seller.

Example 3

Consider a target with 1st-year pro-forma EBITDA of $100 million, growth rate of sales and EBITDA of 5%, initial cash balance of $1.9 million, and senior secured debt making up 35% of total borrowing to be amortized in 5 years. As shown in Section 7.19, such a firm has a debt capacity of about 4.4 times EBITDA. That is, the LBO can borrow 4.4 × $100 million or $440 million, amortize 35% of it, and be left with the $285.5 million of subordinated debt at the end of year 5 and a cash balance of $2.4 million (see Exhibit 7.5 for details).

Assume that the LBO sponsor expects to exit the investment in 5 years at 6 times forward EBITDA. That is, since expected EBITDA for the 6th year is $100 million times 1.05^5 or $128 million, exit enterprise value (EV) would be 6 × $128 million or $768 million.[14] This implies the following residual equity at the end of the 5th year:

Enterprise value	$768
Minus:	
Senior secured debt	0
Subordinated debt minus cash	283
Equity	.$485

Hence, if the sponsor requires 30% return on its investment, equity cannot exceed $485(1.3)^{-5} =$ $131 million and the affordable purchase multiple for the enterprise after fees and expenses of 0.15 x EBITDA, is

[14]From Exhibit 7.5 the free cash flow in year five is expected to be $60.7 million. Hence, a forward 6 times EBITDA multiple is consistent with an exit valuation based upon WACC = $FCF_5(1 + g)/EV_5 + g =$ $(60.7)(1.05)/768 + 5\% = 13.0\%$.

Net debt	$438
Equity	131
	569
Expenses	15
Affordable price	554
EBITDA	100
Affordable multiple	5.5x

This calculation assumes an exit multiple close to the purchase multiple. This is prudent assumption made in practice that puts the burden of value creation in improving operations rather than simply betting on multiple expansion. The reader can iterate on the above calculation to determine that the exit multiple that equates the affordable multiple is 5.3x. Assuming that the exit multiple is the same as the entry multiple, it is no substitute for trying to estimate the multiple that would prevail at exit time given the likely evolution of the industry and the nature of the exit. However, given the uncertainty associated with going public, pricing in public markets and the availability of strategic buyers, assuming that exit would take place at the entry private equity multiple is reasonable.

The above calculation is summarized in the following statement:

Sources		Uses	
	($ millions)		
Senior secured debt	154	Purchase price	554
Subordinated debt	286	Cash	2
Equity	131	Expenses	15
	571		571

The exit time is only an estimate. In fact, even in the case when the sale takes place at the expected time, full liquidity may not be attained until expiration of a lock-up period. Sales restrictions are common in initial public offerings or when part of the sale price is received in another company's shares.

13.7 RETURNS TO INVESTORS AND THE PRIVATE-EQUITY DISCOUNT

LBO investors demand higher returns than investors in public companies with sustainable levels of debt do. Depending on market conditions and the nature of the transaction, high-yield bond-holders demand returns on the 9 to 12% range, private equity requires returns in the mid 20%, and mezzanine-financing demands returns between those of high-yield and private equity. These higher returns are justified because of the higher risk of HLTs and, in the case of the promoters, because of the value they expect to add to the company. In addition, private equity is compensated for the illiquidity it bears. In fact, the sponsor of an LBO makes a highly illiquid investment that can take several years to realize. As discussed in Chapter 3, illiquidity is priced in the market such that less liquid investments require compensation. For example, investors in micro-cap publicly traded firms (with capitalization less than $270 million) demand an additional return of about 3.3% on the average and a total return on equity in the low to mid-teens.[15] Private-equity investors require between 10 and 15% more. More precisely, the additional compensation is usually expressed as a discount on the value the company would have if it were publicly traded instead. That is, in order to value a privately held company, one first values its expected free

---

[15]See Chapter 3, Exhibit 3.7.

cash flows as if it were a public company and then applies the appropriate private-equity discount. This procedure implies an internal rate of return that equates the present value of the free cash flows to the private value of the firm. Such an IRR can be interpreted as the specific all-inclusive cost of capital of the privately held firm.

Calculating the discount for lack of marketability is an inherently imprecise exercise. Ideally, one would like to compare the prices of similar public and private firms at a given point in time. This is difficult, if not impossible, because of the lack of precise data on private sales and the difficulty of finding matching public company transactions. Sometimes, the price of a private company is supplemented with earnouts or other forms of compensation to the seller that are not explicitly accounted by the buyer on the reported price or in its financial statements because they are not considered ascertainable liabilities. Such arrangements can result in underestimation of the price paid for the company and magnification of the discount with respect to the corresponding public value. Thus, the empirical evidence on illiquidity discounts should be considered only indicative. We now review it.

In a series of studies, John Emory (1995) found that the discounts for lack of marketability of private-equity minority interest during 1980 through 1995 were about 45% from their equivalent public market value.[16] Emory compared the price paid for stock prior to going public to its subsequent IPO price. Although he did not adjust for market movement during the period between the private sale and the going public transaction, he restricted the two events to take place during at most 5 months from each other, and his sample covers a variety of market conditions. However, the data is from minority interest transactions rather than from the sale of entire companies, and the estimate is probably subject to selection bias. Only firms that succeeded in going public are considered. While this seems to provide the appropriate discount to apply to the public value of an LBO, the companies in the sample are likely to have experienced a performance superior to that anticipated at the time of the private transaction, and thus showed a larger difference between private and public prices. It should be noted, however, that discounts on private equity of this magnitude can be justified along theoretical lines. Longstaff (1995) has shown that discounts of 50% can result from the opportunity cost of not being able to trade for 5 years.[17]

Another estimate of the lack of marketability discount is provided by the difference between the price of a private placement of unregistered stock and the simultaneous price of the publicly traded stock. Two studies were conducted at the time when SEC Rule 144 restricted the public resale of unregistered securities for 2 years. In one study, Silber (1991) found the discount of restricted stock to average 33.8%.[18] As Silber noted, the sample was dominated by small and rather unprofitable companies. These had discounts in excess of 50%, while the mean discount of the larger firms was only 14%. Also, more recent research suggests that the private placement discount may include compensation for the costs incurred by private investors to assess firm value and for the expected benefits of additional monitoring, particularly in the case of relatively small firms that do private placements.[19] On the other hand, although at the time of Silber's study the illiquidity period was 2 years, it was still less that the average duration of leverage buyouts. Moreover, sponsors do not fully exit at IPO time, and their equity is usually subject to a lock-up period.

---

[16]Similar estimates adjusted for market movements are reported in Pratt (1989).

[17]Longstaff shows that such a maximum cost can be determined as the maximum value of a look-back option. A value of a look-back put depends on the difference between the maximum price attained during the life of the option and the final price. See Hull (2002).

[18]See also Pratt, *op cit.,* for similar results.

[19]Hertzel and Smith (1993) and Wruck (1989).

The discount estimates of Emory and Silber refer to equity. In order to estimate the corresponding discounts on enterprise value, let V and V_r denote the enterprise values based upon the value of the public and private equity, respectively, and u denote the private equity discount. Furthermore, let the debt of the company be dV, which is the same amount in both cases. Then $V_r = (1 - u)(V - dV) + dV$ and the discount on enterprise value is $(V - V_r)/V = (1 - d)u$. For a debt ratio between 30 and 40%, Emory's discount on equity implies a discount on enterprise value between 27% ($0.6 \times 45\%$) and 31.5% ($0.7 \times 45\%$). Silber's result implies a discount on enterprise value between 20 and 24%. Applying these discounts to estimate the enterprise value of truly private firms requires assuming that the pricing of the debt of public and private firms is not significantly different. This seems reasonable given that most of the firms in both studies were relatively small.

A more recent study by Koplin, Sarin, and Shapiro (2000) estimated the discount on enterprise value of private sales and obtains results of the same order of magnitude of those implied by Emory and Silber's studies. Koplin et al. compared the EBITDA multiples paid in private sales of whole companies or sales of controlling interests to the multiples of public companies in approximately the same industry.[20] Although the public companies were larger, the median size of both the private and public companies fell into the microcap class of Exhibit 3.7 of Chapter 3. The attractiveness of this study is that it more closely matches the typical LBO transaction. For 84 U.S. transactions, they found a mean (median) discount of 20% (18%). For 108 foreign transactions covering a variety of countries, they found a mean (median) discount of 54% (23%). Both sets of differences were statistically significant. Although one may expect a higher discount in foreign markets, given the thinness of non-U.S. private equity markets, the mean discount on foreign transactions was too high and out of line with its own median. U.S. private companies had higher EBITDA growth prior to the transaction than the public companies, but foreign companies had much lower EBITDA growth than the public companies. That may account for the differences in discounts between domestic and foreign companies.[21]

We now relate the discount on the public value of equity to the rate of return demanded by LBO sponsors. Let n years be the expected time to exit, E_n be the public value of equity at n, and k be the cost of public equity. Then, the required return on private equity k_r that corresponds to a discount on equity of u satisfies:

Ignore

$$1 - u = \frac{E_n(1 + k_r)^{-n}}{E_n(1 + k)^{-n}} \quad \text{or} \quad k_r - k = [(1 - u)^{-1/n} - 1](1 + k)$$

Hence, for U.S. transactions with u = 30 to 40% and n = 5 years, the premium over the public equity cost of equity is $k_r - k \approx 8.4$ to 12.2% for $k \approx 12\%$, or a required return on private equity of $k_r \approx 20$ to 24%. For non-U.S. transactions, the premium appears to be somewhat higher. For u = 40 to 45%, the premium is between 12.2 and 14.4%, with a required return on private equity of about $k_r \approx 24$ to 26%. These numbers agree with the required return on equity in typical LBO transactions.

Thus, the enterprise value of an LBO can be estimated in two alternative and approximately equivalent ways: (a) Obtaining the enterprise value of a public firm with the same projected leverage as the LBO and reducing it by 18 to 20%. (b) Discounting exit

---

[20]The authors also computed revenue and price-to-book multiples. However, as they recognize, the average of revenue multiples across industries is not meaningful. Averages of price-to-book ratios are also suspect.

[21]See also references in footnote 11 of Chapter 7. Pereiro (2001) reports a discount of 51% in the P/E acquisition multiples of private versus public companies in Argentina.

equity at a rate in the mid-20% and adding the debt capacity of the LBO as outlined in Section 13.6.

13.8 A DETAILED LBO EXAMPLE

Cardinal Oil was a small oil company engaged in the exploration, development, and production of oil and natural gas. In the spring of 1999, its owner, a diversified chemical company, decided to sell Cardinal Oil. The possibility of acquiring Cardinal via a leveraged buyout led by an equity sponsor and Cardinal's management is now examined. First, we need to establish the debt capacity of the company, which depended on the lending terms available in the market: (a) The fraction of the capital that could be borrowed from banks and the rate of interest and the amortization period of secured loans; (b) the availability and terms of subordinated debt; and (c) the minimum equity required by lenders. For the purpose of this illustration, let us assume typical parameters: Banks were willing to lend on a secured basis up to 35% of total debt and required 25% of the purchase price to be equity. They would charge 8% and required their loan to be amortized yearly over 5 years. Subordinated lenders would provide 65% of the total debt at 9.25% cash interest with principal due in 5 years. The sponsor needed to supply the remaining 25% of the capital and required a 25% IRR. Fees and expenses associated with the transaction would be about 2% of the purchase price. Exhibits 13.2 and 13.3 summarize the balance sheet and income statement as of the 12/31/1998. Exhibit 13.4 presents the projection assumptions made in estimating the buyout debt capacity.

Cardinal was assumed to operate on a stand-alone basis such that Exhibit 13.4 does not factor the benefits and financial requirements of possible add-on acquisitions. Exhibit 13.5 presents the calculation of debt capacity following the procedure of Section 7.6. It shows that it was possible to borrow $745 million or 4.9 times EBITDA. The reader can

---

EXHIBIT 13.2	*Cardinal Oil Company Balance Sheet as of 12/31/1998*

($ millions)

Current assets	
Cash and marketable securities	12
Account receivable	70
Inventories	64
	146
Property, plant and equipment	391
Investments	6
Other	93
Total assets	636
Current Liabilities	
Short-term debt	47
Account payable	46
Accrued expenses	29
Other	15
	137
Long-term debt	49
Deferred taxes	37
Shareholders' equity	413
	636

EXHIBIT 13.3	*Cardinal Oil Company Income Statement Year 1998*

($ millions)

Net sales		391
EBITDA margin		38.4%
EBITDA		150
Depreciation		14
Net interest expense		2
Income before taxes		134
Taxes	40%	54
Net Income		81

verify that the same debt capacity results from substituting the average values of the projection percentages into the debt capacity Equation (7.4).[22]

In order to satisfy the lenders' requirement, the sponsor needed to provide at least $745/0.75 – $745 = $248 million of equity. Adding this amount of equity to the debt capacity of $745 million results in a total financing of $993 million. Subtracting fees and expenses of about $20 million yields a feasible bidding price for Cardinal of $973 million. That is, the buyout could finance 6.5 times EBITDA (4.9x of debt and 1.6x of equity), pay fees and expenses of 0.13 times EBITDA, and offer a purchase price of ($973 – $12)/$152 = 6.3 times EBITDA, taking into account the $12 million cash balance.

This is as far as financing is concerned. Next, we need to consider if the lenders' equity requirement satisfies the return required by the sponsor. A quick calculation of the return to the sponsor can be made as follows: Apply the entry (purchase) multiple of 6.3x to 2004 EBITDA calculated assuming 8% growth. This gives the enterprise value at the end of year 2003. That is, ($231)(1.08)(6.3) = $1,572 million. Subtract the amount of net debt projected for the end of 2003 and obtain exit equity. That is, $1,572 – ($484 – $14) = $1,102 million. Then, the IRR to the sponsor would be ($1,102/$248)^{1/5} – 1 = 35%, well in excess of the sponsor's required return.

How much to bid for Cardinal was a decision to be made on the basis of valuation and by gauging the size of competing bids. In fact, depending on the urgency of the seller and the nature of competing offers, the buyout group could decide to start with a bid lower than the feasible amount calculated above. A strategic buyer would be able to offer a higher price than the buyout group if it could capture synergies in the short run, while the LBO would need to make add-on acquisitions to attain them. Also, the cost of capital of a publicly traded strategic buyer is usually not subject to a lack-of-marketability premium.

In summary, strategic buyers are likely to have higher reservation (break-even) prices for targets than buyout groups and typically pay more. Consider, for example, the price that a large strategic buyer could afford to pay for Cardinal without accounting for the value of possible synergies. A rough estimate of such a price is attained multiplying 1999 EBITDA by the forward EBITDA multiple of the publicly traded comparables that could be possible strategic acquirers.[23] The latter was about 6.9x,[24] a depressed value by

---

[22]Debt capacity can be calculated with the Debt Capacity Calculator. See Appendix B.

[23]A multiple commonly used in valuing oil companies is share price to cash flow with cash flow defined as net income plus depreciation, depletion, amortization, non-cash exploration expenses and deferred taxes. EBITDA multiples are more appropriate for the present analysis.

[24]The average 1999 EBITDA multiple of Amerada Hess, Atlantic Richfield, Conoco, Marathon, Occidental, Phillips and Unocal.

EXHIBIT 13.4 *Cardinal Oil Company, Five-Year Projections*

($ millions)

	Actual					
	1998	1999	2000	2001	2002	2003
Sales	391	422	458	495	534	577
EBITDA	150	152	174	198	214	231
Depreciation	14	15	16	18	19	21
Deferred taxes	2	2	2	2	3	3
Capital expenditures	34	3	33	38	51	55
Increase in net working capital including cash	5	1	2	5	5	5
Projection assumptions:						
Crude oil price ($/barrel of West Texas Intermediate)	15	16	17	17	17	17
Natural gas price ($/mcf at wellhead)	2	2	2	2	2	2
Net sales growth	9.0%	8.0%	8.5%	8.0%	8.0%	8.0%
EBITDA margin	38.4%	36.0%	38.0%	40.0%	40.0%	40.0%
Net fixed assets/sales	95.0%	85.0%	82.0%	80.0%	80.0%	80.0%
Net working capital less cash/sales	11.3%	10.5%	10.0%	10.0%	10.0%	10.0%
Cash and marketable securities/sales	3.1%	2.5%	2.5%	2.5%	2.5%	2.5%
Depreciation/sales	3.6%	3.6%	3.6%	3.6%	3.6%	3.6%
Deferred taxes/sales	0.5%	0.5%	0.5%	0.5%	0.5%	0.5%

EXHIBIT 13.5	*Cardinal Oil Company, Debt Capacity of Leveraged Buyout as of 12/31/1998*

($ millions)

Year-end	1998	1999	2000	2001	2002	2003
Net Sales	391.0	422.3	458.2	494.8	534.4	577.2
EBITDA	150.3	152.0	174.1	197.9	213.8	230.9
Depreciation	14.0	15.2	16.5	17.8	19.2	20.8
EBIT	136.3	136.8	157.6	180.1	194.5	210.1
Interest income @	5.25%	0.6	0.6	0.6	0.7	0.8
Senior debt interest @	8.00%	20.8	16.3	13.0	8.9	4.8
Subordinated debt interest expense @	9.25%	44.8	44.8	44.8	44.8	44.8
Income before taxes		71.8	97.1	123.0	141.6	161.3
Provision for tax 40%		28.7	38.8	49.2	56.6	64.5
Net income		43.1	58.3	73.8	84.9	96.8
Deferred taxes		2.1	2.3	2.5	2.7	2.9
Depreciation		15.2	16.5	17.8	19.2	20.8
Capex and incr in net work. capital incl. cash		3.8	35.6	42.6	55.9	60.3
Available for debt retirement		56.6	41.4	51.5	51.0	60.1
Debt amortization						
Senior debt	260.6	204.0	162.6	111.1	60.1	0.0
Subordinated debt	484.0	484.0	484.0	484.0	484.0	484.0
Debt balance	744.6	688.0	646.6	595.1	544.1	484.0
Cash balance	12.0	10.6	11.5	12.4	13.4	14.4
Debt/1999 EBITDA	*Total Debt Capacity* 4.90					
EBITDA net interest coverage		2.3	2.9	3.5	4.0	4.7

historical standards. Hence, a strategic buyer could offer at least $152 × 6.9 = $1,048 million before fees and expenses or about $55 million more than the estimate calculated above for the buyout group.

Exhibit 13.6 calculates the affordable price the equity sponsor could pay for Cardinal and still attain 25% IRR on equity assuming exit at 6.9x EBITDA. It shows that the bid could be as high as $1,142.5 million minus fees and expanses and still yield 25% IRR

EXHIBIT 13.6	*Cardinal Oil LBO Return on Equity and Affordable Bid*

($ millions)

2004 EBITDA with growth @	8%	249.3 (230.9 ×1.08)
EBITDAx		6.9
Enterprise Value		1,720.4
Minus net debt at the end of 2003		469.6 *Debt - Cash Bal*
Exit equity		1,250.9
Present value of equity at	25%	409.9
Return multiple		3.1x
Net debt		732.6 (744.6 - 12)
Equity		409.9
Affordable bid for enterprise		$ 1,142.5
EBITDAx		7.5x

to the sponsor. Although private equity is not likely to win in an auction against deter-mined strategic bidders, the slow approval process followed by many large potential ac-quirers may permit a nimble buyout group to prevail. Moreover, strategic buyers often pay in stock, whereas LBO firms pay in cash. If the seller is seeking cash, an LBO firm could prevail with a lower bid.

13.9   MEZZANINE FINANCING

We now illustrate the use and effect of mezzanine financing. Suppose that the seller would not sell Cardinal Oil for less than $1,100 million approximately and that the lenders had agreed to allow for a junior subordinated layer of debt for $1,100 − $973 = $127 million, and permitted the sponsor to cap its equity investment at $248 million. The mezzanine lenders would require 8% cash interest and an equity kicker sufficient to bring its blended return to 13.5%. That is, these lenders would buy units of note and stock for $127 million. Hence, assuming additional fees and expenses of $3 million, the financial structure of the deal would be as follows:

Sources		Uses	
	($ millions)		
Senior debt	$260.6	Offer price	$1,096.6
Subordinated debt	484.0	Fees and Expenses	23.0
Jr. Subordinated debt	127.0		
Equity	248.0		
	$1,119.6		$1,119.6

The value of the equity kicker necessary to boost the mezzanine return to 13.5% is calcu-lated in Exhibit 13.7. The value of the kicker in year 2003 is the amount that when added to the note cash flow yields an IRR equal to 13.5%. That is, it is the solution to

$$127.0 = \frac{10.16}{1.135} + \frac{10.16}{1.135^2} + \ldots + \frac{10.16 + 127.0 + \text{Kicker}}{1.135^5}$$

which is $45.72 million. In order to express the kicker as a share of the LBO equity, we need to value the latter. The value of the 2003 equity is obtained subtracting the value of net debt at the end of 2003 from the enterprise value. From Exhibit 13.6 we know that, for a 6.9 EBITDA multiple, enterprise value would be $1,720.4 million.

EXHIBIT 13.7   *Cardinal Oil Company LBO Valuation of Unit of Note and Equity Kicker*

($ millions)

Year-end		1998	1999	2000	2001	2002	2003
Junior subordinated note principal		127.00					
Coupon payments @	8.0%		10.16	10.16	10.16	10.16	10.16
Principal repayment							127.00
Note cash flow			10.16	10.16	10.16	10.16	137.16
Equity kicker to yield	13.5%						45.72
Expected cash flow on unit			10.16	10.16	10.16	10.16	182.88
Present value of unit @	13.5%	127.00					

EXHIBIT 13.8 *Cardinal Oil Company LBO Valuation of Junior Subordinated Note and Original Issue Discount Amortization*

($ millions)

Year-end		1998	1999	2000	2001	2002	2003
Junior subordinated note principal		$ 127.0					
Coupon payments @	8.0%		10.2	10.2	10.2	10.2	10.2
Principal repayment							127.0
Note cash flow			10.2	10.2	10.2	10.2	137.2
Present value of note @	11.2%	112.1	114.4	117.1	120.1	123.3	127.0
Original issue discount (OID)		$ 14.9	12.6	9.9	6.9	3.7	—
OID amortization			2.4	2.7	3.0	3.3	3.7

To estimate the outstanding debt, we must recalculate Exhibit 13.5 to incorporate the additional cash interest, the increase in interest deductions for tax computation, and the resulting reduction in the cash available for debt retirement. Mezzanine debt usually gives rise to original issue discount (OID) amortization for accounting and tax purposes. This is so when the cash interest paid is below the interest that would be required by the buyer of the note in the absence of an equity kicker. In fact, in the spring of 1999, a straight junior subordinated issue would have been priced to yield 11.2%. Exhibit 13.8 shows that the value of the note component of the unit would then be $112.1 million with OID over face value of $14.9 million. With the passage of time, the value of the liability increases to the present value of the remaining payments. This increase is charged against income as OID amortization for both financial reporting and income tax determination.[25]

The last line of Exhibit 13.8 is transferred to the income statement in Exhibit 13.9. Exhibit 13.9 shows a debt balance at the end of year 2003 of $638 million. Hence the value of equity in 2003 would be:

$$\text{Enterprise Value} - \text{Net Debt} = 1,720.4 - (638.0 - 14.4) = \$1,096.8 \text{ million,}$$

of which mezzanine investors would receive $45.7/$1,096.8 = 4.17%. The LBO sponsor would retain 95.83%, which would provide an expected return multiple of (1,096.8 − 45.7)/248.3 = 4.2 times and an IRR = 33.5%, before exit fees and expenses, if exit were to take place in 5 years. This means that, in principle, the sponsor could increase its equity investment and still attain a return well above 25%.

In practice, the financial structure has to make room for management incentives in the form of stock options and earnouts.[26] For example, assume the sponsor sets aside approximately 5% of the equity for management stock options. Let the initial equity capitalization consists of ten million shares of which 417,000 shares go to mezzanine investors and 9,583,000 belong to the sponsor. If management receives 500,000 options with a $25.88 exercise price (the "ground floor" price paid by the sponsor equal to $248/9.583), then the initial ownership would need to be adjusted to maintain the return required by mezzanine investors. These adjustments are shown in Exhibit 13.10. Taking into account the proceeds from the exercise of the options, the share value in 2003 would be $105.69.

---

[25]The U.S. Tax Code rules applicable to OID for tax purposes are complex and contain numerous qualifications for specific situations. In the present case OID would be allowed. See footnote 27 in Note N10.1.

[26]Valuation of earnouts is studied in Chapter 10.

EXHIBIT 13.9   *Cardinal Oil Company Cash Flow and Debt Balance with Junior Subordinated Financing*

($ millions)

Year-end		1998	1999	2000	2001	2002	2003
Net Sales		391.0	422.3	458.2	494.8	534.4	577.2
EBITDA		150.3	152.0	174.1	197.9	213.8	230.9
Depreciation		14.0	15.2	16.5	17.8	19.2	20.8
EBIT		136.3	136.8	157.6	180.1	194.5	210.1
Interest income @	5.25%		0.6	0.6	0.6	0.7	0.8
Senior debt interest @	8.00%		20.8	16.7	13.8	10.2	6.5
Sub. debt interest @	9.25%		44.8	44.8	44.8	44.8	44.8
Jr sub note interest @	8.00%		10.2	10.2	10.2	10.2	10.2
Original issue discount amortization			2.4	2.7	3.0	3.3	3.7
Income before taxes			59.2	83.9	109.0	126.9	145.7
Provision for tax	40%		23.7	33.6	43.6	50.7	58.3
Net income			35.5	50.3	65.4	76.1	87.4
Deferred taxes			2.1	2.3	2.5	2.7	2.9
Depreciation and oth non-cash items			15.2	16.5	17.8	19.2	20.8
OID amortization			2.4	2.7	3.0	3.3	3.7
Capex and incr in net work. cap. incl. cash			3.8	35.6	42.6	55.9	60.3
Available for debt retirement			51.4	36.1	46.1	45.5	54.4
Debt amortization							
Senior debt		260.6	209.2	173.0	126.9	81.5	27.0
Subordinated debt		484.0	484.0	484.0	484.0	484.0	484.0
Junior subordinated debt		127.0	127.0	127.0	127.0	127.0	127.0
Debt balance		871.6	820.2	784.0	737.9	692.5	638.0
Cash balance		12.0	10.6	11.5	12.4	13.4	14.4
EBITDA net interest coverage			2.0	2.5	2.9	3.3	3.8

Upon exercise of its options management would end up with 4.76% of the fully diluted number of shares and net out ($105.69 – $25.88) × 500,000 = $39.91 million. Mezzanine investors would need to receive $45.7/$1,109.8 = 4.12% post option exercise, which translates into an initial ownership equal to 4.12%/(1 – 4.76%) = 4.33%. The sponsor would therefore be left with 91.12% at exit time and expect to attain a return multiple equal to 4.1 times its initial investment or an IRR = 32.5%.

Although the calculation made in Exhibit 13.10 is customary, it does not truly reflect the value of the options. For example, the Black-Scholes option pricing formula adjusted for dilution[27,28] for a stock price equal to $105.69/1.2^5 = $34.63, an exercise price equal to $25.88, a riskless rate of 5.5% and volatility of 96%, gives a rough estimate of

---

[27]Technically, these stock options are warrants because they result in dilution upon exercise (see Appendix A). The volatility of Cardinal's equity would be much higher than that of comparables because of higher leverage. Let the rate of return of comparables be $R = (1 - t)(EBIT - rD)/E$, where E denotes equity, etc. We assume that $\Delta E = 0$. Then the variance of the rate of return is $var(R) = [(1 - t)^2/E^2] var(EBIT)$. Consider now a company with the same EBIT and equity E' and solve for the corresponding vol $(R') = [var(R')]^{1/2} = (E/E')vol(R)$. For Cardinal Oil, using the average market equity ratio and volatility of comparables of 65% and 37%, respectively, and reducing the equity ratio to 25% for private equity, yields an estimate of volatility equal to $(0.65)/(0.25)(0.37) = 96\%$.

[28]See Appendix A and Chapter 8 for a discussion of option pricing.

| EXHIBIT 13.10 | *Cardinal Oil Company Ownership with Management Stock Options* |

($ millions, except share value and exercise price)

2003 Enterprise value		1,720.4
Net debt		623.6
2003 Equity value		1,096.8
Options	500,000	
Exercise price	25.88	
Exercise proceeds		12.9
		1,109.8
Diluted shares	10,500,000	
Value per share	105.69	
Management ownership	4.76%	52.8
Mezzanine ownership	4.12%	45.7
Sponsor ownership	91.12%	1,011.2
Total	100.00%	1,109.8
Initial ownership:		
Mezzanine investors	4.33%	432,537
Sponsor	95.67%	9,567,463
	100.00%	10,000,000

$27.33 per option.[29] This value is higher than the present value of the option assumed in Exhibit 13.10: $34.63 − $25.88/1.055^5 = $14.83. Note that the share price is discounted at the sponsor's required return but the exercise price is discounted at the riskless rate because it is a certain amount. A higher value for the management options means that the true expected returns to both the mezzanine investors and the sponsor would be somewhat lower than the returns implied by Exhibit 13.10.

13.10   APV VALUATION

In Exhibit 13.11, we show the DCF valuation Cardinal Oil LBO following the approach outlined in Section 13.6. We first compute its enterprise value as if it were a publicly traded company and then apply to it a 20% private-equity discount. Since the capital structure changes over time, the enterprise value is attained using the adjusted present-value procedure introduced in Chapter 6.

Free cash flows are discounted at the unlevered cost of equity, estimated at 9.45%[30] from comparable data as of 12/1998. The tax shield is based upon the financial structure outlined in Section 13.9 and is discounted at the interest rate paid by the LBO (9.25%).

The enterprise value minus the private equity discount is $1,230 million. This value compares to the enterprise value implicit in the exit valuation made in Section 13.9. The latter can be obtained discounting the exit value of equity estimated there at 25% (the rate required by the sponsor), and adding to it the initial net debt (debt minus cash and OID): 1,096.8/(1.25)^{−5} + 844.7 = $1,204 million.

---

[29]This value was computed with the warrant module of the Financial Options Calculator.

[30]Unlevered beta = 0.65, prospective equity premium = 3%, riskless rate = 5.5% and small cap premium = 2%.

EXHIBIT 13.11	*Cardinal Oil Company, Adjusted Present Value as of 12/31/1998*

($ 000)

Year-end		1998	1999	2000	2001	2002	2003
Net Sales		391.0	422.3	458.2	494.8	534.4	577.2
EBITDA		150.3	152.0	174.1	197.9	213.8	230.9
Depreciation		14.0	15.2	16.5	17.8	19.2	20.8
EBIT		136.3	136.8	157.6	180.1	194.5	210.1
Taxes	40%	54.5	54.7	63.0	72.0	77.8	84.0
Unlevered net income		81.8	82.1	94.6	108.1	116.7	126.1
Defered taxes			2.1	2.3	2.5	2.7	2.9
NOPAT			84.2	96.9	110.5	119.4	128.9
Depreciation			15.2	16.5	17.8	19.2	20.8
Capex & increase in net WC.			3.8	35.6	42.6	55.9	60.3
Unlevered free cash flow			95.6	77.7	85.8	82.8	89.4
Net interest expense			77.6	73.7	71.1	67.7	64.3
Tax shield			31.0	29.5	28.4	27.1	25.7

Unlevered cost of equity	9.45%						
PV FCF 1999-2002 @	9.45%	332.3					
Continuation value @ EBITDAx	6.9x						1,720.4
PV '03 continuation value @	9.45%	1,095.4					
PV Tax shield @	9.25%	110.5					
Enterprise value (EV)		1,538.1					
Private equity discount on EV	20%	307.6					
EV after private equity discount		1,230.5					

13.11 SUMMARY

Buyout specialists enjoy the advantage of speed and focus in the market for corporate control. Once an opportunity is detected, they are able to appraise and structure a transaction in a fraction of the time it takes most large corporations to evaluate and approve a firm bid. The use of high leverage does not permit distraction and forces the sponsor and management to focus on results and cash generation. The ability to execute LBO transactions depends on the level of public prices and the availability of high-yield financing. This explains the fluctuations of buyout activity. However, leverage buyouts are here to stay and have become global in scope. They play an important role in the renewal of the economic system.

The price to bid for an LBO depends on the debt capacity of the company and the return required by investors. The business strategy of the buyout needs to be translated into a financial model with revenue, costs and capital investment projections. This provides the basis for determining how much the company can borrow against its expected cash flow and still be able to amortize senior debt and pay interest to both senior and subordinated debt. Debt capacity use determines how much is left for equity-holders at exit time. The present value of the latter plus debt capacity is the price the sponsor can afford to pay for the acquisition.

The enterprise value of an LBO is affected by a private-equity discount that reflects the temporary lack of marketability of the acquisition. The enterprise value can be determined in two alternative and approximately equivalent ways: (1) Estimating the enterprise value of a public firm with the same leverage as the LBO via the APV valuation technique presented in Chapter 6, and reducing that value by 18 to 20%. (2) Discounting exit equity at a rate in the mid-20% range and adding to it the net debt of the buyout.

PROBLEMS

13.1 Prestige Outlets is a distributor of off-season designer clothing. Gabriella Bucher, the present CEO, came to Prestige 2 years ago and effected an impressive turnaround, reducing distribution costs, eliminating the dividend to conserve cash, speeding up cash-flow realization, and increasing the number of labels. In spite her success, Prestige traded at a 12½ P/E multiple, well below other specialty retailers. She believed that part of the problem was that the market was not interested in the steady non-glamorous cash flow of Prestige. In fact, Prestige was followed by only a couple of analysts, and visible money managers have ignored it since its brush with bankruptcy prior to Ms. Bucher's arrival.

By the fall of 2002, the CEO had concluded that Prestige's low valuation gave management the opportunity to undertake a buyout and provide value to shareholders. The year 2002 was reasonably good for Prestige. While its cash needs were well attended by a credit line, 2002 was expected to generate a substantial amount of cash. This extra financial flexibility added to the optimism of the management team.

Bucher estimated that she could take the company private at a 15% premium to its market price. Prestige was trading at $7¼ a share and had 5 million shares outstanding. There was also the matter of the outstanding $18 million 7¾% secured notes held by American Insurers. The debt indenture stipulated that the notes were due and payable in the event of a change of control at a 10% premium over their face value. In addition, Bucher estimated the need of an additional $1.5 million to cover fees and expenses.

So far, Bucher had obtained the following financing indications: An amortizable secured bank loan at 8.89% on the outstanding balance.[31] Amortization would be flexible based upon a cash sweep (all free cash flow would go to debt amortization), with any remaining balance payable at the end of the seventh year. Inventories, receivables and fixed assets would be pledged as collateral and other standard covenants would apply. The lenders have expressed interest in lending on a secured basis an amount equal to 3x pro-forma 2003 EBITDA.

Bucher thought she could push leverage up to 5.5 times pro-forma 2003 EBITDA that, after secured borrowing, left her 2.5 times to be covered by subordinated lending. She already had an indication for a subordinated non-amortizable 7-year loan at 11.95%. The rest of the purchase price had to come from equity. She and her team already had 311,000 restricted shares from the incentive compensation contract received on joining Prestige. These shares would acquire full rights in the event of a change of control and they would be available for rollover into the LBO. The remaining equity would come from Gladstone Capital Partners, who had expressed interest in filling the financing gap but demanded equity participation sufficient to attain a 30% return. Gladstone had a solid reputation in the retail industry and has already made two successful leveraged build-ups of specialty retailers. Gladstone and Bucher had already agreed on the cash-flow projections shown in the following exhibit and felt that an exit via a sale to a strategic buyer at 10x 2007 EBITDA (minus fees and expenses of about 2%) would be feasible in about 5 years.

Bucher knew management would end up with a minority stake in the LBO but planned to negotiate favorable terms with Gladstone. She would demand a return for management in excess to what it would be entitled by its equity rollover.

---

[31]The interest rate has been grossed up in order to account for the cost of maintaining and using a credit line to cover seasonal cash needs.

Prestige Outlets Proforma Income, Cash Flow and Debt Statements

$ millions			2002	2003	2004	2005	2006	2007
Revenue			49.55	53.51	57.80	62.42	67.41	72.81
EBITDA			6.94	7.49	8.09	8.74	9.44	10.19
Depreciation			0.50	0.54	0.58	0.62	0.67	0.73
EBIT			6.44	6.96	7.51	8.11	8.76	9.46
Senior debt interest			1.62					
Subordinated debt interest			—					
Income before tax			4.82					
Taxes		40%	1.93					
Net income			2.89					
Depreciation			0.50					
Capital expenditures			0.50	0.54	0.58	0.62	0.67	0.73
Ne working capital increase			0.25	0.27	0.29	0.31	0.34	0.36
Free cash flow before financial transactions			2.65					
Debt amortization			———					
Beginning-of-year cash balance			—					
End-of-year cash balance			2.65					

Shares outstanding (millions)	5.00
EPS	$ 0.58
Share price	$ 7.25
P/E	12.53

Capital structure		Current	LBO	
Senior debt		18.00		
	@	7.75%	8.89%	
Subordinated debt				
	@		11.95%	
Total debt				

1. Complete the provided income and cash-flow statements, and debt amortization and debt balance schedules for the LBO for the years 2003 to 2007.
2. Prepare a statement of sources (financing tranches) and uses (total purchase cost) of funds for the LBO. What is the purchase EBITDA multiple?
3. What share of the equity will Gladstone Capital Partners demand?
4. What annual rate of return can management expect to realize on their equity rollover?
5. Prepare a table comparing the equity splits and the returns to the sponsor and to management when: (a) Gladstone gets 30% return; (b) Gladstone gets 25%; and (c) the equity is split according to the value of the initial equity contributions of each party.

13.2 Use the debt capacity Equation (7.4) with the average values of the projections for Cardinal Oil made in Section 13.8 to compute the debt capacity of the company. Hint: You can use the Debt Capacity Calculator.

13.3 Refer to the end of Section 13.8 and compute the return to mezzanine investors and to the sponsor taking into account that the value management's stock options is $27.33 per option.

13.4 Project "Blue Snapper": In April 2000, the board of directors of Cap & Seal agreed to give management an exclusive opportunity to acquire the company at a price determined by an independent appraisal. Cap & Seal held a dominant position in its core business, specialty injection molded plastics, occupying a growing niche in which it controlled an estimated 50% market share. Its product category had not existed 10 years earlier. Demand was growing rapidly as potential users became aware of the product and as new uses were developed. In this environment, the company had achieved annual compound sales growth of nearly 14% over the previous 5 years.

Upon examining an independent appraisal and other offers to purchase Cap & Seal, the Board of Directors approved $420 million as a fair price for the market capital (debt plus equity) of the company. Management was committed to roll over $37.5 million into the equity of Cap & Seal as follows (in 000s $):

Market Capital	$420,000
Less: Existing debt	240,063
Preferred Stock	14,060
Implied Value of Common	165,877
Less: Repurchased Stock	128,377
Equity Rollover	$ 37,500

Management's rollover represented 22.6071% of the 9,259,259 outstanding shares of the company. In addition to refinancing the long-term debt, the new entity would have to repurchase all of the preferred stock but could assume the liability of the unsecured notes ($10.17 million) on the then existing terms. Financing would need to provide for about $19.7 million in fees and other closing costs (including the penalty of prepaying outstanding notes) of which $12.4 million would be capitalized and amortized for accounting and tax purposes over seven years.[32]

The transaction would be structured as an acquisition of stock in order to avoid the reassignment of contracts with existing customers. For accounting purposes, it was decided to account the buyout as a recapitalization so that no goodwill would be recognized.[33]

The rest of the equity was to be provided by FMC's merchant banking unit. Management demanded that the common equity be split with the sponsor in proportion to the value of the equity contributions at closing, with management share valued at $37.5 million.

FMC's Vice President Richard Jones considered that the 14% per annum growth experienced over the previous 5 years, a consequence of rapid market penetration, could not continue in future years. He estimated nominal sales growth of 7.5% per annum for the next 10 years to be reasonable and conservative. Since Cap & Seal's customers were generally in non-cyclical industries sales could be expected to experience smooth growth.

The cost of goods sold was expected to remain at about 55.7% of sales throughout 2010. SG&A and R&D expenses, combined, were to be gradually reduced from 16.2% as a percent of sales in 2000 to 11.6% in 2010. This reflects efficiencies expected to be generated from recent upgrades in systems and one-time expenditures in R&D equipment. In order to support the sales gains, capital expenditures were to increase from $30 million in 2001 to $55 million in 2008 and remain at that level.

The senior debt portion of the financing would be composed of a revolving credit facility and a 5-year term loan. The revolving credit facility, which would provide Cap & Seal with a working capital cushion, would bear interest at prime plus 50 basis points or 9.5% per annum initially. Of the total facility, the company would be able to draw down up to 85% of the value of its accounts receivable and up to 50% of the value of its inventory. Any unused portion would be charged a ½ of 1% per annum commitment fee. The revolving credit facility would mature on June 30, 2004. Thereafter, it would be extendable annually with the consent of the lenders. The interest on the

---

[32]The difference, or $7.3 million, would be charged against equity as part of the cost of repurchasing the shares of the selling shareholders and issuing new shares to the sponsor. This portion of the expenses would not be tax deductible.

[33]See Note N13.2.

term-loan facility would be 9% in the 1st year, and would be 235 basis points above the Libor rate in future years. The term loan would be paid down with a cash sweep of all pre-loan amortization free cash flow by August 31, 2005. The secured term loan would not exceed 55% of total debt (secured debt, assumed subordinated debt and mezzanine financing), and required that 20% of the purchase price be equity (management rollover plus sponsor's equity). Jones was also considering the possibility of fixing the interest rate on the term loan by entering into 5-year interest rate swap. The swap would increase the cost of the term loan by 40 basis points to 9.4%.

Mezzanine financing would have to be structured to yield an expected return of 17% (including the value of the equity kicker) with cash interest on the face value of the security of 10.5% per annum and principal due in 6 or 7 years. Its principal would be callable after 4 years at a 10% premium, which would decline 5% per year.[34]

Exit EBITDA multiples in the range 6 to 8 times were considered conservative at the time of the transaction. However, Jones was determined to not do the deal if FMC could not attain a 35% return on its equity stake at an enterprise value of 5 times 2005 EBITDA and 4% exit expenses. His conservative outlook was influenced by the extreme volatility exhibited by the stock market, the absence of a high-yield market, and the uncertainty concerning oil and resin prices.

Exhibits A to C contain historical financial information as well as the proforma statements as of June 30, 2000, adjusted to account for the effect of the recapitalization of assets and short-term liabilities. Exhibit D contains projections of sales and expenses.

Jones went fishing blue snapper off Montauk Point for the weekend but asked you, the associate assigned to the deal, to have the complete analysis of the transaction on his desk by 8:00 A.M. on Monday. You have the weekend to accomplish the following tasks:

a. Design an appropriate capital structure for the leveraged recapitalization of Cap & Seal with consideration to the paydown requirements of the senior debt facility.
b. Develop pro-forma projections given the operating assumptions and the appropriate capital structure.
c. Calculate the amount of warrants needed to achieve the target return on the mezzanine debt on the basis of a 5-year exit and possible refinancing of the mezzanine debt.
d. Estimate the expected returns to management and the sponsor.

13.5 Notsoblue Chip Corp. wants to issue $50 million of 10-year debt on March 3, 2004. The bonds will be issued at par with 8% annual coupon interest (50,000 bonds of $1,000 par value each, with principal to be repaid in year 10). Notsoblue is willing to attach warrants to the bonds to raise the effective yield to 14%, the yield required by the market on this type of issue. Design the bond-warrant package that would permit the company to implement its financing plan.

So far you have determined that:

- The warrants will expire in 7 years.
- The yield on a 7-year government note is 4.0% (annually compound rate).
- The share value of Notsoblue Chip Corp. is estimated at $14 a share.
- The volatility of the rate of return of Notsoblue is estimated at 65% per annum.
- Common shares outstanding are 5 million.
- Each warrant will entitle the holder to buy one share of Notsoblue stock for an exercise price of $20.
- The company has no other warrants or convertibles outstanding and does not pay dividends.

How many warrants need to be attached to each bond? What is the value of each warrant?

13.6 CWI Communications wants to raise $1 billion by issuing a unit consisting of $1 billion 6.5% 10-year subordinated debentures ($1,000 face value each) with coupon payable semiannually and

---

[34]Jones expected to attain the tax benefits of original issue discount (OID) amortization of the mezzanine note. According to the Federal Tax Code and Regulation Guidelines the note qualified for OID amortization and would be priced at about 13% for determining the allowed OID.

EXHIBIT A	*Cap & Seal Balance Sheets, Historical and Proforma June 2000*		
($000)	Aug-31		Jun-30
	1998	1999	2000
ASSETS:			
Cash	$31,610	$16,010	$23,145
Accounts receivable	36,320	31,730	42,350
Inventory	15,940	27,590	29,143
Other current assets	340	2,840	3,460
Total Current Assets	$84,210	$78,170	$98,098
Net PP&E	75,020	94,440	104,168
Investments	8,320	8,320	4,160
Other assets	14,770	15,940	8,660
Patent value	129,240	117,520	109,009
Total Assets	$311,560	$314,390	$324,095
LIABILITIES:			
Short term debt			
Current portion LT debt	$22,500	$27,520	27,523
Other ST debt			
Trade accounts payable	8,870	14,230	18,760
Accrued expenses	7,290	10,220	12,220
Income tax payable		2,520	
Other current liabilities			
Total Current Liabilities	$38,660	$54,490	$58,503
Long term debt	231,220	212,540	212,540
Other noncurrent liabilities		3,250	
Total Liabilities	$269,880	$270,280	$271,043
Deferred taxes	9,180	7,300	6,050
Preferred stock	14,060	14,060	14,060
Common stock—Class A	3,220	3,220	3,220
Retained earnings	15,220	19,530	29,722
Total net worth	$32,500	$36,810	$47,002
Total Liab. & Net Worth	$311,560	$314,390	$324,095

13 detachable warrants, each entitling the holder to purchase a share of CWI for $76.9231 payable by surrendering the bonds at face value. The warrants would expire in 5 years. Alternatively, CWI is able to issue $500 million of straight subordinated debentures at par with a 12% coupon payable semiannually. Issue fees would be 0.75% of principal amount in each case. CWI does not plan to pay common dividends during the life of the warrants.

The following information is available:

Yield on a 5-year government note	3.77%*
CWI estimated stock value	$47
CWI estimated stock return volatility	54%
CWI common shares outstanding	117.2 million
Issue date	October 31, 2001

* Annually compounded rate.

EXHIBIT B   Cap & Seal Historical Income Statements

($000)	1998	1999	Jun-30 2000*
Net sales	$254,070	$261,070	$237,330
Cost of goods sold	144,420	135,240	134,892
Depreciation & pat. amort.	16,350	29,400	22,108
Gross Profit	$93,300	$96,430	$80,330
SG&A & R&D expenses	47,390	52,530	40,100
EBIT	$45,910	$43,900	$40,230
Interest expense	18,760	26,400	23,671
Other expense/(income)	(3,520)	(2,350)	(3,350)
Unusual items		(9,500)	
Net Profit before Taxes	$30,670	$10,350	$19,909
Income taxes	14,370	4,310	7,987
Net Income	$16,300	$6,040	$11,922
Common dividends		0	0
Preferred dividends	($1,080)	($1,730)	($1,730)
Retained earnings for period	$15,220	$4,310	$10,192

*Pro-forma June 2000 is for 9/1/99 to 6/30/00.

EXHIBIT C   Cap & Seal Historical Cash Flow Statements

($000)	Aug-31 1998	Aug-31 1999	Jun-30 2000
Net Income	$16,300	$6,040	$11,922
Interest expense	18,760	26,400	23,671
Change in taxes payable	(3,570)	2,520	(2,520)
Change in deferred taxes	3,820	(1,880)	(1,250)
Unusual items	0	9,500	0
Depreciation & pat. amort.	16,350	29,400	22,108
Adj cash flow fm ops	$51,660	$71,980	$53,931
Cash interest expense	(18,760)	(26,400)	(23,671)
Current portion—LTD	0	(22,500)	(27,520)
Cash Flow After Debt Service	$32,900	$23,080	$2,740
Capital expenditures	(15,950)	(37,100)	(23,325)
Change in working capital	1,880	(1,270)	(6,263)
Unusual items, change in A/L	(148,520)	(7,420)	8,190
Cash Flow Before Financing	$129,690	($22,710)	($18,658)
Proceeds from disposals	16,860	0	0
Change in ST debt	(7,750)	0	0
Change in LT debt	252,690	8,840	27,523
Change in net worth	(110,490)	0	0
Preferred dividends	(1,080)	(1,730)	(1,730)
Common dividends	0	0	0
Change in Cash	$20,540	($15,600)	$7,135
Reconciliation	$20,540	($15,600)	$7,135

EXHIBIT D *Cap & Seal Projections 2000–2010*

($000 and %)

	2000*	2001	2002	2003	2004	2005	2006	2007	2008	2009	2010
Sales growth rate		7.50%	7.50%	7.50%	7.50%	7.50%	7.50%	7.50%	7.50%	7.50%	7.50%
Sales	64,000	334,800									
CGS/Sales	55.70%	55.70%	55.70%	55.70%	55.70%	55.70%	55.70%	55.70%	55.70%	55.70%	55.70%
(SG&A + R&D)/Sales	16.22%	15.73%	15.14%	14.57%	14.00%	13.50%	12.98%	12.49%	12.05%	11.62%	11.62%
Accounts receivable days out	44.4	44.4	44.4	44.4	44.4	44.4	44.4	44.4	44.4	44.4	44.4
Inventory days on hand	65.0	60.0	60.0	60.0	60.0	60.0	60.0	60.0	60.0	60.0	60.0
Other current assets/Sales	1.0%	1.0%	1.0%	1.0%	1.0%	1.0%	1.0%	1.0%	1.0%	1.0%	1.0%
Accounts payable days out	32.0	32.0	32.0	32.0	32.0	32.0	32.0	32.0	32.0	32.0	32.0
Accrued expenses/Sales	4.2%	4.2%	4.2%	4.2%	4.2%	4.2%	4.2%	4.2%	4.2%	4.2%	4.2%
Plant projections											
Book depreciation	3,376	21,713	23,435	24,626	25,105	26,450	27,240	29,285	29,610	30,000	30,000
Tax depreciation	3,358	21,540	24,560	25,430	30,500	32,980	34,679	38,500	39,230	39,945	40,500
Book patent amortization	1,818	10,906	10,906	10,906	10,906	9,950	9,950	9,950	9,950	9,950	9,950
Tax patent amortization	1,273	7,634	7,634	7,634	7,634	6,965	6,965	6,965	6,965	6,965	6,965
Deferred taxes[#]	(225)	(1,378)	(859)	(987)	849	1,418	1,782	2,492	2,654	2,784	3,006
Capital expenditures	3,333	28,440	25,000	25,400	28,000	35,000	40,000	50,000	55,000	55,000	55,000
Minimum cash balance/Sales	2.5%	2.5%	2.5%	2.5%	2.5%	2.5%	2.5%	2.5%	2.5%	2.5%	2.5%
Amort of cap transactions exp		295	1,771	1,771	1,771	1,771	1,771	1,771	1,476		
Other expense (income)[+]	0.0	0.0	0.0	0.0	0.0	0.0	0.0	0.0	0.0	0.0	0.0
Investments	4,160	4,160	4,160	4,160	4,160	4,160	4,160	4,160	4,160	4,160	4,160
Other assets	8,660	8,660	8,660	8,660	8,660	8,660	8,660	8,660	8,660	8,660	8,660

(continued)

EXHIBIT D Cap & Seal Projections 2000–2010 (continued)

($000 and %)

	2000*	2001	2002	2003	2004	2005	2006	2007	2008	2009	2010
Assumed long-term debt											
Balance remain	10,000	9,330	7,780	5,950	3,880	1,560	150	0.0	0.0	0.0	0.0
Interest rate	12.00%	12.00%	12.00%	12.00%	12.00%	12.00%	12.00%	12.00%	12.00%	12.00%	12.00%
Sr. debt:											
Interest rate	9.00%	9.00%	9.00%	9.00%	9.00%	9.00%	9.00%	9.00%	9.00%	9.00%	9.00%
Sub. Debt (Mezzanine):											
Interest rate	10.50%	10.50%	10.50%	10.50%	10.50%	10.50%	10.50%	10.50%	10.50%	10.50%	10.50%
Tax Payable/Income tax	0.0%	19.0%	19.0%	19.0%	19.0%	19.0%	19.0%	19.0%	19.0%	19.0%	19.0%
Projected current tax rate	40.00%	40.00%	40.00%	40.00%	40.00%	40.00%	40.00%	40.00%	40.00%	40.00%	40.00%

*July and August 2000.
#Deferred taxes are generated by multiplying the difference between tax and book depreciation by Cap & Seal's tax rate.
+Except interest on cash balances, which are projected to earn 6.07% per annum.

a. What price would the $1bn 6.5% debentures trade for without the warrants?

b. What is the value of the warrants?

c. Compare the unit issue with the straight subordinated debenture alternative in terms of cost to CWI and other features you consider relevant.

13.7 The Blindex Corporation is negotiating an 8-year subordinated loan with Good Ground Capital Partners as a first step toward going public the following year. It expects to close the transaction on November 30, 2003. Blindex's investment banker proposes giving the lender 1 million 8-year warrants with a $15 exercise price in exchange for a lower coupon rate. Specifically, Blindex needs to raise $19.9 million net of expenses. It can do so by issuing $20 million subordinated debentures with a 13% annual coupon or with an 11% coupon plus the warrants.

The warrants would expire in 8 years. Blindex has 10 million shares outstanding and has not issued convertibles or warrants in the past. Its stock is valued at $8 a share and the volatility of its stock return is estimated at 40% per year. Blindex is a fast-growth company and does not plan to pay dividends in years to come. The annually compound yield of 8-year government notes is 4%.

a. What is the dollar cost of the warrant sweetener to Blindex?

b. What is the all-inclusive cost of each financing alternative?

13.8 Good Ground wants to insert a safety covenant that provides that if Blindex's stock price falls below $5 at any time during the life of the warrants, the warrants expire and Good Ground receives a $0.73 rebate per warrant. What is the value of this knockout warrant? What is the value of the knockout warrant plus the rebate? (Hint: Use the knockout option module in Financial Options Calculator but adjust output for dilution as in Appendix A, Section A.9).

13.9 On February 25, 2002, the private placement department of Provident Mutual was evaluating a $10 million loan request from Fly-By-Dusk Inc. The loan principal would be repayable in five annual installments of $2 million each. Provident would charge 14% per annum on this type of loan but Fly-By-Dusk was willing to give Provident one million warrants to reduce interest payments. The warrants would have $10 exercise price and would expire in five years. Fly-By-Dusk has 5 million shares outstanding valued at $5 a share with an estimated return volatility of 35%. The stock paid no dividend. Treasury securities traded at the following annually compound yields:

1	year bills	1.30%
3	year notes	1.75
5	year notes	2.50
10	year notes	3.81
30	year bonds	5.87

What is the minimum annual interest rate Provident can charge on the loan if it takes the warrants?

13.10 You are familiar with two approaches to the valuation of warrants. One approach uses present value analysis and exit values to price warrants given as equity kickers in leveraged capitalizations. The second approach uses option-pricing theory (a modified version of the Black-Scholes formula) to price the warrants. What is the relationship between these two approaches? Under what conditions are they consistent with each other?

13.11 You are considering whether to invest $10 million in the 5-year subordinated notes of HTF Inc. on July 1, 2004. The annual coupon of these notes is 8%, and its principal is due at the end of the fifth year. In order to obtain an acceptable return you demand equity participation. HTF's current revenue and EBITDA are $30 million and $5 million, respectively. The EBITDA margin is 20%, and future EBITDA is expected to equal $0.20 \times$ Revenue $- 1,000$, with revenue growing at 12% per year during the following 5 years. Fifth year net debt is projected at $15 million.

a. What equity participation (percent ownership) would you demand if you require 17% expected return from the joint proceeds of the subordinated note and the equity and you assume exit in year 5 at an EBITDA multiple equal to 6x? HTF is not expected to make cash distributions during this period. Under what conditions would your return be more (less) than 17%?

b. Suppose that in order to reduce your equity requirement you are offered a guarantee in the form of a put for your common equity. Under the alternative arrangement, your equity would be puttable to the company at an equity valuation of $35 million at the end of the 5th year. You estimate that the volatility of revenue is 20% per year and that cash flows with the risk characteristics of HTF revenue would be discounted at 20%. The riskless rate is 5%. What equity participation would you demand?

Part Three

Recapitalizations and Restructuring

Chapter 14

Recapitalization of Troubled Companies

14.1 DEALING WITH FINANCIAL DISTRESS

Changes in economic conditions, overoptimistic projections, excessive debt, and managerial errors can precipitate default.[1] How to deal with a company in financial distress depends on if it is worth more as a going concern than in liquidation. Salvaging the going concern requires a recapitalization of the company and the implementation of a turnaround plan directed to conserve cash, reduce expenses, stabilize cash flow, and assure economic viability. Liquidation involves an orderly selling of assets to maximize proceeds.

The purpose of a recapitalization is to reduce the burden of debt on the cash flow of the company to make it consistent with its debt capacity and to maximize the cash recovery of the different claimants. The tools of analysis for recapitalizing and valuing a distressed company are those developed in Chapter 7 on debt capacity and Chapter 13 on leveraged buyouts. Independently of the form of the original company, recapitalizing a distressed company is similar to structuring an LBO in the sense that both use all the debt capacity that can be realistically managed and that the cash flows available to many of the claimants are in the distant future. However, negotiation under distress is more complicated in that creditors attempt to preserve their claims and can force unrealistic amortization schedules. A credible, realistic analysis of debt capacity and a fair valuation of the several instruments offered in exchange for the existing claims are essential components of a sound recapitalization plan.

In this chapter, we present the basic framework for recapitalizations, discuss the options available in and out of court, and examine their tax consequences. We then proceed to discuss two detailed examples: the recapitalizations of Southland and Euro Disney. Between the two of them, we cover the most common valuation issues faced in recapitalization practice.

Most companies that get into financial difficulties have operating problems that often require disposition of assets. Identifying the company's core business, deciding what to keep and what to dispose of, are the basis of a successful turnaround strategy. Asset restructuring is examined in Chapter 15.

14.2 FRAMEWORK FOR RECAPITALIZATIONS

Let us return to the LBO example of Section 13.6, in which the company was bought and financed as follows:

---

[1]See, for example, Wruck (1993).

Sources		Uses	
	($ millions)		
Senior secured debt	154	Purchase price	554
Subordinated debt	286	Cash	2
Equity	131	Expenses	15
	571		571

Assume that the 1st-year cash flow was just enough to pay interest, that the company is in default on senior debt amortization, and that next-year sales and EBITDA are estimated at $1,000 and $100, respectively, with zero nominal growth for the foreseeable future. In addition, capital expenditures and changes in net working capital are to be financed entirely by depreciation and other non-cash items and the cash balance is $2 million. Assume that the original senior debt ($154 million) must now be amortized in 4 years. Then, the new debt capacity is only about 2.8 times EBITDA or $2.8 \times 100 = \$280$ million.[2] Hence, the following reduction or "haircut" in subordinated debt is required:

Original debt	$440
New debt capacity	280
Haircut	$160

such that the recapitalized company will have debt as follows:

Senior	$154
Junior	126
New total debt	$280

Note that now senior debt is 55% of the total debt and that subordinated debt is reduced to $126 million in order to conform to the reduced debt capacity of the company. Similarly, the enterprise value of the company has been reduced because of lack of growth. In fact, expected free cash flow in future years is only $(1 - t)\text{EBIT} = (1 - t)(\text{EBITDA} - \text{Depreciation}) = (0.6)(100 - 15) = \$51$ million, which, for a cost of capital of 13% (see Chapter 13, footnote 14), implies an enterprise value equal to $51/0.13 = \$392$ million or $392/\$100 = 3.9$ times EBITDA at exit time in 4 years. Subtracting net debt (cash balance equal to 0.2% of sales) yields a value of exit equity equal to $392 - (\$124 - \$2) = \$270$ with a present value of $253/(1.3)^4 = \$95$ million, using the sponsor's required return on equity. Hence, the enterprise value of the recapitalized firm is $278 + \$95 = \$373$ million. The valuations at LBO time and after default and recapitalization are:

Equity Valuation

Original		New	
Enterprise value	$569	Enterprise value	$373
Net debt	438	Debt	278
Equity	$131	Equity	$ 95

---

[2]The new debt capacity can be estimated by reproducing Exhibit 7.5 or using Equation (7.4) with the changes in the inputs mentioned above.

And the losses are allocated as follows:

Allocation of Loses

Debt forgone	$160
Minus equity claim	95
Subordinated lenders' loss	65
Old equityholders' loss	131
Total loss = $569 – $373 =	$196

In summary, the secured creditors preserve their original claims, subordinated bond-holders lose $65 million and the original equity-holders are wiped out. Although this is the outcome one would expect according to the absolute priority of the original claims, it represents only a tendency because, in practice, the outcome is the result of bargaining among several parties. In particular, the original LBO promoters (the sponsor and management) may be needed in order to preserve the value of the going concern. Even if they are removed and lose everything, new turnaround management would need to be brought on board, and it would require a share of the equity. Similarly, subordinated holders may be able to offer a common front and demand concessions from the secured holders.[3] When a firm is worth more as a going concern than in liquidation, there is an incentive for other investors to acquire debt and equity claims if in so doing they can resolve conflicts among claim-holders and make a profit. These investors create *de facto* strips and are subject to similar incentives as strip-holders.[4] In some cases, they take outright control of the company.

14.3   OUT-OF-COURT WORKOUTS AND BANKRUPTCY

14.3.1   Out-of-court Workouts

In an out-of-court workout, debtor and creditors negotiate extensions of the time to pay back and/or reductions of the amounts to be paid. Creditors demand a turnaround plan that shows that, with the concessions demanded, they will eventually receive more than from immediate enforcement of their liquidation rights. A successful turnaround plan must be feasible, fair, and better than the alternative of bankruptcy reorganization or liquidation.

Although out-of-court workouts tend to be faster, less expensive, more flexible, and more private than bankruptcy reorganizations, they are subject to the "holdout problem" created by the refusal of some creditors to accept the plan in search for better terms of themselves. Typically, bond indentures require 85% or more acceptance by each class of creditors in order to consummate a recapitalization altering the term of existing debt. Dealing separately with dissident creditors can derail the plan if the other creditors are un-willing to accept that dissidents receive preferential treatment. On the other hand, the very possibility of an in-court reorganization with its consequent delays and costs may be in-centive enough to persuade all or most of the creditors to participate in an out-of-court plan.

---

[3]Weiss (1990) found that absolute priority was violated in 29 out of sample of 37 bankruptcy cases filed during 1979–1986.

[4]See Chapter 13, Section 13.3.

14.3.2   In-court Reorganization

As an alternative, the debtor may seek court relief under the U.S. Bankruptcy Code, either under Chapter 11 reorganization or Chapter 7 liquidation. The purpose of Chapter 11 is the development and court approval of a reorganization plan. The debtor needs to file a petition and complete financial information, including a list of creditors and the nature of their claims. Under Chapter 11 the company becomes a new legal entity referred to as "debtor in possession," but it is usually the same company and operates under the same management. However, there is oversight by the court and a creditor committee, and the court may appoint a trustee. The debtor is granted "automatic stay" when the petition is accepted by the court. This stops any proceedings against the debtor and permits it to operate the business without interference from creditors. In addition, the petition stops interest accruals on unsecured debt and permits the debtor to obtain additional financing by giving priority to the post-petition creditors.

Chapter 11 provides the ability of imposing a reorganization plan binding on all creditors. The reorganization plan must be accepted by at least two-thirds in amount and one-half in number of the creditors within each class. In addition, the court may force ("cram down") the plan upon a class not satisfying these requirements if the court find the plan does not discriminate unfairly against it.[5]

14.3.3   Prepackaged Bankruptcy

The U.S. bankruptcy code permits the debtor to solicit the acceptance of a reorganization plan prior to bankruptcy petition. The plan usually provides for an exchange offer of new securities to current claimholders to be made out of court if the necessary approvals are attained. In addition, the plan provides that a similar proposal be effected under Chapter 11 with the provision that written acceptance of the exchange offer will also constitute acceptance under Chapter 11. This means that by filing a petition under Chapter 11, the debtor can attain binding approval with only two-thirds in amount and 50% in number in each class of creditors and the court can cram down the terms to a dissident class. This is in itself an incentive to elicit a higher level of approval out of court and reduced the holdout problem mentioned above. Even with passage through Chapter 11, a prepackaged bankruptcy plan can reduce the reorganization time to 6 months or less. Another timesaving alternative, called "prearranged bankruptcy," seeks the agreement in principle of at least two-thirds of the creditors prior to entering Chapter 11 and completing the reorganization plan.

14.3.4   Liquidation

Liquidation would usually follow when an in- or out-of-court reorganization fails for lack of a feasible plan or of necessary approval. A court-appointed trustee sells the assets and distributes the proceeds among claimholders under the Chapter 7 rules of the Code in the following priority order: secured creditors, bankruptcy administrative costs and expenses, wages for three months before the filing, employee benefit plan contributions, unsecured customer deposits, taxes, unfunded pension liabilities, unsecured claims, preferred stockholder and common stockholders.

---

[5]See Slaughter and Worton (1991) and Gilson (1993) for more details on the benefits of Chapter 11 protection and Saggese and Ranney-Marinelli (2000) and McConnell and Servaes (1993) and for a comparison of out-of-court restructuring and prepackaged plans.

The liquidation value of the assets depends on which assets can be sold as going-concerns and which assets have to be sold separately, and if the sale is made in an orderly fashion with time to identify potential buyers or in a public auction at a specific date. Piecemeal sales in auctions would normally result in lower proceeds than orderly sales of whole businesses. A reorganization plan needs to include a liquidation valuation of the company to provide creditors with a comparison of the value expected if they approve the recapitalization plan versus the potential recovery under the liquidation option.

14.4   ACCOUNTING TREATMENT

14.4.1   Troubled Debt Restructuring

When a recapitalization involves the restatement of some but not all the liabilities of the company, it often results in accounting for troubled debt restructuring. This involves a modification of the terms of a loan whereby the creditor, for economic or legal reasons related to the debtor's financial difficulties, grants a concession to the debtor that would not otherwise consider.[6] The concession can result in a settlement of the debt at less than the carrying amount or its continuation with reduced interest payments and/or face amount.

When assets or equity are transferred to the creditor in total or partial payment of debt, a restructuring gain equal to the difference between the carrying value of the debt and the fair value of the assets, net of related taxes, is accounted for as an extraordinary gain on restructuring. If the fair value of the assets transferred differs from their carrying value, the difference is accounted for as a separate gain or loss.

When debt restructuring involves only modification of the terms of the debt, its carrying original amount is reduced only if the sum of the new undiscounted cash payments is smaller than the carrying amount and a gain on restructuring equal to the difference is recognized. In that case, future interest payments, if any, do not go through the income statement and will be treated as reduction of indebtedness. This treatment of the implied interest increases reported earnings per share.

If the carrying value of the payable does not exceed the future cash payments, the carrying amount of the payable will not be adjusted, and no gain will be recognized, but future interest expense will be adjusted through the calculation of a new effective interest rate that equates the present value of the new future payments with the carrying value of the payable.

14.4.2   Asset Impairment

Troubled companies often have assets that are no longer worth their carrying amounts. The write-down of such assets is made for the difference between the fair value of its probable future cash flows and the carrying amount. Goodwill is normally reduced or eliminated first, but other assets as well may be written down following SEC guidelines. This results in a reduction of retained earnings and, in the case of write-downs of depreciable assets, an increase in future reported earnings.

14.4.3   Fresh-start Accounting

Fresh-start accounting essentially consists of a revaluation of assets and liabilities. It is required when a bankruptcy reorganization results in a general restatement of liabilities.[7] It

---

[6]Statement of Financial Accounting Standard (SFAS) N° 15. See Delaney et al., *op cit.*

[7]AICPA Statement of Position 90-7. See Delaney et al., *op cit.*

applies to companies operating under Chapter 11 with the expectation of reorganization and to entities emerging from Chapter 11 pursuant of court-confirmed plans, including pre-packaged bankruptcy plans. In the case of out-of-court reorganizations a similar procedure called "quasi reorganization accounting" is applied to the revaluation of assets and liabilities.

Fresh-start accounting applies only to a general restructuring of liabilities. Thus, if some of the liabilities are not subject to compromise during the restructuring, no general restructuring takes place, and debt can be accounted as troubled debt restructuring. Debtors prefer this alternative because it generally avoids running interest (cash or OID amortization) through the income statement, and thus it produces higher EPS (although it results in a higher book value of debt). The net effect of fresh-start accounting on future EPS depends on if the decrease in depreciation is offset by an increase in interest expense.

14.5   TAX CONSIDERATIONS

Debtors are taxed on cancellation of indebtedness (COD) income resulting from debt forgiveness or exchange unless specifically exempted. COD income is the difference between the face value of the debt and the fair value of the asset exchanged. COD income is excluded from taxable income when it results from bankruptcy (Chapter 11) reorganization or in the case of insolvent companies, which are defined as those with a fair value of the assets below the amount of liabilities prior to the reduction of indebtedness. For these debtors, stock for debt exchanges do not produce COD income because the stock is assumed to have the same value as the amount of the debt exchanged.

Under COD exclusion, no tax benefit can be taken from the new interest paid, as principal repayments and interest are both considered repayment of principal. In addition, other tax attributes such as NOLs are reduced by the amount of COD income excluded, which means the COD income is not exempt from tax but offset by other tax attributes usually available in reorganizations. Still, the ability to postpone the tax on COD income has present value to the debtor and facilitates its recapitalization. This is important because in many recapitalizations there is an effective change of control, which results in an annual limit to the use of NOLs equal to the product of the long-term tax-exempt rate times the value of the company immediately prior to its reorganization.[8]

The preferential tax treatment given to bankruptcy reorganizations has diminished the attractiveness of the private exchanges. The latter were the preferred approach to dealing with default during the 1980s prior to the tax changes that penalized them and gave tax preference to Chapter 11 reorganizations.[9] In practice, prepackaged bankruptcy tries to attain some of the benefits of private exchanges with the advantages of Chapter 11.

Merton Miller (1993) has pointed out that taxing a voluntary reapportionment of claims makes no economic sense and is an obstacle to efficient restructuring. We illustrate Miller's argument with the following example: Consider a firm financed with $50 equity and $50 debt that invested in assets valued at $100 at the time of inception. Let the market value fall afterwards to $50 and suppose bond-holders exchange their bonds for 52% of the equity and that there is no COD tax. The new shareholders' stake is worth $26 and the old stockholders retain $24 worth of equity. Each experiencing a capital loss of $24 and

---

[8]U.S. Tax Code Section 382. See Chapter 9, Example 2.

[9]See Gilson, Kose and Lang (1990).

$26, respectively, that eventually, upon the sale of their holdings, may result in a capital gain tax relief.

Let us apply COD tax at 40% corporate tax rate to the exchange "gain" attained by the corporation. The reader can verify that the COD gain becomes $30.30 resulting in a tax of $12.12 and a market value of the equity equal to $50 − $12.12 = $37.88. Thus, the bond-holders' equity stake is worth 52% of $37.88 or $19.70 for a capital loss of $50 − $19.70 = $30.30 (the corporation's COD "gain"). The old shareholders stake is then worth $18.18 for a capital loss of $31.82. Note the irony: The value of the assets has fallen to $50 but the COD tax on the supposed gain further reduces it to $37.88. The bond-holders who lost $24 in the value of their claim to the cash flows are taxed an additional $6.30 for a gain that was their loss. Part of it would be recovered upon the sale of their holdings if the bond-holders are taxable persons or entities, but capital loss deductions cannot often be fully offset against other income and, for individuals, they give credit at a lower rate.

14.6   VALUING RECAPITALIZATION SECURITIES[10]

14.6.1   The Southland LBO

In 1987, Southland, a Texas corporation conducting its business principally under the name 7-Eleven, was the largest convenience store chain in the world. From is founding by J. C. Thompson in 1927, it had grown to almost 13,000 company-operated, franchised, and licensed locations worldwide. On December 15 1987, in response to the threat of a hostile bid, JT Acquisition Corporation (a vehicle of the Thompson family) acquired Southland from its public shareholders via a leveraged buyout transaction. In order to finance the buyout, the company borrowed approximately $2.5 billion under term loans, raised $1.5 billion from the sale of debt securities with attached warrants, and issued preferred stock with a liquidation preference of $247 million. As part of a plan to reduce its indebtedness, the company divested certain convenience stores and substantially all other business units. In addition, Southland sold the Hawaiian properties to an affiliate of 7-Eleven Japan and obtained financing from 7-Eleven Japan (against future royalty payments) for a total of $1.9 billion, of which $1.3 billion went to reduce term loans. An additional $316 term-loan was repaid from cash from operations and borrowing under a revolving credit facility. In April 1990, the company divested of 56 7-Eleven stores in Memphis for a consideration of $12.8 million and signed letters of intent to sell its 68 stores in Kansas City. The company also sold its remaining 50% interest in Citgo Petroleum for $661.5 million. Southland experienced increased competitive pressures from convenience stores built by oil companies, as well as from supermarkets and drug stores offering extended hours and services. These competitors had been able to invest significant amounts of capital in their operations while Southland had had to restrict capital spending. The increased competition, along with changes in demographics and demand, had resulted in slower than anticipated sales growth.

Southland was unable to grow at a rate sufficient to allow it to meet the projections made at the time of the LBO. As of 1989, the company predicted that in the absence of restructuring its debt, EBITDA would need to grow at an average annual rate of at least 22% to be able to meet planned principal and interest payments. In the two full years following the acquisition, EBITDA grew at an annual rate of only 10%. Due to its operating results,

---

[10]This section draws from the case *Southland Corporation, Restructuring (A)*, Columbia Business School, 1992 written by David H. Ford, MBA 1992, and The Southland Corporation, *Proxy Statement-Prospectus*, October 5, 1990.

its debt service requirements and restrictions relating to the bank debt, Southland was forced to decrease its capital expenditures even further.

Notwithstanding the proceeds of the additional asset sales, the company's revised projections based on its post-LBO performance indicated that operating cash flow would be insufficient to conduct normal operations, service debt, and make necessary capital expenditures. Given these circumstances, it was decided that a recapitalization involving renegotiated amounts and amortization schedules of acquisition indebtedness would have to be effected.

14.6.2 The Recapitalization Plans

In March 1990, Southland announced the first in a series of proposed recapitalization plans. At the core of this plan was the purchase of 70% of the equity by 7-Eleven Japan and its parent, Ito-Yokado for $430 million. Ito-Yokado was Japan's second-largest and most profitable retailer. 7-Eleven Japan was by far the largest convenience store operator in Japan and was opening new outlets at the rate of about 300 stores per year. Under the terms of the proposed equity investment, Ito-Yokado was expected to pay about one-third of the $430 million with 7-Eleven Japan paying the balance. In addition, the purchasers would assume control of Southland's board.

The deal involved swapping stock and zero-coupon bonds for the existing acquisition debt and preferred stock. Successful completion of this exchange offer would have, in addition to halving interest expense and providing money for capital spending, resulted in bond-holders owning 10% of the equity while equity-holders would have retained 15%. Bond-holders rejected the offer on the grounds that it was too generous to equity-holders while bond-holders were required to take a "haircut" (debt reduction) in excess of 66%. In fact, bond-holders would have gotten between $0.15 and $0.375 on the dollar and no cash interest, while equity holders would have received $0.30 on the dollar despite their securities ranking lowest in the capital structure.

Negotiations between Southland and a steering committee representing holders of the acquisition indebtedness took place during the summer and fall of 1990. Several plans were considered and revised in successive iterations during which the creditors strove to increase their recovery.

As part of the recapitalization under the revised plan, Southland also decided to solicit approval from its security-holders to file a prepackaged bankruptcy plan. Under the terms of the bond indentures, any out-of-court plan would require approval of at least 95% of each class of security-holders in order to consummate the recapitalization out of court. As seen in Section 14.3, under a bankruptcy court–sanctioned plan, acceptances from debt-holders constituting at least two-thirds in dollar amount and one-half in number were required, and those holders who did not tender their securities would have new securities "crammed-down" by the bankruptcy court, making the completion of the recapitalization easier from Southland's perspective. The main characteristics of the restructuring plan approved in October of 1990 were as follows:

- The purchase by Ito-Yokado of 70% of the company's equity for $430 million; Ito-Yokado would receive 287 million shares out of a total post-restructuring capitalization of 410 million common shares.

- The old shareholders would have their share ownership reduced to 5% of the company.

- The remaining 25% of the shares would be available for distribution to the old unsecured debt holders and old preferred shareholders. Unsecured debt-holders would receive 21.6%. Preferred shareholders would receive 3.4% of the equity in exchange for the shares and unpaid dividends (the liquidation preference plus unpaid dividends amounted to $518 million).

- Unsecured bond-holders would exchange their old debt for bonds paying below market cash interest and amortized at several times depending on their relative seniority.[11,12]
- A new credit agreement would provide for a continuation of the revolving credit facility after consummation of the restructuring plan with a maximum borrowing of $275 million. The applicable rate was 10½% with ½% commitment fee on unadvanced funds. Borrowing under the revolving credit facility would have to be repaid in full for at least 30 consecutive days each year.

Exhibit 14.1 presents the terms of the exchange. Exhibit 14.2 contains a forecast of income and cash-flow statements and Exhibit 14.3 contains the corresponding balance sheets. The forecast assumes nominal growth of sales and EBITDA from 1990 to 1998 of 5% and 8.1%, respectively.

Examination of the cash flow and balance sheet forecast shows that Southland would be able to reduce the recapitalization debt to $1.1 billion by 1997 with most of the amortization going to secured creditors. The distribution of the cash flow in a reorganization is a matter to be negotiated among the parties with the outcome a function of their relative bargaining power. Here, the banks had the upper hand because the liquidation value of Southland was estimated to be sufficient to repay the bank loans but would leave less than $400 million for the unsecured bond-holders or less than 20 cents on the dollar. In fact, in order to continue operations, a significant infusion of cash and the renovation of the credit line were required. This made both Ito-Yokado and the banks essential to the restructuring plan. Ito-Yokado participation was required in order to manage the company and contribute $430 million. This infusion to be applied to repaying suppliers, providing a cash-cushion, and making credible Ito-Yokado's commitment to turn Southland around. The banks's renovation of the credit line was also essential to Southland's survival. Therefore, the banks and the other secured creditors could demand that most of the cash flow go to amortize secured debt before paying subordinated holders.

14.6.3   Valuing the New Debt Securities

To estimate the implications of the plan, we need to value the new debt securities. Since the new subordinated debt pays below-market coupons, the cash flows of the three new securities described in Exhibit 14.1 have to be priced to market at the yields prevailing in the fall of 1990.[13] For example, the 12% New Senior Notes would pay $15.036 million semiannual interest from June 15, 1991 to December 15, 1996, and the principal would be due on the last date. The present value on December 31, 1990 at the semiannual rate of 7% is $232 million. Note that for the case of the First Priority Debentures, one must take

---

[11]The exchange represented an effective partial cancellation of indebtedness that was not taxable in a court-approved reorganization. However, no tax benefits could be taken from the new interest paid. Principal repayments and interest were both considered repayment of principal. See Section 14.5 above.

[12]A cash election for holders of small amounts of debt securities was also offered but it had not material cash flow consequences and is ignored here.

[13]Debt-holders experience a tax loss equal to the difference between the value of the original securities and the value of the new securities. However, they will pay taxes on the yield-to-maturity imputed interest on the new securities. As a consequence, marking to market can be done by discounting pre-tax debt cash flows at the pre-tax rate or discounting after-tax debt cash flows at the after-tax rate. On this equivalence see Notes N2.2 and N10.1.

EXHIBIT 14.1	*Southland Corporation, Exchange Recapitalization. Terms of Exchange Offer*

($000)

For each $1,000 principal amount of:	Holders receive:
13.5% Senior Extendible Reset Notes due December 15, 1995 and extendible to June 15, 1997.	$475 principal amount of 12% Senior Notes due December 15, 1996 ("New Senior Notes").
Total principal amount: $527,581.	Total principal amount: $250,601. 86.5 shares of Common Stock (the "Common Stock") and $57 in cash.
15.75% Senior Subordinated Notes due December 15, 1997 ("Old Senior Subordinated Notes").	$650 principal amount of 5% First Priority Senior Subordinated Debentures* due December 15, 2003 ("New First Priority Debentures").
Total principal amount: $350,000.	Total principal amount: $227,500. 40.5 shares of Common Stock.
16.5% Senior Subordinated Discount Notes due December 15, 1997 ("Old Senior Sub. Discount Notes").	$555 principal amount of 5% First Priority Senior Subordinated Debentures* due December 15, 2003
Total principal amount: $402,440.	Total principal amount: $223,354 35 shares of Common Stock.
16.75% Subordinated Debentures due Dec. 15, 2002 ("Old Subordinated Debentures").	$500 principal amount of 4.5% Second Priority Senior Subordinated Debentures (Series A) due June 15, 2004 ("New Second Priority Series A Debentures").
Total principal amount:$500,000.	Total principal amount: $250,000. 28 shares of Common Stock.
18% Junior Sub. Discount Debentures due December 15, 2007 ("Old Junior Subordinated Debentures").	$257 principal amount of 4.5% Second Priority Senior Subordinated Debentures (Series B) due June 15, 2004 ("New Second Priority Series B Debentures").
Total principal amount: $54,210.	Total principal amount: $14.908. 11 shares of Common Stock.
	*6% sinking fund payments commence Dec.15, 1996.
For each share of:	Holders receive:
15% Cumulative Exchangeable Preferred Stock, Series One, $25 liquidation preference per share ("Old Preferred Stock").	One Share of Common Stock.

---

into account sinking funds payments of 6% of the principal amount from December 15, 1996 to December 15, 2003.

The market value of the new subordinated securities is as follows:

($000)	Face Value	Priced to Yield	Value on 31-Dec-90
12% Senior Notes	$250,601	14%	$232,001
5% First Priority Debentures	450,854	15%	238,001
4.5% Second Priority Debentures	264,908	16%	96,784
	$966,363		$566,784

EXHIBIT 14.2 *Southland Corporation. Forecast Income and Cash Flow Data—Exchange Recapitalization*

($ millions)

	Actual				Years Ending December 31				
	1989	1990	1991	1992	1993	1994	1995	1996	1997
Income Statement Data:									
Net Sales	8,275	8,321	8,252	8,625	9,117	9,735	10,447	11,290	12,261
EBITDA	464	296	367	405	433	462	501	546	602
Interest Income (5%)	0	0	14	16	11	8	9	19	5
Depreciation and Amortization	(277)	(236)	(216)	(210)	(197)	(200)	(202)	(220)	(234)
Write-off of Goodwill	(947)	0	0	0	0	0	0	0	0
Equity in Earnings of Citgo	70	0	0	0	0	0	0	0	0
EBIT	(690)	60	165	211	247	270	308	345	373
Cash Interest Expense[1]	(415)	(302)	(213)	(204)	(191)	(172)	(160)	(162)	(111)
Non-cash Interest Expense	(157)	(129)	0	0	0	0	0	0	0
Gain (loss) on asset sales	(1)	0	0	0	0	0	0	0	0
Extraordinary (charge) Gain	(56)	380	0	0	0	0	0	0	0
Net operating losses carryover		52							
Income (loss) before Taxes	(1,319)	61	(47)	7	56	98	148	183	262
Income Taxes (benefit)	(12)	(143)	6	20	32	45	53	67	88
Net Income (loss)	(1,307)	204	(53)	(13)	24	53	95	116	174
Cash Flow Data:									
Net Earnings (loss)	(1,307)	204	(53)	(13)	24	53	95	116	174
Non-Cash Items	1,360	420	216	210	197	200	209	220	234
(Increase) Decrease in Net Working Cap.	216	(361)	65	(3)	8	8	9	1	3
Cash from operations	269	263	228	194	229	261	313	337	411
Proceeds from Sale of Citgo	(5)	662	0	0	0	0	0	0	0
Dividends from Citgo	55	5	0	0	0	0	0	0	0
Purchase of PP&E	(107)	(44)	(203)	(222)	(177)	(185)	(204)	(236)	(242)
Sale of PP&E	97	117	43	36	38	40	42	44	45
(Increase) Decrease in Other Assets	10	(4)	(2)	(1)	(3)	(5)	(4)	(2)	0
Other Sources (uses) of Cash	50	736	(162)	(187)	(142)	(150)	(166)	(194)	(197)
Increase in Cash before Financing Transactions	319	999	66	7	87	111	147	143	214
Principal repayments and financings[1]	(332)	(724)	(30)	(100)	(147)	(97)	(55)	(414)	(144)
Net cash flow	(13)	275	35	(93)	(60)	14	202	(271)	70

[1]Cash interest payments to the new exchanged securities are treated as reduction of principal.

SOURCE: Based on The Southland Corporation, *Proxy Statement-Prospectus*, October 5, 1990.

EXHIBIT 14.3	*Southland Corporation. Forecast Balance Sheet Data—Exchange Recapitalization*

($ millions)

	Actual	Years Ending December 31							
	1989	1990	1991	1992	1993	1994	1995	1996	1997
Balance Sheet Data:									
Cash and Equivalents	8	283	319	226	166	180	381	110	180
Other Current Assets	922	474	509	527	547	573	602	636	673
Total Current Assets	930	757	828	753	713	753	983	746	853
Net PP&E	1,995	1,710	1,678	1,677	1,640	1,607	1,586	1,577	1,559
Other Assets	399	383	366	347	332	318	303	286	268
Total Assets	3,324	2,850	2,872	2,777	2,685	2,678	2,872	2,609	2,680
Revolving Credit Facility	215	0	0	0	48	250	0	114	127
Current Portion of LTD	467	127	190	288	395	291	356	194	77
Other Current Liabilities	696	569	684	705	739	774	811	845	883
Total Current Liabilities	1,378	696	874	993	1,182	1,315	1,167	1,153	1,087
Total Long-Term Debt	3,381	1,838	1,745	1,547	1,245	1,050	1,290	924	884
Other Liabilities	115	102	88	83	79	79	80	82	85
	4,874	2,636	2,707	2,623	2,506	2,444	2,537	2,159	2,056
Warrants	26	26	26	0	0	0	0	0	0
Preferred Stock	140	0	0	0	0	0	0	0	0
Shareholders' Equity (deficit)	(1,716)	188	139	154	179	234	335	450	624
Total Liabilities and Equity	3,324	2,850	2,872	2,777	2,685	2,678	2,872	2,609	2,680
Secured debt plus revolving credit	2,230	1,398	1,317	1,197	1,026	901	924	740	589
Unsecured debt	1,834	567	617	638	662	690	722	492	499
Total debt	4,063	1,965	1,935	1,835	1,688	1,591	1,646	1,232	1,088

SOURCE: Based on The Southland Corporation, *Proxy Statement-Prospectus*, October 5, 1990.

14.6.4 Valuing Equity

Exhibit 14.4 summarizes a rough, "back-of-the-envelope" valuation of Southland's equity. The enterprise value in 1997 can be estimated capitalizing 1997 EBITDA at 5.8x, which is the median multiple of comparable convenience store companies.[14] This gives an enterprise value equal to 5.8 × $602 million = $3,492 million. Adding the projected cash balance ($180 million) and subtracting total debt ($1,088 million) yields a 1997 value of equity of $2,584 million. Although there was no compelling reason to focus on value in 1997, the projections were made through 1997 to show the long-term survival of Southland and its ability to reduce secured debt and retire the New Senior Notes. In addition, valuation in 1997 is able to capture the improvement in EBITDA attained from a more efficient operation of the company. Note that equity-holders would not receive any intermediate cash flow. Hence, the present value of equity is the discounted value of 1997 equity. However, to do so one would need to allow for the effect of changes in leverage on the cost of equity as discussed in Chapter 6. Based upon comparable data, we know that the

---

[14]Casey's General Store, Circle K, Dairy Mart, Sunshine Jr., and Uni-Marts.

EXHIBIT 14.4	*Southland Corporation. Valuation of Recapitalization Plan*

($ millions)

	Year-end	1990		1997
EBITDA				602
EBITDA multiple				5.8x
Enterprise value				3,492
Cash				180
Secured debt			589	
Unsecured debt value on 12/31/97			499	1,088
Equity				2,584
Present value of equity @	17.4%	841		
Total number of shares (million)		409.6		
Value per share		$2.05		
Unsecured holders claims				
Prior to restructuring		2,130		
Received in exchange				
Value of exchange bonds		567		
Cash		30		
Share of equity	21.7%	182		
		779		
Cents on the dollar		36.6		
Preferred shareholders claims		518		
Share of equity	3.4%	29		
Cents on the dollar		5.5		
Ito-Yokado equity	70%			1,809
Investment		430		
Ito-Yokado's IRR		23%		

unlevered cost of equity of Southland was about 15.2%[15] and that the cost of capital of levered equity had to be higher and decrease over time. As a first approximation, let us discount 1997 equity at 17.4%, the yield on Merrill Lynch High Yield bond index on 12/31/90. This gives a present value of equity equal to $841 million or $2.05 per share. Exhibit 14.5 values Southland with the APV method of Chapter 6. It yields a share price equal to $2.25. Note that the 1997 continuation value was based on 5.8x EBITDA. Solving for the implied growth in the perpetual growth formula (see Chapter 4, Section 4.3) yields 5.5% nominal growth or 2% real growth, somewhat less than the long-term growth of the U.S. economy. Southland's stock traded in the range $0.5 to $2.66 during March of 1991, the first month of trading after the reorganization.

14.6.5   Recovery

Exhibit 14.4 summarizes the value implications of the plan. The subordinated lenders as a class would expect to recover 36.6 cents on the dollar. This is obtained by adding to the

---

[15]The comparables are listed in the previous footnote. Their cost of equity is based upon an average unlevered beta of 0.4, a riskless rate equal to 8.6%, a risk premium equal to 4.8% and a micro-cap premium of 4.5%, with the latter being particularly applicable to the new stock of Southland given the small float expected for its recapitalized equity.

EXHIBIT 14.5 *Southland Corporation. Adjusted Present Value Valuation*

($ millions)

			Years Ending December 31						
		1990	1991	1992	1993	1994	1995	1996	1997
Net Income			(53)	(13)	24	53	95	116	174
Net Interest after Taxes			204	195	184	167	155	151	108
NOPAT			151	181	209	220	250	267	282
Depreciation and Amortization			216	210	197	200	202	220	234
Increase in Net Working Capital			(65)	3	(8)	(8)	(9)	(1)	(3)
Capital Expenditures less disposals			162	187	142	150	166	194	197
Free Cash Flow			270	201	272	278	295	294	322
Tax deductible interest expense			148	140	127	108	96	98	78
Tax shield for tax rate equal to	35%		52	49	44	38	34	34	27
Continuation Valued at EBITDAx	5.8x								3,492
Present Value of FCF @	15.2%	1,112							
Present Value of Continuation Value @	15.2%	1,297							
Present Value of Tax Shield @	10.5%	193							
Enterprise Value		2,602							
Minus Net Debt		1,682							
Equity		920							
Shares outstanding		409.6							
Value per share		2.25							

value of the new debt securities at the end of 1990 the cash received by the Senior Note holders and the value of 22% of the equity. Preferred shareholders would recover 5.5 cents on the dollar. Ito-Yokado would expect to realize an IRR equal to 23% through the end of 1997. But this return ignores the value of protecting the 7-Eleven franchise in Japan, and the value of the global growth opportunities that could become available to Southland if the turnaround is successful.[16]

The recovery of each class of non-secured bond-holders is a follows:

($ millions)	Old Claim as of 12/31/90	New Debt	Cash	Equity	Total Recovery	Cents on the dollar
13.5% Senior Extendible Reset Notes	607.7	232.0	30.0	93.9	355.9	58.6c
15.75% Senior Subordinated Notes	407.8	131.9		29.1	161.0	39.5c
16.5% Senior Sub. Discount Notes	472.1	106.1		28.9	135.0	28.6c
16.75% Subordinated Debentures	587.8	91.7		28.7	120.5	20.5c
18% Junior Sub. Discount Debentures	54.2	5.1		1.3	6.4	11.7c
Total	2,129.6	566.8	30.0	181.9	778.7	36.6c

Recovery goes from 11.7 cents for the junior subordinated holders to 58.6 cents for the senior note holders, for an average recovery of 36.6 cents on the dollar. On March 5, 1999, Southland emerged from bankruptcy. Its recapitalization: (a) permitted secured holders to

---

[16]See Chapter 8 on the value of real options.

recover the value of their original loans; (b) provided subordinated bond-holders with about 36.6 cents on the dollar of their original loans; (c) gave 5.5 cents on the dollar to the preferred shareholders; and (d) provided enough resources for Ito-Yokado and its management team to turn Southland around.

14.7   VALUING RECAPITALIZATION RIGHTS AND OPTIONS

The terms of a recapitalization often includes contingent claims on the equity of the company represented by rights issues, convertible securities, warrants and options given to old creditors, new investors, and management. This section discusses the valuation of a recapitalization plan in the presence of these securities.

In 1987 Euro Disney S.C.A. signed a master agreement with the French government for the location of a theme park in Marme-la-Valle outside Paris. In spite of the high hopes The Walt Disney Company (TWDC) and the French government had for the theme park, Euro Disney had problems from its inception in April 1992. A European recession resulted in low occupancy rates at the hotels and low expenditures per visitor. Less-than-stellar service and poor logistics created image problems and visitor and labor discontent. The property slump impeded the development of commercial and residential property surrounding the park, as well as the sale of some of the new hotels to private investors. Euro Disney simply did not generate enough cash flow to cover debt service and the management fees due to TWDC. As Euro Disney reported a loss of €0.762 billion for fiscal year ending September 10, 1993, its stock, that had traded as high as €25 in March of 1992, fell to €3.7 in November 1993.

A steering committee of the 69 banks holding the syndicated loans was formed to coordinate negotiations with Euro Disney. The outcome of these negotiations was a financial restructuring plan agreed in May of 1994 that was expected to keep Euro Disney in business and give management time to increase revenues and attain operating efficiencies. The plan provided for:

1. A €907 million rights issue (595 million new shares) at €1.5245 per share on the basis of 7 new shares for every 2 existing shares[17] of which: (a) TWDC agreed to subscribe and pay in cash 49% of the new shares; (b) A syndicate comprised essentially of the lenders underwrote the remaining 51%; (c) The United Saudi Commercial Bank (USCB) agreed to act as sub-underwriter for up to €302 million. The rights were to expire on Monday, July 11th, 1994.

2. The old shareholders received a free allocation of 10-year warrants on the basis of one warrant for each existing share (170 million) such that the holder of three warrants was entitled to subscribe for one share at the subscription price of €6.098.

3. The lenders agreed to forgive due interest payments and defer principal payments for 3 years. The lenders received 120 million 10-year warrants with three warrants giving the right to purchase one share at the exercise price of €6.098. The warrants ranked *pari passu* with the warrants described in (2) above.

4. TWDC agreed to waive all royalty and management fees for 5 years, with a lower fee structure beyond the 5th year; to arrange upon the company request for a €167.7

---

[17]That is, for each two shares they had, shareholders could purchase seven shares at €1.5245 or, instead, they could sell their rights in the Paris bourse. A total of 170 million shares were outstanding at the time of the rights issue.

EXHIBIT 14.6 *Euro Disney S.C.A. Pro-Forma Income Statements 1994–2004*

(€ million)

Years ended September 30	1994	1995	1996	1997	1998	1999	2000	2001	2002	2003	2004
Revenues: Theme Park & Resorts	632.2	697.0	770.2	851.1	940.4	1,039.2	1,148.3	1,268.8	1,402.1	1,549.3	1,712.0
Costs and expenses	(626.0)	(627.3)	(664.3)	(702.1)	(740.6)	(779.4)	(861.2)	(951.6)	(1,051.5)	(1,162.0)	(1,284.0)
Operating income	6.3	69.7	105.9	148.9	199.8	259.8	287.1	317.2	350.5	387.3	428.0
Royalties	—	—	—	—	—	15.0	16.5	18.3	20.2	22.3	49.3
Management fee	—	—	—	—	—	10.4	11.5	12.7	14.0	15.5	17.1
EBIT & lease rental expense	6.3	69.7	105.9	148.9	199.8	234.4	259.0	286.2	316.3	349.5	361.6
Lease rental expense	(135.5)	(43.4)	(55.6)	(107.2)	(146.2)	(160.1)	(170.4)	(165.7)	(162.5)	(159.2)	(161.2)
Financial income	82.0	47.1	38.7	54.5	63.9	74.6	86.7	98.7	78.1	89.1	95.6
Financial expenses	(148.2)	(74.5)	(56.4)	(56.3)	(56.3)	(56.3)	(56.1)	(54.5)	(18.5)	(15.8)	(13.0)
New borrowing interest	—	—	—	—	—	—	—	—	(9.8)	(9.8)	(9.8)
Financial charges	(201.7)	(70.8)	(73.3)	(109.0)	(138.6)	(141.7)	(139.8)	(121.6)	(112.8)	(95.8)	(88.5)
Net income bef. extraordinary items	(195.4)	(1.1)	32.6	39.9	61.3	92.7	119.2	164.7	203.5	253.7	273.1
Extraordinary income (loss)	(78.5)	17.1	—	—	—	—	—	—	—	—	—
Income before taxes	(274.0)	15.9	32.6	39.9	61.3	92.7	119.2	164.7	203.5	253.7	273.1
Net operating loss offset	—	(15.9)	(32.6)	(39.9)	(61.3)	(92.7)	(119.2)	—	—	—	—
Taxes @ 33.33%	—	—	—	—	—	—	—	54.9	67.8	84.6	91.0
Net income	(274.0)	15.9	32.6	39.9	61.3	92.7	119.2	109.8	135.7	169.2	182.1

258

EXHIBIT 14.7   *Euro Disney S.C.A. Cash Flow Statements 1994–2004*

(€ million)

Years ended September 30	1994	1995	1996	1997	1998	1999	2000	2001	2002	2003	2004
Net Income	(274.0)	15.9	32.6	39.9	61.3	92.7	119.2	109.8	135.7	169.2	182.1
Depreciation and amortization	44.4	37.4	39.2	41.2	43.2	45.4	47.7	50.1	52.6	55.2	57.9
Other non-cash items	—	(9.2)	3.6	3.6	3.6	3.6	3.6	3.6	—	—	—
Capital expenditures	(121.5)	(35.1)	(36.8)	(38.7)	(40.6)	(42.6)	(44.8)	(47.0)	(49.3)	(51.8)	(54.4)
Change in net working capital.	3.8	(5.3)	(5.6)	(5.9)	(6.2)	(6.5)	(6.8)	(7.2)	(7.5)	(7.9)	(8.3)
Change in other assets	18.9	4.0	—	—	—	—	—	—	—	—	—
Proceeds from sale of PP&E	220.6	5.8	—	—	—	—	—	—	—	—	—
Cash flow before financing	(107.8)	13.5	33.0	40.2	61.3	92.6	119.0	109.3	131.4	164.7	177.3
Financing activities:											
Debt amortization	—	(0.3)	(0.2)	(0.2)	(1.3)	(2.4)	(25.8)	(704.0)	(42.8)	(42.8)	(42.8)
Repurchase of convertible bonds	—	(47.4)	—	—	—	—	—	—	—	—	—
Issue of new shares	880.5	—	—	—	—	—	—	—	—	—	—
New bond issues	152.8	—	—	—	—	—	—	—	—	—	—
Prepayment of borrowings	(236.1)	—	—	—	—	—	—	—	—	—	—
Increase in borrowings	—	—	—	—	—	—	—	103.6	—	—	—
Increase in loans to financing company	(644.4)	—	—	—	—	—	—	—	—	—	—
Debt security deposit	(44.8)	—	—	—	—	—	—	—	—	—	—
Loan repayment from financing company	—	—	—	12.4	29.5	34.2	35.8	35.5	35.5	35.5	35.5
Change in cash	0.2	(34.3)	32.8	52.3	89.5	124.5	129.0	(455.6)	124.1	157.3	170.0
Beginning cash	183.5	183.7	149.4	182.2	234.5	324.0	448.5	577.5	122.0	246.0	403.4
End of period cash	183.7	149.4	182.2	234.5	324.0	448.5	577.5	122.0	246.0	403.4	573.4

million 10-year line of credit; and to cancel receivables due to TWDC for €182.9 million. In addition, TWCD bought €152.45 million of Euro Disney S.C.A. 1% interest bonds mandatorily redeemable by 25 million shares in 2004. TWDC through a specially created vehicle participated in the sale lease-back arrangement and acquired certain tangible fixed assets from Euro Disney for €220.6 million.

5. As part of a retention package, in 1994 Euro Disney granted 19 million 10-year options at an average exercise price of €1.4788 to its employees.

Exhibits 14.6 and 14.7 contain Euro Disney's pro-forma income and cash-flow statements under the recapitalization plan.[18] They provide information for valuing Euro Disney's shares and rights. Euro Disney did not have close comparables but entertainment companies such as Walt Disney, Club Mediteranée, Accor (a leading French hotel operator), Atzar and Bally traded at trailing EBITDAR multiples between 9 and 15 with a median of 13.5 times, and their median unlevered beta coefficient was about 1.1. In the spring of 1994, the long-term French government bond yield was 8%, and the equity-risk premium was estimated at 3.5%.[19] In addition, the volatility of Euro Disney S.C.A. stock during the first 6 months of 1994 was about 29% per year.

WACC valuation is not appropriate in the present case because Euro Disney was not expected to follow a constant debt ratio target during the explicit forecast period. Instead, we compute Euro Disney's enterprise value using the APV method. First, we estimate the value of the tax shield. The tax shield is produced by financial charges and net operating losses (NOLs). The tax shield valued at Euro Disney market cost of debt (9.5%) is shown in Exhibit 14.8 to be worth €298.5 million.[20] Recall that the tax shield is valued only during the explicit forecast period. In the present case, continuation value is computed with an EBITDAR multiple based upon comparables and it already accounts for the value of the tax shield beyond the forecast period.

The next step is to calculate the enterprise value. We use the unlevered cost of equity (11.9%) to discount to present value the unlevered free cash flows and their

---

EXHIBIT 14.8	*Euro Disney S.C.A. Valuation of Tax Shield*

(€ million)

Years ended September 30	1994	1995	1996	1997	1998	1999	2000	2001	2002	2003	2004
Financial charges		70.8	73.3	109.0	138.6	141.7	139.8	121.6	112.8	95.8	88.5
NOLs utilization		15.9	32.6	39.9	61.3	92.7	119.2				
Total offset to taxable income		86.8	105.9	148.9	199.8	234.4	259.0	121.6	112.8	95.8	88.5
Tax shield @ 33.33%		28.9	35.3	49.6	66.6	78.1	86.3	40.5	37.6	31.9	29.5
PV{Tax shield} @ 9.5%	298.5										

---

[18]Euro Disney S.C.A. leased the theme park from Euro Disneyland S.C.N. for 20 years, with lease payments matching debt service, depreciation, and administrative costs such that the financing company generated no net cash flows.

[19]For the 1989 IPO valuation, S. G. Warburg assumed a 12% discount rate based upon the internal rate of return resulting from a forecast of dividends for TWDC, Club Med and Accor. For the initial 3-year development period, Warburg assumed a 20% rate in order to account for the fact that, at that time, Euro Disney was not a going concern.

[20]Since NOLs apply only when the firm has taxable income, one may be tempted to discount them to at the cost of equity, however the total amount of NOLs available is a fixed amount not correlated with future cash flows. NOLs not used in a given year are normally carried forward to future years. In this respect, they are similar to the tax shield of debt.

EXHIBIT 14.9 *Euro Disney S.C.A. APV Valuation*

(€ million)

Years ended September 30	1994	1995	1996	1997	1998	1999	2000	2001	2002	2003	2004
Net income		15.9	32.6	39.9	61.3	92.7	119.2	109.8	135.7	169.2	182.1
Financial charges		70.8	73.3	109.0	138.6	141.7	139.8	121.6	112.8	95.8	88.5
Tax shield		(28.9)	(35.3)	(49.6)	(66.6)	(78.1)	(86.3)	(40.5)	(37.6)	(31.9)	(29.5)
Unlevered net income		57.9	70.6	99.3	133.2	156.3	172.7	190.8	210.9	233.0	241.0
Other non-cash items		(9.2)	3.6	3.6	3.6	3.6	3.6	3.6	—	—	—
NOPAT		48.7	74.2	102.9	136.8	159.9	176.3	194.5	210.9	233.0	241.0
Depreciation and amortization		37.4	39.2	41.2	43.2	45.4	47.7	50.1	52.6	55.2	57.9
Capital expenditures		(35.1)	(36.8)	(38.7)	(40.6)	(42.6)	(44.8)	(47.0)	(49.3)	(51.8)	(54.4)
Change in net working capital.		(5.3)	(5.6)	(5.9)	(6.2)	(6.5)	(6.8)	(7.2)	(7.5)	(7.9)	(8.3)
Change in other assets		4.0	—	—	—	—	—	—	—	—	—
Proceeds from sale of PP&E		5.8	—	—	—	—	—	—	—	—	—
Unlevered free cash flows		55.4	71.0	99.5	133.3	156.2	172.4	190.4	206.6	228.5	236.3
2004 EBITDAR											419.5
EBITDAR multiple											13.5
Continuation enterprise value											5,663

Risk free rate	8.0%	
Risk premium	3.5%	
Unlevered beta	1.1	
Cost of equity	11.9%	
PV {Free Cash Flows} on 7/1/94		750.4
PV {Continuation Value} on 7/1/94		1,797.0
PV {Tax Shield}		298.5
Enterprise Value on 7/1/94		2,845.8

EXHIBIT 14.10   *Euro Disney S.C.A. Valuation of Consolidated Debt*

(€ million)

Years ended September 30	1994	1995	1996	1997	1998	1999	2000	2001	2002	2003	2004
Debt cash flow		137.6	84.24	109.3	174.7	179.2	257.0	820.9	229.4	219.3	220.9
Interest tax shield		23.6	24.4	36.3	46.2	47.2	46.6	40.5	37.6	31.9	29.5
Debt cash flow after taxes		114.0	59.8	73.0	128.5	132.0	210.4	780.3	191.8	187.3	191.4
2004 debt marked to market											609.3
Total debt cash flow		114.0	59.8	73.0	128.5	132.0	210.4	780.3	191.8	187.3	800.7
PV{debt cash flow} @ 6.33%	1,703.8										
Cash and equivalents	228.5										
Net debt	1,475.2										

---

continuation value.[21] Then we add the value of the tax shield. The APV valuation is detailed in Exhibit 14.9.

The value of equity is attained subtracting the value of the consolidated net debt from the enterprise value. Since most of Euro Disney's debt paid below market coupons, it needs to be marked to market, that is, priced by discounting its after-tax cash flows (including lease rental expense) at the after-tax market rate of interest. This is done in Exhibit 14.10.

The value of the Euro Disney's equity is computed in Exhibit 14.11 subtracting from the APV's enterprise value the value of net debt. It gives at €1,370.7 million. From it, we need to subtract the value of the other claims against equity to arrive to the value of common equity. These claims are the value of the employee's stock options, the warrants issued to bond-holders and equity-holders as per the recapitalization plan and the value of the calls embedded in outstanding convertibles. For example, to determine the value of the employees' stock options, we note that, before allowing for the options claims, the value of Euro Disney's share was €1.7351 for a total number of shares of 790 million.[22] Volatil-

---

EXHIBIT 14.11   *Euro Disney S.C.A. Valuation of Equity and Rights*

(€ million except per share values)

Enterprise value		2,845.8
Net debt		(1,475.2)
Equity value		1,370.7
Value of option claims:		
Warrants	32.1	
Convertibles	0.6	
Employee stock options	21.4	(54.1)
Value of common equity		1,316.6
Shares (million)		790.0
Share value		1.667
Right exercise price		1.524
Value of each right		0.142

---

[21]Euro Disney's shares were considered liquid enough to avoid the addition of a small-cap premium to the cost of equity.

[22]The number of shares is the sum of the outstanding shares before the recapitalization (170 million), the shares issued upon the exercise of the rights (595 million) and the 25 million shares that TWDC would receive in 2004 as per item 4 of the recapitalization plan.

ity and interest rate were 29% and 8%, respectively. Using the Financial Options Calculator to value these warrants as of July 1, 1994 yields €1.126 per warrant for a total value of €1.125 × 19 million = €21.4 million. Similarly, the warrants issued to bond-holders and equity-holders are worth €32.1 million, and the conversion option is worth about €0.6 million. (Problems 14.7 to 14.8 ask the reader to verify the value of these options.) Thus, the contingent claims on equity add up to €21.4 + €32.1 + €0.6 = €54.1 million.

Exhibit 14.11 shows that the value of common equity as of July 1, 1994, was €1,316.6 million or €1,316.6/790 million shares = €1.667 per share, and that each right was worth €1.667 − €1.524 = €0.142.[23] Euro Disney shares closed at FF11 or €1.68 on July 31, 1994.

14.8   SUMMARY

Changes in economic conditions, overoptimistic projections, excessive debt, and managerial errors can precipitate default. If the company is worth more as a going concern than under liquidation, a recapitalization plan that recognizes the reduced debt capacity of company may be feasible. Formulating a recapitalization plan and valuing its consequences relies on the same tools and concepts used to plan an original LBO. The main goal is to determine the debt capacity of the company given its new condition, or how much cash flow can be committed for distribution among the several security-holders and still have a viable entity. The specific distribution of the new securities among the several claimants is a matter of negotiation and of the relative bargaining power of the parties.

This chapter surveyed the legal, accounting, and tax aspects of out-of- and in-court recapitalizations and showed how to value recapitalization securities, including residual equity and contingent claims on equity, as well as the calculation of the recovery of each set of claim-holders.

---

[23]Numbers do not add up because of rounding.

PROBLEMS

14.1 Refer to Section 14.2 and use the Debt Capacity Calculator to verify that the debt capacity of the company falls to 2.8.

14.2 Estimate the debt capacity of Southland using the Debt Capacity Calculator with the data in Exhibits 14.2 and 14.3.

14.3 In March 1990, Ingersoll Publications Inc. offered to buy back some of its high-risk (junk) bonds at sharp discounts from face value. The company offered to purchase as much as 80% of its $125 million of 13% reset notes issued by Ingersoll's Community Newspapers Inc. unit for 55% of principal amount. The 13% reset notes have been trading around $390 to $420 for $1,000 notes. It also offered to buy as much as 51% of its $114.9 million of 14.75% discount debentures for 25% of principal amount. The debentures have been trading in the low $200 range for $1,000 notes. Ingersoll Publications Inc. was reportedly negotiating a $600 million bank facility from Chase Manhattan Bank, some of which would be used to fund the tender offer. The offer was subject to several conditions, including receipt of sufficient financing and the tender of 51% of the principal amount of each issue.

To assure buyers of protection of their investments, reset debt promises to adjust the interest rate periodically so that the debt trades around face value.

a. Why would reset notes such as Ingersoll's trade at a discount in spite of an imminent rate reset that would bring them to par?

b. Do you expect bond-holders to balk at the offer? Why?

c. Under what conditions do you expect bond-holders to tender their shares at a discount from par?

14.4 A year ago, the assets of REFC Inc. were purchased by SMP Partners in a leveraged buyout transaction for $1,250 million, financed with $1,100 million debt of which $550 were 12% senior notes and $550 were 14% subordinated notes. The senior notes were to be repaid in 3 years with a minimum annual amortization of $150 million. The subordinated notes were to be repaid with the available cash after repaying in full senior debt with the subordinated notes debt balance paid in full at the end of the 5th year or at the time of ownership change whichever occurred first. Initial EBIT was $250 million and was expected to grow to $380 million during the 1st year and at 10% per year thereafter. The initial cash-flow and debt amortization projections are presented below in Exhibit A. These projections assume that capital expenditures equal depreciation and other non-cash items, that working capital is self-financed, and that the corporate tax rate is 35%.

Soon after the LBO took place, SMP learned that the initial projections were unduly optimistic. In fact, at the present time, which is the end of the 1st year of the LBO, EBIT is down to $200 million and REFC is unable to fully service senior debt. Having fallen $113 million behind the minimum required amortization of $150 million (interest to subordinated holders has already been paid). Moreover, EBIT is not expected to grow beyond 4% per year in the future. The present situation and revised projections are presented below in Exhibit B. These new projections still assume that depreciation will have to be reinvested in the business as initially planned, in spite of the lower rate of growth now being assumed.

You, a recapitalization specialist at the newly established Sour Deals department of First Morningside Corporation, have been retained by the senior lenders to propose a recapitalization plan for the subordinated debt that would assure repayment of all senior notes in 5 years and as much of the subordinated notes as possible in 9 years from the present.

Propose a recapitalization plan for REFC and complete the cash flow projection shown below. What equity participation would subordinated holders receive? What equity participation should be left for the original owners? What is the value lost by each class of security holders? (You estimate that the company assets could be sold at a 4.0 times current EBITDA (depreciation in year 1 was $25 million and was expected to stay at that level during the forecast period).

EXHIBIT A	*REFC Inc. Projected Cash Flow*						
Year		0	1	2	3	4	5
EBIT (g = 10.0%)		250	380	418	460	506	556
Interest expense							
Senior	12.0%		66	48	25	0	0
Subordinated 14.0%			77	77	77	73	34
			237	293	358	433	523
Tax	35.0%		83	103	125	151	183
Net after tax			154	19	233	281	340
Debt amortization:							
Senior			154	191	205	0	0
Subordinated			0	0	28	281	241
Cash balance		0	0	0	0	0	99
Debt balance:							
Senior		550	396	205	0	0	0
Subordinated		550	550	550	522	241	0
		1,100	946	755	522	241	0

EXHIBIT B	*REFC Inc. Revised Projected Cash Flow*											
Year		0	1	2	3	4	5	6	7	8	9	10
EBIT (g = 4.0%)		250	200	208	216	225	234	243	253	263	274	285
Interest expense												
Senior	12.0%		66									
Subordinated 14.0%			77									
			57									
Tax	35.0%		20									
Net after tax			37									
Debt amortization:												
Senior			37									
Subordinated			0									
Cash balance		0	0									
Debt balance:												
Senior		550	513									
Subordinated		550	550									
		1,100	1,063									

14.5 The assets of Super Mart Inc. were acquired by SM-Holdings Corp. in a leveraged buyout transaction for $1,300 million financed with $1,150 million debt of which $650 million were 12% senior notes and $500 million were 15% subordinated notes. The senior notes were to be repaid in 4 years with a minimum annual amortization of $150 million. The subordinated notes were to be repaid with the available cash after repaying in full senior debt with the subordinated debt balance paid in full at the end of the 5th year or at the time of ownership change whichever occurred first. Initial EBIT was $300 million and was expected to grow to $400 million during the 1st year and at 10% per year thereafter. The initial cash flow and debt amortization projections are presented in Exhibit A below. These projections assume that capital expenditures equal depreciation and other non-cash items, that working capital is self-financed, and that the corporate tax rate is 35%.

The initial projections turned out to be optimistic. The recession and delays in the implementation of cost reductions resulted in a 1st-year EBIT of only $160 million. As a consequence,

EXHIBIT A	SM Holdings Projected Cash Flow					
Year	0	1	2	3	4	5
EBIT (g = 10.0%)	300	400	440	484	532	586
Interest expense						
Senior 12.0%		78	59	35	6	0
Subordinated 15.0%		75	75	75	75	38
		247	306	374	451	548
Tax 35.0%		86	107	131	158	192
Net after tax		161	199	243	293	356
Debt amortization:						
Senior		161	199	243	47	0
Subordinated		0	0	0	246	254
Cash balance	0	0	0	0	0	102
Debt balance:						
Senior	650	489	290	47	0	0
Subordinated	500	500	500	500	254	0
	1,150	989	789	546	254	0

SM-Holdings was unable to fully service senior debt, and fell $70 behind the minimum required amortization of $150 million. In addition, it was unable to pay the interest due to subordinated holders ($75 million). Moreover, EBIT was not expected to grow above 5% per year in the future. The present situation and revised projections are presented below in Exhibit B. These new projections still assume that depreciation will have to be reinvested in the business as in Exhibit A, in spite of the lower rate of growth now being assumed.

At this point, SM-II Holdings, a newly incorporated corporation, currently a wholly owned subsidiary of a new limited partnership involving the promoters of the first LBO is offering to exchange all outstanding securities of SM Holdings for securities of SM-II Holdings, which would then become the sole owner of Super Mart. The terms of the exchange are as follows:

EXHIBIT B	SM Holdings Actual and Revised Projected Cash Flow					
Year	0	1	2	3	4	5
EBIT (g = 5.0%)	300	160	168	176	185	194
Interest expense						
Senior 12.0%		78				
Subordinated 15.0%		75				
		7				
Tax 35.0%		2				
Net after tax		5				
Debt amortization:						
Senior		80				
Subordinated		0				
Cash balance	0	0				
Debt balance:						
Senior	650	570				
Subordinated	500	500				
Sub. int. due		75				
	1,150	1,145				

- 12% 4-year senior notes with $570 million nominal amount outstanding: Exchanged for new 9-year senior notes of same nominal amount, 8% annual coupon, and $63.33 million annual amortization of principal.
- 15% 5-year subordinated notes with $500 million nominal amount outstanding and $75 million of interest in arrears: Exchanged for (a) new 9-year subordinated notes of nominal amount equal to 29.91% of the sum of principal and interest arrears amounts. These notes will pay a 10% annual coupon and its principal will be payable in full at maturity. In addition, subordinated note holders will receive (b) common shares giving them as a class 45% equity ownership of SM-II Holdings.
- Common equity: Exchanged for new shares in SM-II Holdings representing 55% ownership.

  Note that the exchange would reduce the value of the creditors' claims and produce taxable capital gains for the corporation. For simplicity, assume that there are asset write-offs associated with the deteriorated condition that produce tax losses that exactly match the capital gains from the exchange. As a consequence, you do not need to deal with the tax effects of capital gains and losses in what follows. As those extraordinary items have no cash flow consequences they are not represented in the cash flow projection and you should ignore them.

  a. Is the proposed recapitalization plan feasible? Change Exhibit B as per the terms of the proposed exchange and complete the columns for years 2 through 5.
  b. In your opinion, what should be the response of each class of creditors (senior and subordinated holders) to the proposed exchange?
  c. What determines the bargaining power of the several parties?
  d. How would you value (i) the new senior notes, (ii) the subordinated notes and the equity participation received by the subordinated holders, and (iii) the equity retained by the original equity-holders. Just explain the procedure to follow without carrying out numerical calculations.

14.6 As of July 1, 1994, Euro Disney S.C.A. had 25.7 million convertible bonds outstanding, each with a par value of €21.3343 plus 10% premium due at maturity, and convertible into 1.361 shares, maturing on 9/30/2001. The bonds were valued as part of the net debt in Section 14.7 ignoring their conversion value. The value of Euro Disney's share as of July 1, 1994, before allowing for option claims, was estimated in Section 14.7 at €1.7351 for a total number of shares of 790 million. Volatility and interest rate were 29% and 8%, respectively. Use the Financial Options Calculator to value the warrants embedded in the convertible bonds.

14.7 In 1994 Euro Disney S.C.A. issued 290 million 10-year warrants to bond-holders and equity-holders, with three warrants giving the right to purchase one share at the exercise price of €6.098. Note that if these warrants end up in the money, the management stock options described in Section 14.7 would have been exercised, increasing Euro Disney equity by the exercise payment of those options. That would amount to €28.1 million and have a present value as of 1994 of €28.1/(1.08)$^{12\frac{1}{2}}$ = €10.7. Also, with the exercise of the management stock options the number of shares would increase by 19 million to 809 million. Use the warrants module of the Financial Options Calculator to value the warrants as of July 1, 1994 with the price and volatility data provided in Problem 14.6.

Chapter 15

Asset Restructuring

15.1 ASSET RESTRUCTURING AND THE VALUE GAP

Asset restructuring involves actions undertaken to realign the asset side of the balance sheet and, as such, it is different from a recapitalization, which involves the realignment of the liability side of the balance sheet and may be done even when the assets of the company remain intact. For example, a firm may decide to increase debt to fund repurchasing its own stock. On the other hand, recapitalizations under distress undertaken to deal with unsustainable debt levels often require the sale of assets to generate proceeds for paying down debt. Recapitalizations were examined in Chapter 14.

Closing the value gap of a company is a common restructuring motive. The value gap can be defined as the difference between the potential value of the company and its current value. For a publicly traded company, the value gap is the difference between its potential value and its market value. For a privately held company, the gap is the difference between the potential value of its future cash flows and the value of its cash flows under present policy. In each case, the potential value is the maximum value attainable by the company itself or by an outsider—strategic buyer, financial buyer, or raider.[1] These may believe they can create value from all or some of the company's assets. In the case of a public company, it is common to think about the value gap as the difference between its takeover value and its present market value.

15.2 IS THERE A DIVERSIFICATION DISCOUNT?

Most large, U.S. and non-U.S. corporations are diversified and involved in several lines of business. That is why the question of whether the value gap results from the underperformance of some particular business unit or from diversification itself needs to be addressed. In other words, does the cost of diversification outweigh its benefits? This is a controversial subject that has not been entirely settled by research.[2]

Firm diversification does not offer risk reduction to shareholders because they themselves can diversify more efficiently than firms. The arguments for firm diversification are more subtle. Diversification may increase the value of the firm in the measure that it reduces the variance of future cash flows, increases debt capacity and the ability of the firm to capture tax shields. A multidivisional firm is better positioned to make use of net operating losses. Similarly, a firm diversified internationally may be able to better manage its tax liabilities although that is more feasible in the case of vertical integration because of the role played by transfer pricing in allocating cost across tax jurisdictions.

---

[1]The typical raider acquires a company in a hostile takeover and profits from splitting up its assets and selling them to buyers that plan to increase their value by operating them. See Biddle (1993).

[2]The literature on this subject is vast and growing. See Martin and Sayrak (2003) for a recent comprehensive survey.

Diversification may also increase the ability of the firm to fund new projects sheltered from fluctuations in the external capital market, creating, in effect, an internal capital market. It can also permit a better access to the public markets.[3] Hubbard and Palia (1999) argue that the benefits of diversification may tend to decrease with gains in the informational efficiency of external capital markets.

The costs of diversification are in part a consequence of the flexibility it provides to managers. The very access to the firm's internal capital may lead managers to overinvest in search of personal objectives related to size and compensation. The allocation of resources in a multi-division firm can be more difficult than in focused firms and result in inefficiencies due to coordination problems.[4]

Empirical research suggests that the costs of diversification outweigh its benefits. Diversified firms trade at a discount of about 15% when compared to portfolios of comparable stand-alone companies, are more likely to be taken over and broken up, and the stock market tends to react positively to increases in their focus.[5] These results have not gone unchallenged however. A number of studies have found that diversified firms were poor performers, lacked growth and sold at a discount prior to their diversification programs which suggests that the discount of diversified firms cannot be attributed to diversification per se. Other studies challenge the very existence of the diversification discount, which they attribute to errors of measurements committed in previous studies particularly due to the limitations of segment reporting.[6]

The international evidence on the effect of diversification on value is also mixed. Lin and Servaes (1999) found no significant diversification discount in Germany but diversification discounts of 10% in Japan and 15% in the United Kingdom. They found that concentrated ownership in hands of insiders enhances the valuation of diversified firms in Germany but not in the other countries. On the other hand, Gibbs (1997) found that the EBITDA margins of divisions of German conglomerates were lower than those of their pure-play peers in 12 of the 16 industry groups studied. Kruse et al. (2002) found that Japanese diversifying mergers that took place between 1969 and 1992 increased operating margins and cash-flow returns (operating cash flows to enterprise value) with respect to the pre-merger aggregate of acquiring and acquired firms.

The lack of depth in emerging markets suggests that diversification may be beneficial in those markets. The evidence is also mixed in this case. Ferris, Kim, and Kitsabunnarat (2003) found that the Korean chaebol-affiliated firms suffer a loss of value relative to nonaffiliated firms, which they attribute to pursuing stability rather than profits, to overinvestment in low-performing industries, and to cross-subsidies to weaker members, and that these costs exceed the benefits associated with the chaebol's greater debt capacity. Chen and Ho (2000) find similar results for Singapore firms but only for firms with low managerial ownership, which they attribute to agency problems.

Although the weight of the evidence supports the conclusion that diversified firms trade at a discount with respect to their stand-alone counterparts, one cannot necessarily conclude that diversification per se is the source of the problem. In fact, firms like General Electric and Buffet's Berkshire Hathaway are well-known examples of successful diversification. On the other hand, the evidence supports the conclusion that diversification is not

---

[3]Hadlock, Ryngaert, and Thomas (2001) found that the market reaction to equity issue announcements is less negative for diversified firms.

[4]Scharfstein (1998) and Rajan, Servaes, and Zingales (2000).

[5]See Berger and Ofek (1995, 1996) and John and Ofek (1995), for example.

[6]See Martin and Sayrak, *op cit.*

a solution for firms in trouble and that those firms tend to trade at a discount before and after their diversification. Similarly, while diversification may offer advantages in emerging markets and may explain why most large firms in those markets are diversified, it seems to lead to inefficiencies that offset the benefits of diversification.

If a firm should restructure itself out of diversification and increase the focus of its operations or it should further it through acquisitions is a question to be answered in each particular instance based upon a careful valuation of its parts and of the benefits of growth through acquisitions. The valuation procedure to apply was presented in Chapter 9 and is further developed below in Section 15.6. We first examine restructuring actions commonly undertaken to close the value gap.

15.3 SHARE REPURCHASES

The actions available to a company for reducing its value gap range from better communications with investors to improving the management of its assets to outright sales of some or all of them. A better articulation of the company's strategy and its implementation may help but is usually not enough. Deeds, especially if in the form of cash, talk louder than words. That is why American and European companies have increasingly resorted to share repurchases.[7] The statistical evidence shows that stock prices react positively to the announcement of share repurchase programs, sometimes with a perdurable price increase of more than 10%.[8] The most effective share repurchase programs are those done via a Dutch auction for more than 15% of the outstanding stock.[9] Share repurchases have been interpreted as signals that the firm expects an increase in its future cash flows,[10] but they can also be interpreted as a recognition that it has fewer investment opportunities with positive net present value. However, if investors had already recognized the latter, disgorging free cash flow rather than misallocating it to negative net present value projects can have a positive effect on stock prices.[11] When share repurchases are financed with debt, the additional tax shield may exceed the risk associated with the increase in leverage and result in a share price increase. However, the empirical evidence is not conclusive on this matter.

15.4 ASSET DISPOSITION

Asset restructuring is a change in the nature of the company business accomplished by total or partial disposition of some of the assets held by the company and the possible acquisition of others. Partial asset disposition is an important part of changes in corporate control. About 4% of U.S. manufacturing plants change control each year through mergers and acquisitions and partial asset disposition. This percentage increases to about 7% in expansion years. Partial asset disposition accounts for half of the ownership changes. The empirical evidence indicates that the transfer of plants and divisions increases total factor productivity and improves the allocation of resources in the economy. This conclusion is also supported by the stock market positive reaction to asset dispositions. In addition, the

---

[7]See Bagwell and Shoven (1989) for an early analysis of this development.

[8]Escherich (2002a) and Gibbs (2001a).

[9]In a Dutch auction shareholders specify the price at which they are willing to sell shares to the firm, and the firm determines what price it must pay to repurchase the desired number of shares.

[10]See Vermaelen (1981) for an early analysis using tender offer data.

[11]As noted in Chapter 13, additional debt can also be interpreted as a pre-commitment to distribute cash to investors. See Jensen (1986) for an articulation of the "free cash flow hypothesis," and Fenn and Liang (1997) and Grullon (2000) for tests of it using open-market share repurchase data.

assets remaining with the seller may also be revalued. Corporate clarity seems to eliminate the discount which conglomerates are often subject to.[12]

A firm can dispose of assets by direct *private sales, initial public offerings (IPOs)*, or *spin-offs*. Partial disposition of a division can be accomplished by *carve-outs* or *tracking stock*. Which alternative to choose depends on the nature of the asset and the state of the capital market. If the value increase depends on the asset being merged into the operations of one of a few possible strategic acquirers, an auction among them may produce the maximum proceeds and the valuation of the asset should take into account the possible synergies of the merger. A business unit capable of competing on its own or becoming attractive to strategic buyers once they have been able to evaluate its stand-alone performance may better be disposed via an IPO, a spin-off, or a carve-out.

An IPO would maximize the proceeds to the seller only if the market impounds its stand-alone value into its share price. If the owner is simply trying to attain corporate clarity, a spin-off, which involves distributing shares to existing shareholders giving ownership in the separate entity, is a direct way of transferring ownership. Empirical evidence shows that the announcement of voluntary spin-offs has a positive effect on the stock of the company doing the spin-off.[13] A spin-off variation is the so-called *split-off* via which the company offers shares of a subsidiary in exchange for its own shares. Its purpose is to reduce the pressure on the spun-off company's stock price because shareholders who exchange their stock are less likely to sell the new stock. It also increases the earnings per share of the distributing company above the level resulting from a complete spin-off.[14]

When the company desires to raise cash for the asset being disposed and a direct sale is not available, a carve-out (partial IPO) with the seller keeping a significant ownership of the company may be a preferred alternative to a complete IPO. A carve-out can reduce the possible drag on value due of the information gap between management and investors mainly because the issuer keeps a significant share of the subsidiary equity. This allows the carve-out to prove itself in the market place. Only later, once investors have had time to evaluate the newly traded company would the rest of the retained stock be offered to the public. In fact, empirical research has found that the market reacts positively to carve-out announcements.[15] However, some empirical evidence on minority carve-outs does not show improved performance of either the parent or the subsidiary,[16] which suggests that if the goal is to attain market recognition for the realignment of the assets the parent should not keep a majority stake in the carve-out.

An alternative to a carve-out is the issuance of tracking stock, the payout of which is tied to the performance of a particular subsidiary of the parent company. This is done if the parent desires to retain the synergies associated with the interrelated operations of the firm. For example, economies of scope can justify maintaining the subsidiary under the control of the parent.[17] However, although on the average the stock price of the parent reacts favorably to the introduction of tracking stock, the latter has been found to underperform a portfolio of comparable firms.[18] Although selling tracking stock is a source of cash

---

[12]On the effects of asset dispositions on productivity and value see, for example, Maksimovic and Phillips (2001), Jain (1985), Hite et al. (1987), Hite and Owers (1987) and Escherich (1997).

[13]Hite and Owers (1983), Schipper and Smith (1983), Gibbs (1999) and Escherich (2002b).

[14]Wasserstein (1998), 673–674.

[15]Schipper and Smith (1986), Escherich (1998b, 2002c) and Gibbs (2000).

[16]Haushalter and Mikkelson (2001).

[17]Arzac (1991).

[18]See, for example, Chemmanur and Paeglis (2001) and Haushalter and Mikkelson (2001).

for the parent, it does do not seem to be the most appropriate way to provide clarity to its operations. It should be recognized, however, that in some cases the purpose of issuing tracking stock is not to attain clarity but to facilitate a merger transaction when there is a difference of opinion about the value of a particular part of the target company. In that case, the relatively poor performance of the tracking stock may be consistent with the prior belief of the acquirer. This subject was examined in Chapter 11.

*15.5   TAX AND ACCOUNTING TREATMENT[19]

15.5.1   Private Sales, IPOs, and Carve-outs

A private sale, often made through an auction, or an IPO provides corporate clarity and proceeds to the seller. Asset and stock sales are subject to corporate tax on the resulting capital gains. The tax treatment to the seller depends on if the transaction is an asset or stock sale and, in the latter case, on if the Code 338 election of treating a stock sale as an asset sale for tax purposes is made. The tax treatments of a sale to the buyer and seller were discussed in Chapter 9, Sections 9.2 and Example 3 of Section 9.3.[20]

For financial reporting, the disposal of a business segment is segregated from recurring operations, and the loss or gain on the disposal net of the applicable tax is reported separately before extraordinary items in the income statement. The gain or loss from the disposal should include the costs and expenses associated with it such as additional pension costs and fees and expenses.

A carve-out offers an attractive way of monetizing the asset while reducing the present value of the tax. For example, the firm may issue 55% of the stock in a first step and pay taxes on the gains associated with those proceeds. However, the remaining 45% of the stock can be monetized without triggering taxes by issuing an exchangeable security. An exchangeable security is a convertible that gives conversion rights into the shares of another company rather than into the stock of the issuer. In this case, the instrument exchanges into the stock of the carve-out. An exchangeable is basically a bond plus a call on the stock of the carve-out. As such, it pays a low coupon interest that is tax deductible. At maturity, if the call is in the money, the exchange would be executed and the issuer would need to pay the capital gain tax on the sale of the remaining 45% interest. In recent years, exchangeables have been issued in the form of mandatory convertibles that force conversion at maturity.[21] Mandatory convertibles receive favorable equity credit from rating agencies.

The accounting treatment of the carve-out depends on if it involves the sale of a minority or majority interest. In the first case, consolidation would continue, and the sale would result in a proportional reduction of the basis at which the subsidiary is carried. A gain or loss computed as the difference between the net proceeds and the proportional reduction of the basis would be reported as an extraordinary item in the income statement with a credit or charge to equity, and a debit to minority interest for the book value of the proportional net worth carved out. A sale of a majority interest would stop consolidation and the seller would carry its remaining stake as an investment (by the equity method of accounting). The seller would recognize a gain or loss on disposal on the proportional interest sold.

---

[19]Sections marked with an asterisk may be skipped on a first reading.

[20]A number of techniques used to postpone the tax on the gain to the seller were overturned in successive changes to the Tax Code and by Treasury decisions made between 1987 and 1990.

[21]See Arzac (1987) for an examination of these instruments. An example of monetization with tax deferral is Cox Communications November 1999 issue of mandatory exchangeables. It was done via a 30-year, $1.1 billion issue of exchangeables into Sprint PCS shares.

15.5.2 Spin-offs

With a spin-off, a company transfers a subsidiary to its shareholders by distributing the shares in its possession if the division was already incorporated or by forming a corporation with newly issued shares otherwise. In either case the shares need to be registered for distribution to public shareholders. The tax treatment of the spin-off to the parent and its shareholders is tax-free in the United States[22] when a number of conditions are fulfilled, including that (a) the distributing corporation must have control of the subsidiary immediately prior to the distribution of stock (must own stock possessing at least 80% voting power and at least 80% of each class of nonvoting stock, including preferred stock, and must distribute either all its stock or a controlling interest, and (b) there must be a business purpose to the distribution and the transaction must not be used principally as a device for distribution of earnings of the distributing corporation or the controlled corporation.[23]

The parent can get cash by levering the subsidiary prior to the spin-off. Alternatively, the parent can sell more than 20% of the stock in a subsidiary and still retain its ability to do a tax-free distribution to its shareholders by creating two classes of shares: low-vote and high-vote shares such that the latter carries at least 80% of the voting power. The low-vote shares are sold to the public, and the high-vote shares are distributed to shareholders. In addition, as per Section 305(e) of the Tax Code and its regulations (the so-called anti–Morris Trust rule), neither the distributing nor the distributed corporation can be part of a plan under which one or more persons acquire stock representing a 50% interest, normally during 6 months after the spin-off.[24]

The accounting treatment of spin-offs depends on the ownership of the disposing entity. If it is a minority stake, it was carried as an investment and its disposal is accounted for as a dividend in kind at the fair value of the shares distributed with charge against the parent's retained earnings. If it is a controlling interest or whole ownership of a division, it was consolidated, and its assets, liabilities, and results from operations need to be eliminated from the parent's consolidated statements from the date of the transfer. In the normal case in which the subsidiary is carried at a positive net book value, its transfer is recorded as a charge against the parent's retained earnings. If the subsidiary is carried at a negative net book value, the transfer is recorded as a credit to paid-in-capital as if shareholders would have made a contribution to the parent by accepting a business with negative book value. None of these transfers pass through the income statement.

15.5.3 Tracking Stock

The tax treatment of tracking stock depends on if it is considered a stock of the issuer or a stock of a subsidiary. A stock of the issuer is one in which the holder votes as shareholder of the issuer, the dividends are declared by the issuer, and liquidation rights apply to the net assets of the issuer and not to specific tracked assets. In that case, the distribution of tracking stock is considered tax-free to the issuer and as a non-taxable stock dividend to the shareholders. Also, a public offering of tracking stock is nontaxable to the issuer.

Tracking stock would be considered a stock of a subsidiary if it does not satisfy the above requirements for consideration as stock of the issuer. In that case, the distribution is

---

[22]In some European countries such as France and Germany spin-offs are not tax-free to shareholders.

[23]See Ginsburg and Levin (2002) for details.

[24]Prior to 1997, a Morris Trust device permitted disposing of a subsidiary tax-free by undertaking a qualified spin-off to the parent shareholders and merging the spun-off entity with an acquirer via a tax-free share exchange. Current law severely restricts the use of this device by excluding prearranged sales and requiring that the value of the subsidiary must be larger than that of the acquirer.

subject to the Tax Code requirements (Section 355) for characterization as a tax-free spin-off, which were discussed above. Otherwise, the issuer would be taxed for the difference between the fair market value of the stock and the basis of the distributed stock.

For accounting purposes, tracking stock is considered equity of the parent and not equity of the subsidiary to which the stock tracks. This means that subsidiary and consolidated financial reports are made in the usual way, with disclosure of the stock issuance done as in the case of accounting for stock compensation to employees (Accounting Principles Board Opinion No. 25). Information about the calculation of the earnings available to each class of stock is provided in a separated statement.

15.6   SUM-OF-THE-PARTS VALUATION

The analysis of restructuring options requires a valuation of the separable assets of the company. This is usually referred to as *break-up* or *sum-of-the-parts valuation*. We used this approach in Section 9.11.4 to estimate the value of an acquisition target. Here we show how to apply valuation analysis to estimate value creation at the business-unit level and how to evaluate restructuring options with respect to individual business units.[25] We concentrate on the fundamental drivers of value creation and the strategic alternatives open to the firm.

Let us begin by considering the sum-of-the-parts valuation of WTT Inc. presented in Exhibit 15.1. There the free cash flow valuation approach introduced in Chapter 2 is applied to each business unit. Note that WACC is different for each business unit. WACC often varies from unit to unit because of differences in business risk and debt capacity. In addition, no allowance for non-allocated headquarter costs is made. It is assumed that the coordination task is carried out by machine tools, the main division, at negligible additional costs. The sum-of the-parts value of WTT Inc. is as follows:

Machine tools	$1,310.9 million
Electronics	236.9
Metal products	117.1
Enterprise Value[26]	$1,664.8

An examination of Exhibit 15.1 does not reveal anything unusual about the value creation potential of each business unit. The reader may note that the free cash flows generated by machine tools tend to decrease over time, but that in itself is not an indication of value destruction. In order to derive meaningful conclusions about each of these assets, one needs to compare their performance under alternative operating and restructuring assumptions that represent the choices available to the firm. A good start is to restate the free cash-flow valuation in terms of economic value-added generation using the approach introduced in Chapter 5. EVA[27] valuation compares the present performance of the unit against the cost of redeploying the capital invested in the unit, assuming that it can yield its cost of capital elsewhere. While this may not be necessarily the case because of the lack of alternative uses for sunk investment, the company can re-deploy the capital expenditures planned for the forecast period. Exhibit 15.2 recalculates the sum-of-the-parts valuation by discounting the EVA generated by each unit. Although the value of each unit

---

[25]This section is based on Arzac (1986).

[26]Numbers do not add up because of rounding.

[27]EVA® is a registered trademark of Stern Stewart & Co.

EXHIBIT 15.1 WTT Inc. Free Cash-Flow Valuation

WTT Inc. Enterprise Value $1,664.8 (in million $)

Machine Tools Unit

	2002	2003	2004	2005	2006	2007	2008	2009	2010	2011	2012
Sales		650.0	702.0	756.4	813.1	872.1	933.1	996.1	1,060.9	1,127.2	1,194.8
Growth of sales		8.0%	7.8%	7.5%	7.3%	7.0%	6.8%	6.5%	6.3%	6.0%	5.8%
EBITDA		195.0	202.6	209.6	216.0	221.7	226.6	230.5	233.3	235.0	235.5
Depreciation		48.0	49.6	51.9	54.2	53.7	58.9	62.9	65.3	67.6	68.3
Operating income		147.0	153.0	157.8	161.8	168.1	167.7	167.6	168.1	167.4	167.2
Taxes @ 40%		58.8	61.2	63.1	64.7	67.2	67.1	67.0	67.2	67.0	66.9
Unlevered net income		88.2	91.8	94.7	97.1	100.8	100.6	100.5	100.8	100.4	100.3
Deferred taxes		3.3	3.5	3.8	4.1	4.4	4.7	5.0	5.3	5.6	6.0
NOPAT		91.5	95.3	98.4	101.2	105.2	105.3	105.5	106.1	106.1	106.3
Depreciation		48.0	49.6	51.9	54.2	53.7	58.9	62.9	65.3	65.3	68.3
Capex and Increase in NWC		60.9	68.8	71.4	49.7	97.6	92.1	82.7	84.8	73.0	101.0
Free cash flow		78.5	76.0	78.9	105.7	61.3	72.1	85.8	86.6	100.7	73.6
Continuation value											2,010.7
WACC	9.62%										
PV{Free cash flow}	508.3										
PV{Continuation value}	802.5										
Business unit value	1,310.9										

Electronics Unit

	2002	2003	2004	2005	2006	2007	2008	2009	2010	2011	2012
Sales		320.0	358.4	400.5	446.6	496.8	551.5	610.7	674.9	744.0	818.4
Growth of sales		12.0%	11.8%	11.5%	11.3%	11.0%	10.8%	10.5%	10.3%	10.0%	9.8%
EBITDA		57.6	62.0	66.5	71.0	75.5	80.0	88.6	94.5	104.2	114.6
Depreciation		24.0	26.5	29.2	32.1	35.2	38.5	42.0	45.6	49.6	53.8
Operating income		33.6	35.5	37.3	39.0	40.4	41.5	46.5	48.9	54.6	60.7
Taxes @ 40%		13.4	14.2	14.9	15.6	16.1	16.6	18.6	19.6	21.8	24.3

	2002	2003	2004	2005	2006	2007	2008	2009	2010	2011	2012
Unlevered net income		20.2	21.3	22.4	23.4	24.2	24.9	27.9	29.3	32.7	36.4
Deferred taxes		1.0	1.1	1.2	1.3	1.5	1.7	1.8	2.0	2.2	2.5
NOPAT		21.1	22.4	23.6	24.7	25.7	26.5	29.8	31.4	35.0	38.9
Depreciation		24.0	26.5	29.2	32.1	35.2	38.5	42.0	45.6	49.6	53.8
Capex and Increase in NWC		40.6	44.4	48.4	52.7	57.3	62.1	65.9	72.3	77.9	88.8
Free cash flow		4.6	4.5	4.3	4.0	3.6	2.9	5.9	4.7	6.7	3.9
Continuation value											570.5
WACC	10.50%										
PV{Free cash flow}	26.7										
PV{Continuation value}	210.2										
Business unit value	236.9										

Metal Products Unit

	2002	2003	2004	2005	2006	2007	2008	2009	2010	2011	2012
Sales		487.0	506.5	526.7	547.8	569.7	592.5	616.2	640.9	666.5	693.2
Growth of sales		4.0%	4.0%	4.0%	4.0%	4.0%	4.0%	4.0%	4.0%	4.0%	4.0%
EBITDA		63.3	67.4	71.6	76.1	80.9	84.1	87.5	91.0	94.6	98.4
Depreciation		36.0	38.7	39.9	41.2	42.5	43.9	45.3	46.8	48.3	49.9
Operating income		27.3	28.7	31.7	35.0	38.4	40.2	42.2	44.2	46.3	48.6
Taxes @ 40%		10.9	11.5	12.7	14.0	15.4	16.1	16.9	17.7	18.5	19.4
Unlevered net income		16.4	17.2	19.0	21.0	23.0	24.1	25.3	26.5	27.8	29.1
Deferred taxes		1.2	1.3	1.3	1.4	1.4	1.5	1.5	1.6	1.7	1.7
NOPAT		17.6	18.5	20.4	22.3	24.5	25.6	26.9	28.1	29.5	30.9
Depreciation		36.0	38.7	39.9	41.2	42.5	43.9	45.3	46.8	48.3	49.9
Capex and Increase in NWC		62.6	51.1	52.7	54.5	56.2	58.1	60.0	62.0	64.0	69.8
Free cash flow		(9.0)	6.1	7.5	9.1	10.7	11.4	12.2	13.0	13.8	10.9
Continuation value											189.3
WACC	10.00%										
PV{Free cash flow}	44.1										
PV{Continuation value}	73.0										
Business unit value	117.1										

EXHIBIT 15.2 *WTT Inc. Economic Value-Added Valuation*

WTT Inc. Enterprise Value $1,664.8 (in million $)

Machine Tools Unit

	2002	2003	2004	2005	2006	2007	2008	2009	2010	2011	2012
EBITDA margin		30.0%	28.9%	27.7%	26.6%	25.4%	24.3%	23.1%	22.0%	20.9%	19.7%
NOPAT margin		14%	13.6%	13.0%	12.4%	12.1%	11.3%	10.6%	10.0%	9.4%	8.9%
Invested capital	400.0	412.9	432.2	451.7	447.2	491.1	524.3	544.0	563.6	569.0	601.7
Capital turnover		1.60	1.70	1.75	1.80	1.95	1.90	1.90	1.95	2.00	2.10
Return on capital		22.51%	23.08%	22.77%	22.40%	23.52%	21.43%	20.13%	19.51%	18.82%	18.68%
WACC		9.62%	9.62%	9.62%	9.62%	9.62%	9.62%	9.62%	9.62%	9.62%	9.62%
Return spread		12.89%	13.46%	13.15%	12.78%	13.90%	11.81%	10.51%	9.89%	9.20%	9.06%
Unlevered net income		88.2	91.8	94.7	97.1	100.8	100.6	100.5	100.8	100.4	100.3
Deferred taxes		3.3	3.5	3.8	4.1	4.4	4.7	5.0	5.3	5.6	6.0
NOPAT		91.5	95.3	98.4	101.2	105.2	105.3	105.5	106.1	106.1	106.3
Capital charge		38.5	39.7	41.6	43.5	43.0	47.2	50.4	52.3	54.2	54.7
EVA		53.0	55.6	56.9	57.7	62.2	58.0	55.1	53.8	51.9	51.6
Continuation EVA											1,409.1
Initial capital	400.0										
PV{EVA}	348.5										
	748.5										
PV{Continuation EVA}	562.4										
Business unit value	1,310.9										

Electronics Unit

	2002	2003	2004	2005	2006	2007	2008	2009	2010	2011	2012
EBITDA margin		18.0%	17.3%	16.6%	15.9%	15.2%	14.5%	14.5%	14.0%	14.0%	14.0%
NOPAT margin		6.6%	6.2%	5.9%	5.5%	5.2%	4.8%	4.9%	4.6%	4.7%	4.8%
Invested capital	160.0	176.6	194.4	213.7	234.3	256.5	280.2	304.0	330.7	359.0	394.0
Capital turnover		2.00	2.03	2.06	2.09	2.12	2.15	2.18	2.22	2.25	2.28
Return on capital		13.20%	12.68%	12.14%	11.57%	10.97%	10.35%	10.62%	10.31%	10.58%	10.84%
WACC		10.50%	10.50%	10.50%	10.50%	10.50%	10.50%	10.50%	10.50%	10.50%	10.50%
Return spread		2.70%	2.18%	1.64%	1.07%	0.47%	-0.15%	0.12%	-0.19%	0.08%	0.34%

	2003	2004	2005	2006	2007	2008	2009	2010	2011	2012
Unlevered net income	20.2	21.3	22.4	23.4	24.2	24.9	27.9	29.3	32.7	36.4
Deferred taxes	1.0	1.1	1.2	1.3	1.5	1.7	1.8	2.0	2.2	2.5
NOPAT	21.1	22.4	23.6	24.7	25.7	26.5	29.8	31.4	35.0	38.9
Capital charge	16.8	18.5	20.4	22.4	24.6	26.9	29.4	31.9	34.7	37.7
EVA	4.3	3.8	3.2	2.3	1.1	(0.38)	0.3	(0.6)	0.2	1.2
Continuation EVA										176.5

Initial capital	160.0
PV{EVA}	11.9
	171.9
PV{Continuation EVA}	65.0
Business unit value	236.9

Metal Products Unit

	2002	2003	2004	2005	2006	2007	2008	2009	2010	2011	2012
EBITDA margin		13.0%	13.3%	13.6%	13.9%	14.2%	14.2%	14.2%	14.2%	14.2%	14.2%
NOPAT margin		4.0%	3.6%	3.9%	4.1%	4.3%	4.3%	4.4%	4.4%	4.4%	4.5%
Invested capital	360.0	386.6	399.0	411.9	425.2	438.9	453.1	467.8	483.0	498.7	518.6
Capital turnover		1.30	1.31	1.32	1.33	1.34	1.35	1.36	1.37	1.38	1.39
Return on capital		5.20%	4.78%	5.10%	5.42%	5.75%	5.84%	5.93%	6.01%	6.10%	6.19%
WACC		10.00%	10.00%	10.00%	10.00%	10.00%	10.00%	10.00%	10.00%	10.00%	10.00%
Return spread		-4.80%	-5.22%	-4.90%	-4.58%	-4.25%	-4.16%	-4.07%	-3.99%	-3.90%	-3.81%
Unlevered net income		16.4	17.2	19.0	21.0	23.0	24.1	25.3	26.5	27.8	29.1
Deferred taxes		1.22	1.27	1.32	1.37	1.42	1.48	1.54	1.60	1.67	1.73
NOPAT		17.6	18.5	20.4	22.3	24.5	25.6	26.9	28.1	29.5	30.9
Capital charge		36.0	38.7	39.9	41.2	42.5	43.9	45.3	46.8	48.3	49.9
EVA		(18.4)	(20.2)	(19.5)	(18.8)	(18.1)	(18.3)	(18.5)	(18.6)	(18.8)	(19.0)
Continuation EVA											(329.3)

Initial capital	360.0
PV{EVA}	(116.0)
	244.0
PV{Continuation EVA}	(127.0)
Business unit value	117.1

and the aggregate enterprise value are the same as those calculated in Exhibit 15.1, examination of EVA at each unit presents a much clear picture of value-creation capability. Machine tool is expected to maintain its positive EVA in spite of diminishing EBITDA margins, which is a natural occurrence in competitive markets. Reduced margins are compensated in part by a gradual increase in capital efficiency as measured by capital turnover. The spread of the return on capital (ROC) over WACC of machine tools decreases over time but stays above 9% at the end of the forecast period. The electronics division, however, is shown to lose its value creation capability and generate break-even returns in the second half of its forecast period.

The metal products division is expected to operate between 4 to 5% negative spread during most of the forecast period and still maintain a 3.8% negative spread after continuous increases in margin and turnover. In conclusion, metal products destroyed value in the past and will do so in the future if it continues to grow and invest as planned.

We have just illustrated the power of EVA valuation for identifying value creation and destruction at the business unit level. We now proceed to use the EVA approach to value the effect of the available restructuring actions. Each unit, even those performing at a positive return spread should be continuously monitored and examined for improvement. In particular, the erosion of the return spread of electronics requires careful consideration. Here, we illustrate the valuation approach by examining possible changes in metal products. A similar analysis should be performed for the other units.

Faced with value destruction in the metal products unit, WTT management has to consider whether it can ever eliminate its negative return spread. A company can justify negative performance only if it expects it to turn positive in the future. Otherwise, it should consider divestment. However, since ROC is based on the book value of invested capital, the spread computation assumes that the company can recoup that value in the open market. It could well be that the proceeds from divestment are below book value, which would mean that the opportunity cost of running the division is actually lower. In that case, the ROC calculated with respect to the divestment value of the unit may be greater than its WACC. Nevertheless, that does not mean that capital expenditures should be maintained. In fact, it may be optimal to harvest the unit for a few years and then liquidate it for scrap.

Let us consider the following potential actions toward metal products:[28]

1. Invest to modernize and gain market share: An additional capital investment of $100 million, financed maintaining the target debt ratio for the unit, to be applied to improving technology and reducing costs, in order to increase the competitiveness of the unit and gain market share.

2. Stop volume growth: Metal products would forgo market share in order to limit value destruction. The unit would limit capital expenditures to maintaining the productive capacity of its assets, which would be done setting capital expenditures approximately equal to depreciation.

3. Harvest: The unit would maximize its cash flow by eliminating investment for replacement and growth. Maintenance expenses and R&D would be curtailed, and production of low-margin product lines would be eliminated as capacity shrinks. After 5 years, the unit's remaining assets, including real estate, would be redeployed to other divisions or liquidated. At that time, the net proceeds would be about 85% of the remaining book value.

---

[28]On restructuring strategies see Porter (1980) and Harrigan (1988).

EXHIBIT 15.3 *WTT Inc. EVA Valuation of Restructuring Actions for Metal Product Unit*

Modernize

(in million $)

	2002	2003	2004	2005	2006	2007	2008	2009	2010	2011	2012
Sales		487.0	511.4	536.9	563.8	592.0	621.5	652.6	685.3	719.5	755.5
Growth of sales		5.0%	5.0%	5.0%	5.0%	5.0%	5.0%	5.0%	5.0%	5.0%	5.0%
EBITDA margin		13.0%	13.7%	14.4%	15.1%	15.8%	15.8%	15.8%	15.8%	15.8%	15.8%
EBITDA		63.3	70.1	77.3	85.1	93.5	98.2	103.1	108.3	113.7	119.4
Depreciation		36.0	46.0	46.3	46.6	47.0	47.5	48.0	48.6	49.3	50.1
Operating income		27.3	24.1	31.0	38.5	46.5	50.7	55.1	59.6	64.4	69.3
Taxes @ 40%		10.9	9.6	12.4	15.4	18.6	20.3	22.0	23.9	25.7	27.7
Unlevered net income		16.4	14.4	18.6	23.1	27.9	30.4	33.0	35.8	38.6	41.6
Deferred taxes		1.2	1.3	1.3	1.4	1.5	1.6	1.6	1.7	1.8	1.9
NOPAT		17.6	15.7	19.9	24.5	29.4	32.0	34.7	37.5	40.4	43.5
NOPAT margin		3.6%	3.1%	3.7%	4.3%	5.0%	5.1%	5.3%	5.5%	5.6%	5.8%
Capex and Increase in NWC		136.0	49.4	49.4	50.5	51.7	52.9	54.1	55.5	56.8	75.1
Invested capital	360.0	460.0	463.4	466.4	470.3	474.9	480.3	486.4	493.3	500.8	525.8
Capital turnover		1.06	1.11	1.16	1.21	1.26	1.31	1.36	1.41	1.46	1.51
Return on capital		3.83%	3.4%	4.30%	5.25%	6.25%	6.73%	7.22%	7.71%	8.19%	8.68%
WACC		10.00%	10.00%	10.00%	10.00%	10.00%	10.00%	10.00%	10.00%	10.00%	10.00%
Return spread		−6.17%	−6.59%	−5.70%	−4.75%	−3.75%	−3.27%	−2.78%	−2.29%	−1.81%	−1.32%
NOPAT		17.6	15.7	19.9	24.5	29.4	32.0	34.7	37.5	40.4	43.5
Capital charge		36.0	46.0	46.3	46.6	47.0	47.5	48.0	48.6	49.3	50.1
EVA		(18.4)	(30.3)	(26.4)	(22.1)	(17.6)	(15.5)	(13.4)	(11.2)	(8.9)	(6.6)
Continuation EVA											(138.9)
Initial capital	360.0										
PV{EVA}	(114.8)										
	245.2										
PV{Continuation EVA}	(53.5)										
Business unit value	191.6										

EXHIBIT 15.4 WTT Inc. EVA Valuation of Restructuring Actions for Metal Product Unit

Stop Volume Growth

(in million $)

	2002	2003	2004	2005	2006	2007	2008	2009	2010	2011	2012
Sales		487.0	499.2	511.7	524.4	537.6	551.0	564.8	578.9	593.4	608.2
Growth of sales		2.5%	2.5%	2.5%	2.5%	2.5%	2.5%	2.5%	2.5%	2.5%	2.5%
EBITDA margin		13.0%	13.3%	13.6%	13.9%	14.2%	14.2%	14.2%	14.2%	14.2%	14.2%
EBITDA		63.3	66.4	69.6	72.9	76.3	78.2	80.2	82.2	84.3	86.4
Depreciation		36.0	38.1	38.8	39.4	40.1	40.8	41.5	42.3	43.0	43.8
Operating income		27.3	28.3	30.8	33.5	36.2	37.4	38.7	39.9	41.3	42.6
Taxes @ 40%		10.9	11.3	12.3	13.4	14.5	15.0	15.5	16.0	16.5	17.0
Unlevered net income		16.4	17.0	18.5	20.1	21.7	22.5	23.2	24.0	24.8	25.6
Deferred taxes		1.2	1.2	1.3	1.3	1.3	1.4	1.4	1.4	1.5	1.5
NOPAT		17.6	18.2	19.8	21.4	23.1	23.8	24.6	25.4	26.2	27.1
NOPAT margin		3.6%	3.6%	3.9%	4.1%	4.3%	4.3%	4.4%	4.4%	4.4%	4.5%
Capex and Increase in NWC		57.0	44.7	45.5	46.3	47.1	47.9	48.8	49.7	50.6	54.7
Invested capital	360.0	381.0	387.6	394.3	401.2	408.1	415.3	422.5	430.0	437.6	448.5
Capital turnover		1.30	1.31	1.32	1.33	1.34	1.35	1.36	1.37	1.38	1.39
Return on capital		4.70%	4.78%	5.10%	5.42%	5.75%	5.84%	5.93%	6.01%	6.10%	6.19%
WACC		10.00%	10.00%	10.00%	10.00%	10.00%	10.00%	10.00%	10.00%	10.00%	10.00%
Return spread		−5.30%	−5.22%	−4.90%	−4.58%	−4.25%	−4.16%	−4.07%	−3.99%	−3.90%	−3.81%
NOPAT		17.6	18.2	19.8	21.4	23.1	23.8	24.6	25.4	26.2	27.1
Capital charge		36.0	38.1	38.8	39.4	40.1	40.8	41.5	42.3	43.0	43.8
EVA		(18.4)	(19.9)	(19.0)	(18.0)	(17.0)	(17.0)	(16.9)	(16.8)	(16.8)	(16.7)
Continuation EVA											(227.8)
Initial capital	360.0										
PV{EVA}	(110.0)										
	250.0										
PV{Continuation EVA}	(87.8)										
Business unit value	162.2										

278

EXHIBIT 15.5	*WTT Inc. Valuation of Restructuring Actions for Metal Products Unit*

Harvest (in million $)

	2002	2003	2004	2005	2006	2007
Sales		487.0	424.4	384.9	349.1	316.5
Growth of sales		–12.9%	–9.3%	–9.3%	–9.3%	–9.3%
EBITDA margin		13.0%	13.5%	14.0%	14.5%	15.0%
EBITDA		63.3	57.3	53.9	50.6	47.5
Depreciation		36.0	32.4	29.2	26.2	23.6
Operating income		27.3	24.9	24.7	24.4	23.9
Taxes @ 40%		10.9	10.0	9.9	9.7	9.5
Unlevered net income		16.4	14.9	14.8	14.6	14.3
Deferred taxes		1.2	1.1	1.0	0.9	0.8
NOPAT		17.6	16.0	15.8	15.5	15.1
NOPAT margin		3.6%	3.8%	4.1%	4.4%	4.8%
Capex and Increase in NWC		0.0	0.0	0.0	0.0	0.0
Invested capital	360.0	324.0	291.6	262.4	236.2	212.6
Capital turnover		1.30	1.31	1.32	1.33	1.34
Return on capital		4.70%	4.9%	5.42%	5.90%	6.40%
WACC		10.00%	10.00%	10.00%	10.00%	10.00%
Return spread		–5.30%	–5.06%	–4.58%	–4.10%	–3.60%
NOPAT		17.6	16.0	15.8	15.5	15.1
Capital charge		36.0	32.4	29.2	26.2	23.6
EVA		(18.4)	(16.4)	(13.4)	(10.7)	(8.5)
Capital loss at exit						(31.9)
Initial capital	360.0					
PV{EVA}	(52.9)					
	307.1					
PV{Continuation EVA}	(19.8)					
Business unit value	287.26					

4. Sell out: Metal products could be sold at a 70% discount of book value or for $252 million net proceeds.

The shareholder value impact of actions 1 to 3 is calculated in Exhibits 15.3 to 15.5.

Exhibit 15.6 summarizes the impact of the four possible actions. It shows that any of them increases the value of the metal products unit. Harvest would result in a value improvement of $170 million or $17 a share, with sale, modernization, and stopping growth following in decreasing order of value creation. Note that here the increase in the enterprise value of the division accrues to equity-holders. This would not be the case if the company were forced to restructure under distress in a recapitalization done for the benefit of bond-holders, as in Chapter 14.

15.7   HEADQUARTER COSTS AND BENEFITS

When valuing a multidivisional firm, the treatment of headquarter costs and benefits often arises. Headquarter costs are those costs that cannot be allocated to the different business units according to a transfer price mechanism that mimics market prices. The cost of centralized accounting, treasury operations, tax planning, and information systems are

---

EXHIBIT 15.6   *WTT Inc. Shareholder Value Impact of Restructuring Actions toward Metal Products Unit*

(in million $)

Strategy	Unit Enterprise Value	Gain with respect to Baseline	Per WTT Inc. Share Gain
Baseline	117.1		
Modernize	191.6	74.6	7.5
Stop growth	162.2	45.1	4.5
Harvest	287.3	170.2	17.0
Sell out	252.0	134.9	13.5
Outstanding shares (millions)	10.0		

---

commonly allocated according some criteria of usage. Those costs would need to be borne by the business units even when operating alone. Cost associated with top management salaries and office space cannot be allocated via transfer pricing and presumably would be avoidable if the units operated independently and already have sufficient managerial depth. Other costs are more difficult to determine. For example, directors' fees would likely be incurred if the units operated as stand-alone public companies but are often not allocated. The magnitude of true headquarter costs is difficult to determine because it depends on the number of activities that headquarter performs on behalf of its units, and it varies from firm to firm.

In practice, one allocates all costs that have to be borne by the divisions operating independently using transfer prices. The non-allocated costs are discounted at the blended cost of capital of the corporation and subtracted from the sum-of-the-parts valuation to yield the total value of the firm.[29]

It should be noted the value of the non-allocated costs is not a measure of the increase of the value of the firm that would result from its break-up. A true valuation of the benefits from headquarters should begin by comparing the cost to each unit of acquiring the services provided by headquarters in the market place to the cost of performing them at headquarters. Additional benefits to take into account are the value of the tax shields produced by the higher debt capacity and other possible tax advantages of the diversified firm, and the lower cost of capital likely to result from the higher liquidity of the stock of the consolidated company. The value of these benefits can then be compared to the value of the non-allocated costs of headquarters.

15.8   SUMMARY

The technique for evaluating the performance of business units and the impact of restructuring decisions consists of the following steps:

1. **Baseline valuation:** For each unit on the basis of estimates of revenues, operating costs, capital expenditures, working capital, noncash items, debt financing and the cost of capital.

---

[29]WACC should be used to account for the change in debt capacity caused by such costs or benefits but the unlevered cost of capital should be used in APV, in which case the tax shield of debt would be valued separately.

2. **Value creation/destruction analysis:** Value each unit using the economic value added approach to identify those units that create shareholder value and those units that destroy it.

3. **Valuing the impact of restructuring options:** Evaluate potential actions for each individual unit, such as changes in production and marketing, alternative investment and growth rates, and harvest and sale options.

4. **Synergy analysis:** Consider the possible synergies, such as economies of scope that are generated by the joint operation of several business units, and estimate the effect of divestment on such synergies.

5. **Complete financial modeling and testing:** As in merger analysis (Chapter 9), construct a financial model with complete financial statements and valuation schedules for each of the restructuring options to be considered and do sensitivity testing under different scenarios about the economy, competition and managerial implementation capabilities.

PROBLEMS

15.1 Review Equations (5.1) and (5.2) of Chapter 5 and verify the calculation of continuation value added made for each unit in Exhibit 15.2.

15.2 Refer to Section 15.6 and value the "stop volume growth" action for the metal products division of WTT by discounting free cash flows. (Hint: You should get the same result as that obtained in Exhibit 15.2 using the EVA approach.)

15.3 Value the "harvest" action toward WTT by discounting free cash flows.

15.4 On November 15, 1990, the Chairman and CEO of Racal Electronics, Sir Ernest Harrison announced a de-merger (break up) plan for two of its three main business units. Sir Ernest's purpose was not clear. One observer suggested that he might have been trying to avert a possible takeover directed to taking control of Racal's profitable cellular business. Racal was one of the fastest growing U.K. companies in the 1970s, reaching in 1990 a level of sales and pre-tax profits estimated at £2.0 billion and £201 million, respectively. Racal's three business units were: (1) Racal Telecom, the successful operator of the Vodafone cellular phone business, 80% of which was owned by Racal Electronics and the rest was publicly traded; (2) Racal Chubb Security, the security business, and (3) the "rump" of Racal Electronics, the main business of which was defense electronics, data communications and networks.

Sir Ernest planned to distribute to Racal's shareholders: (1) The 80% shares of Racal Telecom it still owned and (2) new shares to be issued for the whole of Racal Chubb. The old Racal Electronics shares would continue to trade and would represent the rump. After the break-up, shares of three different companies would be traded. Sir Ernest also said that he intended to lead a management buyout of the rump after "an appropriate time" once the market established its proper value.

Racal Electronics had 1.3 billion shares outstanding, which traded at 190 pence. Racal Telecom had 1 billion shares outstanding (including the 80% owned by Racal Electronics) and traded at 275 p. Analysts estimated the value of Racal Chubb Security in £400 million, before allocation of any debt. The debt of Racal Electronics was £375 million. This debt did not apply to the quoted Racal Telecom that had its own set of accounts.

In addition to its defense electronics business, the rump had won major contracts with the British government: the Government Data Network (GDN) service, which linked government departments, and the still under negotiation Government Telephone System (GTS). While these businesses were potentially lucrative, the rump had been a cash user and would require significant capital investments and R&D in the future. GTS was expected to require an investment of about £200 million and would not become profitable before 1995. The rump attained operating income of £30 million on sales of £942 million during the fiscal year ended March 31, 1990. Profits were depressed because of development costs associated with new business, including the GDN.

   a. What do you make of the valuations of Racal's units given above? How do you explain them? What do you think was Sir Ernest's motivation?

   b. How feasible was his demerger and buyout plan?

   c. What other actions were available to Racal?

15.5 On July 11, 1989, Sir James Goldsmith's bidding vehicle Hoylake Investments Ltd. launched an offer of 850 pence per share for BAT Industries, the U.K.-based tobacco conglomerate.[30] The initial bid was to be financed through a variety of securities including bank debt, junk bonds, and equity in Anglo Group, the entity that would subsequently control BAT through its 75% interest in Hoylake Investments. For each 1,000 shares of existing BAT Industries 1.53 billion common stock, investors would receive £4,250 of Hoylake senior secured notes, due 1992, $4,182 of Hoylake subordinated (junk) notes due 1993, and the equivalent of 387 Anglo Group common shares. Just prior to launching its bid, the consortium purchased 18.89 million shares of BAT at the average price of 590 pence a share.[31]

---

[30]This problem is based on the case *Unbundling Bat (A)*, Graduate Business School, Columbia University, 1993, written by Craig S. Wo, MBA 1993.

[31]These shares were not owned by Hoylake but by the members of the consortium.

The reason for Hoylake's initial non-cash offer laid in British takeover panel regulation. In the U.K., any cash portion of a takeover bid must be fully underwritten, which would imply fees of up to 3% with no guarantee of success. Investors expected that the offer would eventually contain a cash component. Goldsmith's plan was to unbundle BAT, subsequently selling off its non-tobacco assets in order to reduce the £10 billion of proposed debt financing to more manageable levels.

The structure of the bid was as follows:

BAT Shares Outstanding:		1.53 billion
Bid Value		850 pence per share
Financing:		
Senior Notes due 1992		£6.5 bn @ 12%
Subordinated Notes due 1993	$6.4 billion	£3.9 bn @ 16%
Anglo Group shares		£2.6 bn
Total Bid Value		£13.0 bn

Existing shareholders would receive shares equivalent to a 90% equity stake in Anglo Group, which in turn held a 75% interest in Hoylake Investments. The bidding consortium would hold the other 25% of Hoylake in exchange for their £868 million subscription. In effect, existing BAT shareholders would retain about a 67.5% ownership interest in BAT Industries, although they would yield control to the consortium.

While the response to Sir James's non-cash 850 pence per share bid was not very enthusiastic, the FTSE 100 index jumped 55.7 points (2.5%) from 2,195.2 to 2,250.9, and BAT shares soared almost 30% from 694 pence per share to 900 pence per share.

In July 1989, BAT Industries operated in four distinct areas: tobacco, retail, paper, and financial services. For the year ending December 31, 1988, tobacco operations accounted for about 40% of revenues and 46% of operating profits. It included Brown & Williamson Tobacco, the third-largest cigarette manufacturer in the United States and British-American Tobacco, which produced cigarettes for domestic consumption in over 40 countries. BAT's retail interests included Saks Fifth Avenue and Marshall Fields in the U.S., and Argos, a large retailer of small electrical appliances, toys and jewelry.

BAT had two pulp and paper subsidiaries: Wiggins Teape, the U.K.-based pulp, paper mill and paper merchant, and Appleton Paper. Appleton was the world's largest producer of carbonless paper, and the leading producer of thermal paper in the U.S.

BAT's financial services operations were comprised of three primary subsidiaries, two based in the United Kingdom and one in the United States. Eagle Star was a leading competitor in the United Kingdom and Republic of Ireland general insurance markets. Allied Dunbar was the largest combined life assurance and unit trust group in the United Kingdom. Farmers Insurance was the third-largest automobile and home insurer in the United States, and the eighth-largest property and casualty insurer.

The sum-of-the-parts valuations of BAT Industries' assets ranged from £14 billion to £20 billion. BAT's market capitalization on July 10, 1989, the day before the Hoylake bid was announced, was £10.5 billion. Just a few months earlier, BAT's market capitalization was at £8.5 billion and following the bid the stock traded past £13 billion. The following are estimates made by analysts at the time of the offer:

UBS Phillips & Drew, 7/89

Tobacco	£ 6.97 bn
Financial Services	8.97
Retailing	2.52
Paper	1.87
Enterprise Value	20.33
Debt Net of Cash & Other	(2.77)
Net Asset Value	£17.56

Survey of 10 British and US Analysts, 8/89

Tobacco Net Assets	£4.6	to	£6 bn
Financial Services	5.7	to	8
Retailing	2	to	3.6
Paper	2	to	2.5
Non-Tobacco Net Assets	9.7	to	14.1
Net Asset Value	£14.3	to	£20.1 bn

SOURCES: *Wall Street Journal* and analysts' reports.

a. Hoylake's expenses were expected to be 1.5% of the total value of the acquisition and 3% of subsequent break-up proceeds. What return would the Hoylake group expect to realize assuming it would be able to exit the transaction via sales, spin-offs and public offerings within a year? Disposals would generate between £2 and £3.5 billion of capital gains depending on the break-up proceeds, taxable at the corporate level at a 40% rate. Note that the operation of the tobacco business during that year was expected to generate £1.077 billion of free-cash flow.

b. Examine Hoylake's proposal from the point of view of BAT shareholders. What value would they expect to realize as per Hoylake's offer?

c. BAT decided that the appropriate response to Goldsmith was to abandon its diversification strategy and to focus on tobacco and financial services. Accordingly, it considered selling the U.S. retail business and using the proceeds to repurchase up to 10% of its shares and part of the tobacco cash flow to increase its dividend from 20.1 pence to 30 pence a share. It also planned to divest the U.K. catalog business (Argos) and the paper business made up of Wiggins Teape and Appleton (WTP). However, selling them was not tax efficient as both groups were carried at a low tax basis. The pro-forma information is provided below. What do you recommend?

BAT Industries Pro-Forma 1989 EPS for Stand-Alone
Argos and Paper Business

Company	Shares	EPS 1989E
Argos	296.8 m	14.3 pence
WTA	494.4 m	21.9 pence

BAT Industries Retail and Paper Business Pro-Forma Balance Sheet Items,
Dec. 1989

Business	Assets	Liabilities	Net Assets	Tax Basis
	£ millions			
Retailing (except Argos)	1,924	1,010	914	890
Argos (UK catalog)	300	73	227	68
Paper (Wiggings Teape Appleton)	1,151	533	618	316

d. Consider the proposal for the sale of BAT's retail business based upon the lowest value of the analysts' consensus (except Argos, the U.K. catalog retailer, which analysts priced at 12x P/E). The tax basis of the equity in the retail business (except Argos) was £0.914 bn. Extraordinary profits from the sale were to be taxed at a 40% rate. Furthermore, the expenses associated with the sale would be about 3% of gross proceeds. Estimate the net proceeds from the sale.

e. Summarize the shareholder value expected from BAT's plan based upon your recommendations and estimates in c and d. Rely on the low end of the analysts' consensus as needed. Take into account that the combined effect of restructuring, share repurchase and dividend increase can be expected to raise the pre-bid share price of 694 pence by about 15%. Compare the value of BAT plan to that of Sir Goldsmith's bid.

Appendix A

Financial Options

A.1 FINANCIAL OPTIONS IN M&A VALUATION

A number of applications presented in this book require the computation of options values that are provided by formulas developed for the pricing of financial options. The file Financial Options Calculator included in the Valuation Aids CD-ROM contains a number of easy-to-use Excel spreadsheets for computing the value of these options. This appendix summarizes the nature of each spreadsheet and gives references to the sources where the original formulas were derived. The general reference on financial options is Hull (2002). Note NA.2 shows the code of a program for valuing options using the Hewlett-Packard HP19-BII calculator. Although it does not incorporate some of refinements included in the Financial Options Calculator, it permits valuing European calls, puts and warrants. The problem section includes practice problems that can be solved using the calculators.

A.2 EUROPEAN CALLS AND PUTS AND AMERICAN CALLS

European options can be exercised only at expiration. European calls are valued with the Black-Scholes (1973) formula:

$$c(P,t) = PN(d_1) - Xe^{-r(T-t)}N(d_2) \tag{A.1}$$

where P is the stock price, X is the exercise price, T is the expiration date, t is time, r is the riskless rate, N(d) is normal distribution

$$d_1 = [\ln(P/X) + (r + \tfrac{1}{2}\sigma^2)(T - t)]/[\sigma(T - t)^{1/2}], \text{ and } d_2 = d_1 - \sigma(T - t)^{1/2} \tag{A.2}$$

and σ is the volatility (standard deviation of the rate of return) of the stock.

An outline of the original derivation of this formula is provided in Note NA.1. Most programs in the Financial Options Calculator distinguish between calendar time and trading-days time.[1] Calendar time is applied to compute the present value of the exercise price. Trading-days time is applied to calculate the volatility for the duration of the option. Empirical evidence has shown that volatility is better measured as a function of trading days than of calendar days.[2] However, the calculator also allows the use of calendar-day volatility. The difference is not material for most options considered in this book.

The calls sheet computes the value of European calls and puts and American calls. For dividend-paying stocks, the stock price is adjusted subtracting the present value of the dividends forgone, which is calculated as the present value of quarterly dividends until the expiration of the call. European puts are valued via the put-call parity (see Section A.7 below). American calls can be exercised at any time. The Financial Options Calculator

---

[1] See French (1984) and Hull (2002).

[2] That is, the Financial Options Calculator computes d_1 and d_2 as follows: $d_1 = [\ln(P/X) + r(T - t) + \tfrac{1}{2}\sigma^2 t_D]/[\sigma t_D^{1/2}]$, and $d_2 = d_1 - \sigma t_D^{1/2}$, where t_D are the trading days in [t, T].

values them using the approximation suggested by Black (1975): The European calls corresponding to maturities on the days before each ex-dividend date and the expiration date are priced and the value of the American call is set at the maximum value of the European calls so calculated. This procedure is widely used and works well in most cases. It will, however, undervalue the call slightly as it assumes that the exercise date is decided at valuation time although the exercise decision remains open until just before each dividend date.

The program allows solving for the volatility implied by the price of a traded option. It calculates the implied volatility of European calls and puts and of American calls using Excel's Solver tool. This is a practical way of estimating forward-looking volatilities from traded options.

A.3   AMERICAN PUTS

The American puts sheet of the Financial Options Calculator values American puts with the analytic approximation due to MacMillan (1986) and Barone-Adesi and Whaley (1987). It assumes that the stock pays a continuous dividend yield as in Merton's (1973b). Because of this assumption, it yields values of European options that are slightly different from those given by the calls sheet. (In valuing European options on dividend paying stocks, the more exact values given by the call sheet should be preferred.) The program also allows solving for the implied volatility of American and European puts using Excel's Solver tool. The American put formula is as follows:

$$p_{Am}(P) = p(P) + A_1(P/P^{**})^{\gamma_1} \text{ when } P > P^{**} \text{ and } p_{Am} = X - P \text{ when } P \le P^{**} \quad (A.3)$$

p_{Am} and p denote the values of the American and European puts, respectively, with the European put value given by the Black-Scholes formula, P^{**} is the critical stock price below which the put is exercised, and A_1 and γ_1 are parameters to be defined below. We adopt Hull's (2002) notation and define

$$\tau = T - t, \quad h(\tau) = 1 - e^{-r\tau}, \quad \alpha = 2r/\sigma^2, \quad \beta = 2(r - q)/\sigma^2,$$

where q is the continuous-time dividend yield rate. The rest of the variables in Equation (A.3) are as follows: P^{**} is the solution to the equation

$$X - P^{**} = p(P^{**}) - A_1$$
$$A_1 = -(P^{**}/\gamma)\{1 - e^{-q(T-1)}N[-d_1(P^{**})]\}$$
$$d_1 = [\ln(P/X) + (r - q)(T - t) - \tfrac{1}{2}\sigma^2 t_D]/(\sigma t_D^{1/2})$$
$$d_2 = d_1 - \sigma t_D^{1/2}.$$
$$\gamma_1 = -\tfrac{1}{2}(\beta - 1) - \tfrac{1}{2}[(\beta - 1)^2 + 4\alpha/h]^{1/2}$$

and t_D are the trading days in [t, T].

A.4   WARRANT PRICING MODEL

European warrants are valued with the Black-Scholes formula modified for continuous dividend yield as in Merton (1973b). American call and put warrants are valued with the MacMillan/Barone-Adesi and Whaley analytic approximation. The formula for American calls used to value warrants is similar to the American put formula given in A.3 above:

$$c_{Am}(P) = c(P) + A_2(P/P^*)^{\gamma_2} \text{ when } P < P^* \text{ and } p_{Am} = X - P \text{ when } P \ge P^* \quad (A.4)$$

c_{Am} and c denote the values of the American and European call values, respectively. P^* is the stock price above which the call is exercised. P^* is the solution to the equation

$$P^* - X = c(P^*) - \{1 - e^{-q(T-t)}N[-d_1(P^*)]\}P^*\gamma_2^{-1}$$
$$A_2 = -(P^*/\gamma_2)\{1 - e^{-q(T-1)}N[-d_1(P^*)]\}$$
$$\gamma_2 = -\tfrac{1}{2}(\beta - 1) + \tfrac{1}{2}[(\beta - 1)^2 + 4\alpha/h]^{1/2}$$

The valuation of American warrants assumes that warrants are widely held or that a single individual must exercise all the warrants simultaneously. Otherwise, there are situations in which a single monopolist holder can follow an optimal sequential exercise strategy. In such a case, the value given by the program will underestimate the value of the warrants. On this point, see Emmanuel (1983) and Constantinides and Rosenthal (1984).

The program adjusts for dilution and for the current value of the warrants if the warrants are already outstanding (see Section A.7 below).

A.5 ASIAN OPTIONS

The Financial Options Calculator values Asian options on the arithmetic average using the analytic approximation developed by M. Curran (1992). The program values calls and puts before, at and in the averaging period. The formula for Asian puts is based upon the put-call parity condition that holds for Asian options as well (Levy and Turnbull, 1992).

Curran's formula for Asian calls is as follows:

$$c_A = \exp(-rT)\{n^{-1}\sum_{i=1,n}\exp(\mu_i + \tfrac{1}{2}\sigma_i^2)N[(\mu - \ln K^\wedge)/\sigma_x + \sigma_{xi}/\sigma_x]$$
$$- KN[(\mu - \ln K^\wedge)/\sigma_x]\}$$

where N(.) is the normal distribution and

r = risk-free rate

d = dividend payout

T = time to expiration

K = exercise price

P_0 = initial price

n = number of averaging periods

t_1 = time of first averaging point

Δt = time between averaging points

$t_i = t_1 + (i - 1)\Delta t$

σ = volatility

$\mu_i = \ln P_0 + (r - d - \tfrac{1}{2}\sigma^2)\, t_i$

$\sigma_i^2 = \sigma^2(t_1 + (i - 1)\Delta t)$

$\sigma_{xi} = \sigma^2\{t_1 + \Delta t[(i - 1) - i(i - 1)/(2n)]\}$

$\mu = \ln P_0 + (r - d - \tfrac{1}{2}\sigma^2)(t_1 + (n - 1)\tfrac{1}{2}\,\Delta t)$

$\sigma_x^2 = \sigma^2[t_1 + \Delta t(n - 1)(2n - 1)/(6n)]$

$K^\wedge = 2K - n^{-1}\Sigma_{i=1,n}\exp(\mu_i + \sigma_{xi}/\sigma x^2)(\ln K - \mu) + \tfrac{1}{2}(\sigma_i^2 - \sigma_{xi}^2/\sigma_x^2)]$

A.6 KNOCKOUT (BARRIER) OPTIONS

The Financial Options Calculator includes a sheet for valuing knockout options. A knockout call option is a European call that ceases to exist if the price of the underlying asset goes *down* to the knockout barrier. A knockout put is a European put that ceases to exist if the price of the underlying asset goes *up* to the knockout barrier. Similarly, a down-and-in-call (an up-and-in put) is a European call (put) that comes into existence when the price reaches the barrier. Some barrier options stipulate the payment of a rebate. A rebate is a fixed payment made to the holder of a knockout option when the asset price reaches the barrier. In the case of down-and-in or up-and-in options, the holder pays the rebate to the writer of the option.

The value of a down-and-in call is given by

$$D = Pe^{-qT}(H/P)^{2\lambda}N(y) - Xe^{-rT}(H/P)^{2\lambda-2}N(y - \sigma T^{1/2})$$

and an up-and-in put is given by

$$U = Xe^{-rT}(H/P)^{2\lambda-2}N(-y + \sigma T^{1/2}) - Pe^{-qT}(H/P)^{2\lambda}N(-y)$$

where

$$\lambda = \tfrac{1}{2} + (r - q)/\sigma^2 \qquad \text{and} \qquad y = \ln[H^2/(PX)]/(\sigma T^{1/2}) + \lambda\sigma T^{1/2}.$$

The values of a knockout call and a knockout put are

$$K_c = c - D \qquad \text{and} \qquad K_p = p - U,$$

respectively, where c and p are the corresponding regular European call and put, respectively. The value of a knockout call with rebate is given by the following formulas

$$K_c = c - D + R_c, \qquad R_c = [(H/P)^{2\lambda-1}N(z) + (P/H)N(z - \lambda\sigma T^{1/2})$$

where R_c is the value of the rebate and $z = \ln(H/P)/(\sigma T^{1/2}) + \lambda\sigma T^{1/2}$. Similarly, the value of a knockout put with rebate is

$$K_p = p - U + R_p, \qquad R_p = [(H/P)^{2\lambda-1}N(-z) + (P/H)N(-z + \lambda\sigma T^{1/2}),$$

where R_p is the value of the rebate. Finally, a down-and-in call with rebate is worth $D - R_c$ and an up-and-in put is worth $U - R_p$.

For additional details see Cox and Rubinstein (1985), Rubinstein and Reiner (1991), and Hull (2002).

A.7 THE PUT-CALL PARITY

The put-call parity permits valuing European puts as a function of the value of European calls. Consider the following portfolios involving European options: {1 share, 1 put} and {1 call, PV[X]}, where PV[X] is the present value of the exercise price of both the call and the put. Note that, at exercise time (in this case, at expiration), both portfolios give the same payoff: either X when the stock price is less or equal to X, or the stock price when the latter is greater than X. Hence, both portfolios have the same value. That is,

$$\text{share price} + \text{put value} = \text{call value} + PV[X].$$

From this fundamental parity relation one can compute the value of a put from the value of a call as follows:

$$\text{put value} = \text{call value} - \text{share price} + PV[X].$$

Moreover, the payoff of a put can be attained synthetically by constructing the portfolio {buy 1 call, short 1 share, invest P[X]}. Similarly, a put can be written (sold) via the following portfolio {sell 1 call, buy 1 share, borrow P[X]}.

The put-call parity does not hold for American options. Numerical methods or an analytic approximation such as that described in Section A.3 need to be used to value American puts.

A.8   STOCK OPTIONS PAYING A KNOWN DIVIDEND YIELD

Here we present the treatment of dividends in all the spreadsheets except the one described in Section A.2. Consider a stock paying no dividend. Its expected price at time T is $P_t = P_0 e^{kT}$, where P_0 is the current price and k is the expected rate of return on the stock. Note that P_0 is an input to the Black-Scholes formula for valuing non-dividend–paying European options.

Now consider a stock paying a continuous dividend yield at the known constant annual rate y. Then, the stock price ex-dividend will drop by the amount of the dividend. That is, the expected ex-dividend price of the stock will grow at the rate $k - y$, or $P_T = P_0 e^{(k-y)T} = [P_0 e^{-yT}]e^{kT}$. Furthermore, a non-dividend–paying stock with expected rate of return k and initial price $P_0 e^{-yT}$ will also grow to equal P_T. Let $P_0^{ADJ} = P_0 e^{-yT}$ and note that the price of a non-dividend–paying stock with price P_0^{ADJ} and the ex-dividend price of a stock paying a known dividend yield y with price P_0 will exhibit the same paths. Hence, the value of a European option on a stock with dividend yield y has the same value as a European option on a non-dividend–paying stock with price $P_0^{ADJ} = P_0 e^{-yT}$.

A perhaps more intuitive argument is as follows: The holder of a European call forgoes the dividends paid until expiration time T. Thus, the present value of the stock price to prevail at time T equals

$$P_0^{ADJ} = P_0 - PV\{\text{forgone dividends}\}$$
$$= P_0 - \int_{0,T} y P_0 e^{(k-y)t} e^{-kt} dt$$
$$= P_0[1 + e^{-yt}]_{0,T} = P_0 e^{-kT}.$$

Example

Let the dividend yield $y = 6.61\%$, the initial price $P_0 = \$15.125$ and the time to expiration $T = 5$ years, then the European call should be valued substituting $P_0^{ADJ} = P_0 e^{-yT} = 15.125 \ e^{-(0.0661)(5)} = \$10.8683$ for the stock price in the Black-Scholes equation.

A.9   DILUTION ADJUSTMENT IN WARRANT VALUATION

A warrant is a call option issued by the firm. However, warrants have special features that do not permit the direct use of the call formulas. The exercise of a warrant dilutes the equity claim of existing stockholders. In addition, the exercise price of the warrant may change over time and, as with some call options, dividends may be paid before expiration. The dividend adjustment was discussed in the previous section. Exercise price changes can be treated in the same way as dividends valuing the warrant at each exercise price change and choosing its maximum value. Here we deal with the adjustment for dilution.

Consider the issue of m warrants with exercise price X for a price $\hat{w}$ each. The total proceeds are $m\hat{w}$. These proceeds increase the value of equity. Hence, the present value of the equity to be received by the holder of a warrant upon exercise is

$$P_A = \frac{nP + m\hat{w}}{n + m} = \frac{P + \lambda\hat{w}}{1 + \lambda}$$

where P and n are the pre-warrant issue stock price and the shares outstanding, respectively, and $\lambda = m/n$ is the dilution ratio.

On the other hand, the effective exercise price paid by the holder is

$$X_A = X - \text{warrant-holder recovery via dilution}$$
$$= X - \frac{m}{n + m}X = \frac{n}{n + m}X = \frac{X}{1 + \lambda}.$$

X_A is the part of the exercise price that accrues to the "old" shareholders. Therefore, the value of the warrant is the value of a call with adjusted stock and exercise prices. Denoting by $c = c(P, X)$ the value of a standard option given by the Black-Scholes formula, the value of the warrant can be obtained by substituting into c the price of the stock and the exercise price adjusted for dilution, that is,

$$w = c(P_A, X_A; \sigma, r, t) = (1 + \lambda)^{-1}c(P + \lambda\hat{w}, X; \sigma, r, t).$$

If the warrants are issued at the fair value, $\hat{w} = w$ and the latter is the solution to the following equation:

$$w = (1 + \lambda)^{-1}c(P + \lambda w, X; \sigma, r, t).$$

These adjustments are already included in the warrant module of the Financial Options Calculator. The same procedure is applied to the valuation of outstanding warrants. One uses the market price of the warrant in order to calculate its theoretical value. The role of the current price of the warrant is to permit computing the *total* value of equity. The calculation assumes that the total value of equity is correctly priced, and tests if its split between common equity and the outstanding warrants is correct. If not, one would expect a future adjustment in the prices of the stock and warrants making up the split.

PROBLEMS

A.1 Value the following Dell Computer call as of July 9, 1999.

Stock Price	Expiration	Strike Price	Volatility	Premium
$42^{13}/_{16}$	Jan 20, 2001	70	62.26%	$7^7/_8$

Dell was not expected to pay dividends during the period of the option. The compound yield on a government note maturing January 2001 was 5.60%. The volatility was estimated using 52-week price data. What was the implied volatility?

A.2 Consider the following closing prices of XYZ Corp. The call has 18 days to expiration and the Treasury bill with the same maturity yields 4.65%.

Option	Stock Price	Strike Price	Call Price	Historical Volatility
XYZ	$51.125	$50	$1.625	20%

a. Compute the value of the call by direct computation of the Black-Scholes formula.
b. Compute the value of a put with the same exercise price using the put-call parity.

A.3 Value Xidex's warrants on November 5, 1986 using the Financial Options Calculator and compare your result to the actual warrant price. Use the following data:

Exercise price	$20.42	Expiration date	April 4, 1993
Stock price	$15.00	Warrant price	$ 4.44
Warrants outstanding	4.6 million	Shares per warrants	1
Shares outstanding	42 million	Volatility	26.5%
BEY Yield of 4/93 US note	7.16%*	Dividend yield	0

*Bond equivalent yield. That is, 7.16%/2 per semester or $(1 + 7.16\%/2)^2 = 7.29\%$ compound.

A.4 You are the Treasurer of ABC Inc. preparing a presentation to the board of directors on the company's executive stock option plan. In particular, you are attempting to determine the value of the Stock Appreciation Rights (SARs) included in the plan because the directors will want to know the value of the SAR grants they are being asked to approve.

A SAR is a right used to compensate executives that resembles a stock option but gives no right to purchase stock and does not requires payment for exercise. When the SAR is exercised the holder receives cash equal to the amount by which the price of the stock exceeds the stock price at the date of the grant adjusted for any new issue of common stock that took place since the date of the grant. In addition, the strike price of ABS's SARs is reduced by 5% per year to account for forgone dividends by the SAR-holders and to provide an incentive to hold to the SARs rather than to exercise them prematurely. The SARs can be exercised each year on the anniversary of the grant date or the first trading day following the anniversary date and expire 10 years after the date of the grant. The current price of ABC is $30.00. In addition, ABC's current dividend per share is $1.50 per year and its stock volatility, that is, the standard deviation of its rate of return is 22%. On February 7 of 2003 the compound yields on Treasury securities were as follows:

Maturity	Yield	Maturity	Yield
1 year	1.17%	8 years	3.72
2	1.60	9	3.89
3	2.13	10	3.99
4	2.62	15	4.68
5	2.96	20	4.93
6	3.23	29	5.01
7	3.54		

a. It is meaningful to value the SARs as if they were regular options? Why or why not?

b. Irrespective of your answer to (a), explain how to use option pricing to determine the optimal time for ABC executives to exercise their SARs. Briefly explain the procedure, but do not carry out computations.

c. Assume that the optimal time to exercise the SRAs is at their expiration, and use option valuation to determine the value of a SAR assuming the grant date is February 7, 2003.

d. What do you think about reducing the strike price of the SARs by 5% per year in order to discourage premature exercise? Is it necessary?

e. Compare SARs to regular stock options (i) from the point of view of the executives receiving them, and (ii) as a performance incentive.

A.5. On May 22, 1989, The RJR Nabisco Holding Corp. issued warrants with an exercise price of $0.07 per share, exercisable during a 1-year period beginning on May 22, 1998. At that time, those warrants represented 5.2% of the fully diluted equity of the firm. A curious situation arose in connection with the valuation of the newly issued warrants. They traded on the NYSE but the common they represented did not since all of it was held by Kolberg, Kravis and Roberts (65.3%), management, other investors, and convertible preferred holders (who had not converted their holdings into common). The market, however, managed to price the warrants at $5\frac{1}{4} (on Nov. 28, 1990).

a. What difficulties would you encounter in trying to price the warrants using option-pricing theory?

b. How do you think investors priced these warrants or how would you price them yourself?

A.6 Assume you are Telmex's CFO and that you are considering the issuance of a 5-year US$500 million bond to take place on May 1, 1996. The bond would pay an annual coupon of 8% (450 basis points below the required yield for a straight Telmex bond). The principal would be due in full at the end of the 5th year. In order to make up for the difference in yields, Telmex would attach 10 million 3-year European warrants to the issue, each warrant giving the right to purchase one Telmex ADR[3] for a cash exercise price. Price the issue as of May 1, 1996, and determine the required strike price for the warrants.

Additional information: Telmex's ADRs and LEAPS (long-term equity anticipation security) prices on May 1, 1996 were as follows:

Stock Price	Strike	Expiration	Volume	Call	Volume	Put
$34	$35	Jan 18 '97	264	$3½	4	$4⅛
34	40	Jan 17 '98	555	4½		
34	55	Jan 18 '97	80	3/16		

Option volume is expressed in contracts of 100 shares each. Options expire on the Saturday following the third Friday of each month.

---

[3]ADRs are American Depository Receipts that represent shares of a foreign company. Telmex's ADRs are registered with the SEC and trade on the NYSE as regular shares.

Telmex annual dividend was US$0.87 per ADR. Dividend dates were: March 31, June 30, September 30, and December 31. Yields on U.S. Treasury notes per maturity date were as follows: January '97: 5.47%; January '98: 5.98%; May '99: 6.22% expressed in BEY (bond equivalent yield, that is, the semiannual rate multiplied by 2). The yield on Telmex straight dollar-denominated bonds with 3 to 5 years of maturity paying annual interest was 12.5%. There were 483 million shares of Telmex outstanding (expressed in ADR equivalents).

Hints:

1. Find the present value of the 8% bond.
2. You need to estimate the implied volatility of the Leap options. Verify that the volatility implied by the price of the January '98 calls (the most liquid) was 34.45%.

A.7 Mandatory convertibles are equity-linked securities that pay a higher dividend than the common stock for a number of years, convert into common stock at a pre-specified date and have limited appreciation potential. One such mandatory convertible is a PERCS (short for Preferred Equity Redemption Cumulative Stock),[4] which converts in 3 years into common at a one-to-one exchange ratio as long as the value of the common received does not exceed a cap value. Above the cap value, the conversion ratio decreases such that the holder receives a fraction of a common s. ⌐ ⌐ with value equal to the cap. Thus, the value of a Percs is made up of (a) a dividend cash flow received until the Percs maturity, (b) a common share to be received at maturity, and (c) a call option on the company's common stock written by the Percs holder to the issuer.[5] Percs are issued at the same price as the common stock. Mandatory convertibles have been used as part of the stock consideration in a number of acquisitions.[6]

An issuer who wishes to signal strong belief about the future performance of its stock may do so by adding a floor to the Percs value. A floor is equivalent to giving investors a put with exercise price at the floor. In this problem, you are asked to design a puttable Percs for IBM as of the issue date July 1, 1994, with and without a knockout barrier. In order to do so, you will be guided in how to apply the option valuation models included in the Financial Options Calculator.

The following data are available: On June 30, 1994, IBM common stock and Leap option prices closed at:

Stock Price	Dividend	Strike	Expiration	Call Price
$62	$0.25/qt	$70	Jan 18, 1997	$9⅛

In addition, IBM bonds maturing in 1997 traded at a 6.5% yield, and the yields on Treasury notes were: 6.17% for January '97 and 6.26% for June '97. The yield of the May '04 Treasury note was 7.17%. All yields are quoted as bond equivalent yields (i.e., the semiannual rate times 2).

Task: Design a (three-year) puttable Percs for IBM as of July 1, 1994, with and without a knockout barrier and summarize its characteristics. Discuss the pros and cons of a puttable Percs for the issuer. In order to simplify the valuation of the options, make the number of shares to be received by the holder a function of the closing price on June 30, 1997 (not of an average). Alternatively, you can make it a function of the 5-trading day average ending on June 30, 1997 and use the Asian option program included in the Financial Options Calculator.

Designing Mandatory Convertibles—Guideline

Step 1: Design a Percs

1. Choose a preferred dividend as of July 1, 1994, say 6% of the stock price and obtain its present value. Dividend dates are Sept. 30, Dec. 31, March 31, and June 30.

---

[4]PERCS™ is a trademark of Morgan Stanley.

[5]For a detailed discussion of Percs and other mandatory convertibles see Arzac (1997).

[6]See Wasserstein (1998), 419–421.

2. Value the common dividend foregone. In practice you will want to check the consensus EPS growth forecast and payout in order to forecast dividend growth. In June of 1994 IBM was expected to keep is annual dividend of $1 for years to come. Obtain the present value of the dividend foregone. Same dividend dates as in 1. For 1 and 2 you should use the IBM bond rate with the same approximate maturity[7] because both dividends have negligible systematic risk. On this point see Arzac (1997).

3. Since you want to price the Percs at the common stock price, the increase in value of the Percs produced by the difference in the present value of 1 and 2 has to be offset by the Percs cap. Since the cap is a call, you first need to obtain the stock volatility. Solve for the implied volatility in the IBM Leaps option. The time to expiration and the interest rate are given in the assignment. Note that Leaps are American options. You can use the Financial Options Calculator to compute the implied volatility.

4. Now you can solve for the cap X necessary to offset the higher Percs dividend. The cap is a European call such that

$$\text{Value of cap} = \text{call } (P, X; \sigma, r, t)$$

for which all the data except X are already available including the value of the cap. Solve this equation for X using the call sheet of the Financial Options Calculator. Note that you should input the common dividend into the call valuation program.[8]

5. If X is too low to provide enough upside, you need to reduce the Percs dividend. Thus, in designing the traditional Percs you have only one degree of freedom.

Step 2: Make the Percs puttable

6. Choose a floor and value it. Note that the floor is a European option. You have all the information necessary to value it.

7. Attaching a floor increases the value of the Percs designed in Step 1 above the common stock price (why?). So, in order to decrease its value to the common price, you have to reduce the dividend and/or the cap. In designing a puttable Percs you have two degrees of freedom.

Step 3: Attach a knockout barrier to the puttable Percs

8. Attach a knockout barrier at some percentage above the current common stock price such that the put disappears if the price reaches the barrier. Now you have introduced an additional degree of freedom and you can increase the dividend, the cap or the floor. Whatever you do, the price of the Percs should still equal the price of the common. Use the knockout sheet of the Financial Options Calculator.

9. An alternative: Rather than introducing a knockout barrier, you can still attain three degrees of freedom by simply reducing the depth of the floor: That is, by providing a price guarantee for only a percentage price reduction from the floor value. Fix the floor at $55 and provide a guarantee for the first 9.35% reduction from the floor. That is, the company would paid min(max($55 − P, 0), 0.0935 × $55 = $5.14). The value of this guarantee is given by the difference: Put(X = $55) − Put(X = $55 − $5.14 = $49.86). Value the two puts using the Financial Options Calculator, interpret your result and compare this alternative to the previous designs for the puttable Percs. Make any necessary adjustment to price the issue at $62.

---

[7]The rate to use should have the same duration as the dividend streams but simple maturity is a reasonable approximation for this exercise. Duration is a weighted average of the time to the occurrence each cash flow with its present value as weight.

[8]Strictly, the adjustment for dividends should take into account the Percs dividends as well as the number of Percs to issue and the number of common shares outstanding. To do so one would enter the weighted average annual dividend into the call formula if the dividends dates of Percs and common stock are the same or close to each other. Otherwise, a present value adjustment would be required [see Arzac (1997), ftn 17]. Here, however, you can ignore this refinement. This adjustment would be material only when the Percs issue is relatively large and that is not likely to be so in IBM's case given its large market capitalization

Of course, further refinements are possible. For example, you can make the thinner floor disappear if the stock price reaches a knockout barrier or make mandatory conversion a function of an average, but let us not get carried away. By this time, you would have realized that the possibilities in designing derivatives are limited only by your imagination and the willingness of the investors and issuers to buy your idea.

A.8 On October 7, 1988, the board of directors of Irving Bank approved the Bank of New York's (BONY) offer for each and all Irving shares. BONY offered $15 cash, 1.675 BONY shares and a warrant for each Irving share. The warrant entitled the holder, during a 10-year exercise period, to purchase one share of BONY at the exercise price of $62 a share. BONY common closed at $35³/₄ on October 7. The shares outstanding of BONY and Irving were 33.092 and 18.391 million, respectively. On October 7, 1988, the compound yield on government bonds maturing in 1998 was 8.68%, and the volatility of BONY stock was estimated at 28% per annum. Your task is to value the warrants in BONY's offer. One problem with the valuation of BONY's warrants is that BONY paid dividends ($0.45 per quarter or a 5.035% annual yield). As you know, for a non-dividend–paying stock, the warrant is worth more alive than dead and will be exercised only at maturity if it pays to do so. On the other hand, it may pay to exercise the warrant on a dividend paying stock prematurely, that is, before expiration, in order to capture the dividends. In other words, the holder of a warrant incurs the extra cost of forgone dividends by carrying the warrant alive. That is why, at each dividend date the holder would compare the value of the warrant kept alive by forgoing the dividend to the proceeds from exercising the option right away plus the dividend. As seen in Section A.8, one way of accounting for the cost of forgone dividends in pricing the warrant is to reduce the price of the stock by the factor e^{-yt}, where y is the dividend yield and t is the time to expiration of the option. For example, the relevant share price for a BONY warrant holder planning to exercise the warrant in ten years is $35.75e^{-0.503} = $21.62. (If you use the Financial Options Calculator to value this warrant, you would not need to worry about the dividend yield adjustment because the calculator would do it for you. The calculator also takes into account that the warrant is American, and it may pay to exercise it before expiration.)

Appendix **B**

Valuation Aids Software

The enclosed Valuation Aids CD-ROM contains a number of Excel spreadsheets written to assist the reader in applying the models presented in this book. It includes:

- **Equity Premium Calculator:** This spreadsheet calculates the prospective equity premium implied by the one-year forward P/E multiple of the S&P500 index. Additional inputs required are: 5-year consensus growth rate of earnings, the long-term growth rate of earnings, present and long-term payout ratios, and the compound yield on the 10-year government note benchmark. The prospective equity premium is defined as the difference between the rate required by investors on a market portfolio and the long-term government yield. The required return on equity is the rate that equates the present value of the future dividends of the market portfolio to the value of the portfolio. See Chapter 3 for details.

- **Equivalent Multiple Calculator:** This workbook calculates equivalent forward or trailing valuation multiples from any given multiple and parameters values characterizing the earnings of the firm. It permits calculating a different multiple form a known multiple, checking a given multiple against another known multiple, and adjusting comparable multiples for different debt ratios and growth rates. In each case, the corresponding common-size income statements (for $100 revenues) are calculated to facilitate interpretation of the results. It also decomposes multiples into their no-growth value and the franchise and growth factors. For a discussion of the formulas used in this workbook see Chapter 4.

- **Debt Capacity Calculator:** Computes the debt capacity of a company for a given period of amortization of senior debt principal under assumptions about sales growth, EBITDA margins, non-cash items, capital expenditures, changes in working capital, proportions of senior and subordinated debt, and interest rates. Its use is shown in Chapters 7 and 13.

- **HLF Value Calculator:** Computes the enterprise and equity values of a highly leveraged firm that plans to reduce its leverage over a number of years by applying its free cash flow to paying interest and debt reduction. Two models are provided: a recursive adjusted present value model and an option-pricing model. Both models are described and applied in Chapter 6.

- **Financial Options Calculator:** Provides programs for calculating the values of European, American, Asian and knock-out options, and European and American warrants. These options are used in Chapters 6, 8, 10, 11, 13, and 15. Appendix A provides additional details and review problems.

- **Real Options Calculator I:** Provides an algorithm for valuing firms with entry and exit options. Examples of its use are provided in Chapter 8, Sections 8.4 and 8.5, and Chapter 10, Section 10.7.

- **Real Options Calculator II:** Values firms with foothold and growth options using a version of the explicit finite difference algorithm. Applications are discussed in Chapter 8, Sections 8.6 and 8.7. The algorithm is described in Note N8.7.

Appendix C

Answers to Selected End-of-Chapter Problems

CHAPTER 2

2.1. After-tax cash flow = $135,000.

2.4. (a) Applying the comparable EBITDA multiple to Fleet's 2004 EBITDA yields: $56.7 \times 5.6 = \$318$ million.

(b) Cost of debt = 7%, cost of equity = 4.5% + (1.32)(5%) + 3.3% = 14.4%, WACC = 9.30%.

Discanted Back using WAAC

PV of FCF	$ 63.09 million
2009 continuation value at 3% growth rate	$411.14
PV of continuation value	263.57
Enterprise value on 1/1/2005	$327.35

$411.14 = \dfrac{(1.03)}{(.093 - .03)}$

24.684

$\dfrac{411.14}{(1.093)^5} = 263.5$

2.5. Cost of equity = 4.5% + (0.66)(5%) + 3.3% = 11.1%.

PV of FCF	$ 60.93 million
2009 continuation value at 3% growth rate	$319.78
PV of continuation value	188.92
Enterprise value on 1/1/2005	$249.25

1.2

2.8. (b)

Enterprise value	$1,164.7 million
Debt	650.0
Equity	514.7
Shares	35
Value per share	$ 14.71

(c)

	2005	2009
P/E	22.3	9.9

2.11. $EPS_{2013} = (0.99)(1.185)^5(1.09)^5 = \$3.6$

$Dividend_{2014} = (0.51)(3.6)(1.04) = \$1.9$

$Share\ value_{2013} = 1.9/(0.10 - 0.04) = \$31.7$

$Share\ value_{2002} = \$31.7/(1.12)^{10} = \$10.2.$

Different ← This is wrong.
should have g = 4%

Share Value$_{2013}$ = $\dfrac{1.9(1.04)}{(.12 - .04)}$

CHAPTER 3

3.3. Required return on the S&P500 index: $k = 9\% + (4\%)(1) = 13.0\%$.

(a) $P/E_0 = \text{Payout}(1 + g)/(k - g)$ or

$$k - g = \text{yield}(1 + g), \text{ where yield} = \text{Payout}/(P/E_o) = 2.9\%$$
$$g = (k - y)/(1 + y) = (13\% - 2.9\%)/1.029 = 9.8\%$$
$$\text{and } g_{\text{Real}} = (9.8 - 4.5)/1.045 = 5.1\% \text{ or } g_{\text{Real}} \approx 9.8 - 4.5 = 5.3\%,$$

versus a compound growth rate of earnings during the post-war period of about 2%.

(b) The long-term nominal growth of earnings and dividends would be about $(1.02)(1.045) - 1 = 6.6\%$. Hence,

$$\frac{P}{E_0} = \sum_{1,5} \frac{D_0(1.16)^t}{E_0(1 + k)^t} + \frac{1}{(1 + k)^5} \frac{D_0}{E_0} \frac{(1.16)^5(1.066)}{k - 0.066}$$

where $D_0/E_0 = 0.614$ and $P/E_0 = 21.2$. Solving for k, it yields $y = 11.17\%$. This implies a premium over long-term bonds of 2.17%.

3.5. k is the solution to:

$$21.8 = 0.608(1 + k)^{-1} + 0.612(1 + k)^{-2} + 0.624(1 + k)^{-3} + 0.641(1 + k)^{-4}$$
$$+ 0.660(1 + k)^{-5} + 0.715(1 + k)^{-6} + 0.763(1 + k)^{-7} + 0.803(1 + k)^{-8}$$
$$+ 0.832(1 + k)^{-9} + 0.848(1 + k)^{-10} + 0.865(1 + k)^{-10}(k - 0.02)$$

k is the prospective required real return equal to 5.55% or $(1.0555)(1.0255) = 8.24\%$ nominal. The equity premium is $8.24\% - 5.16\% = 3.08\%$.

3.6. The equity premium equals 5.08%.

3.7. $\beta_U = 1.32/(1 + 0.50/0.50) = 0.66$.

CHAPTER 4

4.1. (a) Value of equity = 61.05. Initial P/E = 12.2 (forward). Continuation value P/E = 10.9 (trailing).

(b) $g = 9.7\%$, forward continuation value P/E = 9.9.

4.3.

	(a)	(b)	(b)	(c)
Debt ratio	30%	20%	40%	35%
P/E	18.00	17.10	21.00	8.93
EBITDAx	6.53	6.25	6.85	3.92
EBITx	10.89	10.42	11.41	6.53
RevenueX	0.65	0.63	0.68	0.39

4.4. P/E = No-growth term + Franchise factor $\times$ Growth factor = $8.33 + (4.76)(1.40) = 15x$.

4.6. Price per share = 128 pence or $15.6 per ADR.

CHAPTER 5

5.1.

PV of EVA	$ 23.13 million
PV of continuation value	140.25
Total PV of EVA	163.38
Beginning capital	70.00
Enterprise value	233.38

5.3. Enterprise value = $174.4 million. Value of equity = $134.4.

5.5. Enterprise value = $268 million. During the first 10 years NOPAT and capital will grow at 15% and ROC = 25%, so capital invested would equal 15%/25% or 60% of NOPAT.

5.8. Great Dane Capital can pay a maximum price of $4.9 billion for the equity of North American Labels or $49 a share. The sum-of-the-parts valuation follows:

	Pinkerton	Pipedream
Invested capital (millions)	$2,000	$1,000
Growth rate	5%	10%
ROC first ten years	10%	20%
ROC thereafter	10%	12.8%
WACC	6.54%	7.21%
Enterprise value/Invested capital	3.25	2.34
Enterprise value at exit in 6 months (millions)	$6,500	$2,340
Minus net debt	2,275	702
Net proceeds at exit	$4,225	$1,638
Present value of net proceeds @ 20%	$3,521	$1,365

CHAPTER 6

6.2.

PV of FCF at unlevered cost of equity = 15.20%	$ 42.00 million
PV of 2009 continuation value at WACC = 14.42%	184.07
PV of tax shield at cost of debt = 8%	9.28
Enterprise value	235.34
Net debt	59.05
Equity before fees and expenses	176.29
Fees and expenses	3.48
Value of equity	172.81
Shares (million)	15.00
Value per share	$11.52
IPO proceeds:	$ 57.60 million
Fees and expenses	3.48
Available for debt retirement	54.12

6.5. $V_0 = \$1906.2$.

6.6. Entering the data from Exhibit 6.5 into the HLF Value Calculator yields the following values:

Volatility			
Revenue	Option	V_0	S_0
10%	22%	$1,948	$448
15%	30%	1,997	497
20%	39%	2,952	552
25%	48%	2,109	609
30%	57%	2,167	667

CHAPTER 7

7.1. The capital required to finance 7.02% growth is $73.7 million. A target debt ratio of 40% requires an increase in debt of 40% of $73.7 or $29.50. Furthermore, a net income margin of 5% would produce a net income equal to 5% of $1,102.5 + $77.40 or $59.0, which after a 25% dividend payout leaves $59.0 – $14.75 = $44.2 million of retained earnings.

7.3. For Wotsaf's estimates: g = 30%, σ = (65% + 5%)/6 = 11.67% the EBIT coverage ratio is $[1 - 3.09\sigma/(1 + g)]^{-1}$ = 1.4x, for a 0.1% probability of shortfall. (Note that for normally distributed growth, a range $\pm 3\sigma$ about the mean has 99% probability, which means that 1/6 the range provides an estimation of σ. For more on this see Section 8.2.) For Wirst's estimates: g = 5%, σ = (65% + 55%)/6 = 21.67%, the coverage ratio is $[1 - 3.72\sigma/(1 + g)]^{-1}$ = 4.3x, for a 0.01% probability of shortfall. Note that in this case the coefficient of σ has been changed to 3.72 because a deviation below –3.72σ has a probability of 0.01% for a normally distributed growth rate.

7.5. Substituting the data into the Debt Capacity Calculator yields a debt capacity of 4.28x EBITDA or 4.48 × $3.058 million = $13.5 million. This means that Watt needs to raise $2.5 million of equity.

CHAPTER 8

8.1. NPV = $300.

8.2. NPV = $363.64.

8.5. c = $363.64.

8.7. Consider the transaction: {buy 800 units of the traded asset, sell the option to invest, borrow (or short bills) at 10%}

This results in the following payoffs:

	Now	Year 1 FCF = $100	Year 1 FCF = $200
Buy 800 units	($1,090.91)	800.00	1,600.00
Sell the call	400.00	0	(800.00)
	(690.91)		
Borrow @ 10%	727.27	(800.00)	(800.00)
Arbitrage profit	$ 36.36	0	0

The arbitrage profit is the difference between the value of the option calculated in 8.5 and its price: $400 – $363.64 = $36.36. This means that no rational investor would price the option above its arbitrage-free value of $363.64.

8.10. (a) The expected free cash flows in years 1 through 5 are:

Year	1	2	3	4	5
Expected free cash flow	5.00	5.36	5.75	6.17	6.62

(b) Enterprise value = $18.28 million. NPV = –$11.73 million.

8.11. The Real Option Calculator I gives $16.23 million as the value of the entry option, with entry threshold at $16.67 million of revenues.

8.14. The Real Options Calculator I gives $212.5 million as the value of the acquisition, with exit when revenue falls below $42 million.

CHAPTER 9

9.1. In a stock purchase the proceeds to the seller would be $63. In an asset purchase the proceeds to the seller would be $47 and the buyer would be able to step up the basis of the assets by $50 to $70. Goodwill amortization would be $3.333 per year over 15 years. The tax shield would be $1.333 and have a present value of $10.74.

9.5. (a) $V_{G+S} = [(1.2)(6) + (0.6)(2)](1 + g)/(k - g) = \$88.2$ million for $g = 5\%$ and $k = 15\%$.
(b) Exchange ratio = 0.6/1 or $2 \times 0.6 = 1.2$ m shares issued

$$P = \text{Price paid for SS} = [1.2/(6 + 1.2)]V_{G+S} = \$14.7 \text{ million}$$

$$\text{GLD stockholders' gain} = V_{G+S} - V_G - P = 88.2 - 60 - 14.7 = \$13.5 \text{ million}$$

$$\text{SS stockholders' gain} = P - V_S \qquad\qquad = 14.7 - 10 \qquad = \underline{4.7 \text{ million}}$$

$$\text{Value created} = \$18.2 \text{ million}$$

9.7. (a) Gould's gain = –$63.4 million. AM's gain = $63.4 million.
(b) Required synergy = $77.0 million.
9.11. Real WACC = 7.58%. Maximum bid = $84.6/share.
9.12. Maximum bid = $67/share.

CHAPTER 10

10.2. (a) NPV = $0.5 million and the VC would demand 80% of the equity.
(b) NPV = $1 million and the VC would demand 60%.
10.3. 84.25% and 75.38%, respectively.
10.6. (a) VC required ownership = 39.4%.
(b) New Shares = 325,100 shares.
(c) Price per share = $6.152.
(d) Post-money valuation = $5.08 million
10.9. (a) Subordinated note worth = $6.730 million.
(b) Value of earnout = $ 2.863 million.
(c) Value of offer for enterprise = $29.393 million.
10.10. The earnout is worth $2.863 million. But this earnout pays only when EBITDA exceeds the threshold of $6 million.
10.12. Value of the earnout = $1.514 million. The earnout multiple needs to be increased to 7.305x.
10.14. The earnout equals $(2.5)(0.15) = 0.375$ times the difference between (a) three yearly calls on revenue, each based upon the present value of the respective expected revenue and an exercise threshold equal to $50 million and (b) three yearly calls (the caps), each with exercise price equal to $50 + 2/0.375 = \$55.333$ million. The value of the earnout is $2.2 million.
10.20. (a)

NetServices Inc. Capitalization Table Prior to DesignPlus Acquisition

Shareholder	$ Invested	Post-money Valuation	Pre-money Valuation	Ownership	Shares	Price Per Share
Morningside	$75,000,000			44.78%	11,194,030	$6.7000
STL	$70,000,000			41.79%	10,447,761	$6.7000
Letts	$22,500,000			13.43%	3,358,209	$6.7000
Total	$167,500,000	167,500,000	$0	100.00%	25,000,000	$6.7000

(c)

Return to Georgetown Group

	7/30/97	2/15/98	11/20/98	10/27/99	10/15/00	6/30/03
Investment	(3,000,000)	(4,000,000)	(4,000,000)	(4,000,000)		
Sale of DesignPlus					19,000,000	
IPO:						
Enterprise value						810,000,000
Net debt						25,000,000
Equity						785,000,000
Fully diluted number of shares						30,000,000
Per share						26.17
Proceeds						42,152,170
Cash flow	(3,000,000)	(4,000,000)	(4,000,000)	(4,000,000)	19,000,000	42,152,170
IRR	**44.88%**					

CHAPTER 11

11.3. The value of the gold price guarantee is 5 million times the difference between two Asian puts minus 2.5 million times an Asian call. The common inputs for the option are:

> Initial price = $277.45
>
> Valuation date = August 17, 2001
>
> Expiration = August 16, 2002
>
> Number of averaging point (trading days) = 252
>
> Volatility = 10.45%
>
> Annual risk-free rate = 3.38%
>
> Storage costs = $2/year

The exercise prices of the long put and the short call are $260 and $300, respectively. The exercise price of the short put is 265 – 75/5 = $250. These options are valued with the Financial Options Calculator over 365 calendar days with 1.448413 days between averaging points. This approximation permits generating the 252 days average points throughout the year. The results are: Put(265) = $1.109, Put(250) = $0.108 and Call (300) = $1.587. Hence, the value of the guarantee is: 5(1.109 – 0.108) – 2.5(1.587) = $1.04 million.

11.4. Two alternative interpretations of Borland's offer are

> **1.** 0.398 P – 0.398 Call(X = $43.97) + 0.346 Call(X = $50.58)
>
> **2.** 0.346 P + 0.346 Put(X = $50.58) – 0.398 Put(X = $43.97),

where P is the price of Borland.

11.6. Long 1 Canada Dry and short 0.55 Hunt Foods. Gross spread = $152 per 100 Canada Dry shares.

CHAPTER 12

12.4. Petöfi's free cash flows are computed in the following exhibit. Petöfi's financial policy does not produce a tax shield in every year except 1995. Note that it enjoys a tax holiday until 1995 at the time it has debt, and its debt goes to zero after 1995. In 1995, it pays an average tax rate of 4% (16% on the last quarter) and interest expense is only HUF56 million such that the tax shield has negligible present value. Hence, the value of the enterprise can be computed with the APV procedure, discounting the free cash flows at the unlevered cost of capital.

Petöfi Printing Company Ltd. Projected Free Cash Flows 1992–2000

HUF (Hungarian Forint) millions

Fiscal year ending December 31	1991	1992	1993	1994	1995	1996	1997	1998	1999	2000
EBITDA	354	475	949	1,308	1,553	1,744	1,714	1,697	1,759	1,865
Net income		287	682	1,092	1,342	1,424	1,454	1,485	1,592	1,632
Net interest after tax		52	57	(1)	(75)	(173)	(249)	(316)	(392)	(454)
NOPAT		339	739	1,091	1,267	1,251	1,205	1,169	1,200	1,177
Depreciation and amortization		118	234	244	262	286	313	341	367	394
Sale of assets		0	52	0	0	0	0	0	0	0
CAPEX & Net WC increase		(1,516)	(509)	(450)	(548)	(516)	(479)	(463)	(468)	(504)
Unlevered free cash flow		(1,059)	517	885	982	1,021	1,039	1,046	1,099	1,068
HUF inflation rate		24.0%	14.0%	11.0%	9.0%	7.5%	6.5%	5.5%	5.0%	5.0%
HUF accumulated inflation rate		24.0%	41.4%	56.9%	71.0%	83.9%	95.8%	106.6%	116.9%	127.8%
Real unlevered free cash flow		(854)	365	564	574	555	530	506	507	469

12.6.

Petőfi Printing Company Ltd.

HUF (Hungarian Forint) millions

Fiscal year ending December 31	1991	1992	1993	1994	1995	1996	1997	1998	1999	2000
Discounting (nominal) dollar cash flows										
Unlevered free cash flows in HUFs		(1,059)	517	885	982	1,021	1,039	1,046	1,099	1,068
Continuation value in HUFs										13,616
Exchange rate HUF/$	78.3									
US expected inflation	3.3%									
Estimation of future exchange rate		94.0	103.7	111.5	117.6	122.4	126.2	128.9	131.0	133.1

Future exchange rate = Previous year exchange rate $\times$ (1 + HUF inflation)/(1 + US\$ inflation)

	1991	1992	1993	1994	1995	1996	1997	1998	1999	2000
Unlevered free cas flows in US$		(11.3)	5.0	7.9	8.3	8.3	8.2	8.1	8.4	8.0
Continuation value in dollars										102.3
PV of FCF @	18.5%	$ 16.0								
PV of continuation value @	18.5%	22.2								
Enterprise value in US$		$ 38.2								
Enterprise value in HUFs @	78.3	2,990								

CHAPTER 13

13.3. Taking into account that the present value of the management options is $27.33 per option, and compounding it at 25% one gets an exit value of $83.4 or a total value of $83.4 × 500,000 options = $41.7 million. Subtracting its value from the exit value of equity yields the amount available to common equity and results in lower values for the stakes of the mezzanine investor and the sponsor. The sponsor should expect to get about $1,009.5 million or an IRR = $(1,009.5/248)^{1/5} - 1 = 32.4\%$.

13.5. Warrant value = $7.73 and 40.62 warrants need to be attached to each bond.

13.7. (a) Cost of warrant kicker = 2.63 × 1 million = $2.63 million.

(b) The all-in cost (AIC) of the debt plus warrant package is 13.9% vs. the AIC of the straight debt issue that is 13.1%.

13.9. The minimum rate is 11.28%. Verify that 11.28% coupon interest plus the warrants yields 14% to Provident.

CHAPTER 14

14.6. (a) The following exhibit shows that the proposed recapitalization is feasible.

SM Holdings Revised Projected Cash Flows

Year	0	1	2	3	4	5
EBIT (g = 5.0%)	300	160	168	176	185	194
Interest expense						
Senior 8.0%		78	46	41	36	30
Sub 10.0%		75	17	17	17	17
		7	105	118	138	147
Tax 35.0%		2	37	41	46	51
Net after tax		5	68	77	86	96
Debt amortization:						
Senior		80	63	63	63	63
Subordinated		0	0	0	0	0
Cash balance		0	5	19	42	75
Debt balance:						
Senior	650	570	507	444	381	318
Subordinated	500	172	172	172	172	172
	1150	742	679	616	553	490

(b) Senior bond-holders are likely to demand faster amortization of principal if they are going to accept a below-market coupon. Subordinated bond-holders will also attempt to obtain better terms and demand more equity. Shareholders' attempt to keep 55% of the equity will most likely be rejected by bond-holders.

14.8. The value of the equity per share is (€1,370.7 + €10.7)/809 = €1.7075, the exercise price is €6.098. The value of three warrants is €0.3317 or €0.3317 × 96.667 million = €32.1 million in total.

CHAPTER 15

15.3.

WTT Inc. FCF Valuation of Restructuring Actions for Metal Products Unit

Harvest	(in million $)					
	2002	2003	2004	2005	2006	2007
Sales		487.0	424.4	384.9	349.1	316.5
Growth of sales		−12.9%	−9.3%	−9.3%	−9.3%	−9.3%
EBITDA margin		13.0%	13.5%	14.0%	14.5%	15.0%
EBITDA		63.3	57.3	53.9	50.6	47.5
Depreciation		36.0	32.4	29.2	26.2	23.6
Operating income		27.3	24.9	24.7	24.4	23.9
Taxes @ 40%		10.9	10.0	9.9	9.7	9.5
Unlevered net income		16.4	14.9	14.8	14.6	14.3
Deferred taxes		1.2	1.1	1.0	0.9	0.8
Capex and Increase in NWC		0.0	0.0	0.0	0.0	0.0
Depreciation		36.0	32.4	29.2	26.2	23.6
Free cash flow		53.6	48.4	45.0	41.7	38.7
Recovery at exit						180.7
WACC	10.00%					
PV{Free cash flows}	175.1					
PV{Recovery}	112.2					
Business unit value	287.26					
Invested capital	360.0	324.0	291.6	262.4	236.2	212.6

15.4. (a) Valuation of Racal Electronics

	Share Price	Shares	Units	Total
Racal Electronics	190 p	£1.3 bn		£2.5 bn
Plus debt				0.4
Total assets				2.9
Break up:				
Racal Telecom	275 p	0.8 bn	£2.2 bn	
Racal Chubb			0.4	2.6
Rump assets				0.3

Note: p = pence, bn = billion

15.5. (d)

BAT Restructuring: Sale of retail business and share repurchase (Billion £, except per share numbers)

Value of net assets in retail business			2.000
Argos valuation			
Pro-forma EPS (pence)		14.3	
P/E		12.0	
Shares		296.8	0.509
Gross proceeds			1.491
Expenses		3.0%	0.045
Net proceeds			1.446
Tax basis		0.914	
Taxable profits		0.532	
Taxes on sale profits	40.0%		0.213
Net proceeds after taxes			1.233
BAT shares (million)	1,530		
Repurchase price (pence)		1,000	
Repurchase (million)	10.0%	153.0	1.530
Deficit financed with funds from operations			(0.297)

APPENDIX A

A.1. Dell Computer call value = $7.39. Implied volatility = 64.58%.

A.3. The Financial Options Calculator gives a value for the warrants of $4.72. The computed price is higher than the actual price of $4.44. This may be caused by the Black-Scholes formula, which tends to over-price high volatility and long maturity options. On the other hand, the formula tends to underprice deep out-of-the-money options like Xidex's. At that time, CS First Boston valued Xidex warrants at $4.70 and concluded that the warrants were underpriced and that those holding Xidex stock should swap it for its warrants.

A.6.

Year	0	1	2	3	4	5
Cash flow (millions)		$40.00	$40.00	$40.00	$40.00	$540.00
Face value	$ 500.00					
Coupon	8.0%					
Market rate	12.5%					
Value of bond	$ 419.89					
Required value of warrants	$ 80.11					
Number of warrants (millions)	10.00					
Per warrant	$ 8.01					

Imputs for warrant valuation:	
Warrant value (value of equity kicker from above)	$ 8.01
Stock price	$34.00
Implied volatility (from call program)	34.45%
Expiration	3 years
Interest rate	6.22% BEY
Annual dividend on common	$ 0.87
Number of shares outstanding (millions)	483
Increase in common shares upon exercise of warrants	10
Implied exercise price (from warrant program)	**$35.85**

A.8. Enter the following input into the warrant sheet of the Financial Options Calculator: stock price = $35.75, annual dividend = $1.80, dividends per year = 4, strike price = $62, number of warrants = 18.391, shares outstanding = 63.897, current warrant price = 0, interest rate = 8.68%, volatility = 28%, current date = 7/10/1988, expiration date = 1/10/1998, trading days to expiry = US. The value of the American call is $6.28 or $6.28 × 18.391 = $115.5 million in total. (The *Wall Street Journal* reported on 10/10/1988 that the warrants were being valued at $5 or more and so did *Value Line* on 12/16/1988.)

Technical Notes

NOTES TO CHAPTER 2

N2.1 Projecting Financial Statements Line Items

This note provides details about the line-item projections of Packtech for each year t as shown in Exhibits 2.2–2.4.

Income Statements

$\text{Sales}_t = \text{Sales}_{t-1} \times (1 + \text{Growth Rate of Sales}_t)$

$\text{Cost of Sales}_t = \text{Cost of Sales as \% Sales}_t \times \text{Sales}_t$

$\text{Gross Profit}_t = \text{Sales}_t - \text{Cost of Sales}_t$

$\text{Sales, General and Adm. Expenses}_t(\text{SG\&A}_t) = \text{SG\&A as \% of Sales}_t \times \text{Sales}_t$

$\text{Research and Development}_t(\text{R\&D}_t) = \text{R\&D as \% of Sales}_t \times \text{Sales}_t$

$\text{EBITDA}_t = \text{Gross Profit}_t - (\text{SG\&A}_t + \text{R\&D}_t)$

$\text{Depreciation}_t = \text{Depreciation as \% PP\&E}_t \times \text{PP\&E}_t \text{ (PP\&E from balance sheet)}$ *(handwritten: Book Dep. (Net PPE)(% Net PPE))*

$\text{EBIT}_t = \text{EBITDA}_t - \text{Depreciation}_t$ *(highlighted)*

$\text{Interest Expense}_t = \text{Interest Rate on Debt}_t \times \text{Debt}_{t-1}\text{(Debt from balance sheet)}$

To simplify, interest expense is based upon the level of interest at the beginning of the year. An alternative computation is to base it on the average debt balance during the year. The effect on valuation is usually immaterial.

$\text{Interest Income}_t = \text{Interest Rate on Cash and Marketable Securities}_t(\text{C\&MS})$
$$\times \text{C\&MS}_{t-1} \text{ (C\&MS from balance sheet)}$$

$\text{Pretax Income}_t = \text{EBIT}_t - \text{Interest Expense}_t + \text{Interest Income}_t$

$\text{Current Income Tax}_t = \text{Tax Rate on Income}_t \times \text{Pre-Tax Income}_t - \text{Deferred Tax}_t$

$\text{Deferred Tax}_t = \text{Tax Rate on Income}_t \times (\text{Tax Depreciation}_t - \text{Book Depreciation}_t)$

$\text{Net Income}_t = \text{Pre-Tax Income}_t - (\text{Current Income Tax}_t + \text{Deferred Tax}_t)$

Balance Sheets

$\text{Cash and Marketable Securities}_t = \text{End of Year C\&MS}_t \text{ (from cash flow statement)}$

$\text{Accounts Receivable}_t (\text{AR}_t) = \text{AR as \% of Sales}_t \times \text{Sales}_t$

$\text{Inventories}_t = \text{Inventories as \% of Cost of Sales}_t \times \text{Cost of Sales}_t$

$\text{Other Current Assets}_t = \text{Other Current Assets as \% Sales}_t \times \text{Sales}_t$

$\text{Total Current Assets}_t = \text{C\&MS}_t + \text{AR}_t + \text{Inventories}_t + \text{Other Current Assets}_t$

$\text{Net PP\&E}_t = \text{Net PP\&E as \% of Sales}_t \times \text{Sales}_t$

$\text{PP\&E}_t = \text{Net PP\&E}_t + \text{Depreciation}_t$

$\text{Other Noncurrent Assets}_t = \text{Other Noncurrent Assets}_{t-1}$

$\text{Total Assets}_t = \text{Total Current Assets}_t + \text{Net PP\&E}_t + \text{Other Noncurrent Assets}_t$

$\text{Short-term Debt and Current Portion of LTD}_t = 1/6 \text{ of Total Debt (20\% of Long-term Debt}_t)$

$\text{Accounts Payable}_t (\text{AP}_t) = \text{AP as \% of Cost of Sales}_t \times \text{Cost of Sales}_t$

$\text{Accrued Expenses}_t (\text{AE}_t) = \text{AE as \% of Sales}_t \times \text{Sales}_t$

$\text{Taxes Payable}_t = \text{Tax Payable as \% of Current Income Tax}_t \times \text{Current Income Tax}_t$

$\text{Other Current Liabilities}_t = \text{Other Current Liabilities as \% of Sales}_t \times \text{Sales}_t$

$$\text{Total Current Liabilities}_t = \text{Short-term Debt and Current Portion of LTD}_t + \text{AP}_t + \text{AE}_t$$
$$+ \text{Taxes Payable}_t + \text{Other Current Liabilities}_t$$

$$\text{Lont-term Debt}_t = \text{Total Debt}_t - \text{Short-term Debt and Current Portion of LTD}_t$$

$$\text{Total Debt}_t = \text{Total Debt as a multiple of next year EBITDA}_t \times \text{EBITDA}_{t+1} \text{ (with}$$
$$\text{EBITDA}_{2007} = \text{EBITDA}_{2006} \times (1 + \text{Growth Rate of Sales}_t))$$

$$\text{Deferred Income Taxes}_t = \text{Deferred Income Taxes}_{t-1} + \text{Deferred Tax}_t \text{ (from income}$$
$$\text{statement)}$$

$$\text{Total Liabilities}_t = \text{Total Current Liabilities}_t + \text{Long-term Debt}_t + \text{Deferred Income}$$
$$\text{Taxes}_t$$

$$\text{Common Stock and Retained Earnings}_t = \text{Common Stock and Retained Earnings}_{t-1}$$
$$+ \text{Net Income}_t - \text{Dividends}_t$$
$$\text{(from cash flow statement)}$$

Cash-flow Statements

Net Income, Depreciation and Deferred Tax from income statement.

$$\text{Decrease in Current Assets}_t = \text{AR}_{t-1} + \text{Inventories}_{t-1} + \text{Other Current Assets}_{t-1}$$
$$- (\text{AR}_t + \text{Inventories}_t + \text{Other Current Assets}_t)$$

$$\text{Increase in Current Liabilities except Debt}_t = \text{AP}_t + \text{AE}_t + \text{Taxes Payable}_t - (\text{AP}_{t-1}$$
$$+ \text{AE}_{t-1} + \text{Taxes Payable}_{t-1})$$

$$\text{Decrease in Net Working Capital}_t = \text{Decrease in Current Assets}_t + \text{Increase in Current}$$
$$\text{Liabilities except Debt}_t$$

$$\text{Funds from Operations}_t = \text{Net Income}_t + \text{Depreciation}_t + \text{Deferred Tax}_t + \text{Decrease}$$
$$\text{in Net Working Capital}_t$$

$$\text{Capital Expenditures}_t = \text{Net PP\&E}_t - \text{Net PP\&E}_{t-1} + \text{Depreciation}_t$$

$$\text{Decrease in Debt}_t = \text{Total Debt}_{t-1} - \text{Total Debt}_t$$

$$\text{Dividends}_t = \text{Funds from Operations}_t - \text{Capital Expenditures}_t - \text{Decrease in Debt}_t$$
$$- (\text{Cash Balance as \% of Sales}_t \times \text{Sales}_t - \text{Cash Balance as \% of Sales}_{t-1}$$
$$\times \text{Sales}_{t-1})$$

$$\text{Total Funds to Financing}_t = \text{Decrease in Debt}_t + \text{Dividends}_t$$

$$\text{Increase in Cash}_t = \text{Fund from Operations}_t - \text{Capital Expenditures}_t - \text{Total Funds to}$$
$$\text{Financing}$$

$$\text{End-of-Year C\&MS}_t = \text{End-of-Year C\&MS}_{t-1} + \text{Increase in Cash}_t$$

*N2.2   Debt Valuation[1]

We show that the value of the cash flow to debt for any future change in debt that pays a coupon rate equal to the cost of debt is always equal to the value of the initial debt. First, consider the case in which debt stays constant at its initial level D_0 and is paid back at the end of the year n, the value of the cash flow to debt is then

$$\frac{(1 - t)rD_0}{R} + \frac{(1 - t)rD_0}{R^2} + \ldots + \frac{(1 - t)rD_0}{R^n} + \frac{D_0}{R^n}$$

Where $R = 1 + (1 - t)r$. Note that the first n terms are the present value of an annuity and hence we can rewrite the above expression as

$$\frac{-(1 - t)rD_0(1 - R^n)}{(1 - t)rR^n} + \frac{D_0}{R^n} = D_0.$$

---

[1]Sections marked with an asterisk may be skipped on a first reading.

Now consider an increase in debt ΔD_t repaid in m years. The change in the cash flow to debt and its present value are

$$-\Delta D_t + \frac{(1 - t)r\Delta D_t}{R} + \frac{(1 - t)r\Delta D_t}{R^2} + \ldots + \frac{(1 - t)r\Delta D_t}{R^m} + \frac{\Delta D_t}{R^m} = 0.$$

This expression adds up to zero because, by the same argument used above, the sum of the second-to-last terms equals ΔD_t. Therefore, for any arbitrary set of debt increases or decreases that pay or save coupon interest equal to the cost of debt, the present value of the debt cash flows equals the value of the initial debt.

Finally, note that this result is valid for arbitrary interest and tax rates including $t = 0$. This case corresponds to discounting the pre-tax interest received by debt-holders at the pre-tax rate r. That is, the value of the cash flow to debt-holders evaluated from their perspective is also equal to the initial value of debt, independently of future changes in the amount of debt.

*N2.3   Enterprise Valuation

We now show the equivalence between valuing the free cash flow at WACC and valuing its separate components. We first start with the valuation of the equity cash flow and then show that it implies the valuation of the total free cash flow at WACC. Consider an n-year cash flow projection. The value of equity at the end of year $n - 1$ can be written as:

$$S_{n-1} = \frac{FCF_n - (1 - t)r_n D_{n-1} + \Delta D_n + V_n - D_n}{1 + k_n} \tag{N2.3.1}$$

where $FCF_n = (1 - t)EBIT_n + D\&NC_n - (Capex_n + \Delta NWC_n)$, $D_n = D_{n-1} + \Delta D_n$ and V_n denotes the continuation value of the enterprise. $D\&NC_n$ denotes depreciation and other non-cash items and ΔNWC_n denotes increase in net working capital. This expression can be written as follows

$$(1 + k_n)S_{n-1} + [1 + (1 - t)r_n]D_{n-1} = FCF_n + V_n$$

or

$$S_{n-1} + D_{n-1} = \frac{FCF_n + V_n}{1 + w_n} \tag{N2.3.2}$$

where $w_n = WACC_n = [k_n S_{n-1} + (1 - t)r_n D_{n-1}]/(S_{n-1} + D_{n-1})$. We can now go to the end of year $n - 2$ and write

$$S_{n-2} = \frac{FCF_{n-1} - (1 - t)r_{n-1}D_{n-2} + \Delta D_{n-1} + S_{n-1}}{1 + k_{n-1}} \tag{N2.3.3}$$

or

$$(1 + k_{n-1})S_{n-2} + [1 + (1 - t)r_{n-1}]D_{n-2} = FCF_{n-1} + \Delta D_{n-1} + D_{n-2} + S_{n-1},$$

which can be written as

$$S_{n-2} + D_{n-2} = \frac{FCF_{n-1} + D_{n-1} + S_{n-1}}{1 + w_{n-1}} = \frac{FCF_{n-1}}{1 + w_{n-1}} + \frac{FCF_n + V_n}{(1 + w_{n-1})(1 + w_n)} \tag{N2.3.4}$$

Proceeding recursively to time zero yields:

$$S_0 + D_0 = \frac{FCF_1}{1 + w_1} + \frac{FCF_2}{(1 + w_1)(1 + w_2)} + \ldots + \frac{FCF_n + V_n}{(1 + w_1)\ldots(1 + w_n)} \tag{N2.3.5}$$

which is the valuation of the free cash flow at the WACC rates $w_1, \ldots, w_n$. Thus, we have established the equivalence between equity valuation and total free cash flow valuation. Although the formal equivalence holds for time varying rates and debt ratios, valuation under changing leverage can be best done via alternative approaches such as the adjusted present value method.[2] In fact, it is recommended to discount the free cash flow at WACC only when the target debt ratio is constant and expected to be approximately met over time. In that case, assuming constant costs of debt and equity, the valuation expression becomes

$$S_0 + D_0 = \frac{FCF_1}{1 + w} + \frac{FCF_2}{(1 + w)^2} + \ldots + \frac{FCF_n + V_n}{(1 + w)^n} \qquad (N2.3.6)$$

which represents the approach followed in Chapter 2 to value Paktech International.

*N2.4   Enterprise Valuation with Pre-tax WACC

In Section 2.4 the debt-holder component of the free cash flow was written as $(1 - t)rD - \Delta D$. It was also shown there that adding this after-tax cash flow to the cash flow to equity-holders results in the after-tax free cash flow *paid* by the enterprise to its security-holders, the value of which resulted from discounting it at the after-tax WACC. An alternative but equivalent valuation approach starts with the cash flow *received* (RCF) by security holders:[3]

$$RCF = [NI + D\&NC - (Capex + \Delta NWC) + \Delta D] + [rD - \Delta D].$$

The first term in brackets is the cash flow to equity, which was shown to yield the value of equity when discounted at its cost. The second term is the cash flow received by debt-holders. From N2.2 we know that discounting it at r yields the value of debt. Since the sum of their values yields the value of the enterprise, one can discount the received cash flow by the weighted average of the *pre-tax* cost of debt and the cost of equity:

$$\text{Pre-Tax WACC} = \frac{rD + kS}{D + S}$$

To show that this is in fact the case, we note that $RCF = FCF + trD$ and express S_{n-1} in Equation (N2.3.1) as follows

$$S_{n-1} = \frac{RCF_n - r_n D_{n-1} + \Delta D_n + V_n - D_n}{1 + k_n}$$

or,

$$(1 + k_n)S_{n-1} + (1 + r_n)D_{n-1} = RCF_n + V_n$$

or,

$$S_{n-1} + D_{n-1} = \frac{RCF_n + V_n}{1 + w_n'},$$

where $w_n' = \text{Pre-Tax WACC}_n = (k_n S_{n-1} + r_n D_{n-1})/(S_{n-1} + D_{n-1})$. Hence, proceeding as in N.2.2 we attain for $w_n' = w'$:

---

[2]See Chapter 6.
[3]See Arditti (1973).

$$S_0 + D_0 = \frac{RCF_1}{1 + w'} + \frac{RCF_2}{(1 + w')^2} + \ldots + \frac{RCF_n + V_n}{(1 + w')^n}$$

That is, discounting the cash flows received by security-holders at pre-tax WACC is equivalent to discounting the free cash flow paid to security-holders at after-tax WACC. This equivalence is illustrated using the data for Paktech:

Year-end			2003	2004	2005	2006	2007
Free cash flow			4,564	2,788	4,106	5,156	5,685
Interest tax shield			1,791	1,898	2,031	2,162	2,294
Free cash flow plus tax shield			6,355	4,686	6,137	7,318	7,979
Pre-tax WACC	9.48%						
PV{FCF+ tax shield}		24,557					
Continuation value growth	6.0%						
Continuation value							242,855
PV{Continuation value}		154,391					
Enterprise value		178,948					

Paktech's free cash flows and interest expense are from Exhibit 2.8 and the interest tax shield results from multiplying interest expense times the tax rate. The present value computations are done as in Exhibit 2.4. The pre-tax cost of capital is computed as follows:

$$w' = (0.35)(9.5) + (0.65)(11.0) = 10.47\%.$$

It should be noted that 10.47% is the cost of capital of an unlevered firm with the same asset risk as Paktech.[4] In fact, it is shown in Chapter 6 that this is a general result. The pre-tax weighted average cost of capital of a leveraged firm for any debt ratio is a constant equal to the cost of capital of the corresponding unlevered firm.[5]

*N2.5   Personal Taxes and WACC

So far we have accounted only for the effect of corporate taxes on valuation. However, investors care about returns after corporate *and* personal taxes. In this appendix we show that WACC discounting is still valid when personal taxes are incorporated into the analysis.

Consider the after-personal tax cash flow plus continuation value corresponding to equity holders. The value of equity at the end of year $n - 1$ can be written as

$$S_{n-1} = \frac{(1 - t_S)[FCF_n - (1 - t)r_n D_{n-1} + \Delta D_n] + V_n - D_n - t_S(V_n - D_n - S_{n-1})}{1 + k_n} \quad (N2.5.1)$$

where S_{n-1} on the right-hand side is the tax basis of equity. In addition to the definitions of Note N2.2,

$$k_n = (1 - t_B)r_{f,n} + \beta[(1 - t_S)R_{m,n} - (1 - t_B)r_{f,n}]$$

---

[4]The unlevered cost of capital of Paktech is computed in Chapter 6, Section 6.3.

[5]This result is a restatement of Modigliani and Miller's (1958) proposition that the cost of capital of a firm is constant in the absence of corporate taxes.

is the after-personal taxes required return on equity, $r_{f,n}$ is the riskless rate, t_S is the personal tax on stock income, t_B is the personal tax on interest income and t is the corporate tax rate.

Equation (N2.5.1) can be written as

$$(1 - t_S + k_n)S_{n-1} + (1 - t_S)[1 + (1 - t)r_n]D_{n-1} = (1 - t_S)(FCF_n + V_n)$$

or

$$S_{n-1} + D_{n-1} = \frac{FCF_n + V_n}{1 + w_n}$$

where $w_n = WACC_n = [k_n S_{n-1} + (1 - t)r_n D_{n-1}]/(S_{n-1} + D_{n-1})$, and

$$k_n = \frac{(1 - t_B)}{(1 - t_S)}r_{f,n} + \beta[R_{m,n} - \frac{(1 - t_B)}{(1 - t_S)}r_{f,n}] \qquad (N2.5.2)$$

We can now go to the end of year n – 2 and write

$$S_{n-2} = \frac{(1 - t_S)[FCF_{n-1} - (1 - t)r_{n-1}D_{n-2} + \Delta D_{n-1}] + S_{n-1} - t_S(S_{n-1} - S_{n-2})}{1 + k_{n-1}}$$

or

$$(1 - t_S + k_{n-1})S_{n-2} + (1 - t_S)[1 + (1 - t)r_{n-1}]D_{n-2} = (1 - t_S)[FCF_{n-1} + D_{n-1} + S_{n-1}],$$

which can be written as

$$S_{n-2} + D_{n-2} = \frac{FCF_{n-1} + D_{n-1} + S_{n-1}}{1 + w_{n-1}} = \frac{FCF_{n-1}}{1 + w_{n-1}} + \frac{FCF_n + V_n}{(1 + w_{n-1})(1 + w_n)}$$

that is equal to Equation (N2.3.4). Proceeding recursively to time zero yields Equation (N2.3.5). Note, however, the cost of equity in WACC is now defined by Equation (N2.5.2).

NOTES TO CHAPTER 3

*N3.1   Geometric Versus Arithmetic Averages of Returns and Premiums

This note provides information about the use of alternative statistical estimates of the equity premium. It is relevant to those deciding to relay on historical estimates rather than on the prospective approach suggested in Section 3.2.5.

Ibbotson Associates (2002) and most finance textbooks recommend the use the risk premium derived from arithmetic averages of historic returns on stock and bonds.[6] This view is not shared by other authors, such as Copeland *et al.* (2000) who support the use of a geometric-based risk premium in order to estimate the cost of equity applicable to long-term valuations.

Arithmetic mean returns are higher than geometric mean returns, and their difference increases with the variance of returns. Exhibit 3.1 shows the arithmetic estimate of the risk premium is significantly higher than the geometric estimate (4.38% vs. 3.01%). The choice between arithmetic and geometric risk premia is therefore an important one. For a stationary process, the arithmetic mean of past returns is an unbiased estimator of

---

[6]The arithmetic mean return in defined as $n^{-1}\Sigma_{1,n}R_t$ and the geometric mean return is defined as $[\Pi_{1,n}(1 + R_t)]^{1/n} - 1$. The geometric mean return is the holding period compound return over the sample.

expected returns over the estimation interval. For example, if *annual* observations are used, the arithmetic mean is an unbiased estimator of expected *annual* returns. Moreover, if returns are time-independent, the arithmetic mean is the best (minimum variance) estimator of expected returns. However, while stock returns do not exhibit short-term auto-correlation, they do exhibit significant negative long-term autocorrelation,[7] and the arithmetic mean is an inefficient estimate in the presence of autocorrelation.[8] Even if the arithmetic mean is the best estimator of single-period returns and thus of the single-period equity premium, compounding it for multiyear discounting can lead to underestimation of the present value of distant cash flows. This is because compounding one plus the arith-metic mean of yearly returns overestimates the expected return over the compounding pe-riod.[9] On the other hand, compounding one plus the geometric mean of n yearly returns underestimates all returns except the expected return over n years. In fact, the best estima-tor of the expected return over any m years between 1 and n is the arithmetic mean of the observed compound return over all m-year overlapping periods in the sample. Blume (1974) has recommended the following approximation based upon a weighted average of the arithmetic and geometric means:

$$\frac{n-t}{n-1}(1 + r_A)^t + \frac{t-1}{n-1}(1 + r_G)^t$$

where r_A is the one-period arithmetic mean and r_G is the geometric mean. n is the length of the sample and t is the time of the cash flow being discounted. Simulation experiments have shown that Blume's proposal yields less biased results than either the arithmetic or the geometric mean.[10,11] Blume's weighted average reduces the yearly discount rate slowly toward the geometric mean. For example, for the proverbial 99-year going concern with a riskless rate of 5% and $\beta = 1$, $r_A = 4.38\%$, $r_B = 3.01\%$ as in Exhibit 3.1, the average equity premium during the period is 3.70%.

*N3.2   Share Repurchases and the Prospective Equity Premium

The expected payout rates do not include share repurchases. To see why, consider the case of an individual company. Let n, P, D, E, and m denote the number of shares, the stock price, dividend per share, earnings per share, and the number of shares repurchased, re-spectively. Thus, before repurchase, market capitalization is nP, total dividends are nD and total earnings are nE. Furthermore, let $R = E/P$ denote earnings return with respect to share price. Then, accounting for the fact that a repurchase reduces the number of shares and the earnings assets of the company, per-share dividends will tend to remain the same, total earnings will decrease and payout will be $(n-m)D/[R(n-m)P] = D/E$, as before re-purchase. If share repurchases are expected to alter R, because the company would divests from unprofitable assets to fund the repurchase for example, the greater profitability will be captured in the consensus forecast of growth and be incorporated into Equation (3.7).

---

[7]See, for example, J. Porterba and L. Summers, *op cit.*

[8]But the post-1959 period exhibits no autocorrelation, and the equity premium based on the arithmetic mean of post-1959 is a minimum variance estimator for that sample size. See Chinebell et al., *op cit.*

[9]Blume (1974).

[10]Indro and Lee (1997).

[11]There is another source of bias in present values computed on the basis of the arithmetic mean. The present value is higher than the true value by a factor involving the variance of the estimation error of the mean return but this error is likely to be more than offset by the underestimation produced by compounding the arithmetic mean return over a long horizon. See Butler and Schachter (1989) and Grinblatt and Titman, *op cit.*

Similarly, if repurchases are expected to be financed with debt, its impact on earnings would also be captured in the consensus forecast. Moreover, any effect on value perceived by investors would also be registered in the stock price and the P/E ratio of Equation (3.7).

Since the computation of the prospective equity premium assumes that dividend payout and earnings regress to their means in the long run, we need to consider the recent increase in the number of firms that make share repurchases and pay no dividends [Fama and French (2001)]. Even if this were to result in a permanent change in the dividend payout ratio of the S&P 500 index, it would not invalidate Equation (3.7). Dividends and share repurchases are alternative means of distributing the free cash flow corresponding to equity holders. In fact, Equation (3.6) holds for a cash distribution $p_t E_t$ made of any mixture of dividends and repurchases and a model that assumes that all the distribution is made in dividends will yield the same required discount rate as a model that allow of a mixture of repurchases and dividends. That would be so even if repurchases made in lieu of dividends take place at irregular intervals.

NOTES TO CHAPTER 4

N4.1   Relationships Among Valuation Multiples

This note develops the relationships among the various multiples commonly used in valuation practice (PE, EBITDA, EBIT and Revenues multiples). The following notation is used:

S	sales, initial sales denoted S_0
N	net income
m	EBITDA/sales, EBITDA margin
D	value of net debt
E	value of equity
d	$D/(D + E)$, debt ratio
g	growth rate of sales
t	corporate tax rate
δ	depreciation/sales
κ	capital expenditures and increase in net working capital to sales
η	other non-cash items to sales
r	interest on debt
M_{pe}	PE multiple
M_{ebit}	EBIT multiple = $(D + E)/EBIT$
M_{ebitda}	EBITDA multiple = $(D + E)/EBITDA$
M_{rev}	revenue multiple = $(D + E)/revenue$
M_d	debt multiple = $D/EBITDA$

The EBITDA multiple is the ratio of enterprise value (net debt plus market equity) to EBITDA. Consider its relation to the price-earning multiple using accounting definitions. M_{ebit} (trailing or forward) can be expressed in terms of M_{pe} (trailing or forward, respectively) as follows: First note that

$$M_{ebitda} = \frac{D + E}{EBITDA} = \frac{D}{EBITDA} + \frac{M_{pe}N}{EBITDA} \qquad (N.4.1)$$

Substituting M_d and $N = (1 - t)(EBIT - rD) = (1 - t)[(1 - \delta/m)EBITDA - rD]$ into Equation (N4.1) yields:

$$M_{ebitda} = M_d + (1 - t)[(1 - \delta/m) - rM_d] M_{pe} \qquad (N.4.2)$$

which expresses the EBITDA multiple in terms of the price-earnings multiple and the EBITDA debt multiple. The latter can be replaced by the debt ratio taking into account that $M_d = d\, M_{ebitda}$. Substituting this expression and solving explicitly for M_{ebitda}, yields

$$M_{ebitda} = \frac{(1 - \delta/m)\, M_{pe}}{(1 - d)/(1 - t) + rdM_{pe}} \qquad (N.4.3)$$

Equations (N.4.2) and (N.4.3) can be inverted to solve for M_{pe} in terms of M_{ebidta}. For example, from Equation (N.4.3) one obtains

$$M_{pe} = \frac{(1 - d)\, M_{ebitda}}{(1 - t)(1 - \delta/m - rdM_{ebitda})} \qquad (N.4.4)$$

Similarly, Equations (N.4.2) and (N.4.3) can be restated to give M_{ebit} and M_{rev}. For example, from Equation (N.4.2) and $EBIT = (1 - \delta/m)\, EBITDA$, one gets $M_{ebit} = M_{ebitda}/(1 - \delta/m)$, and from Equation (N.4.3) and $EBITDA = mS$, one gets $M_{rev} = mM_{ebitda}$.

N4.2   The Effect of Leverage and Growth on Multiples

In this note, we derive Equation (4.11) of the main text. Let us first write the enterprise value of a levered firm that grows at a rate g:

$$D + E = (1 - t + t\delta/m + (\eta - \kappa)/m)EBITDA(1 + g)(w - g)^{-1} \qquad (N.4.5)$$

where EBITDA corresponds to the last twelve months. Substituting Equation (N.4.5) into the definition of the trailing EBITDA multiple yields

$$M_{ebitda} = \frac{D + E}{EBITDA} = \frac{(1 - t + t\delta/m + (\eta - \kappa)/m)\,(1 + g)}{(w - g)} \qquad (N.4.6)$$

From this expression we can derive the adjusted multiple for the company being valued. Call it company B, with cost of capital w^B and growth rate g^B. Let the comparable's multiple, cost of capital and growth rates be M^A_{ebitda}, w^A, g^A, respectively. The other characteristics such as depreciation and capital expenditures to sales are assumed to be equal in the two firms. Then, the multiple of B can be calculated as follows:

$$M^B_{ebitda} = \frac{M^A_{ebitda}(w^A - g^A)/(1 + g^A)}{(w^B - g^B)/(1 + g^B)} \qquad (N.4.7)$$

which is Equation (4.10) of the main text. The forward multiple can be estimated as $M^B_{ebitda}/(1 + g^B)$. Alternatively, one can start with an original forward estimate of M^A_{ebitda}, then B's forward multiple adjusted for leverage and growth is $M^B_{ebitda} = M^A_{ebitda}(w^A - g^A)/(w^B - g^B)$.

NOTES TO CHAPTER 5

N5.1 Adjustments to Accounting Data

A number of mainly non-cash accounting entries done for the purpose of financial reporting are eliminated in order to compute EVA. The capital invested is the accounting value of common equity, preferred stock, minority interest, and interest-bearing liabilities plus: the present value of noncapitalized leases; reserves including deferred taxes; cumulative amortization of goodwill; unrecorded goodwill from pooling accounting;[12] cumulative extraordinary losses after taxes; cumulative expenses in R&D and other intangibles; LIFO reserves; and less marketable securities. The purpose of these adjustments is to estimate the capital actually invested in the business. From the balance sheet identity, it follows that capital invested is also equal to the sum of net working capital adjusted by adding FIFO and bad-debt reserves, fixed assets including capitalized operating leases, goodwill or implied goodwill from pooling accounting, capitalized R&D and other intangibles, less marketable securities.

The following additions are made to NOPAT: increase in reserves including deferred taxes; goodwill amortization when applicable; extraordinary losses after taxes; expenses in R&D and other intangibles; increase in LIFO reserve; and amortization of R&D and other intangibles is subtracted (from NOP when tax deductible).[13] Exhibit N5.1 summarizes these adjustments and compares them to the adjustments made in free cash flow valuation. An examination of EVA adjustments shows that non-cash adjustments to NOPAT and Capital not made in FCF valuation, such as those related to R&D expenses or using a different depreciation method for EVA computation,[14] cancel each other in present value and have thus no value consequences. For example, consider intangible adjustments such as R&D and let ΔRD_0 be the R&D expense of time 0, and a_t be R&D amortization of time t such that $\Sigma_{1,T}\, a_t = \Delta RD_0$, then

$$
\begin{aligned}
\Sigma_{1,\infty}\Delta EVA_t(1+w)^{-1} &= \Delta RD_0 - a_1(1+w)^{-1} - a_2(1+w)^{-2} \ldots - a_T(1+w)^{-T} \\
&\quad - w\Delta RD_0(1+w)^{-1} - w(\Delta RD_0 - a_1)(1+w)^{-2} \\
&\quad \ldots - w(\Delta RD_0 - a_1 - \ldots - a_{T-1})(1+w)^{-T} \\
&= \Delta RD_0 - \Sigma_{1,T}a_t(1+w)^{-t} - \Delta RD_0[1 - (1+w)^{-T}] \\
&\quad - \Sigma_{1,T-1}\, a_t[(1+w)^{-t} - (1+w)^{-T}] = 0.
\end{aligned}
$$

*N5.2 Initial Capital and Continuation Value

One question that sometimes arises in practice is the measurement of the initial capital. It turns out the amount of initial capital assigned to an activity or division has not effect on valuation and thus can be chosen arbitrarily. In order to show this, one needs to write explicitly the present value of future EVAs:

$$
\Sigma_{1,\infty}EVA_t(1+w)^{-t} = \Sigma_{1,\infty}[NOPAT_t - w(C_{t-2} - B_{t-1} + \Delta C_{t-1})](1+w)^{-t}
$$

---

[12]The Financial Accounting Standard Board has decided that all business combinations completed after June 30, 2001 should use purchase accounting and that goodwill should not be amortized but should instead be tested for impairment.

[13]See Stewart (1991) for a discussion of these adjustments.

[14]As long as tax computation is consistent with FCF valuation.

| EXHIBIT N5.1 | *EVA and Free Cash Flow Adjustment to Accounting Numbers* |

EVA		FCF
NOPAT	CAPITAL	NOPAT
+ Increase in deferred taxes	+ Deferred tax reserve	+ Increase in deferred taxes
+ Increase in other reserves	+ Other reserves	+ Increase in other reserves
+ Goodwill amortization[a]	+ Cumulative goodwill amortization and unrecorded goodwill from pooling accounting	+ Goodwill amortization – Cost of acquisitions with shares exchanges valued at market
+ R&D expenses[b] – R&D amortization[b]	+ R&D expenses[b]	
– Extraordinary gains + Losses after taxes	– Cumulative extraordinary gain and losses after taxes	– Extraordinary gains + Losses after taxes
	– Proceeds from asset disposition	+ Proceeds from asset disposition
	+ Capital expenditures	– Capital expenditures
	+ Net working capital increases	– Net working capital increases
+ Increase in LIFO reserve	+ LIFO reserve	+ Increase in LIFO reserve
+ Interest component of operating leases after taxes	+ Non-capitalized leases	+ Interest component of operating leases after taxes
	– Marketable securities[c]	

[a]See footnote 14.
[b]Non-cash EVA adjustments not made in computing FCF offset each other in present value and have no value consequence.
[c]Marketable securities are usually not considered part of capital expenditures in FCF valuation.

where B_t denotes depreciation in year t and ΔC_t denotes capital expenditures and change in net working capital in year t, and $C_{-1} - B_0 + \Delta C_0 \equiv C_0$ is the initial capital. Summing the depreciation and capital expenditures terms on the right-hand-side of this expression yields:[15]

$$\sum_{1,\infty} EVA_t(1 + w)^{-t} = \sum_{1,\infty}(NOPAT_t + B_t - \Delta C_t)(1 + w)^{-t} - C_0$$

$$= \sum_{1,\infty} FCF_t(1 + w)^{-t} - C_0,$$

which implies that the present value of free cash flows is

$$\sum_{1,\infty} FCF_t(1 + w)^{-t} = \sum_{1,\infty} EVA_t(1 + w)^{-t} + C_0$$

$$= \sum_{1,\infty}(NOPAT_t + B_t - \Delta C_t)(1 + w)^{-t}.$$

[15]Note that C_0, B_1, B_2, etc. appear as perpetuities with present values C_0/w, $B_1/[w(1 + w)]$, $B_2/[w(1 + w)^2]$, etc.

That is, valuation of a firm or business unit according to the EVA method is independent of the initial capital assumed in the computation of the yearly EVAs. Incidentally, the above is a general proof of the equivalence between EVA and FCF valuation illustrated in Section 5.2. It also follows that the present value of future FCFs and the present value of future EVAs differ only by the arbitrary constant C_0 and, therefore, that maximizing of the present value of future EVAs is equivalent to maximizing the present value of future FCFs irrespective of the initial capital assumed in the implementation of the first criterion.

NOTES TO CHAPTER 6

N6.1   Enterprise Value and Leverage Fluctuations

Here we show that fluctuations around the target debt ratio do not have a significant effect on the value of the firm. We use the APV property presented in Section 6.2 and the following notation:

Y   the expected yearly unlevered free cash flow of the firm

ρ the cost of capital of the unlevered firm

D   the amount of debt

d   the debt ratio

r   the interest on debt

τ the corporate tax rate

θ the absolute value of the yearly percent fluctuation of debt amount

Then, the value of the firm is

$$V = Y\rho^{-1} + TS$$

That is, the value of the levered firm equals the value of the unlevered firm plus the value of its tax shield TS. Assume the firm maintains a constant level of debt D. Then, the value of the tax shield is $TS_0 = \sum_{t=1,\infty} \tau r D(1 + r)^{-t} = \tau r D/r = \tau D$ because $\tau r D$ is a perpetuity. Denote the value of the firm in this case by V_0. This implies a constant leverage $d = D/V_0$.

Instead, let debt alternate each year between $(1 + \theta)D$ and $(1 - \theta)D$. Then,

$$TS = \sum_{t=1,\infty} \tau r[1 \pm (-1)^{-t}\theta]D(1 + r)^{-t} = \tau r D \sum_{t=1,\infty}[1 \pm (-1)^{-t}\theta](1 + r)^{-t},$$

which reduces to

$$TS = \tau D[1 \pm \theta r/(2 + r)].$$

That is, TS will be larger or smaller than TS_0 depending on if debt is increased or reduced in the first year. Moreover, $|TS - TS_0|/V_0 = \theta r \tau d/(2 + r)$, which is small even for large θ and d. For example, let $r = 12\%$, $\tau = 40\%$, $\theta = 50\%$ and $d = 40\%$. Then, $|TS - TS_0|/V_0 = 0.0045$ or 0.45%.

*N6.2   Compressed APV

In this note, we examine the valuation of a firm that keeps a constant target debt ratio within each year but let it change over time. We show that the enterprise value can be computed by discounting free cash flows plus tax shields at the unlevered cost of capital.

As in Miles and Ezzell (1980) we value the firm by backward iteration starting from the last period T:

$$V^L_{T-1/n} = \frac{FCF_{T-1/n,T}}{(1 + \rho)^{1/n}} + \frac{\tau[(1 + r_T)^{1/n} - 1]L_TV^L_{T-1/n}}{(1 + r_T)^{1/n}} + \frac{V^L_T}{(1 + \rho)^{1/n}} \qquad (N6.2.1)$$

where $V^L_{T-1/n}$ is the value of the firm at time $T - 1/n$, $FCF_{T-1/n,T}$ is the expected unlevered free cash flow during subperiod $(T - 1/n,T)$, τ is the corporate tax rate, r_T is the interest rate on debt during period T, L_T is the leverage ratio during period T, and ρ is the unlevered cost of capital. Note that each period $t = 1, 2,\ldots,$ T is divided into n subperiods. L_t stays constant during each period and so does r_t. At the beginning of each subperiod $t - m/n$ the firm borrows $B_{t-m/n} = L_tV^L_{t-m/n}$. That is, debt and the tax shield are fixed for the length of that subperiod until debt is readjusted at the beginning of the following subperiod $t - (m + 1)/n$. Thus, the tax shield has the same risk as interest expense and has to be discounted at $(1 + r_t)^{1/n} - 1$ for the subperiod.

At time $T - 2/n$, the value of the firm is

$$V^L_{T-2/n} = \frac{FCF_{T-2/n, T-1/n}}{(1 + \rho)^{1/n}} + \frac{\tau[(1 + r_T^{1/n}) - 1]L_TV^L_{T-2/n}}{(1 + r_T)^{1/n}} + \frac{V^L_{T-1/n}}{(1 + \rho)^{1/n}} \qquad (N6.2.2)$$

Substituting Equation (N6.2.1) into Equation (N6.2.2) yields

$$V^L_{T-2/n} = \frac{FCF_{T-2/n, T-1/n}}{(1 + \rho)^{1/n}} + \frac{FCF_{T-1/n, T}}{(1 + \rho)^{2/n}} + \frac{\tau[(1 + r_T)^{1/n} - 1]L_TV^L_{T-2/n}}{(1 + r_T)^{1/n}} \qquad (N6.2.3)$$
$$+ \frac{\tau[(1 + r_T)^{1/n} - 1]L_TV^L_{T-1/n}}{(1 + \rho)^{1/n}(1 + r_T)^{1/n}} + \frac{V^L_T}{(1 + \rho)^{2/n}}$$

Continuing backward iteration and substitution results in the following expression at the beginning of period $T - 1$:

$$V^L_{T-1} = \sum_{j=1,n} \frac{FCF_{T-(n-j+1)/n, T-(n-j)/n}}{(1 + \rho)^{j/n}}$$
$$+ \sum_{j=1,n} \frac{\tau[(1 + r_T)^{1/n} - 1]L_TV^L_{T-(n-j+1)/n}}{(1 + \rho)^{(j-1)/n}(1 + r_T)^{1/n}} + \frac{V^L_T}{(1 + \rho)} \qquad (N6.2.4)$$

Note that when the number of subperiods n increases, the adjustment of the debt level is almost continuous and $(1 + r_T)^{1/n}$ approaches 1. This means that the discount factors in the denominators of Equation (N6.2.4) both approach $(1 + \rho)^{j/n}$. In addition, $FCF_{T-(n-j+1)/n,T-(n-j)/n}$ and $V^L_{T-(n-j+1)/n}$ approach $FCF_{T-(1-j/n)}$ and $V^L_{T-(1-j/n)}$, respectively. However, the sum of the tax shield terms does not vanish for large n. Now we can write

$$V^L_{T-1} \rightarrow \sum_{j=1,n} \frac{FCF_{T-(1-j/n)} + \tau[(1 + r_T)^{1/n} - 1]L_TV^L_{T-(1-j/n)}}{(1 + \rho)^{j/n}} + \frac{V^L_T}{(1 + \rho)} \qquad (N6.2.5)$$

Having established that FCF and tax shield can both be discounted at the unlevered cost of capital, we simplify Equation (N6.2.5) by assuming that all the cash flow occurs at the end of the period and by writing $D_T = L_TV_{T-1}$, such that

$$V^L_{T-1} = \frac{FCF_T + \tau r_TD_T + V^L_T}{(1 + \rho)} \qquad (N6.2.6)$$

and, by successive substitutions, we obtain the value of the firm at time zero:

$$V_0 = \frac{FCF_1 + \tau r_1 D_1}{1 + \rho} + \frac{FCF_2 + \tau r_2 D_2}{(1 + \rho)^2} + \ldots \qquad \text{(N6.2.7)}$$

From Note N2.3 we know that for any period t we can also write

$$V^L_{t-1} = \frac{FCF_t + V^L_T}{1 + w_t} \qquad \text{(N6.2.8)}$$

where w_t is the weighted average cost of capital that corresponds to a debt ratio L_t, which implies

$$V_0 = \frac{FCF_1}{1 + w_1} + \frac{FCF_2}{(1 + w_1)(1 + w_2)} + \ldots \qquad \text{(N6.2.9)}$$

Thus, the value of a firm that changes the debt ratio in a known way can be established by discounting the free cash flows at WACC that changes from period to period according to the changing debt ratio or by discounting the free cash flows plus the corresponding tax shield (the cash flow *received* by investors) at the cost of capital of the unlevered firm. Furthermore, combining the result of the present note with that of Note N2.4, where we showed that the cash flow received by investors could also be discounted at the pre-tax cost of capital, shows that the latter is constant and equal to the unlevered cost of capital of the firm.

*N6.3 Recursive APV

In this note, we obtain Equations (6.1) and (6.2) of the main text. The variables are defined as in Section 6.7. We assume that (a) ρ and r, the cost of capital of the unlevered firm and the interest rate on debt are constant over time, and (b) the risk characteristics of debt and the tax shield conditional on the level of debt are the same.

The cash flow of the levered firm is

$$Z_t = Y_t + \tau r D_{t-1} \qquad \text{(N6.3.1)}$$

and, since the firm expects to reduce debt by the amount $(1 - \phi)Z_t - rD_{t-1}$ at time $t = 1, \ldots$ T, successive substitutions of this expression into D_{t-1} yield:

$$D_{t-1} = (1 + r)^{t-1} D_0 - (1 - \phi) \sum_{j=1,t-1} (1 + r)^{t-j-1} Z_j, \qquad \text{(N6.3.2)}$$

and

$$Z_t = Y_t + \tau r [(1 + r)^{t-1} D_0 - (1 - \phi) \sum_{j=1,t-1} (1 + r)^{t-j-1} Z_j], \, t = 2, \ldots, T, \quad \text{(N6.3.3)}$$

where $Z_1 = Y_1 + \tau r D_0$.

In order to obtain the present value of Equation (N6.3.3), one first notes that the uncertainty about the cash flow $(1 + r)^{t-j-1} Z_j$ on the right-hand side of Equation (N6.3.3) is resolved at time j and should be discounted at r from $t - 1$ to j. Thus, $P_0[\sum_{j=1,t-1} (1 + r)^{t-j-1} Z_j]$ $= (1 + r)^{-1} \sum_{j=1,t-1} P_0[Z_j]$ and

$$P_0[Z_t] = \frac{E_0[Y_t]}{(1 + \rho)^t} + \frac{\tau r}{1 + r} (D_0 - (1 - \phi)P_{0,t-1}), \, t = 2, \ldots, T, \quad \text{(N6.3.4)}$$

where $P_{0,1} = P_0[Z_1] = E_0[Y_1](1 + \rho)^{-1} + \tau r D_0 (1 + r)^{-1}$.

Summing Equation (N6.3.4) over t gives Equation (6.2) for the present value of the first t cash flows. Adding to $P_{0,T}$ the present value of the continuation value V_T yields Equation (6.1) for the value of the firm at time 0.

NOTES TO CHAPTER 7

N7.1 Debt Capacity in LBOs

This note derives Equation (7.4) for computing the debt capacity of a highly leveraged firm. Recall the parameters and symbols introduced in Section 7.7 and denote sales, senior debt, and subordinated debt at the end of year t by S_t, R_t, and B_t, respectively. Then, senior debt at the end of the 1st year can be written as follows:

$$R_1 = R_0 - [(1 - t)[(m - \delta)S_1 - r_R R_0 - r_B B_0 + r_c h S_1/(1 + g)] + [\delta + \eta - \kappa - hg/(1 + g)]S_1 \tag{N7.1.1}$$

That is, senior debt at the end of year 1 equals the initial debt minus the cash sweep. The latter equals net income plus depreciation and other non-cash items minus the planned increase in the cash balance. Net income equals EBIT minus interest paid plus interest earned minus taxes. After regrouping terms, Equation (N7.1.1) can be written in the following more manageable form:

$$R_1 = \tau R_0 - \gamma S_1 + (1 - t)r_B B_0,$$

where

$$\tau = 1 + (1 - t)r_R$$
$$\gamma = (1 - t)m + t\delta + \eta - \kappa + (1 - t)r_c h/(1 + g) - hg/(1 + g)$$

Now the senior debt balance at the end of year 2 can be expressed as follows:

$$\begin{aligned} R_2 &= \tau R_1 - \gamma S_1(1 + g) + (1 - t)r_B B_0 \\ &= \tau[\tau R_0 - \gamma S_1 + (1 - t)r_B B_0] - \gamma S_1(1 + g) + (1 - t)r_B B_0 \\ &= \tau^2 R_0 - \gamma[\tau + (1 + g)]S_1 + (1 + \tau)(1 - t)r_B B_0 \end{aligned}$$

Then, successive substitutions yield the expression for the senior debt balance at the end of year n:

$$R_n = \tau^n R_0 - \gamma S_1[\tau^n - (1 + g)^n]/(\tau - 1 - g) + (1 - t)r_B B_0(1 - \tau^n)/(1 - \tau) \tag{N7.1.2}$$

The debt capacity of the firm is defined here as the maximum initial debt $R_0 + B_0$ such that $R_n = 0$, that is, such that senior debt is fully amortized in n years. It is convenient to normalize debt capacity as a multiple of 1st-year EBITDA. In order to so, define the debt capacity multiple as $q = (R_0 + B_0)/EBITDA_1 = (R_0 + B_0)/(mS_1)$. This permits writing $R_0 = fqmS_1$ and $B_0 = (1 - f)qmS_1$. Now, dividing Equation (N7.1.2) by mS_1, the condition that $R_n = 0$ becomes

$$\tau^n fq - \gamma m^{-1}[\tau^n - (1 + g)^n]/(\tau - 1 - g) + (1 - t)r_B(1 - f)q(1 - \tau^n)/(1 - \tau) = 0 \tag{N7.1.3}$$

Finally, solving for q yields Equation (7.4) for computing the EBITDA debt capacity multiple:

$$q = \frac{\gamma m^{-1}[\tau^n - (1 + g)^n]/(\tau - 1 - g)}{\tau^n f + (1 - t)r_B(1 - f)(1 - \tau^n)/(1 - \tau)} \tag{N7.1.4}$$

N7.2   Computing Debt Capacity with the HP19BII Calculator

As an alternative to the spreadsheet Debt Capacity Calculator, debt capacity can be expediently calculated via Equation (N7.1.4) on a Hewlett-Packard HP19BII or similar programmable calculator using the following program:

PROGRAM	INPUT	OUTPUT
DEBTCAP:1+(1–TAX)×SRATE=TAU	TAX,SRATE	TAU
Now start another program line for a different equation. The values of TAX, SRATE and TAU will be carried forward by the HP19, *do not enter them anew!*		
(1–TAX)×M+TAX×DELTA+ETA–KAPPA+(1–TAX)×CRATE×H/(1+G)–H×G/(1+G)=GAMMA	M,DELTA, ETA,KAPPA, CRATE,H,G	GAMMA
GAMMA÷M×(TAU^N–(1+G)^N)÷(TAU–1–G)÷(TAU^N×SLEV+(1–TAX)×JRATE×(1–SLEV)×(1–TAU^N)÷(1–TAU))=MULT	N,SLEV,JRATE	MULT

Definitions:

TAX   = tax rate

SRATE = interest rate on senior debt

M   = EBITDA/sales

DELTA = depreciation/sales

ETA   = other non-cash items/sales

KAPPA = capital expenditures and increase in net working capital (except cash)/sales

CRATE = interest rate earned on cash balance

H   = cash balance/sales

G   = annual growth rate of sales

N   = required senior amortization period in years

SLEV   = senior debt as a fraction of senior and sub debt

JRATE = interest rate on subordinated rate

MULT = debt capacity (senior + sub debt) as a multiple of EBITDA

TAU and GAMMA are intermediate values used to simplify the program.

The program computes the debt capacity of a company for a given period of amortization of senior principal and given data on interest rates, sales growth, tax rate and senior-junior debt mix. It assumes that EBITDA, depreciation, other non-cash items, capital expenditures, and working capital increases are proportional to sales, and assumes a 100% cash sweep to principal amortization.

Example of debt capacity calculation: The multiple computed on the spreadsheet of Exhibit 7.9 is calculated on the HP19BII as follows:

INPUT	OUTPUT	
TAX = 0.40, SRATE = 0.085,	TAU = 1.05	
M = 0.1, DELTA = 0.015,		
ETA = 0.002, KAPPA = 0.02,		
CRATE = 0.045, H = 0.002, G = 0.05	GAMMA = 0.048	
N = 5, SLEV = 0.35, JRATE = 0.10	MULT = 4.39	

NOTES TO CHAPTER 8[16]

*N8.1   Ito's Lemma

Continuous time valuation makes use of a result about differentiation of functions of geometric Brownian motion called Ito's Lemma. Consider the geometric Brownian motion $V(R, t)$ and express its differential dV as a Taylor series expansion up to terms of second-order in R:

$$dV = \partial V/\partial R dR + \frac{1}{2}\partial^2 V/\partial R^2 (dR)^2 + \partial V/\partial t dt$$

$$= \partial V/\partial R(\alpha R dt + \sigma R dz) + \frac{1}{2}\partial^2 V/R^2 (\alpha R dt + \sigma R dz)^2 + \partial V/\partial t dt.$$

Note that $(\alpha R dt + \sigma R dz)^2 = \alpha^2 R^2(dt)^2 + 2\alpha R^2 dt dz + \sigma^2 R^2(dz)^2 \rightarrow \sigma^2 R^2 dt$ for dt small because $(dt)^2$ and $dtdz = \varepsilon(dt)^{3/2}$ go to zero faster than dt. Recall that $dz = \varepsilon\sqrt{t}$ and $(dz)^2 = \varepsilon^2 dt$. Furthermore, the variance of $\varepsilon^2 dt$ is of order dt^2 so $\varepsilon^2 dt$ becomes non-stochastic and equal to its expected value dt as $dt \rightarrow 0$. In addition, all terms of third and higher order omitted in the Taylor expansion vanish faster than dt. Taking these results into account yields Ito's Lemma as it applies to $V(R, t)$ with R following Equation (8.1):

$$dV = [\alpha R \partial V/\partial R + \frac{1}{2}\sigma R^2 \partial^2 V/\partial R^2 + \partial V/\partial t]dt + \sigma R \partial V/\partial R dz.$$

*N8.2   Valuation of a Going Concern in Continuous Time

Here we derive the solution to Equation (8.6)

$$[bR + a_{ce} - n^*(w - \alpha)R]dt + dV - n^* dR = r_f(V - n^* R)dt \quad (N8.2.1)$$

Let us express dV in terms of R. By Ito's lemma from Note N8.1:

$$dV = [\alpha R V_R + \frac{1}{2}\sigma R^2 V_{RR}]dt + \sigma R V_R dz, \quad (N8.2.2)$$

where $V_R = \partial V/\partial R$ and $V_{RR} = \partial^2 V/\partial R^2$. Note that the going concern is modeled as an asset with infinite life, the value of which is independent of time as such. Thus, t drops out of $V(R, t)$. $V(R)$ does depend on the value of the state variable R_t at any given point in time but not on its calendar date. This implies that $\partial V/\partial t = 0$. This simplification applies to all the valuation models considered in Chapter 8 because the options considered do not have expiration date.

Substituting Equation (N8.2.2) into $dV - n^* dR$ yields

$$dV - n^* dR = \alpha R(V_R - n^*)dt + \frac{1}{2}\sigma^2 R^2 V_{RR}dt + \sigma R(V_R - n^*)dz$$

where n^* is set equal to V_R to eliminate the term in dz and make the portfolio riskless. Its total return is

$$dV - n^* dR + [Y - n^*(w - \alpha)R]dt = \frac{1}{2}\sigma^2 R^2 V_{RR}dt + [bR + a_{ce} - V_R(w - \alpha)R]dt \quad (N8.2.3)$$

This is the left-hand side of Equation (N8.2.1). Substituting $n^* = V_R$ into the right-hand side and simplifying expresses Equation (N8.2.1) as the following differential equation

$$\frac{1}{2}\sigma^2 R^2 V_{RR} + (r_f - w + \alpha)R V_R - r_f V + bR + a_{ce} = 0 \quad (N8.2.4)$$

---

[16]Notes N8.1 to N8.7 provide non-rigorous sketches of the derivations of the valuation formulas used in this chapter and the algorithms programmed in Real Options Calculator I and Real Options Calculator II. Chapters 3 and 4 of Dixit and Pindyck (1994) summarize the mathematical background needed to follow the argument.

Consider now the solution AR^λ to the homogeneous part of the equation

$$\tfrac{1}{2}\sigma^2 R^2 A\lambda(\lambda - 1)R^{\lambda-2} + (r_f - w + \alpha)RA\lambda R^{\lambda-1} - r_f AR^\lambda = 0 \quad \text{(N8.2.5)}$$

Equation (N8.2.5) requires that λ be a root to the quadratic equation

$$\tfrac{1}{2}\sigma^2\lambda(\lambda - 1) + (r_f - w + \alpha)\lambda - r_f = 0 \quad \text{(N8.2.6)}$$

The two roots of Equation (N8.2.6) are:

$$\lambda_1 = \tfrac{1}{2} - (r_f - w + \alpha)/\sigma^2 + \{[(r_f - w + \alpha)/\sigma^2 - \tfrac{1}{2}]^2 + 2r_f/\sigma^2\}^{1/2} \quad \text{(N8.2.7)}$$

$$\lambda_2 = \tfrac{1}{2} - (r_f - w + \alpha)/\sigma^2 - \{[(r_f - w + \alpha)/\sigma^2 - \tfrac{1}{2}]^2 + 2r_f/\sigma^2\}^{1/2} \quad \text{(N8.2.8)}$$

Note that $\lambda_1 > 1$ and $\lambda_2 < 0$. So the general solution of the homogenous part of Equation (N8.2.4) is $A_1 R^{\lambda_1} + A_2 R^{\lambda_2}$. $bR/(w - \alpha) + a/[(1 - \tau)r_d]$ is a particular solution to the complete equation. In fact, for this solution, $V_R = b/(w - \alpha)$, $V_{RR} = 0$ and Equation (N8.2.4) is satisfied. Thus the solution to the complete equation is

$$V(R) = A_1 R^{\lambda_1} + A_2 R^{\lambda_2} + bR/(w - \alpha) + a/[(1 - \tau)r_d] \quad \text{(N8.2.9)}$$

The constants A_1 and A_2 are determined by the boundary conditions given by the economic nature of the problem. We require that $V(0) = 0$. That is, if revenue reaches zero, it will remain at that level given that R follows geometric Brownian motion [Equation (8.1)], and the value of the firm will be negligible. But, since $\lambda_2 < 0$, this requires that $A_2 = 0$. Otherwise $V(R)$ would go to infinity as R goes to zero. Similarly, A_1 must be zero if $V(R)$ is not to exceed its fundamental value computed in Equation (8.5) of the main text. That is,

$$V(R) = bR/(w - \alpha) + a/[(1 - \tau)r_d] \quad \text{(N8.2.10)}$$

Letting $A_1 = 0$ means that the value of the enterprise is determined on fundamentals and rules out speculative bubbles.[17] However, we shall see next that the constant A_1 has a role in valuing the deferral option.

*N8.3   Valuing the Entry Option

As in N8.2 we construct a riskless portfolio that yields the riskless rate of interest. The portfolio is long one option to invest (acquire) the firm $F(R)$ and short n units of R.

Proceeding as in N8.2, we apply Ito's Lemma to $F(R)$ and obtain

$$\tfrac{1}{2}\sigma^2 R^2 F_{RR} + (r_f - w + \alpha)RF_R - r_f F = 0 \quad \text{(N8.3.1)}$$

Equation (N8.3.1) differs from Equation (N8.2.4) in that the deferral option has no cash flow. Since Equation (N8.3.1) is homogeneous it has solution

$$F(R) = A_1 R^{\lambda_1} + A_2 R^{\lambda_2}, \quad \text{(N8.3.2)}$$

with $\lambda_1 > 0$ and $\lambda_2 < 0$ being the solutions of the quadratic equation (N8.2.6). Note that when $R \to 0$ we must require $F(R) \to 0$, so $A_2 = 0$. This results in $F(R) = A_1 R^{\lambda_1}$. Thus, there are three unknowns to be determined A_1, λ_1, and R_H. R_H is the threshold above which it pays to acquire the firm at a price I. λ_1 is calculated from Equation (N8.2.6). A_1 and R_H result from the following two additional conditions

$$F(R_H) = V(R_H) - I \quad \text{(N8.3.3)}$$

$$F_R(R_H) = V_R(R_H) \quad \text{(N8.3.4)}$$

---

[17]For more on this point, see Dixit and Pindyck (1994), pp. 181–182.

Equation (N8.3.3) requires that the value of the option equal the net value obtained by exercising it. This condition is called the *value-matching* condition. Equation (N8.3.4) requires that F(R) and V(R) – I meet tangentially at R_H. This is called the *smooth-pasting* condition. These two conditions must be satisfied by the optimal policy.[18] Using Equation (N8.3.2) for F(R) and Equation (N8.2.10) for V(R), Equations (N8.3.3) and (N10.3.4) can be written as

$$A_1 R_H{}^{\lambda_1} = \frac{bR_H}{w - \alpha} + I - \frac{a}{[(1 - \tau)r_d]}$$

$$\lambda_1 A_1 R_H{}^{\lambda_1 - 1} = \frac{b}{w - \alpha}$$

Solving these two equations for R_H and A_1 yields

$$R_H = \lambda_1(\lambda_1 - 1)^{-1}(I - a/[(1 - \tau)r_d])(w - \alpha)/b$$

$$A_1 = (\lambda_1 - 1)^{\lambda_1 - 1}(I - a/[(1 - \tau)r_d])^{-(\lambda_1 - 1)}b^{\lambda_1}[\lambda_1(w - \alpha)]^{-\lambda_1}.$$

*N8.4 Entry and Exit Options

Consider the exit option of a going concern. Recall the general solution in Equation (N8.2.9)

$$V(R) = B_1 R^{\lambda_1} + B_2 R^{\lambda_2} + bR/(w - \alpha) + a/[(1 - \tau)r_d].$$

From Equation (N8.2.10), we know that the last two terms represent the value of the firm when there is no exit option. This means that the first two terms account for the value of the option to exit the business when R is too low. Note that the value of the exit option tends to zero as $R \to \infty$. Hence, $B_1 = 0$, and

$$V(R) = B_2 R^{\lambda_2} + bR/(w - \alpha) + a/[(1 - \tau)r_d]. \tag{N8.4.1}$$

Let R_L be the exit threshold such that the firm stops operations when R falls to R_L. In addition, let $\hat{E}$ denote the lump-sum cost of exit.

In order to solve of R_L and B_2, we use the following boundary conditions:

$$V(R_L) = V^o(R_L) - \hat{E} \tag{N8.4.2}$$

$$V_R(R_L) = V^o{}_R(R_L) \tag{N8.4.3}$$

where V^o denotes the value of the abandoned firm.

Consider now the value of the entry (acquisition) option with acquisition price I. We have seen in N8.3 that

$$F(R) = A_1 R^{\lambda_1} \tag{N8.4.4}$$

In addition, conditions (N8.3.3) and (N8.3.4) must be satisfied at the entry threshold R_H. Let us further assume that the abandoned firm can be restarted or reacquired for \$I. The re-entry option implies that $V^o(R) = F(R)$. Thus, the following conditions must be satisfied at R_L and R_H:

$$V(R_L) = F(R_L) - \hat{E}$$

$$V_R(R_L) = F_R(R_L)$$

$$F(R_H) = V(R_H) - I$$

$$F_R(R_H) = V_R(R_H),$$

[18]See Dixit and Pindyck (1994), pp. 130–132 and Dixit (1993).

Substituting (N8.4.1) and (N8.4.4) into these conditions yields Equations (8.13) to (8.16) in Section 8.4.

   The solution algorithm is programmed into the Excel spreadsheet Real Options Calculator I. It proceeds in two stages. It starts with enumeration to solve for the values of the constants A and B in each pair of Equations (8.13) and (8.14) as well as (8.15) and (8.16) by assuming pairs of values of (R_H, R_L). For any pair of these values, the equations are linear in A and B. The solution of each pair of equations generates a pair (A, B). Then, the solutions with the minimum absolute difference between these (A, B) pairs are selected over contiguous search regions. The search is carried out over 100 values of R_L, spaced between 0 and three times the estimated value of expected potential revenue. R_H is allowed to assume values between the expected potential revenue and three times its value, at values spaced at 1% of its initial value. The average of the selected pairs (A, B) over each region is taken, and the one with the smallest absolute deviation from the right hand of the equations to be solved is chosen as the enumeration solution. This solution is used as the starting point of the improvement provided by the Excel Solver solution. Solver searches locally for the solution using a variation of the Newton method.[19]

   Dixit and Pyndick (1994), p. 223, show that when the exit and entry costs approach zero, the exit and entry thresholds both converge toward –a/b, the fixed cost component of the cash-flow defined in Section 8.2 divided by the cash-flow margin. They also show that the thresholds become extremely sensitive to small changes in the costs when the latter assume small values. Because of this, the threshold values may not converge to –a/b in those applications with zero entry and exit costs. Fortunately, the value of the entry option computed by the algorithm is not sensitive to such discrepancies in the solution thresholds. Furthermore, one can force the thresholds to be equal to –a/b after the solution has been attained and reiterate the algorithm in order to confirm the stability of the option value. The algorithm with zero entry and exit costs is used in Chapter 10, Section 10.6.5, for valuing perpetual earnouts.

*N8.5   Valuing Foothold and Expansion Options

Recall the dynamics of K(t) and R(t) from Equations (8.17) and (8.19):

$$dK = -I_1 dt \tag{N8.5.1}$$

$$dR = \alpha R dt + \sigma R dz \tag{N8.5.2}$$

The differential equation for $F_1(R_1, K)$ is obtained considering the following portfolio: long the option to invest in the foothold and short n units of R_1. The value of this portfolio is $F_1(R_1, K) - nR_1$. Thus,

$$dF_1(R_1, K) - ndR_1 = F_{1R} dR_1 + \tfrac{1}{2} F_{1RR} (dR_1)^2 + F_{1K} dK - ndR_1 \tag{N8.5.3}$$

We let $n = F_{1R}$ to render the portfolio riskless and obtain the instantaneous change

$$dF_1(R_1, K) - ndR_1 = \tfrac{1}{2}\sigma^2 (R_1)^2 F_{1RR} dt - I_1 F_{1K} dt \tag{N8.5.4}$$

   In addition, the buyer of the short position requires compensation equal to $(w - \alpha)F_{1R} Rdt$, and there is an outflow $I_1 dt$ when investment takes place. Equating the total return on the portfolio to the riskless return yields

$$\tfrac{1}{2}\sigma^2 (R_1)^2 F_{1RR} dt - I_1 F_{1K} dt - (w - \alpha)F_{1R} R_1 dt - I_1 dt = r_f(F_1 - F_{1R} R_1)dt \tag{N8.5.5}$$

---

[19]A more efficient algorithm is described in Press et al. (1992), pp. 365–381.

Substituting Equation (N8.5.2) for dR_1, simplifying and rearranging terms produces the following differential equation for $F_1(R_1, K)$

$$\tfrac{1}{2}\sigma^2R^2F_{1RR} + (r_f - w + \alpha)R_1F_{1R} - r_f F_1 - I_1 F_{1K} - I_1 = 0 \quad (N8.5.7)$$

Equation (N8.5.7) must satisfy the following boundary conditions

$$F_1(R_1, 0) = F_2(R_1) \quad (N8.5.8)$$

$$F_1(0, K) = 0 \quad (N8.5.9)$$

$$\lim_{R\to\infty}F_{1,R}(R_1,K) = \lim_{R\to\infty} F_2(R_1)R_1^{-1}\lambda_1e^{-(w-\alpha\lambda_1)K/I_{max}} \quad (N8.5.10)$$

and the value matching and smooth pasting conditions that F_1 and $F_{1,R}$ be continuous at R_1^*.

Equation (N8.5.8) says that at completion, i.e., when $K = 0$ the firms gets the option to invest I_2 and operate the firm in the second-stage. Equation (N8.5.9) says that value of the foothold option is negligible when $R_1 = 0$. Equation (N8.5.9) recognizes that when R_1 is very large the probability of interrupting the investment is very low. Since the time to completion would still be K/I_{max}, $F_1(R_1, K)$ equals the present value of $F_2(R_1) = A_1R_1^{\lambda_1}$, or $F_1 = A_1[R_1e^{\alpha K/I_{max}}]^{\lambda_1}e^{-wK/I_{max}} = A_1R_1^{\lambda_1}e^{-(w-\alpha\lambda_1)K/I_{max}}$. Hence, $F_{1R} = A_1R_1^{\lambda_1-1}\lambda_1e^{-(w-\alpha\lambda_1)K/I_{max}} = F_2(R_1)R_1^{-1}\lambda_1e^{-(w-\alpha\lambda_1)K/I_{max}}$.

Equation (N8.5.7) shows that dF_1 is linear in I_1 with slope $-F_{1K} - 1$. Hence, the rate I_1 that maximizes the value of the foothold option is either its maximum value I_{max} or zero.

Note that when $R_1 < R_1^*$, $I_1 = 0$ and Equation (N8.5.7) becomes

$$\tfrac{1}{2}\sigma^2 R_1^2F_{1RR} + (r_f - w + \alpha)R_1F_{1R} - r_fF_1 = 0 \quad (N8.5.11)$$

which has the same form as Equation (N8.4.4) and, therefore, has solution $F_1(R,K) = A(K)R^{v_1}$, where,

$$v_1 = \tfrac{1}{2} - (r_f - w + \alpha)\sigma^{-2} + \{[(r_f - w + \alpha)\sigma^{-2} - \tfrac{1}{2}]^2 + 2r_f\sigma^{-2}\}^{1/2},$$

and $A(K)$ has values provided by the solution of Equation (8.20) along the boundary $R_1 = R_1^*$. The numerical procedure is simplified by eliminating $A(K)$ using the value-matching and smooth-pasting conditions:

$$F_1(R_1^*, K)_{I=I_{max}} = F_1(R_1^*, K)_{I=0}$$

$$F_{1R}(R_1^*, K)_{I=I_{max}} = Av_1R_1^{*v_1-1} = (v_1/R_1^*)AR^{*v_1}$$

or

$$F_1(R_1^*, K) = (R_1^*/v_1)F_{1R}(R_1^*, K) \quad (N8.5.12)$$

The value of the foothold option can be obtained solving equation (N8.5.7) for $I_1 = I_{max}$ subject to Equations (N8.5.8), (N8.5.10), and (N8.5.12). Note that Equation (N8.5.9) does not apply when $I_1 = I_{max}$. The solution algorithm is outlined in Note N8.7 and has been programmed into the Excel spreadsheet Real Options Calculator II.

*N8.6   Foothold Option with Uncertain Costs

Recall the dynamics of $K(t)$ and $R(t)$ for the case of a foothold with uncertain costs:

$$dK = - I_1dt + v(I_1 K)^{1/2}d\zeta \quad (N8.6.1)$$

$$dR = \alpha Rdt + \sigma Rdz \quad (N8.6.2)$$

The differential equation for $F_1(R_1, K)$ is obtained considering the following portfolio: long the option to invest in the foothold and short n units of R_1. The value of this portfolio is $F_1(R_1, K) - nR_1$. In addition, the buyer of the short position requires compensation equal to $(w - \alpha) F_{1R} R dt$, and there is an outflow $I_1 dt$ when investment takes place. Equating the total return on the portfolio to the riskless return yields

$$dF_1 - F_{1R}dR_1 - (w - \alpha)F_{1R}R_1dt - I_1dt = r_f(F_1 - F_{1R}R_1)dt \qquad (N8.6.3)$$

Using Ito's Lemma, we write dF_1 as

$$dF_1 = F_{1R}\,dR_1 + F_{1K}\,dK_1 + \tfrac{1}{2}F_{1RR}\,(dR_1)^2 + \tfrac{1}{2}F_{1KK}(dK_1)^2 + \tfrac{1}{2}F_{1RK}\,dR_1dK \qquad (N8.6.4)$$

Substituting this expression into Equations (N8.6.3), (N8.6.1) for dK_1 and (N8.6.2) for dR_1, simplifying and rearranging terms produces the following differential equation for $F_1(R_1, K)$:[20]

$$\tfrac{1}{2}\sigma^2 R^2 F_{1RR} + \tfrac{1}{2}\,v^2 I\,K\,F_{1KK} + (r_f - w + \alpha)R_1 F_{1R} - r_f F_1 - I\,F_{1K} - I_1 = 0 \qquad (N8.6.5)$$

Equation (N8.6.5) must satisfy the following boundary conditions

$$F_1(R_1{}^*, 0) = F_2(R_1{}^*) \qquad (N8.6.6)$$

$$F_1(0, K) = 0 \qquad (N8.6.7)$$

$$\lim_{K \to \infty} F_{1,R}(R_1, K) = 0 \qquad (N8.6.8)$$

$$\tfrac{1}{2}v^2\,K\,F_{1KK}(R_1{}^*, K) - F_{1K}(R_1{}^*, K) - 1 = 0 \qquad (N8.6.9)$$

and the value matching conditions that F_1 be continuous at $R_1{}^*$, that is, that $F_1(I_1 = 0) = F_1(I_1 = I_{max})$.

Equation (N8.6.6) says that at completion, i.e., when $K = 0$, the firms gets the option to invest I_2 and operate the firm in the second stage. Equation (N8.6.7) says that value of the foothold option is negligible when $R_1 = 0$. Equation (N8.6.8) recognizes that when K is very large the value of the foothold option is negligible. Equation (N8.6.9) is the smooth-pasting condition that $F_{1,R}$ be continuous at $R_1{}^*$, that is, that $F_{1,R}(I_1 = 0) = F_{1,R}(I_1 = I_{max})$.

Equation (N8.6.5) shows that dF_1 is linear in I_1 with slope $\tfrac{1}{2}v^2\,KF_{1KK}(R_1{}^*, K)$ $- F_{1K}(R_1{}^*, K) - 1$. Hence, the rate I_1 that maximizes the value of the foothold option is either its maximum value I_{max} or zero. That is,

$$I^* = I_{max} \text{ for } \tfrac{1}{2}v^2\,K\,F_{1KK}(R_1{}^*, K) - F_{1K}(R_1{}^*, K) - 1 > 0 \quad \text{and} \quad I^* = 0, \text{ otherwise.}$$

The solution $R_1{}^*$, $F_1(R_1{}^*,K)$ has to be found by numerical methods as noted in Section 8.7.

*N8.7   The Explicit Finite Difference Algorithm for Valuing Foothold Options

In this note, we outline the algorithm used to solve Equation (N8.5.7). The solution method consists in approximating derivatives by first differences and solving the resulting difference equation iteratively. This method is known as the *explicit finite difference method*. The present version is an adaptation of the procedure outlined in Dixit and Pindyck (1994), pp. 353 to 356, for the valuation of the time-to-build option. Here, we need to allow for the changes in the boundary conditions resulting from the compound nature of the foothold valuation model. The algorithm has been programmed into the Excel spreadsheet Real Options Calculator II.

We first eliminate R from the coefficients of Equation (N8.5.7) by substituting the following transformation $F_1(R,K) \equiv e^{-r_f K/I_{max}}G(X, K)$, where $X \equiv \log R$.

---

[20]The covariance of $dzd\zeta$ is of the order $(dt)^2$ and tends to zero faster than dt. This means that $dR_1 dK$ approaches its expected value as $dt \to 0$ but dR_1 and dK are uncorrelated. Hence $dR_1 dK \to 0$ as $dt \to 0$.

$$\tfrac{1}{2}\sigma^2 G_{RR} + (r_f - w + \alpha - \tfrac{1}{2}\sigma^2)G_R - I_{max}G_K - I_{max}e^{-r_f K/I_{max}} = 0 \tag{N8.7.1}$$

The boundary conditions of Equations (N8.5.8), (N8.5.10), and (N8.5.12) then become:

$$G(X, 0) = A_1 e^{\lambda_1 X} \tag{N8.7.2}$$

$$\lim_{R \to \infty} F_{1,R}(R_1, K) = \lim_{R \to \infty} A_1 R_1^{\lambda_1 - 1}\lambda_1 e^{-(w - \alpha\lambda_1)K/I_{max}}$$

or

$$\lim_{X \to \infty} [e^{-r_f K/I_{max}} e^{-X} G_X(X, K)] = \lim_{R \to \infty} A_1\lambda_1 e^{(\lambda_1 - 1)X - (w - \alpha\lambda_1)K/I_{max}}$$

hence,

$$\lim_{X \to \infty} G_X(X, K) = \lim_{R \to \infty} A_1\lambda_1 e^{\lambda_1 X + (r_f - w + \alpha\lambda_1)K/I_{max}} \tag{N8.7.3}$$

$$G(X^*, K) = (1/\nu_1)\, G_X(X^*, K) \tag{N8.7.4}$$

We are now ready to transform the continuous variables X and K into discrete variables and obtain a difference equation that can be solved numerically. Proceeding as in Dixit and Pindyck (1994), we let $G(X, K) \equiv G(i\Delta X, j\Delta K)$ where $-b \le i \le m$ and $0 \le j \le n$ and approximate the derivatives in Equation (N8.7.1) by following finite differences:

$$G_{XX} \approx [G_{i+1,j} - 2G_{i,j} + G_{i-1,j}]/(\Delta X)^2$$
$$G_X \approx [G_{i+1,j} - G_{i-1,j}]/(2\Delta X)$$
$$G_K \approx [G_{i+1,j+1} - G_{i,j}]/\Delta K.$$

Substituting these expressions into Equation (N8.7.1) yields

$$G_{i,j} = p^+ G_{i+1,j-1} + p^0 G_{i,j-1} + p^- G_{i-1,j-1} - \eta_j, \tag{N8.7.5}$$

where

$$p^+ = [\sigma^2/\Delta K + r_f - w + \alpha - \tfrac{1}{2}\sigma^2]]\Delta K/(2I_{max}\Delta X)$$
$$p^0 = 1 - \sigma^2\Delta K/[I_{max}(\Delta X)^2]$$
$$p^- = [\sigma^2/\Delta K - r_f + w - \alpha + \tfrac{1}{2}\sigma^2]]\Delta K/(2I_{max}\Delta X)$$
$$\eta_j = \Delta K e^{r_f \Delta K/I_{max}}$$

Equation (N8.7.2) becomes

$$G_{i,j=0} = A_1 e^{\lambda_1 i\Delta X} \tag{N8.7.6}$$

and Equation (N8.7.3) becomes

$$G_X(m\Delta X, K) = A_1\lambda_1 e^{\lambda_1 m\Delta X + (r_f - w + \alpha\lambda_1)j\Delta K/I_{max}}$$

or

$$G_{m+1,j} = 2\Delta X A_1\lambda_1 e^{\lambda_1 m\Delta X + (r_f - w + \alpha\lambda_1)j\Delta K/I_{max}} + G_{m-1,j}$$

Substituting this expression into Equation (N8.7.5) yields:

$$G_{m,j+1} = p^+[2\Delta X A_1\lambda_1 e^{\lambda_1 m\Delta X + (r_f - w + \alpha\lambda_1)j\Delta K/I_{max}}] + p^0 G_{m,j} \tag{N8.7.7}$$
$$+ (p^+ + p^-)G_{m-1,j} - \eta_j.$$

The free-boundary condition of Equation (N8.7.4) becomes

$$G_{i*,j} = (1/\nu_1)\,(G_{i*+1,j} - G_{i*,j})/\Delta X,$$

or

$$G_{i*,j} = G_{i*+1,j}/(1 + \nu_1\,\Delta X), \tag{N8.7.8}$$

where $i*\Delta X = X^*$.

The algorithm is computed in Real Options Calculator II on a table. First, the values of G are computed on the right hand side of the table from the terminal boundary condition of Equation (N8.7.6). Then, for j = 1, 2, … n the values of $G_{m,1}$ and $G_{m-s,j}$ for s = 1, 2, … are calculated using Equations (N8.7.7) and (N8.7.5), respectively. The resulting values of G are checked for equality with Equation (8.7.8) within an error $|\varepsilon|$ in order to identify the critical value i^* (which yields $R^* = e^{i^* \Delta X}$). Once the free boundary has been identified, the coefficient A(K) of $F_1(R,K) = A(K)R^v{}_1$ for I = 0 is calculated at i^* for each K, and G is made equal to $A(K)R^v{}_1$ for $i < i^*$.

*N8.8   Modeling the Return Distribution of the HLF Option-pricing Model

In this section, we formulate a model for computing the volatility of the option-pricing model used in Chapter 6, Section 6.7, for valuing highly leveraged firms. We derive the moments of the distribution of the continuation value V_T and the debt balance D_T. These moments are expressed as a function of the volatility of revenues and are used for solving for the underlying volatilities of V_T and D_T.

As in Section 8.2, we assume that free cash flow at time t is a linear function of revenue. Here,

$$Y_t = a_t + bR_t \tag{N8.8.1}$$

$$dR/R = \alpha dt + \sigma dz \tag{N8.8.2}$$

$$dY = b\alpha R dt + b\sigma R dz \tag{N8.8.3}$$

where, as before, α is the continuous growth rate and σ is the *volatility* of R.

The expression for the continuation value V_T was obtained in Section 8.3 as

$$V_T = \frac{a_T}{(1 - \tau)\acute{r}} + \frac{bR_T}{\acute{w} - \alpha} \tag{N8.8.4}$$

where $(1 - \tau)\acute{r}$ and $\acute{w}$ are the continuous time equivalent rates $(1 - \tau)\acute{r} = \ln(1 + (1 - \tau)r)$ and $\acute{w} = \ln(1 + w)$ corresponding to the annual compound rates $(1 - \tau)r$ and w, and we assume that a_T remains constant after time T.[21] Hence, the expected value of V_T is

$$E[V_T] = \frac{a_T}{(1 - \tau)\acute{r}} + \frac{bR_0 e^{\alpha T}}{\acute{w} - g} \tag{N8.8.5}$$

Furthermore, the present value of V_T is

$$P_0[V_T] = \frac{a_T}{(1 - \tau)\acute{r}[1 + (1 - \tau)r]^T} + \frac{bR_0 e^{\alpha T}}{(\acute{w} - \alpha)(1 + \rho)^T} \tag{N8.8.6}$$

Turning now to D_T and relying on Note N6.3, we have

$$D_t = D_{t-1} - (1 - \phi)(Y_t + \tau \acute{r} D_{t-1}) + \acute{r} D_{t-1} \tag{N8.8.7}$$

and

$$P_0[D_T] = D_0 - (1 - \phi) \sum\nolimits_{t=1,T} P_0[Z_t] \tag{N8.8.8}$$

where, from Equation (N6.3.3),

---

[21]We mix continuous and discrete compounding in order to maintain this model notation close to that of recursive APV. Both models are included in HLF Value Calculator and use common inputs.

$$P_0[Z_t] = \frac{E[Y_t]}{(1 + \rho)^t} + \frac{\tau r}{(1 + r)}[D_0 - (1 - \phi)\sum_{j=1,t-1}P_0[Z_j]] \quad \text{for } t > 1$$

and $P_0[Z_1] = E[Z_1]/(1 + \rho) + \tau r D_0/(1 + r)$. Furthermore, $P_T[V_T] = V_T$ and $P_T[D_T] = D_T$.

We assume that the distribution of (V_T, D_T) is well approximated by a lognormal distribution and that $P_t[V_T]$ and $P_t[D_T]$ follow the Ito processes:[22]

$$dP[D_T] = \mu_1 P[D_T]dt + \nu_1 P[D_T]dz_1 \tag{N8.8.9}$$

$$dP[V_T] = \mu_2 P[V_T]dt + \nu_2 P[V_T]dz_2 \tag{N8.8.10}$$

with $\nu_{12} = \text{cov}(dz_1,dz_2)$. μ_1, μ_2, ν_1, ν_2 and ν_{12} are the moments of the normal distribution of (dz_1,dz_2).[23]

From Equations (N8.8.4) and (N8.8.7) we derive the following expressions for the covariances of the distribution of (V_T, D_T):

$$\text{var}[V_T] = (\acute{w} - \alpha)^{-2}b^2R_0^2\exp(2\alpha T)\exp[(\sigma^2 T) - 1] \tag{N8.8.11}$$

$$\text{var}[D_T] = (1 - \phi)^2 b^2 R_0^2 \sum_{t=1,T}[(\tau r)^2(1 - \phi)^2 \tag{N8.8.12}$$
$$+ (1 + r)^2]^{T-t}\exp(2\alpha t)\exp[(\sigma^2 t) - 1]$$

$$\text{cov}[V_T, D_T] = -(\acute{w} - \alpha)^{-1}(1 - \phi)b^2R_0^2\exp(2\alpha T)\exp[(\sigma^2 T) - 1] \tag{N8.8.13}$$

Therefore, ν_1, ν_2 and ν_{12} can be solved as a function of σ from the following equations for the moments of the lognormal distribution:

$$\exp(\mu_1 T) = E[D_T]/P_0[D_T] \tag{N8.8.14}$$

$$\exp(\mu_2 T) = E[V_T]/P_0[V_T] \tag{N8.8.15}$$

$$\exp(2\mu_1 T)[\exp(\nu_1^2 T) - 1] = (1 - \phi)^2 b^2 R_0^2 \sum_{t=1,T}[(\tau r)^2(1 - \phi)^2 \tag{N8.8.16}$$
$$+ (1 + r)^2]^{T-t}\exp(2\alpha t)\exp[(\sigma^2 t) - 1]/(P_0[D_T])^2$$

$$\exp(2\mu_2 T)[\exp(\nu_2^2 T) - 1] = \tag{N8.8.17}$$
$$(\acute{w} - \alpha)^{-2}b^2R_0^2\exp(2\alpha T)\exp[(\sigma^2 T) - 1]/(P_0[V_T])^2$$

$$\exp[(\mu_1 + \mu_2)T][\exp(\nu_{12}T) - 1)] = \tag{N8.8.18}$$
$$-(\acute{w} - \alpha)^{-1}(1 - \phi)b^2R_0^2\exp(2\alpha T)\exp[(\sigma^2 T) - 1]/(P_0[D_T]P_0[V_T])$$

Suppose instead that the continuation value is based upon an EBITDA multiple M applied to projected EBITDA such that $V_T = M \times \text{EBITDA}_T$. Let $\text{EBITDA}_t = h + mR_t$, then

$$E[V_T] = M\,E[\text{EBITDA}_T] = M(h + mR_0e^{\alpha T})$$

$$P_0[V_T] = M[h(1 + r)^{-T} + mR_0e^{\alpha t}(1 + \rho)^{-T}]$$

$$\text{var}[V_T] = M^2m^2R_0^2\exp(2\alpha T)\exp[(\sigma^2 T) - 1]$$

$$\text{cov}[V_T,D_T] = -Mm(1 - \phi)bR_0^2\exp(2\alpha T)\exp[(\sigma^2 T) - 1],$$

which provide the appropriate substitutions on the right-hand side of Equations (N8.8.15), (N8.8.17), and (N8.8.18).

---

[22]For the properties of the lognormal distribution see Aitchison and Brown (1966).

[23]μ_1 and ν_1 are the average moments over $[0,T]$ because the $P[D_T]$ process has time-varying (nonstochastic) drift and variance rates.

EXHIBIT N9.1	*Capitalization of Operating Leases*					

($000) Fiscal Year Ending 1/31

		2002	2003	2004	2005	2006	2007
CDH Group							
Operating Lease Payments			48,625	51,834	55,255	58,902	62,487
Capitalized Operating Leases @	11%	442,042	471,217	502,318	535,470	568,067	599,737
Implied Net Capex			29,175	31,100	33,153	32,597	31,670
Implied Interest Expense @	9%		39,784	42,410	45,209	48,192	51,126
Capitol Designs							
Operating Lease Payments			10,019	12,585	15,480	19,041	22,444
Capitalized Operating Leases @	11%	91,084	114,413	140,729	173,096	204,037	218,549
Implied Net Capex			23,329	26,315	32,368	30,941	14,512
Implied Interest Expense @	9%		8,198	10,297	12,666	15,579	18,363

NOTE TO CHAPTER 9

N9.1 Operating Leases

Operating leases are valued in Exhibit N9.1 each year capitalizing future lease payments. The lease payments of both CDH and Capitol Designs were about 11% of the value of the leased properties on the average.[24] The difference between the lease payment and the implied interest expense is made up of depreciation and a put premium. (The lessee pays for the cancellation option implied by the renewal option commonly contained in the lease contract.) These additional costs make the capitalization rate higher than the company's borrowing cost. Retail operating leases are valued as perpetuities in order to account for the lease payments of their renewal. If the company does not intend to renew a particular lease and replace it for another, it would be appropriate to discount only the projected lease payments disclosed in footnotes in the companies financial reports. This is not so for retail going-concerns. As far as computing free cash flows, the implied interest expense computed at the company's cost of debt plus an estimate of the cost of the cancellation option, both computed after taxes, should be added to net income to attain unlevered net income.[25] This leaves out the deduction of the depreciation contained in the lease payments. However, since depreciation should be added to both unlevered net income and to net capital expenditures, it does not change the free cash flows and there is not need to estimate it for valuation purposes. On the other hand, capital expenditures are increased by the net increase in the value of the leases. This item does not account for replacement, which is implicitly funded by depreciation.

NOTES TO CHAPTER 10

N10.1 Debt Valuation with OID Amortization

In Section 10.5, we noted that when OID amortization is allowed for tax purposes the value of the loan to the issuer could be valued discounting the pre-tax cash flows at the

---

[24]A rule of thumb for estimating the capitalization rate is to add about 300 basis points to the dividend yield of retail REITS.

[25]The cancellation option is a put, the purchase of which is an approximately zero net present value transaction such that its cost is offset by the value of the put. Adding its cost to net income allows for this offset. Correcting for the value of the put will not materially effect enterprise value and can be ignored in practice.

pre-tax market rate instead of discounting the after-tax cash flows at the after-tax market rate. In the following table, we show that doing the latter gives the same result.

($000)		2003	2004	2005	2006	2007
Balance		5,000	3,750	2,500	1,250	0
Amortization			1,250	1,250	1,250	1,250
Interest @	8%		400	300	200	100
Payout			1,650	1,550	1,450	1,350
Present value @	9%	4,894	3,685	2,467	1,239	0
OID		106	65	33	11	0
OID amortization			40	32	22	11
Total interest			440	332	222	111
Tax shield	40%		(176)	(133)	(89)	(45)
After-tax cash flow			1,474	1,417	1,361	1,305
PV @ $(1-40\%)(9\%)=$	5.4%	4,894				
After tax cash flow			1,474	1,417	1,361	1,305
Equivalent loan		4,894	3,685	2,467	1,239	0
Interest @	9%		440	332	222	111
Tax shield @	40%		176	133	89	45
Amortization			1,210	1,218	1,228	1,239

The top panel computes the OID each year as the difference between the present value of the loan cash flows at the market rate (9%) and the loan balance. For example, the initial OID is equal to $5,000 – $4,894 = $106. At the beginning of the second year OID = $3,750 – $3,685 = $65. That is, with the passage of time the value of the principal increases and the difference between the market value of the remaining cash flows and the balance due decreases until it becomes zero in 2007. The decrease of the discount represents an accrued interest that is deductible for tax purposes. Subtracting the tax shield on the total (cash and accrued) interest from the cash outflows of the issuer gives the after-tax cash flow. Discounting it at 5.4%, the after tax cost of debt, yields $4,894 as the value of the issuer's liability. This is the value calculated in Exhibit 10.3.

The bottom panel confirms that discounting the after-tax cash flow at the after-tax cost of debt results in the equivalent loan that the issuer could attain at 9%, the market rate.

Proceeding in a similar way, we illustrate in the following table the value of the loan to the issuer when all OID amortization is disqualified.[26]

---

[26]In the present case, OID amortization would be allowed under the "applicable high yield discount obligations" (AHYDO) provisions of the U.S. Tax Code. Essentially, to be considered a AHYDO, a debenture has to have *all* of the following characteristics: (1) it is issued by a corporation and the acquiring corporation is an LBO, (2) it has more than five-year maturity, (3) the yield to maturity exceeds by five percentage points or more the applicable federal rate, and (4) it has significant OID. The latter itself determined after a complex test. See Ginsburg and Levin (2002). When a debenture is determined as a AHYDO, its OID is divided into an allowed part and a disallowed part, with the first deductible only when actually paid.

($000)		2003	2004	2005	2006	2007
Balance		5,000	3,750	2,500	1,250	—
Amortization			1,250	1,250	1,250	1,250
Interest	8%		400	300	200	100
Tax shield	40%		(160)	(120)	(80)	(40)
After-tax cash flow			1,490	1,430	1,370	1,310
PV @ (1 – 40%)(9%) =	5.4%	4,932				
After tax cash flow			1,490	1,430	1,370	1,310
Equivalent loan		4,932	$3,709	$2,479	$1,243	$0
Interest @ 9%			444	334	223	112
Tax shield			178	134	89	45
Amortization			1,224	1,230	1,236	1,243

Discounting the after-tax cash flows at the after-tax cost of debt gives a value of the liability of $4,932, which is higher than when OID is allowed because the issuer has a smaller tax shield and needs to pay higher after tax cash flows.

N10.2   Gauging the Probability of Default from Yield Spreads

In this note, we use a result from Pye (1974) about the relation between the probability of default and the default premium in order to estimate the first. Consider a bond equally likely to default in every year with probability of default p_d. Assume that recovery is $1 - \lambda$ of the previous year price. Pye showed that the yield to maturity of this bond is given by the following formula $y = (r + \lambda p_d)/(1 - p_d)$, where r is the bond's expected return prior to default. Pye pointed out that historically about 2.3% of medium-grade bonds defaulted per year and holders lost about 50% of their par value. In order to estimate the probability of default, note that the expected return should be close to the yield on default free securities such as Treasury bonds, ignoring differences in liquidity and systematic risk. Let the interest on the seller's note be 9% and the yield of a similar Treasury security be 6%. Then, assuming 50% recovery under default, $p_d = (y - r)/(\lambda + y) = (0.09 - 0.06)/(0.50 + 0.09) = 5.1\%$.

NOTES TO CHAPTER 11

Note 11.1   Valuing a Contingent Value Right Extension Option

This note gives additional details about the computation of the value of the CVR extension option examined in Section 11.2. It is done following the risk neutral valuation procedure. Risk neutral valuation is a fundamental result of option-pricing theory that says that option prices attained by assuming risk neutrality are valid in general.[27] In a risk neutral world stock prices yield the riskless rate of return and option payoffs are discounted at the riskless rate.

Generating Price Sequences

The CVR extension option is an option to exchange an asset for another. To value it, one first simulates the stock price path for the trading days included in the period of the first

---

[27]See Hull (2002) for a discussion of risk neutral valuation.

CVR. This can be done on an Excel spreadsheet using the Rand() function to generate random numbers between 0 and 1. A sum of 12 of these random numbers minus 6 is an approximate sample from the standard normal distribution. This value is denoted ε_t and is made to correspond to a day t. ε_t is transformed into the rate of appreciation of the stock price for that particular day. This is done by adding to the daily rate of appreciation the normal deviate times the daily volatility. Since we are assuming risk neutrality, the stock is allowed to grow at a riskless rate of return minus its dividend yield. That is, at $\ln(1.0783) - \ln(1 + 0.36/25.175) = 6.06\%$ per year or $6.06/254 = 0.024\%$ per trading day. In addition, the volatility of the daily prices is $27.97\% \sqrt{254}^{-1} = 1.75\%$. Hence, the stock price on day t is $P_t = P_{t-1}(1 + 0.00024 + 0.0175\varepsilon_t)$. A simulation trial contains the prices corresponding to the 466 trading days in the period 11/14/89 to 9/18/91.

Computing the CVR Payoff

The last 63 days of each trial correspond to the trading days in the 90 days ending on 9/18/91. Let their average be P_{avg}. The CVR payoff for each trial is $S = \min[\max(45.77 - P_{avg}, 0), 15.77]$. This is the number to be compared to the value of the extended CVR that is the function of the last price P_{466} in the trial.

Valuing the Extended CVRs

The possible CVR values as of 9/18/91 are generated by attaching an Excel Data Table to the Asian program of the Financial Options Calculator.

The table replaces values of P_{466} into the initial stock price and uses $50.23 and $30 as the strike prices of the puts. The difference between the two puts is the CVR value corresponding to P_{466}. Denote it V(CVR). The table is computed for 1,000 values of P_{466}, from $0.1 to $100.0 with $0.1 increments. The $[P_{466}, V(CVR)]$ pairs are then copied to the simulation spreadsheet in order to retrieve them via the Lookup function of Excel.

Valuing the Exchange Option

On the simulation spreadsheet for each simulation trial, the CVR value corresponding to P_{466} is retrieved via the lookup function and compared to S, the settlement value of the first CVR. The value of the exchange options that allows Dow Chemical to extend the guarantee for another year is $\max[S - V(CVR), 0]$ for each simulation trial. This value is computed over 10,000 simulation trials via a data table that prompts the generation of new sequences of random numbers. The present value of the average over the trials computed using the riskless rate of interest is the value of the option to extend the guarantee:

$$(10,000)^{-1} \sum_{j=1, 10,000} \max[S_j - V_j(CVR), 0] (1.0783)^{-673/365} = \$0.17.$$

N11.2   Valuing Collars by Simulation

In this note, we describe the simulation experiment used to value the collar described in Section 11.3. We generate price sequences as in N11.1 for the 65 trading days in the period 7/10/91 to 10/10/91 and take the average price P_{avg} of the 20 days ending 10/10/91. If $P_{avg} > \$50.58$, we set $c = P_{65} - \$50.58$ or zero otherwise. If $P_{avg} < \$43.97$, we set $p = \$43.97 - P_{65}$ or zero otherwise. P_{65} is the price generated for 10/10/91. Note that c and p are not necessarily positive in each trial. The averages of c and p are computed over

10,000 simulations trials via a data table. Their present value on 7/10/91 computed at the riskless rate gives the values c(50.58) = $4.50 and p(43.97) = $3.48.

N11.3   Risk Arbitrage

This note summarizes basic concepts of risk arbitrage.[28] Consider the case in which an acquirer A announces a 2 for 1 exchange bid for all the shares of a target B. Assume that after the announcement, the price of A's stock is $40 and the price of B's stock is $70. Given these prices, one would think about acquiring one share of B at $70 in order to eventually get two shares of A valued at $80 and make a profit of $10. However, in doing so one would face two types of risks: (1) The merger may not go through and (2) the stock market may go down and bring down the price of A.

The arbitrageur specializes in obtaining and evaluating information pertaining to the deal and therefore is prepared to face the risk of type (1). However, he or she does not desire to undertake market risk and hedges risk by taking a short position in the securities to be received upon consummation of the merger. In the present case, the arbitrageur takes a long position in B shares and a short position in A shares. In this way, the spread on the deal is fixed under any market condition as it is shown in the following table for two alternative prices of A:

	Events at Closing	
	$P_A = \$35$ ($P_B = \$70$)	$P_A = \$45$ ($P_B = \$90$)
Shares of A short = 2	$10	($10)
Shares of B long = 1	0	20
Arbitrage profit	10	10

More generally, at consummation of the merger the profit from the position is $-2(40 - P_A) + (2P_A - 70) = \$10$ for any P_A. Assume the deal takes 3 months to close, then the gross return on investment is (10/70) = 14.3% over the quarter. A more relevant calculation is the return on the arbitrageur equity after carrying costs. This calculation is a function of the admissible leverage under current regulations. The return to a New York exchange member doing arbitrage can be three times as high as the gross return on investment.

Note that the arbitrageur hedges the position by creating a liability (a short position) that decreases in value in the same amount as his or her asset (the long position) as the market goes down. The number of shares to short is the *hedge ratio* times the number of shares held long. The hedge ratio in this case is the share *exchange ratio*, which for the present example is 2. Thus, the hedged position is attained shorting twice as many shares of A as the arbitrageur buys of B.

The main downside risk of an arbitrage is that the deal may not go through. In building the position on the target the arbitrageur is already assuming part or most of the premium being offered. Suppose the merger of the previous example fails and that the price of A goes up to $45 and the price of B goes down to $65. In that case the arbitrageur would lose $20 ($10 on each position). Other risks include a change in the exchange ratio that leaves a previously hedged position partly at risk and a competing bid that forces the arbitrageur to cover his or her short position at a loss.

A partial cash tender offer exposes the arbitrageur to the after-market risk on the shares tendered but not purchased by the acquirer. Consider, for example, the case in

---

[28]See Wyser-Pratte (1982) for a detailed exposition of risk arbitrage techniques and examples.

which company A offers $80 a share in cash for 51% of company B and 2 shares of A for each remaining shares of B. That is,

Shares sought in first stage	51%
Price offered	$80
Exchange ratio for second stage	2
Company A stock price (after tender)	$40

Hence, under the assumption that the offer will succeed, the value of B's stock would be

$$(0.51)\,(80)\, +\, (0.49)\,(2)\,(40)\, =\, \$80$$

Assume that B shares close at $70 upon the announcement. The arbitrageur should buy one share of B common at $70 and sell short $0.49 \times 2 = 0.98$ shares of A. These are the shares of A to be received in exchange for each shares of B held.

The gross spread of this position is $80 – $70 = $10, which is assured under any market condition as long as the deal goes through. This is shown in the following payoff table:

	Events at Closing	
	$P_A = \$35$ ($P_B = \$70$)	$P_A = \$45$ ($P_B = \$90$)
Shares of A short = 0.98	$4.9	($4.9)
Shares of B long = 1	5.1	14.9
Arbitrage profit	$10.0	$10.0

Where the profit from the long position is $(0.51)(80) + (0.49)(2)(35) – 70 = \$5.1$ for $P_A = \$35$ and $(0.51)(80) + (0.49)(2)(45) – 70 = \$14.9$ for $P_A = \$45$.

The previous calculation assumes everybody would tender. Otherwise, more shares of the arbitrageur would be sold at $80 cash, and less shares of A would be received. Suppose, for example, that only 65% of the shares are tendered. Then the arbitrageur would receive $80 cash for 72.86% of its shares, and 2 shares of A for each of the remaining 27.14%. Assume $P_A = \$45$ at closing and that, as before, 0.98 shares of A were shorted. The loss in the short position would be $4.9, and the gain the long position would be $(0.7286)(80) + (0.2714)(2)(45) – 70 = \$12.71$ with a net profit of $7.81. Had the arbitrageur shorted 0.5428 shares of A, the loss on that position would have been $(0.5428)(\$5) = \$2.71$, and the arbitrage profit would have been locked at $10 for any price of A. This is why the estimation of the number of shares to be tendered to a partial cash offer is essential. This requires subtracting estimates of the so-called "stationary blocks": (1) shares held by the public but not be tendered, (2) shares already held by the acquirer and, in the case of a hostile bid, (3) the shares held by insiders and loyal institutions.

Suppose, for example, that 75% shares are tendered. The arbitrageur tenders 100% of his or her shares and gets cash for 51%/75% = 68% of the shares tendered. Hence, he or she must short $0.32 \times 2 = 0.64$ shares of A for each share of B held long. Note that, according to the SEC Short-Tendering Rule adopted in 1968, only shares held long can be tendered. Otherwise, the arbitrageur could tender $1/0.68 = 147.1\%$ of the long position in the target and get 100% cash. The acquirer is bidding for 51% of the total, so it is going to take 51%/75% = 68% of the shares tendered for cash, and the arbitrageur would be able to sell for cash $68\% \times 147.1\% = 100\%$ of the long position in the target. The possibility of short-tendering would be particularly beneficial to the arbitrageur in the case of a partial cash tender offer that is not followed by a merger as the only transaction available at a premium would be for the cash offer. However, estimation of the amount to be tendered would become more complicated because the arbitrageur has to estimate short-tendering by arbitrageurs and other market participants. Prior to the prohibition of short-tendering, there were instances in which the amount tendered exceeded the total number of outstanding shares. It has been argued that the absence of short-tendering reduces arbitrage activity and depresses the price at which the non-arbitrageurs may cash out before the consummation of the merger.

NOTES TO CHAPTER 13

N13.1   The Simple Algebra of LBOs

From Debt Capacity to Purchase Multiple

Let q be the debt capacity multiple with respect to first-year EBITDA such that

$$\text{Debt Capacity} = q\,\text{EBITDA}.$$

Consider now the value of equity when secured debt has been fully retired:

$$\text{Exit Equity} = M_x\,\text{EBITDA}(1 + g)^T - \text{Exit Debt} = M_x\,\text{EBITDA}(1 + g)^T - (1 - f)q\text{EBITDA}$$

where M_x is the enterprise value exit multiple, T is the exit year, g is the growth rate of EBITDA, and f is the secured percentage of debt. Cash and marketable securities are assumed to be negligible.

Ignore fees and expenses and denote the initial enterprise value by EV. Then, for a required IRR:

$$\text{Entry multiple} = \frac{\text{EV}}{\text{EBITDA}} = \frac{\text{Exit Equity}}{(1 + \text{IRR})^T\text{EBITDA}} + \frac{q\text{EBITDA}}{\text{EBITDA}}$$

$$= \frac{M_x(1 + g)^T - (1 - f)q}{(1 + \text{IRR})^T} + q$$

Let the exit multiple equal the entry multiple and solve for it:

$$M = \frac{[(1 + \text{IRR})^T - (1 - f)]q}{(1 + \text{IRR})^T - (1 + g)^T} = \frac{[1.30^5 - (1 - 0.35)](4)}{1.30^5 - 1.05^5} \approx 5\,x$$

So, entry equity is $1 \times \text{EBITDA}$ or 20% for IRR = 30%, f = 35%, T = 5 years, g = 5%, and q = 4.

From Debt Capacity and Equity Requirement to IRR

Let d = 0.8 be the debt ratio (Debt/EV). Then,

$$\text{Purchase price} = \frac{\text{Debt}}{d} = \frac{q\text{EBITDA}}{d} = (4/0.8)\,\text{EBITDA} = 5 \times \text{EBITDA}$$

That is, the entry multiple is M = q/d. Let the exit multiple equal the entry multiple:

$$(1 + \text{IRR})^T = \text{Exit Equity/Entry Equity}$$

$$= \frac{M\,\text{EBITDA}(1 + g)^T - (1 - f)q\text{EBITDA}}{(1 - d)M\,\text{EBITDA}} = \frac{(1 + g)^T - (1 - f)d}{(1 - d)}$$

Hence,

$$IRR = [((1 + g)^T - (1 - f)d)/(1 - d)]^{1/T} - 1$$

Let d = 80%, q = 4, T = 5, f = 35%, and g = 5%. Then,

$$IRR = [(1.05^5/0.2 - (0.65)(0.8))/0.2]^{1/5} - 1 \approx 30\%.$$

Also,

$$\text{Interest coverage} = \frac{\text{EBITDA}}{\text{Interest Expense}} = \frac{\text{EBITDA}}{rq\text{EBITDA}} = \frac{1}{rq} = \frac{1}{(0.1)(4)} = 2.5$$

for interest rate r = 10%.

That is, the interest coverage ratio is the reciprocal of the debt capacity multiple times the average interest rate on debt.

N13.2   Recapitalization Accounting

The Financial Accounting Standard Board Emerging Issues Task Force, Issue 99-16, May 19, 1989, "Basis in Leveraged Buyout Transactions" establishes that purchase accounting should be used if there is a change in the control group (essentially in the majority voting power) of the target. Purchase accounting usually requires the creation of goodwill and its test for impairment. However, effecting a leveraged recapitalization (leveraged recap) allows for change of control without changing the accounting basis of assets and liabilities. In order to effect a leveraged recapitalization, the following steps must be followed: (1) issuance of shares to the new investors, (2) issuance of debt, and (3) stock redemption (repurchase) from existing shareholders. After these steps, the new investors effectively obtain control of the recapitalized company.[29] Stock repurchase is accounted for as a repurchase of treasury stock. This is useful for acquirers that do not publish consolidated financial statements (such as LBO funds). If the acquirer is an operating company that must use purchase accounting and consolidate the target, the benefit of recapitalization accounting applies only if the parent plans a future sale of the target into the public market. This is because the statements of the latter will be free of goodwill.

Under certain conditions, it is possible to structure the transaction to achieve recapitalization accounting for reporting purposes and to permit the Tax Code 338 election, which permits stepping-up the assets and amortizing goodwill for tax purposes (see Sections 9.2 and 9.3).

NOTES TO APPENDIX A

*NA.1   The Black-Scholes Formula

Here we provide an outline of the original derivation of the Black-Scholes formula using Ito's Lemma introduced in Chapter 8. An alternative derivation that does not require differential calculus is provided in Cox and Rubinstein (1985). Assume the stock price P follows the geometric Brownian motion

$$dP = \mu Pdt + \sigma Pdz, \tag{NA.1.1}$$

where dz is a Wiener process. Let C = F(P, t) be the price of a call option on P. Then by Ito's Lemma

---

[29]In allowing recap accounting the SEC staff considers whether there are other parties participating in the transaction whose ownership interest should not be combined with the acquiring entity. Otherwise, the target will be deemed to be "substantially wholly owned" and recap accounting may be disallowed.

$$dF = [\mu P\, \partial F/\partial P + \tfrac{1}{2}\sigma P^2\partial^2 F/\partial P^2 + \partial F/\partial t]dt + \sigma P\partial F/\partial P dz.$$

Consider a portfolio of $n = \partial F/\partial P$ shares of the stock and a short position in the call C: $\partial F/\partial P\, P - C$. Then the change in this portfolio is $\partial F/\partial P dP - dC$ or

$$\partial F/\partial P dP - [\mu P\, \partial F/\partial P + \tfrac{1}{2}\sigma P^2\partial^2 F/\partial P^2 + \partial F/\partial t]dt + \sigma P\partial F/\partial P\, dz$$

which, upon substitution of (NA.1.1) yields

$$\partial F/\partial P\, (\mu Pdt + \sigma P\, dz) - [\mu P\, \partial F/\partial P + \tfrac{1}{2}\sigma P^2\partial^2 F/\partial P^2 + \partial F/\partial t]dt + \sigma P\partial F/\partial P\, dz$$
$$= -\tfrac{1}{2}\sigma P^2\partial^2 F/\partial P^2 - \partial F/\partial t]dt.$$

This is a riskless portfolio, and, therefore, it has to yield the riskless rate r_f on its investment. Hence,

$$[\tfrac{1}{2}\sigma P^2\partial^2 F/\partial P^2 + \partial F/\partial t]dt = r_f[C - (\partial F/\partial P)P]dt$$

or

$$\tfrac{1}{2}\sigma P^2\partial^2 F/\partial P^2 + r_f P\partial F/\partial P + \partial F/\partial t - rC = 0 \qquad \text{(NA.1.2)}$$

This is the Black-Scholes differential equation [Black and Scholes (1973)]. For a call that can be exercised only at maturity t* (European call) and has exercise price X, the boundary conditions are

$$F(P, t^*) = P - X, \quad P \geq X$$
$$= 0, \qquad P < X.$$

Black and Scholes (1973) showed that, after a change of variables, Equation (NA.1.2) is the heat-transfer equation of physics with a known solution that in the present case can be written as Equations (A.1) and (A.2) of the main text.

NA.2   Valuation of Calls, Puts, and Warrants with the HP19-BII Calculator

PROGRAM	INPUT	OUTPUT
WARRANT:(LN((P+M÷N×W)÷X)+(R+SQ(SD)÷2)×T)÷	P,M,N,W,X	
(SD×SQRT(T))=D	R,SD,T	D
((P+M÷N×W)×IF(ABS(D)>3.5:0:sgn(D)÷2+.5:.5+(1÷SQRT(PI))		
×Σ(I:1:15:1:–(D÷SQRT(2))^(2×I-1)×(–1)^I÷(FACT(I-1)×(2×I-1))))		
–X×EXP(–R×T)×IF(ABS(D–SD×SQRT(T))>3.5:sgn(D-SD×SQRT		
(T))÷2+.5:.5+(1÷SQRT(PI))×Σ(I:1:15:1:–((D-SD×SQRT(T))÷		
SQRT(2))^(2×I-1)×(–1)^I÷(FACT(I-1)×(2×I-1)))))÷(1+M÷N)=WARR		WARR
PUT:WARR–P+X×EXP(–R×T)=PUT		PUT

Input Definition

P = stock price

M = number of warrants (set to zero for simple calls)

N = number of shares (set to unity for simple calls)

W = current warrant price or proceeds per warrant for new warrants (set to zero for simple calls)

X = exercise price

R = continuously compound yield on same-maturity government security. That is, R = ln(1 + r), where r is the compound interest rate

SD = volatility (standard deviation of stock return)

T = time to expiration in years

Output Definition

WARR = warrant value (call value for simple calls)

PUT = put value (based upon WARR giving simple call value for put inputs)

Example of Warrant Valuation

Input: P = 15, M = 4.6, N = 42, W = 4.4, X = 20.42, R = .0716, SD = .265, T = 6.4.

Output: WARR = 4.63.

Comments

1. Implied volatility can be computed by iterating between the first two equations until WARR equals the current warrant or call price (the volatility of puts is obtained by first solving for WARR in the put equation and then iterating the first two equations).

2. The area under the normal function is computed using the first 15 terms of the following series expansion of the error function:

$$\text{erf}(z) = (2/\sqrt{\pi}) \sum_{I} [(-z^{2I-1})(-1)^{I}]/[(I - 1)!(2I - 1)] \quad \text{and} \quad N(z) = 0.5 + \text{erf}(z/\sqrt{2})/2.$$

References

Adler, M. and B. Dumas, "International Portfolio Choice and Corporation Finance: A Synthesis," *Journal of Finance*, 38, 1983, 925–984.

Aitchison, J. and J.A.C. Brown, *The Lognormal Distribution*, Cambridge: Cambridge University Press, 1966.

Alberts W. and J. McTaggart, "The Divestiture Decision: An Introduction," *Mergers & Acquisitions,* Fall 1979, 18–25.

Altman, E., "Measuring Corporate Bond Mortality and Performance," *Journal of Finance*, 44, 1989, 909–922.

Amihud, Y. (ed.), *Leveraged Management Buyouts*, Homewood, IL: Dow Jones-Irwin, 1989.

Amihud, Y., "Leveraged Management Buyouts and Shareholder Wealth," in Y. Amihud (1989), 3–34.

Amihud, Y., "Illiquidity and Stock Returns: Cross-Section and Time-Series Effects," *Journal of Financial Markets*, 5, 2002, 31–56.

Amihud, Y. and H. Mendelson, "Asset Prices and the Bid-Ask Spread," *Journal of Financial Economics*, 17, 1986, 223–249.

Amihud, Y. and H. Mendelson, "Liquidity and Asset Prices: Financial Management Implications," *Financial Management*, 1988, 17, 5–15.

Ang, A. and J. Liu, "How to Discount Cash Flows with Time-Varying Expected Returns," working paper, Columbia Business School, 2002.

Arditti, F.D., "The Weighted Average Cost of Capital: Some Questions on its Definition, Interpretation, and Use," *Journal of Finance*, 28, 1973, 1001–1007.

Arzac, E.R., "Do Your Business Units Create Shareholder Value," *Harvard Business Review*, January-February 1986, 121–126.

Arzac, E.R., "Class Shares and Economics of Scope," *Journal of Economic Theory*, 54, 1991, 448–459.

Arzac, E.R., "On the Capital Structure of Leveraged Buyouts," *Financial Management*, 21, 1992, 16–26.

Arzac, E.R., "In Search for the Cost of Equity," manuscript, Columbia University, 1993.

Arzac, E.R., "Valuation of Highly-Leveraged Firms," *Financial Analysts Journal*, July/August 1996, 42–50.

Arzac, E.R., "Percs, Decs, and Other Mandatory Convertibles," *Journal of Applied Corporate Finance*, 10, 1997, 54–63.

Arzac, E.R. and V. Bawa, "Portfolio Choice and Equilibrium in Capital Markets with Safety-First Investors," *Journal of Financial Economics*, 4, 1977, 277–288.

Arzac, M.G., "Takeovers and Equity Derivatives," *The American Economist*, 42, 1998, 101–107.

Asquith, P. and D.W. Mullins, "Signaling with Dividends, Stock Repurchases and Equity Issues," *Financial Management*, 15, 1983, 61–89.

Asquith, P., D.W. Mullins and E.D. Wolff, "Original Issue High Yield Bonds: Aging Analyses of Defaults, Exchanges, and Calls," *Journal of Finance*, 44, 1989, 923–952.

Auerbach, A.J., Testimony before the Senate Finance Committee, January 26, 1989, reprinted in *Journal of Applied Corporate Finance*, Spring 1989, 52–57.

Bagwell, L. and J.B. Shoven, "Cash Distribution to Shareholders," *Journal of Economic Perspectives*, 3, 1989, 129–140.

Bailey, W. and P. Chung, "Exchange Rate Fluctuations, Political Risk and Stock Returns: Some Evidence from an Emerging Market," *Journal of Financial and Quantitative Analysis*, 30, 1995, 541–561.

Bansal, R. and M. Dahlquist, "Sovereign Risk and Returns in the Global Equity Markets," Discussion Paper No. 3024, Center for Economic Policy Research, London, 2001.

Bansal, R. and C. Lundblad, "Market Efficiency, Market Returns and Size of the Risk Premium in Global Equity Markets," manuscript, Fuqua School of Business, Duke University, 2002.

Banz, R.W., "The Relationship between Return and Market Value of Common Stock," *Journal of Financial Economics*, 9, 1981, 3–18.

Barone-Adesi, G. and R.E. Whaley, "Efficient Analytic Approximations of American Option Values," *Journal of Finance*, 42, 1987, 301–320.

Bartholdy, J. and P. Peare, "The Relative Efficiency of Beta Estimates," manuscript, Aarhus School of Business, 2001.

Baskin, J., "An Empirical Investigation of the Pecking Order Hypothesis," *Financial Management*, 18, 1989, 26–35.

Bekaert, G. and C.R. Harvey, "Foreign Speculators and Emerging Equity Markets," *Journal of Finance*, 55, 2000, 565–613.

Berger, D.G. and E. Ofek, "Diversification's Effect on Firm Value," *Journal of Financial Economics,* 37, 1995, 39–65.

Berger, D.G. and E. Ofek, "Bustup Takeovers of Value—Destroying Firms," *Journal of Finance,* 51, 1996, 1175–1200.

Berk, J.B., "A Critique of Size-Related Anomalies," *The Review of Financial Studies*, 8, 1995, 275–286.

Biddle, A., "The Causes and Consequences of Hostile Takeovers," in Chew (1993).

Biddle, G.C., R.M. Bowen, and J.S. Wallace, "Evidence on EVA," *Journal of Applied Corporate Finance*, 12, 1999, 69–79.

Biddle, G.C., R.M. Bowen, and J.S. Wallace, "Does EVA Beat Earnings? Evidence on Associations with Stock Returns and Firm Values," *Journal of Accounting and Economics*, 24, 1997, 301–306.

Black, F., "Capital Market Equilibrium with Restricted Borrowing," *Journal of Business*, 44, 1972, 444–455.

Black, F., "Facts and Fantasy in the Use of Options," *Financial Analysts Journal*, July-August, 1975, 36–41, 61–72.

Black, F., M. Jensen, and M. Scholes, "The Capital Asset Pricing Model: Some Empirical Tests," in M. Jensen, ed., *Studies in the Theory of Capital Markets*, New York: Praeger, 1972.

Black, F. and M. Scholes, "The Pricing of Options and Corporate Liabilities," *Journal of Political Economy*, 81, May-June 1973, 637–659.

Blanchard, O., "Movements in the Equity Premium," *Brooking Papers on Economic Activity*, No. 2, 1993, 74–138.

Blume, M.E., "On the Assessment of Risk," *Journal of Finance*, 26, 1971, 1–10.

Blume, M.E., "Unbiased Estimates of Long-Term Expected Rates of Return," *Journal of the American Statistical Association*, September 1974, 634–638.

Blume, M.E. and D.B. Keim, "Lower Grade Bonds: Their Risks and Returns," *Financial Analysts Journal,* July/August 1987, 26–33.

Bogner, S., M. Frühwirth, and M.S. Schwaiger, "Business Valuation with Attention to Imputed Interest on Equity Increase," Vienna University of Economics and Business Administration, Vienna, 2002.

Bolton, P. and D. Scharfstein, "A Theory of Predation Based on Agency Problems in Financial Contracting," *American Economic Review*, 80, 1990, 93–106.

Bradley, M.H. and G.A. Jarrell, "Inflation and the Constant-Growth Valuation Model: A Clarification," Working Paper 03-04, Simon Graduate School of Business Administration, University of Rochester, February 2003.

Brealey, R.A. and S.C. Myers, *Principles of Corporate Finance*, 7th ed., New York: McGraw-Hill, 2003.

Brennan, M.J. and L. Trigeorgis, eds., *Project Flexibility, Agency, and Competition*, New York: Oxford University Press, 2000.

Brennan, M.J., T. Chordia, and A. Subrahmanyam, "A Reexamination of Some Popular Security Return Anomalies," manuscript, November 1996.

Bronson, P., *The Nudist on the Late Shift*, New York: Random House, 1999.

Brown, S.J., W.N. Goetzmann, and S.A. Ross, "Survival," *Journal of Finance*, 50, 1995, 853–854.

Bruner, R.F., *General Mill's Acquisition of Pillsbury from Diageo PLC*, Darden Graduate School of Management, University of Virginia, 2001a.

Bruner, R.F., *Technical Note on Structuring and Valuing Incentive Payments in M&A: Earnouts and Other Contingent Payments to the Seller*, UVA-F-1322, Darden Graduate School of Business Administration, University of Virginia, 2001b.

Bruner, R.F., K.M. Eades, R.S. Harris, and R.C. Higgins, "Best Practices in Estimating the Cost of Capital: Survey and Synthesis," *Finance Practice and Education*, Spring/Summer 1998, 13–28.

Bull, I., "Management Performance in Leveraged Buyouts: An Empirical Analysis," in Y. Amihud (1989), 69–94.

Butler, J.S. and B. Schachter, "The Investment Decision: Estimation Risk and Risk Adjusted Discount Rates," *Financial Management*, 18, 1989, 13–22.

Butler, K.C. and L.H.P. Lang, "The Forecast Accuracy of Individual Analysts: Evidence of Systematic Optimism and Pessimism," *Journal of Accounting Research*, 29, 1991, 150–156.

Chan, K.C., and N-fu Chen, "An Unconditional Asset-Pricing Test and the Role of Firm Size as an Instrumental Variable for Risk," *Journal of Finance*, 43, 1988, 309–325.

Chemmanur, T.J. and I. Paeglis, "Why Issue Tracking Stock? Insights from a Comparison with Spin-Off and Carve-Outs," *Journal of Applied Corporate Finance*, 14, 2001, 102–114.

Chen, N-F, R. Roll, and S.A. Ross, "Economic Forces and the Stock Market," *Journal of Business*, June 1984, 323–346.

Chen, S-S. and K.W. Ho, "Corporate Diversification, Ownership Structure, and Firm Value: The Singapore Evidence," *International Review of Financial Analysis*, 9, 2000, 315–326.

Chen, Z. and P. Xiong, "Discount on Illiquid Stocks: Evidence from China," Yase ICF Working Paper No. 00–56, Yale School of Management, 2001.

Chew, D.H. (ed.), *The New Corporate Finance*, New York: McGraw-Hill, 1st ed., 1993.

Chinebell, J., D.R. Kahl, and J.L. Stevens, "Time-Series Properties of the Equity Risk Premium," *The Journal of Financial Research*, 17, 1994, 105–116.

Chordia, T., R. Roll, and A. Subrahmanyam, "Commonality in Liquidity," *Journal of Financial Economics*, 56, 1, 2000, 3–28.

Claus, J. and J. Thomas, "Equity Premia as Low as Three Percent? Evidence for Analysts' Earnings Forecast for Domestic and International Stocks," *Journal of Finance*, 56, 5, 2001, 1629–1666.

Cochrane, J.H., "Where Is the Market Going? Uncertain Facts and Novel Theories," *Economic Perspectives,* Nov./Dec. 1997, XXI (6), 3–37.

Constantinidis, G.M. and R.W. Rosenthal, "Strategic Analysis of the Competitive Exercise of Certain Financial Options," *Journal of Economic Theory*, 32, 1984, 128–138.

Constantinidis, G.M., J.B. Donaldson, and R. Mehra, "Junior Can't Borrow: A New Perspective on the Equity Premium Puzzle," Working Paper, May 1998.

Cooper, I. and E. Kaplanis, "Home Bias in Equity Portfolios, Inflation Hedging and International Capital Market Equilibrium," *Review of Financial Studies*, 7, 1994, 45–60.

Cooper, I. and E. Kaplanis, "Home Bias in Equity Portfolios and the Cost of Capital of Multinational Firms," *Journal of Applied Corporate Finance*, 8, 1995, 95–102.

Cooper, I. and K.G. Nyborg, "Discount Rates and Tax," manuscript, London Business School, 2000.

Copeland, T.E. and J.F. Weston, *Financial Theory and Corporate Policy*, Reading, MA: Addison-Wesley, 3rd ed., 1988, 472–480.

Copeland, T.E. and Y. Joshi, "Why Derivatives Don't Reduce FX Risk," *The McKinsey Quarterly*, 1, 1996, 66–79.

Copeland, T.E., T. Koller, and J. Murrin, *Valuation*, 3rd ed., New York: John Wiley & Sons, 2000.

Cornell, B., "Spot Rates, Forward Rates, and Market Efficiency," *Journal of Financial Economics*, 5, 1977, 55–65.

Cornell, B. and K. Green, "The Investment Performance of Low-Grade Bond Funds," *Journal of Finance*, 46, 1991, 29–48.

Cornell, B., J.I. Hirshleifer, and E.P. James, "Estimating the Cost of Equity Capital," *Contemporary Finance Digest*, 1, 1997, 5–26.

Council of Economic Advisers, *Economic Report of the President*, Washington D.C., 2001.

Cox, J.C. and M. Rubinstein, *Option Markets*, Englewood Cliffs, NJ: Prentice-Hall, 1985.

Curran, M. "Beyond Average Intelligence," *Risk*, November 1992, 60–62. Reprinted in R. Jarrow, ed., *Over the Rainbow*, London: Risk Publications, 1995, 167–168.

Daniel, K. and S. Titman, "Evidence on the Characteristics of Cross Sectional Variation in Stock Returns," *Journal of Finance*, 52, 1997, 1–34.

DeAngelo, H. and R. Masulis, "Optimal Capital Structure and Corporate and Personal Taxation," *Journal of Financial Economics*, 8, 1980, 5–29.

DeAngelo, H. and L. DeAngelo, "Management Buy-out of Publicly Traded Corporations," *Financial Analysts Journal*, 43, 1987, 38–49.

Delaney, P.R., B.J. Epstein, R. Nach and S. Weiss Budak, *Wiley GAAP 2002*, New York: John Wiley & Sons, 2001.

De Santis, G. and B. Gérard, "How Big Is the Premium for Currency Risk," *Journal of Financial Economics*, 49, 1998, 375–412.

Dewing, A.S, *The Financial Policy of Corporations*, 5th ed., New York: The Ronald Press, 1953.

Dimson, E., "Risk Measurement when Shares are Subject to Infrequent Trading," *Journal of Financial Economics,* 7, 1979, 197–226.

Dimson, E., P. Marsh, and M. Stanton, *Triumph of the Optimistic*, Princeton, NJ: Princeton University Press, 2002.

Dixit, A.K., "Entry and Exit Decisions under Uncertainty," *Journal of Political Economy*, 97, 1989, 620–638.

Dixit, A.K., *The Art of Smooth Pasting*, Vol. 55, in J. Lesourne and H. Sonnenschein, eds., *Fundamentals of Pure and Applied Economics*, Chur, Switzerland: Harwood Academic Publishers, 1993.

Dixit, A.K. and R.A. Pindyck, *Investment under Uncertainty*, Princeton, NJ: Princeton University Press, 1994.

Donaldson, G., *Corporate Debt Capacity*, Boston, MA: Harvard Graduate School of Business Administration, 1961.

Donaldson, G., "Strategies for Financial Emergencies," *Harvard Business Review*, November-December 1969, 67–70.

Dumas, B. and B. Solnik, "The World Price of Foreign Exchange Risk," *Journal of Finance*, 50, 1995, 445–479.

Durbin, E. and D. T-C. Ng, "Uncovering Country Risk in Emerging Markets Bond Prices," International Finance Discussion Paper No. 639, Board of Governors of the Federal Reserve System, 1999.

Eaton, P., T. Harris, and J. Ohlson, "Aggregate Accounting Earnings Can Explain Most of Security Returns: The Case of Long Return Intervals," *Journal of Accounting and Economics,* 15, 1992, 119–142.

Elton, E.J. and M.J. Gruber, *Modern Portfolio Theory and Investment Analysis*, 4th ed., New York: John Wiley & Sons, 1991.

Elton, E.J., M.J. Gruber, and J. Mei, "The Cost of Capital Using Arbitrage Pricing Theory," *Financial Markets, Institutions and Instruments,* 3, 1994, 46–73.

Emmanuel, D.C., 1983, "Warrant Valuation and Exercise Strategy," *Journal of Financial Economics*, 12, 1983, 28–138.

Emory, J.D., "The Value of Marketability as Illustrated in Initial Public Offering of Common Stock," *Business Valuation Review*, 1995, 155–160.

Engels, C. and J.D. Hamilton, "Long Swings on the Dollar: Are They in the Data and Do Markets Know It?", *American Economic Review*, 1990, 689–713.

Escherich, R., "Corporate Clarity Still a Strong Theme in the U.S. M&A Market," *Global Mergers & Acquisition Review*, New York and London: J.P. Morgan, October 1997, 19–22.

Escherich, R., "Selected Results from Our Survey of U.S. Valuation Techniques," *Global Mergers & Acquisition Review*, New York and London: J.P. Morgan, January 1998a, 31.

Escherich, R., "Equity Carve-outs and Shareholder Value," *Global Mergers & Acquisition Review*, New York and London: J.P. Morgan, July 1998b, 12–18.

Escherich, R., "Market Reaction to U.S. Share Repurchases," *Global Mergers & Acquisition Review*, New York and London: J.P. Morgan, July 2002a, 47–54.

Escherich, R., "U.S. Spin Offs: Welcomed by Investors and Still Contributing Significantly to M&A Activity," *Global Mergers & Acquisition Review*, New York and London: J.P. Morgan, October 2002b, 31–37.

Escherich, R., "U.S. Equity Carve-outs: Continued Strength Even in a Weaker Equity Market," *Global Mergers & Acquisition Review*, New York and London: J.P. Morgan, October 2002c, 39–43.

Fama, E.F., "Risk Adjusted Discount Rates and Capital Budgeting Under Uncertainty," *Journal of Financial Economics*, 5, August 1977, 3–24.

Fama, E.F., "Forward and Spot Exchange Rates," *Journal of Monetary Economics*, 14, 1984, 319–338.

Fama, E.F. and J. MacBeth, "Risk, Return, and Equilibrium: Empirical Tests," *Journal of Political Economy*, 91, 1973, 607–636.

Fama, E.F. and K.R. French, "The Cross-Section of Expected Stock Returns," *Journal of Finance*, 47, 1992, 427–466.

Fama, E.F. and K.R. French, "Common Risk Factors, in the Returns on Stocks and Bonds," *Journal of Financial Economics*, 33, 1993, 3–56.

Fama, E.F. and K.R. French, "Industry Costs of Equity," *Journal of Financial Economics*, 43, 1995, 153–193.

Fama, E.F. and K.R. French, "Multifactor Explanations of Asset Pricing Anomalies," *Journal of Finance*, 51, 1996, 55–84.

Fama, E.F. and K.R. French, "The Equity Premium," *Journal of Finance*, 57, 2002, 637–659.

Fama, E.F. and K.R. French, "Disappearing Dividends: Changing Firm Characteristics or Lower Propensity to Pay," *Journal of Financial Economics,* 60, 2001, 3–43.

Fenn, G.W. and N. Liang, "Good News and Bad News About Share Repurchases," Milken Institute, December 1997.

Ferris, S.P., K.A. Kim, and P. Kitsabunnarat, "The Costs (and Benefits) of Diversified Business Groups: The Case of Korean Chaebols," *Journal of Banking and Finance*, 27, 2003, 251–273.

Fisher, I., *The Theory of Interest*, reprinting from 1930 edition, New York: A.M. Kelly, 1985.

Fisher, L. and J.H. Lorie, "Rates of Return on Investments in Common Stock," *Journal of Business*, 37, 1964, 1–21.

Fisher, S., "Call Option Pricing When the Exercise Price Is Uncertain and the Valuation of Index Bonds," *Journal of Finance*, 33, 1978, 169–176.

French, D.W., "The Weekend Efffect on the Distribution of Stock Prices: Implications for Option Pricing," *Journal of Financial Economics*, 13, 1984, 547–559.

Fruhan, W.E., *Financial Strategies,* Homewood, IL: Irwin, 1979.

Fuller, K.P., "Why Some Firms Use Collar Offers in Mergers," *The Financial Review,* 38, 2003.

Gibbs, P., "German Conglomerates: Lower Operating Profitability than Pure-play Peers," *Global Mergers & Acquisitions Review*, New York and London: J.P. Morgan, October 1997, 31–36.

Gibbs, P., "European Spin-off Market," *Global Mergers & Acquisitions Review*, New York and London: J.P. Morgan, April 1999, 37–47.

Gibbs, P., "European Equity Carve Outs: Win-Win for Those Who Pay by the Rules," *Global Mergers & Acquisitions Review*, New York and London: J.P. Morgan, July 2000, 37–52.

Gibbs, P., "Share Repurchases Have Positive Stock Price Impact in Continental Europe but Negative in the U.K.," *Global Mergers & Acquisitions Review*, New York and London: J.P. Morgan, July 2001a, 57–65.

Gibbs, P., "Value Creation in M&A," *Global Mergers & Acquisitions Review*, New York and London: J.P. Morgan, October 2001b, 49–64.

Gilson, R.J., *The Law and Finance of Corporate Acquisitions*, Foundation Press, New York: Mineola, 1986.

Gilson, R.J., M. Scholes, and M. Wolfson, "Taxation and the Dynamics of Corporate Control: The Uncertain Case for Tax Motivated Acquisitions," in J. Coffee, L. Lowenstein, and S. Rose-Ackerman, eds., *Knights, Raiders and Targets: The Impact of Hostile Takeovers*, New York: Oxford University Press, 1988.

Gilson, S.C., "Managing Default: Some Evidence on How Firms Choose Between Workouts and Chapter 11," in Chew (1993), 645–653.

Gilson, S.C., K. John, and L. Lang, "Troubled Debt Restructuring: An Empirical Study of Private Reorganizations of Firms in Default," *Journal of Financial Economics*, 26, 1990, 315–354.

Ginsburg, M.D. and J.S. Levin, *Mergers, Acquisitions and Buyouts*, New York: Panel Publishers, A Division of Aspen Publishers, Inc., 2002 edition.

Glosten, L.R., R. Jagannathan, and D.E. Runkle, "On the Relationship between the Expected Value and the Volatility of the Nominal Excess Return on Stocks," *Journal of Finance*, 48, 1993, 1779–1801.

Goetzmann, W.N. and P. Jorion, "Re-Emerging Markets," *Journal of Financial and Quantitative Analysis*, 34, 1999, 1–32.

Gordon, M., *The Investment, Financing and Valuation of the Corporation*, Homewood, IL: Irwin, 1962.

Graham, B., and D. Dodd, *Security Analysis*, New York: McGraw-Hill, 1934.

Graham, J.R., "Proxies for the Corporate Tax Rate," *Journal of Financial Economics*, 42, 1996, 187–221.

Graham, J.R., M.L. Lemmon, and J.S. Schallheim, "Debt, Leases, Taxes, and the Endogeneity of Corporate Tax Status," *Journal of Finance*, 53, 1998, 131–162.

Graham, J.R. and C.R. Harvey, "Expectations of Equity Risk Premia, Volatility and Asymmetry from a Corporate Finance Perspective," manuscript, Duke University, 2001.

Greenwald, B.C.N., J. Kahn, P.D. Sonkin, and M. van Biema, *Value Investing*, New York: John Wiley & Sons, 2001.

Grinblatt, M. and S. Titman, *Financial Markets and Corporate Strategy*, 2nd ed., New York: Irwin-McGraw-Hill, 2002.

Grullon, G., "The Information Content of Share Repurchase Programs," Jesse H. Jones Graduate School of Management, Rice University, January 2000.

Hadlock, C., M. Ryngaert, and M. Thomas, "Corporate Structure and Equity Offerings: Are There Benefits from Diversification?" *Journal of Business*, 74, 2001, 613–636.

Hamada, R.S., "The Effect of the Firm's Capital Structure on the Systematic Risk of Common Stock," *Journal of Finance*, 27, 1972, 435–452.

Hamada, R.S. and M.J. Scholes, "Taxes and Corporate Financial Management," in E.I. Altman and M.G. Subrahmanyan, eds., *Recent Advances in Corporate Finance*, Homewood, IL: Irwin, 1985, 187–226.

Harrigan, K., *Managing Maturing Businesses*, Lanham, MD: Lexington Books, 1988.

Harris, R. and F. Martson, "Estimating Shareholder Risk Premium Using Analysts' Growth Forecasts," *Financial Management*, 21, 1992, 63–70.

Harris, R. and F. Martson, "The Market Risk Premium: Expectation Estimates Using Analysts' Forecasts," Working Paper No. 99-08, Darden Graduate School of Business, University of Virginia, 1999.

Harvey, C., "The World Price of Covariance Risk," *Journal of Finance*, 46, 1991, 111–159.

Haushalter, D. and W. Mikkelson, "An Investigation of the Gains from Specialized Equity: Tracking Stock and Minority Carve-Outs," Lundquist College of Business, University of Oregon, 2001.

Hawawini, G. and D.B. Keim, "On the Predictability of Common Stock Returns: World Wide Evidence," in R.A. Jarrow, W.T. Ziemba, and V. Maksimovich, eds. *Finance*, Amsterdam: North Holland Publishing Co., 1993.

Hawawini, G. and D.B. Keim, "The Cross Section of Common Stock Returns: A Review of the Evidence and Some New Findings," in D.B. Keim and W.T. Ziemba, eds., *Security Market Imperfections in World Wide Equity Markets*, Cambridge: Cambridge University Press, 2000.

Hertz, D.B. "Risk Analysis in Capital Investment," *Harvard Business Review*, 42, 1964, 95–106.

Hertzel, M. and R.L. Smith, "Market Discounts and Shareholder Gains for Placing Equity Privately," *Journal of Finance*, 48, 1993, 459–485.

Herzel, L. and R. Shepro, *Bidders and Targets: Mergers and Acquisitions in the U.S.*, New York: Basil and Blackwell, 1990.

Higgins, R.C., "How Much Growth Can Your Company Afford?" *Financial Management*, 6, 1977, 7–16.

Higgins, R.C., "Sustainable Growth Under Inflation," *Financial Management*, 3, 1981, 36–40.

Hillier, F.S., "The Derivation of Probabilistic Information for the Evaluation of Risky Investments," *Management Science*, 9, 1963, 443–457.

Hite, G., J.E. Owers, and R.C. Rogers, "The Market for Interfirm Asset Sales: Partial Sell-offs and Total Liquidations," *Journal of Financial Economics*, 18, 1987, 229–252.

Hite, T. and J.E. Owers, "Security Price Reactions around Corporate Spin-off Announcements," *Journal of Financial Economics*, 12, 1983, 409–436.

Hong, H., G. Mandelker, and R.S. Kaplan, "Pooling vs. Purchase: The Effects of Accounting for Mergers on Stock Prices," *Accounting Review*, 53, 1978, 31–47.

Houston, J.F. and M.D. Ryngaert, "Equity Issuance and Adverse Selection: A Direct Test Using Conditional Stock Offers," *Journal of Finance,* 52, 1997, 197–219.

Hubbard, R.G. and D. Palia, "A Reexamination of the Conglomerate Merger Wave in the 1960s: An Internal Capital Market View," *Journal of Finance*, 54, 1999, 1131–1152.

Huberman, G. and D. Halka, "Systematic Liquidity," manuscript, Columbia University, 1999.

Hull, J., *Options, Futures and Other Derivatives*, 5th ed., Upper Saddle River, NJ: Prentice-Hall, 2002.

Husmann, S., L. Kruschwitz and A. Löffler, "WACC and a Generalized Tax Code," Discussion Paper 243, Hannover University, 2001.

Ibbotson, R.G. and R.A. Sinquefield, "Stocks, Bonds, Bills, and Inflation: Year-by-Year Historical Return (1926–1974)," *Journal of Business*, 49, 1976, 11–47.

Ibbotson, R.G., P.D. Kaplan and J.D. Peterson, "Estimates of Small Stock Betas are Much Too Low," *Journal of Portfolio Management*, 23, 1997, 104–112.

Ibbotson Associates, *Stock, Bonds, Bills and Inflation*, Valuation Edition 2002 Yearbook, Chicago, IL: Ibbotson Associates Inc., 2002.

Indro, D.C. and W.Y. Lee, "Biases in Arithmetic and Geometric Averages as Estimates of Long-Run Expected Returns and Risk Premia," *Financial Management*, 26, 1997, 81–90.

Inselbag, I. and H. Kaufold, "How to Value Recapitalizations and Leveraged Buyouts," *Journal of Applied Corporate Finance*, 1989, 2, 87–96.

Jackson, A., "The How of EVA® at CS First Boston," *Journal of Applied Corporate Finance*, 9, 1996, 98–103.

Jagannathan, R. and Z. Wang, "The Conditional CAPM and the Cross-section of Expected Returns," *Journal of Finance*, 39, 1996, 3–53.

Jagannathan, R., E.R. McGrattan and A. Scherbina, "The Declining Equity Premium," *Federal Reserve Bank of Minneapolis Quarterly Review*, 24, 2000, 3–19.

Jain, P.C., "The Effect of Voluntary Sell-offs Announcements on Shareholder Wealth," *Journal of Finance*, 40, 1985, 209–224.

Jarrell, G. and M. Bradley, "The Economic Effect of Federal and State Regulation of Cash Tender Offers," *Journal of Law and Economics*, 1980, 371–407.

Jensen, M.C., "Agency Costs of Free Cash Flows, Corporate Finance, and Takeovers," *American Economic Review*, 76, 1986, 323–329.

Jensen, M.C. and W. Meckling, "The Theory of the Firm: Managerial Behavior, Agency Costs and Ownership Structure," *Journal of Financial Economics*, 3, 1976, 323–329.

Jensen, M.C. and R.S. Ruback, "The Market for Corporate Control: The Scientific Evidence," *Journal of Financial Economics*, 11, 1983, 5–50.

John, K. and E. Ofek, "Asset Sales and Increases in Focus," *Journal of Financial Economics*, 1995, 105–126.

Johnson, R., "Term Structures of Corporate Bond Yields as a Function of Risk of Default," *Journal of Finance*, 22, 1967, 313–345.

Jones, C.M., "A Century of Stock Market Liquidity and Trading Costs," manuscript, Graduate School of Business, Columbia University, May 2002.

Jorion, P. and W.N. Goetzmann, "Global Stock Markets in the Twentieth Century," *Journal of Finance*, 54, 1999, 953–980.

Kaplan, S., "Sources of Value in Management Buyouts," in Y. Amihud (1989a), 95–101.

Kaplan, S.N., "Management Buyouts: Evidence on Taxes as a Source of Value," *Journal of Finance*, 44, 1989b, 611–632.

Kaplan, S.N., "The Staying Power of Leveraged Buyouts," *Journal of Applied Corporate Finance*, 6, 1993, 15–24.

Kaplan, S.N. and J.C. Stein, "How Risky Is the Debt of Highly Leveraged Transactions," *Journal of Financial Economics,* 27, 1990, 215–245.

Kaplan, S.N. and R.S. Ruback, "The Valuation of Cash Flow Forecasts: An Empirical Analysis," *Journal of Finance*, 50, 1995, 1059–1093.

Karolyi, G.A. and R.M. Stulz, "Are Financial Assets Priced Globally or Locally," manuscript, Ohio State University, 2001.

Kim, D., "A Reexamination of Firm Size, Book-to-market, and Earnings in the Cross-section of Expected Stock Returns," *Journal of Financial and Quantitative Analysis*, 32, 1997, 463–489.

Kocherlakota, N.R., "The Equity Premium: It's Still a Puzzle," *Journal of Economic Literature,* 34, 1996, 42–71.

Koedijk, K., C.J.M. Cool, P. Schotman and M.A. Van Dij, "The Cost of Capital in International Financial Markets: Local or Global," Discussion Paper No. 3062, Centre for Economic Policy Research, London, 2001.

Kohers, N. and J.S. Ang, "Earnouts in Mergers: Agreeing to Disagree and Agreeing to Stay," *Journal of Business*, 73, 2000, 445–476.

Koplin, J., A. Sarin and A.C. Shapiro, "The Private Equity Discount," *Journal of Applied Corporate Finance*, 12, 2000, 94–101.

Korajczyk, R. and C. Viallet, "An Empirical Investigation of International Asset Pricing," *Review of Financial Studies*, 2, 1989, 553–585.

Kothari, S.P., J. Shanken and R.G. Sloan, "Another Look at the Cross-section of Expected Stock Returns," *Journal of Finance*, 50, 1995, 185–224.

Kothari, S.P. and J. Shanken, "Beta and Book-to-Market: Is the Glass Half Full or Half Empty," Working Paper, University of Rochester, December 1998.

Kruse, T.A., N.Y. Park, K. Park and K. Suzuki, "The Value of Corporate Diversification: Evidence from Post-merger Performance in Japan," unpublished manuscript, 2002.

Lakonishok, J, A. Schleifer and R.W. Vishny, "Contrarian Investment, Extrapolation, and Risk," *Journal of Finance*, 49, 1994, 1541–1578.

Lebowitz, M.L. and S. Kogelman, "Inside the P/E Ratio: The Franchise Factor," *Financial Analysts Journal*, Nov.-Dec. 1990, 17–35.

Leibowitz, M.L., S. Kogelman and E.B. Lindenberg, "A Shortfall Approach to the Creditor's Decision: How Much Leverage Can a Firm Support?", *Financial Analysts Journal*, May-June 1990, 43–52.

Lessard, D.R., "Evaluating Foreign Projects: An Adjusted Present Value Approach," in D.R. Lessard, ed., *International Financial Management*, Boston: Warren, Gorham & Lamont, 1979.

Lessard, D.R., "Incorporating Country Risk in the Valuation of Offshore Projects," *Journal of Applied Corporate Finance*, 9, 1996, 52–63.

Levy, E. and S.M. Turnbull, "Average Intelligence," *Risk*, February 1992, 53–59. Reprinted in *From Black-Scholes to Black Holes*, London: Risk Publications, 1992, 157–164.

Li, H. and Y. Xu, "Survival Bias and the Equity Premium Puzzle," *Journal of Finance*, 57, 5, 2002.

Lichtenberg, F. and D. Siegel, "The Effect of Leveraged Buyouts on Productivity and Related Aspects of Firm Behavior," *Journal of Financial Economics*, 27, 1990, 165–194.

Lins, K. and H. Servaes, "International Evidence on the Value of Corporate Diversification," *Journal of Finance,* 54, 1999, 2215–2239.

Lintner, J., "The Valuation of Risk Assets and the Selection of Risky Investments in Stock Portfolios and Capital Budgets," *Review of Economics and Statistics,* 47, 1965, 13–47.

Litwin, S.M., "The Merger and Acquisition Process: A Primer on Getting the Deal Done," *The Financier: ACMT*, 2, 1995, 6–17.

Liu, J., D. Nissin and J. Thomas, "International Equity Valuation Using Multiples," manuscript, Graduate School of Business, Columbia University, 2002.

Lo, A. and C. MacKinlay, "Stock Market Prices Do Not Follow Random Walks: Evidence from Simple Specification Test," *Review of Financial Studies*, Spring 1988, 41–66.

Loderer, C. and L. Roth, "The Pricing Discount for Limited Liability: Evidence from Switzerland," manuscript, Universität Bern, 2001.

Logue, D.E., "When Theory Fails: Globalization as a Response to the (Hostile) Market for Foreign Exchange," *Journal of Applied Corporate Finance*, 8, 1995, 39–48.

Longstaff, F.A., "How Much Can Marketability Affect Security Values?," *Journal of Finance*, 50, 1995, 1767–1774.

Loughran, T. "Book-to-market Across Firm Size, Exchange, and Seasonality: Is There an Effect," *Journal of Financial and Quantitative Analysis*, 32, 1997, 249–268.

Luehrman, T.A., "MW Petroleum Corporation (B)," Case No. 9-295-045, Harvard Business School Publishing, Boston, MA, 1995.

Lundholm, R. and T. O'Keefe, "Reconciling Value Estimates from the Discounted Cash Flow Model and the Residual Income Model," *Contemporary Accounting Research*, 18, Summer 2001, 311–335.

MacMillan, L.W., "Analytic Approximation to the American Put Option," *Advances in Futures and Options Research*, 1, 1986, 119–139.

Mahesh, S., *Hotmail*, Case No. 9-899-165, Harvard Business School, 1999.

Majd, S. and R.A. Pindyck, "Time to Build, Option Value, and Investment Decisions," *Journal of Financial Economics*, 18, 1987, 7–27.

Maksimovic, V. and G. Phillips, "The Market for Corporate Assets: Who Engages in Mergers and Asset Sales and Are There Efficiency Gains?" *Journal of Finance*, 56, 2001, 2019–2065.

Malkiel, B.G., "The Capital Formation Problem in the United States," *Journal of Finance*, 1979, 291–306.

Marcus, A.J. and D.L. Modest, "Futures Markets and Production Decisions," *Journal of Political Economy*, 92, 1984, 409–426.

Margrabe, R., "The Value of an Option to Exchange One Asset for Another," *Journal of Finance*, 33, 1978, 177–186.

Martin, J.D. and A. Sayrak, "Corporate Diversification and Shareholder Value: A Survey of the Literature," *Journal of Corporate Finance*, 9, 2003, 37–57.

Mayers, D., "Nonmarketable Assets and Capital Market Equilibrium," in Jensen, M., ed., *Studies in the Theory of Capital Markets*, New York: Praeger, 1972.

Mayfield, E.S., "Estimating the Market Risk Premium," manuscript, Harvard University, 1999.

McConnell, J.J. and H. Servaes, "The Economics of Pre-packaged Bankruptcy," in Chew (1993), 676–680.

McDonald, R.L., and D. Siegel, "The Value of Waiting to Invest," *Quarterly Journal of Economics,* 101, 1986, 707–727.

McDonald, R.L., "Real Options and Rules of Thumb in Capital Budgeting," in M.J. Brennan, and L. Trigeorgis, eds., *Project Flexibility, Agency, and Competition*, New York: Oxford University Press, 2000.

Megginson, W.L., "The Purchase vs. Pooling Controversy: How the Stock Market Responds to Goodwill," *Journal of Applied Corporate Finance*, 9, 1996, 50–59.

Mehra, R. and E. Prescott, "The Equity Premium: A Puzzle," *Journal of Monetary Economics,* 15, 1985, 145–161.

Merrill Lynch, Pierce, Fenner & Smith Inc., *Security Risk Evaluation,* December 1998.

Merton, R.C., "An Intertemporal Capital Asset Pricing Model," *Econometrica*, 41, 1973a, 867–888.

Merton, R.C., "Theory of Rational Option Pricing," *Bell Journal of Economics and Management Science*, 4, 1973b, 141–183.

Merton, R.C., "On the Pricing of Contingent Claims and the Modigliani-Miller Theorem," *Journal of Financial Economics*, 5, 1977, 241–249.

Merton, R.C., "On Estimating the Expected Return on the Market: An Exploratory Investigation," *Journal of Financial Economics*, 8, 1980, 321–361.

Miles, J.A. and J.R. Ezzell, "The Weighted Average Cost of Capital, Perfect Capital Markets, and Project Life: A Clarification," *Journal of Financial and Quantitative Analysis*, 15, 1980, 719–730.

Miles, J.A. and J.R. Ezzell, "Reformulating Tax Shield Valuation: A Note," *Journal of Finance*, 40, 1985, 1485–1492.

Miller, M., "Debt and Taxes," *Journal of Finance*, 32, 1977, 261–275.

Miller, M., "Tax Obstacles to Voluntary Corporate Restructuring," in Chew (1993), 641–644.

Miller, M. and F. Modigliani, "Dividend Policy, Growth, and the Valuation of Shares," *Journal of Business*, 34, 1961, 411–433.

Miller, M. and M.S. Scholes, "Dividend and Taxes," *Journal of Financial Economics*, 6, 1978, 333–364.

Milunovich, S. and A. Tsuei, "EVA® in the Computer Industry," in *Journal of Applied Corporate Finance*, 9, 1996, 104–115.

Modigliani, F. and R.A. Cohn, "Inflation, Rational Valuation and the Market," *Financial Analysts Journal*, March-April 1979, 24–44.

Modigliani, F. and M. Miller, "The Cost of Capital, Corporation Finance, and the Theory of Investment," *American Economic Review*, 48, 1958, 261–297.

Modigliani, F. and M Miller, "Corporate Income Taxes and the Cost of Capital: A Correction," *American Economic Review*, 53, 1963, 433–443.

Modigliani, F. and F.J. Shiller, "Coupon and Tax Effects on New and Seasoned Bond Yields and the Measurement of the Cost of Debt Capital," *Journal of Financial Economics*, 1979, 7, 297–318.

Morck, R., A. Schleifer and R.W. Vishny, "Do Managerial Objectives Drive Bad Acquisitions?" *Journal of Finance*, 45, 1990, 31–48.

Mossin, J., "Equilibrium in a Capital Asset Market," *Econometrica*, 34, 1966, 768–783.

Myers, S.C., "Interactions of Corporate Finance and Investment Decisions—Implications for Capital Budgeting," *The Journal of Finance*, 29, 1974, 261–297.

Myers, S.C., "A Framework for Evaluating Mergers," in S.C. Myers, ed., *Modern Developments in Financial Management*, New York: Praeger, 1976, 633–645.

Myers, S.C., "The Capital Structure Puzzle," *Journal of Finance*, 39, 1984, 575–592.

Myers, S.C., "Still Searching for Optimal Capital Structure," Stern and Chew (1998), 120–130.

Myers, S.C. and N.S. Majluf, "Corporate Financing and Investment Decisions When Firms Have Information That Investors Do Not Have," *Journal of Financial Economics*, 13, 1984, 187–221.

O'Brien, T.J., "The Global CAPM and a Firm's Cost of Capital in Different Currencies," *Journal of Applied Corporate Finance*, 12, 1999, 73–79.

O'Byrne, S.F., "EVA® and Market Value," *Journal of Applied Corporate Finance*, 9, 1996, 116–125.

O'Byrne, S.F., "EVA and Its Critics," *Journal of Applied Corporate Finance*, 12, 1999, 92–96.

Ohlson, J., "Earnings, Book Values, and Dividends in Equity Valuation," *Contemporary Accounting Research*, 12, Spring 1995, 661–687.

Pástor, L. and R.F. Stambaugh, "The Equity Premium and Structural Breaks," *Journal of Finance*, 56, 2001, 1207–1239.

Pástor, L. and R.F. Stambaugh, "Liquidity Risk and Expected Stock Returns," manuscript, University of Chicago, 2001.

Penman, S., "On Comparing Cash Flow and Accrual Accounting Models for Use in Equity Valuation," *Contemporary Accounting Research*, 18, Winter 2001.

Penman, S. and T. Sougiannis, "A Comparison of Dividend, Cash Flow, and Earnings Approaches to Equity Valuation," *Contemporary Accounting Research*, 15, Fall 1998, 343–383.

Pereiro, L.E., "The Valuation of Closely-held Companies in Latin America," *Emerging Market Review*, 2, 2001, 330–370.

Pereiro, L.E., *Valuation of Companies in Emerging Markets*, New York: John Wiley & Sons, 2002.

Pindyck, R.A., "Investment of Uncertain Cost," *Journal of Financial Economics*, 34, 1993, 53–76.

Pnegar, J.M. and L. Wilbricht, "What Managers Think of Capital Structure Theory: A Survey," *Financial Management*, 18, 1989, 82–91.

Porter, M., *Competitive Strategy,* New York: The Free Press, 1980.

Porterba, J. and L. Summers, "Mean Reversion in Stock Prices," *Journal of Financial Economics*, 1988, 27–59.

Pratt, S.P., *Valuing a Business*, 2nd ed., Homewood, IL: Irwin, 1989.

Press, W.H., S.A. Teukolsky, W.T. Vetterlling and B.P. Flannery, eds., *Numerical Recipes in Fortran 77*, 2nd ed., Cambridge: Cambridge University Press, 1992.

Pye, Gordon, "Gauging the Default Premium," *Financial Analysts Journal*, 30, 1974, 49–52.

Rajan, R., H. Servaes and L. Zingales, "The Cost of Diversity: The Diversification Discount and Inefficient Investment," *The Journal of Finance*, 60, 2000, 35–80.

Rappaport, "Selecting Strategies That Create Shareholder Value," *Harvard Business Review,* 1981, 139–149.

Ritter, J.R. and R.S. Warr, "The Decline of Inflation and the Bull Market of 1982 to 1997," paper presented at *The 11th Annual Australasian Finance and Banking Conference*, The University of New South Wales, December 1998.

Rogalski, R.J. and J.D. Vinso, "Price Variations as Predictors of Exchange Rates," *Journal of International Business Studies*, Spring-Summer 1977, 71–83.

Roll, R., "A Critique of the Asset Pricing Theory's Tests: Part I: On Past and Potential Testability of the Theory," *Journal of Financial Economics*, 4, 1977, 129–176.

Roll, R., "Violations of the 'Law of One Price' and Their Implications for Differentially Denominated Assets," in M. Sarnat and G. Szego, eds., *International Finance and Trade*, vol. 1, Cambridge, MA: Ballinger, 1979.

Roll, R. and S. Yan, "An Explanation of the Forward Premium 'Puzzle'," *European Financial Management*, 6, 2, 2000, 121–148.

Ross, S.A, "The Arbitrage Theory of Capital Asset Pricing," *Journal of Economic Theory*, 13, 1976, 341–360.

Ross, S.A. and M. Walsh, "A Simple Approach to the Pricing of Risk Assets with Uncertain Exchange Rates," in R. Hawkins, et al., eds., *Research in International Business and Finance* 3, JAI Press, 1983, 39–54.

Ruback, R.S., "Calculating the Market Value of Risk-free Cash Flows," *Journal of Financial Economics*, 15, 1986, 323–339.

Ruback, R.S., "Capital Cash Flows: A Simple Approach to Valuing Risky Cash Flows," *Financial Management*, 31, 2002, 85–103.

Rubinstein, M. and E. Reiner, "Breaking Down the Barriers," *Risk*, 1991, 23–35.

Rydqvist, K., "Empirical Investigation of the Voting Premium," Working Paper No. 35, Northwestern University, November 1987.

Saggese, N.P. and A. Ranney-Marinelli, eds., *A Practical Guide to Out-of-court Restructuring and Prepackaged Plans of Reorganization*, 2nd ed., 2000 Supplement.

Sahlman, W.A., "Aspects of Financial Contracting in Venture Capital," *Journal of Applied Corporate Finance*, 1988, 23–36.

Sarig, O. and A. Warga, "Some Empirical Estimates of the Risk Structure of Interest Rates," *Journal of Finance*, 44, 1989, 1351–1360.

Scharfstein, D.S., "The Dark Side of Internal Capital Markets II: Evidence from Diversified Conglomerates," National Bureau of Economic Research, No. 6352, Boston, MA, 1998.

Schipper, K. and A. Smith, "Effects of Recontracting on Shareholder Wealth: The Case of Voluntary Spin-offs," *Journal of Financial Economics*, 12, 1983, 437–467.

Schipper, K., "A Comparison of Equity Carve-outs and Seasoned Equity Offerings: Share Price Effects and Corporate Restructuring," *Journal of Financial Economics*, 15, 1986, 153–186.

Schneider, E., *Industrielles Rechnungswesen,* Tubingen: J.C. Mohr, 1954.

Schramm, R.M. and H.N. Wang, "Measuring the Cost of Capital in an International Framework," *Journal of Applied Corporate Finance*, 12, 1999, 63–72.

Scholes, M.S., M.A. Wolfson, M.M. Erickson, E. Maydew and T. Shevlin, *Taxes and Business Strategy*, 2nd ed., Englewood Cliffs, NJ: Prentice Hall, 2001.

Schwartz, E.S. and M. Moon, "Evaluating Research and Development Investments," in M.J. Brennan and L. Trigeorgis, eds., *Project Flexibility, Agency, and Competition*, New York: Oxford University Press, 2000.

Schwert, W.G., "Indexes of US Stock Prices from 1802 to 1987," *Journal of Business*, 63, 1990, 399–426.

Shaefer, S.M., "The Problem with Redemption Yields," *The Financial Analysts Journal*, May-June 1977, 59–67.

Sharpe, W.E., "Capital Asset Prices: A Theory of Market Equilibrium under Conditions of Risk," *Journal of Finance*, 19, 1964, 425–462.

Sick, G.A., "Tax-Adjusted Discount Rates," *Management Science*, 1990, 26, 1432–1450.

Siegel, J., "The Real Rate of Interest from 1800–1990," *Journal of Monetary Economics*, 29, 1992, 227–252.

Siegel, J., "Comments and Discussion," *Brooking Papers on Economic Activity*, 1993, 138–140.

Siegel, J., *Stocks for the Long Run*, 3rd ed., New York: Irwin, 2002.

Silber, W.L., "Discount on Restricted Stocks: The Impact of Illiquidity on Stock Prices," *Financial Analysts Journal*, 1991, 60–64.

Simon Hodrick, L. and P. Moulton, "Liquidity," manuscript, Graduate School of Business, Columbia University, October 2002.

Sirower, M.L., *The Synergy Trap*, New York: Free Press, 1997.

Slaughter, W.A. and L.G. Worton, "Workout or Bankruptcy," in D. DiNapoli, S.C. Sigoloff and

R.F. Cushman, eds., *Workouts and Turnarounds*, Bur Ridge, IL: Irwin, 1991.

Smith, D.J., "The Arithmetic of Financial Engineering," *Journal of Applied Corporate Finance*, 1, 1989, 49–58, reprinted in Chew (1998), 534–543.

Solnik, B., "An Equilibrium Model of the International Capital Market," *Journal of Economic Theory*, 8, 1974, 500–525.

Solomons, D., "Divisional Performance: Measurement and Control," Financial Executives Research Foundation, Charlottessville, VA, 1965.

Statman, D., "Book Values and Stock Returns," *The Chicago MBA: A Journal of Selected Papers*, 4, 1980, 25–45.

Stern, J.M., "Earnings Per Share Don't Count," *Financial Analysts Journal*, July-August 1974, 39–40, 42–43, 67–75.

Stern, J.M., *Measuring Corporate Performance*, New York and London: The Financial Times Ltd., 1975.

Stern, J.M. and D.H. Chew (eds.), *The Revolution in Corporate Finance*, 3rd ed., New York: Blackwell, 1998.

Stewart, G.B., *The Quest for Value*, New York: Harper, 1991.

Stulz, R.M., "A Model of International Asset Pricing," *Journal of Financial Economics*, 9, 1981, 383–406.

Stulz, R.M., "Globalization of the Capital Markets and the Cost of Capital: The Case of Nestlé," *Journal of Applied Corporate Finance*, 8, 1995, 30–38.

Stulz, R.M., "Globalization, Corporate Finance, and the Cost of Capital," *Journal of Applied Corporate Finance*, 12, 1999, 8–25.

Summers, L.H., "Investment Incentives and the Discounting of Depreciation Allowances," in M. Feldstein, ed., *The Effect of Taxation on Capital Accumulation*, Chicago: Chicago University Press, 1987.

Sundaresan, S.M., *Fixed Income Securities and Their Derivatives*, 2nd ed., Boston, MA: South-Western Pub., 2001.

Taggart, Jr., R.A., "Consistent Valuation and the Cost of Capital Expressions with Corporate and Personal Taxes," *Financial Management*, 20, 1991, 8–20.

Tobin, J., "A General Equilibrium Approach to Monetary Theory," *Journal of Money, Credit and Banking*, 1, 1969, 15–29.

Titman, S. and R. Wessels, "The Determinants of Capital Structure Choice," *Journal of Finance*, 43, 1988, 1–19.

Treynor, J., "Toward a Theory of the Market Value of Risky Assets," unpublished manuscript, 1961.

Trigeorgis, L., ed., *Real Options in Capital Investment*, Wesport, CT: Praeger, 1995.

Vermaelen, T., "Common Stock Repurchases and Market Signaling: An Empirical Study," *Journal of Financial Economics*, 1981, 9, 129–183.

Wasserstein, B., *Big Deal*, New York: Warner Books, 1998.

Weiss, L.A., "Bankruptcy Resolution: Direct Costs and Violation of Priority of Claims," *Journal of Financial Economics*, 27, 1990, 285–314.

Williams, J.B., *The Theory of Investment Value*, Cambridge, MA: Harvard University Press, 1938.

Wilson, J.W. and C.P. Jones, "An Analysis of the S&P 500 Index and Cowles's Extensions: Price Indexes and Stock Returns, 1870–1999," *Journal of Business*, 75, 2002, 505–534.

Wruck, K.H., "Equity Ownership Concentration and Firm Value: Evidence from Private Equity Financings," *Journal of Financial Economics*, 23, 1989, 3–28.

Wruck, K.H., "What Really Went Wrong at Revco," *Journal of Applied Corporate Finance*. Reprinted in Chew (1993), 654–667.

Wyser-Pratte, G.P., *Risk Arbitrage II*, Monograph Series in Finance and Economics, Salomon Brothers Center for the Study of Financial Institutions, New York University, 1982.

Index

A

Absolute priority, 245
Accounting
  asset impairment, 247
  asset restructuring, 269–271
  fresh-start, 247
  goodwill in EVA, TN10
  goodwill, 148
  mergers, 147–148
  negative goodwill, 148
  pooling, 147, TN10
  purchase, 147
  recapitalization, TN33
  troubled debt restructuring, 247
Accretion-dilution analysis, 155–156,
  161, 168
Adjusted present value (APV), original,
  89–95, 239–240
Adjusted present value
  compressed, 97–99
  HLF calculator, A7
  leverage above target, 94–95
  recursive, 99–102
American depository receipts (ADRs),
  196
Appraisal rights, 144
Arbitrage pricing theory, 53–54
Arbitrage pricing, 124
Asset disposition, 267–269
Asset purchase. *See* Mergers and acqui-
  sitions
Asset restructuring, 265, 267–271
Asset turnover ratio, 17, 108

B

Balance sheet adjustments, 27–30
Balance sheet, 10–12, 165–166,
  TN1–TN2

Beta, 16, 36, 47
  adjusted, 47
  estimation, 47, 51, 55
  levering/unlevering, 47–50
Black-Scholes formula, A1,
  TN33–TN34
Break-even synergies, 153–154
Brownian motion, 126, 135, TN17

C

Cancellation of indebtedness (COD),
  248–249
Capital assets pricing model (CAPM),
  36, 50–51
Capital expenditures
  in debt capacity, 116
  in economic value added, 81
  in free cash flow, 14
Capital leases, 64
Carve outs, 268–269
Cash and marketable securities,
  28–29
Cash flow statement, 13, TN2
Cash flow to equity, 21–23
Changing capital structure, 89–90
  recursive WACC, 95–97
Class shares. *See* Tracking stock
Collars, 195–196, 200–203
Comparables, 63–65
Conglomerates, 266
Consensus forecasts, 43–45
Constant growth perpetuity, 16, 22
Contingent value rights (CVRs), 181,
  196–200
Continuation value, 15–21, 81–82
Continuous-time model, 124–127
Convertible bonds, 61
Convertible preferred, 61, 182

Cost of capital, 15–16, 35–62, 233
  and inflation, 214
  and personal taxes, 25–27
  in developed markets, 206–208
  in emerging markets, 216–217
  in private equity, 229–232
Cost of debt, 15, 58
  in emerging markets, 213
Cost of equity, 16, 36
  a detailed example, 58
  and leverage, 47–50
  and the equity premium, 38–47
  and the riskless rate, 36–38
  country risk, 212–213
  in developed markets, 206–207
  of large capitalization companies, 47
  of small cap companies, 55–58
Country betas, 207
Country risk premium, 216–217
Coverage ratio, 110
  and debt capacity multiple, TN33
  and debt ratio, 110
  and shortfall probability, 113
  and WACC, 113–114
Curran Asian call formula, A3

D

Deal making
  earnouts. *See* Earnouts
  risk shifting, 181–182
  source of disagreement, 179
  staged financing, 182–183
Debt capacity, 107–120
  and affordable price, 227–229
  and diversification, 265
  and financial distress, 244
  calculator, A7, TN16
  in LBOs, 114–119, TN15
  multiple, 116, 117–119
Default probability, TN28
Deferred taxes, 14, 79–80
Depreciation, 14, 79
Dilution adjustment
  in collars, 201
  in warrant valuation, 226–227,
    A5–A6
Discounted cash flow (DCF). *See* Enter-
    prise valuation
  and balance sheet adjustments, 27–29

and multiples, 21, 63, 63–68
  and real options, 121–122
Diversification discount, 265–267
Dividend growth model, 42–43
Dividends, 23–24
  in preferred stock, 61
  in trust-preferred stock, 61
Dixit-Pindyck entry-exit models,
    130–133
Duration
  of an asset 58
  of competitive advantage, 85–86

E

Earning power, 31–32
Earnings per share, 63–64, 247, 268,
    TN7–TN8
Earnout agreements, 184–185
Earnout valuation, 185–193
Economic value added (EVA), 77–87
  and market value, 84–87
  defined, 78
  relation to free cash flow, 78–80
Emerging market betas, 217
Enterprise valuation, 14–17, TN3–TN4
  and pre-tax WACC, TN4–TN5
Entry and exit options. *See* Real options
Equity kicker, 224–227, 236
Equity premium, 16, 35–47
  calculator, A7
  historical analyses, 38–40
  in the global market, 206–207
  prospective, 41–47
  survivorship bias, 40
  time varying, 41
Equity valuation, 22–23
Equity-linked securities, 29
Equivalent loan, TN27
Exit value, 15, 225, TN32–TN33
Explicit finite difference algorithm,
    TN22–TN24

F

Fama-French three-factor model, 51–53
Financial distress, 243
  costs, 112
  and debt ratio, 89
  in emerging markets, 216

Financial interdependencies, 107–108
Financial sponsor. *See* Sponsor
Fisher-Margrabe formula, 104
Fixed exchange ratio with collar, 203
Floating rate debt, 60
Forecast period, 15, 19
Foreign currency translation, 205–206,
    209–212
Forward merger. *See* Mergers and ac-
    quisitions
Forward or prospective multiples. *See*
    Valuation multiples
Franchise and growth, 30–32, 82–84
Franchise factor, 73–75
Free cash flow valuation. *See* Enterprise
    valuation
Free cash flows
    continuous time, 124–127
    correction in emerging markets,
        216–217
    decomposition, 21–22
    forecasting, 9–14
    incremental, 156–157
    unlevered, 90–91

G

Generally accepted accounting princi-
    ples (GAAP). *See* Accounting
Global capital market, 205–208
    capital asset pricing model, 206
    company beta, 207
Goodwill
    accounting. *See* Accounting, goodwill
    tax treatment, 144, 146
Growth opportunities. *See* Franchise
    and growth

H

Harvest, 83, 276–279
Headquarter costs and benefits, 279–280
High yield debt, 221, 223–224
Holdbacks. *See* Mergers and acquisi-
    tions

I

Income statement, 10–12, TN1
    common size, 69

Inflation
    and nominal and real rates, 214
    forecast, 44
    in continuation value, 20
    in return on capital, 17–18
    premium in Treasury note, 16
Interest coverage. *See* Coverage ratio
Interest expense and unlevered net in-
    come, 10
Interest rate parity. *See* Translating for-
    eign currency cash flows
Internal rate of return (IRR), 225–226

L

LBOs. *See* leveraged buyouts
Leases
    and cost of debt, 28, 60
    and EBITDAR multiple, 64
    capital, 64
    operating, 64, TN26
    retail companies, 157
Leveraged buyouts (LBOs), 221–240
    affordable price, 227–229
    and leveraged changes, 89
    debt capacity, 114–119
    rationale, 221–223
    signaling hypothesis, 99
    simple algebra, TN32–TN33
Leveraged recapitalization. *See* Recapi-
    talizations
Libor, 38
Liquidation, 243, 245, 245–247
Liquidity
    and expected returns, 54
    and private equity return, 229–232
    beta, 54, 58
    premium proxy, 16, 51, 55–58
Lognormal distribution, 116, TN25

M

Majd-Pindyck time-to-build model, 135
Management buyout, 221
Market risk premium. *See* Equity pre-
    mium
Marketable securities, 28–29
Mergers and acquisitions, 143–177
    accounting. *See* Accounting
    asset purchase, 144, 146

Mergers and acquisitions (*cont.*)
  financial model, 9–14, 161–167
  forward merger, 144
  holdbacks, 144
  iron law, 148–154
  reverse subsidiary merger, 144, 147
  stock purchase, 143–146
  tax considerations, 143–147
  terms, 148, 151–153, 160–162,
    179–181
  triangular merger, 144
  winners' course, 151
Metrics, 63–64, 110
Mezzanine financing, 224, 236–239
Mid-year discounting, 29
Miles and Ezzell's analysis, 49, 95
Miller-Modigliani valuation model, 82
Minority interest, 29
Modigliani-Miller Proposition I, 48
Monte Carlo simulation. *See* Simulation
Morris trust, 147, 270
Multiples. *See* Valuation multiples
Myers APV rule, 90

N

Net debt, 15–17
  negative, 49–50
Net operating losses (NOLs), 144–196
  tax shield, 260
Net operating profits (NOP), 78
Net operating profits after taxes
  (NOPAT), 14
NOLs. *See* Net operating losses
Nominal and real
  cost of capital, 214
  free cash flows, 214–215
  growth, 18, 82
  rates, 18
Nondiversifiable risk, 36

O

Options
  American, A1–A2
  and net present value, 121–123
  Asian option, 188, 197–202, A3
  calculators, A7, TN34–TN35
  calls, 103–104, 123, A1–A2
  dividend paying, A1–A2, A5

  European, 186, A1–A2
  exchange, 104, 198, TN29
  implied volatility, A2, TN35
  knockout option, A4
  put-call parity, A5–A6
  puts, 197–198, A1–A2
Original issue discount (OID), 185, 237,
  TN26–TN28

P

Payout ratio, 43, 107–108
Pecking order, 99, 112
Pension liabilities, 28, 246
Personal taxes, 25–27, 49, 90–91,
  93–94, TN5–TN6
Pindyck uncertain cost model, 137
Portfolio beta, 48
Preferred stock, 29, 60–61, 115, 182,
  246
Pre-packaged bankruptcy, 246, 248
Price guarantees, 195–200
Price-to-book ratio. *See* Valuation multi-
  ples
Private sales, 268
Purchasing power parity (PPP). *See*
  Translating foreign currency cash
  flows

Q

Q ratio, 84

R

Real options, 121–140, 186–193
  calculators, A8
  compound, 135
  deferral, 130–133, TN18–TN19
  entry and exit options, 121–124,
    131–138, TN18–TN20
  foothold and expansion, 133–138,
    TN20–TN22
  in earnouts, 186–193
  Ito process, 126, TN17
  return distribution of the HLF pricing
    model, TN24–TN25
Recapitalization
  accounting for troubled companies.
    See Accounting

accounting. *See* Accounting
debt capacity, 114–119
  of troubled companies, 243–263
  framework, 243–245
  leveraged, 114, 221–223
  plans, 243, 250–251, 257–258
  recovery by claimants, 255–257
  rights and options, 257–263
  tax considerations, 248–249
  valuing plan securities, 251–255
Regression toward the mean, 47
Reorganizations
  in-court, 246
  out-of-court workouts, 245
  Section 368. *See* Reorganizations, tax
    free
  tax free, 146–147
  types A to C, 147
Reproduction value, 30–32
Restructuring. *See* Asset restructuring
  accounting treatment. *See* Accounting
  expenses, 29–30
  IPOs, 268
  tax considerations, 269–271
Return on capital (ROC), 18, 74, 82–84,
    276
Revenue multiple. *See* Valuation multiples
Risk analysis, 172–174
Risk arbitrage, 195, TN30–TN32
Risk neutral valuation, TN28–TN29
Risk shifting, 181–182
Risk-free (riskless) rate, 16, 36–38
Ruback's capital cash flow method,
    97–99

S

Scenario analysis. *See* Sensitivity and
    scenario analyses
Section 338 election, 144, 269
Senior debt, 58, 60, 227–228, 244
  amortization period, 115–116
  cash sweep, 117
Sensitivity and scenario analysis,
    171–176
Share repurchases, 267
  and the equity premium, TN7
Simulation, 173, 198, 200–201
Size premium, 16, 55–58

Small capitalization. *See* Size premium
Small company beta, 55, 57
Special offer structures, 195–203
Spin-offs, 268, 270
Sponsor, 115, 221
Spot exchange rate, 205–206
Staged financing. *See* Deal making
Stern valuation model, 20
Stock purchase. *See* Mergers and acquisitions
Stranded costs, 180
Subordinated debt, 60, 115, 224–225,
    251–252
Sum beta, 55
Sum-of-the-parts valuation. *See* Valuation
Survivorship bias, 40
Sustainable debt, 111–113
Synergies, 151–154
Systematic risk. *See* Nondiversifiable
    risk

T

Target debt ratio
  and APV, 89–90
  and coverage ratio, 110–111,
    113–114
  and WACC, 15
  fluctuations, TN12
Tax considerations
  in asset restructuring, 269–271
  in leveraged buyouts, 143–146
  in mergers and acquisitions,
    143–146
  in trouble company recapitalizations,
    248–249
Tax imputation, 27, 91, 94
Tax shield, 10, 14–15, 90–91, 222–223,
    260
Term premium, 36
Top-up rights, 203
Tracking stock, 180, 190–193, 268–271
Trailing multiples. *See* Valuation multiples
Transfer pricing, 265, 279–280
Triangular merger. *See* Mergers and acquisitions
Troubled debt restructuring. *See* Accounting

U

Uncertain costs in foothold investments, 137–138
Unconditional equity premium, 40
Unlevered net income, 10

V

Valuation Aids, A7–A8
Valuation multiples, 63–76
   calculator, A7
   EBITDA, 21, 64, 65–68
   EBITDAR, 64
   price-to-book, 64–65
   price-to-earnings, 43, 63–64, 76
   revenue, 64
   trailing/forward, 64
Valuation
   business units, 271–281
   choosing the method, 24–25
   enterprise. *See* Enterprise valuation
   equity. *See* Equity valuation
   sum-of-the-parts, 169–170, 271–281
   tax shield. *See* Tax shield

Value gap, 265–267
Valuing equity as an option, 102–105
Venture capital, 179, 181–183
Volatility, 104–105, 126, A1–A2

W

WACC. *See* Weighted average cost of capital
Walk-away rights, 202
Warrants, 61, 224, 227, A2–A3, A5–A6, TN34–TN35
Weighted average cost of capital (WACC), 15, 24–27, 61–62, 89–90, 95–97
Working capital, 14, 29, 33, TN2
Workouts, 245

Y

Yield to maturity, 60

Z

Zero-beta asset, 36, 38